Gender and Development: Theoretical, Empirical and Practical Approaches
Volume II

The International Library of Critical Writings in Economics

Series Editor: Mark Blaug

Professor Emeritus, University of London, UK
Professor Emeritus, University of Buckingham, UK
Visiting Professor, University of Amsterdam, The Netherlands
Visiting Professor, Erasmus University of Rotterdam, The Netherlands

This series is an essential reference source for students, researchers and lecturers in economics. It presents by theme a selection of the most important articles across the entire spectrum of economics. Each volume has been prepared by a leading specialist who has written an authoritative introduction to the literature included.

A full list of published and future titles in this series is printed at the end of this volume.

Wherever possible, the articles in these volumes have been reproduced as originally published using facsimile reproduction, inclusive of footnotes and pagination to facilitate ease of reference.

For a list of all Edward Elgar published titles visit our site on the World Wide Web at
http://www.e-elgar.co.uk

Gender and Development: Theoretical, Empirical and Practical Approaches Volume II

Edited by

Lourdes Benería

Professor of City and Regional Planning
Cornell University, USA

with

Savitri Bisnath

Doctoral Candidate
Cornell University, USA

THE INTERNATIONAL LIBRARY OF CRITICAL WRITINGS IN ECONOMICS

An Elgar Reference Collection
Cheltenham, UK • Northampton, MA, USA

Published by
Edward Elgar Publishing Limited
Glensanda House
Montpellier Parade
Cheltenham
Glos GL50 1UA
UK

Edward Elgar Publishing, Inc.
136 West Street, Suite 202
Northampton
Massachusetts 01060
USA

A catalogue record for this book is available from the British Library.

Library of Congress Cataloging in Publication Data

Gender and development : theoretical, empirical, and practical approaches / edited by Lourdes Benería with Savitri Bisnath.
    p. cm. — (The international library of critical writings in economics) (An Elgar reference collection)
Includes bibliographical references and index.
1. Women in development. 2. Economic development—Social aspects. 3. Women—Developing countries—Economic conditions. I. Benería, Lourdes. II. Bisnath, Savitri, 1965- III. Series. IV. Series: An Elgar reference collection

HQ1240 .G43 2001
305.4'091724—dc21   2001023010

ISBN   1 84064 194 0 (2 volume set)

Printed and bound in Great Britain by MPG Books Ltd, Bodmin, Cornwall

Contents

Acknowledgements

The editors and publishers wish to thank the authors and the following publishers who have kindly given permission for the use of copyright material.

Lourdes Benería for her own excerpt: (1999), 'Structural Adjustment Policies,' in Janice Peterson and Margaret Lewis (eds), *Elgar Companion to Feminist Economics*, 687–95.

Frank Cass & Company Ltd for articles: Bina Agarwal (1986), 'Women, Poverty and Agricultural Growth in India', *Journal of Peasant Studies*, **13** (4), July, 165–220; Adrian Wood (1991), 'North-South Trade and Female Labour in Manufacturing: An Asymmetry', *Journal of Development Studies*, **27** (2), January, 168–89.

CEPAL Review and United Nations Economic Commission for Latin America and the Caribbean for article: Irma Arriagada (1994), 'Changes in the Urban Female Labour Market', *CEPAL Review*, **53**, August, 91–110.

Elsevier Science for articles: Carmen Diana Deere (1985), 'Rural Women and State Policy: The Latin American Agrarian Reform Experience', *World Development*, **13** (9), September, 1037–53; Nilüfer Çağatay and Günseli Berik (1990), 'Transition to Export-Led Growth in Turkey: Is There a Feminization of Employment?', *Review of Radical Political Economics*, **22** (1), Spring, 115–34; Jean Larson Pyle and Leslie Dawson (1990), 'The Impact of Multinational Technological Transfer on Female Workforces in Asia', *Columbia Journal of World Business*, **25** (4), Winter, 40–8; Nan Wiegersma (1991), 'Peasant Patriarchy and the Subversion of the Collective in Vietnam', *Review of Radical Political Economics*, **23** (3 & 4), Fall/Winter, 174–97; Gillian Hart (1992), 'Household Production Reconsidered: Gender, Labor Conflict, and Technological Change in Malaysia's Muda Region', *World Development*, **20** (6), June, 809–23; Bina Agarwal (1994), 'Gender and Command Over Property: A Critical Gap in Economic Analysis and Policy in South Asia', *World Development*, **22** (10), October, 1455–78; Lawrence Haddad, Lynn R. Brown, Andrea Richter and Lisa Smith (1995), 'The Gender Dimensions of Economic Adjustment Policies: Potential Interactions and Evidence to Date', *World Development*, **23** (6), June, 881–96; Diane Elson (1995), 'Gender Awareness in Modeling Structural Adjustment', *World Development*, **23** (11), November, 1851–68; Nilüfer Çağatay and Şule Özler (1995), 'Feminization of the Labor Force: The Effects of Long-Term Development and Structural Adjustment', *World Development*, **23** (11), November, 1883–94; William Darity, Jr. (1995), 'The Formal Structure of a Gender-Segregated Low-Income Economy', *World Development*, **23** (11), November, 1963–8; Anne Marie Goetz and Rina Sen Gupta (1996), 'Who Takes the Credit? Gender, Power, and Control over Loan Use in Rural Credit Programs in Bangladesh', *World Development*, **24** (1), January, 45–63; Gita Sen (1996), 'Gender, Markets and States: A Selective Review and Research Agenda', *World Development*, **24** (5), May, 821–9; Nilüfer Çağatay (1996), 'Gender and International Labor Standards in the

World Economy', *Review of Radical Political Economics*, **28** (3), September, 92–101; Amy Lind (1997), 'Gender, Development and Urban Social Change: Women's Community Action in Global Cities', *World Development*, **25** (8), August, 1205–23; Guy Standing (1999), 'Global Feminization Through Flexible Labor: A Theme Revisited', *World Development*, **27** (3), March, 583–602.

Diane Elson and Ruth Pearson for excerpt: Ruth Pearson (1991), 'Male Bias and Women's Work in Mexico's Border Industries', in Diane Elson (ed.), *Male Bias in the Development Process*, Chapter 6, 133–63.

Journal of Developing Areas for article: Maria Sagrario Floro and Kendall Schaefer (1998), 'Restructuring of Labor Markets in the Philippines and Zambia: The Gender Dimension', *Journal of Developing Areas*, **33** (1), Fall, 73–98.

Koninklijke Brill N.V. for excerpt: Valentine M. Moghadam (2000), 'Gender and Economic Reforms: A Framework for Analysis and Evidence from Central Asia, the Caucasus, and Turkey', in Feride Acar and Ayşe Günes-Ayata (eds), *Gender and Identity Construction: Women of Central Asia, the Caucasus and Turkey*, 23–43.

Macmillan Press Ltd for excerpt: Catherine Hein (1986), 'The Feminisation of Industrial Employment in Mauritius: A Case of Sex Segregation', in Richard Anker and Catherine Hein (eds), *Sex Inequalities in Urban Employment in the Third World*, Chapter 7, 277–311.

Routledge, Taylor & Francis Books Ltd, for excerpts: Cecile Jackson (1998), 'Rescuing Gender from the Poverty Trap', in Cecile Jackson and Ruth Pearson (eds), *Feminist Visions of Development: Gender, Analysis and Policy*, Chapter 2, 39–64; Barbara Harriss-White (1998), 'Female and Male Grain Marketing Systems: Analytical and Policy Issues for West Africa and India', in Cecile Jackson and Ruth Pearson (eds), *Feminist Visions of Development: Gender, Analysis and Policy*, Chapter 9, 189–213; Mieke Meurs (1998), 'Imagined and Imagining Equality in East Central Europe: Gender and Ethnic Differences in the Economic Transformation of Bulgaria', in John Pickles and Adrian Smith (eds), *Theorising Transition: The Political Economy of Post-Communist Transformations*, Chapter 14, 330–46.

State University of New York Press for excerpt: Linda Y.C. Lim (1983), 'Capitalism, Imperialism, and Patriarchy: The Dilemma of Third-World Women Workers in Multinational Factories', in June Nash and Marie Patricia Fernandez-Kelly (eds), *Women, Men, and the International Division of Labor*, Chapter 3, 70–91.

Taylor & Francis Ltd (http://www.tandf.co.uk/journals/) for article: Carmen Diana Deere (1995), 'What Difference Does Gender Make?: Rethinking Peasant Studies', *Feminist Economics*, **1** (1), Spring, 53–72.

University of Chicago Press for article: Aline K. Wong (1981), 'Planned Development, Social Stratification, and the Sexual Division of Labor in Singapore', *Signs: Journal of Women in Culture and Society*, **7** (2), Winter, 434–52.

Every effort has been made to trace all the copyright holders but if any have been inadvertently overlooked the publishers will be pleased to make the necessary arrangement at the first opportunity.

In addition the publishers wish to thank the Marshall Library of Economics, Cambridge University, the Library of the London School of Economics and Political Science, B&N Microfilm, London, and the Library of Indiana University at Bloomington, USA, for their assistance in obtaining these articles.

Part I
Women's Access to Resources, Gender and Poverty

[1]

Women, Poverty and Agricultural Growth in India

Bina Agarwal*

This article explores the interlinkages between gender, poverty and agricultural growth in India. It shows how women and female children of poor rural households bear a disproportionately high share of the burden of poverty. This is manifest especially in a systematic bias against females in the intra-household distribution of food and health care. However, there are significant cross-regional differences in the extent of the bias which is much higher in the north-western states relative to the southern. Some of the likely factors – economic, social, historical – underlying these differences are discussed here. The specific problems of female-headed households are separately considered. Also, the on-going debate on the relationship between rural poverty and agricultural growth is critically examined. In addition, a detailed quantitative analysis is undertaken of the differential effects of the new agricultural technology, and associated growth, on the employment and earnings of female and male agricultural labourers (who constitute the bulk of the rural poor). The association between changes in these economic variables and others, such as in the incidence and pattern of dowry payments, is also examined, as are the implications of both these aspects for the situation of rural women in poverty in different geographic regions.

INTRODUCTION

Over the past two decades a vast amount of literature has accumulated both on the incidence of rural poverty in India and on agricultural growth-related aspects. In recent years, studies which have examined the association between these two aspects, in the context of an on-going debate, have also expanded to respectable numbers. But somewhere in this mass of information, rural women, like the poor in real life, remain invisible.

This article, on the basis of available literature and an analysis of secondary data, seeks to highlight (a) why the issue of women and poverty requires a special consideration and indeed needs to be an integral part of poverty

* Reader, Institute of Economic Growth (IEG), Delhi University. An earlier version of this article was presented at the IEG Silver Jubilee Seminar, April 1984. I am grateful to Raghav Gaiha and Terry Byres for comments on the earlier version.

studies, and (b) what direct and indirect implications the existing patterns of agricultural growth are likely to have for the economically underprivileged rural women.

The article is divided into four broad sections. Section I examines the question of inequalities within the rural household, of the possible economic factors underlying gender discrimination, and of the relative poverty-proneness of female- and male-headed households. Section II focuses on the debate on rural poverty and agricultural growth. Section III attempts to bring together all the three aspects, namely, women, rural poverty and agricultural growth; and the last section, IV, contains concluding comments.

I. WOMEN AND RURAL POVERTY

Does the burden of rural poverty fall equally on women and men? In particular, does it fall equally on female and male members of poor households? In much of the 'poverty literature' in India, neither at the level of general discussion nor in attempts to estimate poverty are these questions admitted, let alone addressed. (Exceptions to this are recent and rare.) Estimates of absolute poverty, for instance, although often expressed in terms of the numbers of the poor (head-count ratio), relate to numbers which are usually obtained by multiplying the count of households below the poverty line by the average household size. Sometimes actual figures of females and males in poor households are provided. In either case, the attempt is to first identify the poor households and then look at the numbers involved, the implicit assumption being that *all* members of a poor household are poor. Estimates of economic inequality among the poor further assume (again implicitly) that all members of a poor household are *equally* poor.

However, if we were to admit the possibility of a systematic sex-bias in the distribution of income/consumption within households, then household-specific estimates of poor persons would no longer suffice. We could, for example, have poor women among households in which the average income/consumption level puts the household above the poverty line, and not-poor men among households which are below the poverty line. Also, estimates of inequality among the poor may need to be revised significantly.

The accuracy of estimates apart, a focus on the gender dimensions of poverty is also necessary for the designing and directing of more effective state policies or programmes, and for a more specific thrust in non-governmental grassroots efforts to organise and empower the rural poor.

Here I shall be examining the issue of women and rural poverty in terms of: (1) inequalities in the distribution of the burden of poverty between male and female household members, especially in the context of male-headed households; and (2) poverty and female-headedness.[1]

(1) Intra-Household Distribution of the Burden of Poverty in Rural Households

The burden of poverty embodies multiple privations and complex forms of oppression. While it relates first and foremost to the problem of basic physical survival, it also has additional dimensions, such as those stemming from the social relations (in the family and outside) within which the struggle for survival takes place. In this part of the article, while focusing primarily on the issue of sex-based differentials in access to basic necessities such as food and medical care, I also briefly touch upon some of the other dimensions of poverty as they affect women in particular. In addition, the question – why are females discriminated against? – is addressed.

Since food is the most important item of consumption among poor households to begin with, it is important to examine the evidence on the intra-household distribution of food. Another aspect closely related to the survival chances of the poor is access to medical care. The evidence on these is of two kinds: (a) actual estimates of food intakes *vis-à-vis* requirements; and (b) *ex-post* indicators of inadequacies in food and medical care as apparent in the incidence of malnourishment, morbidity (the incidence of disease) and mortality. Let us consider each in turn.

(i) Inequalities in food intake relative to requirements: There is today a fair amount of literature from different parts of the Third World which points to the unequal sharing of food within the family – with female members getting a much lower share than male members in food quality and quantity (see Schofield's [1979] survey of studies relating to Asia, Africa and Latin America). However, most studies do not go beyond mentioning that there are male–female differentials in food intake (with food distribution favouring the males); they give no assessment of the degree of differentials, nor provide quantitative information based on an actual measurement of intakes.

The measurement of intra-household food intake is of course extremely difficult since it means very close observation by the data collector of the amounts consumed. Also, as Sen [1981] points out, the very fact that someone is observing food intakes may alter consumption behaviour. However, to what extent it does alter that behaviour would depend a good deal on the extent of rapport and familiarity the observer has with the household members observed. Again, to estimate food 'requirements' for different household members is tricky. The need can vary according to height, weight, age, activity level and, for women, whether pregnant or lactating.[2] Among the more commonly-used measures for requirements are those recommended by WHO/FAO experts for various activity levels for women and men. The Indian Council of Medical Research (ICMR) provides similar recommendations for the Indian context. (There continues to be a controversy as to whether recommendations from both these sources are too high – for example, see Lipton [1983].)

In particular, there is a danger of a gross underestimation of *women's* needs due to (a) an underestimation, in most available statistics, of women's work participation outside the home (see Agarwal [1985]), and a lack of adequate information on women's work in the home, and (b) the often misinformed classification of home-bound work as 'sedentary'. An additional dimension of underestimation in women's caloric requirements is introduced where the extra needs during pregnancy and lactation are ignored.

Keeping these problems in mind, let us examine some of the existing studies. Estimates on the relative male – female food intake to requirement that relate specifically to the Indian context are extremely few. However, those that do exist provide interesting pointers. Also, some carefully done studies from other parts of South Asia can be taken as indicative on grounds of close cultural/ geographic proximity.

Gulati [1978] in her study of an agricultural labour household in Kerala compares the daily caloric intake of the household head and of his wife (both of whom are engaged in agricultural wage work) with ICMR recommendations. She notes that on days when both the man and the woman are employed, the woman's shortfall *vis-à-vis* recommendations is 20 per cent and the man's 11 per cent; when both are unemployed the relative short-falls are 50 per cent and 26 per cent respectively. Gulati's observations of food intake, as of other aspects of the household, are based on her intensive interaction with the family over an extended period, but she does not spell out her method of measuring the respective female and male intakes. Another India-based study which focuses on this issue is Batliwala's [1983]. Her data relate to 560 households in six villages of Karnataka, and were gathered by observers living in the villages in question. Batliwala compares caloric intake with a measure of requirements based on basal metabolic rate (BMR) needs and activity levels, for male and female household members. She finds that while the women have a shortfall of 100 calories per day, the men have a surplus of 800 calories per day. Batliwala's relative food intake data are based on the village women's answers on how they distribute the staple diet of *ragi* among family members.[3] Another study in Western Uttar Pradesh notes that both the protein and caloric intakes of females are far below those of males among all socio-economic groups [*Mathur et al.*, 1961]. All these studies in the Indian context can of course be taken only as indicative since none is based on systematically measured food intake levels.

However, one of the more careful studies to emerge from South Asia is that by Chen *et al.* [1981] relating to Bangladesh, which can be taken as indicative at least for parts of India in geographic and cultural proximity to Bangladesh. The data, collected in Matlab Thana, include information on nutrition, morbidity and health service utilisation. The nutrition data were of two types: those relating to the level of malnourishment among a sample of 882 children, and those obtained by a dietary survey of 130 families in four villages. The latter incorporated a meticulous 24-hour measurement of household and individual food intake, twice a month, over three months.[4] Here I will discuss only the results of the dietary survey.[5]

Chen *et al.* found that per capita food intake by males consistently exceeded that by females in every age group, the average for all ages being 1,927 for males and 1,599 for females (Table 1). Disaggregated by age groups, the excess of male consumption over female is the highest (61 per cent) in the group 45 + and second highest (29 per cent) in the group 15–44. The ratio of male to female protein intake closely follows that for calories. When Chen *et al.* adjusted the intakes by body weights and by the extra caloric needs of pregnancy and lactation for women, the sex differential (apparent in the unadjusted intake levels) disappeared in the age group 5–14 but remained in the other age groups, although to a lesser extent.

TABLE 1

DAILY INTAKE OF CALORIES AND PROTEIN BY AGE AND SEX IN
MATLAB, BANGLADESH, JUNE–AUGUST 1978

Age Group	Calories (Number)			Protein (grams)		
	Male	Female	Ratio M/F	Male	Female	Ratio M/F
0– 4	809	694	1.16	23.0	20.2	1.14
5–14	1,590	1,430	1.11	50.9	41.6	1.22
15–44	2,700	2,099	1.29	73.6	58.8	1.25
45 +	2,630	1,634	1.61	71.8	46.9	1.53
All ages	1,927	1,599	1.20	55.0	45.5	1.21

Source: Chen, Lincoln *et al.* [1981].

The reduction in differential stemmed essentially from the body weight adjustments, since males, on average, weigh more than females and are therefore assumed to have higher calorie needs. However, there is a danger of circular reasoning here in that if a person is underweight because of past undernourishment, the assumed calorie needs will also be low, in a sense justifying the maintenance of a person in a state of chronic underweight (see also Sen [1981]). Hence women who might be underweight because of a lower initial access to food will be 'measured' too as requiring less food.

Chen *et al.* also undertook a further adjustment by activity level using WHO/FAO guidelines on the needs of males and females for various work intensities, and data on the male/female labour force participation rates in Bangladesh. Not surprisingly, this adjustment brought male and female intake/requirement ratios close to parity. As the researchers themselves note [1981: 63]:

> The various activity adjustments are flawed because of their reliance on national statistics providing information on the percentage of the labour force involved in heavy agricultural work. The extra energy requirements of women cannot be estimated accurately because of definitional problems and inadequacies in the data.

Also, irrespective of what adjustments are made, in the 0–4 and 45+ age groups the intake/requirement ratio in the Chen *et al.* study continues to be lower for females than males. In the Indian context, detailed data on activities of men and women are extremely scarce. Among the few studies which provide time-allocation data by gender are those by Jain and Chand [1982] and Batliwala [1983]. A further lacuna is the inavailability of energy cost figures for each of the activities and especially for women's home-based work.

(ii) Malnourishment, morbidity and mortality: The noted difficulties in obtaining reliable food intake data and, further, in making accurate adjustments for 'requirements' make it necessary (and in some senses preferable) to consider the *ex-post* results of sex-specific dietary shortfalls and sex-differentials in health care, on the male/female incidence of malnutrition, morbidity and mortality.

Two of the recent and carefully done pieces of research on malnutrition among children in the Indian context are those by Sen and Sengupta [1983] in West Bengal, and the Narangwal action-research experiment in Punjab (see Taylor and Faruque [1983]). Sen and Sengupta on the basis of primary data from two villages find a systematic sex bias, manifest in the higher deprivation (in diet) of girls *vis-à-vis* boys. This is apparent both in the greater prevalence of undernourishment of various degrees among girls than boys (Table 2), and in the lower growth dynamics of girls relative to boys. A further disaggregation by landless and landed households indicates that, in general, girls from landed households are less undernourished than those from landless households in both villages. Sex-based differentials are found to exist among both classes of households (being sharper among the landless) in one village, and only among the landless in the other village. In other words, the study indicates that while sex differentials are not confined to the poor they are more closely associated with poverty.

Again, in the Narangwal study in ten villages of Ludhiana district, clinical responses of Punjabi children under age five in July 1970 revealed that 15 per cent of the males and 25 per cent of the females were malnourished (Table 2). Caste (and related class) was also noted to be a significant determinant of child nutrition, but a cross-classification by caste and sex was not given. Another Punjab-based study where an in-depth nutritional survey of children aged 2–24 months was conducted among two caste groups in 17 villages, sex was found to be the most significant determinant of nutritional status. Also female infants were breastfed for a shorter time and given less supplementary milk and solid food [*Levinson*, 1974].

Further, as Sen [1981] notes, the extent of discrimination against female children sharpens in times of economic distress: for instance a UNICEF nutrition survey carried out after the 1978 floods in rural Bengal, revealed that the incidence of malnutrition was much higher for girls than boys, in each year of age from one to six.

The more severe the nutritional deficiency the greater the susceptibility of the child to infection. Hence we would expect a much higher incidence of illness

Women, Poverty and Agricultural Growth in India   171

TABLE 2
PERCENTAGE OF UNDERNOURISHMENT OF CHILDREN
BELOW THE AGE OF FIVE BY SEX

	West Bengal				
	Degree of malnourishment*				
	Below I	Below II	Below III	Below IV	Undernourishment Index
Sahajahanpur boys	94	71	39	6	53
Sahajahanpur girls	92	73	44	9	55
Kuchli boys	79	52	19	7	39
Kuchli girls	90	75	48	8	55
	Punjab			
	Marasmus	Undernourished	Sub-total	Normal
Boys (1108)	1.7	13.4	15.1	84.9
Girls (924)	2.5	22.7	25.2	74.8

Sources: West Bengal: Sen and Sengupta [1983: 856];
      Punjab: Taylor and Faruque [1983: 150].

Notes: *Below I = slightly undernourished
      Below II = moderately undernourished
      Below III = severely undernourished
      Below IV = disastrously undernourished
      Figures in brackets give the sample size.

among female children. Several studies on morbidity and health care indicate that women and female children are worse off than men and male children. For instance, Dandekar's [1975] health survey of six rural communities in the then Bombay State (present-day Maharashtra and Gujarat) in 1957 revealed that among children below 15 years of age, a much higher percentage of girls than boys was ailing, but a much lower percentage of girls than boys received medical treatment. Among adults too, significant sex-based differences were noted in the extent and type of treatment received: a greater percentage of women than men received no treatment, and among those treated, reliance on domestic traditional medicines or on *Mantriks* (witch doctors) was much more for women than men. Men also received more expensive medical treatment.

Similarly, Chakraborty et al.'s [1978] survey in Singur (West Bengal) revealed 25 per cent females relative to 22 per cent males (not separated by adults and children) in a state of ill health. The percentages were found more or less equal (around 11 per cent) in a prior survey of the region in 1957. In the Narangwal experiment in rural Punjab, 48 per cent of female children relative to 64 per cent male children received care in the first 24 hours of their terminal illness. Again, in a recent study by Khan et al. [1983] among 20 families which were watched for a year in rural Uttar Pradesh, there were 207 incidences of sickness among women relative to 192 among men; and 32 of the women relative to only 27 of the men had suffered from some disease or other for over 15 days. It was also noted that women often tend to hide their sickness in order not to disrupt household work, to save on medical expenses, or out of shyness. Hence even the noted high female morbidity is likely to be an underestimate. Some of the doctors who were interviewed mentioned that women's ailments usually tend to be ignored in the initial stages and medical attention is made available only when the disease becomes serious or chronic [*Khan et al.*, 1983]. This last observation is corroborated by Chatterjee [1983] in her survey article on women's access to health care. Miller [1981] also refers to several studies which point to discrimination against females in the medical care they receive.

Hospital admissions data are again revealing, and several studies based on information from city hospitals in different parts of the country note lower rates of admission for females than males [e.g., *Kynch and Sen*, 1983; *Miller*, 1981; *Ghosh*, 1985]. Ghosh also observes that the incidence of severe malnutrition is much higher among female than male children attending hospitals. While the hospitals studied are urban based, some proportion of the patients would come from the rural areas. The data presented in the studies mentioned do not give the background of the patients (rural or urban) but one would expect higher male/female differentials in admissions among the rural patients as the costs of bringing a child to hospital are greater. Miller's analysis also brings out regional differences in hospital admissions. She finds that while in the northern states there is a heavy weightage in favour of boys − two boys admitted to one girl; in the South although boys are still favoured, the weightage is less, namely, 1.2 boys to 1 girl.

It is the mortality-related figures, however, which highlight sex differentials most strikingly. First, despite the biological advantage that women are known to have over men, apparent in women's higher expectation of life at birth in most parts of the world, Indian women today have a lower life expectancy than Indian men, and (as seen from Table 3) since the decade 1921−30, the *difference* between male and female life expectancy has been *increasing* consistently. Prior to 1921 on the other hand, female life expectancy was higher than male. Second, there is the much-mentioned low and *declining* (since 1901) sex ratio (females per 1000 males). This suggests that although in *absolute* terms both women and men are better off since the turn of the century, in that they both now live longer on average, in *relative* terms women are in fact worse off. A glance at the 1981 census also reveals that the north-western states have the most adverse sex ratios and the southern states have the least adverse (Table 4). Third, information on death rates in rural India for 1978−80 indicates that for all ages taken together the rates are higher for females than males. An age-specific breakdown further shows that the rates for females exceed those for males up to the age of 34 and are lower in subsequent age groups [*Kynch and Sen*, 1983].

There are however noteworthy state-wise differences. Gordon *et al.* [1965], for instance, provide information on death rates and their causes, by sex and age, based on a detailed survey of 11 villages carried out over an extended

Women, Poverty and Agricultural Growth in India   173

TABLE 3

EXPECTATION OF LIFE AT BIRTH BY SEX FOR ALL INDIA
(1881–90 to 1961–70)

Decade	Life Expectancy at birth (years)		
	Males	*Females*	*difference**
1881–1890	24.6	25.5	0.9
1891–1900	23.6	24.0	0.4
1901–1910	22.6	23.3	0.7
1911–1920	19.4	20.9	1.5
1921–1930	26.9	26.6	– 0.3
1931–1940	32.1	31.4	– 0.7
1941–1950	32.5	31.7	– 0.8
1951–1960	41.9	40.6	– 1.3
1961–1970	46.4	44.7	– 1.7

Source: Jain [1982: 137].

Note: * Female life expectancy minus male life expectancy.

TABLE 4

SEX RATIO (FEMALES PER 1000 MALES): INDIA

All India		State-wise	
Year	*Sex Ratio*	*State*	*Sex Ratio (1981)*
1901	972	Kerala	1032
1911	964	Orissa	981
1921	955	Tamil Nadu	977
1931	950	Andhra Pradesh	975
1941	945	Karnataka	963
1951	946	Bihar	946
1961	941	Gujarat	942
1971	930	Madhya Pradesh	941
1981	933	Maharashtra	937
		Rajasthan	919
		West Bengal	911
		Assam	901
		Jammu & Kashmir	892
		Uttar Pradesh	885
		Punjab	879
		Haryana	870

Source: Census of India [1981a: 4, 5], Series I, paper 2 of 1983.

period, 1957–59. In its extent of detail this is a rare study. They found that death rates were higher for females than males in every age group except for those over 65. A disaggregation by cause of death further revealed that the rates were higher for females than males in the case of almost all cases. In particular, deaths due to diarrhoeal diseases which were a major cause of death among very young children, were twice as frequent among girls as boys. The earlier-mentioned Narangwal study relating to Punjab also noted a higher mortality among girls than boys of 0–3 years of age.

Again, an examination of child mortality in rural India by states, in 1978, reveals a high male–female differential. In nine out of the 15 states listed in Table 5, the ratio of female to male mortality rates in the 0–4 age group is greater than one. Most of the high differential states are in the northern and western belt, the ratio being close to or less than one in the southern and eastern region. This regional pattern, suggested in Table 5, is in fact very strikingly highlighted by Miller's [1981] analysis in which she brings together a large amount of anthropological and ethnographic evidence from across India to

TABLE 5

CHILD MORTALITY BY STATE AND SEX IN 1978
(0–4 YEARS; RURAL)

Region/State	Deaths per 1000 population		
	Female	Male	Ratio F/M
North-Western			
Haryana	39.6	31.0	1.28
Punjab	42.2	35.6	1.18
Rajasthan	66.9	55.3	1.21
Uttar Pradesh	80.4	57.0	1.41
Western			
Gujarat	47.5	38.4	1.24
Maharashtra	24.4	25.4	0.96
Central			
Madhya Pradesh	60.9	52.3	1.16
Eastern			
Bihar	34.6	34.8	0.99
Orissa	44.6	43.3	1.03
West Bengal	25.6	25.6	1.00
Southern			
Andhra Pradesh	38.1	43.6	0.87
Karnataka	28.7	30.1	0.95
Kerela	13.6	12.6	1.08
Tamil Nadu	45.8	42.5	1.08
All India	54.3	54.0	1.01

Source: Government of India [1981a].

bear on the issue of sex differentials in child care (feeding, medical attention, etc.) and mortality. The overall pattern noted is of much greater discrimination of all types against females in the northern states relative to the southern. Of particular interest is her mapping of the rural juvenile sex ratios (that is, of children under ten) by district, using the 1961 census data. This reveals a distinct pattern of deficit of females relative to males in the North, especially the North-West, while the southern states show sex ratios which are either favourable to females or less unfavourable than in the north. That this regional pattern in the juvenile sex ratio (JSR) is related to differences in juvenile mortality is supported by studies from north and south India which Miller quotes: two Punjab-based studies show female mortality rates among children and infants to be almost twice as high as for males; while in the southern study for Kerala the rates are only slightly higher for females.

(iii) Why are females discriminated against? Clearly, underlying the geographic differences in the extent of discrimination against females are a variety of historical, cultural and economic factors. Historically, for instance, female infanticide is noted to have been practiced widely in the northern and western (Gujarat upwards) belt, especially the states of Rajasthan, Uttar Pradesh, Punjab and Haryana, with very few and scattered instances being noted elsewhere. Records from British India in the nineteenth century (quoted in Miller [1981]) indicate that in some villages and tribes in the north-west not a single female child was to be found. The practice was noted to be most common among the upper castes (whom Miller also terms 'the propertied').[6] The explanations commonly given for its existence are hypergamy and heavy dowry expenditures. A more recent explanation for the practice in relation to the *Kanbi Patidars* of Gujarat is that by reducing their numbers the practice helped the group consolidate its hold on land and prevented excessive land fragmentation [e.g., *Clark*, 1983]. However, the issue needs much more probing, and questions such as why was the practice essentially concentrated in the northern and western parts of the country and what were its underlying material causes, have yet to be answered satisfactorily.

Among cultural factors an important one would be marriage patterns. In the South, marriages are often between close relatives, especially cross-cousins, and within or close to the natal village; this facilitates social contact and reciprocity between the bride's and groom's families. In the North, and especially the North-West, women are more commonly married to total strangers at much greater distances from their parental homes. In many communities in the North-West, there are also strict social taboos against parents accepting even a meal in the homes of their married daughters; hence most parents can expect no material support from their daughters after marriage. This would impinge on the relative care that male and female children receive.

What are of particular interest here, however, are the economic factors and the interlinks between the economic and the cultural. An aspect explored in different ways in several studies is the earning capacity of females which would affect the economic value placed on women and female children in the house-hold [e.g., *Bardhan*, 1984; *Rosenzweig and Schultz*, 1982; *Miller*, 1981]. It is worth considering this issue in some detail.

Bardhan hypothesises that the differential survival chances of the female child would relate to the expected employment or earning opportunities of female adults, and these in turn are hypothesised to relate to ecological variations in cropping patterns. The North–South difference in discrimination against females is thus seen by him to relate to the greater demand for female labour generated under rice cultivation which characterises much of south and east India, relative to primarily wheat cultivation whcih characterises the North. He also draws support for this hypothesis from Rosenzweig and Schultz's [1982] study. In a two-state regression analysis based on an all-India sample of 1331 rural households in 1971, these authors note, in the first stage, a positive correlation between normal district-level rainfall (and hence presumably with wet-rice cultivation) and the probability of women being employed, and in the second stage a negative correlation between female employment rates (given male employment rates) and male/female survival differentials.

However, Bardhan's rice/wheat dichotomy in explaining differences in female employment is problematic, in that while female labour force partici-pation rates (female workers to total female population) are generally lower in the traditionally wheat-growing belt of the North-West (especially in Punjab-Haryana) relative to the rice-growing southern states, there are also consider-able variations between the rice regions in the extent of involvement of women in agricultural production. For instance, female labour participation (FLP) in the eastern states is lower than in the southern states and close to that in the wheat-growing northern. Women's relative labour contribution in agri-cultural field work also varies regionally: while in large parts of the southern states, as in Tamil Nadu and Andhra Pradesh, women are found to contribute half or over half of total labour time in rice cultivation [*Agarwal*, 1984] in many eastern states it is men who make the primary labour contribution in rice cultivation (see Agarwal [1984], for Orissa, and Miller for West Bengal). Also as Miller notes from her mapping of district-level FLP* (defined by her as female workers in the age group 15–34 to total female population in that age group) on the basis of the 1961 census data, a large set of low FLP* districts include both wheat and rice regions. Further, areas of millet-growing such as the northern hilly tracts are noted by her to have high FLP* rates.

However, whether or not closely related to paddy cultivation, women's participation in economic activity does appear to be related to differentials in male and female survival, as found in Rosenzweig and Schultz's study (already noted) and suggested by Miller's analysis (discussed below).

Miller finds a high correlation between JSR and FLP*: districts where FLP* is high are also those where the JSR is less unfavourable to female children, although where FLP* is low the JSR is not necessarily more adverse to females. (For example, in states such as West Bengal, Assam, Orissa and Kerala where she finds JSR are less unfavourable to females than in the North-West, FLP* rates are noted to be almost as low as in the North-West.) Again when Miller looks at *disparities* in male/female participation rates and JSR, she notes that where disparities in participation are low the JSR is never unfavourable to females, but where disparities are high the JSR is not necessarily more adverse. In other words higher FLP* and lower disparities in male/female participation are associated with less unfavourable female to male survival chances but not in a one-to-one relationship.

Also related to the issue of the economic valuation of women and female children is the question of marriage costs, especially as reflected in the custom of dowry. Miller's survey of ethnographic studies relating to different parts of rural India reveals some interesting patterns. Among the propertied, dowry marriages are noted to predominate in both north and south India, but in the North they imply asymmetrical payments and expenditures, with much of the 'giving' being done by the bride's kin and much of the 'receiving' by the groom's kin; in the South dowry weddings are characterised by much greater reciprocity in the exchange of gifts and a greater equality in expenditures. The practice of cross-cousin marriages is also more prevalent in the South, which encourages reciprocity. Among the unpropertied, a combination of dowry and bridewealth predominate in the North, while in the South bridewealth is the typical practice and dowry the exception. In general, the North is characterised by much greater differences in male/female marriage costs than the South. And dowry-related high marriage costs for girls, as noted, was one of the factors observed to be associated with the practice of female infanticide historically.

Miller also notes some correspondence (although not one-to-one) between marriage costs and JSRs − high marriage costs being associated with highly adverse JSRs and low marriage costs with less adverse JSRs. It is noteworthy too that in regions and groups where Miller finds a greater prevalence of dowry and comparatively high female marriage costs, she also finds low FLP* and vice versa: in this the correspondence is very close.

The patterns that emerge from Miller's analysis are summarised in the table below:

Categories	FLP*	Marriage costs	JSR[+]
Northern Propertied	low	high	low
Southern Propertied	low-medium-high	low-medium-high	high
Northern unpropertied	high	low	medium
Southern unpropertied	high	low	high-medium

Note: [+] Miller defines sex ratios as males per 1,000 females; in the above chart, however, the sex ratio refers to females per 1,000 males in accordance with the definition used in India.

Miller while noting these associations does not examine the factors that may underlie dowry itself. Bardhan [1984] argues that dowry is in some sense a compensation for a low female participation in the labour force.[7] This would provide a part of the explanation but other explanations are also needed since (among other things) from the patterns observed today (especially in the North-West) dowry is often given even when the women are employed. In fact a complex intermesh of factors is likely to underlie the practice, some relating to the historical antecedents of the practice such as its association wtih hypergamy; and others with contemporary changes such as the impact of agricultural modernisation on differentials in male/ female participation in the labour force and in earnings, rather than on female participation *per se*; the role of modern media in the spread of a consumer culture and upper class values; the association of dowry with social prestige and the emulation of this by the relatively less well-off,[8] etc. These are all aspects which clearly need greater exploration. Also needing attention and explanation are the factors which lead to regional variations, especially between north and south India, in the content of dowry (for example, the giving of land as dowry is not unknown in the South [*Gulati*, 1984] while almost never noted in the North); and in the degree of control that the woman can exercise over her dowry. The specific changes observed in dowry-giving patterns in recent years as associated with the process of agricultural modernisation will be discussed further on.

Let us now examine the question: is discrimination against females greater or less under conditions of poverty? From our reasoning so far we would expect such discrimination to be less in poor (unpropertied) households since in such households (a) female labour force participation tends to be higher [*Miller*, 1981; *Gaiha*, 1981], and (b) marriage costs are low or even negative [*Miller*]. Also, other reasons which are noted to be associated with a son-preference, such as the transmission of family property and name [*Millier*, 1981; *Wyon and Gordon*, 1971], or the need for sons to provide power by their presence in rivalries between families and between village factions [*Wyon and Gordon*, 1971], would be weak or non-existent among the poor.

The actual evidence on this is, however, contrary to expectation. To begin with, Miller's analysis as summarised in the earlier-given table does not indicate any clear association between property ownership and the degree to which the JSR is adverse to females, especially not in the southern region. Further, Rosenzweig and Schultz's household-level analysis, relating to all-India, shows that male/female differences in child survival rates (measured by the sex ratio below ten years of age) are higher among the landless (those owning no land) than the landed, holding the adult female employment rate constant (which, as noted, is negatively associated with male/female survival differentials).[9] Bardhan suggests that this may be because the *fatality* rate of female children among the propertied classes is less despite the likely *greater* relative *neglect* of female children among such classes. However, Sen and Sengupta's [1983] study for West Bengal, which gives a more direct measure of discrimination, shows (as noted earlier) that even in terms of the *nutritional* status of children, the male/female difference is higher among the landless households relative to the landed households.

There can be several possible reasons why this pattern is different from the expected, such as those discussed below:

(a)   FLP *per se* is only a very crude indicator of women's likely economic contribution. It basically implies that women are working but not to what extent or intensity (in terms of days, etc.). The actual economic worth of working would depend on the *realised* economic contribution of women to the household income. Hence even if the women in poor households have a higher FLP, this, in itself, may not reduce discrimination if underemployment is high. Sen and Sengupta, unfortunately, do not indicate the extent of underemployment among women by class of household, but West Bengal does rank high in terms of 'current status' unemployment of women by the 32nd NSS round information (see Sen [1983]). Rosenzweig and Schultz's measure of expected female unemployment also does not take account of the intensity of work participation.

(b)   For a rise in *women's* employment to make an impact on the survival chances of *female children* (relative to male children) there would need to be a *sustained* increase in employment, such that the advantages are clearly perceivable and can affect behaviour and attitudes towards girls.

(c)   Neither FLP rates, nor the expected female employment measure used by Rosenzweig and Schultz, distinguish between on-farm and home-based economic activity, or between 'working' and 'earning'. In this context, it is significant to note that in both villages studied by Sen and Sengupta, boys are more involved in 'earning' activities while girls spend more time in 'collecting' (cow-dung, paddy after harvest, etc.), although the *total* time spent in both activities taken together does not differ much between girls and boys. Also, in the village where discrimination against girls is sharper, the differentials in girl/boy involvement in 'earning' is greater. In other words, the economic worth of females to the household is likely to be related not merely to whether or not they work in productive tasks but whether or not they *earn* (which would make their work more *economically* visible). The *physical visibility* of women's work, that is, whether field-based or home-based, could also be important in so far as this affects the social recognition accorded to it.

(d)   In households where both men and women are earning, the *differential* in their earnings is also likely to impinge on the relative valuation of males to females in the household.

Hence, while I would still argue that there would be a lesser tendency towards discrimination against females among the unpropertied, this tendency could get modified and even reversed in a situation where there is a high and sustained underemployment among women, where the productive work done is not visible, especially economically, or where male/female earnings differentials are high. This tendency would also vary in degree, inter-regionally, since the ideology justifying female neglect would to some extent tend to permeate all classes in the region, as for instance in the north-western states. In either case, the argument for increasing the employment opportunities for women of the poorer households and of reducing differentials in male and female earnings remains strong.

(iv) Some additional dimensions of intra-household inequities in the burden of poverty: So far our primary focus has been on differentials in nutrition, morbidity and mortality between male and female household members. There are, however, several additional dimensions to the question of the intra-household distribution of poverty, such as those mentioned below:

(a)   The time devoted to work and rest by women and men.
       Issues relating to the *energy* expended by women and men in the tasks they undertake have already been discussed. However, the time dimension of work done has significance *in itself*, because it determines the period available for leisure activity of any kind. Existing time-allocation studies in India are few but those that exist indicate that rural women of poor households put in long hours of work, often longer than put in by men when domestic work, other home-based work and labour outside the home is counted [*Jain and Chand*, 1982; *Batliwala*, 1983; *Khan, et al.*, 1983]. Anecdotal evidence and personal observation from across the country also indicates that rural men, more often than rural women, have the leisure to smoke a cigarette, drink liquor or play cards, while women usually do not. In any case, women in such households can rarely enjoy 'leisure' in any real sense because of their almost sole responsibility for childcare. Hence they are constantly surrounded by young children demanding attention, even in the moments when they are not engaged in specific tasks.

(b)   The nature of women's domestic work, particularly their specific responsibility for collecting fuel, fodder and water under conditions of increasing deforestation and ecological deterioration.
       In most rural households in India, the bulk of the energy consumed, especially in the domestic sector, comes from firewood. In poor households this fuel is typically gathered by women and female children mainly from forest land or village common land. In recent years with depleting forests many of these households are facing a fuelwood crisis,[10] the burden of which has fallen mainly on the women.
       For instance, there has been a substantial increase in the time and energy spent by them to gather firewood. In parts of Bihar where seven to eight years ago women of poor rural households could get wood for self-consumption or sale within a distance of one-and-a-half to two kilometres they now have to trek eight to ten kilometres every day [*Bhaduri and Surin*, 1980]. In some villages of Gujarat, women, even

after spending several hours searching, can no longer get enough for their needs and have to depend increasingly on the roots of trees and on weeds and shrubs; these do not provide continuous heat, thus also increasing women's cooking time [*Nagbrahman and Shreekant*, 1983].

Where adequate fuel is not obtainable despite the extra time and effort spent there can be changes in consumption patterns. While information on this is not available for India, evidence from other Third World countries provides significant pointers. In Bangladesh, for instance, poor families in some areas have had to decrease the number of meals cooked per day [*Briscoe*, 1979]. In parts of Africa, families have had to shift from two to one cooked meal a day, or to eat food raw or half-cooked with the danger of it being toxic [*Hoskins*, 1979]. A trade-off between the time spent in gathering fuel and that spent in cooking is also noted to adversely affect the nutritional quality of meals as in the context of Peru (see Skar [1982]). As one observer put it: 'None of the principal foodcrops in the tropics is palatable unless it is cooked first. Lack of fuel can be as much a cause of malnutrition as a lack of food' [*Poulsen*, 1978: 13]. While the adverse nutritional effects would impinge on the whole household, women bear an additional burden because of the noted biases in the distribution of food in the family. Also the extra energy expended by them to collect the fuel is unlikely to be made up in most cases by the required consumption of food.

Further, for an estimated two to three million poor rural people, most of whom are women, the sale of firewood to the urban areas is the main source of livelihood − the availability of which has been affected adversely by deforestation as has the availability of minor forest produce [*Agarwal and Deshingkar*, 1983]. Additionally, deforestation has been noted to lower the water-table, compounding the difficulties that women face in obtaining water for domestic use, especially during the dry season. In the hills of Uttar Pradesh, in fact, a woman grassroots activist has noted several cases during the past three years of young women committing suicide because of the growing hardship of their lives with ecological deterioration: in one year seven such cases were observed − four in a single village where shortages were especially acute [*Bahuguna*, 1984].

(c)   The nature of women's work in agriculture which exposes them to particular health hazards.

In several states, especially in south India, rice transplanting is done primarily by women. This increases their susceptibility to a number of ailments such as intestinal and parasitic infections, arthritis, rheumatic joints, leech bites, etc. [*Mencher and Saradamoni*, 1982]. A UNDP [1980] report further notes that there is observed to be an association between gynaecological infections and working in rice fields, among rural women in Asia.

(d)   Women's unequal access to and control over cash and its implications
       for female consumption.

       In male-headed households, women often have little control over cash
income, even when they are significant earners. For example, in a study
of three Indian states, Chakravarty and Tiwari [1977] note that wages
for agricultural work, even when paid to the women are usually taken
over and controlled by the household men. However, other studies
indicate that where the women have some control over the money they
earn, they usually spend the bulk of it on the family's basic needs,
especially food, while the men are often observed (even in very poor
families) to spend a fair amount of what they earn on their specific needs
such as liquor, cigarettes, etc. [*Mencher and Saradamoni*, 1982; *Gulati*,
1978]. Hence the issue of control over household income can be a crucial
factor affecting the nutritional levels of women and children.

       Here Gulati's [1978] and Kumar's [1978] findings are noteworthy.
Gulati found that the children's nutritional shortfalls in an agricultural
labour household were much more directly related to whether or not the
mother was employed, than to the father's employment; daughters, in
particular, were left much worse off than the sons on the mother's non-
working days. Likewise, Kumar in his study of a sample of low income
households (where both men and women were in the labour force) in
Trivandrum district, Kerala, noted a much stronger positive relationship between the children's nutritional levels and the mother's wages than
the father's wages.

       It is relevant to note here that the effect of the mother's employment
on the children's health and nutritional status would be the net result
of two opposite effects: a positive income effect because a better diet
is possible, and a negative time effect as less attention and child care
is possible. This conflict is especially important in poor households where
alternative child care possibilities are few and is highlighted in Kumar's
[1978] analysis: Kumar finds though that the *net* effect of the mother's
employment on the children's nutrition is positive.

(e)   The seasonal variation in poverty.

       That the incidence of poverty fluctuates by agricultural seasons has
been noted in several studies [e.g., *Chambers, et al.*, 1981]. It is during
the lean season that the family is also most vulnerable to becoming
indebted and bonded. In a sense this would affect the household as a
whole. However, it would tend to affect women more than men because
women's employment is much more seasonal in nature, due to the
relatively greater task-specificity of women's work (female labour tends
to be concentrated in specific operations, for example, transplanting,
weeding and harvesting and to some extent in threshing) while male
labour is much more evenly spread across operations [Table 6; and
Harriss, 1977a]. This would mean that female agricultural labourers
would have access to wage income only in certain times of the year;

Women, Poverty and Agricultural Growth in India 183

TABLE 6

PERCENTAGE USE OF FEMALE LABOUR AND TOTAL MALE LABOUR*
BY OPERATIONS

Operation	Andhra Pradesh				Tamil Nadu			
	Female Labour			Male Labour	Female Labour			Male Labour
	Family	Casual	Total	Total	Family	Casual	Total+	Total+
Ploughing*	1.3	1.2	1.2	15.0	0.1	0.0	n	30.6
Sowing/ Transplanting	19.6	31.2	30.7	12.3	9.9	19.2	18.4	6.1
Manuring	9.8	0.4	0.8	8.8	4.3	2.3	2.4	4.4
Interculture***	33.4	30.8	31.0	10.4	42.9	38.7	39.1	8.4
Irrigation	0.8	n	0.1	11.9	3.5	n	0.3	14.4
Plant Protection	0.3	n	n	1.3	0.0	n	n	0.5
Harvesting	15.9	28.3	27.7	14.7	18.1	32.7	31.5	20.9
Threshing	17.0	7.9	8.3	23.3	21.0	6.8	8.0	14.0
Miscellaneous	1.9	0.1	0.2	2.3	0.1	0.3	0.3	0.6
All Operations	100.0	100.0	100.0	100.0	100.0	100.0	·100.0	100.0

Notes: * For details of the operation-wise use of male labour by type see Agarwal [1981].

   + Does not include exchange labour

   n = negligible

   ** 'ploughing' also includes other subsidiary functions associated with seed-bed preparation.

   *** mainly weeding.

and during the slack period they would be exposed much more to the risk of undernourishment and starvation, than men. This is especially likely given both the noted positive association of women's access to independent income with the family's expenditure on basic needs such as food, and the reduced possibility of food-at-work (since part of the wages are often in kind). The seasonal dimension of work also has adverse implications for pregnant and lactating women workers who have been noted to lose weight during peak seasons, and for infants who are often weaned during the busy periods [*Palmer*, 1981].

(f)   Sexual exploitation stemming from poverty.

Among bonded labour households it has been noted that women often have to provide sexual favours to the landlord/creditor to whom the household is indebted (see, for example, Devi and Ghosh [1981]). In fact in one study [*Gupta*, 1985] relating to the Jaunsar Bawar region of Uttar Pradesh, women from bonded labour households are routinely sent into prostitution to repay the debts incurred by the husbands, typically for subsistence. The brothel owner pays the husband an advance which the latter uses for debt repayment, while the wife puts in several years as a prostitute. Historically, a polynyandrous form of family (two or more brothers married to two or more wives) has emerged among the labouring households in the region, and at times all but one wife are sent to the brothel, sometimes immediately after marriage.

In the mass of information on rural indebtedness, and even on bondage, the aspect of women's sexual exploitation is seldom mentioned; and the gender dimension of questions such as who controls the money borrowed, in whose interests is it spent, by whom and in what form is it repaid, requires much greater attention than it has received to date.

(g)   The caste dimension.

The considerable overlap of low caste position and poverty affects women in particular ways. Untouchability, as manifest in separate drinking water wells for the lowest castes, burdens especially the women if their (often sole) well dries up during a drought and water has to be fetched from long distances; rape is frequently used as a weapon by upper caste landlords to stem militancy among low caste tenants and agricultural labourers (for recent incidents see Kishwar and Vanita [1984]).

(h)   Violence in the family.

There is today a fair amount of evidence indicating that liquor drinking and even alcoholism among men is widely prevalent in poor rural families. Further, the main brunt of men's violence, especially under the influence of alcohol, falls on their wives [see *Horowitz and Kishwar*, 1982; *Jain*, 1980; and *Mies*, 1983). Attempts by the village women to counter this problem by organising night patrols or in other ways have also been documented [*Jain*, 1980; and *Mies*, 1983].

(2) Female-headedness and Poverty

So far we have essentially emphasised discrimination against females as observed in male-headed households, which is likely to lead to a greater burden of poverty falling on the women and female children of such households (although the noted discrimination against female *children* need not be confined to male-headed households). A large number of households in India are, however, female-headed. By the 1971 census, 9.6 per cent of rural households were so classified — the head of the household being defined in the Indian census as basically a person on whom falls the chief responsibility for the economic maintenance of the household members.[11] Technically, this definition would cover both those households where a male adult may be totally absent (as may be the case with widowed, divorced, separated, or deserted women) and those where the male adult has migrated or is unable to provide for the family due to extended unemployment, physical disability, etc. (that is, *de facto* female-headed households: FHHs).[12] However, a range of biases in actual data collection is likely to lead to an underestimation of female-headedness in census data. In the section below we will first examine existing estimates of the incidence of female-headedness, including possible factors

Women, Poverty and Agricultural Growth in India   185

which would affect the accuracy of the estimates, and then consider whether FHHs (as identified in available data) are more poverty-prone than others.

(i) Incidence and trends: Attempts to estimate the incidence of female-headedness in India have been few. Visaria and Visaria [1983] provide figures from the 1971 census which, as noted, indicate that 9.6 per cent of all rural households in India are headed by women. The percentages vary a great deal between regions – the figures range from 5.9 per cent in Jammu and Kashmir to 21.3 per cent in Meghalaya and are generally higher in the southern states relative to the north-western (Table 7). An estimate of female-headedness is provided also by Dandekar and Unde [1964] for West Bengal, based on the 1951 census sample survey of 12 districts. They found that ten per cent of households (rural plus urban) were headed by women, 16 per cent of whom were married, seven per cent widowed and four per cent single. Also, the percentage of widows who were heads of households in the rural areas was as high as 26.5, while only 1.4 per cent of the married rural women and 0.3 per cent of the single rural women were household heads.

TABLE 7

PERCENTAGE OF FEMALE-HEADED HOUSEHOLDS IN RURAL INDIA BY STATES

State	1961	1971
Andhra Pradesh	13.34	12.45
Assam	6.69	5.97
Bihar	10.41	8.27
Gujarat	8.26	8.08
Haryana	n.a.	5.98
Himachal Pradesh	9.97	15.29
Jammu & Kashmir	7.66	5.86
Karnataka	13.71	13.13
Kerala	16.23	17.09
Madhya Pradesh	7.84	7.45
Maharashtra	11.46	11.17
Manipur	11.67	10.76
Meghalaya	n.a.	21.31
Nagaland	13.41	12.92
Orissa	9.37	9.29
Punjab	6.92	7.24
Rajasthan	5.98	6.33
Sikkim	6.21	10.72
Tamil Nadu	14.51	14.57
Tripura	5.15	6.39
Uttar Pradesh	7.88	7.21
West Bengal	8.14	7.76
All India	10.02	9.58

Source: Visaria and Visaria [1983].

Notes: (1) n.a. = not available
        (2) The table is based on census data.

It is noteworthy, too, that 40.2 per cent of rural female heads were found to be living alone while only 8.3 per cent of male rural heads were living alone.

Census data are, however, likely to underestimate the incidence of female-headedness because of biases in data collection. These biases would stem from a variety of factors such as the enumerators and respondents being typically male, the definitions used, and the instructions given to the enumerators. Buvinic and Youssef [1978] provide several examples (which although taken largely from Africa and Central America would not be atypical for India) to indicate that in countries where male supremacy is the norm, both the enumerators and the respondents are predisposed to identify a man rather than a woman as the household head. Sometimes the census instructions themselves are biased, as in the 1951 Indian census, where the instructions were as follows:

> The head of the household is a person on whom falls the chief responsibility for the maintenance of the household. *You need not, however, make any enquiry about this and you should treat as the head any person who is actually acknowledged as such* [*Census of India*, 1971: 636; emphasis mine].

In other censuses, too, the enumerators are noted to have been told (see Visaria and Visaria [1983]) not to 'make any elaborate enquiry' (1961 Census), or not to 'enter into any long argument' (1971 Census). With these instructions, existing cultural biases would readily ensure that any household with an adult male will tend to be classified as male-headed even if the prime economic responsibility for the household's survival might be the woman's. This is also likely where adult males have migrated out for extended periods or are disabled, or have been unemployed over long stretches. This may be one reason too why such a low percentage of those identified as female heads of households are found to be married women. It would also be one of the factors explaining why in Dandekar and Unde's study such a large proportion of female heads were found to be living alone (that is, without adult males). A woman living alone clearly has a greater likelihood of being classified as the head. However, even a 9.6 per cent incidence of female-headed households in 1971 gives us a substantial figure of over 7.5 million such households in rural India.

An additional question that arises of course is whether the incidence of female-headedness is increasing over time. Two types of factors may be expected to impinge on this: economic, such as job-induced, individual migration of men and women, and social, such as the break-up of marriages manifest in divorce and separation. With industrialisation and economic development, we may expect the incidence of female-headedness to increase as a result of both these types of factors.

The economic factor is perhaps obvious in that structural changes in the economy may be expected to be accompanied by rural—urban, inter-industry and inter-sectoral shifts in population, in terms of a movement of individuals and not necessarily of families. Also, we may expect that as capitalist relations develop in agriculture there would be a breakdown of traditional patron—client relationships between landowners and labouring families, thus reducing the chances of all members of wage labour households finding wage employment within the village, and leading to the separation of family members with job-search migration. Further, to the extent that economic growth is accompanied by the impoverishment of some sections of the rural population, and with over-all changes in village attitudes accompanying modernisation, we could expect there to be a greater reluctance on the part of male relatives (especially those now economically worse off) to support female dependants who have been widowed, divorced or separated, as noted in the context of Bangladesh.[13] Socially, again, with industrialisation, as labour moves into conditions of factory production and the possibilities of contact between men and women increase, or because of the noted individual job-search migration, we may expect a reduction in the duration of marriages and a greater incidence of marriage dissolution. These are, however, hypotheses which need testing.

Visaria's census-based figures for 1961 and 1971 do not show any noticeable inter-temporal change either for all-India or at the state-level. The only state where there is a noteworthy change – an increase – is Himachal Pradesh, probably due to male out-migration to cities. Micro-studies, however, do indicate an increase in the incidence of *de facto* female-headedness in certain regions as in the agricultural underdeveloped district of Ratnagiri in Maharashtra, from where men migrate to Bombay in search of industrial employment [*Desai*, 1982].

It would be worth researching what the nature of the relationship is between the incidence of female-headedness and factors such as the rate of agricultural growth, the level of industrialisation, the incidence of landlessness, and the levels of unemployment, etc., across districts or states.

(ii) The poverty-proneness of female-headed households: Let us now examine whether female-headed households are more prone to poverty. While this is a relatively unexplored area, a useful beginning is still provided by Visaria's [1980a] analysis of National Sample Survey (NSS) data for Gujarat and Maharashtra. He examines both the percentage of female-headed households (FHHs) among different decile groups ranked by per capita and total monthly household expenditure; and the mean per capita and total monthly expenditure of FHHs and male-headed households (MHHs). As regards the first exercise, he finds a distinct over-representation of women in the low total expenditure deciles in both rural Gujarat and rural Maharashtra. However, the average size of FHHs is considerably smaller than of MHHs, so that in terms of per capita expenditure women are underrepresented in the low expenditure deciles in rural Gujarat, while no distinct pattern is found for rural Maharashtra.

As regards the second exercise, Visaria notes that the mean total monthly expenditure of FHHs is less than half that of MHHs in both rural Maharashtra and rural Gujarat. The mean per capita monthly expenditure of FHHs relative to MHHs is also lower (90 per cent) in rural Maharashtra; but somewhat higher (107 per cent) in rural Gujarat (Table 8). In other words, these data suggest some linkages between poverty and female-headedness but not a very strong linkage.

TABLE 8

MONTHLY HOUSEHOLD AND PER CAPITA EXPENDITURE
BY SEX OF HOUSEHOLD HEAD (1972–73)

	Gujarat (Rural)	Maharashtra (Rural)
(1) *Monthly household expenditure (Rs)*	293.4	218.1
Male-headed households (MHHs)	302.0	230.7
Female-headed households (FHHs)	150.7	109.8
FHHs/MHHs (%)	49.9	47.6
(2) *Monthly per capita expenditure (Rs)*	50.4	41.0
Male-headed households	50.3	41.2
Female-headed households	54.0	37.5
FHHs/MHHs (%)	107.3	90.9
(3) *Average household size*	5.8	5.3
Male-headed households	6.0	5.6
Female-headed households	2.8	2.9
FHHs/MHHs (%)	46.4	52.3

Source: Visaria [1983].

Note: Data base is the *National Sample Survey*, 27th round, 1972–73.

However, a more in-depth analysis of FHHs in a recent paper by Visaria and Visaria [1983] provides stronger evidence. In addition to the NSS data for Gujarat and Maharashtra, they use the 1961 and 1971 census to identify some characteristics of FHHs and of female heads of households. From the census data, for example, some idea is gained of the occupational and other characteristics of female- and male-headed households as indicated below:

(a)   A classification of households by three occupational categories, namely, cultivation, household industry and 'other' indicates that the percentage of FHHs engaged in the former two occupations is much lower than of MHHs, in all states except Manipur. The category 'other' is likely to include both those female heads with no occupation and those working as wage labour (agricultural and non-agricultural).

(b)   Among cultivating households, the percentage of FHHs in a given land size class to total households in that size class, is much higher in the smallest holding size of less than one acre, and decreases consistently as the holding size increases, both at the all-India level and for most states.

(c)   Female heads of households are on average older than male heads.

The NSS data-based analysis by Visaria and Visaria corroborates the above observations and also provides additional information.[14] It is noted that a larger proportion of FHHs relative to MHHs either have no land or a nominal amount of land per capita and have a lower child-dependency ratio (that is, those 14 years or less of age to those in the 15–59 age group). Many FHHs

Women, Poverty and Agricultural Growth in India   189

have no children, and some six to seven per cent have no members in the working age bracket. Also, a significantly higher percentage of female heads of households relative to male heads:

  - are in the higher age groups, especially that of over 60;
  - depend on wage labour, as versus self-employment in non-agricultural activities;
  - report no participation or full participation in the labour force by current weekly status (due no doubt to the higher proportion among FHHs of elderly heads or of single member households);
  - report unemployment during the reference week, or report inability to find work on any day when they sought work or were available for work;
  - have a low education level and a high illiteracy rate.

Further, the study notes that female heads of households are usually the widowed, separated or divorced; 81.4 per cent of the sample for rural Gujarat, and 67.8 per cent for rural Maharashtra are so classified. (The likely reasons for this as relate to biases in identification of FHHs have already been noted.)

A multi-classificatory analysis was also undertaken by Visaria and Visaria for explaining differences in monthly per capita expenditure among FHHs. This indicated that in the rural Gujarat sample, the per capita land operated, the child-dependency ratio and the household size were the three most important explanatory factors (the first being related positively and the latter two negatively to per capita expenditure). In the rural Maharashtra sample, the usual occupation, usual industry, educational attainment and usual activity of the household head were the four most important explanatory variables, although the household size and per capita land operated were also significant.

The overall picture one therefore obtains is that FHHs relative to MHHs have poorer survival chances, given their lower control over land resources and their greater dependency on wage income, their higher rate of involuntary unemployment, and the lower levels of education and literacy of the household heads. Also, many female heads, as noted, are over the working age of 59. The smaller size of FHHs, while an advantage in that it makes for a larger per capita income, also implies a lower availability of household labour and overall less labour at the command of female household heads. This can negatively affect the ability of female heads to be successful in self-employment ventures. All those aspects when viewed in conjunction with the observation that a higher percentage of FHHs are in the lower income deciles, indicates that FHHs are more poverty-prone.

A study by Parthasarthy [1982] provides additional pointers on this count. This study, based on a household survey carried out in 1980 in a district in Andhra Pradesh notes that:

(a) A much larger percentage of FHHs relative to MHHs in the sample (90.6 per cent relative to 87.9 per cent) are below the poverty line (defined at Rs.700 per capita per year at 1980 prices). Also the percentage of FHHs in the bottom-most income group of less than Rs.175 (which the author terms 'the poorest of the poor') is higher than of MHHs. This holds for every caste group when the data are cross-classified by caste groups.

(b) A much larger percentage of households among the scheduled castes have female heads relative to other caste groups.

(c) Among households in the bottom-most decile, 57.5 per cent of FHHs are dependent on wage labour for a livelihood (47.7 per cent of them being dependent on agricultural wage labour), while only 36.0 per cent of all heads (male plus female) are so dependent (Table 9).

In other words, FHHs are seen to constitute a much more marginalised group even among 'the poorest of the poor'.

TABLE 9

FEMALE-HEADED HOUSEHOLDS BY OCCUPATIONAL GROUPS (percentages)

Occupational Group	*Poorest of the Poor**		Total house-holds in all income groups
	Female heads	All heads	
Agricultural Labour	47.7	31.3	29.8
Non-agricultural Labour	9.8	4.7	5.5
Marginal Farmers	15.5	24.8	16.1
Small Farmers	3.5	11.8	16.1
Large Farmers	–	1.4	12.7
Others	23.5	26.0	19.8
Total	100.0	100.0	100.0

Source: Parthasarthy [1982].

Notes: The data base is a sample survey in Vizag. district, Andhra Pradesh.

* Relates to households with a per capita monthly income of less than Rs.175/ – at 1980–81 prices.

As part of the survey, the household heads of the poorest groups were also asked what their preferences were in terms of development programmes. While the majority of both the FHHs and the MHHs showed a preference for dairy, a striking feature about the women's responses was the high percentage – 16.1 – that mentioned 'no need', while only 6.3 per cent of the male household heads so responded [*Parthasarathy*, 1982]. This may reflect a greater lack of confidence among female heads regarding the possibility of a development programme reaching them; or it may be related to the age of the female head: as Visaria's data suggest, a much larger percentage of FHHs than MHHs is over 60 years of age, and the 'no need' response may thus reflect an age-inability to handle an income-generating scheme.

All in all, both Visaria's and Parthasarathy's work points to the greater vulnerability to poverty of FHHs, although much more in-depth data from other micro-regions is necessary for a more definitive understanding.

Further, studies which examine in particular *de facto* FHHs as a result of male out-migration over extended periods, indicate that such migration greatly increases the women's work burden and compounds their difficulties of basic survival (see Desai [1982]; Krishna Raj and Ranadive's [1984] village survey in Thana district of Maharashtra; and Jetley's [1984] study in eastern Utter Pradesh). However, much more analytical and empirical work in this area needs to be done. It would be useful, for example, to examine questions such as: what is the relatively poverty-proneness of FHHs *by type* – for example, absence of male adult, short-term and long-term male migration, and resident male's incapacity to provide for the family? To what extent does the woman's role as main economic provider link with her role in the decision-making in the household? What are the socio-economic processes which lead to the increased incidence of FHHs? And so on.

II. RURAL POVERTY AND AGRICULTURAL GROWTH

We know from the previous section that the burden of poverty falls disproportionately on women and female children. The question which then arises is: are present patterns of agricultural growth and development likely to exacerbate or diminish this burden? The answer would relate partly to the changes in the *overall* incidence of rural poverty in the recent period and its association with agricultural production, which would affect women *and* men, and partly to the gender specificities of particular effects. In this section, I shall consider the former aspect and in the next section the latter.

(1) Time Trends in Rural Poverty

Recent debate on the question of poverty and agricultural growth has centred around the existence or otherwise of a time trend in absolute poverty and on whether growth in agricultural production has led to a decline in absolute poverty through the 'trickle down' effect, or to an increase, or to a neutral effect. Among the initial protagonists in this debate, two prominent ones have been Ahluwalia [1978] and Saith [1981].

Ahluwalia has computed the incidence of absolute poverty (using the headcount ratio and the Sen index) in rural India from National Sample Survey data for the period 1956–57 to 1973–74, reproduced in Table 10. From the table, three different directions of change in the incidence of rural poverty are discernible over this period. Between 1956–57 and 1960–61 there is a decline in poverty; between 1960–61 and 1967–68 there is an increase; and after 1967–68 there is again a decline. Ahluwalia fits a linear time trend to the entire series and finds no evidence of trend increase or decrease in absolute poverty at the all-India level. A time trend line fitted for each state, further

TABLE 10

THE INCIDENCE OF RURAL POVERTY IN INDIA

Year	Percentage of Rural Population in Poverty			Size of Population in Poverty (millions)	
	Estimate I	Estimate II	Sen's Poverty Index	Derived from Estimate I	Derived from Estimate II
1956–57	54.1	n.a.	0.23	181.0	n.a.
1957–58	50.2	53.4	0.22	171.0	182.0
1958–59	46.5	n.a.	0.19	162.0	n.a.
1959–60	44.4	48.7	0.17	158.0	173.0
1960–61	38.9	42.0	0.14	141.0	152.0
1961–62	39.4	42.3	0.14	146.0	157.0
1963–64	44.5	49.1	0.16	171.0	189.0
1964–65	46.8	50.4	0.17	184.0	198.0
1965–66	53.9	51.1	0.21	216.0	205.0
1966–67	56.6	57.4	0.24	231.0	235.0
1967–68	56.5	57.9	0.24	235.0	241.0
1968–69	51.0	53.5	0.20	217.0	227.0
1970–71	47.5	49.1	0.18	210.0	217.0
1973–74	46.1	47.6	0.17	214.0	221.0

Source: Ahluwalia [1978].

Notes: (1) The poverty line used here relates to a consumer expenditure level of Rs.15/– per person per month.

(2) Estimate I has been obtained by applying the all-India poverty line for various years to the NSS consumption distribution for rural India.

Estimate II is obtained as a weighted sum of the estimated percentages in poverty in individual states, obtained from the NSS distributions for individual states, and the state-specific poverty line.

(3) n.a. = not available.

indicates that in only three states out of 14 is there a discernible trend: in Assam and West Bengal there is an increase over time in the percentage of rural population in poverty and in Andhra Pradesh there is a decrease.

Ahluwalia's time trend results for all-India have been questioned by Saith [1981] essentially *vis-à-vis* the reference period used. Saith points out that if some of the earlier observations of Ahluwalia's series are dropped and the analysis done for 1960–61 to 1973–74 then there is a significant positive time trend in the incidence of rural poverty. Further, if the last observation is also dropped, the statistical significance of the equations improves considerably.[15]

Griffin and Ghose [1979] challenge Ahluwalia's state-level results again in terms of the time period used. Using a truncated NSS series, namely, 1960–61 to 1973–74, they find that of the 13 states studied, 12 have a positive time trend in poverty; in five of these the coefficients are statistically significant at the five per cent level. Andhra Pradesh is the only state for which there is noted to be a decline in poverty over time. The authors give no reasons for dropping the observations prior to 1960–61, although, as noted, Saith [1981] does do so. Mundle [1983] also uses the NSS data but for the period 1963–64 to 1973–74 (that is, the period beginning just before the new agricultural technology was introduced and extending over the main phase of its spread), and computes simple correlations to ascertain the time trends in poverty by states, and finds no statistical significance (at the ten per cent level) in 12 out of the 15 states considered.

Gaiha [1981] using all-India level panel data (that is, data relating to the same set of households) for 1968–69 and 1970–71, collected by the National Council for Applied Economic Research (NCAER), finds that over this period there has been a decrease in the head-count ratio and in the income-poverty gap (namely, the difference between the average income of the poor and the poverty line), but an increase in the gini coefficient of the poor. The Sen index of poverty (see Sen [1976]) which takes account of all three aspects, also shows a decrease. The noted decrease in the overall incidence of absolute poverty over the period 1968–69 and 1970–71 found by Gaiha is consistent with the decline noted in other studies from the NSS data.

Finally, studies undertaken for individual states, also based on the NSS data, indicate an increase in the percentage below the poverty line over 1960–61 and 1970–71 (e.g., see Rajaraman [1977] for Punjab; Nayyar [1977] for Uttar Pradesh and Bihar; Kurien [1977] for Tamil Nadu; and Bardhan [1981] for West Bengal).

Clearly the period over which the exercises are done makes a crucial difference to the results. In such a situation there need to be cogent reasons for choosing one period rather than another. Ahluwalia's choice of period is dependent essentially on the availability of the NSS consumer expenditure data. Saith's justifications for truncating the series are basically 'negative' ones such as the dropping of some of the 1950s observations because their accuracy is doubtful. While this may be a valid step to take, the choice of period also needs to be based on 'positive' reasons such as that of capturing the initial effects of the 'green revolution'. Further, given the observed change in direction in the incidence of poverty, first at 1960–61 and then at 1967–68, it would be worthwhile to explore why the directions changed as they did. As Kurien [1977] also notes, these two turning points are of special interest because they underline the effects of particular strategies of agricultural development and sources of agricultural growth.

In this context, for studying the effects of the new agricultural technology (high yielding variety (HYV) seeds, chemical fertilisers, mechanical equipment, etc.), it may be more appropriate to look at the series over 1967–68 to 1973–74 rather than 1963–64 to 1973–74 as Mundle has done, since the former period would help avoid the bias introduced by the two drought years (namely, 1965–66 and 1966–67) of poor agricultural performance. Also, it may be worth considering whether what is being captured in the data up to 1970–71 or even 1973–74 relates only to the early period of the 'green revolution'. If, as is being argued by some, the underlying time trend reflects a particular kind of growth process, then we may well find a change in the trend in more recent years. This argument would also apply to the question of the relationship between agricultural growth and rural poverty, to which I shall now turn.

(2) The Relationship Between Agricultural Growth and Poverty

Ahluwalia's analysis indicates that at the all-India level, for the entire NSS series (1956–57 to 1973–74), there is a significant negative relationship between the percentage of rural population below the poverty line and the index of agricultural production per head, there being no time trend. His state-wise analysis gives a more varied picture: here he finds a statistically significant negative relationship between rural poverty and agricultural growth in seven of the 14 states studied, and an insignificant relationship in the others. Giving an overall greater weightage to the all-India figures he concludes that the evidence indicates a 'trickle down' of benefits associated with agricultural growth.

Saith fits a regression equation, with the percentage of rural population below the poverty line as the dependent variable, and three independent variables: the percentage deviation of the Index of Agricultural Production (IAP) around its fitted trend value, the percentage deviation of the Consumer Price Index of Agricultural Labour (CPIAL) around its trend value, and the time trend (over the period 1960–61 and 1970–71). His results support Ahluwalia's in terms of a negative relationship between changes in agricultural production and the incidence of poverty. At the same time the price deviations are positively related to the incidence of poverty; and in explaining fluctuations in the level of poverty the price variable is found to be considerably more significant than the production variable. Also, the coefficient of the time trend variable is found to be significant and positive, after taking account of the price and production variables. Hence, in Saith's view the apparently beneficial effect of agricultural growth in terms of alleviating poverty, has been more than negated by the positive price changes and the underlying positive time trend.

Griffin and Ghose [1979] also test the relationship between the percentage change in absolute rural poverty and the trend rate of growth of (a) per capita agricultural output and (b) per capita foodgrain production, over their truncated reference period (from the average for 1960–64 to the average for 1970–74), and note that the relationships are essentially neutral. They thus find no evidence to support the 'trickle down' hypothesis. Mundle [1983] who, as noted, limits his period to 1963–64 to 1973–74 finds that the simple correlations between the incidence of poverty and per capita foodgrain production are statistically significant and negative in only six of the 15 states and insignificant in the others. He takes the view that the production performance of agriculture is not a decisive factor underlying trends in rural poverty though it may have an ameliorating effect on poverty.

However, Bardhan's [1981] state-level, cross-sectional analysis for West Bengal based on the NSS 32nd round data, indicates a significant *positive* relationship between the district-level rate of growth of agricultural production and the probability of both agricultural labour and culitvator households sliding below the poverty line.

Taking an overview of the studies reviewed, the broad picture that emerges is that agricultural growth has had no significant impact in *reducing* the incidence of absolute poverty in rural India. At best it may have helped, through its output-increasing effect, to stem further increases in poverty incidence in certain areas. And even this may not be a lasting effect in so far as the increases in agricultural production have been accompanied by other less favourable changes in the agrarian economy. Both Saith and Bardhan in fact emphasise this aspect. They contend that whether or not agricultural growth has a poverty-reducing effect depends on the nature of the growth process; and argue that the growth process in Indian agriculture has unleashed certain forces which have negated or are likely to negate the positive effects.

What would be these poverty-increasing effects of agricultural growth? Before turning to this question, we need to consider too: who are the poor? Has their composition been changing over time?

(3) Who are the Poor?

Several studies have sought to identify the characteristics of poor rural households, although most do not go beyond attempts to classify the poor by occupational groupings.

(i) Occupation: Taking first the studies relating to the early 1960s, there is a broad agreement that the majority of the rural poor in that period were constituted of agricultural labour and small cultivator households, though a good deal of conjecturing is involved in these studies, often due to data shortcomings (Minhas [1974], Dandekar and Rath [1971], Vaidyanathan [1974], and Bardhan [1981], provide all-India assessments; and Rajaraman [1977] and Kurien [1977] provide state-specific assessments). There is also a broad consensus that among the poor, the poorest were constituted primarily of agricultural labour households – the majority of which were landless (for example, see Dandekar and Rath [1971]; and Vaidyanathan [1974]). In terms of the farm size of the poor cultivator households, both Minhas, and Dandekar and Rath put it as less than five acres. There was some disagreement, however, as to whether a large percentage of the rural poor belong to the agricultural labour or the small cultivator category. By the estimates of Minhas, for example, about 54–57 per cent of the poor belonged to the small cultivator households and about 30.5 per cent to the agricultural labour households, while Bardhan assesses that the majority (52 per cent) of the poor households belonged to the latter category. Dandekar and Rath, and Vaidyanathan also give greater weight to agricultural labour households. In any case, these two occupational categories cannot be viewed as dichotomous, since they relate to the primary source of income, and a large number of small cultivator households also depend on agricultural wage labour as an important supplementary source of income.

Studies relating to the end-1960s and early 1970s again support the view that agricultural labour and small cultivator households continue to account for the bulk of the poor (see Bhatty [1974]; Gaiha [1981]; and Rajaraman [1977]). These derive their conclusions from a relatively stronger data base and all of them also agree that among the poor, agricultural labour households constitute the single most important category. Also, Bhatty [1974] finds that at the all-India level, whatever be the specification of the poverty line (he uses five different specifications), a larger proportion of the agricultural labour households are below the poverty line than either cultivator households or non-agricultural worker households. This is also largely true at the state-level.

Some of these studies record changes over time as well. Bardhan [1981] notes a small increase in the percentage of the agricultural labour households below the poverty line in rural India as a whole, from 52 in 1963–64 to 56 in 1977–78. Rajaraman, for Punjab alone, notes a much more dramatic shift, with agricultural labour and small cultivator households constituting 40.5 per cent and 31.4 per cent of the rural poor in 1970–71 relative to 22.6 per cent and 47.1 per cent respectively in 1960–61. Gaiha's [1981, 1984 and on-going] analysis, however, is the most detailed and even though limited in its time coverage and relating to the not-so-recent period, has the unique feature, as noted, of being based on panel data. He computes changes in the poverty status of the same set of households (also disaggregated by cultivator and daily wage labour categories) for 1968–69 and 1970–71, using two alternative cut-off points to define the poverty line. His estimates for the second cut-off point are given in Table 11. We note from the table that between 1968 and 1970, 12 per cent of all rural households in the sample which were not poor in the earlier year became poor by 1970; 22 per cent of those which were poor in 1968 remained at the same level of poverty, while another 12 per cent of those which were poor in 1968 became *poorer* still in 1970. Hence a significant percentage of the rural households were worse-off in 1970 than they were in 1968. An occupational disaggregation into daily wage labour and cultivator households indicates that the shift to greater poverty among those which were poor was much more among the former than the latter category. The observation that some of the poor became poorer is important *in itself* since it highlights that *whatever may be happening vis-à-vis the incidence of poverty at the aggregative level, a significant majority is getting further impoverished.*

At the aggregate level, in fact, Gaiha's own data shows that a certain percentage of those who were below the poverty line in 1968 also rose above it by 1970, so that the poverty incidence declined over the period, even while inequality among the poor increased. This movement of a substantial percentage of the rural households across the poverty line (from poor to not poor and vice versa), within a short span of three years, also indicates that divisions on either side of the line cannot be seen as representing entirely separate categories. The risk of poverty extends much above the poverty line, so that many of those who manage to stay above in a particular year

Women, Poverty and Agricultural Growth in India   197

TABLE 11

CHANGES IN POVERTY STATUS AMONG RURAL HOUSEHOLDS IN INDIA,
1968–69 to 1970–71

Nature of Change in Poverty Status over 1968–69 to 1970–71	Cultivating Households	Daily Wage Labour Households	Erstwhile Cultivating households	All Rural Households
(1) Poor who remained poor	17.06	30.98	31.31	22.50
(2) Poor who became poorer	6.01	22.66	11.86	12.25
(3) Not-poor who became poor	12.42	12.69	15.61	12.22
(4) Poor who became not-poor	24.57	19.59	16.06	24.73
(5) Not-poor who remained not-poor	39.94	14.08	25.16	28.30
All households	100.00	100.00	100.00	100.00

Source: Gaiha [1984].

Notes: (1) Cultivating households are those whose primary source of income derived from cultivation in 1968–69. Daily wage labour households are those whose primary source of income derived from wage labour (agricultural and non-agricultural) in 1968–69. Erstwhile cultivating households are those whose primary source of income was from cultivation in 1968–69 but ceased to be so in 1970–71. This is a subset of the cultivating households.

(2) The data source is the Additional Rural Incomes Survey (1968–70) carried out by the National Council of Applied Economic Research, New Delhi.

The total sample size is 4,118 rural households.

could fall below it in another. Gaiha [1981] also measures the probability of a household falling below the poverty line ('risk of poverty') and notes that the possibility is higher among households depending on wage income – especially agricultural – than among those which derive their income primarily from other work (Table 12).

(ii) Other characteristics: Studies that have examined characteristics other than occupation note that poor rural households tend to be larger in size than the not-poor [*Dandekar and Rath*, 1971; *Gaiha*, 1981], have a higher child-dependency burden (the ratio of children in the age group 0–14 to all household members: Gaiha, [1981]) and a higher overall dependency burden (ratio of non-earners to earners: Bardhan [1981]). Gaiha also finds that the level of illiteracy as well as the male and female labour force participation rates (defined as the number of earners to total adults) are higher among the poor households than among the not-poor. Despite their higher participation rates, the members of poor households do not necessarily find adequate work in terms of days of employment, and Visaria [1980b] notes a clear association between poverty and the person-days of unemployment, unemployment being much higher among those falling in the lower monthly per capita deciles. None of the studies discussed so far traces the gender characteristics of the poor, although Visaria [1980a], and Visaria and Visaria [1983], as noted in the last section, do go into this question with reference to female-headed households.

TABLE 12

RISK OF POVERTY AND DISTRIBUTION OF POOR HOUSEHOLDS
BY PRIMARY SOURCE OF INCOME

Primary Source of Income	Risk of Poverty*		Percent of all Poor Households	
	I	II	I	II
Agricultural and allied pursuits	46.56	47.81	38.09	35.88
Agricultural wages	72.50	77.73	42.72	41.98
Non-agricultural wages	41.91	73.39	4.06	6.48
Salaries and permanent wages	29.76	49.33	3.34	5.05
Business, craft and professions	61.31	59.55	9.59	8.53
Transfer income, pension, dividends etc.	46.06	47.18	2.20	2.08
			100.00	100.00

Source: Gaiha [1981].

Notes: * Risk of poverty refers to the share of poor households with a given characteristic in the total number of households possessing that characteristic.

Col. I refers to actual income and Col. II to actual expenditure. The poverty line has been defined as Rs.16 per month per person, at 1960–61 prices.

(iii) Regional aspects: As seen from Table 13, while the incidence of absolute poverty in rural India as a whole comes to 47.6 per cent in 1973–74, there is considerable variation across states. The highest incidence is found in the three eastern states of West Bengal, Bihar and Orissa and the lowest incidence in the north-western states of Punjab, Haryana and Rajasthan.

(4) Growth Processes

Let us now return to the issue of agricultural growth and poverty. As noted, both Bardhan and Saith have argued that while agricultural growth and an improvement in agricultural productivity may potentially have an income-raising and poverty-reducing effect, certain types of growth processes, in the context of pre-existing economic inequalities, may generate forces which over time have a negative effect on the poor. Both authors maintain that the new agricultural technology has unleashed precisely such forces. Gaiha [1983] in a recent paper argues along the same lines. Among the factors listed by Bardhan as likely to prevent the benefits of growth from reaching agricultural wage labourers, and possibly impoverishing them further, are those below:

(a) the adoption of labour-displacing machinery by the landed;
(b) the rise in administered prices of foodgrains (of which agricultural labourers are not buyers) due to an increase in the political bargaining power of the rich farmers (following the prosperity associated with the new agricultural strategy), with wages typically lagging behind prices.
(c) the heavy influx of labour from other occupational groups into the agricultural labour market (and the consequent depressing of wage

Women, Poverty and Agricultural Growth in India   199

TABLE 13

PERCENTAGE OF RURAL POPULATION IN POVERTY BY STATES
(1957–58 to 1973–74)

Region/State	1957–58	1959–60	1960–61	1961–62	1963–64	1964–65	1965–66	1966–67	1967–68	1968–69	1970–71	1973–74
North-Western												
Punjab & Haryana	28.0	24.2	18.8	22.3	29.4	26.5	26.5	29.5	33.9	24.0	23.6	23.0
Rajasthan	33.4	n.a.	32.3	33.0	32.6	31.8	30.8	37.1	35.9	41.4	41.8	29.8
Uttar Pradesh	52.3	36.7	37.9	35.4	56.6	53.7	47.1	55.2	60.2	46.4	40.6	47.3
Western												
Gujarat	n.a.	41.5	31.6	39.7	45.7	49.8	50.7	54.1	50.8	42.8	43.8	35.6
Maharashtra	n.a.	54.5	48.4	43.6	48.2	59.1	57.8	63.2	57.2	54.8	46.6	49.8
Central												
Madhya Pradesh	57.7	46.4	43.8	40.0	43.6	42.1	47.2	58.3	62.3	56.0	52.9	52.3
Eastern												
Bihar	59.7	55.7	41.5	49.9	52.3	54.3	59.4	74.4	70.9	59.4	59.0	58.4
Orissa	66.6	63.4	62.4	49.3	60.0	61.9	62.1	64.2	64.7	71.2	65.0	58.0
West Bengal	62.3	61.4	40.4	58.3	63.3	64.0	56.5	64.3	80.3	74.9	70.1	66.0
Southern												
Andhra Pradesh	53.5	48.8	50.1	47.2	45.6	41.5	45.4	47.9	46.0	47.3	41.0	39.8
Karnataka	41.3	48.9	39.1	35.4	50.5	55.1	63.9	59.5	56.9	58.8	47.2	46.9
Kerala	59.6	62.3	57.8	50.3	52.8	60.7	70.7	67.1	63.4	64.6	62.0	49.3
Tamil Nadu	67.8	64.4	53.9	51.0	52.0	57.4	59.5	62.7	58.1	60.6	57.3	48.3
All India	53.4	48.7	42.0	42.3	49.1	50.4	51.1	57.4	57.9	53.5	49.1	47.6

Source: Ahluwalia [1978].

Notes: (1) The data source is the National Sample Survey, various rounds.
(2) The states have been rearranged by me according to regions to facilitate comparisons with other state-level tables.

income) – the influx being due to factors other than natural increases in population, such as the eviction of small tenants by big landlords as self-cultivation becomes more profitable; increased need for purchased inputs and private irrigation, leading those small farmers who have limited access to credit and resources to seek supplementary income in agricultural labour markets; decreased productivity of traditional lift irrigation techniques as big farmers appropriate ground-water through tubewells and water tables fall, as well as the poor maintenance by big farmers of old irrigation channels – leading to small farmers being driven out of cultivation; and the displacement of village artisans who also join the agricultural labour markets, as demand patterns shift to mass-produced factory products.

Bardhan also includes growth-induced, in-migration of agricultural labour from the backward areas as a factor, but this would operate as an explanation only at the regional level and not at the all-India level. Factors listed under (b) and (c) above would also be applicable in explaining any increase in poverty among small cultivators.

Saith's [1981] stress is largely on the foodgrain price factor where, like Bardhan, he notes the significance of the large-farmer lobby in bringing about high increases in the administered prices of foodgrains, and the consequent effect on the real incomes of those who are net buyers of foodgrains.

Neither author provides adequate direct evidence on the variables listed. However, evidence on some of these aspects gleaned from other studies does provide pointers in support of the view extended by these authors. Several studies, for instance, point to tenant eviction both in the wheat areas [*Bhalla*, 1977] and the rice areas [*Bardhan and Rudra*, 1978] in recent years. The total land under tenancy is also noted to have declined at the all-India level from 20 per cent in 1953–54 to less than 11 per cent in 1970–71 [*Singh*, 1981], and the proportion of this tenanted land which is under cash-renting is noted to be increasing [*Dasgupta*, 1977]. In both senses, therefore, there appears to be a tightening of the land-lease market.

There is also evidence of an increase in the incidence of landlessness (in terms of those operating no land): Gaiha [1983], for instance, notes an increase from 25 per cent to 35 per cent between 1968 and 1970 among the same set of households, on the basis of the NCAER data. He also observes a significant decline in the share in total gross cropped area of the bottom 50 per cent of his sample households ranked on the basis of cropped acreage. He suggests that the favourable effects of the new agricultural technology operating through higher yields and new employment opportunities in the *initial years*, is likely to have weakened *over time* as a direct consequence of the increasing landlessness. Additionally, Gaiha's [1984 and on-going] analysis shows that, on average, among the rural cultivating households of his sample that were poor in 1968 and became poorer in 1970, the contribution of wage income to total income increased significantly. At the same time, in absolute terms their increase in wage income did not make up for the decline in income from cultivation, leading to an overall decline by 57 per cent in their average real income per capita.

The growing dependence of the rural population on the agricultural wage labour market is also indicated by the sharp increase in the numbers of agricultural labourers over 1964–65 and 1974–75 (noted in the Rural Labour Enquiry (RLE) Reports for these years) which cannot be attributed to population increase alone. Over the noted period the proportion of agricultural labour households to total rural labour households increased from 21.7 per cent to 25.3 per cent for rural India; and according to Bardhan's [1981] estimate from the NSS 32nd round data, this proportion had increased to 30 per cent by 1977–78.

In other words, the available evidence points to a growing dependence of rural households on agricultural wage income either as a sole source of income, or as a primary source or a supplementary source. We also know from Gaiha [1981] that households whose primary source of income is agricultural wage labour tend to have the highest risk of poverty. At the same time, the average number of days of employment from agricultural wage work for agricultural labourers (male and female) are noted to have declined at the all-India level over 1964–65 and 1974–75 by the RLE data [*Agarwal*, 1981]. Also Bardhan's [1981] computations of the annual wage income (from farm and non-farm work) of all the earning members (men, women and children) in an average agricultural labour household, by state, indicate that between 1964–65 and 1974–75 the income declined in all states (including the highest growth states of Punjab and Haryana) except Uttar Pradesh. The decline was 16 per cent for rural India as a whole (Table 14). It is noteworthy that the decline was especially high in some of the eastern States such as Orissa (44 per cent) and West Bengal (34 per cent).

The issue that we now need to consider is whether these growth processes have affected women and men differently.

III. WOMEN, RURAL POVERTY AND AGRICULTURAL GROWTH: INTER-
   RELATIONSHIPS

From the points raised in the previous two sections we can deduce that the *direct* impact of agricultural growth on female poverty is likely to depend crucially (although not exclusively) on what effect agricultural growth has on the access of rural women (especially those belonging to the most poverty-prone of rural households, namely, the agricultural labour households) to income-earning opportunities. This is apart from the *indirect* impact mediated through changes in the *household's* economic position as a whole. To reiterate, this is essentially because of the following factors:

   (a) In poor female-headed households, survival depends crucially on the women's earnings; and a priori reasoning suggests that the incidence of such households may well grow over time, partly due to the agricultural growth process itself.

TABLE 14

ANNUAL WAGE INCOME PER AGRICULTURAL LABOUR HOUSEHOLD (Rs.)

Region/State	Annual Wage Inome*			
	1964–65	1974–75	1974–75 at 1964–65 prices	Col. 3 as % of Col. 1
	(1)	(2)	(3)	(4)
North-Western				
Punjab & Haryana	992.38	2146.00	886.78	0.89
Rajasthan	617.17	1552.13	554.33	0.90
Uttar Pradesh	385.12	1081.85	470.37	1.22
Western				
Gujarat	845.12	1495.65	623.19	0.74
Maharashtra	630.91	1214.01	503.74	0.80
Central				
Madhya Pradesh	620.19	1152.14	385.33	0.62
Eastern				
Bihar	475.76	1094.49	419.34	0.88
Orissa	498.39	780.98	280.93	0.56
West Bengal	767.23	1252.32	502.94	0.66
Southern				
Andhra Pradesh	434.97	999.43	387.38	0.89
Karnataka	506.40	1183.16	501.34	0.99
Kerala	664.41	1440.08	496.58	0.75
Tamil Nadu	445.89	1005.58	343.20	0.77
All India	536.53	1164.59	453.15	0.84

Source: Bardhan [1981].

Notes: (1) *This is the total annual wage income earned by usually occupied workers (men, women and children) in the agricultural labour households.

(2) The data source is the Government of India, Rural Labour Enquiry Reports for 1964–65 and 1974–75.

(3) The states have been rearranged by me according to regions to facilitate comparisons with other state-level tables.

(b) In male-headed households, access to such independent earnings for women becomes important in so far as it can give women greater control over cash which, in turn, is noted to have implications for the pattern of household expenditure. For instance, expenditure on basic necessities, especially food (and hence the family's nutrition) is often found among poor households to be linked more closely to women's earnings than to men's earnings, where both women and men earn.

(c) The extent of sex-bias within the household in access to consumption items, health care etc., is noted to be related negatively, *inter alia*, to women's contribution to household earnings and hence to women's employment/income-earning opportunities. Further, women's greater participation in employment/income-earning activities also appear to be associated negatively to marriage costs (especially via dowry payments), even if not in a one-to-one relationship; and the relative male/female marriage cost, in turn, has implications for the extent of sex-bias against females in the household.

An additional point noted earlier but not elaborated is that the entry of rural women into wage labour is essentially a result of poverty. Gaiha [1981], for example, finds for all-India that the female labour force participation is much higher among the households below the poverty line than among those above it. Miller's review of ethnographic literature also reveals that female work participation is higher among the unpropertied than the propertied in both north and south India. Further, the 1981 census data reveals that the dependence on agricultural wage work as the main source of employment is twice as much for rural women than men. All said, therefore, when considering the issue of female poverty and agricultural growth, we need to closely examine the impact on rural women's wage earning opportunities, especially among agricultural labour households.

In assessing this impact, to begin with, it is noteworthy that the dependence of rural women on agricultural wage work for a livelihood has been increasing rapidly and faster than for men. For instance, according to census figures, in 1961, 25.6 per cent of rural women workers were classified as agricultural labourers; by 1981 this had almost doubled to 49.6 per cent. By contrast, in both years, rural male workers were noted to be primarily cultivators with 16.2 per cent and 24.3 per cent being agricultural labourers in 1961 and 1981 respectively.[16] This sex-related difference also highlights women's lack of independent access to land.

Evidence from the Rural Labour Enquiries (RLE) of 1964−65 and 1974−75 further reveals that over this period, while the number of both female and male agricultural labourers in agricultural labour households increased in India,[17] the percentage increase was substantially greater for women than men − being 57.5 per cent for women and 43.6 per cent for men. Chatterji [1982] using the same data source finds a close positive correspondence between the ranks of regions (the RLE divides India into five geographic regions) in terms of the growth in numbers of female agricultural labourers over 1964−65 and 1974−75, and the ranks of regions in terms of the changes in the incidence of rural poverty (as assessed in Ahluwalia [1978] over the same period.[18] The highest growth in the numbers of female agricultural labourers and in the incidence of rural poverty is found in the eastern region (covering Bihar, Orissa and West Bengal) of the country.

In this context it is relevant to note that the 1964−65 and 1974−75 RLEs

are a valuable data source because they cover the broad period over which
the new agricultural technology gained a foothold in India and helps provide
an idea of its impact.[19] It may also be mentioned here that although agricultural growth in particular regions need not *necessarily* be associated with
the introduction of HYVs, etc. yet in the overall Indian context the new
agricultural technology *has* served as the principal vehicle for agricultural
growth in recent years; and the impact of the one can thus be taken as indicative
of the impact of the other. Also, we have a specific interest here in the process
underlying increases in agricultural production, and for this again a focus on
the new agricultural technology-related effects, especially on employment and
earnings, becomes useful.

With regard to the relative availability of agricultural wage work for female
and male agricultural labourers, and to changes in availability over time, the
evidence from the RLE Reports is mixed. Tables 15 and 16 indicate that at
the all-India level:

- the average number of days of employment are lower for women than
  men in both survey years;
- the average number of days not worked during the year due to want
  of work are higher for women than men in both years;
- over the period, the average number of days of employment have
  decreased for both women and men, but the decline is somewhat more
  for men than for women;
- over the period the average number of days of involuntary unemploy-
- ment have increased equally for both women and men.

State-wise, as seen from the same tables, we find that in terms of the average
number of days of employment, except for Uttar Pradesh and Rajasthan where
there has been an increase for both women and men, and Andhra Pradesh
where the increase is for women alone, in all the other states (including those
which have had high agricultural growth rates and are among the principal
adopters of HYVs) there has been a decrease for both sexes.[20, 21] Also, the
days of involuntary unemployment have increased in all the states, other than
Tamil Nadu, for both women and men; but in most states (including Punjab)
the increase is more for women than men.

Changes in the aggregate days of agricultural wage employment over the
period, however, mask noteworthy differences in the impact of different
components of the new agricultural technology. Conceptually, we can separate
the new technology into two components: (a) bio-chemical inputs such as HYV
seeds and chemical fertilisers used with an assured water supply (provided
through pumpsets or other means) or what could be termed the 'HYV-
irrigation package'; and (b) mechanical equipment (other than irrigation-
related), such as tractors, combine harvesters and threshers. Even though in
practice these two components have tended to go together, they have done
so in varying degree in different regions. Also, at the conceptual level such
a separation is useful for gaining a better understanding of the new technology,
since the effects of the two components on labour use often tend to move in

Women, Poverty and Agricultural Growth in India   205

TABLE 15

EMPLOYMENT OF AGRICULTURAL LABOURERS IN AGRICULTURAL LABOUR
HOUSEHOLDS BY STATES

Region/State	Average annual full days of agricultural wage work					
	Women			Men		
	1964–65	1974–75	Change	1964–65	1974–75	Change
North-Western						
Haryana	} 173	131	− 42	} 282	203	− 79
Punjab		170	− 3		233	− 49
Rajasthan	153	163	+ 10	210	239	+ 29
Uttar Pradesh	102	124	+ 22	189	200	+ 11
Western						
Gujarat	240	160	− 80	278	206	− 72
Maharashtra	183	180	− 3	239	221	− 18
Central						
Madhya Pradesh	147	125	− 22	212	198	− 14
Eastern						
Bihar	127	114	− 13	198	186	− 12
Orissa	165	111	− 54	224	164	− 60
West Bengal	216	147	− 69	269	210	− 59
Southern						
Andhra Pradesh	104	138	+ 34	204	193	− 11
Karnataka	192	175	− 17	228	204	− 24
Kerala	147	108	− 39	173	138	− 35
Tamil Nadu	146	118	− 28	194	148	− 46
All India	149	138	− 11	217	193	− 24

Source: Government of India; [1981b: 140, 143], Tables 3.3(a).1M and 3.3(a).1W.

opposite directions: the 'HYV-irrigation package' is generally associated with
an increase in the demand for labour time, and mechanical equipment
(especially harvest and post-harvest technology) with a decrease. This is
revealed even at the aggregate level in the RLE reports. Table 17 gives the
operation-wise employment of female and male agricultural labourers of
agricultural labour households, at the all-India level. We find an increase in
the annual average number of labour days worked by both women and men
in sowing/transplanting, weeding and harvesting, that is, the three main
operations which are likely to need more labour with the introduction of the
'HYV-irrigation package'.[22] However, what the table also brings out is the
divergent effects of HYVs and mechanisation. In two operations, namely,
ploughing and 'others' (which would include basically the post-harvest
operations), there is a decrease in the use of hired labour time. It is these very
operations which, in a number of areas, have been mechanised through the
introduction of tractors and threshers. The decline in overall terms, that is,

TABLE 16

UNEMPLOYMENT AMONG AGRICULTURAL LABOURERS IN AGRICULTURAL
LABOUR HOUSEHOLDS BY STATES

Region/State	Average annual days not worked due to want of work					
	Women			Men		
	1964−65	1974−75	Change	1964−65	1974−75	Change
North-Western						
Haryana	} 59	88	+ 29	} 27	88	+ 61
Punjab		111	+ 52		64	+ 37
Rajasthan	81	97	+ 16	41	49	+ 8
Uttar Pradesh	108	114	+ 6	35	57	+ 22
Western						
Gujarat	82	111	+ 29	44	67	+ 23
Maharashtra	44	90	+ 46	32	57	+ 25
Central						
Madhya Pradesh	75	141	+ 66	27	70	+ 43
Eastern						
Bihar	103	155	+ 52	70	90	+ 20
Orissa	105	158	+ 53	40	92	+ 52
West Bengal	73	166	+ 93	37	88	+ 51
Southern						
Andhra Pradesh	99	103	+ 4	16	61	+ 45
Karnataka	8	81	+ 73	44	58	+ 14
Kerala	120	162	+ 42	106	126	+ 20
Tamil Nadu	155	142	− 13	106	98	− 8
All India	96	124	+ 28	48	76	+ 28

Source: Government of India [1981b: 206, 212], Tables 3.6(a).1M, 3.6(a).1W.

TABLE 17

OPERATION-WISE EMPLOYMENT OF AGRICULTURAL LABOURERS
IN AGRICULTURAL LABOUR HOUSEHOLDS: ALL INDIA

Operations	Average Full Days Worked During the Year					
	Women			Men		
	1964−65	1974−75	Change	1964−65	1974−75	Change
Ploughing	7	2	− 5	48	36	− 12
Sowing	4	5	+ 1	5	5	0
Transplanting	12	13	+ 1	7	8	+ 1
Weeding	22	33	+ 11	13	22	+ 9
Harvesting	45	49	+ 4	40	46	+ 6
Others	48	36	− 12	85	76	− 9
Unclassified	11	−	− 11	19	−	− 19
All operations	149	138	− 11	217	193	− 24

Source: Government of India [1981b: 158], Table 3.4(a)1.

for all operations taken together, may thus be seen to be accounted for largely by mechanisation. (Unfortunately, the RLE reports provide information only in terms of labour time and not in terms of the numbers of labourers employed. Hence it is not possible to say how the changes in labour time requirements have been shared between people.)

The positive labour demand effects of the 'HYV-irrigation package' taken on its own, appear to have been shared somewhat unevenly between women and men. As the table shows, there is a rise in the use of both male and female labour time in the three mentioned operations linked wtih the 'package', but in two of the operations (sowing/transplanting and weeding) taken separately and for all three operations taken together the increase is more for female labour.

The negative effects of mechanisation on employment also appear to have been shared unevenly between men and women. Tractorisation *so far* has affected largely male labour; this is because tractors have been used mainly for ploughing[23] which is an almost exclusively male-specific operation. By contrast, with the mechanisation of post-harvest operations such as paddy processing, it is women who have been displaced disproportionately, as noted in several micro-studies on the introduction of rice milling in India (for example, see Harriss [1977b]; and Acharya and Patkar [1983]). This is also indicated by Table 17 where, for the operations included in 'others', the decline is more for female labour days than for male labour days. In net terms, however, the decline in male employment in ploughing plus 'others' is greater than of female employment in these operations.[24] At the same time given the noted task specificity of women's work, as and when the use of tractors or other mechanical equipment spreads to operations such as sowing/transplanting and weeding, in many states (especially in the South) we would expect primarily female labour to be displaced. Finally it may be noted that in both survey years, the aggregate employment across all operations taken together is less for women than men.

Now let us consider what has been happening to the earnings of agricultural labourers from agricultural wage work. The RLE data reveal that although the daily *money* wage earnings have increased for both women and men in all the states, the increase has not kept pace with the rise ir prices. Hence as seen from Table 18 in *real* terms in almost all states, the *daily* wage earnings have declined. The only state where there has been an increase for both male and female labour is Uttar Pradesh, while in Madhya Pradesh, Kerala and Haryana there has been a slight increase in earnings for female labour alone, and in Punjab for male labour alone.

When we consider the employment information together with the daily wage earnings information to gain an idea of the *annual* real earnings of female and male agricultural labourers, from agricultural wage work (see Table 19), we find, first, that for women the earnings have increased in Uttar Pradesh and Andhra Pradesh and have decreased in all the other states, while for men they have increased in Uttar Pradesh and Punjab and have declined in every other state. Second, when we examine the *differentials* in male to female

TABLE 18

DAILY REAL EARNINGS FROM AGRICULTURAL WAGE WORK OF WOMEN
AND MEN IN AGRICULTURAL LABOUR HOUSEHOLDS (Rs.)

Region/State	ACPI	Women		Men	
		1964−65	1974−75	1964−65	1974−75
North-Western					
Haryana	} 242	} 1.45	1.63*	} 2.13	2.00
Punjab			1.41		2.65*
Rajasthan	280	1.09	0.92	1.76	1.30
Uttar Pradesh	230	0.93	1.07*	1.10	1.39*
Western					
Gujarat	240	1.19	1.05	1.47	1.35
Maharashtra	241	0.77	0.63	1.47	1.09
Central					
Madhya Pradesh	299	0.86	0.91*	1.11	0.82
Eastern					
Bihar	261	1.20	1.05	1.39	1.23
Orissa	278	0.89	0.66	1.33	0.95
West Bengal	249	1.36	1.14	1.81	1.40
Southern					
Andhra Pradesh	258	0.85	0.76	1.21	1.03
Karnataka	236	0.79	0.77	1.21	1.21
Kerala	290	1.23	1.48*	2.11	2.08
Tamil Nadu	293	0.85	0.79	1.39	1.24
All India	257	0.95	0.88	1.43	1.26

Source: Government of India [1979: 102, 103, 162], Tables 3.1(a).1 and 3.4.

Notes: ACPI = Agricultural Consumer Price Index with 1964−65 = 100, relating to a fixed
basket of goods and services consumed by agricultural labour households.

* denotes an increase over 1964−65; the absence of * denotes a decrease or constancy.

earnings from agricultural wage work, it is noted that at the all-India level
there has been some narrowing down of differentials over the period being
considered. State-wise, however, the picture varies. In six out of the 14 states
listed in the table, there has been an *increase* in earning differentials. This
includes the agriculturally backward eastern states of Bihar, and Orissa and
also West Bengal, as well as the high growth/high new technology-adopting
north-western state of Punjab. The increase is especially high in the case of
Punjab where the differential is also the highest among all the states in
1974−75. The state where the differential is the least and has declined is
Madhya Pradesh; and much of the southern region also shows a decline (the
increase in differential in the case of Karnataka being slight). The decline is
noted to be especially high in the case of Andhra Pradesh. Also, the degree
of differential is generally lower in the southern states compared with the north-
western ones in 1974−75.

Women, Poverty and Agricultural Growth in India   209

TABLE 19

ANNUAL REAL EARNINGS FROM AGRICULTURAL WAGE WORK OF
AGRICULTURAL LABOURERS IN AGRICULTURAL LABOUR HOUSEHOLDS (Rs.)

Region/State	Annual Real Earnings@ Per Person				Differential: Ratio of Male to Female Earnings	
	Women		Men			
	1964–65	1974–75	1964–65	1974–75	1964–65	1974–75
North-Western						
Haryana	} 250.8	213.3	} 600.7	406.8	} 2.39	1.91
Punjab		239.5		618.1*		2.58*
Rajasthan	166.8	150.2	369.6	310.7	2.22	2.07
Uttar Pradesh	94.9	133.2*	207.9	277.4*	2.19	2.08
Western						
Gujarat	285.6	168.0	408.7	278.1	1.43	1.66*
Maharashtra	140.9	114.3	351.3	241.2	2.49	2.11
Central						
Madhya Pradesh	126.4	114.1	235.3	162.9	1.86	1.43
Eastern						
Bihar	152.4	119.7	275.2	229.5	1.81	1.92*
Orissa	146.8	73.1	297.9	155.7	2.03	2.13*
West Bengal	293.8	167.1	486.9	294.3	1.66	1.76*
Southern						
Andhra Pradesh	88.4	104.8*	246.8	198.2	2.79	1.89
Karnataka	151.7	134.2	275.9	246.4	1.82	1.84*
Kerala	180.8	159.4	365.0	286.5	2.02	1.80
Tamil Nadu	124.1	93.4	269.7	183.9	2.17	1.97
All India	141.6	121.9	310.3	243.3	2.19	2.00

Sources: (1) Table 14

(2) Government of India [1979: 102, 103, 162], Tables 3.1(a).1 and 3.4.

Notes: @ Money earnings have been deflated by the Agricultural Consumer Price Index with
1964–65 = 100.

* denotes an increase over 1964–65; the absence of * denotes a decrease.

Underlying the regional variations in the changes in earning differentials, there is likely to be a complex set of factors, including differences in the demand for female labour created by HYVs in the predominently wheat-growing states relative to the predominantly rice-growing states. In absolute terms, in all the states, the differentials are substantial in both survey years, with women's earnings being about half or less than half of men's earnings in most cases.

Further, if we consider the *total* wage earnings (that is, earnings from agricultural *and* non-agricultural wage employment) of agricultural labourers, we note that the male to female differentials are higher than for earnings from agricultural wage work alone, in almost all the states, in both survey years (see Table 20). In terms of changes over the period, the pattern is broadly similar to that observed in the instance of agricultural wage earnings.

On the whole, therefore, over the period 1964–65 and 1974–75, female agricultural labourers in virtually all the states have suffered a decline in absolute real wage earnings; in some states this decline has been less than that suffered by male agricultural labourers, but in several others it has been more.

Let us now, as a summing up exercise, try to put together some of the significant pointers *vis-à-vis* female poverty and the agricultural growth process that have emerged in the last two sections and in this section. Since the regional dimension has been noted all along as being an important factor impinging on the issues discussed, it would be useful to consider this question by region.

TABLE 20

ANNUAL REAL EARNINGS FROM ALL WAGE WORK OF AGRICULTURAL
LABOURERS IN AGRICULTURAL LABOUR HOUSEHOLDS (Rs.)

Region/State	Annual real earnings per person				Differential: Ratio of male to female earnings	
	Women		Men			
	1964–65	1974–75	1964–65	1974–75	1964–65	1974–75
North-Western						
Haryana	} 261.5	245.8	} 648.3	448.3	} 2.48	1.82
Punjab		244.3		649.6*		2.66*
Rajasthan	178.5	155.7	404.6	330.6	2.27	2.12
Uttar Pradesh	105.3	136.9*	260.8	310.8*	2.48	2.27
Western						
Gujarat	294.0	188.3	426.6	314.3	1.45	1.67*
Maharashtra	148.8	126.0	391.5	269.8	2.63	2.14
Central						
Madhya Pradesh	146.2	126.7	277.6	189.3	1.90	1.49
Eastern						
Bihar	158.8	125.9	312.4	252.8	1.97	2.01*
Orissa	155.2	82.7	346.6	180.0	2.23	2.18
West Bengal	323.2	174.5	533.6	324.5	1.65	1.86*
Southern						
Andhra Pradesh	98.8	113.4*	281.7	221.0	2.85	1.95
Karnataka	161.4	144.3	301.9	281.2	1.87	1.95*
Kerala	191.8	165.1	408.2	309.1	2.13	1.87
Tamil Nadu	127.6	98.9	291.1	211.8	2.28	2.14
All India	151.7	131.0	348.8	271.3	2.30	2.07

Sources: (1) Government of India [1981b: 140, 143], Tables 3.3(a).1M and 3.3(a).1W.
         (2) Government of India [1979: 102, 103, 114, 162], Tables 3.1(a).1, 3.2(a).1 and 3.4.

Note: * denotes an increase over 1964–65; the absence of * denotes a decrease.

I shall focus basically on the north-western, eastern and southern regions, since these can be linked with the broad regional profiles of the incidence of sex-discrimination in the home, of the FLP rates, and of the practice of dowry that were highlighted in the discussion in section I.

The north-western states, especially Punjab and Haryana, as noted, rank among the highest in terms of increases in agricultural production and the adoption of the new agricultural technology. Punjab and Haryana also have the lowest incidence of absolute poverty in India. Rajasthan, again, has a low incidence of absolute poverty and it too has had relatively high agricultural growth rates, although its adoption of the new technology is still limited. However, it is precisely the north-western region where discrimination against females is most apparent, as seen both historically and in the recent period. Historically, as noted in section I, the region has been associated closely with the practice of female infanticide. In the recent period too it is from the Punjab that the demand for sex-determination tests on unborn babies and the abortion of female foetuses has been most commonly reported [see *Deshpande*, 1982; and *Manushi*, 1982]. Again, it is in the north-west – in the state of Rajasthan – that *Sati* was most prevalent historically, and where occasional incidents continue to be reported today. While *Sati* and sex-selective abortions would both be associated with relatively well-off families, the ideology underlying sex-selectiveness and discrimination against females tends to permeate and affect all classes (even if in varying degree). The same is true of the practice of dowry. In general, a daughter's birth is seen here as an unwelcome event and son preference among all classes is found to be strong. In other words, while the overall incidence of poverty may be lower in the north-western states than elsewhere, among the poor households we would expect a sharper anti-female bias in this region than elsewhere.

Now if we were to take the view that the growth process associated with the new technology has unleashed forces which, over time, will have a negative effect on the poor, then we would expect an increase in the overall incidence of poverty, or at least a worsening of the economic position of a significant section of the poor. Either way it would have a greater negative effect on women and female children because of the noted unequal distribution of income, etc. within the household. Further it is possible that the level of discrimination against females may strengthen in parts of this region, especially in the Punjab where (a) employment opportunities for female agricultural labour have not been rising as much as the supply of such labour, and the consequent increase in involuntary unemployment has been more for female than for male labour; and (b) differentials in male/female real earnings have increased in relation to both agricultural wage work and all wage work.

Even if we were to take the more optimistic view of some 'trickle down' effect of agricultural growth on poverty (although, as noted, much of the existing literature relating to long-term trends does not support this view), we could still have a worsening of the economic situation of a significant section of the poor. This is because the overall incidence of poverty (head-count ratio *and* Sen index) can decline even while inequality among the poor increases and some sections of the poor become further impoverished. This, as noted in section II, was found by Gaiha [1981, 1984] to have happened between 1968–69 and 1970–71 at the all-India level. Further, for those households that may benefit in any such 'trickle down', women and female children are likely to benefit less than men for reasons already noted. There is also a chance that they may be as badly-off as before in that an improvement in the household's economic position may be accompanied by a worsening of the relative position of females in the household. This could happen if the now not-poor households aspire to the social status of the better-off by confining the women to home-bound work and adopting customs such as dowry, where it was not practiced before. (This is found to have happened in rural Karnataka by Epstein [1973] in her study of social change in two villages which she first visited in 1955 and again in 1970. In one of the villages dowry has replaced bride-wealth altogether and in the other partially.)[25] In the Punjab in fact (as also in Himachal Pradesh) Sharma [1980] in her village study notes that in recent years there has been a total shift from bride-price to dowry amongst all but the lowest castes, and not only among those where women have withdrawn from outdoor labour. The amounts paid in dowry even among agricultural labourers are also noted to have increased several-fold in Punjab with expenditures in marriage celebrations and dowry being as high as Rs.10,000 today, compared to about Rs.200 in 1909 and about Rs.6000 in 1968 [*Horowitz and Kishwar*, 1982]. Underlying these trends would be several factors including the increase in differentials in male/female earnings in parts of the region, and the ideological spread of upper caste and upper class prestige norms and consumerism to all groups, aided especially by the visual mass media. These trends are likely to further strengthen the view that women and female children are economic liabilities, and have consequent negative implications for the survival of female children over time.

The eastern states, especially Orissa and Bihar, in contrast to the north-western states, have been characterised by agricultural stagnation. This region also has the highest incidence of absolute poverty in the country. Here again women and female children would be bearing a disproportionately higher burden of poverty. This is not merely because of a sex-bias against females in access to food, etc. (although relative to the north-west such discrimination appears to be less, at least as reflected in the overall sex ratios), but also because of the likely increase in female-headed households with increased male out-migration to the North-West. The sizeable increase in female agricultural labourers in the eastern states, which was noted to be higher than in other states, could well be a reflection partly of the increase in female-headed households which are dependent primarily or solely on the women's income, and partly of the overall higher poverty incidence in these states. On the whole, therefore, regional imbalances in agricultural growth in the country may be seen as having affected the women in poor households in agriculturally stagnant regions much more negatively than the men in these regions. Also, given the rise in male/female differentials in wage earnings in this region, and the relatively greater decline in the average days of employment for women than men in states such as Bihar and West Bengal, the existing sex-based discrimination could get further strengthened over time.

The southern states fall somewhere in-between the eastern and the northwestern ones in the adoption of the new technology and in the incidence of absolute poverty. They have an advantage over the eastern and the northwestern states in terms of a lower intra-household discrimination against women and female children. The noted trend towards a reduction of male/female differentials in agricultural wage earnings in states such as Tamil Nadu, Andhra Pradesh and Kerala, if sustained, could well help further reduce the existing sex-bias. Also, at least in Andhra Pradesh, the annual real wage earnings have increased for female labour, even while they have declined for male labour. (Andhra Pradesh is also the one state *vis-à-vis* which two otherwise divergent studies, namely, Ahluwalia [1978], and Griffin and Ghose [1979] agree that there has been a negative time trend in the incidence of rural poverty.) However, the threat from future mechanisation in operations such as transplanting, weeding, etc. is higher for female than male labour in the southern states (including Andhra Pradesh), since these operations are noted to employ primarily female labour here, and these are also the operations in which female labour is primarily concentrated. An additional aspect of concern is the increase in the incidence of dowry even among households in south India as noted by Epstein [1973, discussed earlier] in Karnataka, and Gulati [1984] in Kerala.

IV. CONCLUDING COMMENTS

From the analysis in the article we get a complex and mixed picture of the implications of agricultural growth for rural women in poverty. But, by and large, the picture is a pessimistic one, in that unless present trends can be countered, the burdens of poverty of a significant section of poor rural women may be expected to increase in most regions.

Existing state policies and programmes (even those aimed at alleviating poverty) offer little scope for optimism that these trends will be countered through them. The point of hope, however, lies in the growth of consciousness among rural women in recent years of the need to organise and unite for fighting against oppression, both outside the home and within it. In the present paper, it is not possible to discuss in any detail the nature and scope of such struggles but it is necessary to take note of them. A development of particular interest is the growing recognition within several left mass organisations of the rural poor (especially outside the political party context) of the need to wage a struggle against women's oppression, in addition to their ongoing struggle and mobilisation against class and caste oppression. Women's specific concerns – both economic, such as their independent need for employment, income and land rights, and other, such as the violence they face from husbands, employers and landlords, etc. – are finding a voice usually via women's committees within these organisations.

Some noteworthy examples of such struggles launched via non-party, non-governmental organisations are the assertion by landless women of their independent right to land in the *Bodhgaya Movement* for land rights in Bihar initiated by the *Chhatra Yuva Sangharsh Vahini*; the agitation by tribal women of agricultural labour households against low and unequal wages, inadequate employment, wife-beating and rape through the *Shramik Sangathan* (toilers organisation) in Maharashtra; the struggle by poor women for higher wages and land, and against wife-beating in Andhra Pradesh via the Comprehensive Rural Operations Service Society (CROSS); the revolt of low caste poor rural women via *Mahila Sangams* (Women's Groups) against exploitation by upper caste landlords in some parts of the Telengana region of Andhra Pradesh; women's resistence to deforestation and their concerted effort for environmental development and against alchoholism through the *Chipko Andolan* in the hills of Uttar Pradesh, and so on.

In addition, there has been a growth too of solely women's organisation such as the Self-Employed Women's Association which began by taking up the problems of economic survival of women in the urban informal sector in Ahmedabad city but has since branched out into the rural areas of Gujarat as well; the Working Women's Forum in Tamil Nadu which too is organising poor women in the informal sector in Madras city and the rural areas around; the women's groups fighting to curb liquor-associated wife-beating in the villages of Manipur (called the 'Night Patrollers of Manipur'), and so on.

In this context, it is also relevant to take note of the emergence of several urban-based women's groups which are raising a voice against issues such as dowry, violence against women, the negative portrayal of women in the media, etc., and are pressurising too for changes in existing laws and legal processes. The efforts of such groups are of significance beyond their immediate urban context, that is, for rural women as well, in so far as they can affect the law and also make an impact on existing ideological biases.

It is in the growth and development of consciousness and unity through such grassroots struggles that the potentials and possibilities of change lie, both within the immediate local context and at the wider level, through the countervailing pressures exerted on existing state policies and structures.

NOTES

1. The gender-specific implications of *caste*-based discrimination faced by the poor (there being a considerable overlap of low caste position with poverty) are discussed at various points in the paper, although the class and caste effects have not been separated empirically.
2. In addition, there is the issue of the individual's ability to 'adapt' to differential intakes as emphasised by Sukhatme [1978, 1981].
3. The cereal, cooked to a dough, is separated into balls for eating and the division among family members is stated to be two balls for the man, 1.5 for the woman and one for the child. These ratios have been used by Batliwala as rough approximations of the way in which other food items too are distributed among family members. She computes energy requirements for different tasks done by women and men in the sample, by using

Women, Poverty and Agricultural Growth in India   215

norms of energy costs where available in the literature, and imputing values where they are not.

4. The procedure followed was to measure the weight of all food items consumed in the household over 24 hours before and after cooking. The post-cooked food was converted to volume units and measured in the cooking pots before and after serving. During meals the number of spoonfuls of food served to each individual was closely observed.

5. In Chen *et al.*'s malnourishment survey (using a weight-for-age standard) the incidence of both severe and moderate malnourishment was much higher among females than males.

6. Miller attempts to broadly translate castes into classes, on the assumption that the upper castes are composed predominantly of people who are propertied, and the lower castes primarily of people who are unpropertied. Hence the *Jats, Rajputs* and *Ahirs* are termed by her as the 'northern propertied' and the *Kurmis, Chamars* and *Mallahs* as the 'northern unpropertied'.

7. The 'compensation' argument also implies that a lower value is placed on a woman's contribution to housework and childcare than that placed on the expenditure incurred for her maintenance in her marital family. For a discussion on some related aspects also see Rajaraman [1983].

8. On this last also see Sharma [1980].

9. Rosenzweig and Schultz's *district-level* analysis based on 1961 census data, by contrast, indicates that in districts where a greater proportion of households are landless, female child survival relative to male child survival is higher. However, such a district-level analysis would be affected by intervening factors, such as whether the districts with more landless households fall mainly in the southern or in the northern states, the employment opportunities for women in these districts, etc. Unfortunately, the authors do not undertake a household-level analysis by *regions*.

10. For a detailed discussion on the nature and causes of this crisis see Agarwal [1986].

11. This definition is broadly the same in the 1951, 1961 and 1971 censuses.

12. For a useful discussion on definitions and concepts relating to female-headed households also see Youssef and Hetler [1981].

13. Cain *et al.* [1979] found in their study of a Bangladeshi village that only 54 per cent of all widows in the village had the security of being integrated members of their sons' households. They also note a weakening in the bonds of obligation of male relatives, either within or outside the joint family set-up, to support women whose husbands were dead or had left them.

14. There are some variations in the NSS results for Gujarat and those for Maharashtra but the broad pattern is as indicated here.

15 Saith provides several justifications for dropping the years prior to 1960–61 in the series, such as it being misleading to use a single linear trend for the entire period, since the few initial observations overturn the experience of the following 15 years; and that the consumer expenditure data in the early part of the series are not comparable with those for subsequent years because of differences in the duration of the reference period, the geographic coverage and the valuation procedure used.

   Saith's justification for dropping 1973–74 is, first, the data gap in the series which is of two years prior to 1973–74 and of one year prior to 1970–71, so that from 1969–70 to 1973–74 there are only two observations: This, he argues, gives too much weight to the end year. Second, he points out that the relative prices of the inferior and superior foodstuffs did not alter significantly until 1970–71 but shifted dramatically in the following three years, with prices of the inferior foodstuffs (consumed by the poor) increasing much more rapidly. He thus concludes that the most appropriate period for the analysis would be 1960–61 to 1970–71.

16. The 1981 figures relate to 'main workers' classification. However, the figures obtained from the five per cent sample census results, which relate to main plus marginal workers, give percentages very close to the above. 1961 and 1981 have been chosen for the comparison and not the interim 1971 census because definitional changes in this census led to considerable underestimation of the female work force and reduced its comparability with the 1961 census. However, the total worker classification for 1981 census is broadly comparable to the worker classification in the 1961 census.

17. Female and male agricultural labourers belonging to agricultural labour households constituted 95.8 per cent and 98.4 per cent respectively of female and male agricultural labourers in all rural labour households in 1974–75.
18. Strictly speaking, Chatterji's poverty comparisons relate to 1963–64 and 1973–74, presumably because poverty estimates for 1974–75 are not available from Ahluwalia's study.
19. 1974–75 as compared with the previous year and subsequent years was not a particularly good year in terms of agricultural production. Nevertheless, relative to 1964–65 it represented a noteworthy increase of 11.6 per cent in the total quantum of foodgrains produced.
20. In the north-western states of Punjab and Haryana, while the decrease in days of employment is noted in Table 15 to be more for male than for female labour, more recent evidence suggests that some substitution of female casual labour in these states by male migrant labour from other states, has been taking place (see Dasgupta [1977: 327]).
21. A more direct quantification of the state-wise effects of HYVs on labour use for Tamil Nadu, Andhra Pradesh and Orissa, is undertaken by Agarwal [1984] through a regression analysis. This indicates that HYV rice has had a significant positive effect on the use of casually hired labour time in all three states. Sex-wise, the increase is found to be only for male casual labour in Tamil Nadu, only for female casual labour in Andhra Pradesh, and for both sexes in Orissa.
22. For a detailed spelling-out of reasons for expecting such an operation-wise increase in labour use see Agarwal [1984].
23. See, for example, Agarwal [1983] for the effect of tractor use in the Punjab.
24. The female labour under 'ploughing' in Table 17 is likely to be essentially labour involved in other functions associated with seed-bed preparation.
25. One of the factors to which she attributes this shift is the withdrawal of women from field work due to prestige considerations, among peasant families whose economic position has improved. The bride, unused to such labour, is thus seen by the groom's family as a liability and the dowry she brings as a compensation; earlier, the bride's father *received* compensation from the groom's family for having lost a productive worker. Epstein notes too that the adoption of the practice of dowry among the peasants also represents an attempt by them to imitate Brahmin customs, in the hope of raising their social status.
     The withdrawal of family women from manual work in the fields when the economic status of the cultivating household improves has also been noted by Agarwal [1984].

REFERENCES

Acharya, Sarthi and Pravin Patkar, 1983, 'Employment Conditions of Women in Rice Cultivation Areas', mimeo, Tata Institute of Social Sciences, Bombay.
Agarwal, Anil and Priya Deshingkar, 1983, 'Headloaders: Hunger for Firewood – I', CSE Report No. 118, Center for Science and Environment, Delhi.
Agarwal, Bina, 1981, 'Agricultural Modernization and Third World Women: Pointers from the Literature and an Empirical Analysis', World Employment Programme Research Working Paper No. WEP 10/WP 21, International Labour Organization, Geneva.
Agarwal, Bina, 1983, *Mechanization in Indian Agriculture: An Analytical Study Based on the Punjab*, Delhi: Allied Publishers.
Agarwal, Bina, 1984, 'Rural Women and the High Yielding Variety Rice Technology', in *Economic and Political Weekly* (Review of Agriculture), Vol. 19, No. 13, 31 March.
Agarwal, Bina, 1985, 'Work Participation of Rural Women in the Third World: Some Data and Conceptual Biases', *Economic and Political Weekly* (Review of Agriculture), Vol. 20, Nos. 51 and 52, 21–28 Dec.
Agarwal, Bina, 1986, *Cold Hearths and Barren Slopes: The Woodfuel Crisis in the Third World*, Delhi: Allied Publishers and London: Zed Books.
Ahluwalia, 1978, 'Rural Poverty and Agricultural Performance in India', *Journal of Development Studies*, Vol. 14, No. 3, April.

Women, Poverty and Agricultural Growth in India   217

Bahuguna, Sunderlal, 1984, 'Women's Non-Violent Power in the Chipko Movement', in Madhu Kishwar and Ruth Vanita (eds.), *In Search of Answers: Indian Women's Voices from Manushi*, London: Zed Press.

Bardhan, Pranab, 1981, 'Poverty and 'Trickle Down' in Rural India: A Quantitative Analysis', Working Paper, University of California, Berkeley.

Bardhan, Pranab, 1984, 'On Life and Death Questions: Poverty and Child Mortality' in *Land Labour and Rural Poverty: Essays in Development Economics*, Delhi: Oxford University Press, forthcoming.

Bardhan, Pranab and Ashok Rudra, 1978, 'Interlinkage of Land, Labour and Credit Relations: An Analysis of Village Survey Data in East India', *Economic and Political Weekly*, Vol. 13, Nos. 6 and 7, Feb.

Batliwala, S., 1983, 'Women in Poverty: The Energy, Health and Nutrition Syndrome', paper presented at a workshop on 'Women and Poverty' at the Center for Studies in Social Sciences, Calcutta, 17–18 March.

Bhaduri, T. and V. Surin, 1980, 'Community Forestry and Women Head-Loaders', in *Community Forestry and People's Participation*, Seminar Report, Ranchi Consortium for Forestry, 20–22 Nov.

Bhalla, Sheila, 1977, 'New Relations of Production in Haryana Agriculture', *Economic and Political Weekly* (Review of Agriculture), Vol. 11, No. 13, 27 March.

Bhatty, I. Z., 1974, 'Inequality and Poverty in Rural India', in T. N. Srinivasan and P. K. Bardhan (eds.), *Poverty and Income Distribution in India*, Calcutta: Statistical Publishing Society.

Briscoe, John, 1979, 'Energy Use and Social Structure in a Bangladeshi Village', *Population and Development Review*, Vol. 5, No. 4, Dec.

Buvinic, Mayra and Nadia H. Youssef, 1978, 'Women-Headed Households: The Ignored Factor in Development Planning', Report submitted to AID/WID, International Centre for Research on Women, Washington, DC, March.

Cain, Mead, Syeda Rokeya Khanam and Shamsun Nahar, 1979, 'Class, Patriarchy and the Structure of Women's Work in Rural Bangladesh', Working paper No. 43, Center for Population Studies, The Population Council, New York, May.

Census of India, 1971, 'Indian Census Through a Hundred Years, Part I', Census Centenary Monograph No. 2, by D. Natarajan, Office of the Registrar General, Ministry of Home Affairs, New Delhi.

Census of India, 1981a, Series 1, Paper 2 of 1983, 'Key Population Statistics based on 5 per cent Sample Data', by P. Padmanabha, Registrar General and Census Commissioner, India.

Census of India, 1981b, Series 1, Paper 3 of 1981, 'Provisional Population Totals, Workers and Non-workers', by P. Padmanabha, Registrar General and Census Commissioner, India.

Chakraborty, A. K. *et al.*, 1978, 'Health Status of Rural Population of Singur as Revealed in Repeat General Health Survey 1975', *Indian Journal of Medical Research*, Vol. 68, Dec.

Chakravarty, Kumaresh and G. C. Tiwari, c. 1977, 'Regional Variation in Women's Employment: A Case Study of Five Villages in Three Indian States', mimeo, Programme of Women's Studies, Indian Council for Social Science Research, New Delhi.

Chambers, Robert, Longhurst, Richard and Arnold Pacey (eds.), 1981, *Seasonal Dimensions to Rural Poverty*, London: Frances Pinter.

Chatterji, Ruchira, 1982, 'Marginalisation and the Induction of Women into Wage Labour: A Case Study of Female Agricultural Wage Labour in India 1964/5 to 1974/5', mimeo, forthcoming as a World Employment Programme Research Working Paper, International Labour Organisation, Geneva.

Chatterjee, Meera, 1983, 'Women's Access to Health Care: A Critical Issue for Child Health', mimeo, Center for Policy Research, Delhi, forthcoming in *Proceedings of ICMR Workshop in Issues for Child Health, Nutrition and Family Planning*.

Chen, Lincoln C., Huq Emdadual and Stan D'Souza, 1981, 'Sex Bias in the Family Allocation of Food and Health Care in Rural Bangladesh', *Population and Development Review*, Vol. 7, No. 1, March.

Clark, Alice, 1983, 'Limitations on Female Life Chances in Rural Central Gujarat', *Indian Economic and Social History Review*, Vol. 20, No. 1.

Dasgupta, Biplab, 1977, *Agrarian Change and the New Technology in India*, Report No. 77.2, United Nations Research Institute for Social Development, Geneva.

Dandekar, Kumudini and D. B. Unde, 1964, 'Households in West Bengal and their Headship', *Artha Vijnana*, Vol. 6, No. 1, March.

Dandekar, Kumudini, 1975, 'Has the Proportion of Women in India's Population Been Declining', *Economic and Political Weekly*, 18 Oct.

Dandekar, V. M. and N. Rath, 1971, 'Poverty in India', *Economic and Political Weekly*, Vol. 6, Nos. 1 and 2, 2 and 9 Jan.

Desai, Rajni X, 1982, 'Migrant Labour and Women: the Case of Ratnagiri', World Employment Programme Research Working Paper No. WEP 10/WP 28, International Labour Organisation, Geneva.

Deshpande, Anjali, 1982, 'A New Menace', *Mainstream*, 24 July.

Devi, Mahasweta and Nirmal Ghosh, 1981, *Bonded Labour in India* (in Hindi), New Delhi: Radhakrishna Publishers.

Epstein, T. Scarlett, 1973, *South India: Yesterday, Today and Tomorrow*, London: Macmillan.

Gaiha, Raghav, 1981, 'Aspects of Poverty in Rural India', *Economics of Planning*, Vol. 17, Nos. 2–3.

Gaiha, Raghav, 1983, 'Poverty, Technology and Infrastructure in Rural India', paper delivered to the European Econometric Society Meeting, Pisa, Aug.

Gaiha, Raghav, 1984, 'Impoverishment, Technology and Growth in Rural India', mimeo, Faculty of Management Studies, Delhi University.

Ghosh, Shanti, 1985, 'Discrimination Begins at Birth', UNICEF, mimeo.

Government of India, 1979, 'Rural Labour Enquiry 1974–75, Final Report on Wages and Earnings of Rural Labour Households', Labour Bureau, Ministry of Labour, Chandigarh.

Government of India, 1981a, 'Survey of Infant and Child Mortality, 1979', Office of the Registrar General, India.

Government of India, 1981b, 'Rural Labour Enquiry 1974–75, Final Report on Employment and Unemployment of Rural Labour Households', Labour Bureau, Ministry of Labour, Chandigarh.

Gordon, John, E., Singh, Sohan and John B. Wyon, 1965, 'Causes of Death at Different Ages by Sex and by Season in a Rural Population of Punjab 1957–59: A Field Study', *Indian Journal of Medical Research*, Vol. 53, No. 9, Sept.

Gulati, Leela, 1978, 'Profile of a Female Agricultural Labourer', *Economic and Political Weekly* (Review of Agriculture), Vol. 13, No. 12, 25 March.

Gulati, Leela, 1984, *Fisherwomen on the Kerala Coast: Demographic and Socio-Economic Impact of Fisheries Development Project*, International Labour Office, Geneva.

Gupta, Jayoti, 1985, 'Himalayan Polynyandry: Bondage Among Women in Jaunsar Bawar', in Utsa Patnaik and Manjari Digwaney (eds.), *Chains of Servitude: Bondage and Slavery in India*, Hyderguda, Hyderabad: Sangam Books (Orient Longman).

Griffin, Keith and Ajit Kumar Ghose, 1979, 'Growth and Impoverishment in the Rural Areas of Asia', *World Development*, Vol. 7, Nos. 4/5.

Harriss, John, 1977a, 'Implications of Changes in Agriculture for Social Relationships at the Village Level: The Case of Randam', in B. H. Farmer (ed.), *Green Revolution? Technology and Change in Rice-Growing Areas of Tamil Nadu and Sri Lanka*, London: Macmillan.

Harriss, Barbara, 1977b, 'Paddy-Milling: Problems in Policy and the Choice of Technology', in B. H. Farmer (ed.), *op. cit.*

Horowitz, B. and Madhu Kishwar, 1982, 'Family Life – The Unequal Deal: Women's Condition and Family Life Among Agricultural Labourers and Small Farmers in a Punjab Village', *Manushi*, No. 11.

Hoskins, Marilyn, 1979, 'Women in Forestry for Local Community Development: A Programming Guide', paper prepared for the office of women in development, AID, Washington, DC, Sept.

Jain, Devaki, 1980, 'The Night Patrollers of Manipur', in *Women's Quest for Power: Five Indian Case Studies*, in Sahibabad (UP): Vikas Publishing House.

Jain, Devaki and Malini Chand, 1982, 'Report on a Time-Allocation Study – Its Methodological Implications', paper presented at a 'Technical Seminar on Women's Work and Employment', Institute of Social Studies Trust, 9–11 April.

Women, Poverty and Agricultural Growth in India   219

Jain, S. P., 1982, 'Mortality Trends and Differentials' in *Population of India – Country Monograph Series No. 10*, Economic and Social Commission for Asia and the Pacific, Bangkok, Thailand.

Jetley, Surinder, 1984, 'India: Eternal Waiting', in *Women in the Villages, Men in the Towns*, Paris: UNESCO.

Khan, M. E., Ghosh, S. K. Singh, Dastidar and Ratanjeet Singh, 1983, 'Nutrition and Health Practices Among the Rural Women – A Case Study of Uttar Pradesh, India' Working paper No. 31, Operations Research Group, Delhi.

Kishwar, Madhu and Ruth Vanita, 1984, *In Search of Answers: Indian Women's Voices from Manushi*, London: Zed Books.

Krishna Raj, Maithreyi and Jyoti Ranadive, 1984, 'The Rural Female Heads of Households – Hidden from View', in Murali Manohar (ed.), *Women's Status and Development in India*, Society for Women's Studies and Development, Warangal.

Kumar, Shubh K., 1978, 'Role of the Household Economy in Child Nutrition at Low Incomes', Occasional paper No. 95, Dept. of Agricultural Economics, Cornell University, Dec.

Kurien, G. T., 1977, 'Rural Poverty in Tamil Nadu', in *Poverty and Landlessness in Rural Asia*, Geneva: International Labour Organisation.

Kynch, Jocelyn and Amartya Sen, 1983, 'Indian Women: Well-Being and Survival', *Cambridge Journal of Economics*, Vol. 7, No. 3/4, Sept.–Dec.

Levinson, J. F., 1974, *Morinda: An Economic Analysis of Malnutrition Among Young Children in Rural India*, Cornell/MIT International Nutrition Policy Series.

Lipton, Michael, 1983, *Poverty, Undernutrition and Hunger*, World Bank Staff Working Paper No. 597, Washington, DC.

Manimala, 1984, 'Zameen Kenkar? Jote Onkar!', in Madhu Kishwar and Ruth Vanita (eds.), *In Search of Answers: Indian Women's Voices from Manushi*, London: Zed Press.

Manushi, 1982, 'A New Form of Female Infanticide', No. 12.

Mathur, K. S., Wahi, P. N., Srivastava, S. K., and D. S. Gahlaut, 1961, 'Diet in Western Uttar Pradesh' *Journal of Indian Medical Association*, Vol. 37, No. 2, 16 July.

Mencher, Joan and K. Saradamoni, 1982, 'Muddy Feet and Dirty Hands: Rice Production and Female Agricultural Labour,' *Economic and Political Weekly* (Review of Agriculture), Vol. 17, No. 52, 25 Dec.

Mies, Maria, 1983, 'Landless Women Organize – A Case Study of an Organisation in Rural Andhra', *Manushi*, Vol. 3, No. 3, March–April.

Miller, Barbara, 1981, *The Endangered Sex – Neglect of Female Children in Rural North India*, Ithaca and London: Cornell University Press.

Minhas, B. S., 1974, 'Rural Poverty, Land Distribution and Development Strategy: Facts', in Poverty and Income Distribution in India, op. cit.

Mundle, Sudipto, 1983, 'Effect of Agricultural Production and Prices on Incidence and Rural Poverty: A Tentative Analysis of Inter-State Variations', *Economic and Political Weekly* (Review of Agriculture), Vol. 18, No. 26, 25 June.

Nagbrahman D. and Shreekant Sambrani, 1983, 'Women's Drudgery in Firewood Collection', *Economic and Political Weekly*, 1–8 Jan.

Nayyar, Rohini, 1977, 'Wages, Employment and Standard of Living of Agricultural Labourers in Uttar Pradesh', and 'Poverty and Inequality in Rural Bihar', in *Poverty and Landlessness in Rural Asia*, op. cit.

Palmer, Ingrid, 1981, 'Seasonal Dimensions of Women's Roles' in *Seasonal Dimensions to Rural Poverty*, London: Frances Pinter.

Parthasarathy, G., 1982, 'Rural Poverty and Female Heads of Households: Need for Quantitative Analysis', paper presented at the Technical Seminar on 'Women's Work and Employment', Institute of Social Studies Trust, 9–11 April.

Poulsen, Gunnar, 1978, *Man and Trees in Tropical Africa*, Publication No. 1010, International Development Research Council, Ottawa.

Rajaraman, Indira, 1977, 'Growth and Poverty in Rural Areas of the Indian State of Punjab', in *Poverty and Landlessness in Rural Asia*, op. cit.

Rajaraman, Indira, 1983, 'Economics of Bride-Price and Dowry', *Economic and Political Weekly*, Vol. 18, No. 8, 8 Feb.

Rosenzweig, Mark R. and T. Paul Schultz, 1982, 'Market Opportunities, Genetic Endowment and Intrafamily Resource Disttribution: Child Survival in Rural India', Center Paper No. 323, Economic Growth Center, Yale University.

Saith, Ashwani, 1981, 'Production, Prices and Poverty in India', *The Journal of Development Studies*, Vol. 17, No. 2, Jan.

Schofield, Sue, 1979, *Development and the Problems of Village Nutrition*, London: Croom Helm.

Sen, Amartya, 1976, 'Poverty: An Original Approach to Measurement', *Econometrica*, Vol. 44, No. 2, March.

Sen, Amartya, 1981, 'Family and Food: Sex-Bias in Poverty', mimeo, forthcoming in P. Bardhan and T. N. Srinivasan (eds.), *Rural Poverty in South Asia*.

Sen, Amartya and Sunil Sengupta, 1983, 'Malnutrition of Rural Children and the Sex Bias', *Economic and Political Weekly*, Annual Number, May.

Sen, Gita, 1983, 'Inter-Regional Aspects of the Incidence of Women Agricultural Labourers (District-Level), Employment and Earnings', paper presented at the workshop on 'Women and Poverty', Center for Studies in Social Sciences, Calcutta, 17–18 March.

Singh, I. J., 1981, *Small Farmers and the Landless in South Asia*, Chapter II, monograph, World Bank, Washington, DC.

Sharma, Ursula, 1980, *Women, Work and Property in North-West India*, London and New York: Tavistock Publishers.

Skar, Sarah Lund, 1982, 'Fuel Availability, Nutrition and Women's Work in Highland Peru', World Employment Programme Research Working Paper No. WEP 10/WP 23, ILO, Geneva.

Sukhatme, P. V., 1978, 'Assessment of Adequacy of Diets at Different Income Levels', *Economic and Political Weekly*, Special Number, Aug.

Sukhatme, P. V., 1981, 'On Measurement of Poverty', *Economic and Political Weekly*, Vol. 16, No. 32, 8 Aug.

Taylor, Carl E. and Rashid Faruque, 1983, *Child and Maternal Services in Rural India: The Narangwal Experiment*, Part I Baltimore and London: John Hopkins University Press.

UNDP, 1980, *Rural Women's Participation in Development*, Evaluation Study No. 3, United Nations Development Programme, New York, June.

Vaidyanathan, A, 1974, 'Some Aspects of Inequalities in Living Standards in Rural India', in *Poverty and Income Distribution in India*, op. cit.

Visaria, P., 1980a, *Poverty and Living Standards in Asia: An Overview of the Main Results and Lessons of Selected Households Surveys*, Working Paper No. 2, The World Bank, October.

Visaria, P., 1980b, *Poverty and Unemployment in India*, World Bank Staff Working Paper No. 417, April.

Visaria, Pravin and Leela Visaria, 1983, 'Indian Households With Female Heads: Their Incidence, Characteristics and Level of Living', paper presented at a workshop on 'Women and Poverty', op. cit.

Wyon, John B. and John E. Gordon, 1971, *The Khanna Study: Population Problems in the Rural Punjab*, Cambridge, MA: Harvard University Press.

Youssef, Nadia and Carol Hetler, 1981, *Women-Headed Household and Rural Poverty: What Do We Know?*, International Labour Office, Geneva.

[2]

World Development, Vol. 20, No. 6, pp. 809–823, 1992
Printed in Great Britain.

0305–750X/92 $5.00 + 0.00
© 1992 Pergamon Press Ltd

Household Production Reconsidered: Gender, Labor Conflict, and Technological Change in Malaysia's Muda Region

GILLIAN HART
University of California, Berkeley

Summary. — The notion of the farm-household as a bounded unit of production and consumption has become enshrined as a category of analysis, and as a policy ideal. This article points to the limitations of the neoclassical theory of the farm-household for understanding technological and economic change, and suggests an alternative, politicized approach that focuses on gender relations within and among households. Evidence to illustrate these arguments comes from the Muda region of Malaysia, often regarded as the archetypical farm-household economy.

1. INTRODUCTION

Over the past 20 years or so, the "farm-household" has replaced "the farmer" or "the peasant" in many analyses of agrarian questions. For neoclassical economists, the significance of farm-household resides in its role as a unit of both production and consumption. Thus, Barnum and Squire (1979a, p. 3) assert, the outcomes of technological change in agriculture "can only be assessed by reference to a model that integrates the decision-making process of the farm household with respect to both production and consumption" (see also Singh, Squire and Strauss, 1986).

Within such models, "the household" is treated as a solidary unit, undifferentiated by gender or age. In response, an extensive critique of unitary models of the household has now developed in the context of technological change in agriculture. The central thrust of this critique has been the unequal impact of Green Revolution technology on women and men, and the way unitary household models mask these differential effects. In particular, a number of researchers have shown how poor rural women often bear a disproportionate share of the costs of technological change. When confronted with this critique, economists often draw a distinction between "the household" as a production issue, and gender (or, more often, "women in development") as a distribution issue.

In fact, the neoclassical farm-household model obscures not only the gender-differentiated *effects* of technological change, but also some of the key forces responsible for bringing about shifts from labor-intensive, seed-fertilizer technology to mechanization. I will illustrate this argument with reference to Muda, the main rice-producing region of Malaysia — the locus of one of the first econometric estimates of the farm-household model (Barnum and Squire, 1979a; 1979b).

Muda is a particularly dramatic example of the transition from labor-intensive, seed-fertilizer technology to mechanization. In their review of South and Southeast Asian experience with the Green Revolution, Jayasuria and Shand (1986) observe that in the first phases of the Green Revolution, the new seed-fertilizer technology initially increased labor demand in wheat and rice production. More recently, many producers have adopted labor-saving chemical and mechanical innovations. The switch to labor-saving technology has been taking place even in the most labor-abundant areas of South and South-

*This research was supported by a fellowship from the Rockefeller Foundation under the "Changing Gender Roles" program, and was carried out in affiliation with the Centre for Policy Research, Universiti Sains Malaysia. For helpful comments and discussion, I am grateful to Bina Agarwal, Sara Berry, Pauline Peters, Michael Watts, and three reviewers. They of course bear no responsibility. Final revision accepted: July 30, 1991.

east Asia where real wages have in some cases declined (Jayasuria and Shand, 1986). Policies that cheapened the price of capital played a role in some cases, but they cannot fully explain the spread of labor-saving technology.

On the face of it, the explanation for mechanization in Muda seems quite straightforward from a neoclassical point of view. Although the relative factor price of labor (i.e. the wage divided by the price of padi) did not increase very much in the first phase of technological change in Muda, the real return to employment (i.e. the wage divided by the consumer price index) rose significantly. According to Barnum and Squire (1979a, p. 24), these patterns suggest both a competitive labor market and a relatively inelastic labor supply. This inelastic labor supply is, they maintain, a reflection of high leisure preferences. Increasing farm incomes in the first phase of technological change enabled farm-households to indulge their consumption preferences for leisure. Labor supply therefore failed to keep pace with rising labor demand, and placed upward pressure on wages.

This interpretation overlooks some of the key forces at work in the Muda countryside during the 1970s. Rather than just the growing indulgence of leisure preferences, I will show how a major dynamic during the first phase of technological change was escalating conflict over the mobilization and control of labor. Of the multiple loci of labor conflict within and among domestic groups, the most important was the growing capacity of poor women to organize collectively and to challenge the interests of rich men. From this perspective, mechanization was not simply a price-induced response to relative factor scarcities; it was also part of an effort by large landowners and the irrigation authorities to bring recalcitrant women workers under control.

Although the model of the farm-household bears little resemblance to the realities of production organization, it has continued to inform policy thinking in the postmechanization era. In the period immediately following mechanization, key state agencies claimed that mechanization would finally *create* the conditions for farm-household production. More recently, the World Bank has once again invoked the farm-household as the solution to problems in Malaysia's rice economy. In section 4, I will draw on recent longitudinal evidence from Muda to show how the unified farm-household has remained a chimera from the viewpoint of policy makers, and a misleading theoretical construct. I will also suggest how a direct understanding of poor women's capacity to organize collectively opens the way for innovative approaches to agrarian reform.

2. MODELS OF "THE HOUSEHOLD" AND LABOR PROCESSES: NEOCLASSICAL VS. POLITICIZED APPROACHES

(a) *The farm-household model in the Muda Region*

The farm-household model invokes two crucial assumptions. First is that the preferences of all household members can be aggregated in a single joint utility function, so that the household can be treated as if it acts like an individual. Second is the existence of a perfectly competitive labor market. This assumption is particularly important for econometric applications, because it permits the separate estimation of production and consumption segments of the model, with all prices taken as exogenous to the household.[1]

In one of the first econometric applications of the farm-household model, Barnum and Squire (1979a; 1979b) used data from a 1972–73 survey of 534 Muda households. The Muda Irrigation Scheme, which came into operation in 1970, is a large-scale system of canal irrigation and water control that made possible the application of seed-fertilizer technology and a switch from single to double cropping. Muda is widely regarded as one of the most successful instances of Green Revolution technology. During 1965–74, rice production rose from 277,000 tons to 678,000 tons. In contrast to the situation in many other parts of Asia, even the smallest producers gained access to seed-fertilizer technology. Two rice crops a year, tight irrigation schedules, and high-yielding varieties combined to produce large annual increases in labor demand, and much sharper patterns of seasonality in labor use.

According to Barnum and Squire, Muda is the quintessential farm-household economy comprised of tightly-bounded units of production and consumption linked together by a perfectly competitive labor market. They adduce two sets of evidence to support the argument that Muda labor markets conform to the perfectly competitive ideal. First, survey data suggest that most padi households participate in the labor market as buyers, sellers, or both, particularly in peak seasons of rice production. Second is the upward trend in real agricultural wages following the construction of the Muda Scheme. From a base of 100 in 1970, nominal transplanting wages rose to 245 and harvesting wages to 201 by 1976. The consumer price index rose to 140 over the same period.

These wage increases are, they claim, a reflection of inelastic labor supply in the face of increasing demand. Figures from the 1972–73 survey pointed to a very low level of labor deployment: in the average household containing 3.1 adults, each adult worked 723 hours a year (1,793 hours plus 449 hours divided by 3.1 adults per household), of which 578 hours per year was in income-generating activities (Barnum and Squire, 1979a, p. 19). In their view, such a low level of labor utilization may reflect either an absence of employment opportunities, or a strong preference for leisure. Since labor could be sold freely in a competitive market, low levels of labor supply could only reflect high leisure preferences.

Although Barnum and Squire do not address the question of mechanization, their analysis accords neatly with the theory of induced innovation. This theory posits that innovations emerge in response to relative factor scarcities, which in turn are reflected in prices. In this view, it was Malay households' leisure preferences that played a major role in ushering in mechanization by driving up wages.

In fact, the organization of production in Muda diverges quite sharply from the assumptions of the farm-household model. Far from being solidary units, Muda households are marked by internal conflicts which render the mobilization and control of "family" labor heavily problematic. In addition, the assumption of a uniform wage rate to measure the opportunity cost of labor is violated by the growing organization of women's labor on a group basis. To comprehend the broader significance of these patterns and their implications for dynamic processes, we require a fundamentally different conceptualization of relations within and among households.

(b) *Politicizing the household and labor relations*

The neoclassical assumption of a joint utility function has become the target of growing criticism in recent years. In response, some economists have drawn on game theory to construct bargaining models of the household that incorporate both cooperation and conflict among household members (e.g., Manser and Brown, 1981; McElroy and Horney, 1981; Jones, 1983; see also Folbre, 1984 and 1986). Initial objections to these models were cast in terms of their being "less parsimonious" than the unified model, and therefore less convenient (Rosenzweig and Schultz, 1984). Others have sought to avoid the complexities of a bargaining approach by assuming Pareto efficiency (Chiappori, 1988a and 1988b; but see also McElroy (1990) for a defence of the Nash-bargained household model). Empirical tests of neoclassical vs. bargaining models lend some support to the latter,

although they have had to rely heavily on indirect inferences (Schultz, 1990; Thomas, 1990). These efforts have concluded with calls for a better theory of marriage (Schultz, 1990), and for an expanded information base (Kooreman and Kapteyn, 1990).

In fact, the recognition of intrahousehold conflict entails additional complexities. As Sen (1990) has pointed out, the rules governing intrahousehold distribution are made to appear natural and legitimate even though they often embody spectacular inequalities, and gendered perceptions tend to support and sustain such rules. These perceptions, however, are not immutable: "the process of politicization — including a political recognition of the gender issue — can itself bring about sharp changes in these perceptions" (Sen, 1990, p. 126), and hence in the rules of intrahousehold allocation.

As I have argued more fully elsewhere (Hart, forthcoming), these and other considerations lead one to a politicized conceptualization of the household. Rather than a bounded unit, the household is more usefully seen as a political arena constituted by particularly dense bundles or rules, rights, and obligations governing relations between men and women, and elders and juniors (see Guyer, 1981). The rules defining property rights, labor obligations, resource distribution, and so forth are potentially subject to contestation, and must be constantly reinforced and reiterated. Accordingly, we need to ask not only what these rules are, but also how they are reinforced or redefined in daily practice. Ideologies of gender figure prominently in these "intrahousehold" negotiations and struggles, often in conjunction with conflicting notions of family unity (see for example Lem, 1988; Carney and Watts, 1990; Yanagisako, 1990). Domestic politics — in other words, the influence that different household members can wield in negotiations and struggles over the mobilization and deployment of "family" labor and resources — are reciprocally linked with the organization of labor and conditions of access to resources (both material and symbolic) in nondomestic spheres. As Berry (1984, p. 20) puts it, "The questions we need to ask are not what do 'households' decide and how, but rather how does membership in a household affect people's access to resources, obligations to others, and understanding of their options — and vice versa?" These connections and interactions can only be understood longitudinally and in relation to larger configurations of economic and political power.

This politicized approach helps to clarify a key dynamic at work in the Muda countryside during the 1970s — namely, an intensifying set of struggles over labor mobilization and control, and a shift in the chief locus of conflict. Historically, the most problematic relationship in terms of labor control had been between parents and children, particularly sons. As labor requirements escalated, the locus of conflict increasingly came to center upon the relationship between wealthy male employers and women workers. A key element in the upward pressure on wages was poor women's capacity to organize collectively.

In the discussion that follows, I will also show how gender-differentiated labor conflict in Muda did not follow in an automatic way from the characteristics of the technology. Rather, the terrain of struggle was set in critically important ways by the conditions of access to resources, which in turn were shaped by larger political-economic struggles.

3. FORCES LEADING TO MECHANIZATION: A REINTERPRETATION OF MUDA EXPERIENCE

(a) *Property and labor relations in the domestic arena*

Muda exemplifies those areas of Southeast Asia in which bilateral kinship is practiced by the numerically dominant Malay population. To outside observers, at least, such areas present a picture of remarkable symmetry in relations between women and men:

> The cultural manifestations of this sexual equality are, for example, a bilateral kinship structure; equal inheritance rights of sons and daughters; post-marital residence patterns emphasizing neolocality and/or residence (often temporary) with either set of parents according to considerations of convenience; the lack of substantial material transactions in marriage contracts and approximately equal contributions to marriage costs from both parties; a large element of free choice of marriage partners; tolerance (but rarely approval) of pre-marital and extra-marital sexual relations; male-female equality in social intercourse; and the lack of strong preference for children of one [sic] sex (Moore, 1973, p. 912).

In fact, this appearance of gender symmetry masks important conflicts between genders and generations.

To comprehend how "family" labor was mobilized and organized in the past, one must begin with marriage — which was how wealthier parents gained access to their children's (especially sons') labor. Upon marriage, a young couple would move in with either the husband's or the wife's parents, depending mainly on the resource endowments and labor needs of the respective families. After contributing their labor for a few years, the couple would then set up a separate residence at which time the parents assigned them a piece of land to cultivate. Such land was not granted permanently; it was regarded as a special contribution to get the young family started, and could be reclaimed. Although the young couple often paid little or no rent, they were expected to contribute labor services to the parental family. In this way, apparently autonomous nuclear households can in practice be bound together by complex transfers of land, labor, and often other resources.

In later years, when the parental family was too old to engage in cultivation, the younger couple would often rent their land. One of the key issues in disputes over inheritance is which sibling took best care of elderly parents, and the net direction of intergenerational resource transfers.

Although these changing patterns of access to land over the course of the life cycle have a somewhat Chayanovian air, they are by no means a reflection of simple demographic differentiation. Poorer parents who lacked the property with which to bind their children generally lost them to migration — which probably accounts for the historically high levels of migration from the region (Jegatheesan, 1977), as well as the small numbers of people who neither own nor farm land.

There was, however, a particularly important way in which marriage was sometimes associated with social mobility in rural society. Wong's (1983) and my own research in Muda revealed a marked tendency for comparatively wealthy parents to marry at least one child to a notably poorer spouse. Family histories indicated that both sons and daughters had married "down" in terms of wealth, although most of the wealthier women who married poorer men were young divorcees. Discussions of such marriages produced a consistent theme: a poor spouse tended to be *lebih patuh* — more compliant and malleable to the needs and wishes of the parents of the wealthier party. As we will see later, there have been significant shifts in the intergenerational balance of power in the postmechanization period.

A persistent theme in intergenerational relations is the low level of parental control over unmarried sons: "Children of poor farm households go away to work when they reach fifteen or sixteen years old, while the young men from the wealthier families loiter around in front of the coffee shop dressed in a clean western-style shirt and sharply creased slacks" (Kuchiba *et al.*, 1979, p. 47; see also Wong, 1983). If young men living at home do earn income they may make some contribution to their up-keep, but neither their income nor their labor is automatically available to "the household." Considerable tension often ensues. Not all parents were as explicitly resentful as the woman in Sungai Gajah who, when asked what work her son did, replied angrily "He works at eating" (*"Dia kerja makan"*); but problematic relationships with adolescent sons was the theme of many lively discussions. Several fathers attributed the problems to their own permissive treatment of their sons, which they wistfully contrasted with the discipline exercised by Chinese patriarchs.

A very different set of rules governs the treatment of daughters: "Malay girls (unlike boys) are brought up to be shy and retiring (*malu*), obedient to their parents (*ikut parentah bapamak*), and timid/fearful (*takut*) of strangers and unfamiliar surroundings" (Ong, 1983, p. 5). By confining young, unmarried women to the home, parents sought in the past to control not only the gendered subjectivity of their daughters, but also their domestic labor. The purported relative autonomy of older women derived at least in part from their ability to consign domestic labor to their daughters and, in some instances, daughters-in-law: "Control over the labour of unmarried daughters is rigidly exercised but [this labor] is applied almost exclusively to the domestic sphere and not made available for paddy cultivation [most of which is undertaken by women beyond their childbearing years]" (Wong, 1983, p. 173; for a similar account see Kuchiba *et al.*, 1979; Maznah, 1984; Banks, 1984; McLellan, 1984).

Age-gender hierarchies and the asymmetrical treatment of sons and daughters are crucial to understanding the low average working hours mentioned earlier. They reflect, in essence, low labor force participation rates. Barnum and Squire's assertion of high "household" leisure preferences fails to take into account both domestic work by young women, and the incapacity of parents to mobilize and control the labor (or the earnings) of their unmarried sons.

Over the course of the 1970s there were important shifts in the intergenerational balance of power, particularly between unmarried daughters and their parents. As discussed more fully later, the intensification of labor demand in rice agriculture coincided with the New Economic Policy (NEP) that generated both massive increases in government spending and important changes in the structure of the economy. Spending on higher education in rural regions such as

Muda was particularly rapid, and the average years of schooling of both boys and girls rose sharply. In addition, expansion of export-oriented industrialization in free-trade zones generated large increases in the demand for the labor of young, unmarried women. Ong (1987) has shown how fundamentalist Islamic groups and factories have both taken an active hand in adapting, elaborating, and restructuring mechanisms of control over young women. In terms of intergenerational relations, however, the balance of power has shifted significantly and parental control is now far more tenuous (McLellan, 1984). As I will argue more fully later, the greater mobility of young women has contributed to the withdrawal from agricultural labor of older married women from wealthier households.

The massive social and economic dislocations brought about by the NEP helped to precipitate the *dakwah* (Islamic revivalist) movement. In addition to challenging the new structures of privilege created by the NEP, the Islamic movement in Malaysia sought to redefine Malay-Muslim identity by invoking a mythic, homogeneous Islamic past (Ong, 1990). These efforts to promote "Arabization" demanded a rigid separation between public roles as male and female ones as private, a separation which, as Ong (1990) notes, is quite contrary to indigenous arrangements. Under threat from the Islamic movement, the coalition in control of the state launched an Islamicization campaign of its own. In the process, it appropriated and elaborated key *dakwah* ideologies of women's rightful position in the home, men's moral and intellectual superiority to and responsibility for women and, through pronatalist "family development" policies aimed at middle class Malays, women's role as reproducers of the racial stock.

These efforts to redefine the domestic sphere and women's position have exercised a particularly strong influence on the emergent urban middle class, but they have had far less impact on working-class women (Ong, 1990). Processes of domestication have been more uneven in rural areas, but they follow an essentially similar class-differentiated pattern (Hart, 1990b, 1991). As I will now try to show, working-class women's capacity to organize collectively *vis-à-vis* their employers is crucial to understanding technological and economic change.

(b) *Labor intensification and the reorganization of work*

The organization of agricultural labor in Muda diverges in important ways from the perfectly competitive labor market ideal on which the farm-household model is crucially contingent. Interestingly, Barnum and Squire do recognize this point. In presenting some "descriptive" background information on Muda, they observe that

> Transplanters and harvesters usually work in groups and are paid by the area completed. As a result, groups that work more efficiently can earn a higher daily wage. Unfortunately, no information is available either on the formation of the groups or on the way the group divides its earnings. It is probably safe to assume, however, that the effective wage rate per unit of time per worker varies considerably, especially among groups but probably also within groups. Wage data calculated from the FAO-IBRD survey confirm that the earnings per unit of time from employment in the padi sector do vary considerably among individuals (Barnum and Squire, 1979a, p. 24).

This point, however, drops out of sight in the econometric application of the model, which requires a uniform wage rate to measure the opportunity cost of labor.

There are several ways in which the organization of labor in groups is particularly significant. First, it blurs the line between family and hired labor. For key agricultural operations performed by women it is the work group (discussed more fully later) and not the "household" that is the salient unit of production. Second, the organization and logic of women's work groups changed significantly over the 1970s. Broadly speaking, there was a shift from an elaborate system of exchange labor based on principles of reciprocity to collectively organized labor gangs that reflected escalating conflicts between workers and employers. More than leisure preferences, it was poor women's capacity to organize collectively and resist efforts by large landowners to break up

these gangs that was responsible for increasing labor costs. The third significant point is that men did not organize collectively, despite all apparent indications that it would have been in their short-term material interests to do so. Questions of gender must therefore figure prominently in any effort to understand labor market developments.

Table 1 summarizes data from the Muda Agricultural Development Authority (MADA) showing the increase in hired labor relative to both family and exchange labor. Exchange labor is nominally organized on a group basis (known as *kumpulan derau*, or exchange labor groups). In fact, it comprises a set of individual contracts. The *kumpulan derau* refers to a very loosely organized grouping of women which can vary enormously in size. When any one member wishes to transplant a plot, she invites as many people as are necessary to complete the job in a morning. She then owes each of them an equivalent amount of labor, which can be settled either with reciprocal work, or with a cash payment. This system therefore entails an implicit wage at which labor is valued per unit of time. The increase in hired labor in transplanting and harvesting reflects a move to smaller, more tightly organized groups (at least on a season-by-season basis) which undertake piece-rate jobs for which they are paid by the area. Even if payment is equally divided within the group, the payment per unit of time is likely to vary among groups. The coexistence of multiple arrangements at any one time has been noted in a number of village studies (e.g., Barnard, 1981; Emby, 1977; de Koninck, 1979; Kuchiba and Tsubouchi, 1967; Scott, 1985; Wong, 1983), leading one observer to note that "the respective responsibilities and modes of operation of traditional-style *derau* groups and of salaried labor gangs is becoming

Table 1. *Distribution of labor arrangements*

		All Muda			ACRBD4 Region	
	1970	1974	1979		1979	
			T*	H†	T*	H†
Family	34	39	26	16	12	16
Hired	32	59	69	70	22	84
Exchange	34	2	5	14	66	0
	100	100	100	100	100	100

Source: Yamashita *et al.* (1981), tables 19 and 20.
*Transplanting.
†Harvesting.

increasingly complex and confused" (de Koninck, 1979, p. 6).

This unevenness is also evident in different parts of the Muda region. One particularly striking pattern in Table 1 is the apparently high incidence of exchange labor in the the ACRBD4 subregion compared with the whole of Muda. This subregion contains the village of Sungai Gajah studied by Md. Shadli in 1976–77 (Md. Shadli, 1978), Wong in 1979–80 (Wong, 1983), and myself in 1987.[2] Of the 227 households in the MADA sample, 35 were from Sungai Gajah. Wong (1983) confirms that *derau* was still widespread in Sungai Gajah in 1979. Her evidence and my own field research reveal a system known as *kontrek* (literally contract labor) by which certain poor women had long-standing contracts to transplant and harvest specific plots belonging to women from households with large landholdings. The recipients of contracts, who were typically poorer relatives of the landowner, would undertake to mobilize the necessary labor through some combination of calling on women who still owed them labor, and hiring additional workers.

A key factor responsible for the persistence of dyadic arrangements in Sungai Gajah was that a comparatively high proportion of women from large landholding households remained actively involved in mobilizing and organizing agricultural labor, and in allocating contracts to poorer women for transplanting and harvesting particular plots. The contract system appears to have forestalled the development within the village of labor gangs composed of poor women. Some poor women, however, with no long-standing contracts did form gangs for wage work outside the village. By the early 1980s, virtually all of the women from large landholding households had relinquished their roles in organizing agricultural labor. Only then did women who remained in the agricultural workforce form share groups, which were differentiated according to landholdings. As discussed more fully later, women with medium landholdings worked mainly on members' land, whereas poor women's groups were collective gangs geared primarily to wage labor.

Studies in other villages (Barnard, 1981; de Koninck, 1979; Scott, 1985) suggest that the formation of labor gangs was far more fully developed by the late 1970s elsewhere in Muda. There are also a number of indications of escalating conflict between gangs of poor women and their employers during the 1970s in the period prior to the spread of mechanization. One particularly interesting example concerns efforts by employers to break up labor gangs and replace them with individual daily wages. Even in periods of relatively slack labor demand, women refused to transplant or harvest on an individual basis (or, as they put it, to *"makan kupang"*; literally, to "eat shillings," one of the smallest denominations of Malaysian currency). As Scott notes, "they understand that this is another way of reducing their wage and breaking their rudimentary organization." In areas where labor gangs had become the dominant organizational form, strikes were not unusual. The "trade union mentality" that was developing in some areas became clearly evident in the latter part of the 1970s when the use of combine harvesters began spreading, initially among large landowners. In a number of different places, women's work groups tried to resist displacement by refusing to transplant the land of employers who used the combine for harvesting. These boycotts typically failed because large landholders called in work gangs from other parts of the region who effectively acted as strike breakers, but they attest to growing labor conflict.

These actions by poor women's work groups assume additional significance when contrasted with the organization of male labor. In the case of threshing, the main labor-intensive task performed by men prior to the spread of the combine harvester, village studies document a consistent trend toward individualized labor relations. In the past, men worked in threshing groups that were paid on a per area basis. Following the intensification of rice production, there was a shift to individual piece rate payment on a per sack basis (Md. Shadli, 1978; Kuchiba, 1979; Barnard, 1981; Wong, 1983; Scott, 1985). By promoting competition among workers, this system operated strongly to the advantage of employers.

Men did not try to organize collectively as women did, despite all indications that collective organization would have increased their returns to labor (Hart, 1991). Gender differences in labor organization were evident in other ways. For example, female labor groups would strike as a unit, whereas male workers tended to walk out as individuals. Scott notes that "pressure is brought to bear on those [men] who would remain in the walkout" (Scott, 1985, p. 260), but men were notably less inclined than women to act collectively *vis-à-vis* their employers. Moreover, in contrast to the open boycotts that poor women tried to organize in an effort to sanction employers for using the combine harvester, men expressed their resistance in individual and largely clandestine acts of sabotage.

The differential involvement of women and men in political patronage relations is one of the major reasons for gender differences in labor

816   WORLD DEVELOPMENT

arrangements. As mentioned earlier, technological change and labor intensification coincided with the New Economic Policy, which vastly accelerated the flow of resources into rural regions like Muda. The chief political threat to the ruling party (UMNO or the United Malays National Organization) comes from these regions in the form of PAS (Partai Islam), the fundamentalist Islamic opposition. To maintain their position and ensure continued access to state resources, UMNO rural party bosses had to consolidate a base of political support among the poorer peasantry. Large landowners belonging to PAS were similarly concerned with ensuring a loyal following. These patronage relations are intertwined with religious practices, and operate largely to the exclusion of women. Poorer women's capacity to organize collectively and engage in direct confrontation grows partly out of their exclusion from the main arenas in which power and influence are exercised. Conversely, it is precisely because men are more closely incorporated into larger structures of power and privilege that poorer men are subject to a wider array of controls through religious and political institutions (Hart, 1991).

Official gender ideologies that stress female domestication and men's responsibility for women are also important to understanding differential politicization in the labor process (Hart, 1991). As mentioned earlier, these ideologies figured prominently in political struggles sparked by the NEP during the 1970s. Poor men's inability to live up to official ideals of masculinity undermined their bargaining position both in the domestic sphere as well as in the labor process. At the same time, poor women's capacity to question male responsibility in the domestic sphere — the product in part of the burden of daily provisioning in the harsh material circumstances in which they found themselves — is, as I have argued more fully elsewhere (Hart, 1990, 1991), reciprocally linked with their capacity to organize collectively and confront their employers.

These gender-differentiated patterns of labor relations underscore the limitations of Barnum and Squire's contention that leisure preferences were driving up the price of labor in a perfectly competitive market. Over the course of the 1970s, shifts in labor supply — such as the withdrawal from agricultural labor of women from wealthier households — may well have contributed to increasing labor costs. Wage increases however, were a reflection not simply of the aggregate labor market conditions, but also the changing forms of struggle and contestation within the domestic domain, and between workers and employers.

(c) *Pressures for mechanization*

The capacity of poor women to organize collectively not only confronted large landowners with problems of labor mobilization and control; in addition, it disrupted efforts by key state agencies to control the conditions of production. Although the Muda scheme is not, strictly speaking, a contract-farming system, it operates according to similar principles of highly centralized control. The Muda Agricultural Development Authority (MADA) is responsible for access to inputs, water release, extension services, the timing of planting, and the promotion of technology. MADA's concern with ensuring production and procurement has meant that even the smallest producers have had access to subsidized production inputs. In questions of labor control, however, MADA's interests are closely congruent with those of the large operators who dominate the Farmers' Associations through which MADA operates (Scott, 1985).

From the inception of the Muda scheme, MADA officials contended that labor problems were acute, and advocated large-scale mechanization and other labor-saving technologies (e.g., Afifuddin, 1974; Jegatheesan, 1974; Tamin and Noah, 1974). These official efforts focused particularly on harvesting and transplanting — the tasks carried out mainly by women. For example, MADA actively promoted combine harvesters that perform both harvesting and threshing operations rather than the small, portable threshing machines that were widely used in other parts of Southeast Asia. MADA has also played a major role in developing and refining direct seeding techniques to replace transplanting.

MADA's efforts to promote combine harvesters through Farmers' Associations in the early 1970s failed. Subsequently, syndicates of wealthy Chinese capitalists started experimenting with combines and by the mid-1970s were beginning to reap extremely high profits from the rental of combine services. The number of combines in the Muda region shot up from 57 in 1977 to nearly 400 in 1981, and wealthy Malays also entered the market for combine services (Mustafa, 1985). Finance companies were the chief source of loans for the purchase of combines (Mustafa, 1985), and subsidies played only an indirect role in stimulating mechanization.[3]

Despite the centrality of market mechanisms, combine harvesters and other labor-saving technologies were not simply "induced" by increases in the relative price of labor, and by narrowly defined considerations of profitability. They are also the means by which both large landowners and state agencies sought to reassert control over recalcitrant women workers.

MADA viewed mechanization and direct seeding not only as a means for eliminating disorderly and disruptive labor markets, but also as the lever by which large numbers of "non-viable" households would be displaced from agriculture. According to the official vision, complex systems of labor mobilization would give way to Chayanovian farm households. This patriarchal ideal, laid out most explicitly in a joint project between MADA and the Japanese Tropical Agricultural Research Centre (Yamashita *et al.*, 1981, p. 5), defined a "viable farm" as follows: "Income from double cropping of paddy enables the farmer to support his [sic] family, and to accumulate some surplus", and "Farm units will consist of private farms operated by one farmer with assistance from his [sic] family labour." The study concluded that "large farms (above 15 relongs or 4.4 ha) and the lower medium size farms (5–10 relongs or 1.5–3 ha) bring about good income and can fit into the concept of 'viable farms' . . . which is necessary for optimal farming" (Yamashita *et al.*, 1981, p. 75).

No indication was given of what was to become of those displaced from agriculture. Apparently they were expected to move into nonagricultural sectors of the economy which at that time were growing fairly rapidly, at least in urban areas. A broad indication of the extent to which the creation of "viable farms" was predicated on large-scale proletarianization comes from a census of Muda conducted in the mid-1970s by the Centre for Policy Research at Universiti Sains Malaysia (Gibbons *et al.*, 1981). According to this census, the smallest farm size category (less

than four relongs or 1.1 ha) contained 47% of cultivating households (Table 2), but only 17% of rice land.

In fact, these plans have failed to materialize. Instead, as we will now see, there have developed multiple systems of part-time farming. "Intrahousehold" shifts in conjugal and intergenerational power relations are essential to explaining the emergence of part-time farming, and to grasping its implications.

4. AFTERMATHS OF MECHANIZATION: THE ELUSIVE "FARM-HOUSEHOLD"

(a) *Part-time farming in the post-mechanization period*

By the early 1980s, virtually the whole of the Muda region was being harvested by combines. Even the smallest cultivators purchased combine services with the cash coupon component of the rice subsidy, which was simply being passed on to the owners of capital. Despite the creation of some new jobs for men, labor displacement by combines has been massive. MADA data indicate that combines reduced labor demand dramatically; when direct seeding is used together with combines, average labor requirements fall by 80% (Table 3). The proportion of land that was direct seeded rose from 20% in 1982 to 65% in the first season of 1986, although it has since fallen to about 50% (MADA, 1987). Apart from some transplanting, the manual labor involved in rice production is now very limited.

Mechanization has thus eliminated the managerial diseconomies of scale that Bray (1983,

Table 2. *Size distribution of operated padi farms, Muda irrigation scheme*

Size class (hectare)	Percentage of Farms		Percentage of Area	
	1955	1975/76	1955	1975/76
0.01–0.57	13.6	20.7	2.2	4.2
0.58–1.15	18.8	25.9	7.9	12.8
1.16–1.72	20.3	19.5	14.0	16.7
1.73–2.30	15.0	11.1	14.5	13.4
2.31–2.87	14.4	8.3	18.4	13.0
2.88 and above	17.9	14.5	43.0	39.9
Totals	100.0	100.0	100.0	100.0
Total farms	46,547	61,164		
Total area (hectare)			95,950	99,002

Source: Gibbons *et al.*, 1981.

Table 3. *Labor use before and after mechanization: Muda Region*
(Labor days per hectare)

Field activity	1974	1979	1982*	1982†	1986
Nursery	4	2	2	0	1
Land preparation	6	4	1	1	3
Transplanting/seeding	19	13	19	4	15
Crop management	8	4	6	6	6
Harvesting	32	20	3	3	1
Postharvest	8	5	1	1	1
Total	77	48	32	15	27

Source: MADA.
*Hand transplanting.
†Direct Seeding.

1986) and others regard as necessitating small-scale units of production in wet-rice agriculture. In addition, rice subsidies escalated sharply in the late 1970s. Research by Md. Ikmal (1989) revealed a small but significant category of agricultural capitalists who combined machine rental operations with rice production, and who expanded their scale of rice cultivation when labor-displacing technology became available.

In general, however, the degree of land concentration and displacement of "subviable" holdings following mechanization appears to have been far more limited than many expected. This observation was stated most forcefully in a 1988 World Bank report which asserted that small farm size is the major structural problem of the Malaysian rice industry. The World Bank identified rice subsidies as the key culprit constraining the development of viable farms "because owners of small lots are induced to retain ownership in order to keep their claims on subsidies" (World Bank, 1988, p. 17). In addition, the World Bank claimed, the growth of off-farm employment has severed the relationship between small farm size and poverty (World Bank, 1988, p. 30). At the same time, the availability of contracted mechanized services has sharply reduced the time needed to manage and work a farm, and has facilitated the growth of part-time farming which leads to inefficiency (World Bank, 1988, p. 16): "When total farm income cannot be increased by enlarging farm size and when other, more remunerative work is available for the slack period of almost 200 working days a year, padi growing becomes a secondary job and cultivation standards necessarily fall" (World Bank, 1988, p. iii–iv).

In time-honored fashion, the Bank invoked the "viable family farm" as the solution to the related problems of small farm size, part-time farming, and declining yield. This ideal was to be accomplished by "orderly departures from the [rice] sector" (World Bank, 1988, p. 33) so as to increase farm size and reduce the number of claimants on padi income while simultaneously lifting subsidies. "Farm size could be increased by providing assistance to promising young [full-time] farmers by buying out salaried siblings or pensioning older, part-time growers who are not interested in farm expansion" (World Bank, 1988, p. 33).

In the case of Muda, the evidence that the Bank adduces to support its assertions of small farm size and part-time farming consists of a table showing an inverse relationship between farm size and the proportion of income from nonagricultural sources in 1982 (World Bank, 1988, Table 3.5). In fact, there are no data for the region as a whole on trends in landholdings in the postmechanization period. The only longitudinal evidence of which I am aware consists of panel data from my own study of changes during 1977–87 in the village of Sungai Gajah.[4] These data cannot, of course, be taken as representative of the region as a whole, but they help to illustrate a number of important points.

First, these data show an increase in both land concentration and landlessness during 1977–87, along with remarkable stability in the distribution of land among cultivating households (defined, as in the census data, as the residential unit) (Table 4). Land concentration is evidenced by a decline of 13% in the land cultivated by villagers, although total population increased slightly from 616 in 1977 to 629 in 1987. A large proportion of that land passed into the hands of a wealthy urban businessman who hired a manager. The increase in landlessness is partly a reflection of

Table 4. *Sungai Gajah: Distribution of rice land ownership and operation, 1977–87*

Farm size group (relong)*	1977				1987			
Ownership:	Households		Area		Households		Area	
	No.	%	Re.	%	No.	%	Re.	%
0	39	29.8	—	—	49	34.0	—	—
0.1–3.99	47	35.9	96.0	21.2	57	39.6	105.50	25.6
4–9.99	31	23.7	188.50	41.6	26	18.1	163.50	39.7
10+	14	10.6	168.75	37.2	12	8.3	143.00	34.7
	131	100	453.25	100	144	100	412.00	100
Operation:	Households		Area		Households		Area	
	No.	%	Re.	%	No.	%	Re.	%
0	11	8.4	—	—	31	21.5	—	—
0.1–3.99	54	41.2	114.75	17.2	54	37.5	106.25	18.4
4–9.99	45	34.4	274.00	41.2	42	29.2	248.50	43.2
10+	21	16.0	276.75	41.6	17	11.8	221.50	38.4
	131	100	665.50	100	144	100	576.25	100

*1 relong (Re.) = 0.28 ha.

more elderly people living alone, although there was also an increase in proletarianization. What is most striking, however, is that the number of "nonviable" cultivating households (or, more accurately, residential units) remained identical over the 10 years in which mechanization took hold. As in the aggregate data, there is a strong inverse relationship between farm size and nonagricultural income.[5]

Second, the Sungai Gajah data show that "part-time farming" can encompass quite different sets of "intrahousehold" arrangements with very different implications. The rise in part-time farming by "nonviable households" in Sungai Gajah since the late 1970s reflects the emergence of a new middle class, together with the proletarianization of a substantial segment of the rural population — although in ways that are quite at odds with official intentions. In middle class households, women were fully domesticated. Men held lucrative nonagricultural jobs through connections with government and supravillage capitalists, which they combined with occasional visits to the rice fields. In contrast, for poor men and women "the household" became a more spatially and sectorally divided sets of arrangements. Women took over agriculture which they organized along the lines of the labor gangs described earlier, while men moved into low-wage nonagricultural jobs and many engaged in circular migration. These jobs were sporadic and unreliable, however, and poor men depended

heavily on their wives' agricultural labor — both in retaining hold over tiny plots of land, and in generating agricultural wage labor income through labor gangs.

To appreciate the significance of part-time farming, one needs to understand why it has assumed these multiple forms. Mechanization has facilitated part-time farming, but cannot in itself explain the diverse patterns observed in Sungai Gajah. Nor is the increase in part-time farming a reflection of a self-sustaining regional growth process, by which agricultural growth generates nonagricultural activities through production and consumption linkages (Hart, 1989). In fact, the regional economy has remained remarkably undiversified (Wong and Anwar, 1987). Much of the increase in nonagricultural employment is in government services (Wong and Anwar, 1987), and has been driven by large increases in government spending in the region which reflect heightened political tensions at the national level. Following the dismissal of PAS from the UMNO-dominated National Front in 1978, the coalition in control of the state escalated spending in regions like Muda where PAS is influential. In addition, these resources were channelled to strategically placed UMNO supporters through mechanisms such as the dismissal of PAS members from local government positions.

The new middle class in Sungai Gajah has been shaped in critically important ways by the conditions of access to state resources. Men with lucrative nonagricultural occupations were all linked to large village landowners, most of whom formed the main base of UMNO support, through actual or fictive kinship ties. These kinship ties meant that the sons and sons-in-law of wealthy UMNO villagers were strategically placed to gain access to state resources. Several of them returned to the village in late 1970s and early 1980s to secure lucrative government jobs, while others acquired lucrative licences and contracts. In one way or another, men belonging to the emergent middle class had used their kinship connections to take advantage of the opportunities generated by state spending.

That most of these men also operate small holding reflects shifts in intergenerational power relations. Mechanization has meant that wealthy parents no longer depend on the labor of their children, and can delay handing over land to them. When large landowners retire or die, their land is likely to pass into the hands of their "part-time farming" sons and sons-in-law. Given the lucrative nature of their nonagricultural pursuits, it is difficult to see how a subset of these men could be persuaded to transform themselves into the yeoman farmers envisaged by the World Bank. The far greater likelihood is that they would continue to farm on a part-time basis as long as it were still profitable, and that cultivation practices would deteriorate still further.[6]

The system of "part-time farming" practiced by poor men and women represents the multiplication of income sources in the face of economic insecurity that is pervasive in many other contexts.[7] If the situation in Sungai Gajah is at all indicative of conditions in the region more generally, this group constitutes in the vicinity of 25% of the population, many of them couples in their 30s and 40s who would need full-time nonagricultural jobs which are unlikely to materialize in the regional economy. Employment in the national economy contracted sharply after 1984 with the slump in commodity prices and structural adjustment programs. Aggregate economic activity picked up in the late 1980s, but Standing (1989) has shown how a "labor flexibilization" process is underway, involving a shift away from employment security, and a shift of employment risk from employers to workers. In these conditions, the capacity to retain access to a small piece of land represents an important source of security for the poor. Any effort to displace these "part-time farmers" in line with World Bank recommendations would undoubtedly provoke a costly political backlash in the form of support for PAS.

There is an additional reason that the World

Bank recommendations may well have been greeted with some dismay in official circles. Most of the middle class "part-time farmers" are connected with the village government, and they have become, in effect, brokers of state resources who exercise considerable influence on the coalition in control of the state. At the time of my research, many of the poor men engaged in low-wage nonagricultural jobs depended on the contracts and resources controlled by these brokers, on whom the ruling party in turn relied for delivering the rural vote. Accordingly, these brokers are in a position not only to press for the continuation of agricultural subsidies, but also for a range of nonagricultural state supports.

In the case of Sungai Gajah — and possibly many other parts of the Muda region — the World Bank's invocation of full-time family farmers is as divorced from the reality of production relations and power struggles as was Barnum and Squire's application of the neoclassical household model. Other than elderly large landowners, most of those with "viable" holdings were resentful PAS supporters whose political affiliations deprived them of access to state resources and opportunities in nonagricultural spheres. Just as the neoclassical household model yielded a distorted understanding of the first phase of technological change in Muda, efforts to conjure up "farm-households" in the postmechanization period represent little more than the pursuit of a mirage.

(b) *Women's work groups: An alternative approach to agrarian reform*

Some interesting possibilities emerge if, instead of invoking "the household," one focuses concretely on the organization of production. At least in Sungai Gajah, the "share groups" organized by poor women for work on their own farms and as labor gangs are, in fact, well-functioning collectives. If these groups were able to expand their control over land and capital, they could capture a substantially larger share of the surplus.

In 1987, there were 6–7 share groups in Sungai Gajah, each composed of between 6–8 women. The character and organization of the groups varied. At one extreme was a set of older women who only worked on one another's farms. At the other extreme were two highly commercialized groups of landless and very small landholding women who functioned primarily as labor gangs working both inside and outside the village. In between were two groups comprising women from medium to small-landholding households who mainly worked on one another's land but who also did a certain amount of contract work for wages. In addition to these fairly stable groups, there were several smaller groups of women who would get together more informally on a season-by-season basis.

Poorer groups in particular were very highly organized. There was considerable emphasis on the mutual compatibility of group members, as well as a great deal of mutual assistance in the form of transfers of goods and cash to members in need. In a very real sense, poor share groups operate like stereotypic "households"; they are essentially units of production with highly developed sharing mechanisms. Some of the women in these groups were either widowed or divorced, but the married women also operated in considerable independence from their husbands. Even when husbands were present in the village, these women maintained separate budgets (and, where possible, savings) rather than pooling their income into a common fund.

In 1987, work groups transplanted an average of 30–35 relong (8.5–10 ha) per season. The time available for transplanting was severely constrained by the simultaneous planting of contiguous plots necessitated by the combine harvester. If, as I will suggest presently, the combine harvester were to be replaced with mobile threshing technology, the time available for transplanting would increase. Under these conditions, each group could probably handle at least 50 relong (14.5 ha).

The key problem that poor groups confront is the nature of the land market. Throughout the Muda region, there exists a very active rental market. Although nominal rents per season appear to have remained fairly stable, economic rents have increased sharply. The mechanism through which this has happened is a system of long-term leasing known as *pajak*, which entails an upfront cash payment for as much as 5–10 years. A number of studies documented a sharp increase in *pajak* leases in the period following the spread of mechanization. In addition, the number of seasons covered by these leases has been increasing. Only wealthy cultivators who can afford these large cash payments can compete in the rental market. If credit were made available, it is possible that poor women's work groups could enter the rental market.

A second possibility is the substitution of the combine harvester with small mobile threshing machines, a technology which is well-developed and widely used in the Philippines. This substitution would involve women's work groups' resuming hand harvesting, but threshing the padi mechanically. In addition to being small and relatively cheap, these machines are comparatively easy to maintain and transport. Ownership and operation of threshing machines could, in principle, contribute the share groups' expanding quite significantly their income generating capacity.

To put these ideas into practice would, of course, require research in other parts of Muda. Most importantly, it would call for the direct involvement of the work groups themselves. What these suggestions do illustrate, however, is that a critical disaggregation of "the household" is necessary not only for explanatory purposes, but also in order that alternative institutions can be recognized and supported.

NOTES

1. In econometric applications of the farm-household model, the integration of production and consumption is accomplished by inserting a profit function derived from the production segment into the consumption equation. Profits are then determined endogenously within the model.

2. This research was supported by a fellowship from the Rockefeller Foundation's program on "Changing Gender Roles," and was carried out in affiliation with the Centre for Policy Research at Universiti Sains Malaysia.

3. The spread of hired machine services has been facilitated by the cash coupon component of the rice price subsidy, which is now simply passed on to machine owners.

4. Raw data from a 1977 census of the village were made available by Md. Shadli Abdullah. With the help of two very able research assistants from the village, I was able to trace demographic and occupational information on each person during 1977–87, as well as data on changes in landholdings. Tabulations of the quantitative information are available from the author.

5. A more detailed discussion of these patterns can be found in Hart (1990a).

6. The majority of men with lucrative jobs used direct seeding. In principle, direct seeding does not lower yields as long as there is very careful water control and heavy use of herbicides. In practice, these conditions were not met. The second season of 1987 was particularly dry, and yield data from Sungai Gajah

are therefore difficult to interpret. MADA officials, however, noted that the decline in rice yields since the early 1980s are probably attributable in part to inadequate direct seeding practices.

7. The multiplication of income sources is often associated with notions of the household as an income-pooling unit (e.g., Wallerstein, 1984). Drawing on her research in Sungai Gajah in the late 1970s, Wong (1984, p. 60) notes that "a closer examination of the pattern of transfers and exchange reveals a system more indicative of a network pattern with different rules for different kinds of goods and services than of 'isololated', tightly bounded, internally coherent household units with little to do with one another." As discussed more fully later, by the time of my research in the late 1980s, poor women's work groups had become important mechanisms of resource transfer and consumption guarantees.

REFERENCES

Afifuddin bin Haji Omar, "Some implications of farm mechanization in the Muda Irrigation Scheme," in M. Barnett and H. Southworth (Eds.), *Experience in Farm Mechanization in Southeast Asia* (New York: Agricultural Development Council, 1974).

Banks, D., *Malay Kinship* (Philadelphia: Institute for the Study of Human Issues, 1984).

Barnard, R., "Recent developments in agricultural employment in a Kedah rice-growing Village," *The Developing Economies*, Vol. 19, No. 2 (1981), pp. 207–228.

Barnum, H., and L. Squire, *A Model of an Agricultural Household: Theory and Evidence* (Baltimore: The Johns Hopkins University Press, 1979a).

Barnum, H., and L. Squire, "An econometric application of the theory of the farm-household," *Journal of Development Economics*, Vol. 6, No. 1 (July 1979b), pp. 79–102.

Berry, S., "Households, decision-making, and rural development: Do we need to know more?" Development Discussion Paper No. 167 (Cambridge, MA: Harvard Institute for International Development, 1984).

Bray, F., *The Rice Economies* (Oxford: Basil Blackwell, 1986).

Bray, F., "Patterns of evolution in rice growing societies," *Journal of Peasant Studies*, Vol. 11, No. 1 (October 1983), pp. 431–433.

Carney, J., and M. Watts, "Manufacturing dissent: Work, gender, and the politics of meaning in a peasant society," *Africa*, Vol. 60, No. 2 (May 1990), pp. 207–241.

Chiappori, P., Nash-bargained household models: A comment," *International Economic Review*, Vol. 29, No. 4 (November 1988a), pp. 91–796.

Chiappori, P., "Rational-household labor supply," *Econometrica*, Vol. 56, No. 1 (January 1988b), pp. 63–89.

De Koninck, R., "Of rice, men, women and machines in Malaysia," Mimeo (1979).

Emby, Z., "The commercialization of padi farming in putat," PhD dissertation (Melbourn: Monash University, 1977).

Folbre, N., "Hearts and spades: Paradigms of household economics," *World Development*, Vol. 14, No. 2 (February 1986), pp. 245–255.

Folbre, N., "Market opportunities, genetic endowments, and intrafamily resource distribution: Comment," *American Economic Review*, Vol. 74, No. 3 (June 1984), pp. 518–520.

Gibbons, D., *et al.*, *Hak Milik Tanah di Kawasan Perairan Muda* (Penang: Universiti Sains Malaysia, Centre for Policy Research, 1981).

Guyer, J., "Household and community in African studies," *African Studies Review*, Vol. 24, Nos. 2/3 (June/September 1981), pp. 87–137.

Hart, G., "The dynamics of diversification in an Asian rice region," in B. Koppel *et al.* (Eds.), *The Future of Work in Rural Asia* (forthcoming a).

Hart, G., "Imagined unities: Constructions of "The Household in Economic Theory," in S. Ortiz (Ed.), *Understanding Economic Process* (Lanham: University Press of America, forthcoming b).

Hart, G., "Engendering everyday resistance: Production, patronage and gender politics in rural Malaysia," *Journal of Peasant Studies*, Vol. 19, No. 1 (1991), pp. 93–121.

Hart, G., "The growth linkages controversy: Some lessons from the Muda Case," *Journal of Development Studies*, Vol. 21, No. 4 (July 1989), pp. 571–575.

Jayasuria, S., and R. Shand, "Technical change and labor absorption in Asian agriculture: Some emerging trends," *World Development*, Vol. 14, No. 3 (March 1986), pp. 415–428.

Jegatheesan, S., "The green revolution and the Muda Irrigation Scheme" (Alor Setar: Muda Agricultural Development Authority, 1977).

Jegatheesan, S., "The economics of mechanization in rice double cropping in the Muda Irrigation Scheme," in M. Barnett and H. Southworth (Eds.), *Experience in Farm Mechanization in Southeast Asia* (New York: Agricultural Development Council, 1974).

Jones, C., "The mobilization of women's labor for cash crop production: A game-theoretic approach," *American Journal of Agricultural Economics*, Vol. 65, No. 5 (May 1983), pp. 1049–1054.

Kooreman, P., and A. Kapteyn, "On the empirical implementation of some game theoretic models of household labor supply," *Journal of Human Resources*, Vol. XXV, No. 4 (Fall 1990), pp. 584–98.

Kuchiba, M., and Y. Tsubouchi, "Paddy farming and social structure in a Malay Village," *The Developing Economies*, Vol. 5, No. 3 (August 1967), pp. 463–485.

Kuchiba, M. *et al.*, *Three Malay Villages: A Sociology of Padi Growers in Malaysia* (Honolulu: The University Press of Hawaii, 1979).

Lem, W., "Household production and reproduction in

rural Languedoc," *Journal of Peasant Studies*, Vol. 15, No. 4 (July 1988), pp. 500–529.

MADA (Muda Agricultural Development Authority), *Matlamat dan Pencapaian* (Alor Setar, Indonesia: MADA Pejabat Pengurus Besar, 1987).

Manser, M., and M. Brown, "Marriage and household decision-making: A bargaining analysis," *International Economic Review*, Vol. 21, No. 1 (February 1981), pp. 31–44.

Maznah Mohammad, "Gender, class and the sexual division of labour in a rural community in Kedah," *Kajian Malaysia* Vol. II, No. 2 (December 1984), pp. 101–122.

McElroy, M., "The empirical content of nash-bargained household behavior," *Journal of Human Resources*, Vol. XXV, No. 4 (Fall 1990), pp. 559–583.

McElroy, M., and M. Horney, "Nash bargained household decisions: Toward a generalization of the theory of demand, *International Economic Review*, Vol. 22, No. 2 (July 1981), pp. 333–350.

McLellan, S., "Mothers and daughters in the changing economy of Rural Kedah," *Manusia dan Masyarakat*, Vol. 5 (New Series 1984), pp. 1–11.

Md. Ikmal Said, "Large farmer strategies in an undiversified economy," in G. Hart *et al.* (Eds.), *Agrarian Transformations: Local Processes and the State in Southeast Asia* (Berkeley: University of California Press: 1989).

Md. Shadli Abdullah, "The relationship of the kinship system to land tenure," Masters thesis, School of Comparative Social Science, Universiti Sains Malaysia, 1978.

Moore, M., "Cross cultural studies of peasant family structures," *American Anthropologist*, Vol. 75, No. 3 (June 1973), pp. 911–915.

Mustafa Md. Najimuddin, "The political economy of mechanization: The case of combine harvesters in the Muda Area, Kedah," Rural Poverty Study Series, Pusat Penyelidikan Dasar, Universiti Sains Malaysia, 1985.

Ong, A., "State versus Islam: Malay families, women's bodies, and the body politic in Malaysia," *American Ethnologist*, Vol. 17, No. 2 (May 1990), pp. 258–275.

Ong, A., *Spirits of Resistance and Capitalist Discipline: Factory Women in Malaysia* (Albany: State University of New York Press, 1987).

Ong, A., "Japanese factories, Malay workers: Industrialization and the construction of gender in West Malaysia," Paper prepared for the Social Science

Research Council conference on the Cultural Construction of Gender in Southeast Asia (1983).

Rosenzweig, M., and T. Schultz, "Market opportunities and intrafamily Resource Distribution: Reply," *American Economic Review*, Vol. 74, No. 3 (June 1984), pp. 521–522.

Schultz, T., "Testing the neoclassical model of family labor supply and fertility," *Journal of Human Resources*, Vol. XXV, No. 4 (Fall 1990), pp. 599–634.

Scott, J., *Weapons of the Weak: Everyday Forms of Peasant Resistance* (New Haven CT: Yale University Press, 1985).

Sen, A., "Gender and cooperative conflicts," in I. Tinker (Ed.), *Persistent Inequalities: Women and World Development* (New York: Oxford University Press, 1990).

Singh, I., L. Squire, and J. Strauss (Eds.), *Agricultural Household Models* (Baltimore: Johns Hopkins Press, 1986).

Standing, G., "The growth of external labour flexibility in a nascent NIC: Malaysian labour flexibility survey," World Employment Working Paper (Geneva: ILO, 1989).

Tamin, Md., and R. Noah, "Rice mechanization: Some technical and policy issues," in M. Barnett and H. Southworth (Eds.), *Experience in Farm Mechanization in Southeast Asia* (New York: Agricultural Development Council, 1974).

Thomas, D., "Intra-household resource allocation: An inferential approach," *Journal of Human Resources*, Vol. XXV, No. 4 (Fall 1990), pp. 635–664.

Yamashita, M. *et al.*, *MADA-TARC Cooperative Study* (Alor Setar: Muda Agricultural Development Authority, 1981).

Yanagisako, S., "Capital and gendered interest in Italian family firms," in D. Kertzer and R. Sallers (Eds.), *The History of the Italian Family* (New Haven, CT: Yale University Press, 1990).

Wong, D., "The social organization of peasant production: A village in Kedah," PhD dissertation (Bielefeld, Germany: University of Bielefeld, 1983).

Wong, D., "The limits of using the household as a unit of analysis," in J. Smith *et al.* (Eds.), *Households and the World-Economy* (Beverley Hills, CA: Sage Publications, 1984).

Wong Poh Kam and Anwar Ali, *Economic Base Study* (Alor Setar, Indonesia: Majis Pebandaran Kota Setar, 1987).

World Bank, *Review of the Rice Industry* (Washington, DC: World Bank, 1988).

[3]

WHAT DIFFERENCE DOES GENDER MAKE? RETHINKING PEASANT STUDIES

Carmen Diana Deere
Department of Economics, University of Massachusetts at Amherst

ABSTRACT

This article argues that gender analysis has challenged and enriched many of the standard assumptions and concepts utilized in the analysis of Third World peasantries. Drawing primarily on the literature regarding Latin America, the impact of gender analysis on seven assumptions and concepts of peasant studies is illustrated: the family farm as the basic unit of production; the undifferentiated return to family labor; peasant household strategies; the competitive edge of peasant farms in capitalist markets; peasant social differentiation; the class analysis of peasantries; and the determinants of peasant household reproduction.

KEYWORDS

Peasants, gender, Latin American rural women, concepts, peasant studies

The multitude of ways in which rural women contribute to the economic support of households and to local, regional, and national economies has been well documented over the past several decades.[1] Moreover, the mechanisms through which women's subordination to men is created, reproduced and/or challenged have also been well illustrated. The genesis of the field of women and development has made women's work in production and reproduction visible, while focusing attention on the gender division of labor as a policy variable and clarifying a number of concepts and debates in the social sciences (June Nash 1985).

This article considers the contribution of the field of women and development to the field of peasant studies. My aim is to show how gender analysis has challenged and enriched many of the standard assumptions and concepts utilized in the analysis of Third World peasantries. Drawing primarily on the literature regarding Latin America, I illustrate the impact of gender analysis on the following seven assumptions and concepts of peasant studies: (1) the family farm as the basic unit of production; (2) the undifferentiated return to family labor; (3) peasant household strategies; (4) the competitive edge of peasant farms in

Feminist Economics **1(1)**, 1995, 53–72

1354–5071 © IAFFE 1995

capitalist markets; (5) peasant social differentiation; (6) the class analysis of peasantries; and (7) the determinants of peasant household reproduction.[2] In developing these points, I also demonstrate how the women and development field has contributed new concepts – such as the "gender division of labor" and "household relations" – concepts which provide a different and deeper understanding of how peasant households reproduce themselves over time.

The peasant-studies literature, theoretically, spans the gamut from functionalist, rural sociology to Marxist political economy. My concern in this paper is less with the contending constructs of these paradigms than with the assumptions that they have in common. It is these commonalities which I re-examine here through the lens of Marxist–feminist analysis.

1. THE FAMILY FARM AS THE BASIC UNIT OF PRODUCTION

Most definitions of the peasantry begin with the family farm as the basic unit of production and consumption. The family farm is posited to rely primarily on family labor for its productive and reproductive activities (Alexander Vasilevich Chayanov 1966; Diane Wolf 1966; Teodor Shanin 1971).[3] Implicit, if not explicit, is the assumption that peasant family farms are synonymous with male-headed households and that, with respect to farm activities, men are the primary agriculturalists, assisted by women and children.

Ester Boserup (1970) was among the first to challenge this assumption demonstrating that, cross-culturally, peasant men are not always the principal farmers. Drawing on census data, she argued that an important distinction must be drawn between male and female farming systems, with the latter prevailing in many parts of Africa prior to colonization. While Boserup's work was path-breaking in illustrating that one could not assume that farmers were always men, her reliance on census statistics to characterize farming systems was soon challenged.[4]

The deficiency of census data in capturing women's economic participation has been amply demonstrated, particularly in the case of rural women in Latin America.[5] Census data led to the conclusion that Latin American peasant agriculture was male-based; moreover, this data suggested that over the course of the twentieth century women were being displaced from agricultural activities. While Latin America thus seemed to conform to Boserup's main propositions – that male farming systems were associated with plow agriculture, and that mechanization often resulted in displacing women from agricultural work – field research in the 1970s and 1980s revealed a much more complex picture.

54

RETHINKING PEASANT STUDIES

Prior to the rapid development of agrarian capitalism in Latin America in the 1950s and 1960s, peasant agriculture was generally family-based, rather than characterized by a male farming system. Nonetheless, women's participation in agriculture was most heterogeneous, varying, for example, by region and with race and ethnicity (Carmen Diana Deere and Magdalena León 1987: 3–5). Women's participation in agriculture was much more important in the Andean countries and Central America – regions characterized by an indigenous peasantry – than in the Southern Cone – where the peasantry was predominantly white or mestizo. Women's participation in agriculture was also quite high in the Caribbean, where the peasantry is predominantly Afro-American.

Probably the most important contribution of the new generation of field research was to demonstrate that the family-based farm is often characterized by a division of labor by gender, not only in terms of farm activities (agriculture versus animal raising or agricultural processing) but also with respect to given tasks (plowing versus seeding). The concept of the gender division of labor was increasingly employed to stress the social, rather than biological, construction of men's and women's roles.[6] The gender division of labor in agriculture was found to vary not only cross-culturally and regionally in accordance with cultural constructions of femininity and masculinity (Susan Bourque and Kay Warren 1981; Olivia Harris 1978), but also, within given regions in accordance with the prevailing social relations of production and income-generating opportunities, as well as with peasant social differentiation, suggesting the importance of material conditions in changing social constructs (León 1980, 1982; Deere 1982; Lynne Stephens 1991).

Given this heterogeneity, it is difficult to establish any linear relationship between women's participation in agriculture and the degree of capitalist development (Deere and León 1987). Nevertheless, there is sufficient evidence to suggest that, over time, rather than decreasing, as census statistics imply, women's participation in peasant agriculture in a number of Latin American countries has been increasing – a product of growing land shortage and male migration in search of wage work, and women's lower opportunity cost in the labor market, among other factors (Deere and León 1982; María de los Angeles Crummet 1987; Francis Pou *et al.* 1987; M. Soledad Lago 1987).[7]

Feminist research in Latin America uncovered not only a heterogeneous gender division of labor in agriculture and heterogeneous family farming systems, but also drew attention to the existence of female-headed households in rural areas, households that do not have an adult male in permanent or even temporary residence. Far from an aberration, rural female-headed households and female farming systems were found to be a historical feature of some regions, such as the

ARTICLES

English-speaking Caribbean, while associated with capitalist development, proletarianization and male migration in other areas.[8]

The research effort on the gender division of labor and the variations in family farming systems also led to two other contributions. Gender analysis enriched the definitions of activities encompassed in the categorization of farming systems and raised the issue of the relationship between women's participation in production and women's status in the household. In addition to field labor, animal care and processing and transformation activities, it was shown that a gender-based understanding of farming systems had to also include farm decision-making and control over the outcome of productive activities on the farm.

Taking into account this broader set of variables to pursue the relationship between women's participation in production and women's status, Magdalena León and I (1982) differentiated among patriarchal and egalitarian family farming systems. Patriarchal farming systems are characterized by women's participation in agricultural field work and animal raising, but male control over decision-making and the product of family labor; egalitarian farming systems, in contrast, are those where there is a corresponding association between men's and women's participation in farm labor, decision-making and disposition of the product. We found that, in the Andean case, the rich peasant strata most clearly corresponded to a patriarchal family farming system whereas more egalitarian family farming systems tended to predominate among the poorer strata of the peasantry. This research led us to challenge a second major assumption of peasant studies, discussed subsequently, the undifferentiated return to family labor.

In sum, the basic contribution of gender analysis has been to demonstrate that the male-headed peasant family farm cannot always be assumed to be the basic unit of production; moreover, while family farms do rely upon family labor, these are differentiated both by the gender division of labor within them and by whether they correspond to patriarchal or egalitarian family farming systems.

2. THE UNDIFFERENTIATED RETURN TO FAMILY LABOR

Chayanov's (1966) influential theory of the family-labor farm was based on the argument that such was a uniquely non-capitalist unit which could not be analyzed with the toolkit of neoclassical economics.[9] Since the category of wages did not exist, it was impossible to calculate the category of profits and to posit, as for capitalist firms, that the objective of family-labor farms was to maximize profits. Rather, according to Chayanov, the peasant family maximized the undifferentiated return to family

RETHINKING PEASANT STUDIES

labor subject to the drudgery constraint and the consumer/worker trade-off.

Underlying the concept of an undifferentiated return to family labor is the assumption that the family labor product goes into a household fund and that it benefits those who produced it; that is, it assumes income pooling and shared consumption. A growing feminist literature has demonstrated that not all the income generated by family labor is necessarily pooled; moreover, income pooling does not always result in shared consumption, particularly in equitable consumption among household members (Hans-Dieter Evers *et al.* 1984; Judith Bruce and Daisy Dwyer 1988).

Whether the family labor product is used to benefit all who produce it largely depends on who controls the fruits of family labor. In the Andes, income pooling is more likely the lower the degree of monetization of the economy, with the family labor product stored and consumed over the year. Once the family labor product consists of commodities, sold on the market, women's participation in decision-making and the marketing of farm products is often necessary to assure that the family labor product results in pooled income and shared consumption (Deere 1990). That is, income pooling is more likely in egalitarian farming systems where women participate in field work, decision-making and disposition of the product.

The specialization of household members in given occupations greatly influences the extent to which control over income is individualized rather than socialized. For example, when peasant men in Latin America generate wage income from selling their labor power, they are much more likely to dispose of this income as they so wish – with minimal contributions to the household fund – even though the agricultural unit might be characterized as a relatively egalitarian farming system. Moreover, when income is generated individually, it is much more likely that women pool the income which they have earned from their own independent income-generating activities with their spouses and children as compared to men (Martha Roldán 1982; Cornelia Flora and Blas Santos 1985; Amparo Arango *et al.* 1987). But whether income generated by women in their own independent activities is pooled also depends on women having first access to their own income. As Gunseli Berik (1987) has shown in her study of rural women carpet weavers in Turkey, if men control women's earnings, this income is not necessarily utilized for the benefit of all family members, including the women who generated it.

Other research has demonstrated that there is not a one-to-one correspondence between income pooling and shared consumption. The practice of male preference in protein and caloric consumption is common to many societies, with men either eating first or being served the choice morsels. Nancy Folbre (1986), reviewing a broad range of cross-cultural material, thus concludes that women work more and

57

consume less than men within rural households. This proposition suggests that the assumption of an undifferentiated return to family labor is a problematic building block for a theory of peasant economy.

3. PEASANT HOUSEHOLD STRATEGIES

Recent feminist work on intra-household relations has also questioned the appropriateness of the concept of household strategies. As Diane Wolf (1990) has pointed out, in the peasant studies literature individual and household behaviors are often merged and discussed interchangeably as if households had a logic and an interest of their own. At the very least, the concept of a household strategy implies a unity or coincidence of interests among household members. Nevertheless, until recently, little attention was given within the peasant studies literature to how such a unity of interests might be achieved, imposed, or implemented.

Recent feminist analysis has shown that gender and generational hierarchies and the struggles within and among them are central to an understanding of peasant household economy (Gillian Hart 1986; Berik 1987; Wolf 1990, 1992; Stephens 1991). Household decision-making – whether with respect to farm decisions, labor allocation among different income-generating activities, family size and so on – is rarely democratic. Rather, those with more authority or bargaining power – men and adults – tend to make decisions over those with less – women and children. Women and children often do not participate in how "household" goals are defined.

Moreover, "household strategies" do not necessarily reflect the interests of all household members. For example, the common Andean practice of sending daughters to school at a later age than sons, may be a rational household strategy if young girls are more productive than boys at an earlier age, due to their significant contribution to domestic work and animal care. Moreover, sending girls to school for fewer years than their brothers may represent a rational household strategy, if there is a greater return to education for men than for women due to unequal labor market opportunities. But such "rational" household strategies do not serve the interests of young women very well (Deere 1990).

As Nancy Folbre (1986, 1987) has argued in a more general context, the significant differences in economic welfare among household members in terms of consumption levels, noted earlier, also shed doubt on the assumption that altruism governs household behavior. She contends, instead, that economic self-interest penetrates the most intimate aspects of household life. For Folbre, inequality within the household is linked to differences between men and women in bargaining power.[10] She considers these differences not just culturally determined but directly related to the institutions of patriarchy, such as systematic differences in access to means of production, wealth, and wages.

RETHINKING PEASANT STUDIES

Latin American researchers, such as Beatríz Schmukler (1990), have tended to place greater weight on cultural and ideological factors in structuring systems of authority within households. For women in Latin American households often have bargaining power, based on moral authority, if not material conditions. Male domination within households in this perspective is seen to be a product of cultural and ideological constructs surrounding systems of authority.

Other researchers highlight how gender relations are an arena of potential conflict and constant struggle. Lourdes Benería and Martha Roldán (1987), for example, propose that intra-household relations are characterized by a continuous process of negotiation, contracts, renegotiation, and exchange. However, as Schmukler points out, negotiations between men and women are rarely carried out as equals, but rather, these are constrained by the very system of authority structuring household relations.

There does seem to be general agreement that rather than by cohesion and coherence, as implied by altruism, intra-household relations are governed by relations of domination and subordination, hierarchy and inequality, and struggle and conflict. This suggests that to posit the existence of household strategies, the cultural rules, attitudes and beliefs, and the material conditions which favor the pursuit of altruism rather than self-interest, as well as the conditions which favor negotiation and compromise within the family, must be subject to scrutiny and established as preconditions, rather than assumed.

4.   THE COMPETITIVE EDGE OF PEASANT PRODUCERS IN CAPITALIST MARKETS

The persistence of the peasantry is often explained in terms of peasants' ability to produce cheap food or cheap labor for capitalist markets (Alain de Janvry 1981). Peasants will accept a price less than that which capitalist farmers might accept since peasants do not need to earn a profit to stay in business, but rather, simply a positive return to their labor. Similarly, peasant wage workers can accept a wage less than that needed to reproduce the capacity to labor, since some portion of consumption requirements are met through subsistence production on the household plot (Deere 1976).

It has been argued that what gives peasant units of production their competitive edge in capitalist markets is the non-transferability of family labor (Alexander Schejtman 1980). Specifically, because women, children and the elderly often have a zero or low opportunity cost, the household is better off no matter how low the return to family labor in agricultural production.

Feminist researchers have probed further, asking why this might be the case. They have demonstrated that there is, indeed, a differential social

ARTICLES

valuation of male and female labor, both in the capitalist labor market and among and within peasant households, and that these factors are highly interactive (Roldán 1982; Cheywa Spindel 1987; Jane Collins 1993). In the labor market, the subordination of women allows capitalists to pay women lower wages than men, even for similar tasks and at comparable levels of productivity (Belkis Mones *et al.* 1987). Women earn less than men also because of gender segregation of the labor force and differential wage scales for male and female jobs and tasks (Lourdes Arizpe and Josefina Aranda 1986). Moreover, often the structure of agricultural employment – whereby permanent wage employment is a male domain – limits women's potential income opportunities outside the household, relegating them to either seasonal, labor-intensive tasks, or household-based production – thus rendering their labor "non-transferable."[11]

Not only are rural labor markets often characterized by significant male/female wage differentials, but artisan activities also often exhibit significant differences in returns to male and female labor. Weaving and spinning in the Andes are usually remunerated at a much lower level than are carpentry and shoemaking, for example; and seamstresses earn much less per hour worked than do tailors (Deere 1983).

Another aspect of this non-transferability which must be taken into account in explaining why family labor is cheap, is "joint production" and the gender division of labor which assigns to women the tasks of daily and generational reproduction. An often noted characteristic of rural women's work is that they carry out several activities simultaneously in time, combining productive and reproductive tasks.[12] If we extend the notion of simultaneity to cover the length of the working day, another general characteristic of women's work is the wide range of productive and reproductive activities in which they engage (Pilar Campana 1982). In a typical day, a peasant woman might pasture her animals while spinning and collecting firewood, work three or four hours in the field after cooking for the field hands, in addition to spending six or seven hours on housework, food processing, and child care. Each of these activities taken by itself may be lowly remunerated or unremunerated. But taken together they serve to enhance the household's level of reproduction, mitigating the effects of a low return to family labor implicit in low prices for peasant production or of low wages. In sum, gender analysis has revealed that the competitive edge of peasant units of production may in fact lie in the subordination of women and the undervaluation of female labor in productive and reproductive activities.

5.   PEASANT SOCIAL DIFFERENTIATION

One of the main debates in the field of peasant studies for several decades has been that of the fate of peasantries in capitalist social formations,

RETHINKING PEASANT STUDIES

known in Latin America as the *campesinista/descampesinista* (peasantization/depeasantization) debate.[13] At the heart of this debate is the relevance of the Leninist hypothesis of peasant social differentiation to Third World social formations, and whether social differentiation necessarily produces the two main classes of capitalism, proletarians and capitalists. In the *descampesinista* view, inequality in access to means of production among direct producers, in the context of expanding market relations, produces a growing concentration of means of production among the few while dispossessing the majority, providing the impetus for increased reliance on wage labor by poor peasants and the purchase of wage labor by rich peasants.

The *campesinistas*, in contrast, argue that the agrarian class structure generated by dependent, peripheral capitalism will not resemble that of the advanced capitalist countries because of the very nature of underdevelopment. In their view complete proletarianization of the peasantry is precluded, either because the peasantry is functional to capital – as a source of cheap food production or cheap labor – or because peripheral capitalism cannot absorb a fully proletarian labor force. The *campesinistas* also question whether peasant social differentiation has taken place, citing factors intrinsic to peasant communities that mitigate inequalities (Arturo Warman 1980).

In the Latin American case, the inverse relation between access to land and peasant participation in wage labor has generally held empirically (Deere and Robert Wasserstrom 1981). Nonetheless, while most Latin American countries have seen a dramatic decline in the proportion of their population still classified as rural over the last four decades, the absolute number of rural households, and households that remain as both units of production and reproduction, still continues to increase in absolute terms in most countries (de Janvry 1981; de Janvry *et al.* 1989).

Part of the solution to this paradox comes from the recognition that peasant households often engage in a broad range of economic activities to generate household income. Besides direct agricultural and/or livestock production combined with the other activities complementary to a household-based farming system, household members are often also artisan producers, petty merchants, wage workers and engage in the service trades. Feminist analysis took this basic insight a step further, illustrating that the broad range of income-generating activities was facilitated by and often based upon the gender division of labor (Lago and Carlota Olavaría 1982; Spindel 1982; CIERA *et al.* 1987; Collins 1988; Florence Babb 1989).[14] Moreover, these non-agricultural activities often allowed peasant households to survive as units of production and reproduction; i.e., the income generated by peasant women in marketing activities, artisan production or wage labor allowed households to

61

purchase additional land or complementary means of production, precluding the household's dispossession (Deere 1990).

Feminist analysis also demonstrated that focusing on agricultural and livestock activities, to the detriment of other sources of household income, leads to a distorted vision of peasant social differentiation. In the Latin American literature a common measure of social differentiation is whether the level of farm production is sufficient to reproduce the necessary consumption levels of peasant household members; poor peasant households are defined as those which do not meet this critical level whereas rich peasant households are those which exceed it (Schejtman 1980). However, it has been well established that in peasant units of production of less than three or sometimes even five hectares, farm income is often less than one quarter or at most half of the level of total net household income (Deere and Wasserstrom 1981). Ignoring multiple income sources and their level, could lead to an overestimation of the number of households which are, in fact, poor, and the extent of social differentiation. In a similar fashion, focusing exclusively on the extent of participation in wage labor (or semi-proletarianization) as a measure of social differentiation led to premature conclusions regarding the disappearance of the peasantry. A narrow focus on the productive unit and its productive potential does not go very far in explaining why peasant agricultural production might be a losing proposition, but why peasant households can still reproduce themselves as units of production and reproduction over time. A focus on the multiple sources of peasant household income facilitated by a division of labor by gender and age is much more fruitful in this regard, for it can provide an explanation of how peasant households persist in the face of their impoverishment and diminishing agricultural income (Deere 1990).

6. THE CLASS POSITION OF PEASANTS

What distinguishes peasant households from proletarian households is the former's access to means of production, making it both a unit of production and a unit of reproduction of labor power. This conceptualization of the peasant household, however, is compatible with a number of fundamental class relations – feudal, petty, communal, and capitalist – depending on the form of access to means of production and how surplus is appropriated.[15] Within a rigorous framework of class analysis, there is no direct correspondence between the peasant household as a unit of production and reproduction, its relation to the means of production, and a specific form of surplus labor appropriation.

Class analyses of peasant households have invariably focused on the principal occupation or class position of the male head of household, ignoring the gender and age division of labor within the household itself.

62

RETHINKING PEASANT STUDIES

As Marianne Schmink (1984) has pointed out, it is most problematic to assume that "supplementary" workers who have their own independent economic relations necessarily belong to the class category of the head of household.

Moreover, if peasant household members engage in multiple income-earning activities, as I have argued above, the class content of each of these activities must be taken into account in analyzing the class position(s) of different household members. And if, in fact, individuals occupy different and multiple class positions, the household must be reconceptualized as the potential site of multiple class relations (Deere 1987, 1990).[16]

In contrast to the *campesinista* view that petty production must always be considered the primary activity and objective of peasant households (Warman 1980), gender analysis also suggests that the class position of peasant households can never be given in theory, but rather, its class composition must be the result of careful empirical investigation.

7. THE DETERMINANTS OF PEASANT HOUSEHOLD REPRODUCTION

The field of peasant studies has tended to concentrate on the peasant household as a unit of production with relatively little attention to the conditions which give rise to and support the household as both a unit of production and reproduction. Moreover, as noted earlier, until relatively recently, the nature of relations within the family production unit have been generally assumed to be unproblematic. The result of this myopia has been that the debates over peasant social differentiation and the persistence of the peasantry have been solely focused on the production possibilities of the farm with little attention to how peasant households might dissolve as a result of changing relations between men and women or among kin.

My own recent work (Deere 1990) has focused on the practices which support the constitution of households as the site of reproduction of labor power and the contingency of peasant household reproduction. At the outset, it is important to note that the daily and generational reproduction of labor power is a general condition of existence for all class processes. For necessary and surplus labor to be performed, the capacity to labor must be reproduced on a daily basis through such activities as cooking, cleaning, and washing clothes. And for a class process to be reproduced over time biological reproduction as well as the socialization of the next generation of productive workers must also be ensured through child rearing, education, and so on.

But the specific form and manner of the reproduction of labor power, as well as the sites in which it takes place, are historically contingent.

ARTICLES

Aspects of daily and generational reproduction may be purchased as commodities, performed by direct producers for themselves, or carried out individually or collectively by other persons. The sites of labor power reproduction may include households, the community, the marketplace, or the state.

A number of economic, political, and cultural practices – what I term "household relations" – influence whether or not and to what extent the household is the principal site of labor power reproduction. Such cultural practices include the rules and strategies governing kinship, marriage, and the constitution and dissolution of households. Also important are how individual and collective rights and obligations are structured and how these are ordered by gender and age. Among the economic practices that influence whether the household is the principal site of reproduction of labor power are income pooling and shared consumption. These practices may depend in turn on whether the household is also the main unit of labor allocation, on whether it is a unit of production, and as noted earlier, on the division of labor by gender and age. Other relevant economic practices include the distribution of resources and wealth between men and women, as well as how these resources are transmitted between generations.

Political practices that influence whether the household is the site of reproduction include the manner in which the state intervenes in defining and enforcing the rules of household constitution and dissolution and the rights and responsibilities of individuals within the household to one another or among kin. Marriage and divorce, the ownership of property and inheritance, the mutual responsibilities of parents and children, may all be subject to state regulation. The state, for example, may intervene directly in determining whether the household is a unit of income pooling, legislating that a husband controls a wife's earnings or forcing fathers to contribute to child support. And state provision of services also influences the availability of collective consumption possibilities and thus the degree to which the household is the principal site of labor power reproduction.

These economic, cultural and political practices are highly interrelated and are not independent of the class relations of a given social formation nor of those in which households directly participate. But neither can they be simply derived from the degree of development of capitalist markets or capitalist class relations.[17] Household and class relations are highly interactive. Such intervening variables as household structure and composition may influence the class relations in which given household members participate (Crummet 1987) just as class relations will impact upon the gender division of labor, inheritance and other household practices.

The importance of this line of analysis is that it leads to the conclusion

64

RETHINKING PEASANT STUDIES

that peasant households can disintegrate or differentiate themselves out of existence not only because of class relations, but also as a result of tensions in household relations.[18] The household may cease to be a unit of production, for example, if the degree of surplus extraction and distribution, based on the multiple class relations in which household members participate is so great that household labor power or the means of production cannot be reproduced at the same level. In a similar vein, divorce, abandonment of women by men and vice versa, and the breakdown of income pooling due to the individuation of income sources, may all produce instability and result in the inability of the household to reproduce itself as both a unit of production and consumption. In other words, household relations are relatively autonomous of class relations, and may be just as important as class relations in explaining the persistence of the peasantry as well as its social differentiation.

Let me illustrate this proposition with an example from the Peruvian highlands in the early twentieth century (Deere 1990). Land tenure in the northern department of Cajamarca was characterized by the dominance of the hacienda system, large agricultural estates where feudal class relations predominated. On the haciendas, household relations were largely mediated through this dominant class relation. For example, the constitution of a new household largely depended upon the landlord's permission to marry, since household formation was associated with the creation of a new tenancy relationship. Moreover, feudal class relations were relations among men; only peasant men were given access to land on the hacienda and only they negotiated the rental contracts which determined the amount of family labor services to be provided to the landlord in exchange for access to land.

Without independent access to land for their animal-raising activities, women had little choice but to marry and had little option of divorce. These conditions produced very stable household and class relations, where parents were assured of old-age security and male children guaranteed rental contracts and thus access to land.

Surrounding the Cajamarcan haciendas were communities of independent petty producers, not directly subject to feudal class relations. In these, inheritance was bilateral and women inherited equal land shares to those inherited by men. Since women brought land into the constitution of the household, women in these communities had an economic basis for divorce. If a relationship became too oppressive, a woman could throw out the man and attract a new partner.

In the early twentieth century, households in the independent communities were also not very stable. Even before the region was substantially proletarianized, extra-marital unions (by both men and women), the abandonment of women by men and of men by women, and even the abandonment of children by their mother, were not uncommon

ARTICLES

phenomena. Such practices contrasted starkly with household relations on the haciendas.

The differences between hacienda households and those of the independent communities were accentuated even further, when, as a result of increasing land pressure in the communities, men increasingly migrated to the coastal region of Peru to participate in wage labor. Women, in their absence, took on a growing share of the agricultural work. Although wage income started to exceed the income earned from farm activities, this change was accompanied by a breakdown in income pooling. Men tended to treat the income which they earned through wage labor as their own discretionary income. Sometimes, this independent income source allowed them to set up a new household on the coast, abandoning highland farming altogether, along with their highland household. Not surprisingly, this process was associated with an increasing number of female-headed households in the highlands. Sometimes, without access to male labor for crucial "male only" tasks, such as plowing, these female-headed households would cease to work the land, share-cropping it out to relatives and neighbors. These households thus ceased to be units of production and reproduction; that is, they ceased to be peasant households by the definition we have employed.

In sum, what I hope to have illustrated is that relations between men and women within households and the conditions of household constitution and reproduction are just as important as class relations in explaining peasant social differentiation – that is, the disintegration of peasant households as well as their reproduction over time.

CONCLUSION

Over the last decade feminist scholarship has challenged many of the central assumptions of the field of peasant studies: the composition of the family farm, its very logic and motivation, and the basis of its insertion and persistence in capitalist social formations. Gender analysis has also enriched the basic concept of peasant social differentiation and the class analysis of peasants by demonstrating that attention to the different activities of men and women does make a difference. The field of women and development has also contributed new concepts to peasant studies, such as household relations, which should help recast some of the longstanding debates in peasant studies.

Carmen Diana Deere, Department of Economics,
University of Massachusetts, Amherst, MA 01003, USA
e-mail: deere@oitvms.oit.umass.edu

RETHINKING PEASANT STUDIES

ACKNOWLEDGMENTS

The author is grateful to Simi Afonja, Magdalena León, Beatríz Schmukler, Marjoleen Van der Veen and Diane Wolf for helpful comments on earlier drafts of this article.

NOTES

[1] In the Latin American case, on which this article focuses, see the contributions in the edited volumes by León (1982), June Nash and Helen Safa (1985) and Deere and León (1987), as well as the national level studies in León (1980), Pou *et al.* (1987), CIERA *et al.* (1987) and Paola Pérez (1990).

[2] My concern in this article is with the basic conceptual building-blocks of peasant studies. I will thus not address the contribution of feminist analysis to such processes as migration, rural organization, structural adjustment, etc., all which have been of much concern to peasant studies scholars.

[3] This is also the implicit point of departure of most neoclassical agricultural household models. For example, see Inderjit Singh *et al.* (1986). For a thorough feminist critique of the field of development economics see Elson (1991).

[4] Boserup has been challenged on other grounds as well, ranging from her conceptualization of modernization (Benería and Gita Sen 1981) to her generalization of African agrarian history (Jane Guyer 1991).

[5] See Deere and León (1982) and Stephens (1991). Excellent overviews of the extent of women's participation in agricultural production cross-culturally are provided in Ruth Dixon (1984) and Deniz Kandiyoti (1985). See Benería (1982) for a general discussion of the underremuneration of women in productive and reproductive activities.

[6] Benería and Roldán (1987: 11–12) provide a good definition of the concept of gender: "... a network of beliefs, personality traits, attitudes, feelings, values, behaviors, and activities differentiating men and women through a process of social construction that has a number of distinctive features." Among the latter, they emphasize how ranking, whereby male activities and traits are accorded greater value, is an "intrinsic component of gender construction."

[7] Janet Momsen's (1993) research suggests that in the Eastern Caribbean, where women have traditionally been farmers, the trend until the crisis of the 1980s was for women to move out of agriculture and into the service sector in the most developed islands. The economic crisis may have encouraged a "re-peasantization of women."

[8] See Mayra Buvinic and Nadia Youssef (1978) on the general phenomenon of female-headed households in Latin America. National-level data indicated that 22 percent of rural households in the Dominican Republic were headed by a woman (Pou and Mones 1987) and 18 percent in El Salvador (Lastarria-Cornhiel 1988).

[9] Alexander Vasilevich Chayanov was a Russian agricultural economist writing in the early decades of this century. He is considered by most to be the "father" of peasant studies.

[10] See Amartya Sen (1983) for one of the first developments of the bargaining power approach to the analysis of family relations. In his early development of this approach, bargaining power depends on a number of elements, including a family member's "fall-back position" if family cooperation fails to benefit all members. He also takes into account non-economic (values, emotions, social

ARTICLES

commitments) as well as economic factors in the determination of bargaining power, but does not fully examine the gender inequalities until later writings; see Sen (1990).

[11] Also see Cynthia Truelove (1990) on how Colombian rural women are becoming semi-proletarianized within the context of the home through the growing practice of factories' contracting piecework to them. This contrasts with the Asian case where a growing number of factories moved to rural areas to take advantage of young, cheap female labor (Wolf 1992).

[12] See Maria Sagrario Floro's (1994) recent summary of the incidence of women's work intensification cross-culturally. She defines work intensity as the incidence of overlapping activities or the simultaneous performance of two or more tasks by the same person.

[13] The issue of whether peasant economies were being successfully reproduced or differentiated out of existence fueled debates throughout the Third World (Benjamin White 1989). For summaries of these debates in the Latin American case see Luis Crouch and de Janvry (1979) and Klaus Heynig (1982).

[14] The multiple income-generating activities in which both urban and rural women engage was intensified during the economic crisis of the 1980s. See the articles in Benería and Shelley Feldman (1992).

[15] This was initially pointed out by Judith Ennew *et al.* (1977) with respect to the relations of production encompassed in attempts to construct a peasant mode of production. See Deere (1990) for a more detailed explanation of the concept of class relations drawing on the work of Stephen Resnick and Richard Wolff (1982, 1987).

[16] For a recent analysis of the household as the site of multiple class and non-class processes see Harriet Fraad *et al.* (1994).

[17] Joan Smith *et al.* (1984), who define the household as a system of reproduction of labor power, also argue that it should be considered as a historically contingent site of labor power reproduction. Nevertheless, their analysis is quite essentialist, for they analyze the household totally in terms of its ability to provide cheap wage labor to capital. In Smith and Immanuel Wallerstein (1992), they revise this view, still seeing the household as a unit of income pooling, but recognizing that the boundaries of class, the world market and the state, impact upon the household in an overdetermined manner.

[18] This same point is illustrated by Bina Agarwal (1990) using a bargaining power and entitlement approach to the analysis of famines and natural disasters.

REFERENCES

Agarwal, Bina. 1990. "Social Security and the Family: Coping with Seasonality and Calamity in Rural India." *Journal of Peasant Studies* 17(3): 341–411.

Arango, Amparo, Milagros Dottin and Lidia Grant. 1987. "División del trabajo por sexo y toma de decisiones," in F. Pou *et al.*, *La Mujer Rural Dominicana.* Santo Domingo: Centro de Investigación para la Acción Femenina, CIPAF.

Arizpe, Lourdes and Josefina Aranda. 1986. "Women Workers in the Strawberry Agribusiness in Mexico," in H. Leacock and H. Safa (eds) *Women's Work.* South Hadley: Bergin & Garvey.

Babb, Florence. 1989. *Between Field and Cooking Pot: The Political Economy of Marketwomen in Peru.* Austin: University of Texas Press.

Benería, Lourdes. 1982. "Accounting for Women's Work," in L. Benería (ed.) *Women and Development: The Sexual Division of Labor in Rural Societies.* New York: Praeger.

RETHINKING PEASANT STUDIES

—— and Shelley Feldman (eds). 1992. *Unequal Burden: Economic Crises, Persistent Poverty, and Women's Work.* Boulder: Westview Press.

—— and Martha Roldán. 1987. *The Crossroads of Class and Gender.* Chicago: University of Chicago Press.

—— and Gita Sen. 1981. "Accumulation, Reproduction and Women's Role in Economic Development: Boserup Revisited." *Signs* 7(2): 279–98.

Berik, Gunseli. 1987. *Women Carpetweavers in Rural Turkey: Patterns of Employment, Earnings and Status.* Geneva: ILO.

Boserup, Ester. 1970. *Women's Role in Economic Development.* New York: St. Martin's Press.

Bourque, Susan and Kay Warren. 1981. *Women of the Andes: Patriarchy and Social Change in Rural Peru.* Ann Arbor: University of Michigan Press.

Bruce, Judith and Daisy Dwyer (eds). 1988. *A Home Divided: Women and Income in the Third World.* Stanford: Stanford University Press.

Buvinic, Mayra and Nadia Youssef. 1978. *Women Headed Households: The Ignored Factor in Development Planning.* Washington, D.C.: International Center for Research on Women.

Campana, Pilar. 1982. "Mujer, trabajo y subordinación en la Sierra Central del Peru," in M. León (ed.) *Las Trabajadoras del Agro.* Bogotá: ACEP.

Chayanov, Alexander Vasilevich 1966. *The Theory of Peasant Economy.* Daniel Thorner, Basile Verblay and R. E. F. Smith (eds). Homewood: Irwin.

CIERA, ATC and CETRA. 1987. *Mujer y agroexportación en Nicaragua.* Managua: Instituto Nicaraguense de la Mujer.

Collins, Jane. 1988. *Unseasonal Migrations: The Social Construction and Ecological Effects of Rural Labor Scarcity in Peru.* Princeton: Princeton University Press.

——. 1993. "Gender, Contracts and Wage Work: Agricultural Restructuring in Brazil's São Francisco Valley." *Development and Change* 24(1): 53–82.

Crouch, Luís and Alain de Janvry. 1979. "El debate sobre el campesinado: teoría y significancia política." *Estudios Rurales Latinoamericanos* 2(3): 282–95.

Crummett, María de los Angeles. 1987. "Class, Household Structure, and the Peasantry: An Empirical Approach." *Journal of Peasant Studies* 14(3).

Deere, Carmen Diana. 1976. "Rural Women's Subsistence Production in the Capitalist Periphery." *Review of Radical Political Economy* 8(1): 9–17.

——. 1982. "The Division of Labor by Sex in Agriculture: A Peruvian Case Study." *Economic Development and Cultural Change* 30(4): 795–811.

——. 1983. "The Allocation of Familial Labor and the Formation of Peasant Household Income in the Peruvian Sierra," in M. Buvinic, M. Lycette and W. P. McGreevy (eds) *Women and Poverty in the Third World.* Baltimore: Johns Hopkins University Press.

——. 1987. "The Peasantry in Political Economy: Trends of the 1980s." Program in Latin American Studies, University of Massachusetts, Amherst, Occasional Papers Series No. 19.

——. 1990. *Household and Class Relations: Peasants and Landlords in Northern Peru.* Berkeley: University of California Press.

—— and Magdalena León. 1982. *Women in Andean Agriculture: Peasant Production and Rural Wage Employment in Colombia and Peru.* Geneva: ILO.

—— and Magdalena León (eds). 1987. *Rural Women and State Policy: Feminist Perspectives on Latin American Agricultural Development.* Boulder: Westview Press.

—— and Robert Wasserstrom. 1981. "Ingreso Familiar y Trabajo No Agrícola entre los Pequeños Productores de América Latina y El Caribe," in A. Novoa and J. Posner (eds) *Producción Agropecuaria y Forestal en Zonas de Ladera de America Tropical.* Turrialba, Costa Rica: CATIE.

ARTICLES

de Janvry, Alain. 1981. *The Agrarian Question and Reformism in Latin America.* Baltimore: Johns Hopkins University Press.

——, Elizabeth Sadoulet and Linda Wilcox Young. 1989. "Land and Labour in Latin American Agriculture from the 1950s to the 1980s." *Journal of Peasant Studies* 16(3): 396–424.

Dixon, Ruth. 1984. *Women's Work in Third World Agriculture: Concepts and Indicators.* Geneva: ILO.

Elson, Diane (ed.). 1991. *Male Bias in the Development Process.* Manchester, U.K.: Manchester University Press.

Ennew, Judith, Paul Hirst and Keith Tribe. 1977. "'Peasantry' as an Economic Category." *Journal of Peasant Studies* 4(4): 295–321.

Evers, Hans-Dieter, W. Clauss and Diana Wong. 1984. "Subsistence Reproduction: A Framework for Analysis," in Joan Smith, I. Wallerstein and H. D. Evers (eds) *Households and the World-Economy.* Beverly Hills: Sage.

Flora, Cornelia and Blas Santos. 1985. "Women in Farming Systems in Latin America," in J. Nash and H. Safa (eds) *Women and Change in Latin America.* South Hadley: Bergin & Garvey.

Floro, Maria Sagrario. 1994. "Work Intensity and Time Use: What Do Women Do When There Aren't Enough Hours in a Day?" in G. Young and B. Dickerson (eds) *Color, Class and Country: Experiences of Gender.* London: Zed Books.

Folbre, Nancy. 1986. "Cleaning House: New Perspectives on Households and Economic Development." *Journal of Development Economics* 22(1): 5–40.

——. 1987. "The Black Four of Hearts: Toward a New Paradigm of Household Economics," in J. Bruce and D. Dwyer (eds) *A Home Divided: Women and Income in the Third World.* Stanford: Stanford University Press.

Fraad, Harriet, Stephen Resnick and Richard Wolff. 1994. *Bringing it all Back Home: Class, Gender, and Power in the Modern Household.* Boulder: Westview Press.

Guyer, Jane. 1991. "Female Farming in Anthropology and African History," in M. di Leonardo (ed.) *Gender at the Crossroads of Knowledge: Feminist Anthropology in the Postmodern Era.* Berkeley: University of California Press.

Harris, Olivia. 1978. "Complementarity and Conflict: An Andean View of Women and Men," in J. LaFontaine (ed.) *Sex and Age as Principles of Social Differentiation.* London: Academic Press.

Hart, Gillian. 1986. *Power, Labor and Livelihood: Processes of Change in Rural Java.* Berkeley: University of California Press.

Heynig, Klaus. 1982. "The Principal Schools of Thought on the Peasant Economy." *CEPAL Review* 16: 113–39.

Kandiyoti, Deniz. 1985. *Women in Rural Production Systems: Problems and Policies.* Paris: UNESCO.

Lago, M. Soledad. 1987. "Rural Women and the Neo-Liberal Model in Chile," in C. D. Deere and M. León (eds) *Rural Women and State Policy: Feminist Perspectives on Agricultural Development in Latin America.* Boulder: Westview Press.

—— and Carlota Olavaría. 1982. "La mujer campesina en la expansión fruticola chilena," in M. Leon (ed.) *Las Trabajadoras del Agro.* Bogotá: ACEP.

Lastarria-Cornhiel, Susana. 1988. "Female Farmers and Agricultural Production in El Salvador." *Development and Change* 19(4): 585–616.

León, Magdalena (ed.). 1980. *Mujer y Capitalismo Agrario.* Bogotá: Asociación Colombiana para el Estudio de la Población, ACEP.

—— (ed.). 1982. *Las Trabajadoras del Agro.* Bogotá: ACEP.

Mones, Belkis, Lidia Grant, Taracy Rosado and Pastora Hernandez. 1987. "Proletarización femenina y el limitado mercado laboral agrícola," in F. Pou *et al., La Mujer Rural Dominicana.* Santo Domingo: CIPAF.

Momsen, Janet. 1993. "Development and the Gender Division of Labor in the

RETHINKING PEASANT STUDIES

Rural Eastern Caribbean," in J. Momsen (ed.) *Women and Change in the Caribbean*. Bloomington: University of Indiana Press.

Nash, June. 1985. "A Decade of Research on Women in Latin America," in J. Nash and H. Safa (eds) *Women and Change in Latin America*. South Hadley: Bergin & Garvey.

Pérez, Paola. 1990. *Organización, Identidad y Cambio: Las Campesinas en Nicaragua*. Managua: Centro de Investigación y Acción para la Promoción de los Derechos de la Mujer, CIAM.

Pou, Francis and Belkis Mones. 1987. "Mujer, familia y diferenciación social," in F. Pou *et al.*, *La Mujer Rural Dominicana*. Santo Domingo: CIPAF.

——, B. Mones, P. Hernandez, L. Grant, M. Dottin, A. Arango, B. Fernandez, and T. Rosado. 1987. *La Mujer Rural Dominicana*. Santo Domingo: CIPAF.

Resnick, Stephen and Richard Wolff, 1982. "Classes in Marxian Theory." *Review of Radical Political Economy* 13(4): 1–10.

—— and Richard Wolff. 1987. *Marxist Theory: Epistemology, Class, Enterprise and State*. Chicago: University of Chicago Press.

Roldán, Martha. 1982. "Subordinación genérica y proletarización rural: un estudio de caso en el Noroeste Mexicano," in M. León (ed.) *Las Trabajadoras del Agro*. Bogotá: ACEP.

Schejtman, Alexander. 1980. "The Peasant Economy: Internal Logic, Articulation, and Persistence." *CEPAL Review* 11: 115–34.

Schmink, Marianne. 1984. "Household Economic Strategies: Review and Research Agenda." *Latin American Research Review* 19(3): 87–101.

Schmukler, Beatríz. 1990. "Negociaciones de genero en familias populares." *Revista Paraguaya de Sociologia* XXV Aniversario.

Sen, Amartya. 1983. "Economics and the Family." *Asian Development Review* 1.

——. 1990. "Gender and Cooperative Conflicts," in I. Tinker (ed.) *Persistent Inequalities*. New York: Oxford University Press.

Shanin, Teodor. 1971. "Introduction," in T. Shanin (ed.) *Peasants and Peasant Societies*. London: Penguin.

Singh, Inderjit, Lyn Squire and John Strauss (eds). 1986. *Agricultural Household Models: Extensions, Applications, and Policy*. Baltimore: Johns Hopkins University Press.

Smith, Joan and Immanuel Wallerstein (eds). 1992. *Creating and Transforming Households: The Constraints of the World Economy*. Cambridge, U.K.: Cambridge University Press.

——, Immanuel Wallerstein, and Hans-Dieter Evers. 1984. "Introduction," in J. Smith, I. Wallerstein and H. D. Evers (eds) *Households and the World Economy*. Beverly Hills: Sage.

Spindel, Cheywa. 1982. "Capital, familia y mujer. La evolución de la producción rural de base familiar, un caso en Brasil," in M. León (ed.) *Las Trabajadoras del Agro*. Bogotá: ACEP.

——. 1987. "The Social Invisibility of Women's Work in Brazilian Agriculture," in C. D. Deere and M. León (eds) *Rural Women and State Policy: Feminist Perspectives on Latin American Agricultural Development*. Boulder: Westview Press.

Stephens, Lynn. 1991. *Zapotec Women*. Austin: University of Texas Press.

Truelove, Cynthia. 1990. "Disguised Industrial Proletarians in Latin America: Women's Informal Factory Work and the Social Reproduction of Coffee Farm Labor in Colombia," in K. Ward (ed.) *Women Workers and Global Restructuring*. Ithaca: Cornell University Press.

Warman, Arturo. 1980. *"We Come to Object"* : *The Peasants of Morelos and the National State*. Baltimore: Johns Hopkins University Press.

ARTICLES

White, Benjamin. 1989. "Problems in the Empirical Analysis of Agrarian Differentiation," in G. Hart, A. Turton and B. White (eds) *Agrarian Transformations: Local Processes and the State in Southeast Asia.* Berkeley: University of California Press.

Wolf, Diane. 1990. "Daughters, Decisions, and Domination: An Empirical and Conceptual Critique of Household Strategies." *Development and Change* 21: 43–74.

——. 1992. *Factory Daughters: Gender, Household Dynamics, and Rural Industrialization in Java.* Berkeley: University of California Press.

Wolf, Eric. 1966. *Peasants.* Englewood Cliffs: Prentice-Hall.

[4]

 Pergamon

World Development, Vol. 24, No. 1, pp. 45–63, 1996
Copyright © 1995 Elsevier Science Ltd
Printed in Great Britain. All rights reserved
0305–750X/96 $15.00 + 0.00

0305–750X(95)00124–7

Who Takes the Credit? Gender, Power, and Control Over Loan Use in Rural Credit Programs in Bangladesh

ANNE MARIE GOETZ
Institute of Development Studies, Brighton, U.K.

and

RINA SEN GUPTA*
Dhaka, Bangladesh

Summary. — Special credit institutions in Bangladesh have dramatically increased the credit available to poor rural women since the mid-1980s. Though this is intended to contribute to women's empowerment, few evaluations of loan use investigate whether women actually control this credit. Most often, women's continued high demand for loans and their manifestly high propensity to repay is taken as a proxy indicator for control and empowerment. This paper challenges this assumption by exploring variations in the degree to which women borrowers control their loans directly; reporting on recent research which finds a significant proportion of women's loans to be controlled by male relatives. The paper finds that a preoccupation with "credit performance" — measured primarily in terms of high repayment rates — affects the incentives of fieldworkers dispensing and recovering credit, in ways which may outweigh concerns to ensure that women develop meaningful control over their investment activities.

1. INTRODUCTION

Women in Bangladesh have gained an international reputation for their excellent credit performance in specialized credit institutions. This achievement is all the more remarkable given the extreme sociocultural constraints on women's productivity and their access to capital in Bangladesh. The fact that they are a good credit risk — signalled in particular by their manifestly high propensity to repay loans when properly organized — has made them a priority target group for poverty-oriented credit programs, most of which have seen a reversal over the 1980s in the gender balance of their membership and the flow of credit to favor women. This paper assesses the degree to which women actually control loans once they have gained access to credit institutions. Based on recent research on this issue,[1] it finds that a significant proportion of women's loans are directly invested by their male relatives, while women borrowers bear the liability for repayment. The implications of this process for the assumed connection between access to credit and the empowerment of women are discussed.

2. SPECIAL CREDIT INSTITUTIONS IN BANGLADESH: THE SHIFT TO TARGETING WOMEN

The special credit programs which are justly famous in Bangladesh for their capacity to reach the poor have had notable success in overcoming institutional barriers to lending to women, although with the important exception of the Grameen Bank, these programs were initially slow to address the needs of rural

*Many people have provided helpful comments on various drafts of this paper. We would like to thank in particular Mick Howes, Alison Evans, Naila Kabeer, Martin Greeley, Harold Alderman, Sarah White, Brooke Ackerly, Russell Pepe, Jeanette Adair, Nasreen Huq, and two anonymous reviewers. We are also very grateful to the organizations discussed in this paper (BRAC, the Grameen Bank, TMSS, SNSP, and RD-12) for permission to conduct research on their operations, and for their kind assistance. Thanks also to Rina Roy and Cathy Green for providing research assistance. Final revision accepted: July 6, 1995.

46 WORLD DEVELOPMENT

Table 1. *Increase in women's membership of credit programs in Bangladesh, early 1980s to 1992*

Organization	Women as a % of membership	
	1991–92	1980–83
Grameen Bank	93.3	39
BRAC	74	34*
RPP (RD-12)	59*	8.3

*Figure for 1986
Sources: Grameen Bank, 1992; BRAC, 1992; RD-12/CRT, 1993.

women borrowers. In the 1980s strong gender differentials could be observed in the numbers of women borrowers in these programs compared to men, and, even in the Grameen Bank, in the average size of loans to women compared to men, and in the proportion of overall credit they received in relation to their membership of these programs (Saffilios-Rothschild and Mahmud, 1989, pp. 28–29). From the late 1980s that situation has been changing radically. Over 1989–92, 1.8 million rural women were reached by the three largest special credit programs alone: the Grameen Bank, BRAC (the Bangladesh Rural Advancement Committee, a very large nongovernment organization — NGO), and the government's RPP (Rural Poor Programme, part of the Bangladesh Rural Development Board). When other smaller credit programs are added, the total probably comes to well over two million. This is more than double the number reached during 1985–88 (World Bank, 1990, p. 113), evidence of a very high rate of expansion in women's membership of rural development programs since the mid-1980s. Table 1 gives an indication of the rate of this expansion in a few organizations offering special credit facilities.

Cumulative disbursements to women in these programs have increased both absolutely and relatively over this period, so that the gender differentials

observed in the mid-1980s in the proportion of credit awarded to women compared to men have been substantially reduced. Table 2 summarizes information on the percentage of special institutional credit reaching women relative to their membership numbers in the three largest programs.

In effect, there has been a near-reversal in the gender orientation of special credit programs in Bangladesh since the 1980s; a *de facto* policy shift. Credit provision for women is now seen as a powerful tool for institution-building at the grassroots level, and has become a mainstay of many NGO efforts in rural areas. BRAC has even decided to phase out the formation of new men's Village Organizations (VOs) and now concentrates on forming women's VOs (DLO, 1993). To keep this situation in perspective, however, it is worth remembering that women still receive an extremely small proportion of the cumulative amount of loans which have been disbursed by financial institutions to rural areas — about 5% over the 1980s (World Bank, 1989a, p. xii), and in spite of the above-noted increases, still only just over 5% in 1991 (BBS, 1992, p. 431).

There are a number of reasons for the shift to targeting women through special credit programs. The 1980s brought increasing pressure from promoters of gender-sensitive development policy in Bangladesh's domestic development community and its foreign aid donors for the inclusion of women in rural credit and income-generating programs. Credit, it is argued, delivers a range of particular benefits when targeted to low-income women. It is seen as a critical input for increasing women's employment in small-scale enterprises and is expected to encourage the adoption of improved technology to enhance the productivity of women's homestead-based income-generating and expenditure-saving work. Further, as many studies show, increases in women's incomes improve the unique livelihood enhancement functions women perform for their households as brokers of the health, nutritional, and educational status of other household members. It is also argued that credit represents a form of economic empowerment which can enhance

Table 2. *Comparative information on selected special credit program in Bangladesh period: 1990–mid-1992*

Organization	Number of members		Women as % of total	Credit disbursed (TK 000,000)		% of credit to women
	Women	Men		Women	Men	
Grameen Bank	1,186,826	84,635	93.3	1721*	143*	92.3
BRAC	482,014	167,260	74	1218	602	67
RD-12	204,775	141,547	59	287	247	54

*Data on credit disbursed by the Grameen Bank taken from its 1990 annual report.
Sources: Grameen Bank, 1992; BRAC, 1992; RD-12: CRT, 1993.

women's self-confidence and status within the family, as independent producers and providers of a valuable cash resource to the household economy.

Whatever the reasons for targeting women, the tremendous increase of credit availability for women must be seen as a positive contribution to efforts to challenge gendered terms of access to productive resources and opportunities. The phenomenal membership reach of special credit programs is a success by any standards, and is all the more remarkable given the tight sociocultural constraints on women's market access and on their freedoms and capacities to shift significantly their rate of market engagement in Bangladesh. In these circumstances, how far have women been able to convert access to credit, and membership of credit organizations, into a process of "empowerment"; in what way does women's access to credit affect gender relations?

3. EVALUATING THE IMPACT OF SPECIAL CREDIT PROGRAMS

Evaluations of credit programs in Bangladesh (and elsewhere, see Thomas, 1993) do not typically ask this question directly, but rather, restrict themselves to analyzing financial costs to the program, and monetary benefits to the borrower. Some evaluations do look at the contribution of these projects to enhancing the power positions of the poor — for example, assessing the impact on rural wages of providing the poor with alternative sources of income, or assessing the degree to which the poor's grassroots organizations provide them with an institutional base for challenging the prerogatives of local elites (Atiur Rahman, 1986). Still fewer evaluations assess the impact of credit on power relations of gender in the household and the community.[2] By and large, beneficiary evaluations focus on quantifiable results: days of employment generated, rates of return to investment activities, degree of increase in household incomes.

Where women borrowers are concerned, important strategic gains such as improvements in women's status in a range of institutions, starting with the household, are harder, methodologically, to identify, and therefore less is known about credit impact in these terms. Because most studies take the household as the unit of study, questions about the impact of credit on women in terms of its effects on intrahousehold decision making, resource allocation, and empowerment are more difficult to ask. Compounding this difficulty is uncertainty surrounding the meaning of terms such as "empowerment"; though popular, this is a term which is rarely precisely defined. Does women's empowerment in the context of a credit program imply a demonstrated capacity to invest loans profitably? Or does it imply changed gendered relations, such as women's greater control over

household decision making, greater physical security, reproductive control? Or is the first achievement inseparable from the second? In evaluations of credit programs, women's high demand for loans and regular repayment rates are commonly taken as proxy indicators of empowerment, understood as women's capacity to control loan use effectively. These phenomena, however, do not necessarily reveal patterns of loan control within the household.

Our research approached the issue of the relation of credit to women's empowerment from a perspective which, in relation to standard credit evaluations, was unconventional. We were concerned with women's leadership development — understood as action to institutionalize women's interests in the development process. As a result, the research poses the question of women's involvement in credit programs in a distinctly political light — raising issues of power, not just productivity. This is an important conceptual distinction. To simplify, it represents the difference between asking whether a concern to integrate women in the development process is about harnessing women's labor for development, or whether it is about development for women.[3] Research methods were designed to assess the quality and meaning of women's experience of participation in these programs, both as staff members and beneficiaries. The research focused on BRAC's Rural Development Programme (RDP), and the CIDA-funded component of the government's Rural Poor Programme (RD-12). Comparative samples were drawn from the Grameen Bank, and two women's NGOs: *Thangemara Mahila Sebuj Sengstha* (TMSS), and *Shaptagram Nari Swanivar Parishad* (SNPS).

It is important to stress that the initial focus of the study did not concern actual credit use or control, but rather, the experience of participation. In the course of the research, however, field workers and women beneficiaries alerted us to the phenomenon of women transferring loan control to men within their households. To investigate this issue, we conducted qualitative studies of 275 loans (22 of these to men) across four organizations: BRAC (106 loans to women; 22 to men), Grameen Bank (53), TMSS (39), and RD-12 (55), compiling detailed loan use histories on the basis of discussions with borrowers.[4]

(a) *Methodological issues*

Methodologically, credit impact studies pose notoriously difficult problems to which this study was hardly immune. Whether investigating income or empowerment effects, it is difficult to isolate the effect of credit from other variables such as group membership or training. Methods for measuring profits and changes in household income depend on respondent recall, which may be weak in reporting on an activity which stretched over a year, where numeracy skills are low and records are not kept. Translated into quantitative data it takes on a potentially misleading degree of precision and authority. Women's credit enters general household funds and is used for multiple purposes, while women's income-generating activities are managed in tandem with expenditure-saving work and homestead maintenance, making it difficult to filter out the exact number of days spent "employed," or the exact rate of return to a specific activity. In light of these problems, and given that we lacked the resources to conduct a detailed examination of loan investment patterns over time, we did not attempt to make quantitative evaluations of loan profitability. Instead, we established whether women retained managerial control over the productive activity: from the initial loan proposal, to investment in productive assets, labor inputs, marketing, and use of profits. Resource and time constraints also prohibited an in-depth exploration of questions of women's empowerment within the household and the community, which would have required more anthropological methods. The focus on managerial control is designed to produce insights on one aspect of women's empowerment. It provides, however, a relatively incomplete perspective, and there are many other aspects of women's empowerment which might have been explored. As the subsequent discussion will illustrate, there are many ambiguities surrounding control over loan use — an apparent loss of control may disguise a negotiated transfer, where the nature of the negotiation and transfer, and the rights and privileges gained in return, may indicate a power achievement for the woman borrower.

(b) *Profile of the sample*

Loan histories were compiled with borrowers from credit groups in all four organizations in villages around Mymensingh, Bogra, Dinajpur, Jamalpur, and Rangpur. This was a purposive selection; efforts were made to ensure representation of a variety of group and loan characteristics, such as years of membership in the credit program, and size of loan. Of the sample, 6.3% of the loan histories came from groups which had been established for less than one year, 31.8% from groups aged between one and two years, 38.1% from groups between three and five years old, and 23.8% from groups with six or more years of activity. In terms of loan amounts, 21% had taken loans for up to 1000TK, 38% between 1000–2000TK, 22% between 2000–3000 TK, 7% between 3000–4000 TK, and 19% for 4000 TK or above. This distribution is roughly proportional to the patterns of group maturity and average loan sizes across the four organizations, where rapid expansion means a preponderance of younger village credit groups with women taking

smaller loans in the initial stages of group membership. The most common investment activity of the borrowers surveyed was livestock and milch cow rearing (31.6%), followed by paddy husking and rice trade (18.5%), and small business and rural trade (16%). Other investment activities included crop farming and land mortgaging (7.9%), rickshaw purchase (8%), homestead cultivation (5.5%), construction activities including house building and installing latrines and tubewells (5.5%), poultry, sericulture, and fish culture (4%), and expenditures for illness and dowries (3%). Numbers of borrowers heading their own households were relatively low, with just 13% of the sample widowed, divorced, or separated. This number reflects the participation of female-headed households in special credit programs.

4. WOMEN'S CONTROL OVER LOAN USE

A range of questions were asked about women's control over the productive process, for example, women were asked what activity they invested in, where the inputs and productive assets came from and who procured them, what they cost, how they were put to use, where outputs were marketed, for what price, what were the problems involved in the productive process, who the main user of the loan was in terms of labor input, and in terms of controlling accounts and general management. On the basis of these questions we built up an index of loan control, as follows:

FULL = full control over the entire productive process, including marketing.
SIGNIFICANT = control over every aspect of the productive process with the sole exception of marketing (often the case in livestock or milch cow raising, where men are needed to manage the purchasing and selling process — cattle markets being a strongly masculine territory in Bangladesh).
PARTIAL = loss of managerial control over the productive process, but the provision of substantial inputs of labor (as was often the case in paddy husking, where men provided the raw inputs and women were unable to give an account of the market prices of their products, and felt they had little say over the volume of weekly production).
VERY LIMITED = minimal input to the production process, for example, small labor contributions (as when women wash vegetables for men to sell).
NO INVOLVEMENT = these were the cases where women provided no labor for activities which are culturally ascribed as masculine (for example, carpentry, crop farming, rickshaw peddling), and had no managerial involvement, or cases where women stated that they did not know how their men had used their money.
Figure 1 summarizes findings on women's degree

of loan control aggregated across the four organizations studied. These loans assessments were made for the first or primary activity in which loans were invested, and does not include secondary activities or immediate reinvestment of loan funds after rapid-yielding first investments.

As Figure 1 shows, on average women retained full or significant control over loan use in 37% of the cases, while nearly 22% of respondents were either unable to give details of loan use, or were aware of how their husbands or other male household members had used loans, but were not themselves involved in the productive process. About 63% of the cases fall into the three categories of partial, very limited, or no control; indicating a fairly significant pattern of loss of direct control over credit. Of course, given the Bangladeshi context in which women's rights of control over productive resources are so constrained, the significance of these findings might perhaps more correctly lie in the 37% of cases in which women succeeded in retaining control over their loans. Factors associated with positive rates of loan control will be discussed below, but this paper concentrates on the problem of the loss of loan control in order to assess implications for the presumed relationship between access to credit and empowerment. Patterns of loan control vary among the four organizations studied. These variations are presented later but this paper does not dwell on them. This is in part because the research was not intended to be an evaluation of these credit programs but rather, an investigation of the issue of loan control. In addition, once disaggregated by organization, problems of small sample size, and sample biases by region, group maturity, and patterns of loan investment, make observations for individual organizations unreliable.

The issue of transfer of loan control has not gone entirely unnoticed in other studies. R. Rahman's (1986) study of 151 loans to women in the Grameen Bank found that 77% of women were using up to three-quarters of their loans themselves, while 12% surrendered the entire loan to their husbands or other male guardians (1986, pp. 32–33). White's (1991) study of loan use patterns in 140 ActionAid loans in bola suggests that approximately 50% of loans taken by women are used for men's productive activities,

while another significant proportion are used for activities where gendered patterns of control are more ambiguous, such as consumption, stocking and resale of goods, or on-loaning for interest (1991, p. 29). Ackerly's (1995) study of 826 loans to 613 women borrowers in the Grameen Bank, Save the Children Fund (USA), and BRAC also registers loss of direct control over loans. She details a range of variables indicating involvement in loan use — from labor involvement, involvement in purchasing inputs, selling products, and direct involvement in accounting. Her dependent variable, "women's knowledge of accounting," is roughly equivalent to what is meant in this paper by "managerial control," and includes knowledge of input costs, product yield, and profitability. While she finds 70% or more women investing their labor in loan-funded activities, women who had actual knowledge of accounting for the activity represented 49.2% of the BRAC sample, 52.4% of the Grameen Bank sample, and 62.3% of the SCF sample (Ackerly, 1995).

Variations in levels of loan control (or imputed control) recorded in other studies attest to the difficulty of making assessments about control over resources within the household. The index used here has some advantages in comparison with other methods. R. Rahman's (1986) study calibrates the cash amount of each loan actually used by the borrower herself, but this does not give a full account of the degree of managerial control women retain over their investment activities. For example, in paddy husking, which was the second most important activity in which women in Rahman's study invested, there are a range of possible degrees of women's involvement. Women certainly provide most of the labor involved, but do not have direct control over marketing the product, and may not have full control over the amounts husked each week, given that they must rely upon men to provide inputs.

White's (1991) study identifies the main user on the basis of the investment activity — given that productive activities are strongly gendered in Bangladesh. This method for classifying loan use is more sensitive to issues of loan control, as women are more likely to retain control over activities in which men do not engage. But, as she acknowledges, it is a tentative indicator, "imposing a structure on something which is essentially fluid" (1991, p. 29). Even where loans are used for conventionally male activities, a range of managerial and contractual arrangements can be found through which women retain some control over loan use. In our study, 28% of the loans had been invested in conventionally female productive activities, 56% in male activities, and the rest in "family" investments such as housing, sanitation, rice storage, and payments for dowry or illness. This does not correlate directly with the way the "control" index ranked women's involvement in loan use,

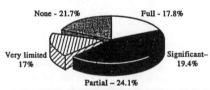

None - 21.7%   Full - 17.8%

Very limited   Significant–
17%   19.4%

Partial – 24.1%

Figure 1. *Degree of women's control over loans (n = 253).*

as the index was able to distinguish variations in control within conventionally gender-typed activities. Thus a woman whose loan had gone toward the purchase of a rickshaw might still retain control over the productive activity if the rickshaw was licensed in her name, and if she had established a contract with the rickshaw-puller for a regular rent from the activity. Cases such as these we classified as showing "Significant" loan involvement on the part of the woman borrower. In cases where loans were invested in nondirectly productive ways — such as payments for dowry or medicine — women were often the decision makers, as they can have the greatest future stake in ensuring a daughter's entry to her in-laws' household is smooth, or in repairing the health of household members, especially if it is their own, and hence less likely to attract scarce general household resources. Similar ambiguities obtained in assessing degrees of women's control of loans when credit is used for a range of consumption activities, such as food or clothing, paying off old debts, housing, sanitation, and safe water supply.

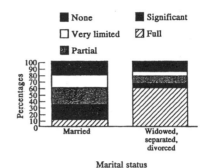

Figure 2. *Degree of loan control by martial status* (*n* = 253).

young daughters-in-law to make loan installments, having forbidden their new household members contact with strangers, especially where the field worker in question was male.

(a) *Marital status*

In this study, a range of circumstances and conditions were identified which correlated with degrees of loan control. Women borrowers were more likely to retain full control over loan use when they were widowed, separated, or divorced, as Figure 2 indicates. This is to be expected, given the more likely absence of productive men in female-headed households. In some of these cases, however, single female household heads had given over their loans to male relatives beyond the immediate household, for example nephews and sons-in-law in exchange for a guarantee of a regular food supply. Again, this illustrates the ambiguity of assessing loan control — these were registered under the "No involvement" category, yet they were not cases of straightforward male appropriation *per se,* as they involved an implicit contract and a viable economic and social survival strategy for the women involved, and could have significant empowerment effects such as increasing confidence and economic security.

Women's capacity to control loan use is likely to vary importantly according to stages in their life cycles, although this study did not examine this set of variables. First wives in polygamous households might have greater control over household investment decisions, as might older married women. It is probable that those least likely to be able to retain control over loans would be young, single and unmarried women, or new brides. In the latter case, there is also a risk of appropriation of loan management by mothers-in-law. In some of the credit societies we visited, mothers-in-law attended meetings in lieu of their

(b) *Nature of investment activity*

As might also be expected, women were also more likely to retain control over loan use where they invested in traditional women's work, particularly livestock and poultry rearing, as shown in Figure 3.

The highest scorer in this respect was the category of poultry, sericulture, and fish culture, followed by livestock and milch cow rearing, homestead cultivation, and paddy husking. The first three of these activities involve women in work whose products (eggs, milk, vegetables) can be marketed from the home, thus allowing women to retain control over the marketing process. In the cases of women investing in fish or sericulture, they had received intensive training from the development program in question (BRAC), and also benefited from program-supplied productive inputs, which eased their reliance on household men for marketing purposes at the front end of the productive cycle. Cocoons produced through sericulture were also purchased in an internal market managed by BRAC. Livestock fattening and milch cow rearing also affords women a greater degree of control than many other forms of investment. Though opportunities for women to actually purchase or sell cattle in the market are restricted, livestock management is one of the few activities over which women hold rights of ownership and control. Women who had used loans for construction, less conventionally seen as women's work, also scored highly to the degree that they were implementing house repairs, or had used credit to build new homes or purchase homestead land registered in their names — a requirement in some special credit programs (in particular the Grameen Bank).

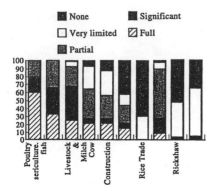

Figure 3. *Degree of loan control by investment activity*
(n = 253).

(c) *Size of loan*

Loss of direct control seems to correlate broadly with increases in the cash size of loans up to a certain point, as Figure 4 indicates. This finding is corroborated in other studies. R. Rahman found that Grameen Bank women loanees retained 100% of the cash amount of small loans (up to 1,000 TK), falling to just 46% of the total amount when loans exceeded 4,000 TK (1986, p. 33). White also found that ActionAid women borrowers were more likely to retain full control over smaller loans than larger ones (1991, pp. 29–30). It would seem that the larger the cash size of a loan, the more likely it is to be used by other household members.

Several explanations for this suggest themselves. Some of women's investment activities are too small

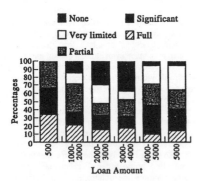

Figure 4. *Degree of control over loan use by amount*
(n = 253).

to absorb larger cash inputs, especially where no investment is being made in an improved technology, as is the case with livestock rearing or paddy husking. It then becomes a more rational household decision to invest a larger cash loan in a potentially higher turn-over and higher yielding male investment activity — such as rice stocking, rural trade, or rural transport. Another explanation may inhere in the gendered nature of rights over particular kinds of resources. Just as small-scale investment activities are strongly distinguished by gender in Bangladesh, so too are different household resources. Resources in kind, such as livestock, rice, and homestead vegetables or animal products can come under women's control. Women's savings habit of reserving a handful of rice — "mushti chal" — before cooking every meal is symbolic of this. This is one reason that informal credit exchanges between women often take the form of loans in kind, particularly rice, as women are able to retain control over this resource and can often bring it into the household without alerting male household members (Blanchet, 1986; Haque, 1989). Cash, however, especially in larger amounts, is more strongly culturally marked as a resource for men to control. It is fungible primarily through the market, a public realm culturally prohibited to women.

As Figure 4 shows, there appears to be an increase in women's loan control at the higher end of the scale, which would contradict suggestions just made regarding the greater vulnerability of larger loans to male control. Unfortunately the data are not robust enough to draw firm conclusions from this finding. Only 30 borrowers in the sample received loans above 4000 TK in value, with 12 cases falling into the "Full" or "Significant" loan use category. Six of the 12, two of them widows, invested in livestock, building on earlier loans for the same activity in which a few had accumulated small herds. One had built a house which was registered in her own name, another had bought a rickshaw for 5,000 TK and had a contractual arrangement with the rickshaw puller for a regular weekly income. Two were using loans of over 5,000 TK for activities benefiting from a high degree of technical support and monitoring from the lending organization (BRAC) — one was managing a chick hatchery and another a cocoon-rearing unit. In these two cases the extremely high degree of management input from the lending organization may have contributed significantly to women's capacity to control loan use — a point to which we will return later. One woman used her loan from the RPP to support a long-term family enterprise in running a tree nursery. This was an extremely successful business, receiving strong support from the local government department of social forestry, and benefiting from a booming market for mulberry saplings to stabilize feeder roads and contribute to environmental and sericulture programs. Finally, one woman had used her loan to cover her daughter's dowry and wedding expenses. Because of insufficient data, it is not possible here to determine whether these cases were unusual or whether they are of a more general significance.

(d) *Years of membership*

It might be expected that women's control over loan use would increase in tandem with years of experience as members of credit societies. As women gain more experience of credit procedures and of managing small-scale enterprises, as their grassroots organizations become institutionalized over time at the village level, and as they gain access to more training opportunities, an overall accretion of competence and confidence in controlling loans would presumably follow. Figure 5 shows that this is true up to a certain point.

Particularly high degrees of loan control are evident in credit societies with three to five years of institutional life, with degrees of loan control increasing steadily with each year of organizational membership up to that point. After that point, however, loan control appears to diminish. Rahman's study also records diminishing loan control over time, with the amount of a loan borrowers themselves use falling from 86.6% of the total loan amount in the first year to 66% in the fifth year of membership in the Grameen Bank, although the drop in actual cases she examines with more than three years of borrowing experience (just 11% of her cases) makes this finding less reliable (1986, p. 35). Since, over time, the cash amount of loans increases to reward good repayment, the drop in loan control over time can be explained, as above, as a reflection of the limitations to expansion of women's productive investments in comparison with the greater profitability of investing in male activities. Patterns of diminishing loan control over time have important

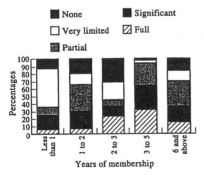

■ None   ■ Significant

□ Very limited ▨ Full

▨ Partial

Figure 5. *Degree of loan control by years of membership in credit society (n = 253).*

policy implications, raising questions about problems in increasing the profitability of women's enterprises with successive loans, problems in ensuring the sustainability of women's credit societies, and questions about building women's capacity to "graduate" from special credit societies to other institutions in the rural financial market.

In sum, our findings raise as a problem the question of male control of a proportion of loans targeted to women. This is in contrast to loan impact evaluations, where the issue of women's actual control of loan use tends to be obscured by the methodological focus on the household and the preoccupation with repayment rates. Supporting evidence for these findings came in anecdotal form and from interviews with fieldworkers and observation of their work. Fieldworkers claimed that the increasing pressure on them to assess creditworthiness of borrowers was prompting them to screen the likely productivity of husbands of women borrowers. In other words, some fieldworkers were assuming *a priori* that loans would be used by other family members. Some field workers were quite candid about this process, admitting that when forming groups, husbands were approached first, and were persuaded to let their wives join in return for the promise of credit — implicitly for the husband. This has worrying implications for the inclusion of women heading their own households in these programs, in spite of the fact that this is the category of borrower most likely to control loans fully.

Most telling of the supporting evidence were the interviews with the 22 male borrowers. In the course of relating loan use histories, many of these men provided detailed accounts of multiple loans they had invested in activities such as livestock rearing or paddy husking, in addition to more conventional male activities such as rickshaw pulling, rice trading, itinerant trading, and so on. When these accounts were checked against group records, no trace could be found of some of the loans which had been described. Asked about this, the men explained that in these cases they had taken "a 'woman's' loan." In other words, no clear distinction in actual rights of ownership over credit was made. Women did not exhibit this kind of conceptual slippage regarding their husband's loans, even though men's loans, just like women's, enter into the household as a new resource for general benefit.

5. LOAN USE WITHIN THE HOUSEHOLD AND LOAN REPAYMENT

The implications of these findings about loan transfer within the household are very complex. It cannot simply be assumed that individual control over a loan is equivalent to empowerment, nor does the phenomenon of transferring a loan in and of itself signal a loss of power for women. To begin with, conventional banking assumptions about individual loan use and responsibility may be misplaced in the context of the prevailing gender division of labor in household production in Bangladesh. The household is a joint venture, and the gender division of labor is such that full, individual control of the productive process is virtually impossible for women given the gendered nature of access to markets. A complementary division of labor which assigns marketing to men makes it virtually inevitable that women's loans will be used jointly by themselves and productive men within the household. In the case of men, though they tend more often to manage loans individually, they too rely on divisions of labor by gender and age to accomplish productive tasks as a joint family process (Montgomery, Bhattacharya and Hulme, 1996, p. 102). Men's near-monopoly of access to the market also means that they have greater economic control over household income-generating activities, and with the main responsibility for cash transactions, they are identified as the earners of family income, regardless of the contributions of other family members. Within this constraint women do have strategies to assert economic control. Village ethnographies have shown that considerable variation in gendered patterns of income and asset control within the household give women control over a certain range of household decisions (often relating to consumption). Women also employ a range of strategies to establish control over assets, through informal lending of cash or paddy to other women as a form of dispersed insurance against future crises, investing in livestock, and saving small amounts of paddy, all of which constitute "female assets" which are out of the immediate sphere of male control (Montgomery, Bhattacharya and Hulme, 1996).

For any household, the gendered division of labor in production, the gender divisions around control of economic activities and cash proceeds, and the consequent gendered differences in consumption patterns, will affect the way credit is used. Because control of cash is so strongly identified as a masculine business, expanded opportunities for women to have access to cash loans could have a profound impact on gender relations. As Montgomery, Bhattacharya and Hulme point out: "[w]omen borrowing cash and generating cash income tend towards a contradiction of existing norms" (1996, p. 99). Without parallel interventions, however, designed to ease women's direct access to the market, improve their productive skills, and access to technology, the role of mediators such as male relatives remains critical, with implications for women's authority over economic decision making. In this context, new cash inputs to the household through women are likely to be identified by household males as a resource for their use. An example of this was given by a 40-year-old widow, Sultana, whose elder son uses her loan to buy paddy, which she parboils and

dries, and which he then takes to the rice mill for processing. When asked about her family's feelings about her membership of a credit organization, she replied: "My sons are happy that I have access to a loan, but they say they have to repay it so their feelings are mixed," in other words, her sons assumed responsibility for managing the loan.

When credit is invested in conventional women's activities, gender role ascriptions are not challenged, and the increase in welfare to the household may be minimal, given the constraints to profitable expansion of most of these ventures. In addition, women's labor burden may be increased without any significant concomitant increase in control over the productive process. As Montgomery, Bhattacharya and Hulme suggest: "[w]hen the division of labour and distribution of authority over resources remains uncontested, it is not easy to argue that there has been a positive change in women's degree of 'empowerment'" (1996, p. 95). They add that the use of credit "for conventional activities, undertaken according to conventional patterns, may actually strengthen the intradomestic distribution of power which is heavily in favour of male members" (1996, p. 104).

There are, nevertheless, a range of plausible benefits to women of transferring loan control from the point of view of enhancing their status within the household. It is often argued in Bangladesh that even when men do control women's loans, women's overall status within the household increases because they are acknowledged as an important new source of revenue. R. Rahman provides some evidence for this. She found that Grameen Bank women borrowers who had transferred their entire loan to a male relative had a higher nutritional status, and had more money spent on their clothing and medical needs, than the wives of male borrowers (1986, p. 60). But inevitably, expenditures on women in the household are lower when men control women's loans than when women have full control. As Rahman's study also shows, 10% less was spent on the medical expenses of women who had transferred their loans to husbands, than on the medical expenses of women controlling their own loans. In cases where men were the direct borrowers, fully 74% less was spent by them on their wives' health (1986, p. 60).

Anecdotal evidence from BRAC suggests familial stability to be an important reflection of women's increased status through loan access, where one of the reasons women give for handing over loans to husbands is the need to preserve their marriages (Jiggins, 1992). It is important not to deride or dismiss these sorts of choices. In a context where women's life chances are directly related to security in marriage, transferring credit to men is an important survival strategy. This is especially so given that small loans and women's low productivity hardly offer the prospects of building an alternative institutional survival base to the marital household. A narrow concern with women's control over loans risks obscuring the importance of the role of women's credit in easing household financial crises and preserving family stability — as when, for example, credit is used to pay off a husband's debts and hence ward off the possibility of his having to leave to avoid creditors (Jiggins, 1992).

In addition, women may use credit as a bargaining chip to allow them access to other opportunities available through credit organizations — opportunities to congregate with other women, to have access to skills training or functional education or health inputs. For example, a BRAC borrower, Farida, whose husband had used her loan to mortgage land and farm it, explained to us: "If I don't give him all the money then I can't stay with BRAC — he makes all the decisions about what to do." For her, waiting to attend a vegetable gardening training session at the BRAC Area Office, this was a worthwhile tradeoff. Other tradeoffs of great value to women include the exchange of control over a loan for a guaranteed food supply from the person controlling the loan (this is especially important to widows), and sometimes, the right to have more household resources spent on their own and their children's health or clothing.

In Bangladesh's poverty context, women's access to credit represents a source of capital acquisition for men, and may induce a revaluing of women's contribution to household survival. The danger is that this may lead to the manipulation of women, putting pressure on them to gain membership of a credit group. Anecdotal evidence about the Grameen Bank suggests that women who are unsuccessful in gaining loan access, or who have to wait too long for their turn to get a loan, are experiencing increases in domestic violence from frustrated husbands (see also Haque, 1993, pp. 60–62). An analogy can be made to the problem of dowry inflation, where some argue that increased competition to raise the price of dowry reflects a qualitative drop in women's status. One field worker made this connection directly, saying: "Actually, it (credit) is just another form of dowry."

The phenomenon of transfer of loan control may be introducing greater tensions within the household, for all that it may enhance men's appreciation of women in the household. Women still have to repay their loans, however and by whomever they are used. If they are not generating cash income themselves, they will have to demand weekly loan repayment funds from their husbands. As White points out, this is something they do not normally do. It can reinforce (or create new) gendered patterns of dependency and may produce new sources of tension (1991, p. 30). Where husbands refuse to repay, or invest credit badly, or abscond altogether with the money, the pressure is on women to find repayment funds from their other homestead activities. Women's high repayment

rates in these cases may attest less to profitable loan use than to their desire to retain membership of one of the few social and public institutions to which they have legitimate access beyond the household.

How do women repay when their loans are not invested by themselves? Evidence from the research suggests a range of strategies.[5]

— Where there is a good relationship between the borrower and her male relative, men supply the installments on a weekly basis. Many women said their male relatives were obliging in this respect, and some spoke of this arrangement in quasi-contractual terms. This situation can result in increased financial responsibility for women and greater respect within the family. Arguably, however, the developmental objectives of targeting credit to women can be eroded if a direct relation between personal loan use and repayment responsibility is ruptured. Aside from the issue of using credit to increase the productivity of women's labor, its role as a tool for institution-building may be lost. In some cases, we observed men coming to women's weekly group meetings and submitting the loan installment on behalf of their absent wives. This deprives women of the benefits of regular group attendance and social contact.

—Where husbands may not be able to supply installments, women may substitute funds from their "expenditure saving" homestead activities. Many borrowers said they paid weekly installments out of sales from eggs, fruit, and homegrown vegetables. Some supplied loan installments from their regular savings habit of reserving a handful of rice before meals. Where loan repayment is coming from other sources of women's domestic income, this may deplete daily consumption resources within the household, as well as resources otherwise kept for savings.

— In a minority of cases, husbands were unwilling, as opposed to unable, to supply weekly installments. In cases where women could not supply repayments from other sources, they were forced into a supplicant relationship to their husbands. Some women borrowers admitted that increased tensions within the household associated with installment recovery from men forced them into pressuring their husbands for money, which resulted in violence. Field workers, especially woman field workers, were aware of this problem and felt that it had worsened, although we were unable to assess the prevalence of domestic violence or any quantitative increase.

As Ackerly notes, in the last two types of situation, women's responsibility for credit is not matched by their economic and political resources in the family (1995, p. 59). Women do have strategies to resist, of course, and as the following story provided by a women field worker shows, the role of lending institutions in supporting their rights of control over loans is important:

> One woman gave her loan to her husband. But he refused to repay the money. She had so many problems getting money from him — and had to repay by selling eggs, chicks, etc. He also beat her when she tried to get loan instalments from him. She managed to repay and asked for another. But she told the field workers that she didn't want money to go to the husband. She said: "Give me the cash, I'll buy a cow." On the loan disbursement day, the husband came to the office to get the money. The woman told the office to forget she had a husband. "Think of me as husband-less and give me the money." When the office tried to give it to the husband she said: "Look, I am under double pressure, from my husband who won't repay and you who want my money back." She went and bought a cow with the husband and the field workers and brought it close to her house in the village so she could control it, in case the husband tries to take it away.

Where men use women's loans, gender relations within the household are in effect (if not intention) providing a tool to ease the work of credit institutions in recovering loans. Women may have a higher incentive than men for loan repayment — it allows them to retain access to village groups, whereas men have many more opportunities for social contact. In addition, women are more vulnerable to pressure to repay. They are easy to locate, being much less able than men to leave a locality temporarily to evade field workers, and they are easier to intimidate into repayment than men, who can always threaten violence. In effect, the household is internalizing the high transaction costs of lending to men. These costs are primarily those of monitoring men's loan use and enforcing regular repayment. Women in effect offset these costs by using intrahousehold gender relations of obligation or persuasion to recover weekly loan repayments.

This does not imply that this is the intention of credit organizations, whose reasons for lending to women are not that they should act as conduits for credit to men. It is important, however, to consider the motivations and practices of field workers, who, distant from top-level policy makers, deal with local realities and mediate program inputs on the basis of their own perception of people's needs and capabilities. The following candid comment from a government field worker illustrates how an instrumental view of the purpose of lending to women can develop: "We are much better at getting our loan money back now that we are using women as middle-men (sic)."

This instrumental approach to women as conduits for credit for the family plays on, and reinforces, traditional cultural notions of womanhood, with women seen as moral guardians of the household and policers of recalcitrant men. The implications of this process for the way men are being constructed culturally in relation to credit operations are also disturbing. In the formal credit system which reaches primarily middle-

class farmers, male defaulting is so endemic as to constitute probably the most significant supply-side transaction cost which discourages formal credit institutions from lending to (male) rural producers. For example, within the nationalized commercial banking system, loan recovery from farmers fell from just below 50% in 1980–81 to 25% in 1985–86, and was just above 40% in 1987 (UNDP, 1989, p. 66). In response to the recovery crisis, the flow of formal credit has been drastically cut back since 1985, while extensive rescheduling and expensive measures of interest remission and interest rate subsidies have been introduced (World Bank, 1989a, p. 132). Between 1987–88 and 1990–91 agricultural credit disbursements by nationalized commercial banks, the Bangladesh Krishi (Agriculture) Bank, the BRDB, and other formal financial institutions shrank by 54%, not taking into account inflation (Bangladesh Bureau of Statistics, 1992, p. 431). On the nongovernmental side, rural development organizations appear to be experiencing difficulties working with men, especially where credit operations are concerned, and as a consequence are shrinking their operations; BRAC's decision to freeze the formation of new men's VOs has already been mentioned. Field workers in development programs justify this on the basis of problems experienced working with men: their lack of commitment to village credit groups, their poor financial discipline when it comes to repaying loans, the difficulty of enforcing loan repayment given men's greater capacity to evade both development agents and the law, and the threat of violence from men. Many fieldworkers described male credit society members as "touts," or petty criminals. Men's higher default rates may owe to the greater risks involved in their investment activities, the demonstration effect of the way wealthier rural borrowers default with impunity, and the greater range of opportunities available to men for squandering their credit which come with urbanization and Westernization: gambling, tobacco, prostitution, and cinemas and restaurants in town. Lower levels of commitment to village-level institutions may owe to men's greater range of choice in participating in institutions beyond the village.

In the context of the general retrenchment in the flow of formal institutional credit to the rural sector, the slow-down in the formation of new credit societies for landless men is contributing to the impression that men's access to formal and special credit opportunities is shrinking in relation to women's (even though in actual fact they still benefit from the lion's share of available rural credit). But this perception may have as corrosive an effect on household well-being and gender relations as the exclusion of women from institutional credit opportunities has had in the past. Unable to gain access to the resources needed to fulfil their traditional functions as family providers, poor men are having to renege on their responsibilities, increasing the rate of family fragmentation. But if poverty and family fragmentation has meant the loss of the tradition of male support for women, exclusionary aspects of male prejudice and control which sustain discrimination in productive opportunities outside the household, as well as in intrahousehold consumption, have adapted to the changed circumstances (Chen, 1990, p. 217; Cain *et al.*, 1979, p. 410; Alam and Matin, 1984, p. 9). One way in which male dominance persists and reconstitutes itself is through the exploitation of women as new sources of labor and capital. It is hardly surprising that women's loans are being treated as a new resource for men in this context.

There is a danger that excluding men from credit opportunities may intensify the exploitation of women within the household, and at the same time, limit the possibilities of achieving broader attitudinal change among men. Policy makers need to bear in mind that in situations of intense competition for scarce resources, gender power conflicts will be aggravated. In a context such as Bangladesh, men retain by far the greater balance of sociocultural power, such that women can hardly defend such small gains as they might make participating in development programs from male control unless men's attitudes change or men perceive a tangible benefit to themselves. This can be achieved through intensive qualitative investments in changing men's perceptions of women's worth, which is often beyond the capacity or commitment of development programs, or through ensuring that men's access to resources is not constrained in proportion to women's increasing access, in an apparently zero-sum manner. Ideally, the two should go together.

6. IMPLICATIONS FOR PROGRAM DELIVERY PATTERNS AND ORGANIZATIONAL INCENTIVES

The concerns raised in this paper call for a policy response to enhance women's control over loan use. It is important to stress that what is at issue here refers not just to credit programs, but to all manner of development inputs targeted to women; the point is that more attention needs to be paid to gender relations as mediators of development resources. This is an extremely difficult area for program interventions as it implies penetrating the household to tackle gender power relations and suggests a degree of social engineering for which methods are unknown, even if a commitment to it existed, which to date has not in the development process. Many other more practical and immediate policy responses suggest themselves, including evening the balance between social development objectives and credit performance, improving women's productivity, opening their access to markets, protecting their rights of ownership over assets, enhancing their managerial skills and control, and

investing in larger scale enterprises in which women's investments might be protected. These measures will be discussed below, and the performance of the organizations studied will be compared in relation to current policy differences between them.

(a) *The balance between social development inputs and credit performance*

Special credit programs vary in their investments in advancing members' perceptions of social issues and in the training they offer for human resource development which can enhance loan use as well as household well-being and structural change at the local level. The Grameen Bank offers the fewest support services for these social goals, beyond the "Sixteen Decisions" about household and community management and social justice which members recite at the beginning of group meetings. It has started, however, to offer credit on special terms for investments in the quality of household life, like loans for tubewells, latrines, and housing. The RPP's RD-12 program also offers social development services and leadership training for women, as do the women's NGOs. BRAC offers an enormous range of supplementary services to bolster leadership and social development in its VOs. These range from paralegal training, health and family planning facilities, a vast nonformal primary education (NFPE) program for members' children, and leadership training for VO management committees. Each group is visited once a month by a range of specialist Program Officers who lead intensive issue-based discussions in these areas. Nevertheless, rapid expansion has forced a cut-back in its preparatory work with borrower groups. The one-year induction period, with literacy training, which BRAC conducted in an earlier incarnation of its credit program has been cut to two months of awareness-raising and functional education.

With the exception of women's NGOs, these inputs are often not sufficiently tailored to women's gender-specific social needs. "Leadership training" in many organizations consists primarily of rules and methods for credit society management, not methods to counter gender-specific constraints to assertiveness, confidence, and power within households and the local community. Few of the large special credit institutions provide Gender and Development training to their staff, although BRAC and RD-12 have recently introduced this training for field managers and headquarters staff. Unsurprisingly, women's NGOs differ in these respects. Consciousness-raising among women borrowers is a central program component, and for TMSS, pursuing cases through local courts of illegal divorce, deprivation of inheritance rights, default on maintenance payments, and rape, represent a significant part of the workload of its staff.

The tangible shift in organizational incentives in larger special credit institutions away from social development and institution-building has been exacerbated by donors' interests in seeing the development of financially self-sustaining credit programs. This 'process is clearly illustrated in the government's RD-12 program. CIDA's support for RD-12 will be phased out over the next three years. The consequent imperative for the program to become self-sufficient prompted the introduction in mid-1993 of a range of new staff incentives to increase the magnitude of loan disbursal and the efficiency of loan recovery. Each Field Officer is expected to distribute a minimum of 625,000TK annually to 250 members (10 groups, 25 members each). Salary bonuses will be supplied on a pro-rata basis to those who distribute greater amounts and achieve a 100% recovery rate. The new incentive system concentrates organizational attention on conventional banking concerns. Pressure on field staff to disburse and recover greater volumes of credit may have negative consequences for women borrowers. They may be encouraged to take larger loans, but without adequate technical backup for improving their productivity and marketing capacity, they may find themselves unable to realise effective profits. Larger volumes of credit coming into households are vulnerable to misrouting for immediate consumption needs, and to appropriation by male relatives, leaving women more heavily indebted than before.

As credit and service delivery come to supplant more qualitative and elusive social change objectives, earlier concerns with developing organizational solidarities among the poor have receded somewhat. BRAC's goal of forming federations of landless groups is now being underplayed, and the meaning of "institution-building" is shrinking to encompass merely the formation and induction of new groups. This is unfortunate, for as women's primary societies grow in number, federating their activities might allow them to take up leadership and decision-making roles in a more public way. The government's system of federating landless groups through the RD-12 Thana Bittoheen Central Cooperative Associations is more promising in this respect, in spite of problems of elite capture. It offers the possibility for women to take decision-making positions within the sphere of credit administration at the local level. In many TBCCAs, women's groups form the majority of the membership; in three, women were elected as Chairpersons in 1993.

Finally, the rush to scale-up credit delivery arguably has some implications specific to the problem of women's capacity to control loans. Pressure to register new borrowers rapidly may lead to relaxed targeting, with better-off women gaining access to loans, while those in more need, but with fewer initial resource endowments, such as women heading their own households or the poorest women, may not be seen as sufficiently creditworthy. Pressure to disburse and recover larger loans may erode a concern with ensuring that women control loans themselves, rather than ceding control to male household members whose investment activities tend to be more productive. The following quotation from a woman field worker illustrates how this can happen:

> One woman who had neither children nor a husband was doing domestic labour, and became a *samity* member and applied for a loan. I supported her loan proposal for a small trade business but the office did not approve it. The office said she has no husband or son so how will she run the business? I think she could have, that's why I proposed her!

(b) *Improving women's productivity*

Low-income women borrowers in Bangladesh invest cautiously in low-risk, familiar, low-productivity enterprises. A recent RD-12 study of loan use shows that rates of return for women's income-generating activities average 145% while rates for men average 211% (Matienzo, 1993, p. 34). By far the bulk of loans taken by women in special credit programs are invested in traditional activities such as paddy husking, petty trade, and livestock rearing, most of which show a negative return to labor when it is imputed to the male agricultural wage rate (Hossain, 1984). Livestock fattening and milch cow rearing are exceptions, because they involve relatively low-intensity labor inputs which can be distributed to other household members, children especially. Nevertheless, livestock rearing offers limited scope for significantly shifting women's rate of market engagement through technological changes or increased employment. Like women's other traditional enterprises, it is a low-maintenance activity which is home-centered and is part of the cultural ascription of low value to women's work.

By and large, none of the larger special credit programs have succeeded in shifting women out of traditional income-generating activities, although most do acknowledge the importance of encouraging more profitable and socially valued nontraditional forms of entrepreneurship for women. The Grameen Bank is the most "minimalist" of all the special credit institutions in terms of its support for skills development, and though it does operate a small subprogram which experiments with improved farming techniques, the majority of its borrowers invest in traditional activities, most often livestock rearing. The RD-12 has regionally-based Technical Resource Teams which promote new technologies to improve the productivity of the enterprises of the landless, and is developing programs to encourage women to make nontraditional investments. BRAC is most comprehensive in supporting higher profit investments, providing training, technical advice, access to inputs, and other services in the following sectors: irrigation, livestock, poultry, fisheries, social forestry and vegetable cultivation, and sericulture. In addition, its Rural Enterprises Project experiments with new businesses such as women-run restaurants, poultry feed mills and chick hatcheries, mechanics workshops, apiculture, warehouses, and pearl culturing. These activities are promoted as integrated packages to borrowers. Credit is tied to specific skills training, some of the credit is provided in kind — for example, as chicks for poultry-rearing units — and in some cases, such as sericulture, backward and forward linkages are made at different points along the production process. Some of these programs train women in occupations which provide paid employment — as paravets, poultry vaccinators, or tree caretakers.

Promoting higher risk, higher skill, and higher profit nontraditional activities for women, however, confronts head-on complex problems relating to the way gender affects the perceived value of different forms of employment. In the first place, where women move into activities which compete with "men's work," gender power conflicts may be exacerbated. In the second, there is no automatic connection between nontraditional occupations for women and improvements in their status relative to men.

When women move into nontraditional forms of enterprise, men may simply assume control over activities which involve higher cash investments and more complex technology. Some evidence of this comes from a BRAC study of women's experience investing in one of the higher profit ventures — women-owned restaurants — encouraged through its Rural Enterprise Project. Khan's study analyzes six women's experiences of managing large loans (on average 6,000 TK) for *Shuruchi* ('Good Food') restaurants. She found that with the exception of one widowed woman, women's male relatives had taken over the management of these restaurants, with none of the married women feeling they owned these enterprises. Just one woman, the only literate woman in the sample, participated in managing accounts (Khan, 1993). Interestingly, the widowed woman in the sample had also lost control of her restaurant, but to her apparently more dynamic married sister (p. 21). This brings up the important issue, mentioned earlier, of power differences between women according to life cycle stages and social status. Investing in shifting women's rate of market engagement, therefore, requires not just the introduction of new technologies and skills training, but strong support for women's rights of ownership over new enterprises. Although limited by its sample size of six, Khan's study hints at the importance of literacy and numeracy in enhancing women's managerial capacities. Accounts keeping, and in some cases, coping with official formalities and interactions with

suppliers and clients, requires levels of education which the majority of the low-income women members of special credit programs lack. Unfortunately, as mentioned in the first section of this paper, few special credit programs are making the long-term investments in literacy and numeracy training which are necessary for the development of effective accounting and management skills.

When women are undertaking new entrepreneurial investments individually, whatever the level of organizational support, their resources are bound to be more vulnerable to male control given women's dependence on maintaining positive relations with men within the household. Where investments are made jointly in enterprises collectively managed by women outside the boundaries of individual households, there may be more potential for protecting women's assets from male relatives, as well as for achieving economies of scale. Larger scale enterprises using new technologies — such as mechanized rice mills — can help develop management skills, and may eventually provide wage employment opportunities for other women. They also have the potential to provide women with a significant nonfarm production base in the rural economy and to develop linkages to other productive sectors. Efforts have been made in this direction by some special credit programs: BRAC offers credit for the joint management of deep tube-wells, the Grameen Bank for fisheries management, and the women's NGO, SNPS, for power tillers. Unfortunately, these efforts, in Bangladesh as elsewhere, have been hobbled by severe management problems and by free-rider problems (Hossain, 1988).

They have also aroused both class and gender hostility. A good example is SNPS's program of providing credit to groups of women for managing power tillers. Women in these groups were able to rent out their equipment and labor for preparing crop land for ploughing, thereby gaining access to a lucrative new form of employment providing a valuable agricultural service, and in the process, making a powerful public statement about women's productive capacities. By the second year of operation in one area, landlords and farmers incensed both by the loss of an important male source of income (from traction ploughing) and by women's transgression of an important symbolic boundary between the home and the field, grouped together to purchase their own power tillers, pushing the women's group out of business.

This speaks to the critical importance of applying an analysis of gendered power relations to policy efforts to enhance women's productivity and access to resources. There is a tendency to assume that changes in sociocultural perceptions of women's worth will follow changes in women's productivity. For example, the economist Adnan comments: "The capacity to earn market incomes has also led to the *re-valuation* of the status of women by their fathers, husbands, and immediate families, as well as the communities to which they belong" (1989, 12, emphasis in text). This underspecifies, however, the importance of gender relations in affecting the perceived value of what women and men do, which is less a function of what the activity is or what income it generates, than of the power relations in which it is embedded. Numerous studies of gender relations in the region show that the cultural discounting of the value of women's work does not necessarily alter when women's work takes place outside of the household or when their contribution to the household takes the form of a cash income (Standing, 1991; White, 1992; Bardhan, 1986; Chen, 1990). This should not be taken as an argument against encouraging nontraditional forms of self- and formal employment for women, but rather, as a reminder of the importance of holistic strategies which support women who take these risks, which build up mutual support networks among women, which provide adequate skills training and other forms of technical backup, and which encourage male support.

(c) *Marketing*

None of the large special credit programs offer facilities to enhance women's access to markets. BRAC has made various experiments with establishing space in local markets for women, but these have been abandoned, although an account of the reasons for this is not available. Women's exclusion from markets is perhaps the greatest constraint to their productivity. It means that they lose control over a critical phase of the production process and are unable to make informed assessments of market demand and new productive opportunities. Improving women's market access might be the single most effective way of enhancing their control over loans, as well as expanding their public presence and their self-confidence. Policy efforts to open rural markets to women will be likely to encounter severe male opposition. As in the case of enhancing women's productivity, it will require considerable investment in support systems — including such measures as providing transportation and indeed, security measures to protect women from physical assault.

(d) *Enhancing managerial control*

Some potential policy responses to enhance women's managerial control are evident from the above discussion. Measures likely to help are greater and continuous investment in literacy and numeracy training, investment in attitudinal change in men, and women too, regarding women's rights over their own resources, skills development and technical inputs directly relevant to the loan investment activity, overcoming constraints to women's access to rural markets, the development of solidarities among women, especially beyond the limited horizons of the individual credit society, effective support for viable collective enterprises, and measures to guarantee women's ownership of productive assets. As will be clear from the discussion so far, however, enhancing women's managerial control in the context of gender relations in Bangladesh is no easy project. It touches on problems which are beyond the scope of any single organization to solve — such as the inadequate legal foundation for women's economic rights, especially as concerns rights of ownership and inheritance. An important issue in this respect is the national religious environment, with many rural development organizations reporting increased levels of opposition from Islamic groups in recent years. Such problems require state-level responses. Since the 1980s, however, the Bangladeshi state has sought to palliate its legitimation anxieties by aligning itself, increasingly, with Islamic interests (Kabeer, 1989; Goetz, 1991), which has meant that an effective public commitment to social change in women's interests is lacking.

Policy efforts to enhance women's loan control may run the risk of introducing a degree of organizational control and surveillance over women's loan investment decisions which unacceptably undermine women's autonomy in decision making over loan use. To dictate and closely monitor loan investment strategies may actually undermine a household survival strategy. Women's credit enters households under conditions which policy cannot predict. It may be desperately needed to mitigate a short-term consumption crisis, which once resolved, can enhance a household's productivity. Other problems might arise if loans are given in kind, rather than cash, or if cash loans to women are kept very small. These measures are likely to ensure women's loan control, but they may also construct women differently as credit clients than men; as not fully individually responsible, as incomplete participants in rural economies, where their organizational membership is experienced as patronizing and tutelary, not empowering. There is an extremely fine line between recognizing constraints on women's freedom of maneuver and reinforcing the terms of those constraints by taking them as givens. It may be tempting for credit organizations to avoid this dilemma altogether by sticking to measures known to be associated with higher degrees of women's control, for example by lending small amounts for fail-safe activities such as livestock rearing. But lending patterns such as these will not contribute to broader goals of empowering women to change the terms of gender relations in the household and the community. In addition, they only modestly contribute to goals of poverty alleviation, where small investments become little more than loan-repayment schemes, not long-term income-accumulation strategies.

The women's NGO TMSS has an interesting policy response to this dilemma. It is aware of the problem of male control of loans, and of its near intractability in the context of contemporary gender relations in Bangladesh, and in response, it makes efforts to ensure that women retain control over decision making and accounts, however the loan is actually used. It requires its women borrowers to provide accurate and continuous accounts of loan use and encourages informal contracts between women and the users of loans if women are not the primary users.

7. DIFFERENCES IN WOMEN'S LOAN CONTROL IN THE FOUR ORGANIZATIONS STUDIED

Differences in women's loan control record in the organizations studied point to the impact of different policy approaches. The small size of the samples, however, once disaggregated by organization, caution against drawing firm conclusions from the findings, raising problems of sample biases by region, different performance records of individual credit societies, group maturity, and more constrained ranges of investment activities and loan sizes.

The best performing sample were the Grameen Bank borrowers ($N = 53$), with 62% of the loan histories showing full or significant loan use, and just 10% of loans in the "Very limited" or "No involvement" category.[6] This most is probably because of the Grameen Bank's strong encouragement of borrowers to invest initial loans in livestock (fully 71.7% of loans in the sample were used for this), and its insistence that productive investments (livestock, land, housing) be registered as women's property. TMSS ($N = 39$) also scored well, with 41% of loan histories showing full or partial involvement, and 25% in the two lowest categories. Here, loan investment strategies were more diverse, venturing into small businesses such as yogurt making (20%) and house construction (17.5%). Higher degrees of loan control here might be due to the organization's insistence on proof of women's managerial control, and to the long periods it invests in institution-building, social development, and consciousness-raising work.

Twenty-eight percent of the loan histories in the BRAC sample ($N = 106$) showed full or significant loan control, while 45% fell into the two lowest categories. The BRAC sample had the largest proportion of women using their loans for forms of rural enterprises in which men normally dominate (10.4% in rickshaw purchasing, 6.6% in crop farming, 9.4% in vegetable trading, 6.6% in rice stocking for resale, 4% in sericulture). It would be unfair to interpret this

result as an indictment of BRAC's strategy of encouraging nontraditional investment for women — following the argument of the previous section, it represents an important strategy for challenging negative ascriptions of the value of women's income-generating activities. The result does, however, point to the importance of accompanying new credit-deployment strategies with adequate social development inputs. Moreover, lesser degrees of women's loan control might be a consequence of the rapid scaling-up of credit delivery.

In RD-12, 31% of the loan histories ($N = 55$) were in the full or significant category, and the majority, 56%, in the two lowest categories. The RD-12 sample showed the greatest diversity in patterns of actual loan use of all the samples, but also, a high concentration in traditionally male-dominated activities (16.4% in rickshaw purchasing, 11% in rice stocking for trade). Lower degrees of loan control may attest to the generally higher socioeconomic status of its women members. A recent study of loan impact in RD-12 found the literacy levels of women members to be 14% over the national average (Matienzo, 1993), which suggests, given the association between women's literacy and household resource endowment, that poorer women are not being targeted effectively. Studies of women's economic activity in Bangladesh have found that women from better-off households tend to have a lesser role in household production decisions than do poorer women (Safilios-Rothschild and Mahmud, 1989, Chapter 1; Rosario, 1992).

On the surface, these findings seem to go against the direction of the suggestions in the previous section regarding enhancing women's loan control, as the most "minimalist" program in terms of social development investments, the Grameen Bank, performed the best in terms of women's control. The implications of this finding can work in several directions. On the one hand, arguably the contribution of Grameen Bank credit to changing gender relations may be minimal insofar as loans are kept relatively small and loan activities remain highly traditional. On the other hand, it provides a few very key forms of program support which may be more effective at strengthening women's rights of asset ownership and social status than many of the other strategies suggested. One of these elements is the intense energy which goes into creating and maintaining a culture of discipline and belonging in each borrowing *kendra* or center, which contributes to institutionalizing women's rights to credit. Another is the insistence that new assets gained through a loan be registered in the woman borrower's name — from the receipt for the purchase of a cow to the registering of land or a house. Nevertheless, there is probably a point beyond which this strategy cannot go as a means of long-term change in gender relations given the neglect of efforts to enhance women's direct market access.

8. CONCLUSIONS

This paper has problemmatized the issue of women's loss of direct control over their loans, although it recognizes the difficulty of establishing clear patterns of loan control once credit enters the rural household. In highlighting the poverty of assumptions that women's high repayment rates and sustained high demand for loans can be assumed to reflect effective loan investment strategies by women, the paper raises a number of issues for further research regarding the empowerment contribution of credit to women. These include the possibility that high degrees of male control of loans can postpone the appearance of the positive social externalities expected from increasing women's control over household income, or worse, that it can undermine household survival strategies where men invest loans badly, forcing women to mobilize repayment funds from resources which would otherwise be used for consumption or savings purposes. Another issue regards the potential of loan transfers to exacerbate gender-related tensions within the rural household.

The discussion in this paper bears importantly on current debates about the transformative capacity of small-scale credit and income-generating programs. The uncertain economic environment in the rural arena over the 1980s has favored an increasing focus on credit and income-generating programs in general — for women as well as men. As Sanyal argues, the failure of rural industries in Bangladesh to absorb growing numbers of landless people has prompted the focus since the late 1970s on informal sector enterprises managed by the poor as alternative sources for income and employment generation. In tandem with this, there has been a shift in the donor environment to favor private initiative capitalism as a better guarantee of efficient market responses than traditional top-down government poverty-alleviation measures (1991, p. 1367). Credit programs have gained even further in popularity to the degree that they promise the possibility of cost recovery; as low-income borrowers demonstrate their repayment capacity at market rates of interest, donors can satisfy their ambitions for financially sustainable development.

Critics of self-employment initiatives claim that the emphasis on informal sector economic enhancements overlooks the structural factors that maintain the economic marginalization of the poor. Credit and income-generating programs frame the problem of poverty as a temporary, and easily remedied, cash-flow problem, instead of one which bears on relations of inequality and their institutionalization in broader economic policy (White, 1991). This critique is particularly germane to assessments of whether these programs can promote women's economic and social empowerment. One of the many lessons of the history of women's involvement in rural development programs has been that unless substitutes are found for women's reproductive work at home, women's experience of participation can be negative, exacting a high cost in terms of intensified demands on women's labor. The promotion of small-scale enterprises gets around this problem by concentrating on improving the productivity of women's homestead-based work — which allows them to fulfill their domestic responsibilities at the same time. This postpones any feminist concerns with redistributing gendered domestic responsibilities — which are, after all, a structural feature of unequal gender relations — and limits the potential for skills acquisition, exposure to the "public" world, and job-based organization associated with gaining formal sector employment. The input-delivery focus of credit and income-generation programs involves an implicit assumption that easing women's access to credit translates unproblematically into their control over its use. Economic empowerment, however, is not as straightforward a process as this; gendered power relations within the household affect the distribution and use of cash resources, and may undermine women's capacity to retain control over the way a loan is invested, or profits used.

The successes of special credit programs in reaching women must be acknowledged as highly impressive, given the sociocultural conditions which they challenge. In some ways, what this paper points to is a "second-generation" problem; the "first-generation" problem having been managing institutional changes in order to provide for women's access to credit in the first place.[7] Most of these programs acknowledge the problems which gender power relations pose for women's control of loans; they offer integrated programs designed to enhance women's institution-building at the grass-roots level, provide technology and training supports for women's investments, and some programs, particularly those managed by women's NGOs, work to raise women's consciousness about gender and class relations.

These laudable interventions run in some respects counter to the implications for program management of the rapid scaling-up of credit delivery and recovery operations. Improvements in women's productivity, mobility, access to markets, literacy, social status, and control of household decisions takes time, requires considerable commitment by development workers, a long-term investment in local-level processes of social change, as well as a willingness to cope with the sometimes violent and disruptive consequences of challenging class and gender privilege. This is even more true when it comes to changing social attitudes toward women's right of ownership over resources and to assigning value to women's contributions to household well-being. The drive for increased credit disbursement and recovery, however, is insensitive to

WORLD DEVELOPMENT

social development needs, and may be particularly insensitive to the special problems women face in developing the capacity to use their loans.

International aid donors bear some responsibility for this process. Donors' interests in seeing the development of financially self-sustaining rural development institutions has resulted in a preoccupation with cost recovery, to the degree that loan repayment rates have become the primary index of success, however much they may obscure the important issue of the quality of loan use. Ironically, this might also be seen as an unintended consequence of the success of gender and development policy lobbies. Women's inclusion in many development sectors, one of the achievements of the gender and development lobby, has

tended to be a quantitative affair; the concern is with increasing numbers, and less with the quality and meaning of women's participation. The latter raises difficult problems about the political orientation of the development process as well as problems about power relations between women and men from the household to the state. That these concerns, which have been at the center of the agenda of gender and development advocates, tend to evaporate in the process of policy implementation, attests to the importance of institutional change in development organizations to bring women's interests into decision-making processes, from the top-level of policy making to the impact level of the household.

NOTES

1. Entitled: "Women's Leadership in Rural Development in Bangladesh," this study was funded by the UK Economic and Social Research Council and conducted under the auspices of the Institute of Development Studies at the University of Sussex, and the Bangladesh Institute of Development Studies in Dhaka. Field work was carried out between February and October 1993.

2. There are exceptions. A landmark evaluation of this type was conducted by Rushidan Islam Rahman, studying the Grameen Bank (1986), in which the definition of "impact of credit" on the beneficiary was extended beyond income and employment questions to women's decision-making role in deciding upon the investment activity, labor inputs, and use of profits, as well as changes in attitudes toward women borrowers on the part of male household members, changes in women's self-perceptions, capacities to invest in personal well-being, capacities to assume control over their physical integrity and reproductive rights, and attitudes toward their daughters' education and future prospects. There is a study currently underway, managed by Jahangir Nagar University and John Snow International, which will likely provide the most comprehensive informa-

tion so far on these issues, most particularly the relation between credit and family planning acceptance (see Schuler and Hashemi, 1992).

3. This question is underwritten by a concern which is most easily defined as a feminist one and has been asked in different ways in a range of feminist critiques of the development process. See, for example, Jaquette (1990) or Kandiyoti (1988b).

4. Loan-use patterns were not recorded for SNPS as its credit facilities are extended not to individual borrowers but to groups, for collective investment.

5. Ackerly's study identifies a similar set of repayment scenarios (1995).

6. Interestingly, this corresponds closely with the finding in Rahman's (1986) study of the Grameen Bank which showed a 12% rate of loan appropriation by male relatives of women borrowers.

7. We are grateful to Harold Alderman for this insight.

REFERENCES

Ackerly, B., "Testing tools of development: Credit programmes, loan involvement, and women's empowerment," *IDS bulletin: Getting Institutions Right for Women in Development*, Vol. 26, No. 3 (1995), pp. 56–68.

Adnan, S., "Birds in a cage: Institutional change and women's position in Bangladesh," *ADAB News*, Vol. 3 (January–February 1989).

Alam, S. and N. Matin, "Limiting the women's issue in Bangladesh: The Western and Bangladesh Legacy," *South Asia Bulletin*, Vol. 4, No. 2 (1984).

Bangladesh Bureau of Statistics, *1992 Statistical Yearbook of Bangladesh* (Dhaka: BBS, Ministry of Planning, 1992).

BRAC (Bangladesh Rural Advancement Committee), *Mid-*

Term Report, June 1992 (Dhaka: BRAC, 1992).

Bardhan, K., "Women's work, welfare and status: Forces of tradition and change in India," *South Asia Bulletin*, Vol. 6, No. 1 (1986).

Blanchet, T., "Rural women, savings and credit: An anthropological view," Mimeo (Dhaka: USAID, 1986).

Cain, M., "The household lifecycle and economic mobility in Bangladesh," *Population and Development Review*, Vol. 4, No. 3 (1979).

Cain, M. *et al.*, "Class, patriarchy and women's work in Bangladesh," *Population and Development Review*, Vol. 5, No. 3 (1979).

Chen, M. A., "Poverty, gender and work in Bangladesh," *Structure and Strategies: Women, Work and Family* (New Delhi: Sage, 1990).

DLO (Donor Liaison Office), "Information on BRAC's Rural Development Programme and Rural Credit Project," Mimeo (Dhaka: BRAC Donor Consortium, 1993).

Goetz, A. M., "The institutional politics of gender in development policy for rural women in Bangladesh," PhD dissertation (Cambridge: University of Cambridge, 1991).

Grameen Bank, "Grameen Bank vital statistics," Mimeo (Dhaka: Grameen Bank, August 1992).

Haque, T., "Women and the rural informal credit market," Research Report No. 104 (Dhaka: BIDS, 1989).

Hossain, M., *The Impact of the Grameen Bank on Women's Involvement in Productive Activities, Bank Credit for Landless Women — A Study Tour of Grameen Bank, Dhaka* (Dhaka: Grameen Bank, 1984).

Hossain, M. and R. Afsar, *Credit for Women: A Review of Special Credit Programmes in Bangladesh* (Dhaka: Bangladesh Institute of Development Studies, 1988).

Jaquette, J., "Gender and justice in economic development," in I. Tinker (Ed.), *Persistent Inequalities* (Oxford: Oxford University Press, 1990).

Jiggins, J., "Gender issues: A contribution to the BRAC mid-term evaluation report," Mimeo (Dhaka: BRAC, 1992).

Kabeer, N., *The Quest for National Identity: Women, Islam and the State in Bangladesh,* Discussion Paper (Brighton: Institute of Development Studies, 1989).

Kandiyoti, D., "Bargaining with patriarchy," *Gender and Society,* Vol. 2, No. 3 (1988a).

Kandiyoti, D., *Women and Rural Development Policies: The Changing Agenda,* Discussion Paper (Brighton: Institute of Development Studies, 1988b).

Khan, M. R., "BRAC's 'Suruchi' restaurants: An assessment," Mimeo (Dhaka: BRAC, 1993).

Lindenbaum, S., *The Social and Economic Status of Women in Bangladesh* (Dhaka: Ford Foundation, 1974).

Matienzo, R., *Loan Profitability and Impact in the RD-12 Project* (Dhaka: Canadian Resource Team, 1993).

McKim, R. C., "Production and employment program inception report," Mimeo (Dhaka: Canadian Resource Team, 1988).

Molyneux, M., "Family reform in socialist states: The hidden agenda," *Feminist Review,* Vol. 21 (1985a).

Molyneux, M., "Mobilisation without emancipation? Women's interests, the state and revolution in Nicaragua," *Feminist Studies,* Vol. 11, No. 2 (1985b).

Montgomery, R., D. Bhattacharya and D. Hulme, "Credit for the poor in Bangladesh: the BRAC Rural Development Programme and the Government Thana Resource Development and Employment Programme," in D. Hulme and P. Mosley (Eds.), *Finance Against Poverty* (London: Routledge, 1986).

Rahman, Atiq *et al., Rural Poor Programme — Mid-Term Operational Review* (Dhaka: CIDA, 1986).

Rahman, Atiur, "Impact of Grameen Bank intervention on the rural power structures" (Dhaka: BIDS, 1986).

Rahman, R. I., *Impact of the Grameen Bank on the Situation of Poor Rural Women* (Dhaka: Bangladesh Institute of Development Studies, 1986).

RD–12/CRT (Rural Development 12, Canadian Resource Team), "Statistics on performance of RD–12 project, 1993" (Dhaka: Canadian Resource Team, 1993).

Rosario, S., *Women and Social Change in a Bangladeshi Village* (London: Zed Books 1992).

Safilios-Rothschild, C. and S. Mahmud, *Women's Roles in Agriculture: Present Trends and Potential for Growth* (Dhaka, UNDPUNIFEM, 1989).

Sanyal, B., "Antagonistic cooperation: A case study of non-governmental organizations, government and donor's relationships in income-generating projects in Bangladesh," *World Development,* Vol. 19, No. 10 (1991).

Schuler, S. R. and S. Hashemi, *Islamic Ideology, Contraception and the Emergence of Women in Bangladesh,* Mimeo (Dhaka: Development Research Centre, 1992).

Standing, H., *Dependence and Autonomy: Women's Employment and the Family in Calcutta* (London: Routledge, 1992).

Standing, H., *Dependence and Autonomy* (London: Routledge, 1991).

Thomas, J. J., "Replicating the Grameen Bank: The Latin American Experience," Mimeo (London: Department of Economics, London School of Economics, 1993).

UNDP, *Bangladesh Agriculture: Performance Policies* (Dhaka: UNDP, 1989).

White, S., *Arguing with the Crocodile: Gender and Class in Bangladesh* (Dhaka: University Press Ltd., 1992).

White, S., *Evaluating the Impact of NGOs in Rural Poverty Alleviation: Bangladesh Country Study* (London: ODI, 1991).

World Bank, *World Development Report* (New York: Oxford University Press, 1990).

World Bank, *Bangladesh Strategy Paper on Women in Development: Towards a Better Understanding of Women's Role in the Development Process* (Washington, DC: World Bank, 1989a).

World Bank, *Bangladesh: Public Expenditure Review — Public Resource Management During the Forth Five-Year Plan, FY1991–95* (Washington, DC: World Bank, 1989b).

World Bank, *Bangladesh: Recent Economic Developments and Short-Term Prospects* (Washington, DC: World Bank, 1989c).

World Bank, "Working paper for the local consultative group on NGOs" (Dhaka: World Bank, 1989d).

[5]

RESCUING GENDER
FROM THE POVERTY TRAP

Cecile Jackson

Introduction

The New Poverty Agenda is seen as incorporating gender within a new broader concept of poverty (Lipton and Maxwell, 1992) capable of measuring, evaluating and redressing gender bias along with poverty reduction policies, based on labour intensive growth, targeted social services and safety nets. Multilateral positions on gender and development (GAD) for their part also stress the poverty of women as a primary justification for development interventions designed to improve the position of women. However, it is argued here that the concept of poverty cannot serve as a proxy for the subordination of women, that antipoverty policies cannot be expected to necessarily improve the position of women and that there is no substitute for a gender analysis, which transcends class divisions and material definitions of deprivation. The instrumental interest in women as the means to achieve development objectives such as poverty reduction may ultimately undermine GAD. Gender appears to have collapsed into a poverty trap; this essay raises a call for help, or at least a discussion about the relative benefits of captivity versus escape.

A retrospective on the past twenty years, since gender became a widespread development concern, would have to acknowledge that gender has been assimilated into development thinking in what appears to be a comprehensive way. Bilateral and multilateral development agencies have gender policies, priorities and strategies, gender units, gender specialists, gender reporting criteria and monitoring. If gender and development (GAD) has moved from the fringe to the mainstream of development, this should be cause for celebration rather than unease about what has been lost in translation. Gender has been assimilated into development thinking in a particular way (Jaquette, 1990), and the many strands of feminist thinking and varieties of gender analysis have not been equally absorbed by development agencies. Any evaluation of how far gender has become incorporated into development institutions needs to enquire not only about whether they have staff with gender responsibilities, how funds are allocated, whether policy documents exist; it also needs to examine the content of how development institutions understand gender issues. This chapter is about one characteristic of this assimilation process – the perception of gender issues in development as a variant of poverty problems. Twenty years ago Huntington

39

FEMINIST VISIONS OF DEVELOPMENT

(1975) published a critique of Ester Boserup which expressed concern about the implications of abandoning the equality argument in favour of an efficiency justification, a concern which this chapter argues was well founded. The next section suggests some common and problematic themes in how most development agencies understand gender questions, the second section remarks on the main prescriptions of the New Poverty Agenda from a gender perspective as a prelude to the third section which discusses the problems with poverty concepts and measurement based upon 'outsider' definitions, and finally the last section extends the critique to subjective definitions of poverty.

Gender stances in multilaterals

Instrumentalism

Moser (1993: 66–9) describes what she calls an 'anti-poverty approach to women' as a strand in WID which sees women's poverty as the consequence of underdevelopment rather than of subordination, and she distinguishes this from the 'efficiency' approach to women, although it seems they have shared assumptions about the causes of, and remedies for, gender disadvantage. The poverty/efficiency approach has remained dominant in multilaterals for some years now, hence the World Bank WID Division focus on 'measures to include women in development that contribute to economic performance, poverty reduction, and other development objectives' (World Bank, 1989: iii) and statements such as '[i]nvesting in women can be a cost-effective route to economic efficiency' and '[e]xpanding women's choices in economic activity . . . can increase output and efficiency by enabling women to find their true comparative advantage, much as international trade can promote efficient specialisation and economic expansion among nations'(World Bank, 1989: iv–v). 'Investing in women is a major theme in the World Bank's two pronged strategy for poverty reduction' (World Bank, 1994: 8), i.e. to labour intensive growth and improved social services, and, furthermore, the Bank justifies concern with women's health on the grounds of the benefit to the family of healthy mothers and the cost effectiveness of women's health interventions.

An instrumental approach is evident in major development agencies like the World Bank where the justifications made for attention to gender are in terms of how this will facilitate other development objectives rather than being an end in itself. Gender issues have been taken on board insofar as they are consistent with other development concerns (including poverty) and insofar as women are seen to offer a means to these, other, ends. Gender concerns are, for the World Bank, justified with reference to economic growth and poverty reduction. Similarly, UNFPA justify gender in relation to population control and environmental agencies in terms of environmental management and conservation. Even women's 'empowerment' is instrumental – UNFPA expects empowered women to have smaller families. Thus women are now the means of controlling population, of achieving sustainable development, of poverty alleviation.

RESCUING GENDER FROM THE POVERTY TRAP

The concern with instrumentalism, however, could be said to be linked to a model of development policy, practice and outcomes which are linear, structuralist and oversimplified. There are at least two ways by which instrumentalist development policies and projects may be confounded. One is via unintended consequences which may not be related to any particular human agency, and the other is through the multitude of ways in which the instrument strikes back. Women as actors and agents have their own priorities and projects which they seek to further through participation in development activities or which emerge in the process of participation. Let us look at three examples. The British ODA funds a poverty-focused agricultural development project in the Chhotanagpur Plateau region of India, the Rainfed Farming Project, which has formed vegetable gardening groups of tribal and low caste women in Orissa. Over a few years they have spontaneously begun to collectively punish male domestic violence and act against alcohol abuse by destroying the equipment of village distillers. Thus an agricultural project distributing improved vegetable seeds to poor women has been enrolled by them in their project of collective action against domestic violence and alcohol related poverty and abuse. The project model of poverty as caused by the deficiencies of agricultural technology was subverted to add social welfare issues into the portfolio of activities undertaken by the groups.

A second example shows women using the vehicle of development interventions, in this case an income generating project, to capture state commitment and turn it to their own ends. A case study in northern Oman (Heath, 1995) demonstrates how, over a decade, rural Muslim women involved with a rather ineffective income generating weaving project, shaped and used the project to improve their gender relations within and beyond the household. These strategies were not based on improved financial independence through weaving but included the establishment of relations of patronage with the state, then used to deflect control by household men and to legitimise new freedoms in behaviour; the assertion by women of their creative identity as weavers, and their 'invention of tradition' (weaving was not a women's activity in the pre-project situation) around weaving and the representation of themselves as sustaining the cultural traditions of the nation; and the gendering of space in the weaving centres in ways which positively changed work legitimacy, veiling and seclusion practices.

A final example comes from the experiences of an NGO worker in rural Mexico observing the interface between a group of women beekeepers, with an initial self-image of themselves as rustic housewives (*mujeres pata rajada* i.e. women with cracked soles) pursuing beekeeping as a hobby, and government implementors of a WID initiative constituting them as entrepreneurs within a project (Villarreal, 1992). In this encounter the government agency sought to label the beekeeping women as needy victims, in line with government discourses on incorporation of peasant women into society whilst local male opinion denied any threat to the gender order by asserting the marginality of the women and the subordination of the beekeeping group to the *ejido*. Meanwhile, 'many of the women beekeepers learned the language of "subordination" in order to extract benefits from it, while

41

FEMINIST VISIONS OF DEVELOPMENT

at the same time to some degree subverting this very ideology' (Villarreal, 1992: 260).

Studies such as these suggest the need for caution in linking policies and outcomes directly. The problem with the poverty trap is less the inevitable negative outcomes for women and more a 'political' one of the consequences for GAD of reliance on the poverty argument. The reasons for project 'misbehaviour' have been sought in the sociology of development organisations (Buvinic, 1986), institutional inertia, the gendered character of organisations and the marginal commitment to GAD by donors and governments (Staudt 1987; Goetz, 1992) but they also lie in the agency of women.

If women too are instrumental and the outcomes of actually existing development activities are a dynamic mixture of interlocking projects (Long and Long, 1992), then does instrumentalism as identified in feminist critiques matter? I think it does, because the 'projects' of actors do not interlock or overlap without struggle, negotiation and compromise, a process in which participants and officials are seldom equal. Where the policy and project objectives differ from those of participants, outcomes are likely to be closer to those of the more powerful bargaining partner, and the opportunities for subversion are uncertain. Goetz (1994: 24) shows why instrumentalism matters in the context of credit programmes (of the Grameen Bank and others) in Bangladesh which have been widely cited as examples of how to, synergistically, tackle gender and poverty issues simultaneously. In reporting evidence for the low level of loan control by women, she concludes that

> Donors' interests in seeing the development of financially self-sustaining rural development institutions has resulted in a preoccupation with cost recovery, to the degree that loan repayment rates have become the primary index of success, however much they obscure the important issue of the quality of loan use. . . . As poor women convincingly demonstrate a high repayment capacity, donors previously recalcitrant on the gender issue have pushed for the inclusion of women in credit programmes, not insensible to the obvious efficiency gains to be made.
>
> (Goetz, 1994: 30)

Thus although predominantly disbursed to women, loans arguably have limited benefits for women because the loans enter into gendered social relations in the household and women largely lose control of the loans. Goetz finds that a significant proportion of women's loans are directly invested by their male relatives, with 'women borrowers bearing the liability for repayment, though not necessarily directly benefiting from loan use' (1994: 1). Here an instrumental poverty programme offering capital to women has transformed many women into loan repayment officers, with uncertain long term consequences for gender relations. Money proves an inadequate currency for changing gender relations.

Synergism is a related feature of development discourses, i.e. the assertion of a positive, mutually beneficial, relationship between gender equity and other

RESCUING GENDER FROM THE POVERTY TRAP

development objectives, and if instrumentalism casts women as the means to other ends, synergism implies that the means/ends distinction is irrelevant. However, this has not gone unquestioned. The antipathy of gender interests and population policy has been analysed by Hartmann (1987), for women's reproductive goals and interests do not necessarily conform with those of family planners. Furthermore, although it has been widely argued that the education of women is linked to declining fertility, and that thus the empowerment of women through education is consistent with population limitation policies, Patricia Jeffery (1994) argues that this link may speak less of empowerment and more of the impact of the nuclear family ideology embodied in the content of much educational material. The clash between women's interests and environmental conservation is another arena in which synergy is debated (Jackson, 1993; Green, 1994).

The entrapment of GAD by poverty reduction presents analogous problems, for the view that it is the concentration of women amongst the poor and vulnerable (the 'feminisation of poverty') which justifies gender and development activity has some policy implications. Does this mean that where poverty is not feminised then there is no justification for GAD? Are there no gender issues amongst those who are not the deserving poor? Must all GAD activity be focused on poor women? Will poverty alleviation improve the position of women? These are some of the questions which deserve wider debate. Part of the struggle against the increasingly instrumental approach to GAD in development agencies requires a demonstration of how gender analysis, interests and issues are distinct from, and sometimes contradictory to, poverty and class.

The arguments which show how women's subordination is not derived from poverty need to be excavated to demonstrate the (liberal) fallacy that poverty alleviation will lead to gender equity. Poverty and gender are not entirely separate social phenomena. Indeed, one of the main features of gender analysis is the insistence that gender identity patterns all social life and that therefore gender awareness is not about 'adding women' but about rethinking development concepts and practice as a whole, through a gender lens. This insight is one of many which appears to have been lost in translation. Thus, the unfortunate term 'the feminisation of poverty' has come to mean not (as gender analysis would suggest) that poverty is a gendered experience, but that the poor are mostly women.

The feminisation of poverty

The term 'feminisation of poverty' suggests that '[w]omen tend to be disproportionately represented among the poor . . . the poorer the family the more likely it is to be headed by a woman' (World Bank, 1989: iv). Gender and development is frequently justified in terms of the poverty of female-headed households, for example the IFAD review on *The State of World Rural Poverty* in estimating the number of rural women below the poverty line in 114 countries makes the calculation on the basis of the number of households headed by women, added to the expected numbers of women in households classified as falling below the poverty

43

FEMINIST VISIONS OF DEVELOPMENT

line (Jazairy *et al.*, 1992: 274), i.e. it is assumed that all women-headed households are poor. This is not the case. Much depends upon the reason for female-headedness, those which are *de facto* household heads and receive remittances from migrant males may often be less poor than male-headed households (Kennedy and Peters 1992), whilst widows, divorced and separated women are indeed often amongst the poorest of rural people, with limited access to male income transfers and property rights. The study by Lloyd and Gage-Brandon (1993) of male- and female-headed households in Ghana is one example which shows that female-headedness is not associated with low incomes, whilst even for India where the heads of female-headed households are more uniformly elderly widows, the link with poverty is not generally strong (Agarwal, 1986: 187).

It is said that between 1965/70 and 1988 there was an increase of 47 per cent in women living below the poverty line compared to a 30 per cent increase for men (Jazairy *et al.*, 1992: 273). However, methodological queries cast doubt on these figures. As well as variability of poverty in female-headed households, the definition of female-headedness was debated, contested and redefined in the period in question. For the earlier dates (1965/70) women-headed households were generally defined in a *de jure* manner, whilst by 1988 gender scholarship in the 1970s and 1980s had been showing that numbers of women-headed households were underestimated because of the exclusion of *de facto* women-headed households. The changing definitions make comparisons over time invalid and what we now see is the belief that all female-headed households are poor combined with a now much more inclusive definition of female headship to suggest the feminisation of poverty. Combining *de facto* and *de jure* female-headed households created problems, one of which was the invalidity of time series comparisons such as those presented by IFAD, but also generated a category with little analytical use for poverty profiles as a result of high intra-group variation (Ahmad and Chalk, 1994: 185). Spurious averages, from populations including both these types of household, will be very misleading. Another methodological problem (Moore, 1994: 9) is that the use of percentage of income spent on food as an indicator of poverty may well also lead to an overestimation of the percentage of female-headed households among the poor since women-headed households seem to spend more on food even at higher income levels. It is arguable that the poverty of *de jure* women-headed households has been obscured by the inclination in GAD discourses to 'talk up' the numbers of women-headed households, and their poverty, to justify GAD in numerical terms.

One example of current poverty orthodoxy which displays some of the problems with assumptions about female-headed households is the World Bank country study on Uganda entitled *Growing out of Poverty* (1993a). This report insists that 'poorer households tend to be larger, have older and less educated household heads, and are more likely to be headed by a woman' (1993a: 5). This could be understood to mean that poorest households are more likely to be headed by a woman *than a man*, which is quite incorrect as Table 2.1 shows. The table reflects the very different meaning that poorest households are slightly more likely *than other households* to be headed by a woman.

44

RESCUING GENDER FROM THE POVERTY TRAP

Table 2.1 Selected characteristics of Ugandan households

Average	All Uganda	Non-poor	Poor	Poorest	Female-headed	Male-headed
Real per capita household expenditure	7,512	11,810	3,485	1,845	7,491	7,517
Household size	5.4	4.8	6.1	6.4	4.5	5.7
Dependency ratio (%)	44	38	51	52	45	44
Average age of household head	42	40	43	43	44	41
Female-headed households (%)	22	21	23	25	100	0
Household heads literate (%)	77	80	74	70	69	79
Percentage shares in total expenditure:						
Food	67	66	67	58	70	66
Drink and tobacco	5	6	5	3	2	6
Clothes	6	6	7	10	6	6
Rent	3	3	4	7	4	3
Fuel	2	2	2	3	2	2
Transport	0.3	0.4	0.2	0.2	0.1	0.3
Health	1	1	2	2	2	1
Education	1	1	1	2	1	1
Food expenditure, as share of total expenditure:						
Market purchases	26	30	23	19	29	26
Own production	40	36	44	39	41	40

Source: Adapted from World Bank (1993a), p.5.

Calculated from data for Household Budget Survey 1989/90 conducted by the Statistics Department of the Ministry of Finance and Economic Planning consisting of a stratified sample of 4,500 households across Uganda, except for eight districts in the North and East which were not sampled due to insecurity. Expenditures were calculated adding the value of purchased goods and the estimated value (at market prices) of the goods consumed out of own production.

The table also indicates other disjunctions between the classification by poverty and by gender of the household head; there are dramatic differences in per capita expenditure for categories of the poor, but virtually none for the gender of house-hold head categories; the poor do indeed have larger households but the female-headed households are small and more similar to those of the non-poor; the dependency ratios across groups of the poor increases but that of households headed by women and men is remarkably similar. This table seems to suggest that female-headed households cannot all be assumed to be poor and that, whilst they are distinct from male-headed households in literacy, age (possibly, although no indication of significance is given) and some aspects of consumption these are not simply poverty differentials but speak of another axis of differentiation.

FEMINIST VISIONS OF DEVELOPMENT

The meaning of female headship is highly contingent and cannot be used as a proxy for material deprivation (see Moore, 1994: 7–13, and Handa, 1994 for Jamaica). Apart from the important question of remittances and intra-household transfers which, as we discuss below, is a feature of women's incomes, the meaning of female headship is strongly related to age and life cycle as well as to cultural patterns such as the probability and acceptability of widow and divorcee remarriage and the levels of support from offspring and kin. Women-headed households are also seen as the victims of nucleation (Bruce, 1989) of extended families, divorce and fragmentation. The implication here is that women are better off in extended male-headed households. However, it is possible to see family fragmentation rather differently, since women-initiated divorce, for example, is often an indicator of relatively strong breakdown positions. Increasing divorce rates in Zimbabwe, the rise of informal unions and the phenomenon of single mothers are as much about the increasing viability of women as individuals as about their vulnerability and poverty (Jackson, 1994). Similarly the nucleation of households can be seen differently, as a process often stimulated by the increasing autonomy of younger women in extended households and their resistance to demands made on them by parents-in-law.[1] It often seems to be the case that women face a trade-off between material well-being, which may be greater in extended families, in conventional marriages, and under the wing of a male household head, and other aspects of well-being such as personal autonomy, independence and personhood.

The situation of female-headed households is extremely geographically variable and difficult to generalise about. There is little doubt that Indian widows, for example, are impoverished and vulnerable (Dreze, 1990) and insofar as they make up a major group of women-headed households in India there is possibly some validity in representing, and counting, such households as poor, but this is not a global truth. One implication of the focus on female-headed households is that it also rather implies that the feminisation of poverty only exists where there are many female-headed households, which is not everywhere. A table such as that in the IFAD study (Jazairy *et al.*, 1992: 279) which states that the percentages of households headed by women in Asia and Sub-Saharan Africa are 9 per cent and 31 per cent respectively suggests, by the feminisation of poverty logic, that Africa has the greater problem, a view which I think would be hard to defend.

Finally, a poverty focus directs attention to female-headed households. But the emphasis on poor female-headed households avoids the more important, and more difficult area of intra-household poverty. The unitary conception of the household goes unchallenged: only the gender of its head has changed.

The combination of an instrumental interest in women as the means to the ends of poverty reduction, and the feminisation of poverty discourse has led to a damaging erosion of the differences between gender disadvantage and poverty. The next section briefly examines the prescriptions of the New Poverty Agenda to suggest that they are unlikely to be gender neutral in their effects and may indeed exacerbate gender differentials.

46

RESCUING GENDER FROM THE POVERTY TRAP

Poverty through a gender lens

The poverty consensus

The New Poverty Agenda of multilateral development agencies claims that the concept of poverty has 'been broadened, beyond the notions of inadequate private income or consumption, toward a more comprehensive perspective: absence of "a secure and sustainable livelihood" [which] allows us to measure and evaluate the *level* and *vulnerability* – and freedom from bias by gender and age – of individuals' access to privately and publicly provided goods and services and to common property' (Lipton and Maxwell, 1992: 10, original emphasis). This section queries whether the new poverty agenda can, or does in practice, deal with gender bias.

Labour intensive growth is the central prescription of the new consensus on poverty. Thus criticism is levelled by Lipton and Maxwell (1992) at the declining additional demand for labour in the HYVs (High Yielding Varieties) being developed currently (by comparison with the 1970s). For them, saving labour is unemploying labour. But is it reasonable to criticise labour saving technology in a static manner such as this? If labour saving technologies are more profitable and are therefore more widely adopted they may increase the absolute levels of employment. For example, in the Rainfed Farming Project (eastern India) described on p.41, the introduction of upland paddy varieties in villages of West Bengal, which tiller (send up multiple stalks) strongly and minimise weeding, has led to large areas of previously semi-cultivated upland being put under paddy. Here, labour saving paddy has been associated with increasing food production and rapidly rising upland land values (mostly owned by poor tribal and low caste farmers) as well as rising agricultural wage rates in the context of expanding labour markets. Labour conserving varieties are popular both with farming household women for reducing drudgery and with women wage workers for stimulating growth in labour markets.

It can also often be the case that increasing labour intensity in agriculture equals greater unpaid work for household women, and therefore a conflict of their interests with those of poor men and women in the labour force, who might gain from increased demand for wage labour. Much depends on the specific tasks in which labour is saved, the gender divisions òf labour and the patterns of payment for tasks. Women are not a uniform group and the costs and benefits of labour saving technologies are class specific, but it is arguable that mechanisation has frequently been beneficial to women in relieving drudgery and that labour intensive agricultural growth is less clearly advantageous to rural women than to men.

The New Poverty Agenda also emphasises safety nets and targeted social welfare, although much of this discussion is about households rather than individuals. Targeting rather than universal benefits is seen as desirable because it allows resources to be concentrated on the needy (World Bank, 1993a, 1993b), but disadvantages include the high costs of administration for narrow targeting and most of the Bank's Program of Targeted Interventions have been broadly targeted

FEMINIST VISIONS OF DEVELOPMENT

(1993b: 18). Means testing as a method of targeting is expensive, so the profiling of poverty aims to identify the characteristics of the poor to serve as a proxy (Ahmad and Chalk, 1994: 182), and this is the context in which the household categorisation by male/female headship has been used as a poverty marker.

Smart safety nets and self-targeted social welfare offer support at levels which are only attractive to the very poor, and the criteria for targeting is poverty, not gender. From a gender perspective one might wonder what poverty targeting will offer the high birth order girl child in a landed rural household in northern India, which may not be very poor but in which such a child may be very much at risk? Even where the targeted individual is a poor woman her gendered identity patterns the extent to which she may benefit from safety nets and social services. Besley and Kanbur (1993: 79) point out that a critical assumption in self-targeting such as workfare is that the opportunity cost of time is lower for target groups, an assumption which may not hold where the targeted individual bears household commitments such as child rearing that prevent them from giving up labour time in return for very low wages. A further objection is that where such work is highly energy intensive, as in construction projects, the health consequences for poorly nourished women may be serious. Kumar (1995) found that women's BMI (Body Mass Index) is negatively affected by participation in a food for work project in Ethiopia, unlike men's, and she suggests that this is because women are less able to substitute food for work labour for other household labour.

It is assumed that poor men and women will be able to respond similarly to safety net provision, but I argue below that the experience of poverty is profoundly different for men and women and that such an assumption may be misguided. Targets bear gender identities. Some people may slip through the safety net where gender norms, of propriety and self-respect for example, mediate responses to safety net provision. Thus in Bangladesh women have been unable to take up food for work opportunities because of disapproval by male kin, and after the Bangladesh floods in 1988 women were very reluctant to leave their rooftops for the relief camps where purdah was difficult to maintain: 'To be seen by strangers while washing, sleeping and especially eating (since a wife is defined as a provider, not a consumer, of food) caused them great shame' (Shaw, 1992: 212). Women refugees experience gendered problems of obtaining separate food rations if they are not attached to a male household and sexual harassment problems are widely documented for women in post-disaster situations. As Mary Douglas (1992) has pointed out, needs and wants are culturally defined and express gender ideologies, thus women consistently do not reliably identify, report and seek attention for their own ill-health. Self-targeting depends upon socially legitimised and individually recognised 'need' as the basis for participation. Where targeting refers to women, e.g. in education of girls, there is often an instrumental core (educated women have smaller families), and targeting of social services and safety nets relies on, in general, the identification of the especially poor. A central flaw with the poverty agenda is that it conceives of poor women as just like poor men, except poorer.

48

RESCUING GENDER FROM THE POVERTY TRAP

The emphasis in the New Poverty Agenda is now on 'secure and sustainable livelihoods' with less weight on income or consumption and more attention to the perceptions of poor people themselves. However, the livelihood concept, when stripped down for measurement, consists of familiar elements – poverty lines defining inadequate incomes, consumption, nutrition, health, life expectancy, assets – and thus the following discussion is structured around some of these poverty indicators. Poverty is defined in a number of different ways, e.g. the World Bank defines poverty as 'the inability to attain a minimal standard of living' (1990: 26), all of which, however, embody gender spin and distortion of various kinds, much of which relates to the use of the household as the unit of analysis. For example, the poverty reduction strategy of the World Bank is based upon the preparation of Poverty Assessments derived from poverty lines, poverty profiles and poverty indicators (Askwith, 1994). Poverty lines identify the proportion of the population with incomes below the level considered necessary to meet minimum nutrition and survival needs, and poverty indicators commonly include GDP per capita, mortality statistics, life expectancy and literacy statistics. The brief examination of poverty indicators below shows that poor women are disadvantaged by a different metric to poor men and that the populist alternative to poverty lines, the definition and assessment of poverty by the poor themselves, fails to transcend dominant gender ideologies which deny disadvantage.

Poverty observed

Food consumption

The poor are frequently defined as those who do not have enough to eat, and food bias against women is alleged. Are women especially poor because of food bias? The questions raised here are whether women are malnourished in relation to their specific needs and to men, and whether women are explicitly and consciously discriminated against in food consumption. Women are usually smaller than men, their physiology and metabolism differs from men's, their work differs and their nutritional needs are different (Harriss, 1990; Kynch, 1994). Studies of intra-household food allocation are beset with methodological problems but the view that adult women are discriminated against in access to food is now seriously questioned (for example see Gillespie and McNeill, 1992; Lipton and Payne, 1994; Svedberg, 1991). A review of nutrition studies in Sub-Saharan Africa found little evidence for food bias (Svedberg, 1991) and in south Asia the evidence for gender bias in anthropometric status of adults is contradictory and geographically limited (Harriss, 1990), whilst increases in mortality during famines affect men more than women (Dreze and Sen, 1989: 55), despite the ways families appear to prioritise male interests during crises, because women seem better able to survive famine conditions. Jocelyn Kynch's study of food and growth amongst the poor in Palanpur found that adult men were more wasted than adult women, and amongst adults the men who were thinnest in relation to their wives were concentrated in

FEMINIST VISIONS OF DEVELOPMENT

childbearing couples, they were 'provisioning men whose authority depends upon the ability to supply the household with food' (Kynch, 1994: 49). A gender analysis of the implications of male roles in Palanpur reveals the costs of the provisioning expectations of men in particular age groups. However, the picture for children was the reverse and girls were much more likely to be wasted and stunted than boys.

The terms 'food access' and 'food allocation' imply a rather mechanistic process whereby rights to food become actual consumption. But consumption is not simply determined by availability; there may be underconsumption without overt and explicit food discrimination, and adequate consumption despite it. Needs are culturally constructed and partly understood in relation to beliefs about work (its intensity and its perceived value) and well-being. In addition, where food is limited, the needs of other household members influence, to a variable degree, the level of consumption of any individual. For example, women within Asian households are socialised into an ideal of self-sacrifice, which begins with food denial, and in Bengal women fast for the welfare of their husbands whilst men do not reciprocate. As Harriss observes, 'male fasts [are] for individual spiritual purposes and female fasts [are] for the auspiciousness of the household collective (i.e. for husband, son or brother)' (1990: 359–60). Self-denial over food is not exclusive to women. Hampshire and Randall writing about Fulani pastoralists observe that 'the concept of Pulaaku – what it is to be a Fulani – involves eating to meet minimal requirements rather than to fill oneself up' (1994: 8), but it is certainly commonly bound up with altruism and prioritising the needs of others as a central element in many feminine identities. Thus food availability at the household level tells us little about the individual experience of food adequacy in either quantity or quality.

It seems paradoxical that at the same time as gender ideologies express gender bias in food access (e.g. in the commonly reported pattern of women eating last after the men and children) we find that in terms of outcomes, i.e. anthropometric measures of nutritional status and ability to survive famines, the evidence for discrimination against women is patchy and women not infrequently fare better than men. Is this partly a consequence of too ready an acceptance (see the World Bank Uganda study, 1993a: 10) by researchers of articulated nutritional norms as reflecting actual food access without any interrogation of how women's agency subverts norms, e.g. by snack food consumption, by eating during food preparation and by consumption of 'leftovers'? If poverty is understood as minimum access to food, and it emerges that women do not generally suffer food bias, then a logical conclusion is that women are not poor and do not suffer deprivation.

When the justification for gender policies in development rests on the poverty allegation, analyses such as these can seriously undermine the case, despite the fact that poverty here only refers to material deprivation. What can be lost from view is not only the food deprivation of some categories of women (in India, the very young and old, and those in the north) but also the myriad other forms of

RESCUING GENDER FROM THE POVERTY TRAP

deprivation experienced by women. Kynch's (1994: 36–7) data on a northern Indian village studied in 1958, 1964, 1974 and 1984 found that for 0–5-year-olds the known deaths of male individuals surveyed fell from 22 per cent to 5 per cent whilst that of females remained at 17–19 per cent: i.e. overall mortality rates declined but the gap between male and female mortality widened.

How too does a Poverty Assessment account for the non-surviving girls and the costs of stunting? The situation of the girl child is particularly worrying for when son-preference damages the survival chances as substantially as occurs in northern India, mainly through unequal health care, what does it mean that surviving girls grow into adult women who do not suffer food bias?

Life expectancy

Life expectancy is another poverty indicator used as a summary measure of lifetime welfare to compare changing levels of well-being within and between countries. Yet in many developing countries women, despite being socially and economically disadvantaged, live longer than men and, notwithstanding high levels of maternal mortality, adult mortality of men outstrips that of women in all income groups (World Bank, 1990: 78). What gender differences in life expectancy tell us is not that most men are discriminated against, but that men and women experience different age-specific mortality risks related to both different physiologies and nutrition and to different divisions of labour, broadly defined. Whether these risks reflect gender inequity depends on how they are generated. For example, not all male mortality risks are the same and the health hazards faced by the wasted male providers in Kynch's study are very different from the health hazards of male overconsumption in the West. Gender analysis suggests that the quantity of life is not a good measure of well-being. As a recent review has pointed out, 'Because women live longer than men, the common belief is that they are healthier. In reality women are more likely to experience ill-health.' Much of this ill-health is women specific; for example 35 per cent of ill-health among women aged 15–44 years is accounted for by reproductive health problems, gender violence and rape (World Bank, 1994: 14). The evidence for gender violence against women spreads across all regions, classes, cultures and age groups and there are no grounds for believing that it is alleviated by increasing prosperity (Richters, 1994).

Assets

Poverty is also defined commonly in terms of household assets and resource access, land and livestock for example, but since patriliny is extremely common, women have widely different property relations to men. Thus, land ownership is seldom as defining of women's socio-economic position as it may be of men's. Patrilocal marriage also places a premium on mobile property for women, who may therefore have different strategies of asset accumulation to men; they may be

FEMINIST VISIONS OF DEVELOPMENT

excluded from land inheritance but accumulate gold. Possessions are often used to indicate poverty and prosperity as if they are gender neutral in their patterns of ownership, but most possessions indices are not relevant to assessing poverty of women, for they are based on typically male owned property. The problem goes beyond gender disaggregation of ownership of the same list of possessions, and requires a rethink of which indicators are used. It might be argued that men and women both benefit from 'household' assets, despite male ownership, and that therefore they are valid indicators of poverty. A woman married to a man with land, with a bicycle or with a radio is in some ways better off, but it is argued below that this may well not be the case.

Approaches to poverty which emphasise the transfer of assets to the poor (land reforms, social forestry, livestock) generally fail to recognise the differing relationship of women to property. Household ownership of land is not necessarily an unambiguous asset for household women. Settlement schemes in which women's labour becomes more deeply exploited abound: e.g. the Small Scale Commercial Farms and the Resettlement Areas of Zimbabwe where communal farmers and the landless have been given larger farms in which labour is scarce and women experience heavier workloads, and in which men recruit labour through extensive polygyny (Cheater, 1981; Jacobs, 1989). Furthermore, the disparity between the assets held by spouses may disadvantage women in bargaining by increasing the gap between the gains from cooperation (marriage) and the losses from breakdown. And of course, in the event of breakdown, few conjugal contracts uphold the rights of wives to a share of joint property (Goody, 1990). The endowing of men with land may adversely affect women's bargaining position within households. This is another poverty indicator which potentially distorts the understanding of gendered deprivation by use of a male yardstick.

Household income

Household income also tells us little about individual access to income and is therefore an unsatisfactory indicator of individual poverty (see Dwyer and Bruce, 1988); and 'there appears to be sufficient intra-household inequality to throw out standard estimates of overall inequality by an order of 30–40 per cent' (Kanbur and Haddad, 1994: 445). Household income is composed of a number of different streams; men and women cooperate in joint production and they engage in separate income earning activities, they consume jointly and as individuals. The variations in men's and women's incomes stem from a number of sources; women have generally poorer wages and lower levels of employment than men, they also have different kin and conjugal entitlements to transfers, different levels and forms of income access and control and different sets of expenditure obligations and responsibilities. The distinctive features of women's incomes affect, and limit, the degree to which household income can serve as an indicator of their wellbeing.

Despite the diversity and complexity of the work on incomes within households

RESCUING GENDER FROM THE POVERTY TRAP

there is one point which has been made much of, and that is the evidence that women spend more of their money on children and household needs than men. This is becoming a much used argument justifying GAD on the grounds of child welfare. It may well be true that women prioritise children's needs, but there is a sense in which one might wish women to be a little less selfless and self-sacrificing. It is the sense that women have to be the 'deserving poor' to earn the attention of development agencies which disturbs. Some recent work (Hopkins *et al.*, 1994) has been investigating, and partly substantiating, the possibility that it is the particular characteristics of women's incomes (their seasonality and their regular nature) rather than women's altruism which explains gender differences in expenditure. One fears that if research shows that women's income expenditure is not as child welfare oriented as currently seems to be the case, the commitment to gender will wane. A real improvement in the position of women may indeed involve a shift to less altruism, yet paradoxically this could undermine the support of development agencies for GAD.

How does rising household income affect women within the household? Haddad and Kanbur's work (on a data set from the Philippines) on the intra-household Kuznets curve (1990) suggests that as household income rises, so too do levels of inequality (measured in this instance by calorie adequacy) amongst members, until relatively high incomes are reached. They conclude that 'it is not simply enough to increase the total resources of a household since, particularly for poor households, the accompanying increase in inequality may well undermine the beneficial effects on the poorest individuals of the total resource increase' (Haddad and Kanbur, 1990: 25).

There seems to be a considerable body of evidence for the argument that gender relations are more equitable in poor Indian households. Poor Indian women engage in labour markets more than wealthier women, they contribute more significantly to total household income, they have greater control over incomes and are less subject to restrictions on their physical mobility than the non-poor. Gender equity often appears to be inversely related to household income (Menscher, 1985; Agarwal, 1986), a situation with parallels in other Asian countries. Studies on women's experience of the green revolution have also shown a pattern of withdrawal of women's labour from farm work and increasing dependence of women on men as household incomes rise.

In reviewing village studies in India, Harriss (1992: 361–3) finds that the greatest excess mortality of girls occurs amongst poor landless groups in some studies, and amongst high caste landed groups in others. Some of the most severe discrimination against the girl child in India is found in high caste rural groups, characteristically also high income (Krishnaji, 1987; Jeffery *et al.*, 1989; Heyer, 1992). My research in Giridih district (1993–4) of rural south Bihar also found dramatic differences in the survival of girls among different caste/income groups: higher caste farmers had very few surviving daughters whilst the juvenile sex ratio in low caste and tribal households of the same village was much more balanced. This village is in a rainfed area where there has been no green revolution and

53

FEMINIST VISIONS OF DEVELOPMENT

where there is virtually no irrigated agriculture. A useful study over some years of fertility and mortality in a village of Uttar Pradesh found that in recent years the mortality of female children of the poor has now begun to rise dramatically, which has been related mainly to reduced employment for women as a result of crop changes (away from those demanding female labour) and mechanisation displacing women, and to rising dowry (Wadley, 1993). What seems to have happened is that as households have become more prosperous, in a context of green revolution generated growth, women have been withdrawn (or displaced) from wage work in order to conform with the strong purdah norms, and dowries have inflated to very high levels for the poor as well as the rich. Differential neglect and higher mortality of girls is thus related both directly and indirectly to the increasing dependence of women in upwardly mobile households where higher incomes bring with them deeper aversion to girl children.

This is not to suggest that women are better off poor, but that there can be something of a trade-off between women's material well-being and their autonomy, a situation which poor men do not seem to face. This is one way of looking at the limited degree to which poverty and gender development can be approached synergistically with the same policy instruments. If rising household income has a perverse effect on women's well-being then poverty reduction policies, even if successful, may well not increase women's well-being in the short run. There is great variation in the degree and manner by which women gain from raising male incomes and poverty reduction, but it seems clear that women within households may not necessarily benefit from higher male incomes; much depends on the transactions and transfers within the household.

The degree to which women benefit from higher personal incomes through, for example, income generating projects, also depends on intra-household transactions and the degree to which women can retain control of additional incomes. Conversely, project failure to reduce poverty through income generation does not signify an absence of change in gender relations. Heath (1995) shows how money earned in an income generating project may be largely irrelevant to changing gender relations, which derive as much from the non-financial leverage gained by women from project participation. Money is neither necessary nor sufficient for transforming gender relations.

Entitlements

Sen's idea of entitlements has been seen as an alternative approach to poverty lines, and these too vary for men and women in households. Naila Kabeer has pointed out, for Bangladesh, that the entitlements of women are 'embedded to a far greater degree than those of men within family and kinship structures. Even where women have independent entitlements, for instance through ownership of assets or sale of labour power, they may prefer to exercise them in ways which do not disrupt kinship-based entitlements, their primary source of survival and security' (1989: 9). Thus women (more than men) can be, and become, poor through

RESCUING GENDER FROM THE POVERTY TRAP

both the condition and deterioration of household entitlements and the character and deterioration of the intra-household social relations upon which they depend. Kabeer calls for the use of more qualitative poverty indicators which recognise how, for example, marriage mediates the experience of poverty for women. Sen's capabilities framework (1987) offers a more flexible approach to well-being since capabilities may be formulated which reflect specifically gendered disadvantage, and include, for example, freedom from violence. However, this leaves the problem of the commensurability of men's and women's well-being and the invalidity of comparison.

The New Poverty Agenda claims to give more attention to the perceptions of poor people themselves, in line with participatory development approaches which acknowledge the rights, and value, of beneficiary involvement with development interventions. Do the perceptions and definitions of poverty elicited from the poor give more adequate representation to gender issues?

Poverty experienced

The turn to qualitative understandings of poverty has not generally been conducive to greater gender awareness and the approach which claims to be based on how the poor themselves define poverty (Chambers, 1988) is in ways even more gender blind than the head-count methods it criticises.[2] Here 'poor people' and 'the poor' are treated as an homogeneous group such that it is possible to speak of the 'knowledge of poor people' and the 'priorities' of poor people. Chambers calls for poor people themselves to be consulted about their own criteria for well-being and the use of Participatory Rural Appraisal (PRA) has been promoted as the relevant mechanism. PRA is no longer the preserve of small NGOs and is now used in poverty assessments by the World Bank (as 'Beneficiary Assessment') and by bilateral agencies (e.g. the Overseas Development Administration, 1995). Do the tools of PRA, such as wealth ranking, reveal critical gender variations in the experience of poverty?

Wealth ranking

Wealth ranking has a number of problematic features: it produces a single hierarchy yet there are multiple orderings reflecting the different dimensions of well-being, and it is static unlike poverty into which people move and escape, precipitated by particular events or simply as a consequence of domestic development cycles. There are at least two gender problems here. First, ranking of the household obscures the situation of women within it. Scoones (1995) has shown how in rural Zimbabwe men and women defined well-being differently and therefore classified people differently (women gave a greater weighting, than men or the research team, to cash incomes, remittances, women's incomes) and he acknowledges that 'Wealth ranking . . . associates wealth with a household, usually through the name of the oldest male resident. Yet "wealth" may be held and controlled by different individuals within the household' (Scoones, 1995: 85). A further objection arises around the gendered cultural internalisation of well-being expectations.

Gendered subjectivities

As Sen (1987) memorably reminds us, there are often large discrepancies between subjective perceptions of well-being and well-being as measured by 'objective' indicators such as some of those discussed. Chambers (1988: 23) illustrates this with reference to the studies of N.S. Jodha in Rajasthan which showed that the group of households who had experienced a fall in income (1964–84) also claimed to have experienced improvement in 37 of 38 aspects of well-being identified by themselves, over the same period. Clearly income is only one element of well-being, and it might be concluded that poverty lines underestimate well-being, but Sen insists that we do need objective measures of poverty as a counterpoint to perceptions which reflect the biases and prejudices inherent in all cultures. Populists such as Beck (1994) take issue with Sen's critique of 'mental-metricism', or subjective perceptions of poverty, on the grounds that it discredits the validity of what poor people say in general and he is at pains to defend the self-definitions of poverty by poor people and to assert solidarity and mutual support as features of poor communities. It is interesting that the example used by Sen to show the problem of mental-metricism is drawn from a 1944 study of the Bengal Famine of 1943 which reported that of widowers asked whether they were 'ill' or in 'indifferent' health 48.5 per cent of widowers said they were 'ill' and 45.6 per cent that they were in 'indifferent' health, whilst 2.5 per cent of widows asked the same question said they were 'ill' and none said they were in 'indifferent' health (Sen, 1987: 53). Beck's 'deconstruction' consists of the following: 'one wonders why a male academician should have chosen poor female famine sufferers as an example of "mental-metricism". Does this choice reveal "mental-metricism" on the part of Sen himself? . . . Could a comparative survey of the health of female and male academics who had just failed to get tenure, lost their house and car, and hadn't eaten for three days, be taken as an accurate reflection of their well-being or would we expect some "mental-metricism" to creep in?' (1994: 30).

Beck seems to have missed the point, the gender differences in perceptions of well-being, and instead has become angry about what he thinks is a slur against the truth of the perceptions of the disadvantaged, but perhaps what needs deconstructing is not Sen's 'mental-metricism' but Beck's populist outrage. In his study of villages in West Bengal, Beck does not confront the problem of his own representation of 'poor people's perceptions' despite the fact that his text repeatedly displays his own beliefs about the causes and nature of poverty (1994: 173–7). However, this apart, if we accepted Beck's version of poor peoples' views of poverty at face value what would it tell us about gender? Women appear as respondents, but they do not speak of gender, and nor do men. Thus, for example, Beck's discussion of violence is entirely in class terms (1994: 168) and says nothing about domestic

RESCUING GENDER FROM THE POVERTY TRAP

violence, whilst Kabeer (1994: 149–50) cites a number of studies on the high levels of suicide, homicide, rape and prostitution amongst Bengali women, many of which implicated male kin, and domestic violence, which invariably did. This absence may therefore derive from the beliefs of the researchers, or may indeed be an absence in the views of 'the poor' because domestic violence is embodied in 'doxa' (Bourdieu, 1977) or because it is not spoken of for other reasons. In reviewing people's own concepts of poverty in India Barbara Harriss concludes '[t]hat people's own criteria [of poverty] do not include longer life, less disease, more freedom for women and makes one suspicious of what Sen (1985) calls "physical condition neglect" as well as outright gender bias in phenomenological enquiry' (1992: 372).³ Anthropological work such as the Jefferys' extended work on childbearing in villages of Uttar Pradesh shows the (gendered) limits of subjective perceptions: '[G]irls' inferior chances of survival [are not] locally perceived. Yet they are manifest almost from birth in the maternity histories. For couples in Dharmnagri and Jhakri, however, it is primarily the unpredictability of sons' deaths that enters their calculations about family size' (Jeffery *et al.*, 1989: 195).

Researchers blinded by populist sympathy for the poor easily overlook gender relations of inequality. There seems to be a strong connection between the view of mutual solidarity amongst the poor and the absence of gender analysis in work which claims to report the perceptions of the poor. According to Beck, 'poverty involves much more than lack of food, shelter and being subject to illness; it also involves the experience of being subordinated and oppressed, and resisting this where possible' (1994: 180). Being subordinated is not only related to poverty, it is also a consequence of being a woman, yet we are offered no discussion of resistance by poor women against poor men possibly because of the 'virtuous peasant' problem (Bernstein, 1990) characteristic of populism. Self-respect is a major feature in Beck's interviews and analysis yet he declines to comment on what this might mean for gender relations, specifically here the ways in which poor women observe purdah norms as an avenue to self-respect and the ways in which men's respect depends in large part upon the behaviour of their wives. There are many gains from moral conformity and observation of the 'patriarchal bargain' (Kandiyoti, 1988) but what are the intended and unintended consequences of such choices for women, in the short- and long-term, and therefore is it responsible to represent women's articulated perceptions as necessarily complete truths?

Cultural, including gender, ideologies pattern the entire business of communication upon which PRA depends. What women *can want*, what it is thinkable to desire, differs from what it is culturally thinkable for men to want; what women *can say*, what a muted 'vocabulary' allows, also differs and finally, what women *will say* in the context of a public PRA exercise bears a gender imprint. For women who are excluded from dominant worldviews and male vocabularies (Ardener, 1975) it is not wise to assume that they can, or will, simply express their priorities as PRA assumes. This is not to suggest that women are social automatons: clearly they actively subvert language and subordination, but only to point out that what all of

FEMINIST VISIONS OF DEVELOPMENT

us say is context dependent, contingent and to varying degrees constrained by identities. Some of the gendered politics of communication affecting PRA in my experience includes the construction of local knowledge in exogamous and patrilocal communities as the preserve of 'insiders' whilst women often appear as outsiders, and in local terminology even as 'strangers' despite their length of marital residence. Women can also be especially sensitive to allegations of gossip, yet PRA invites and requires opinions and information to be expressed publicly about others.

Although a more theorised perspective is developing in PRA and related methods (e.g. Cornwall *et al.*, 1993) there remains a curious paradox in the recognition that communications between researchers and researched are interactive, profoundly shaped by context, intra-community struggles, and the politics of (multiple) identities, and the simultaneous insistence that PRA tools are any better able than other methods to deal with these issues. David Mosse, writing from experience of using PRA on a British ODA agricultural development project in western India, states that 'PRA, far from providing a neutral vehicle for local knowledge, actually creates a context in which the selective presentation of opinion is likely to be exaggerated, and where minority or deviant views are likely to be suppressed' (1993: 11) and in this way the public PRA exercise can offer an avenue for the generalisation of personal, and gender specific, interests.

Whose perceptions and representations?

How does one evaluate the claims of Participatory Rural Appraisal (Mascarenhas *et al.*, 1991; Chambers, 1992) to give voice to the perceptions of local people by approaches which explicitly involve respondents as partners in research and which validate these perceptions and knowledges? Many of these approaches are based on group work, e.g. participatory mapping and modelling, diagramming, wealth ranking, transect walks and matrix ranking, and it is suggested that women are involved in either mixed or single sex groups depending on the context. At a practical level a number of objections can be raised about many of these techniques which claim to be open to all but for which, as always, participation makes certain demands. One is time to participate in lengthy exercises such as modelling, another is the mobility needed to participate in, for example, transect walks, when women are constrained by child care.

Assuming the researcher to be aware of a diversity of opinion within any community, the question of whose voice is represented arises. For example, Cornwall *et al.* recognise that the 'local community' consists of many different people with different power positions, different priorities and perceptions and they raise the question of which of these competing viewpoints are then privileged. For them, 'If truths are relative, choosing a version becomes more a matter of appropriateness or applicability' (1993: 28). Given that the choice of which truth to represent lies with the PRA researchers, who after all are in control of the external representation process, then how can it be claimed that PRA voices local perceptions?

RESCUING GENDER FROM THE POVERTY TRAP

PRA as practised assumes local knowledge to be complete and impartial, yet it seems to be neither. The reliance on PRA and the popularity of the approach in which the poor define their condition can conceal some major issues of inequality. In this regard there is something to be said for the older approaches to research, both long-term research and the much despised survey. Indeed, it was analysis of the Indian census which revealed the sex ratio problem in India (Miller, 1981).

Gender interests cannot be entirely equated with the articulated views of women. Women can be implicated in female foeticide and infanticide, in food and health biases within households, in exploitative relations with other women (e.g. as mothers-in-law) and in dowry deaths (Jeffery *et al.*, 1989: 30–1). Sen is justified in his concern about 'mental-metricism', not because it devalues the perceptions of the poor but because it insists that there is a role for other forms of knowledge than the self-perceptions of the poor.

One problem with measuring men and women by the same poverty yardstick, be it food, income, entitlements, or local perceptions of deprivation, is that it both exaggerates women's poverty in some directions and conceals it in others, for the causes and experience of poverty differ by gender. Another is that the poverty argument is precarious, being exposed to deconstruction and dissolution in its own terms, i.e. of both measured material deprivation as well as perceptions and representations of deprivation, and uncertain to deliver clear gains to women given the instrumentalism inherent in much of the commitment to GAD in development agencies.

Conclusions

This chapter has tried to make the case that gender justice is not a poverty issue and cannot be approached with poverty reduction policies, and that it is important to assert the distinction between gender and poverty in the face of the tendency in development organisations to collapse all forms of disadvantage into poverty. The influences which have resulted in gender issues being so closely identified with poverty are many. WID narratives were, in the 1970s, often constructed around women as victims of development, a trend which was sustained, despite protests from Southern feminists, in much of the critique of structural adjustment. Gender discourses also had to survive within development bureaucracies, which were themselves dominated by men, where it was easier to ring-fence gender issues as a problem of poverty, and to argue for the feminisation of poverty, than to admit a corrosive feminist view of gender disadvantage as crossing boundaries of class and ethnicity, denying the 'otherness' of the poor and directing attention to the gendered character of development agencies themselves.

The debates about targeting versus mainstreaming also possibly reflect these struggles. Special projects for women were the object of extensive GAD critique, on mostly legitimate grounds (e.g. McCarthy, 1984 on Bangladesh) and the anti-targeting stance was avidly taken up by development agencies. Thus the World

FEMINIST VISIONS OF DEVELOPMENT

Bank WID Division states that '[w]omen are viewed too often as "targets" or "beneficiaries", and too rarely as effective "agents" or contributors' (1989: v) and advises that '[i]n general, do not design "women only" programs' (1989: vi).[4] However, one consequence of mainstreaming gender into 'every page of every project document' (as suggested by Chris Patten, the Minister for Overseas Development in Britain in the 1980s) may have been to depoliticise gender analysis and to expose it to the prevailing gender ideologies of project management, of which the most one could expect was the view of women as a resource in meeting other development goals, a position not always consistent with gender interests. It is arguable that mainstreaming has become assimilation in that the possibilities of developing distinct and autonomous GAD discourses have been limited by the absence of women-only activities and institutional bases, and the reduction of gender perspectives to conform with dominant views of deprivation as caused by poverty.

Rescuing gender from the poverty trap means we need poverty independent gender analyses and policies which recognise that poverty policies are not necessarily appropriate to tackling gender issues because the subordination of women is not caused by poverty. Even if smart safety nets are successfully provided for the materially deprived, non-poor women are of interest to GAD for a number of reasons. Women who are not poor, of course, experience subordination of different kinds: domestic violence, personal insecurity, limited opportunities, oppressive gender ideologies, and mortality risks which make them an important category in their own right. But in addition, the position of non-poor women is also relevant to poor women in both positive and negative ways. By changing societal perceptions of women's roles, identities and options the achievements of non-poor women can positively influence gender bargaining, ideologies and opportunities for poor women. Non-poor women also have negative influences on poor women, for example sanskritisation and the dowry problem in India, and it could be argued that tackling dowry practices among middle income groups may be the most important social issue to address in India today. A poverty focus misses the range of interconnected gender issues across classes and socio-economic strata and obscures both the problems of gender bias by women towards other women as well as the possibilities for solidarity across social boundaries.

Acknowledgements

I would like to thank Ruth Pearson for my title and shared ideas, and Anne Marie Goetz, Richard Palmer-Jones and Christine Okali for useful comments and support.

Notes

1 The conditions under which fragmentation occur are clearly significant: for example, the breakup of households under conditions of persistent and acute scarcity are discussed in Harriss, 1992.
2 The well-known critique of gender bias in census data needs no repetition.

RESCUING GENDER FROM THE POVERTY TRAP

3 'Sen (1985)' is the Sen 1987 in the reference list.
4 It is, incidentally, interesting that the term 'agent' is used here to refer to women as positive channels for development rather than to the capabilities of women for action which is not necessarily conducive to development as specified by development agents. Women's agency is, for many gender analysts, about their capacity for disruption, subversion and challenge to structural constraints.

References

Agarwal, B. (1986) 'Women, poverty and agricultural growth in India', *Journal of Peasant Studies*, Vol. 13, No. 4, pp.165–220.
Ahmad, E. and Chalk, N. (1994) 'On improving public policies for the poor: major informational requirements' in van der Hoeven, R. and Anker, R. (eds) *Poverty Monitoring: An International Concern* (London: Unicef, Macmillan), pp.173–90.
Ardener, E. (1975) 'Belief and the problem of women' in Ardener, S. (ed.) *Perceiving Women* (London: Malaby Press), pp.1–15.
Askwith, M. (1994) *Poverty Reduction and Sustainable Development: Semantics or Substance.* Discussion Paper 345 (Brighton, Sussex: Institute of Development Studies).
Beck, T. (1994) *The Experience of Poverty: Fighting for Respect and Resources in Village India* (London: Intermediate Technology Publications).
Bernstein, H. (1990) 'Taking the part of peasants?' in Bernstein, H., Crow, B., MacKintosh, M., and Martin, C. (eds) *The Food Question: Profits Versus People?* (London: Earthscan Publications).
Besley, T. and Kanbur, R. (1993) 'The principles of targeting' in Lipton, M. and van der Gaag, J. (eds) *Including the Poor.* Proceedings of a Symposium organised by the World Bank and the International Food Policy Institute (Washington, DC: IBRD), pp.67–83
Bourdieu, P. (1977) *Outline of a Theory of Practice* (Cambridge: Cambridge University Press).
Bruce, J. (1989) 'Homes divided', *World Development*, Vol. 17, No. 7, pp.979–91.
Buvinic, M. (1986) 'Projects for women in the Third World: explaining their misbehavior', *World Development*, Vol.14, No. 5, pp.653–64.
Chambers, R. (1988) *Poverty in India: Concepts, Research and Reality.* Discussion Paper 241 (Brighton, Sussex: Institute of Development Studies).
Chambers, R. (1992) *Rural Appraisal: Rapid, Relaxed and Participatory.* Discussion Paper 311 (Brighton, Sussex: Institute of Development Studies).
Cheater, A. (1981) 'Women and their participation in commercial agricultural production: the case of medium-scale freehold in Zimbabwe', *Development and Change*, Vol. 12, pp.349–77.
Cornwall, A., Guijit, I. and Welbourn, A. (1993) *Acknowledging Process: Challenges for Agricultural Research and Extension Methodology.* Discussion Paper 333 (Brighton, Sussex: Institute of Development Studies).
Douglas, M. (1992) *Risk and Blame: Essays in Cultural Theory* (London and New York: Routledge).
Dreze, J. (1990) *Widows in Rural India.* Development Economics and Public Research Programme, No. 26 (London School of Economics, Suntory-Toyota International Centre for Economics and Related Disciplines).
Dreze, J. and Sen, A. (1989) *Hunger and Public Action* (Oxford: Clarendon Press).
Dwyer, D. and Bruce, J. (eds) (1988) *A Home Divided: Women and Income in the Third World* (Stanford: Stanford University Press).

FEMINIST VISIONS OF DEVELOPMENT

Gillespie, S. and McNeill, G. (1992) *Food, Health and Survival in India and Developing Countries* (Delhi: Oxford University Press).

Goetz, A. M. (1992) 'Gender and administration', *IDS Bulletin*, Vol. 23, No. 4, pp.6–17.

Goetz, A. M. (1994) 'From feminist knowledge to data for development: the bureaucratic management of information on women and development', *IDS Bulletin*, Vol. 25, No. 2, pp.27–36.

Goody, J. (1990) *The Oriental, the Ancient and the Primitive: Systems of Marriage and the Family in the Pre-industrial Societies of Eurasia* (Cambridge: Cambridge University Press).

Green, C. (1994) *Does 'Synergism' Work for Women?* Poverty, Population and Environment IDS Discussion Paper 343 (University of Sussex, Brighton: Institute of Development Studies).

Haddad, L. and Kanbur, R. (1990) *Is There an Intra-Household Kuznets Curve? Some Evidence from the Philippines.* Development Economics Research Centre, Discussion Paper 101 (University of Warwick).

Hampshire, K. and Randall, S. (1994) 'Migration and household structure: flexibility as a survival strategy for Sahelian agropastoralists'. Conference paper, Population and Environment Research Programme (University of Bradford, Development Project Planning Centre, 14–16 December).

Handa, S. (1994) 'Gender, headship and intra-household resource allocation', *World Development*, Vol. 22, No. 10, pp.1535–47.

Harriss, B. (1990) 'The intrafamily distribution of hunger in south Asia', in Dreze, J. and Sen, A. (eds) *The Political Economy of Hunger. Volume 1: Entitlement and Well-being* (Oxford: Clarendon Press), pp.351–424.

Harriss, B. (1992) 'Rural poverty in India: micro level evidence', in Harriss, B., Guhan, S. and Cassen, R., *Poverty in India. Research and Policy* (Bombay: Oxford University Press), pp.333–89.

Hartmann, B. (1987) *Reproductive Rights and Wrongs. The Global Politics of Population Control and Reproductive Choice* (New York: Harper and Row).

Heath, C. (1995) 'Hidden currencies: women, weaving and income generation in Oman'. PhD dissertation submitted to School of Development Studies, University of East Anglia, Norwich, UK.

Heyer, J. (1992) 'The role of dowries and daughters' marriages in the accumulation and distribution of capital in a south Indian community', *Journal of International Development*, Vol. 4, No. 4, pp.419–36.

Hopkins, J., Levin, C. and Haddad, L. (1994) 'Women's income and household expenditure patterns: gender or flow?' *American Journal of Agricultural Economics*, Vol. 76, pp.1219–25.

Huntington, S. (1975) 'Issues in women's role in economic development: critique and alternatives', *Journal of Marriage and the Family*, Vol. 37, No. 4, pp.1001–12.

Jackson, C. (1993) 'Questioning synergism: win-win with women in population and environment policies?' *Journal of International Development*, Vol. 5, No. 6, pp.651–68

Jackson, C. (1994) 'Changing conjugal contracts in rural Zimbabwean households'. Conference paper to the African Studies Association, UK Conference, Lancaster University, 5–7 September.

Jacobs, S. (1989) 'Zimbabwe: state, class, and gendered models of land resettlement', in Parpart, J. and Staudt, K. (eds) *Women and the State in Africa* (London and Boulder, Colorado: Lynne Rienner Publishers), pp.161-84.

Jaquette, J. (1990) 'Gender and justice in economic development', in Tinker, I. (ed.)

RESCUING GENDER FROM THE POVERTY TRAP

Persistent Inequalities: Women and World Development (Oxford: Oxford University Press), pp.54–69.

Jazairy, I., Alamgir, M. and Panuccio, T. (1992) *The State of World Rural Poverty: An Inquiry into its Causes and Consequences* (London: Intermediate Technology Publications).

Jeffery, P (1994) 'Education and population policy: the implications for women of the supposed relationship between girls' schooling and women's autonomy'. Paper presented at the Conference on Gender Research and Development: Looking Forward to Beijing, School of Development Studies, University of East Anglia, 9–10 September.

Jeffery, P., Jeffrey, R. and Lyon, A. (1989) *Labour Pains and Labour Power: Women and Childbearing in India* (London and New Jersey: Zed Books).

Kabeer, N. (1989) *Monitoring Poverty as if Gender Mattered: A Methodology for Rural Bangladesh.* Discussion Paper 255 (Brighton, Sussex: Institute of Development Studies).

Kabeer, N. (1994) *Reversed Realities: Gender Hierarchies in Development Thought* (London, New York: Verso).

Kanbur, R. and Haddad, L. (1994) 'Are better off households more unequal or less unequal?' *Oxford Economic Papers,* Vol. 46, pp.445–58.

Kandiyoti, D. (1988) 'Bargaining with patriarchy', *Gender and Society,* Vol. 2, No. 3, pp.274–90.

Kennedy, E. and Peters, P. (1992) 'Household food security and child nutrition: the interaction of income and gender of household head', *World Development,* Vol. 20, No. 8, pp.1077–85.

Krishnaji, N. (1987) 'Poverty and sex ratios', *Economic and Political Weekly,* Vol. 22, pp.892–97.

Kumar, S. (1995) 'Intra-household gender aspects of food and agricultural research' personal e-mail communication (7 July).

Kynch, J. (1994) *Food and Human Growth in Palanpur.* The Development Economics Research Programme No. 57 (London School of Economics, Suntory-Toyota International Centre for Economics and Related Disciplines).

Lipton, M. and Maxwell, S. (1992) *The New Poverty Agenda: an Overview.* Discussion Paper 306, (Brighton, Sussex: Institute of Development Studies).

Lipton, M. and Payne P. (1994) *How Third World Households Adapt to Dietary Energy Stress: The Evidence and the Issues* (Washington: International Food Policy Research Institute).

Lloyd, C. and Gage-Brandon, A. (1993) 'Women's role in maintaining households: family welfare and sexual inequality in Ghana', *Population Studies,* Vol. 47, pp.115–31.

Long, N. and Long, A. (eds) (1992) *Battlefields of Knowledge: Theory and Practice in Social Research and Development* (London: Routledge).

Mascarenhas, J., Shah, P., Joseph, S., Jayakaran, R., Devavaram, J., Ramachandran, V., Fernandez, A., Chambers, R. and Pretty, J. (1991) 'Participatory rural appraisal'. Proceedings of the February 1991 Bangalore PRA trainers workshop. RRA Notes No. 13 (London and Bangalore: International Institute for Environment and Development and MYRADA).

McCarthy, F. (1984) 'The target group: women in Bangladesh', in Clay, E. and Schaffer, B. (eds) *Room for Manoeuvre: An Exploration of Public Policy in Agriculture and Rural Development* (Cranbury, New Jersey: Associated University Presses), pp.49–58.

Menscher, J. P. (1985) 'Landless women agricultural laborers in India: some observations from Tamil Nadu, Kerala and West Bengal', in International Rice Research Institute (eds) *Women in Rice Farming* (Manilla), pp.351–71.

FEMINIST VISIONS OF DEVELOPMENT

Miller, B. (1981) *The Endangered Sex: The Neglect of Female Children in Rural North India* (Ithaca: Cornell University Press).

Moore, H. (1994) *Is There a Crisis in the Family?* Occasional Paper No.3 (World Summit for Social Development, Geneva: United Nations Research Institute for Social Development).

Moser, C. O. N. (1993) *Gender Planning and Development: Theory, Practice and Training* (London: Routledge).

Mosse, D. (1993) *Authority, Gender and Knowledge: Theoretical Reflections on the Practice of Participatory Rural Appraisal.* ODI, Agricultural Administration (Research and Extension) Network Paper 44 (London: Overseas Development Institute).

Overseas Development Administration (1995) *A Guide to Social Analysis for Projects in Developing Countries* (London: HMSO).

Palmer-Jones, R. and Jackson, C. (1997) 'Work intensity, gender and sustainable development', *Food Policy,* Vol. 22, No. 1, pp.39–62.

Richters, A., (1994) *Women, Culture and Violence. A Development, Health and Human Rights Issue,* Women and Autonomy Series (Leiden: Leiden University, Women and Autonomy Centre).

Scoones, I. (1995) 'Investigating difference: applications of wealth ranking and household survey approaches among farming households in southern Zimbabwe', *Development and Change,* Vol. 26, No. 1, pp.67–88.

Sen, A. (1987) *Commodities and Capabilities* (Delhi: Oxford University Press).

Shaw, R. (1992) 'Nature, culture and disaster: floods and gender in Bangladesh', in Croll, E. and Parkin, D. (eds) *Bush Base: Forest Farm* (London and New York: Routledge).

Staudt, K. (1987) 'Women's programs, bureaucratic resistance and feminist organisations', in Boneparth, E. and Stoper, E. (eds) *Women, Power and Policy* (New York: Pergamon Press).

Svedberg, P. (1991) 'Undernutrition in Sub-Saharan Africa: is there a gender bias?', *Journal of Development Studies,* Vol. 26, No. 3, pp.469–86.

Villarreal, M. (1992) 'The poverty of practice: power, gender and intervention from an actor-oriented perspective', in Long, N. and Long, A. (eds) *Battlefields of Knowledge. The Interlocking of Theory and Practice in Social Research and Development* (London and New York: Routledge).

Wadley, S. (1993) 'Family composition strategies in rural north India', *Social Science and Medicine,* Vol. 37, No. 11, pp.1367–76.

World Bank (1989) *Women in Development: Issues for Economic and Sector Analysis.* WID Division Working Paper 269 (Washington, DC: World Bank).

World Bank (1990) *World Development Report 1990. Poverty: World Development Indicators* (Oxford and New York: Oxford University Press).

World Bank (1993a) *Uganda: Growing out of Poverty* (Washington, DC: World Bank).

World Bank (1993b) *Implementing the World Bank's Strategy to Reduce Poverty. Progress and Challenges* (Washington, DC: World Bank).

World Bank (1993c) *Poverty Reduction Handbook* (Washington, DC: World Bank).

World Bank (1994) *A New Agenda for Women's Health and Nutrition* (Washington, DC: World Bank).

Part II
Gender, Employment and Labour Markets

[6]

Planned Development, Social Stratification, and the Sexual Division of Labor in Singapore

Aline K. Wong

Singapore, a city republic of 2.3 million, has recently captured the interest of social scientists because of its rapid economic development since 1965. Under British colonial rule, Singapore had thrived as a major commercial center and entrepôt port in Southeast Asia. Shortly after independence and separation from the Federation of Malaysia in 1965, the government of Singapore embarked on extensive programs of industrialization. As a result, the economy has grown rapidly, and Singapore is now ranked among the middle income countries by the World Bank.[1]

As Singapore industrialized, the population experienced a rapid decline in fertility that brought the natural rate of increase from 2.3 percent in 1966 down to 1.2 percent in 1979. Changes in fertility, together with rapid economic development and a rising level of education, have significantly altered the lives of men and women in the republic. While some of the social and economic changes have benefited women, the effects of others are questionable. A number of important issues arise in the following discussion of the role of women in Singapore's development and the impact of development on the sexual division of labor and on women's status. Here, as in other countries, women's roles and women's status are intrinsically linked to their productive and reproductive activities, their class and ethnic affiliations. A brief description of development planning in Singapore must preface discussion of women's roles.

1. In 1977, the per capita GNP for Singapore was $2,880 (U.S.) (see *World Development Report, 1979* [Washington, D.C.: World Bank, 1979]).

[*Signs: Journal of Women in Culture and Society* 1981, vol. 7, no. 2]

Signs   *Winter 1981*   *435*

Planned Development in Singapore

Like most other developing economies, Singapore began with import substitution as a mode of industrial development. The government, however, soon realized the shortcomings of this development strategy, particularly in light of Singapore's lack of natural resources and its small domestic market. Thus, beginning in the early 1970s, it adopted an export-oriented industrialization strategy, with a heavy reliance on the inflow of foreign capital and technology.[2] By offering tax incentives and appropriate factory sites, providing efficient infrastructural and public services, and strictly controlling labor unrest, the government was able to attract the foreign capital that has since laid the foundation for Singapore's industrial growth.[3] In 1978, although foreign-owned or joint-venture firms constituted only 33 percent of manufacturing establishments, they accounted for 82.7 percent of the total output value, and 78.4 percent of the value added. Furthermore, they accounted for nearly 68.7 percent of total industrial employment and 91.8 percent of direct export value of manufactured goods.[4]

The inflow of foreign capital and technology has taken place in Singapore within a broad framework of state economic planning. Initially socialist in orientation, the People's Action Party (PAP) has remained the single dominant political party since 1959. The PAP government has carefully orchestrated the pattern and pace of economic development—investing heavily in the public sector, creating special economic institutions, and directly participating in economic activities. Social planning is also seen as an integral part of national economic planning. The government has centralized education and relocated the majority of lower socioeconomic groups into massive public housing estates. They have instituted a highly successful national family-planning program and have legislated social policies, planning for social development in accordance with population and labor force projections and their perception of the necessary cultural basis for a rugged Asian society. In other words, the government has intervened extensively in almost every sphere of social and economic life, influencing work and the family as well as cultural values and psychological motivations. Political dissent, labor movements, and mass organizations have been effectively con-

2. John Wong, *ASEAN Economies in Perspective: A Comparative Study of Indonesia, Malaysia, the Philippines, Singapore and Thailand* (London: Macmillan Co., 1979), pp. 71–75.

3. Soo Ann Lee, *Industrialization in Singapore* (Victoria: Longman Australia Pty. Ltd., 1973); Goh Keng-Swee, *The Economics of Modernization and Other Essays* (Singapore: Asia Pacific Press, 1972); Kunio Yoshihara, *Foreign Investment and Domestic Response* (Singapore: Eastern Universities Press, 1976).

4. Department of Statistics, *Report on the Census of Industrial Production* (Singapore, 1978).

trolled to provide a stable political climate conducive to the steady inflow of foreign capital. In the process, a majority of the citizens have come to accept the firm, guiding hand of a strong government; they have become increasingly depoliticized.[5]

Even though Singapore owes much of its industrial success to a unique combination of historical, economic, and social factors, as well as to effective political leadership, its experience with development offers a number of instructive lessons to other developing countries. The neighboring countries in Southeast Asia, in fact, look to Singapore as a model of development. Similarly, Singapore's dependence on the industrial West—be it economic, social, or cultural—is a common experience shared by many Third World countries, just as the city-republic shared with them a recent colonial past. And Singapore demonstrates the validity of a widely held belief: that in general, women are adversely affected by strategies for economic development.[6]

Economic Development and Women's Work

There is a consensus developing among social scientists that indicators of women's roles and status should be included in overall measures of socioeconomic development—indicators such as the rate of female labor force participation, marriage age and life expectancy, and rates of fertility and divorce. Any construction of composite socioeconomic indicators has inherent problems and weaknesses. What is questionable here is an underlying assumption that there is a direct ratio between the level of economic development on one hand, and the economic participation of women and women's status on the other. Although a woman's economic activity may bring her a certain measure of economic independence as an individual, the overall pattern of women's participation in the labor force may actually indicate that women's work is not sufficient for autonomous economic development, as in the case of dependent economies, or that it at best reinforces existing class and ethnic cleavages, as in both the developed and developing countries.

The rate of economic activity among women aged fifteen years and above has increased impressively since Singapore began to industrialize in the late 1960s. In 1957, only 21.6 percent of the women were economically active. But by 1970 the rate had risen to 29.5 percent, and by 1979 to 41.9 percent (table 1). Increasingly, women are employed in industry

5. Chan Heng-Chee, "Politics in an Administrative State: Where Has the Politics Gone?" in *Trends in Singapore*, ed. Seah Chee-Meow (Singapore: Singapore University Press, 1975), pp. 51–68. See also Chan Heng-Chee, *The Dynamics of One Party Dominance: The PAP at the Grass-Roots* (Singapore: Singapore University Press, 1976).

6. Irene Tinker and Michele Bo Bramsen, eds., *Women and World Development* (Washington, D.C.: Overseas Development Council, 1976).

Table 1

Female Labor Force Participation Rates in Singapore, 1957–79
(%)

Economically Active Women	1957	1970	1975	1979
As proportion of total female population aged 15 and over...........	21.6	29.5	34.9	41.9
As proportion of total number of women and men employed	17.5	23.5	29.6	33.6

SOURCES.—P. Arumainathan, *Report on the Census of Population 1970* (Singapore: Department of Statistics, 1970), vol. 1. Ministry of Labour, *Report on the Labour Force Survey of Singapore* (Singapore, 1975, 1979).

and commerce. Gains in the manufacturing sector are the most prominent. In 1979, manufacturing accounted for 38.4 percent; commerce, 24.2 percent; and the services, 20.8 percent of the total female labor force (table 2). These changes in women's economic roles are reflected in the occupational structure itself. In 1979, 35.1 percent of the female labor force was engaged in production work, operation of transport equipment, and general labor. Clerical workers made up the next largest occupational category (26.3 percent), while 14.0 percent of the female labor force did service work (table 3).

Singapore's population is young as a result of the postwar baby boom; thus the majority of new entrants into the labor market are young and single women. On the other hand, there has also been an increasing proportion of married women seeking employment. In 1957, the economic activity rate among married women was only 14.0 percent, but it rose to 26.8 percent by 1979 (table 4).

The rates and patterns of economic activity among women no doubt reflect the expanding employment opportunities of a rapidly growing economy. Three other factors for female employment, however, must be noted. First, female economic participation is inextricably bound to the pattern of foreign investment in Singapore. Second, the recent increase in employment of married women is a result of the rising cost of living in Singapore as the economy goes multinational, leaving Singapore wide open to the inflationary tendencies of the world market economy. Third, employment for some married women represents a return to the labor market after an initial loss of independent economic status; many were previously engaged in self-employment, agricultural work, and service jobs. All of these factors have important implications for understanding the role of women in Singapore's economic development, and they indicate as well some adverse effects of development on the women themselves.

Table 2

Distribution of Female Labor Force by Industry, 1957–79

Industry	1957		1970		1975		1979	
	N	%	N	%	N	%	N	%
Agriculture, forestry, fishing	9,819	11.7	4,796	3.1	5,033	2.0	4,305	1.3
Mining, quarrying	165	.2	205	.1	271	.1	291	...
Manufacturing	16,301	19.4	48,121	31.3	86,210	34.9	131,464	38.4
Electricity, gas, water utilities	77	...	533	.4	758	.3	1,061	.3
Construction	1,761	2.1	2,817	1.8	3,085	1.2	4,659	1.4
Commerce	13,246	15.7	28,986	18.9	55,958	22.7	83,129	24.2
Transport, communication	1,112	1.3	3,943	2.6	11,311	4.6	17,158	5.0
Finance, insurance, business services	2,013	2.4	5,305	3.5	17,480	7.1	29,325	8.6
Community, social, personal services	39,551	47.0	58,843	38.3	66,511	26.9	71,129	20.8
Others	165	.2	63	...	379	.2	62	...
All industries	84,210	100.0	153,612	100.0	246,996	100.0	342,583	100.0

Sources.—See table 1.

Table 3

Distribution of Female Labor Force by Major Occupational Groups, 1957–79

Occupational Group	1957		1970		1975		1979	
	N	%	N	%	N	%	N	%
Professional, technical workers	8,328	9.9	21,818	14.2	26,572	10.8	32,777	9.6
Administrative, managerial workers	259	.3	645	.4	1,569	.6	1,789	.5
Clerical workers	5,616	6.7	26,029	16.9	61,586	24.9	90,097	26.3
Sales workers	8,630	10.2	16,433	10.7	30,306	12.3	44,237	12.9
Service workers	30,112	35.7	35,884	23.4	40,318	16.3	47,877	14.0
Agricultural, animal husbandry, fishing industry workers	10,057	11.9	4,950	3.2	6,169	2.5	4,908	1.4
Production workers, transport equipment operators, laborers	21,098	25.1	47,412	30.9	79,337	32.1	120,337	35.1
Other workers	110	.2	441	.3	1,136	.5	562	.2
All groups	84,210	100.0	153,612	100.0	246,993	100.0	342,584	100.0

Sources.—See table 1.

Table 4

Female Economic Activity Rates by Marital Status,
1957–79
(%)

Marital Status	Economic Activity Rates			
	1957	1970	1975	1979
Single	24.8	35.6	39.1	66.5
Married	14.0	14.7	22.1	26.8
Widowed	25.8	15.5	14.8	21.4
Divorced	46.5	47.6	50.0	68.5

SOURCES.—See table 1.

Singapore's industrial success, then, has depended heavily on
foreign investment. The interrelationship between women's employment and Singapore's economic dependence on the industrial West is
clear; the majority of female industrial workers are engaged in light
manufacturing financed by foreign capital, particularly in the electronics, textile, and garment industries. These labor-intensive industries
have traditionally been characterized by a predominance of female
labor, even in advanced capitalist economies. Recently established
branches of such industries in developing countries actually represent a
last stage in the constant search for cheap labor, made possible by the
increasing fragmentation of the labor process and the international free
flow of capital.[7] The semiconductor branch of the electronics industry,
in particular, has literally built a global assembly line encompassing
almost all the countries of Southeast Asia.[8]

In Singapore, as elsewhere in the developing world, foreign corporate managers consider women workers to have special qualities—
docility, diligence, and the "swift fingers" and tolerance necessary for
repetitive tasks—that make them especially suitable for unskilled work in
the export-processing industries. In spite of keen competition among the
firms for female workers, wages are low and employment is unstable,
fluctuating with world market demands for the products. Thus, when
economic recession came in the wake of the world oil crisis, female
workers felt the impact first. In 1974 alone, out of the 16,900 workers
who were retrenched, 79 percent were women. Singapore weathered the
crisis and recovery was quick. But the long-expected American recession
in 1980 again brought about massive layoffs of female electronics workers in large United States firms.[9]

7. Helen I. Safa, "Runaway Shops and Female Employment: The Search for Cheap
Labor," in this issue.
8. Rachael Grossman, "Women's Place in the Integrated Circuit," *Southeast Asia
Chronicle* 66 (1979): 2–17.
9. *Straits Times* (Singapore) (October 21, 1980).

The light-manufacturing industries generally prefer to hire young, single women. Young workers are more easily trained and can be paid less because of their lack of seniority. Older, married workers, then, are easily displaced, even during periods of full employment. This displacement has occurred, although the expanding economy has been able to absorb more married women into the commerce and the service sectors. Married workers, however, encounter discriminatory practices in recruitment as well as promotion. Whether working in the industrial or service sector, married women are generally regarded as less productive and less committed to their work because of their family responsibilities. Yet married women have to seek outside employment because of the rising costs of living, a fact made clear in a number of recent surveys of working mothers. The surveys indicate that married women work out of financial necessity.[10]

The age-specific rates of female economic participation and the historical distribution of the female labor force by industry indicate that it was easier for married women in the past to combine work and family responsibilities. The present pattern of age-specific activity appears to be unimodal (table 5). The highest participation rate is found among young single women between the ages of twenty and twenty-four. The rate steadily declines for every older age group, with no resurgence among women in their early forties, as is typical of developed countries where women with older children return to the work force. In 1957, the activity

Table 5

Age-specific Female Economic Activity Rates, 1957–79 (%)

Age Group (Years)	1957	1970	1979
15–19	23.4	43.0	43.1
20–24	22.9	53.6	76.6
25–29	16.5	30.8	55.3
30–34	17.3	22.7	40.8
35–39	20.8	19.3	37.7
40–44	26.3	17.8	31.7
45–49	30.1	17.5	25.6
50–54	28.8	17.5	19.2
55–59	24.7	16.2	16.2
60–64	17.1	13.4	12.5
65 and over	5.8	6.5	7.5
All age groups	21.6	29.5	41.9

SOURCES.—See table 1.

10. Aline K. Wong, "Women's Status and Changing Family Values," in *The Contemporary Family in Singapore*, ed. Eddie C. Y. Kuo and Aline K. Wong (Singapore: Singapore University Press, 1979).

rates were much more evenly distributed throughout the various age groups, even though the overall rate of participation was much lower than the present. This implies that older women and married women with children were able to find some kind of paid employment in the past. The jobs they held, however, were quite different then. Nearly 50 percent of the women workers in 1957 were in the community, social, and personal services, with another 16 percent in commerce and 12 percent in agricultural activities (table 2). These occupations did not discriminate against older, married women, as manufacturing industries do in the present.

Women who worked on family farms and in small businesses, as domestic servants, or as hawkers and traders were engaged in the informal sector of the economy which, some researchers estimate, provided employment for 23 percent of the 1970 labor force.[11] Although earnings were small and working hours long, women could derive some measure of economic independence from these activities. In most developing economies, the informal sector has persisted and has remained important, especially in providing employment for the urban poor. Development economists used to view the informal sector as backward or marginal—an anomaly caused by the slow growth of the formal sector. Now the more dominant view is that the informal sector serves some very useful functions for the developing economy, and is attractive to the workers themselves, when compared with wage employment in the formal sector. The boundaries of this informal sector are difficult to draw, but there is evidence that its size in Singapore has declined considerably because of development. Several factors have contributed to the decline of the informal sector: the rapid expansion of the formal sector; the increasing emphasis placed on educational training requirements for entry into industrial and commercial jobs; urban renewal and relocation programs, which disrupt traditional trading and marketing activities; and increasing government regulation of formerly unregulated activities, such as hawking. The shrinkage of the informal sector has important implications for the economic activity of women. Informal-sector activities are typically those that require little capital outlay and minimal training or skills. They are further characterized by ease of entry, flexible working hours, and opportunity for self-employment. The shrinkage of this sector may mean that women who could not find jobs in the formal sector because of age, education, or family responsibilities will have fewer opportunities to find employment in what remains of the informal sector. More definite observations await further research on this topic in Singapore.

Because of a tight labor supply and rising wages, the Singapore

11. Chia Lin-Sien and Chia Siow-Yue, "The Informal Sector in Singapore" (paper presented at the Seminar on the Informal Sector, Indonesian Human Resources Development Foundation, Jakarta, 1978).

government realized late in 1978 that its strategy for industrial development had to take a new twist if Singapore was to survive competition from neighboring countries that still offered very cheap labor and equally attractive incentives to foreign capital. Hence, Singapore is embarking on a third stage in its industrialization, one which emphasizes capital-intensive, high-technology, and high value-added industries in place of the former emphasis on labor-intensive processing industries.[12] This strategy calls for the development of indigenous industrial technology and skills, but it does not necessarily reduce Singapore's dependence on the industrial West for continued economic development, at least not in the short run. Singapore will still seek the overseas markets of the industrial West for its industrial products. Foreign expertise will still be required to help upgrade the skills of the Singapore workers. Although the government has set up an industrial skills development fund for retraining workers and upgrading their skills, it is by no means clear how women workers will benefit from such government assistance. In fact, a recently published guideline for applications to use the fund indicates that women workers, most of whom are unskilled, cannot apply, since the fund is earmarked for higher skills development rather than for basic training.[13] It is also easy to predict that women will bear the brunt of Singapore's industrial transformation, as they will be the first victims of industrial layoffs resulting from the structural transformation of industries and the withdrawal of multinational firms to neighboring countries in search of lower wage costs.

The tight labor supply has had another consequence for female labor force participation. Because of the local labor shortage, the government has been admitting large numbers of migrant workers from neighboring countries, primarily Malaysia, on a work-permit basis. A sizable proportion of the work force in Singapore, then, is of foreign citizenship—8.8 percent in 1979.[14] The majority of the migrant workers are men who work in the production and construction industries, but female migrant workers have come to constitute a substantial proportion of the women working in manufacturing and in personal services. In 1979, 9.3 percent of the total number of female workers in manufacturing were not citizens of Singapore. Most of these migrant workers were concentrated in the textile and garment and electrical and electronics industries. As many as 13.0 percent of the female workers in

12. Seah Chee-Meow, "Singapore 1979: The Dialectics of Survival," *Asian Survey* 20 (1980): 144–54.

13. *Straits Times* (September 26, 1980).

14. Ministry of Labour, *Report on the Labour Force Survey of Singapore* (Singapore, 1979). Figures on foreign workers in the survey are typically underestimated due to inadequate coverage of workers in the construction industry, which employs large numbers of foreign men. Official figures on the numbers of work-permit holders are not available, but there are unofficial estimates of 100,000–120,000 foreign workers in Singapore.

personal and household services were also of foreign citizenship. Recently, the government has been issuing work permits to foreign workers other than Malaysians—to Thai women working in the textile and electronics industries, and to Filipino women working in domestic service.[15] Migrant workers are not necessarily discriminated against in pay, but they are subject in greater degrees to unstable employment and low unionization, and are restricted in geographical and job mobility and even in their options regarding marriage and family.[16]

Although the international migration of labor has long been researched by social scientists, the focus on female migrant workers is a recent phenomenon. Studied in the context of developing countries with dependent economies, the international migration of female labor due to activity of multinational corporations contributes to an understanding of women's role in economic development. Apart from a small number of studies on the situation in Singapore and Malaysia, however, this important area of research has yet to be developed.[17]

Class, Status, and Women's Education

In Singapore, educational development has been deliberately geared toward the economy's changing labor force requirements. The educational reforms of the 1960s and those of more recent years have brought both the structure and content of education in line with the government's industrialization strategies. Emphasis on technical training and science is introduced at the junior high school level and, for some students, right after primary education.[18] Under the colonial regime,

15. In 1979 there were about 1,000 Thai female factory workers in Singapore (see Chan Chee-Hoe, "A Study on Thai Female Factory Workers" [Honors thesis, National University of Singapore, Department of Sociology, 1981]). The estimate for Filipinas working as domestics is also around 1,000 (see *Straits Times* [November 3, 1980]).

16. Foreign workers are categorized according to whether they hold professional passes or work permits. Work permits are periodically renewed and can be withdrawn if the holders "job hop." Some foreign workers have only one- or two-day work permits. Permit holders are also required to apply to the Commissioner of Labour for permission to register their marriages to Singapore citizens. If permission is granted, they must sign an agreement to be voluntarily sterilized after having two children.

17. See Linda Lim, *Women Workers in Multinational Corporations: The Case of the Electronics Industry in Malaysia and Singapore*, Michigan Occasional Papers, no. 9 (Ann Arbor: University of Michigan Women's Studies Program, 1978); Noeleen Heyzer, "From Rural Subsistence to an Industrial Peripheral Workforce: Female Malaysian Migrants in Singapore," in *Women and Development: The Sexual Division of Labor in Rural Economies*, ed. Lourdes Benería (Geneva: International Labour Organisation, in press); and Chan Chee-Hoe, "Thai Female Factory Workers."

18. Goh Keng-Swee for the Ministry of Education, *Report on the Ministry of Education* (Singapore: Ministry of Education, 1978). Popularly known as the Goh Report, this document summarizes past developments in education and suggests new reforms.

education in the English language and in the arts and humanities was the prerequisite for entering secure jobs in civil service and the professions. Now education in science and technology provides the certificates to industrial jobs and professional training in management to top positions in business. English proficiency is a basic requirement for most types of occupations in Singapore's open economy.

There is little question that girls and young women have been able to benefit from the expanding educational opportunities. In 1978 they constituted 47.1 percent of the primary school enrollment, 51.6 percent of the secondary enrollment, and 43.0 percent of the university enrollment.[19] But in spite of the almost equal split in the student population between girls and boys, sex-role segregation is very evident in the educational system. Young women tend to elect the academic and vocational streams, rather than the technical stream. In 1978, for example, only 8.3 percent of the students enrolled in technical and vocational institutes were female. At the postsecondary level, while 84.2 percent of the students training at the Institute of Education were women, only 20.1 percent of those at technical colleges were. This lack of technical training means that women with a high school education or less generally become semiskilled or unskilled workers when they enter industry. Women also tend to concentrate in other low-pay, low-status jobs in commerce and the services; they form the majority of the domestic service workers, stenographers and typists, clerks and cashiers, tailors and dressmakers.

In the universities the difference in the subjects chosen by women and men is also obvious. As in many countries, young women in Singapore tend to study the arts, the social sciences, and other science subjects, all of which prepare them primarily for the teaching profession. Although more women have taken up law, accounting, and business administration in recent years, other professions such as medicine, engineering, and architecture remain largely male dominated. Medicine, a field of study that assures the graduate lifelong high income and social status, is restrictive for female students. By explicit policy, the Minister of Health recently declared a 30 percent quota for female entrants into the field beginning in 1979. Among all women workers that year, 9.6 percent were working in professional, technical, or related occupations, and many of them were in the lower-status professions, traditionally assigned to women: teaching, nursing, and social work. Only 0.5 percent were administrative and managerial workers, compared with 3.9 percent of the male work force.

As in other developing countries, education is an important avenue for upward social mobility in the emerging class structure. In Singapore, however, formal education is the most important determinant of initial

19. Department of Statistics, *Yearbook of Statistics* (Singapore, 1978/79).

occupational placement, subsequent career advancement, or lifelong income and social status.[20] A recent survey on the social values and attitudes of young people in Singapore also shows that an education and material wealth are considered the two most important symbols of success in life, and that working hard and getting an education are the two most important ways of achieving success in the local society.[21] Thus, the differing types of education received by women and men take on added significance; the differences tend to widen the income gap between males and females and increase sex inequality in other aspects of socioeconomic life.

Ethnic Stratification and Women's Economic Participation

The population of Singapore is heterogeneous: 76 percent are Chinese, 15 percent Malay, 7 percent Indian, and 2 percent are Eurasian or another ethnicity. Each of the major groups is also divided by dialect, region, and caste. There is no definitive study on social stratification in Singapore, but the available evidence suggests that all the major ethnic groups have achieved a substantial degree of upward mobility as the social structure itself continues to open up into a middle-class society. Development in Singapore has not been accompanied by the widening income disparities that often characterize the initial stages of development in other countries.[22] But though all the ethnic groups are represented in the different social classes, a slight majority of the Chinese and the Indians are middle class, while the great majority of the Malays are lower and working class people.[23]

The economic participation of women from the major ethnic groups has been altered as a consequence of industrialization. In 1957, Chinese women had the highest economic activity rate, 21.8 percent, compared with a rate of 6.3 percent among the Malays and 7.1 percent among the Indians. By 1979, the economic activity rates of the three major groups had leveled out to approximately 42 percent each. Malay and Indian women became economically active later than the Chinese, but at a faster rate (table 6). In the past only the highly educated Malay

20. David H. Clark and Pang Eng-Fong, "Returns to Schooling and Training in Singapore," *Malayan Economic Review* 15 (October 1979): 83–100; and Pang Eng-Fong, *Education, Earnings and Occupational Mobility in Singapore*, World Employment Programme Research Working Paper no. 13 (Geneva: International Labour Organisation, 1976).

21. Tai Ching-Ling, "Survey on Youth Attitudes in Singapore," mimeographed (Singapore: Nanyang University, February 1980).

22. Pang Eng-Fong, "Growth, Inequality and Race in Singapore," *International Labor Review* 3 (1975): 15–28.

23. Peter S. J. Chen, "Social Stratification in Singapore" (Working Paper no. 12, University of Singapore, Department of Sociology, 1973), p. 15.

Table 6

Female Economic Activity Rates by Ethnic Group, 1957–79
(%)

Ethnic Group	1957	1970	1975	1979
Chinese	21.8	27.0	31.5	42.2
Malays	6.3	14.3	22.4	42.0
Indians	7.1	16.0	25.6	42.4

SOURCES.—See table 1.

and Indian women worked as professionals, usually teaching school, while those with little education took jobs in the personal services, working mainly as domestics. The largest proportion of both Malay and Indian women workers in 1979 were engaged in manufacturing; they have entered industrial jobs at a much faster rate than Chinese women. In 1970 the proportions of Malay and Indian female workers in manufacturing were 31.2 percent and 18.9 percent, respectively, compared with 32.2 percent for the Chinese. By 1979 the proportions of Malay and Indian women jumped to 55.3 percent and 41.1 percent, respectively, while the proportion of Chinese women rose only slightly, to 35.3 percent (table 7). Malay and Indian women have experienced a corresponding decline in the proportion of their ranks involved in community, social, and personal services. The large-scale entry of young Malay and Indian women into the manufacturing sector has come about not only as a consequence of expansion in industrial employment but also because older Chinese women are now often seeking the better-paying white-collar jobs in commerce and the services.

As long as social scientists continue to measure social class based on men's occupations, education, and other indices of household socioeconomic characteristics, the effects of women's increased economic participation on social stratification will not be evident. On one hand, women's gainful employment brings additional income to the household, perhaps enhancing its resources for upward social mobility. On the other hand, women's employment among both the working and the middle classes may be necessary for such families simply to maintain their present social class positions. In any case, it is not likely that women's employment has great potential for changing the relative class status of ethnic groups in the near future.

Among the Malays and the Indians in particular, recent rapid entry into the industrial labor force may have serious repercussions for individuals and families, as industrial work brings drastic changes in work routines and life-styles. Periodic press reports of outbreaks of mass hysteria among young Malay women workers in electronics assembly plants bear witness to the psychological adjustment problems faced by such

Table 7

Distribution of Female Labor Force by Industry and Ethnic Group, 1957–79
(%)

Industry	1957			1970			1979		
	Chinese (N=76,217)	Malays (N=3,438)	Indians (N=1,441)	Chinese (N=136,489)	Malays (N=9,737)	Indians (N=4,375)	Chinese (N=268,064)	Malays (N=49,977)	Indians (N=20,424)
Agriculture, forestry, fishing	12.5	8.1	2.8	3.4	1.0	.3	1.5	.2	.5
Mining, quarrying	.2	...	...	.1	...	.1	.1	...	...
Manufacturing	21.0	3.7	2.1	32.2	31.2	18.9	35.3	55.3	41.1
Electricity, gas, water utilities	.1	.1	.6	.4	.2	.6	.3	.3	.6
Construction	2.2	.3	1.2	2.0	.2	.8	1.5	.5	1.2
Commerce	16.0	10.9	8.5	19.6	11.8	12.8	27.3	12.4	13.9
Transport, communication	1.0	.5	2.3	2.4	3.1	3.2	4.8	5.9	5.5
Finance, insurance, business services	2.3	.6	1.7	3.6	.9	2.3	9.1	5.9	6.7
Community, social, personal services	44.5	75.7	80.4	36.2	51.6	60.9	20.1	19.5	30.5
Other	.2	.1	.4	.1	...	.1	...	...	...
All industries	100.0	100.0	100.0	100.0	100.0	100.0	100.0	100.0	100.0

Sources.—See table 1.

workers in a dehumanized work setting. Furthermore, industrial employment may change women's family roles, reproductive behavior, and self-perceptions.

Reproduction and Women's Status

The traditional religiocultural systems of Confucianism, Hinduism, and Islam prescribed a subordinate status to women within the household. Whether born Chinese, Indian, or Malay, a woman was socialized from a young age both to play the roles of wife, mother, and daughter-in-law, and to lead a secluded life. Not much is known about the status of women in premodern Singapore, but there is evidence that immigrant women had a higher social standing than in their native countries due to Singapore's customs and the experience of immigration.[24] Before independence, Singapore was a commercial port. The status of women did not depend only on their cultural background; it also varied according to the social status of their fathers and husbands—whether they were merchants, civil bureaucrats, and skilled artisans, or laborers and farmers. And like so many other stratified societies, women in the lower classes seemed to enjoy more effective control over their own and household activities. Among upper-class women, seclusion was an unavoidable fact of life. It was uncommon for women to be educated; on the other hand many women helped run family businesses, engaged in the sale of farm and fishery products, or controlled the family purses. These were not the fabled manipulative Asian women who were said to wield influence but not power within the household; they were women who, under certain circumstances and by customary practice, had actual control over their households.

As Singapore's economy becomes increasingly urban based and industrialized, the separation of the private and public domains becomes more apparent. Men enter wage-earning occupations, while women forfeit their previous income-earning activities that arose from home production. Women also lose material support from their kin as the individual family unit is disengaged from kin-based economic production. The issue of whether a married woman can successfully combine home and a career arouses a strong emotional reaction from the public, which demonstrates that women's work is now defined as work outside the home and is therefore considered incompatible with family responsibilities.

Over time, the age of marriage in Singapore has risen to an average of twenty-eight years for men and twenty-four years for women. Marriages are now primarily a matter of individual choice, and young

24. A. K. Wong, *Women in Modern Singapore* (Singapore: University Education Press, 1975).

couples generally form independent households right after marriage. Furthermore, small families with two or three children have become the norm. Education and economic employment have had definite effects on the age of marriage for women. Young women now have ample opportunities for paid work. Many postpone marriage in order to enjoy personal freedom, friendship and social activities with other workers, and the release from household chores, as well as to help support their parents and younger siblings. Because the young women do not expect to continue working very long after marriage, especially after childbirth, they are motivated to postpone marriage as long as possible. But marriage remains the single most important life goal.

Among young people in Singapore, the ideal husband-and-wife relationship is identified as the companionship type common in modern Western societies. There is, however, a strong emphasis on the husband being the main provider and the wife being a good mother. A clear-cut conception of separate sex roles is evident.[25] Although some recent studies have shown that husbands and wives share decision making over a large number of family matters, especially when the wives work, housework and child care have remained the wives' main responsibilities even when they work outside the home.[26]

It is difficult to conclude that women in Singapore have made indisputable gains in family status. Education and employment have served to increase role strain and psychological pressure for working women. Well-educated professional women have held their ground and continued their pursuit of independent careers, generally with the help of paid domestic servants and some willing relatives. Lower-class women have little choice but to work in order to augment meager household incomes. They do so by alternating household duties and working shifts and by calling on relatives or child-care workers to watch their children.

Because of the shortage of part-time jobs for women, many have had to do shift work in the manufacturing industries,[27] especially in the electrical and electronics industry, which also hires predominantly female workers. A recent National Productivity Board survey of production workers reveals that 58 percent of a total of 16,017 shift workers in 419 manufacturing firms were women. The survey also shows that Singapore women take up permanent night work nearly three times more often than men.[28] A study on the child-care problems of low-

25. Saw Swee-Hock and A. K. Wong, *Adolescents in Singapore: Sexuality, Courtship and Family Values* (Singapore: Singapore University Press, 1981).

26. Aline K. Wong, "Women's Status and Changing Family Values," and "Working Mothers and the Care of Preschool Children in Singapore—a Research Report" (Singapore: Singapore Girl Guides Association, 1980).

27. In 1979, only 6.5 percent of the women workers were engaged in part-time work (less than forty hours per week) (Ministry of Labour, *Report on the Labour Force Survey of Singapore* [Singapore, 1979]).

28. *Sunday Times* (Singapore) (May 4, 1980).

Signs   *Winter 1981*   *451*

income mothers with preschool children living in public flats found that 43 percent of the working mothers were shift workers. In order to work shifts, many women have had to send their children to relatives, or to professional child-care workers when relatives are unavailable. But even with child-care help, shift workers tire more easily and more often than other working mothers.[29]

Among working mothers as a whole, 23 percent send their preschool children to relatives or child-care workers, and of this 23 percent, as many as 10 percent leave their children with the caretaker for the entire work week or more. In some cases, then, children do not get to see their mothers except on weekends or on even less frequent visits. Work may mean a measure of economic independence for women and give them some say over family matters, but it also means a double day for women who carry the major responsibility for housework and child care.

Conclusion

Development has hardly altered the sexual division of labor in Singapore. Women are now better educated and have expanded economic opportunities; they bear fewer children and enjoy more personal freedom. But they have not benefited fully from the development process. Most of the female workers earn very low wages and are engaged in low-status, dead-end jobs.[30] In all occupational categories women are earning much less than their male counterparts, even when education is held constant. The income differential is the greatest at the upper end of the educational scale.[31] Homemakers and women who work outside the home continue to bear the major burden of reproductive activities— household chores, child care, and family-status maintenance. Even if economic employment has brought personal independence to single or married women, their family status has not been translated into public status.[32]

Many argue that integrating women in development will raise their status. This argument is usually accompanied by a call for expanded

29. A. K. Wong, "Working Mothers and Preschool Children."

30. The median gross monthly income for female workers in 1979 was $290 (see Ministry of Labour, 1979).

31. Ministry of Labour, *Report on the Labour Force Survey of Singapore* (Singapore, 1978).

32. Space permits neither a discussion of women's lack of involvement in politics and mass organizations nor an overview of the sociocultural effects of Singapore's Westernization, particularly the influences of multinational firms. Both have significant implications for the roles and status of women. It should be noted that an embourgeoisement of feminine values is under way; many women are adopting a family-centered life-style and are increasingly emphasizing beauty care, leisure-time activities, and consumerism. Multinational firms also tend to promote Western tastes in consumption and Western social activities among their female workers.

educational and employment opportunities for women. But in Singapore, and in other developing countries as well, it is clear that expanded opportunities have not necessarily altered the sexual division of labor. As long as sexual segregation characterizes the occupational world and women are bound by domestic responsibilities, they will remain a peripheral work force. Singapore's dependent economic development also tends to transform women into a type of reserve labor force. An official comment on a labor force survey made the government's attitude toward female workers very clear. The survey found that nearly half a million married women in 1979 were staying home, and that only 7.6 percent of them would consider taking a job. Government officials responded: "This figure, low as it is, can still go a long way towards relieving the current labour shortage." Those women, the government knew, could fill at least twenty thousand full-time vacancies.[33]

Department of Sociology
National University of Singapore

33. *Straits Times* (September 25, 1980).

[7]

Capitalism, Imperialism, and Patriarchy: The Dilemma of Third-World Women Workers in Multinational Factories

LINDA Y. C. LIM

Introduction

Female employment in multinational factories in developing countries has recently become the subject of much academic and political interest. Studies have been done analyzing the growth and spread of such employment and its impact on women in particular countries and industries.[1] The findings generally point to a central theoretical and political question that as yet remains unanswered: Is the employment of women factory workers by multinational corporations in developing countries primarily an experience of *liberation*, as development economists and governments maintain or one of *exploitation*, as feminists assert, for the women concerned? Does it present a problem or a solution to the task of integrating women into the development of their countries?

This paper examines the theoretical issues raised by the available case study material, in an attempt to resolve this question. It emphasizes economic analysis, and suggests that the interactions between capitalist, imperialist, and patriarchal relations of production are responsible both for the phenomenon of female employment by multinationals and for the dilemma it poses for women workers and for progressive feminist analysis and political action.

70

CAPITALISM, IMPERIALISM, AND PATRIARCHY

Capitalism and the Relocation of Manufacturing Industry to Developing Countries

Capitalism is the economic system prevailing in the parent countries of multinational corporations and in the world market which they dominate. It is a mode of production based on private ownership of capital (the "means of production"), employment of wage labor, and production for exchange on a free market to earn private profit that is accumulated and reinvested for growth and further profit. Whereas the Western nations and Japan are developed economies in a mature or advanced stage of capitalism, many developing countries are embarking on economic programs aimed at further developing the capitalist relations of production first introduced in them by colonialism and world market forces. This colonial heritage, combined with the dominance of the world capitalist system, forces even those new nations that have embraced socialist ideologies of development to tolerate some degree of private enterprise and foreign investment producing for exchange on the world market.

The relocation of manufacturing industry from developed to developing countries by multinational corporations engaged in "offshore sourcing" is part of a new international division of labor and pattern of trade in manufactures.[2] From plants in the Third World, multinational subsidiaries export manufactures to their home countries. From their home countries they import capital and technology in exchange. This is the direct result of two developments in the world capitalist economy which began in the 1960s. First, growth in international trade intensified inter-capitalist competition among the developed nations. In particular, the ascendancy of Japan as a major industrial power and its rapid and highly successful penetration of Western consumer markets led American and European manufacturers to invest in developing countries as a means of reducing costs in competition with the Japanese (Reynis 1976). In the 1970s, the slowing down of growth in Western and world markets further intensified these competitive pressures.

Second, the accelerating development of capitalist relations of production in a number of developing countries resulted in some of their indigenous entrepreneurs manufacturing for export to Western markets, beginning in the 1960s. This placed them in direct competition with Western manufacturers, who were forced to relocate to these same countries in order to be cost competitive in their own home markets. This trend continued through the 1970s on an ever larger and wider scale, particularly in Asian countries like Hong

71

LINDA Y. C. LIM

Kong, Taiwan, South Korea, and Singapore, whose larger local firms have themselves become multinationals operating offshore manufacturing plants in other developing countries.

Thus, Western manufacturers in several industries located plants in developing countries in response to the competitive challenge from other mature capitalist countries, especially Japan, and from newly industrializing developing capitalist countries, mainly in Asia. The crucial factor in the competition was and is the cost of production, which differs between mature and developing capitalist economies according to their stage of development. In the 1960s and early 1970s, the mature Western economies experienced tight domestic labor markets—low unemployment rates, high wages, and chronic labor shortages in many industries. Labor-intensive manufacturing industries—those which employ large numbers of workers in generally unskilled or low-skilled jobs—were the most affected, and these countries began to lose their international comparative advantage in industries such as garments, shoes, plastic toys, and electronics assembly. The developing countries, on the other hand, had relatively abundant supplies of labor, reflected in the rural-urban migration of surplus labor off the farms; high urban unemployment rates; and low wages. Cheap labor, combined in many cases with government-subsidized capital costs, including tax holidays and low interest loans from government banks (Lim 1978), gave these countries a comparative advantage in world trade in labor-intensive products.

It is labor-intensive industries, then, that tend to relocate manufacturing plants to developing countries, thereby becoming multinational in their operations. This is a rational competitive response to changing international comparative cost advantages. In a free world market, factors of production like capital and labor will tend to move to locations where they are most scarce and can therefore command the highest returns from their employment in production. Through the nineteenth and early twentieth centuries, this was reflected in fairly free international migration of labor, but subsequent restrictive national immigration policies together with transportation costs and imperfect market information have increasingly inhibited the mobility of labor across international boundaries, except for the legal and/or illegal immigration of "guest workers." Capital, however, remains internationally mobile, especially from the developed to developing countries, a flow encouraged by policies of the latter's governments that offer profit tax holidays, duty free imports and

CAPITALISM, IMPERIALISM, AND PATRIARCHY

exports, unrestricted remittance of profits, repatriation of capital, and so forth.

The relocation of manufacturing industry from mature to developing capitalist economies is an outcome of the expansion of capitalism on a world scale, reflecting the different rate and degree of development of capitalist relations of production, particularly the wage-labor market, in different nations. It is aided by state policies in both developed and developing countries, but remains largely a market phenomenon.

Imperialism, Nationalism and the Multinational Corporation

Imperialism—the system of military, political, economic, and cultural domination of the Third World by its former colonial masters—was historically the outgrowth of capitalist development in the West. In the economic sphere, it is characterized by the exploitation of natural and human resources in the Third World by Western capitalist enterprises. Although *bourgeois* economists were in agreement with classical Marxists—including Lenin, Luxemburg, and Marx—that imperialism, or Western investment in developing countries, would be an agent of capitalist development in the Third World, modern-day theorists of imperialism—including dependency theorists and "world-system" analysts following André Gundee Frank and Immanuel Wallerstein—argue that it retards such development.

Most of the latter analysis has been applied to the sectors of primary production for export and import-substituting industrialization in developing countries. But manufacturing for export by multinational subsidiaries also has its critics.[3] It is pointed out that workers' wages are much lower and their working conditions worse than in the multinationals' home countries; that few transferable skills or industrial linkages are generated; that there is heavy dependence on foreign capital, technology, skills, inputs, and markets; that few taxes are paid in the host country and high profits that accrue only to foreigners are mostly remitted overseas.

Although the above are true in most situations, it should be noted that manufacturing for export in developing countries is not the sole preserve of multinationals. Many local firms are also involved, and in some countries—such as Hong Kong, Taiwan, and South Korea—and industries, such as garments, they may outnumber the multinationals. In general, Third World enterprises engaged in manufacturing for export to Western markets are smaller, less capital inten-

LINDA Y. C. LIM

sive, and more labor intensive than multinational subsidiaries and are concentrated in simple-technology industries with competitive markets and relatively low profit margins. Wages are usually lower and working conditions worse, sometimes much worse, than in the multinational sector. Skills are low, and there is dependence not only on foreign markets, to which access is less easy than for the multinationals, but also on foreign technology and inputs purchased on the world market. Tax payments and reinvestment rates may be higher than for multinational subsidiaries; but since earnings are less, absolute contributions may be lower.

Comparisons between multinational subsidiaries and local firms in export manufacturing in developing countries suggest that the former may contribute more to the host economy in terms of market access, output growth, total wage-bill, and skill and technology acquisition. Local firms may, however, contribute more to the national development of capitalist relations of production in the long run, in developing a class of indigenous entrepreneurs in the manufacturing sector. They may reinvest more, since they do not remit profits overseas and are less likely to transfer operations. But competition with multinational subsidiaries in factor, input and output markets may inhibit the development of independent indigenous enterprises and entrepreneurs (Lim 1978b; Pang and Lim 1977). A complementary relationship is possible, but it tends to maintain local firms in the dependent position of subcontractors and suppliers to foreign firms and markets.

Despite the validity of many of the criticisms against it, manufacturing for export does enhance the development of capitalist relations of production in developing countries, mainly by spurring the growth of industrial wage labor and an indigenous industrial capitalist class. Multinationals and local firms make somewhat different contributions to this process. Two more questions remain. First, what are the long-run prospects for a multinational-led, export manufacturing sector in a developing country? Second, is it likely to lead to the development of an independent national capitalism in the developing country?

One of the criticisms commonly levelled at manufacturing for export by multinational corporations is that it is likely to be only a temporary phenomenon in developing host countries. Multinationals that relocate manufacturing capacity in these countries are "footloose" because they are not bound to any particular location by a need for local markets or local input sources other than labor, which is abundantly available everywhere. Therefore, it is argued,

74

CAPITALISM, IMPERIALISM, AND PATRIARCHY

they will tend to move away from a location if labor market conditions or government policies change to make it less competitive—that is, if wages rise more in one location than in others or tax holidays expire in one location but are offered in other "newer" locations. Although this has happened in individual firm cases, it has not yet threatened the viability of an entire export–manufacturing sector in any country.

On the contrary, in the less developed countries where most of the export oriented multinational subsidiaries are concentrated—Hong Kong, Taiwan, and Singapore—changing comparative costs, particularly the appearance of tight labor markets, have resulted in an upgrading of the industries producing for export. Multinationals, encouraged by host government policies, have begun relocating more capital-intensive, technology-intensive industrial products and processes from their home countries to these location. Labor-intensive processes are replaced or shifted to more labor-abundant locations as comparative advantages continue to change between developed and developing countries and among developing countries themselves.

This suggests that, at least in some developing countries, the multinational-led export manufacturing sector does mature over time, further developing capitalist relations of production. Wages rise, working conditions improve, more skills are imparted, more local linkages generated, more taxes paid, and more profits reinvested locally. Although the countries where this is happening are still a minority in the Third World, they are the ones that have had the longest experience with multinational subsidiaries in manufacturing for export.

But what about local firms and the development of an independent national capitalism? As previously noted, competition with multinationals may inhibit the growth of indigenous enterprises. But as the multinational subsidiaries continue to grow and to upgrade and diversify their products, they generate more local linkages, make more input purchases from local suppliers, and subcontract some of their simpler products and processes to local manufacturers. This may stimulate the growth of indigenous enterprises, though they remain in a dependent position vis-à-vis the multinationals. But from the point of view of enhancing capitalist development, dependence may not be a problem if it results in accelerated growth and the emergence of an indigenous industrial capitalist class. A nationalist industrial policy that excludes multinationals may result in more independence but less growth and thus a smaller indigenous

LINDA Y. C. LIM

capitalist class since the advantages multinationals possess in stimulating supply sources and in providing technical and managerial training would be lost.

Although dependency theorists and others who argue that multinationals retard the development of capitalism in developing countries are right with respect to their criticisms of the early stages of labor-intensive manufacturing for export, the experience of some important developing countries suggests that bourgeois economists and classical Marxists alike might be right in the longer run. That is, multinationals do foster the development of capitalist relations of production and are often more successful in this than indigenous firms. The relocation of industry between countries continues if firms behave rationally in response to changing comparative advantages. Although multinationals may shift labor-intensive industries out of some developing countries as comparative costs change, so do national firms in these countries, (as in the case of Singapore firms that shifted their labor-intensive processes and products to cheaper-labor countries like Malaysia, Indonesia, Sri Lanka, and Bangladesh); so long as new industries and processes are moved in, capitalist relations of production continue to develop and mature.

Patriarchy and the Female Labor Market

Patriarchy is the system of male domination and female subordination in economy, society, and culture that has characterized much of human history to the present day. In the economic sphere, it is reflected first in the sexual division of labor within the family, which makes domestic labor the sole preserve of women. Their involvement in production activities outside the home varies with different societies and different stages of development, but is, particularly in those countries where capitalist development has penetrated (Boserup 1970), often accorded inferior status and reward compared to the activities of men.

In the pure capitalist model of "bourgeois" economists, conditions of perfect competition prevail in the labor market, where workers are hired solely on the basis of their marginal productivity.[4] Although productivity differences may be correlated with the sex of a worker, sex itself, like race, religion and other *ascriptive* characteristics, is irrelevant in the hiring process. Where there are no productivity differences between the sexes, discrimination cannot exist in a free labor market. The employer who discriminates on the basis of sex

76

CAPITALISM, IMPERIALISM, AND PATRIARCHY

will be less profitable than the one who does not because productivity of the worker is the only relevant criterion (Becker 1957).[5] Thus, competition and the progress of capitalist relations of production should eventually eliminate any differences between the sexes in the labor market.

This model is clearly invalid in the real-world capitalist labor market, where sex differences obviously exist. Not only is participation in the wage-labor force lower for women than for men, but they are also concentrated in a narrow range of occupations characterized by low wages, low productivity, low skill levels, high turnover, insecurity of tenure, and limited upward mobility. One of the most distinctive and persistent features of the capitalist labor market is the segmentation of the labor market and occupational segregation by sex (Blaxall and Reagan, 1976). Productivity differences between male and female workers is one explanation for this phenomenon, but they themselves reflect differential access to the determinants of productivity, such as education and skill training and different levels of technology in the jobs to which they are assigned. In addition, there is an element of pure discrimination by employers, that is, discrimination unrelated to any productivity differences between male and female workers.

Patriarchal institutions and social relations are responsible for the inferior or secondary status of women in the capitalist wage-labor market. The primacy of the sexual division of labor within the family—man as breadwinner and woman as housekeeper and child raiser—has several consequences for the woman who seeks wage employment. Socialized to accept this sex role in life, she has little motivation to acquire marketable skills; is often prevented by discrimination from acquiring such skills; and, even after she has acquired them, may be prevented by discrimination from achieving the employment or remuneration that those skills would command for a man.

Discrimination itself is based on the patriarchal assumption that woman's natural role is a domestic one and that she is therefore unsuited to many kinds of wage employment, either because her productivity will "naturally" be lower than a man's in the same employment or because it will be adversely affected by her domestic responsibilities. Family duties do often reduce a woman's mobility, stability, and efficiency as a worker and most women who participate in the capitalist wage-labor market do so because of the inadequacy of the family income earned by their menfolk in wage employment. Attitudes of families, employers, and the women themselves, do-

LINDA Y. C. LIM

mestic responsibilities, and their own lack of skills limit their employment opportunities and weaken their bargaining position in the labor market.

It is this *comparative disadvantage* of women in the wage-labor market that gives them a comparative advantage vis-à-vis men in the occupations and industries where they are concentrated—so-called female ghettoes of employment. In the manufacturing sector of mature capitalist economies, women are concentrated in labor-intensive industries where the wages earned are often insufficient to support an entire family. It is assumed by employers and society in general that women work only for "pocket money" for luxuries or to make a secondary income contribution to families where the principal breadwinner is a male. In addition, it is believed that women do not have the need or the inclination to be career-minded and upwardly mobile in the job hierarchy and so do not mind dead-end jobs with no prospects of advancement. They also have certain feminine social and cultural attributes that make them suitable to certain kinds of detailed and routine work, such as sewing garments and assembling electronic gadgets. That is, they are careful and conscientious workers, patient enough to endure long hours of repetitive work (Lim 1978b).

Thus, both the demand for and supply of female labor are determined by the culture of patriarchy, which assumes woman's role in the family as natural and consigns her to a secondary and inferior position in the capitalist wage-labor market. Occupational segregation and differential remuneration by sex is explained by an assumed productivity differential between men and women, based in part on this sex role differentiation. Even where women are acknowledged to be more productive than men, they are often paid less; and prevailing wages are always lower in female-intensive than male-intensive industries and occupations even at equivalent skill levels. This is contrary to the prediction of neoclassical economic theory that higher productivity means higher, not lower, wages.

The labor-intensive industries in which women manufacturing workers are concentrated in mature capitalistic economies are the very industries that are losing their comparative cost advantage to newly industrializing countries. It is likely that these labor-intensive industries maintained their comparative advantage as long as they did because they employed the lowest-paid workers in those countries—women, often women of minority races. Thus it is female-intensive industries that have the greatest propensity to "run away" from the developed countries and relocate manufacturing facilities

CAPITALISM, IMPERIALISM, AND PATRIARCHY

in the Third World, where wages are even lower than those of women in the developed countries. In the developing countries as well, traditional patriarchal social relations ensure that women occupy a similarly secondary and inferior position in the wage-labor market and so are the preferred employees of multinational and local employers in labor-intensive export industries.

Although the relocation of manufacturing industry from mature to developing capitalist countries reflects changes in world capitalism, the employment of women in these industries reflects the influence of patriarchy on the female labor market in both mature and developing countries. Women's comparative disadvantage in the capitalist wage-labor market enhances the comparative advantage of firms that employ them in labor-intensive industries producing for the world market. This disadvantage—reflected in low wages—is greatest for women in countries where capitalist relations of production are least developed, since there they have the fewest opportunities for wage employment and the weakest bargaining power in the labor market. Patriarchal social relations are also strongest and most restrictive of female wage employment where precapitalist modes of production, like various forms of feudalism, persist. Thus, female employment in export manufacturing industries is most prevalent in those developing countries where capitalist relations of production are developing most rapidly, but traditional patriarchy is sufficiently strong to maintain women in an inferior labor market position.

Imperialism, Patriarchy and Exploitation

Studies of Third World women workers in multinational export factories tend to focus, explicitly or implicitly, on the exploitation of these women by their multinational employers. Absolutely low wages and poor working and living conditions are often cited as evidence of such exploitation. In an earlier work, I pointed out that the concept of exploitation is an established one in all schools of economics, from the bourgeois to the Marxist, though the particular definition of it may vary. All, however, agree that

> exploitation . . . is a *relative* concept, bearing no direct relation to the *absolute* level of wages paid: so long as the worker does not receive the full value of her product, however defined, she is exploited. A higher wage may also entail a higher rate of exploitation if greater intensity

LINDA Y. C. LIM

of work, longer working hours, better equipment and organization of production, etc. mean that labor productivity, and hence the value of the worker's output, is proportionally greater in the higher-wage than lower-wage situation. [Lim 1978b]

Thus, focussing on absolute conditions faced by workers does not lend itself to useful theoretical or political analysis.

In the economic sense defined above, all workers employed in capitalist enterprises are exploited to produce profits for their employers. But the degree of exploitation differs among different groups of workers. In addition to being paid less than the value of the output they contribute, Third World women workers in multinational export factories are paid less than women workers in the multinationals' home countries and less than men workers in these countries and in their own countries as well, despite the fact that in relocated labor-intensive industries their productivity is frequently acknowledged to be higher than that of either of these other groups. Thus, Third World women workers are the most heavily exploited group of workers, both relative to their output contribution and relative to other groups. Although all are subject to capitalist exploitation, Third World women workers are additionally subject to what might be called imperialist exploitation and patriarchal exploitation.

Imperialist exploitation—the differential in wages paid to workers in developed and developing countries for the same work and output—arises from the ability of multinationals to take advantage of different labor market conditions in different parts of the world—a perfectly rational practice in the context of world capitalism. In the developing countries,

high unemployment, poor bargaining power vis-a-vis the foreign investor, lack of worker organization and representation and even the repression of workers' movements, all combine to depress wage levels, while the lack of industrial experience, ignorance and naivete of workers with respect to the labor practices in modern factory employment enable multinational employers to extract higher output from them in certain unskilled operations. [Lim 1978b:11–12]

Patriarchal exploitation—the differential in wages paid to male and female workers for similar work and output—derives from women's inferior position in the labor market, discussed in the previous section of this paper.

Although multinational employers of women factory workers in developing countries do practice all of the above forms of exploi-

CAPITALISM, IMPERIALISM, AND PATRIARCHY

tation, they do so only in response to labor market forces, specifically the international and sexual segmentation of labor markets. Differences in the degree of development of capitalist relations of production and natural restrictions on the international mobility of labor are responsible for differential wage rates between countries whereas patriarchal institutions and attitudes limiting the employment opportunities open to women are responsible for differential wage rates between the sexes. Multinationals may, consciously, attempt to preserve these differentials from which they benefit; but in general they merely take advantage of them since they exist.

In fact, it may be argued that the activities of multinationals in labor-intensive export manufacturing in developing countries might in the long run contribute to a reduction of national and sex wage differentials—in other words, a reduction of the imperialist and patriarchal components of capitalist exploitation of Third World women workers. To the extent that these multinationals contribute to the development of capitalist relations of production, particularly to the growth of demand for wage labor and to the upgrading of skills, wages will rise in the developing countries. If at the same time the relocation of industry from the developed countries reduces demand for labor in those countries, wage increases there will decline. Both factors will reduce over time the wage differential between the developed and developing countries—that is, the degree of imperialist exploitation.

Because multinationals engaged in export manufacturing in the developing countries employ mostly women workers, they increase the demand for female labor more than the demand for male labor. Female wages will then rise relative to male wages, and female unemployment rates will fall. Sex wage differentials, reflecting the degree of patriarchal exploitation of women workers, will narrow. In some countries governments have already expressed concern about the lack of employment creation for men—whom they consider to be the principal breadwinners—in multinational export firms.

So far, the narrowing of national and sex wage differentials has been imperceptible in most cases. In most developing host countries, multinationals manufacturing for export constitute too small a sector of the economy to have a significant impact on the national labor market. Even where, as in a handful of Asian countries, they are an important sector of the economy and have contributed to rising wages, wages have increased just as rapidly in the developed countries with generalized inflation. Furthermore, the relocation of industry has not reduced the overall demand for labor in the developed

LINDA Y. C. LIM

countries, where capitalist development continues in different sectors. With respect to sex wage differentials, although female wages have risen, high turnover of labor and the short average working life of women factory workers keeps their average wages low. The countries in which female wages have risen most rapidly are also those where male employment creation has been proceeding apace, and male wages have often increased even more rapidly in other sectors of the economy.

Continued imperialist and patriarchal exploitation in multinational factories in developing countries does not, however, imply that the women employed in these factories are worse off than they would have been without such employment. On the contrary, the vast majority are clearly better off, at least but not only in a narrow economic sense, for being subject to such exploitation. For one thing, wages and working conditions are usually better in multinational factories than in alternative employment for women in indigenous capitalist enterprises. Although in the relative economic sense defined previously they may be more exploited in the multinationals, in terms of producing a greater surplus or marginal product over and above the wage they receive, than in indigenous enterprises, in an absolute sense their incomes tend to be higher and they are better off. This is true also when compared with women's traditional economic roles as housewives and unpaid family labor in farms and shops.

Capitalist Development and Liberation from Patriarchy

In developing as in mature industrial economies, the state of development of capitalist relations of production defines the employment opportunities available to wage labor. Patriarchal social structures and cultures divide these opportunities by sex, typically limiting female wage labor to a narrow range of inferior jobs. In this situation the entry of labor-intensive export manufacturing industries and of multinational corporations in particular into sex segregated local labor markets has two somewhat contradictory effects. On the one hand, multinational *and* local employers can take advantage of women's inferior position in the labor market to employ them at lower wages and poorer working conditions than exist for men in the same country and for women in developed countries. This is what I have termed patriarchal and imperialist exploitation. Both local firms and multinationals benefit from the gap between

CAPITALISM, IMPERIALISM, AND PATRIARCHY

workers' wages in the developing country and final product prices in markets of developed countries.

On the other hand, the expansion of employment opportunities for women in these industries does improve conditions for women in the labor market. In however limited a way, the availability of jobs in multinational and local export factories does allow women to leave the confines of the home, delay marriage and childbearing, increase their incomes and consumption levels, improve mobility, expand individual choice, and exercise personal independence. Working for a local or foreign factory is for many women at least marginally preferable to the alternatives of staying at home, early marriage and childbearing, farm or construction labor, domestic service, prostitution, or unemployment, to which they were previously restricted. Factory work, despite the social, economic, and physical costs it often entails, provides women in developing countries with one of the very few channels they have of at least partial liberation from the confines and dictates of traditional patriarchal social relations.

Given their lack of access to better jobs, women workers usually prefer multinationals as employers over local firms since they offer higher wages and better working conditions and often have more "progressive" labor practices and social relations within the firm [Lim 1978b]. Indeed, the more multinationals there are in any one country and the longer they have been established, the stronger becomes the workers' bargaining position. Exclusive employment of female production workers in labor-intensive export industries creates occasional labor shortages, resulting over time in rising wages, greater job security, and improved working conditions for women in indigenous as well as multinational enterprises.[6] Greater competition for female laborers will tend to reduce the degree of exploitation found in women's work.

Whether or not market forces alone will expand women's employment alternatives beyond the traditional "female ghettoes" of low wage, low skill, dead end jobs depends on the state and rate of development of capitalist relations of production in the economy as a whole. In an economy that is rapidly growing, diversifying, and upgrading itself in all sectors, high demand for labor might eventually propel women into skilled industrial and nonindustrial jobs from which they have previously been excluded by custom, education, or employment discrimination. This will improve the wages and working conditions of women who remain in factory employment as production workers, given the reduction in the numbers of women available for work.

Linda Y. C. Lim

So far, such a situation is an exceptional one among the many developing countries that host multinational corporations in female-intensive industries. Even where rapid growth occurs, employers may escape the tightening labor market by importing migrant labor, by automation, and by shifting labor-intensive processes to other countries, as they have done in the home countries of the multinationals and are now doing in rapidly developing countries like Singapore. In this latter country, growth in other industries and sectors has prevented these actions from having a depressing effect on wages, and the government's high wage policy has furthermore forced firms to shed or shift their labor-intensive activities. Also, when women ascend the job hierarchy, it is usually to take jobs vacated by male workers who have since advanced even higher in the hierarchy of skills and incomes. That is to say, although rapid growth may enable women to improve their position in the labor market in absolute terms, relative to men they remain in an inferior position.

Employment of women in modern capitalist industrial enterprises in developing countries does contribute to an expansion of employment opportunities and thus to some economic and social liberation for women in patriarchal societies that customarily restrict them to a domestic role in the family. But such wage employment on its own or combined with generally rapid capitalist development throughout an economy cannot significantly undermine the patriarchal social relations responsible for women's inferior labor market position on which their very employment is predicated. In other words, capitalism cannot wipe out patriarchy, though exploitation in capitalist enterprises can provide some women with an at least temporary escape from traditional patriarchal social relations.

Exploitation and Liberation: A Dilemma for Political Action

The above analysis has identified the relocation of manufacturing industry from mature to developing capitalist countries as the outcome of the expansion of capitalism on a world scale,, reflecting differences in the development of capitalist relations of production between nations, particularly of the wage labor market. The relocation is carried out by multinational corporations, whose export manufacturing activities in developing host countries can and do enhance the development of capitalist relations of production. The almost exclusive employment of female labor in many relocated industries is based on women's inferior position in the wage labor market,

CAPITALISM, IMPERIALISM, AND PATRIARCHY

resulting from patriarchal social relations. Although women workers in these multinational factories are exploited relative to their output, to male workers in the same country, and to female workers in developed countries, their position is often better than in indigenous factories and in traditional forms of employment for women. The limited economic and social liberation that women workers derive from their employment in multinational factories is predicated on their subjection to capitalist, imperialist, and patriarchal exploitation in the labor market and the labor process. This presents a dilemma for feminist policy towards such employment: because exploitation and liberation go hand in hand, it cannot be readily condemned or extolled.

Many of the studies of female employment in multinational export factories in developing countries focus their criticism on the multinational corporation as chief perpetrator of all the forms of exploitation that these women workers are subject to in their employment. But although the multinational does take advantage of national and sexual wage differentials and sometimes reinforces them, it is not responsible for creating them and cannot by its own actions eliminate them. National wage differentials are the result of differences in the development of capitalist relations of production between nations, whereas sex wage differentials originate in indigenous patriarchy.

Removing the multinational—the logical if extreme conclusion of an antiimperialist political stand—will, in the absence of a credible alternative form of development, drastically reduce employment opportunities for women in developing countries. This will weaken their labor market position and subject them to even greater exploitation by indigenous capitalists and continued subordination to traditional patriarchy. This is clearly undesirable for the economic and social liberation of women. A less radical solution—attempting to reduce imperialist exploitation by imposing reforms on the multinational or local employer—is unlikely to succeed even if host governments were willing, which is doubtful. Export manufacturers operate in highly competitive international markets with generally elastic supply and, in important industries like garments and shoes, inelastic demand. Host governments and workers can neither demand nor enforce better wages and working conditions in profit-oriented multinationals that are mobile between countries. Local firms are often less competitive than multinationals in the world market and, with their lower profits, are unlikely to be able to absorb the costs of such reforms.

LINDA Y. C. LIM

Another possibility for reducing imperialist exploitation is through international action to restrict multinationals from exploiting market wage differentials between nations—for example, by standardizing certain terms and conditions of work in particular industries or occupations. This is clearly unrealistic, given the different stages of development of capitalism and different labor market conditions in different countries. Furthermore, workers in developed and developing countries tend to have opposing interests vis-à-vis the relocation of manufacturing industry. National interests inhibit the development of international labor solidarity. For example, protectionist groups of employers and labor unions in the multinationals' home countries have furthered their own self interest by citing exploitation of women workers overseas as a reason why goods made by these workers should be prevented from reaching their destined markets by means of tariffs, quotas, and other restrictive trade practices. This has the effect of pitting workers in mature and developing capitalist countries against each other.

Because patriarchal social relations are at the bottom of women's subjection to imperialist exploitation, it is logical to turn to an attack on traditional patriarchy as a means of improving the position of women. The successful elimination of patriarchal institutions and attitudes, discrimination, differential socialization by sex, and the sexual division of labor within the family would equalize male and female employment opportunities and incomes, ending the sex segregation of the capitalist labor market. This is also difficult to envisage, given the deep cultural and psychological as well as economic and social foundations of patriarchy, which is found in advanced as well as developing capitalist countries and in socialist countries as well. Furthermore, in developing countries, national identity is very much bound up with a traditional, often feudal, patriarchal culture. An attack on traditional patriarchy may be construed as an attack on national identity and thus arouse the forces of a reactionary nationalism against the liberation of women. Indeed, one of the dangers of multinational exploitation of Third World women workers is that it arouses local antiimperialist sentiment that becomes identified—as in fundamentalist Islamic ideology in Iran—with traditionalism and opposition to wage employment by women.

Even if traditional patriarchy is successfully undermined and equality in the capitalist labor market achieved for women workers, they will remain subject, together with male workers, to capitalist exploitation in a capitalist economy. Capitalist employers themselves are unlikely to be indifferent to the elimination of sex differences

CAPITALISM, IMPERIALISM, AND PATRIARCHY

in the labor market. Although employers of predominantly female workers may be expected to oppose sex equalization because it would reduce the supply and thus raise the wages of women workers in low skill, labor-intensive and dead end jobs, employers in male-intensive industries where labor is scarce may welcome the entry of female labor as a means of increasing the labor supply and reducing wages. The balance between these opposing interests and the attitude of male workers themselves, depends on the state and rate of development of capitalist relations of production. A nation that is rapidly growing and upgrading into high skill, high wage industries and occupations and experiences rising demand relative to supply of labor is likely to have greater sex equalization in the labor market than one which is only slowly growing or stagnating, with high unemployment and a dependence on low wage, labor-intensive industries. In other words, rapid capitalist development is more conducive to sex equalization in the labor market but by itself cannot be expected to bring about such equalization.

Elimination of worker exploitation altogether can only occur if capitalism itself is eliminated. This presents enormous difficulties for the small developing country in a world dominated by capitalism and imperialism. Domestically, a necessary precondition is the unity of the working class, which is hampered by sex, race, regional, and other differences within the labor force. So long as patriarchal relations of production persist, male and female workers remain divided by occupational segregation and by the tendency for male workers to assume the position of a labor aristocracy. If development is slow and mainly in low skill industries, male unemployment and low wages will limit this aristocracy to a small segment of the male work force, rather than creating a male elite that opposes female workers. Thus, the elimination of patriarchy would facilitate the elimination of capitalism itself. However, the elimination of capitalist exploitation does not necessarily facilitate the elimination of patriarchal exploitation, as the experience of present-day postcapitalist societies indicates. In all the "socialist" countries, including the USSR, China and eastern Europe, women occupy an inferior position in the labor force and in social and political life relative to men (though the difference may be less than in mature capitalist countries). Indeed, in some cases, the struggle against a capitalism identified with imperialist exploitation can lend itself to a reinforcement of traditional patriarchy and opposition to women's participation in the labor force. Finally, to the extent that socialist societies are likely to be less materially successful than capitalist societies—at least in the

Linda Y. C. Lim

short and medium run—the elimination of all forms of exploitation
may be achieved at the cost of lower absolute wages and standards
of living and working for both men and women.

Conclusion

This paper has sought to spell out the complexities involved in
an analysis of female employment in multinational export factories
in developing capitalist countries and in any attempt to formulate
policy or political action on behalf of these women workers. The
interplay of capitalist, imperialist, and patriarchal relations of production and the simultaneously exploitative and liberating consequences of this form of wage employment for women, point out the
inadequacy of simplistic anti-capitalist, anti-imperialist or anti-pa-
triarchal analyses and strategies to relieve exploitation.

Within the existing structure of economy and society, pro-capitalist
and pro-imperialist strategies—for example, encouraging maximum
investment by labor-intensive multinational factories—may serve an
antipatriarchal aim—by increasing the demand for female labor and
raising female wages absolutely and relative to male wages where,
as in many developing countries, male wage employment is growing
more slowly. Multinationals generally offer a better employment
alternative to women than local enterprises in modern and traditional
sectors of the economy and also provide a limited escape from the
domestic roles imposed by traditional patriarchy. But there are
limitations to the success of this strategy in raising women's wages
permanently. Because female employment creation in multinational
factories is based on patriarchal exploitation—low absolute and relative wages for women workers—the elimination of these conditions
may well bring about an elimination of the jobs themselves, given
the international mobility of multinational capital and the availability
of exploitable female labor in other countries. A similar limitation
faces attempts to impose reforms on the multinationals through
government policy actions or worker organization and labor union
activity on an enterprise, national, or international scale.

In the larger national context, a pro-capitalist, pro-imperialist strategy on behalf of women workers can generate a "backlash" response
from traditional patriarchy, making a general and genuine liberation
for women more difficult. It also weakens worker solidarity where
anti-imperialist and anti-capitalist struggles exist. On the other hand,
these struggles are unlikely to succeed so long as the labor force and

CAPITALISM, IMPERIALISM, AND PATRIARCHY

labor market remain divided by sex, and so these struggles would be strengthened by the undermining of patriarchal relations of production.

Ultimately, it is the existing structure of the economy and society that has to be changed if the exploitation of women in the labor force is to be eliminated. Capitalist market forces and employment based on imperialist exploitation cannot liberate women from patriarchal exploitation that is the very condition for their entry into wage labor in multinational factories producing for the world market. In the long run, capitalism and imperialism only perpetuate and may even reinforce patriarchal relations of production, which in turn reinforce capitalist and imperialist relations of production. Although the liberation of women workers as women and as workers can only come about through some combined struggle against capitalist, imperialist, and patriarchal exploitation, the specific strategies to be undertaken depend on the particular historical, social, economic and political circumstances of each national unit in the context of an international capitalism.

Notes

1. For a few examples of relevant case studies, see Snow 1977, Lim 1978b, Paglaban 1978, Grossman 1979, Fernández Kelly 1980, United Nations Industrial Development Organization (UNIDO) 1980.

2. See, for example, Leontiades 1971, Adam 1975, Moxon 1974, UNIDO 1979, Fröbel, Heinrichs, and Kreye 1980.

3. See, for example, Nayyar 1978, Fröbel, Heinrichs, and Kreye 1978, Takeo 1978; Landsberg 1979, Sivanandan 1980.

4. Marginal productivity is a theoretical concept central to neoclassical economic doctrine: it is the addition to a firm's total output value resulting from the employment of one additional worker or unit of labor.

5. In neoclassical economic theory, this is true in all but the pure and unattainable case of perfect competition in both product and labor markets, where labor is paid exactly the value of its marginal product. In Marxist economic theory, even the "normal profit" or "zero economic profit" earned by perfectly competitive firms—the return just necessary to maintain them in their line of production, which includes a return to capital—represents "surplus value" exploited off labor.

6. Indigenous firms have to compete with multinationals in the labor market; multinationals are the leaders in setting wages and working conditions. In Singapore, the improvement of wages and working conditions in the female labor market are illustrated by the following facts: Starting wages have more than doubled in five years (ahead of inflation); fringe benefits have improved (for example, the extension of paid holiday time to

Linda Y. C. Lim

two weeks in the year); part-time shifts have been instituted to suit housewives; the desired age of workers has risen from sixteen to twenty-three years to up to fifty years; there has been a dramatic reduction in rotating shifts and microscope work in electronics factories; and a five-day week is typical. Singapore workers have become a "labor aristocrary" in the Southeast Asian region.

References

Adam, Gyorgy. 1975. "Multinational Corporations and Worldwide Sourcing." In *International Firms and Modern Imperialism*, ed. Hugo Radice. Hamondsworth, England: Penguin.

Becker, Gary Stanley. 1957. *The Economics of Discrimination.* Chicago: University of Chicago Press.

Blaxall, Martha and Barbara Reagan, ed., 1976. *Women and the Workplace: The Implications of Occupational Segregation.* Chicago: University of Chicago Press.

Boserup, Ester. 1970. *Woman's Role in Economic Development.* London: Allen and Unwin.

Fernández-Kelly, María Patricia. 1982. "Mexican Border Industrialization, Female Labour Force Participation and Migration." Working Paper. Center for the Study, Education and Advancement of Women. University of California, Berkeley.

Fröbel, Folker; Heinrichs, Jürgen; and Kreye, Otto. 1978. "Export-Oriented Industrialization of Underdeveloped Countries." *Monthly Review* 30, no. 6, pp. 22–27.

———.1980. *The New International Division of Labour: Structural Unemployment in Industrialised Countries and Industrialisation in Developing Countries.* Cambridge and New York: Cambridge University Press.

Grossman, Rachel. 1979. "Women's Place in the Integrated Circuit." *Southeast Asia Chronicle, Pacific Research,* Issue, 9 nos. 5–6.

Landsberg, Martin. 1979. "Export-led Industrialization in the Third World: Manufacturing Imperialism." *Review of Radical Political Economics* 11, no. 4, pp. 50–63.

Leontiades, James. 1971. "International Sourcing in the Less-developed Countries." *Columbia Journal of World Business* 6, no. 6, pp. 19–26.

Lim, Linda Y. C. 1978a. "Multinational Firms and Manufacturing for Export in Less-developed Countries: The Case of the Electronics Industry in Malaysia and Singapore." Ph.D. Dissertation, University of Michigan, Ann Arbor.

———. 1978b. *Women Workers in Multinational Corporations: The Case of the Electronics Industry in Malaysia and Singapore.* Michigan Occasional Papers, no. 9. Ann Arbor, Michigan: University of Michigan, Women's Studies Program.

Moxon, Richard W. 1974. "Offshore Production in Less-developed Countries—A Case Study of Multinationality in the Electronics Industry." *Bulletin,* nos. 98–99 (July). New York University: Graduate School of Business Administration, Institute of Finance.

CAPITALISM, IMPERIALISM, AND PATRIARCHY

Nayyar, Deepak. 1978. "Transnational Corporations and Manufactured Exports from Poor Countries." *Economic Journal* 88:58–84.

Paglaban, E. 1978. "Philippines: Workers in the Export Industry." *Pacific Research* 9, Nos. 3–4.

Pang Eng Fong and Lim, Linda Y. C. 1977. *The Electronics Industry in Singapore: Structure, Technology and Linkages*. Economic Research Centre, University of Singapore, Research Monograph Series, no. 7.

Reynis, Lee Ann. 1976. "The Proliferation of U.S. Firm Third World Sourcing in the Mid-to-Late 1960's: An Historical and Empirical Study of the Factors Which Occasioned the Location of Production for the U.S. Market Abroad." Ph.D. dissertation, University of Michigan, Ann Arbor.

Sivanandan, A. 1980. "Imperialism in the Silicon Age." *Monthly Review* 32, no. 3, pp. 24–42.

Snow, Robert. 1977. "Dependent Development and the New Industrial Worker: The Export Processing Zone in the Philippines." Ph.D. dissertation, Harvard Universilty.

Takeo, Tsuchiya. 1978. "Free Trade Zones in Southeast Asia." *Monthly Review* 29 no. 9, pp. 29–39.

United Nations Industrial Development Organization (UNIDO). 1979. "Redeployment of Industries from Developed to Developing Countries." Industrial Development Conference. 419 (October 3).

    1980. "Women in the Redeployment of Manufacturing Industry to Developing Countries." UNIDO Working Papers on Structural Change, no. 18, UNIDO/ICIS. (July 8).

[8]

The Feminisation of Industrial Employment in Mauritius: A Case of Sex Segregation

CATHERINE HEIN

One 'female' job which has recently become of some importance in certain Third World countries is that of production worker in export-oriented labour-intensive industries. Mauritius is an example of such a country. The Export Processing Zone (EPZ) created in 1970 has employed mainly women workers despite persistent high unemployment among men. The research reported in this chapter investigates the operation of the labour market in Mauritius, and the reasons why these jobs have gone to women, using data from interviews conducted with a representative sample of women factory workers along with data from interviews conducted with factory employers. [Editors' note]

7.1 INTRODUCTION

Various studies in this volume have shown the greater difficulties encountered by women as compared to men in obtaining formal employment in the organised sector of Third World countries. Women's opportunities are said to be restricted by ideas among employers and in society that only certain limited jobs can be performed by women. Women are thus said to be 'crowded' into certain segments of the employment market where wages are relatively low. Accordingly, sex segregation in employment can usually be seen as clearly to the advantage of men who benefit from lack of competition from

278   *Industrial Employment in Mauritius*

women in certain protected segments of the employment market and to the advantage of employers who benefit from lower wages paid to the female work force.

The country study in this chapter presents an example of sex segregation where it is debatable whether women are or are not disadvantaged by this segregation. In Mauritius[2] there has been rapid growth of employment in export manufacturing in recent years, and women have obtained the vast majority of the jobs despite high levels of unemployment among men.

In 1970, the Government of Mauritius created an Export Processing Zone (EPZ) with the express purpose of providing employment opportunities for the approximately 20 per cent of the labour force who were then unemployed. According to the 1971–5 development plan (Government of Mauritius, 1971) promotion and selection of projects in manufacturing would be based on maximisation of employment rather than on productivity. At that time, women constituted only about one-fifth of the unemployed.

The EPZ grew rapidly during the 1970s such that by 1980 there were about 100 factories in various parts of the island employing 22 000 people. This employment constituted about 11 per cent of employent in large establishments (i.e. establishments employing more than 10 persons which can roughly be considered as the formal sector). It is remarkable that despite high unemployment among men, about 80 per cent of EPZ employment has been feminine throughout the 1970s (Government of Mauritius, Ministry of Economic Planning and Development, 1978).

The use of mainly female labour in export assembly industries appears to be a fairly widespread phenomena in developing countries and is often seen as part of the international search for cheap labour by industries which are labour intensive (Safa, 1980). This interpretation is compatible with the Mauritian situation where labour legislation and practice explicitly provide for lower wages of women in factory employment as compared to men. However, there are additional factors favouring the employment of women which should not be overlooked; these, like lower wages, emanate from the subordinate position of women within society as a whole.

The first part of this chapter discusses the limited economic opportunities for women that have existed until recently within the traditional economy of the island. The chapter then goes on to look at both the supply and demand side of the industrial employment market, particularly as these affect women. The socio-economic background and motivations of women factory workers are analysed in Section 6.3 using results of a survey of 380 workers conducted by the author in 1977. The reasons why industrial employers in Mauritius have preferred to utilise female labour are discussed in Section 7.4 on the basis of interviews with a sample of employers.

7.2 LABOUR FORCE PARTICIPATION AND INDUSTRIAL EMPLOYMENT OF WOMEN

The Mauritian economy has been based traditionally on the export of sugar, and its society – composed of ethno-religious groups of various origins – has been structured around the sugar-producing activity. It may be termed a 'plantation society', with many parallels to other plantation islands such as Jamaica, Trinidad and Fiji (Beckford, 1972).[3]

The official labour force participation rate of women as recorded by regular censuses has always been low; at the time of the 1972 Population Census,[4] 17.5 per cent of women aged 15 years and over were reported as being employed and a further 2.9 per as cent unemployed. In contrast, 69.7 per cent of the men aged 15 and over were reported as being employed and 14.1 per cent as unemployed. This latter figure may be considered to underestimate male unemployment since 11 per cent of male employment in 1972 was in a government work creation programme called 'relief' work. This programme was only for men, the objective being 'to provide employment and incomes for those families whose breadwinners cannot immediately find work elsewhere in the economy' (Government of Mauritius, 1971, p. 40). 'Breadwinners' were and still are assumed to be men.

7.2.1 Age, marital status and education

The labour force participation rate of women 15 years and over (including the unemployed) in 1972 was low for both married women (15.4 per cent) and single women (24.5 per cent). In comparison, women who were separated or divorced had relatively high rates of activity (47.3 per cent) reflecting the greater economic need of separated women. It is important to note that at that time, widowed and separated women – i.e. women who could be considered as primary earners – comprised one-quarter of the female labour force.

280   *Industrial Employment in Mauritius*

The traditional pattern in Mauritius was for women *not* to take employment before marriage. In 1972, women's labour force participation rate increased with age, reaching a peak of 28 per cent for women in their late forties. Only 14.5 per cent of 15 to 19 year old women were economically active and 20 per cent were still in school. The remaining two-thirds were recorded as housewives or relatives helping in the house. Since few women aged 15 to 19 years were married in 1972 (only 13 per cent) it can be deduced that approximately half were single women who had left school, who were not working nor officially looking for work.

Within the plantation economy, most employment is for wages or salary – 89 per cent of women and 86 per cent of working men are employees. For women, there is little tradition of home industries or of self-employment in selling. In 1972, 37 per cent of working women were field labourers in agriculture as compared to 29 per cent of working men. Another 29 per cent of working women were in domestic service. Most of the remaining working women were in white-collar occupations which require secondary education such as teachers (11 per cent), clerical workers (7 per cent) and shop assistants (3 per cent). By 1972, completed primary education was fairly widespread among younger women but completion of secondary school much more rare. In the 20–24 age group, 38.9 per cent had completed primary or had some secondary schooling while only 7.7 per cent had completed secondary school.

It is noticeable that for clerical jobs, secondary education appears to be a more important qualification for access to employment for women than for men: in 1972, about two-fifths of male clerical workers had not gone beyond primary school compared to only 8 per cent of the females. Opportunities for the majority of women who had not been to secondary school were thus limited to very menial tasks of agricultural labour or domestic service, acceptable mainly to those in financial difficulties such as separated or widowed women.

Given the pattern of employment opportunities in 1972, it is not surprising to find that women's employment rates do not increase monotonically with educational level but show a J-shaped relation (Table 7.1). This is not an unusual phenomenon and has been found by Youssef (1974) for Chile; Youssef (1976–7) for Egypt and Syria; and Peil (1979) for various West African towns.

The high proportion of women with completed secondary education who are working (Table 7.1) reflects the expansion of opportunities for employment at this level and the willingness of educated

TABLE 7.1 *Percentage of women not attending school who were employed, by age and education, 1972*

Age (yrs)	Education				
	None	*Lower primary*	*Complete primary*	*Lower secondary*	*School certificate or above*
15–19	10.1	9.0	7.9	11.9	31.9
20–24	13.3	11.1	10.3	19.3	63.8
25–34	19.4	14.2	11.6	23.0	68.2
35–44	28.9	21.6	17.1	28.3	59.1
45–54	29.9	24.3	19.4	23.8	54.8

SOURCE   Central Statistical Office (1975), Tables 17, 29, 44 and 53.

women to work even in the main child-bearing ages. The problem of the care of children is solved either by leaving them with another member of the family or by hiring a servant to look after them since the wife's earnings are much greater than the salary for a servant. At the white-collar level a wife's salary may be about as much as her husband's, so that the addition to the household income is considerable and allows them to buy luxuries which they otherwise could not afford. At this level, the status of the family tends to go up rather than down if she works. It is often suggested that when looking for a bride, Mauritian men who have finished secondary school tend to prefer a women who works in a white-collar job and can contribute to the family budget.

In 1972, women with primary schooling are least likely to be working. It is possible that the husbands and/or fathers of women with some education have better jobs than those of women with little or no education so there is less need to work particularly in the jobs available at that time which may be regarded as too demeaning. However, the creation during the 1970s of industrial employment for women with an intermediate level of education has probably increased their participation and thus changed the relationship of women's education to their rate of employment from J-shaped to positive.

7.2.2   White-collar occupations

Despite the high employment rates of educated women in 1972, women constituted a very small minority (6.4 per cent) of administrative/managerial workers in 1972 and their share of both professional and clerical jobs had in fact declined in the previous 20 years. The proportion of professional workers who were women has oscillated around 40 per cent throughout this century, but it dropped from a peak of 46.2 per cent in 1952 to 41.6 in 1962 and 36.0 in 1972. This decreasing proportion of women among professionals is mainly the result of a decline in women's share of teaching jobs from 55 per cent in 1952 to 41 per cent in 1972. This was a period of considerable expansion of education, but clearly women did not profit from the new employment opportunities in teaching to the same extent as men.

Between 1962 and 1972 women's share of clerical posts also declined, though less than in the case of teaching, from 23 per cent to 20 per cent.[5] With the expansion of government service, the number of clerical posts increased rapidly, more than doubling between 1962 and 1972 but, as in the case of the expansion of employment in teaching, the expansion of clerical jobs led to a decline in women's share of this type of employment.

Women's declining share of white-collar jobs cannot be attributed to a lack of suitable candidates as unemployment is high among young women with at least secondary education. (In 1972, 43 per cent of women aged 15–19 with secondary schooling declared themselves unemployed and 17 per cent in the 20–24 age group.) These trends in white-collar employment illustrate the disadvantage of women in a society with high unemployment and with the underlying belief that employment is much more important for a man who must support his family than for a woman who normally has a husband or father to support her. It is in this context of restricted opportunities for women that the creation of export manufacturing industries utilising mainly female workers must be viewed.

7.2.3 Women in industry

In 1972, the EPZ[6] was just starting operation and so had little effect on the employment figures of the census given in the previous section. However figures from bi-annual surveys of employment in large establishments document the rapid increase in industrial employment of women during the 1970s.

As can be seen in Table 7.2, the proportion of women among employees in the manufacturing sector increased rapidly during the 1970s and continued to increase in the early 1980s. Women's share of

Catherine Hein 283

TABLE 7.2 *Employment in large establishments by sex, Mauritius, 1971, 1974, 1977, 1982*

	Total employment			Manufacturing			Manufacturing
Year	Men	Women	% Women	Men	Women	% Women	as % total
1971	114 161	28 007	19.7	7189	2 592	26.5	6.9
1974	130 062	37 156	22.2	10 576	10 019	48.6	12.3
1977	149 158	45 498	23.4	14 037	16 904	54.6	15.9
1982	140 659	51 878	26.9	15 654	22 326	58.8	19.7

SOURCE   Central Statistical Office (1971–1983)

total employment in large establishments has also continued to rise, particularly since the decline in the number of men employed which started at the end of the 1970s.[7] At the same time, the proportion of total employment which is in the manufacturing sector has continued to increase. Within the manufacturing sector, the EPZ accounts for a large proportion of employment – 59 per cent in 1977 and 62 per cent in 1982.

Employment within the various industries of the manufacturing sector shows a clear pattern of sex segregation. Some industries such as printing, machinery repair and furniture have a high proportion of male employees, whereas others such as wearing apparel and electrical machinery have mainly female employees (see Table 7.3). Since wearing apparel firms (mainly EPZ factories) provided 42 per cent of the employment in manufacturing in 1977, the concentration of women in this type of industry accounts considerably for the overall high proportion of women in the manufacturing sector. The other main industry with a high concentration of women (84 per cent of employees) was electronics assembly plants in the EPZ which accounted for 7 per cent of manufacturing employment in 1977.

Wearing apparel factories can be roughly divided into two types: knitting and sewing factories. Knitting factories manufacture sweaters usually of wool. The knitting itself is done on a machine which is not power assisted. The other main tasks in knitting factories are looping (done on an electric machine which attaches sleeves, collars and seams), mending (done by hand), inspection, ironing and packing. Sewing or confection factories in Mauritius make blouses, skirts, pants, gloves and dresses. Many of the workers in these factories work on electric sewing machines, while some do less skilled jobs

284   *Industrial Employment in Mauritius*

TABLE 7.3 *Employment within the manufacturing sector by industrial group and sex of worker, March–June 1977*

Industrial group	Males	Females	Total	% female
Food	1511	646	2157	29.9
Beverages and tobacco	1702	479	2181	22.0
Textiles	1654	937	2591	36.2
Wearing apparel	2010	11 022	13 032	84.6
Wood and furniture	763	169	932	18.1
Printing and publishing	803	100	903	11.1
Rubber and leather products	374	419	793	52.8
Non-metallic mineral products	1209	93	1302	7.1
Metal products	744	14	785	1.8
Repairs of machinery	805	20	825	2.4
Repairs of electrical machinery[1]	377	1916	2293	83.9
Transport equipment	655	8	663	1.2
Miscellaneous	799	739	1538	48.0
Total	14 037	16 904	30 941	54.6

[1] This category includes factories doing electronic assembly.
SOURCE Central Statistical Office (1978).

such as turning collars, clipping threads, ironing and packing. In electronics assembly factories, much of the work involves very fine manipulations using a microscope.

Women are concentrated in production jobs within the manufacturing sector and constitute the majority of production workers (see Table 7.4).

The use of female labour at the production level combined with employers' belief in the appropriateness of sex segregation has resulted in employment opportunities for women in clerical occupations and to some extent in administrative/managerial and professional/technical jobs. Compared to all other sectors of the economy, the percentage of women in clerical posts is highest in manufacturing. In construction, agriculture and transport where the majority of workers are men, women clerical workers are relatively rare. In these sectors, jobs such as pay clerk or personnel assistant are occupied by men, as interaction of women with the workers is felt to be inappropriate. Conversely, in the industrial sector, these clerical posts tend to be occupied by women; in most factories employing women workers, the clerical staff of the personnel department is almost entirely female.

TABLE 7.4 *Female share of employment in large establishments (percentages), by major occupational groups and selected major industrial groups, June 1977*

Occupational group	Industrial group					All industrial groups
	Manufacturing	Agriculture	Construction	Transport	Services¹	
Professional, technical and related workers	12.9	6.3	3.4	5.7	39.1	35.9
Administrative and managerial	6.2	1.1	0	0	6.1	4.5
Clerical and related workers	45.0	20.8	15.7	7.1	32.7	28.8
Sales workers	11.5	0	0	–	0.6	16.9
Service workers	11.8	1.5	0	6.4	10.3	9.9
Agricultural workers	19.0	30.9	–	–	8.2	28.6
Production workers, transport equipment operators and labourers	58.9	0.4	0.8	0	3.2	19.4
All occupations	54.6	25.4	0.8	2.7	18.3	23.4
Total employment (N)	30 941	61 845	7309	10 115	54 583	194 656

¹ Include development workers employed by central government.
The sign – in the table indicates there were no workers in the category.

SOURCE Central Statistical Office (1978), Table 5.

286   *Industrial Employment in Mauritius*

For administrative and technical posts, the figures in Table 7.4 suggest a slightly greater proportion of women in industry as compared to other private sector activities, although men are still the vast majority at these higher levels. The relative paucity of women in high level production jobs which are normally filled by outside recruitment rather than internal promotion is probably the result of a lack of Mauritian women with the required technical background, rather than any employer bias against women. In fact, two employers interviewed for the employer survey (see Section 7.4) indicated that they would favour female over male candidates given equal qualifications.

In industry there is some possibility of a woman being in charge of the personnel department. There were 12 factories in the employer sample which had a personnel manager and which employed mainly female workers; of these 12 personnel managers, three were women. One manager explained that women could understand better the problems of women workers and gain their confidence more easily than a man. Another suggested the need for a certain amount of 'maternalism' within the factory; given the youth of the majority of the workers, they needed the social support of a 'mother' or 'big sister' within the factory environment. In the male dominated sectors of agriculture, construction and transport, on the other hand, women personnel managers are non-existent.

In the past, when male workers formed the vast majority in all sectors, the practice of segregation tended to limit opportunities for women in white-collar jobs, and continues to do so in sectors such as agriculture, construction and transport. However, in the new industrial sector, where many factories employ almost exclusively female labour, the belief in the appropriateness of sexual segregation has created opportunities for women above the level of worker, particularly in jobs involving interaction with workers. The position of first-line supervisor is the most influenced by this tendency since most factories use women promoted from the worker level, as will be discussed below.

7.3 SURVEY OF WOMEN FACTORY WORKERS[8]

Regular surveys of employment serve to document the high participation of women in Mauritian industry and provide some overall figures on type of industry and occupations. However, they are not meant to provide the micro-level information required to answer such questions as: Who are the women workers? Why were they attracted to factory work? What do they think of their work?

In order to obtain this type of information, the author conducted a survey of women factory workers in 1977 using a two-stage sample design. At the first stage, 10 factories were selected with probability proportional to size from a list of all factories in Mauritius employing at least 50 women.[9]

Half of the factories selected were knitting factories, three did sewing, one was an electronic assembly plant and one was none of these types (and was the only one not in the EPZ). Two were located in rural areas and size varied from 90 to 1800 female employees. The majority of the factories were between two and six years old. Within each selected factory, a systematic sample of 45 production workers (excluding trainees) was taken from personnel lists provided by the management. This procedure ensured an adequate representation of workers in different types of jobs and of varying seniority since lists were by section in the factory, or date of entry, or both. This two-stage sample design with probability proportional to size in the first stage meant that the sample was reasonably representative of women factory workers in Mauritius.

Selected workers were interviewed in their homes so they would feel more free to talk. Of the 428 who were contacted by interviewers, 9 per cent had left the factory where their name had been obtained and 2 per cent refused, so that the actual number of workers interviewed was 380.

The median length of employment of workers in their current factory was about two years. In terms of the type of job the representativity cannot be checked but is probably reasonable – 25 percent were working on knitting machines, 31 per cent on sewing machines, 5 per cent in ironing, 16 per cent in jobs outside the wearing apparel sector and 22 per cent in unskilled jobs in wearing apparel factories.

7.3.1 Background characteristics of workers

The results of the survey of women factory workers indicate the emergence of an important new group of workers within the Mauritian labour force. The majority of factory workers are under age 25 years (70 per cent), are single (77 per cent) and have completed, or almost completed, primary school (74 per cent). In constrast, the majority of women employed in 1972 were over 25 years (75 per cent) and not single (71 per cent); many had no education at all (41 per cent), while a few (11 per cent) had secondary schooling or better. Young single girls with some basic primary education have thus been the main source of female labour for the factories which opened during the 1970s.

The low proportion of married women among factory workers does not appear to be the result of any systematic discrimination against married women on the part of employers. Three of the employers interviewed even expressed a preference for married women, whom they thought were more conscientious workers than single women. Nevertheless, the general tendency among single workers is to leave factory employment around the time of their marriage, even before they are pregnant or have any children to look after. The reasons for this trend are investigated in another study (Hein, 1982) which reveals that husbands' opposition to their wives' working, particularly in a factory, is a crucial factor in these withdrawals.

Consideration of the occupations of the workers' fathers indicates the socio-economic groups from which workers are most likely to come. About half the fathers were skilled manual workers such as masons, electricians or carpenters, while another quarter were engaged in unskilled manual work outside agriculture. The agricultural milieu was under-represented among factory workers since only 15 per cent had fathers who worked in agriculture, yet according to the Population Census of 1972, 30 per cent of the male labour force was composed of agricultural workers. As might be expected, almost no workers came from families where the father was a white-collar worker.

One possible explanation for the low proportion of workers from agricultural families is geographical distance from the factories. However, five of the 10 factories in the sample were located in rural areas or near sugar estates, and therefore this explanation is incomplete. Evidence from a question concerning parental reactions to the factory employment of their daughter suggests that attitudes about young girls going out to work were more conservative in agricultural families. 43 per cent of the workers from agricultural backgrounds reported some family opposition to their working as compared to 29 per cent among the other workers ($X^2 = 4.3$, $p < 0.05$).

Family reluctance about allowing their daughter to work in a factory was clearly limiting the supply of female labour. Among all religious groups in Mauritius, families are concerned about the reputation of their daughter since it affects her marriage prospects. In Mauritius, as elsewhere (Boserup, 1970; Youssef, 1974; Reynolds and Gregory, 1965) women working in factories have acquired a reputation for 'loose morals' and are considered to be 'bad company' for one's daughter. The survey finding that Hindu girls tend to start factory work at age 17 or 18 whereas Christian girls are more likely to start at age 15 or 16 was explained by Hindu interviewers in terms of concern for the daughter's reputation; only after a Hindu girl has reached a certain age and a good marriage is not in view is she allowed to participate in what is often perceived as a compromising activity.

Industrialisation is often associated with an increase in migration from rural to urban areas. However, in Mauritius there has been no massive departure from the countryside to the towns and the results of the present survey reflect this relative stability of the population. Among workers currently living in an urban area, only 10 per cent had lived in a rural area as a child. Girls residing in rural areas and working in urban factories (in fact, not very numerous) either commuted from their home or stayed with a relative on weekdays. Furthermore, the geographical dispersion of the EPZ has meant that girls residing in rural areas and wishing to work often had some opportunities in their own area. In any case, in the Mauritian context, it would be socially inconceivable and practically impossible for a young single girl to live on her own outside the family circle. Her ability to work depends on the existence of job opportunities within commuting distance of her family residence. This type of labour force does not move to areas where jobs are available, and puts pressure on factories to locate in areas with a good potential supply of labour.

In summary, the women who have participated in factory work in Mauritius are mainly young, single women who have completed their primary education. The existence of a large supply of such women was the result of historically low female labour force participation rates, women's relatively late age of marriage and their widespread acquisition of primary education. In addition, Mauritian women are not secluded as in some other countries; although parents are sometimes reluctant to allow daughters to work in factory, there are no norms which actually forbid this activity. Finally, factory employment appeals to girls with primary education much more than the main alternatives, domestic servant or agricultural labourer, as will be seen below.

290   *Industrial Employment in Mauritius*

TABLE 7.5 *Reasons for starting work, by marital status, percentages*

Reasons for starting work	Single	Married	Separated/ widowed	All
Money for family	54	80	64	59
Money for self	35	13	36	31
Something to do[1]	31	13	7	27
Total[2]	120	106	107	117
N	292	60	28	380

[1]'Something to do' is a rather rough translation of the Creole expression 'ène bon distraction'.
[2]Total exceeds 100 percent because of multiple replies.

SOURCE   1977 survey of women factory workers.

7.3.2 Reasons for working

The process by which sampled women workers joined the industrial labour force suggests that the creation of these particular types of jobs was, in itself, responsible for increasing the participation rate of women. Almost half (42 per cent) of the workers interviewed claimed that they had not been looking for work just before entering their first factory job. The typical scenario for two-thirds of the workers was that a friend or relative told them that factory X was looking for workers and encouraged them to go and see. Factory employment had been the first job for 95 per cent of the interviewees. Given the number who said they were not looking for work before joining the industrial labour force, it seems unlikely that many of these workers would have sought employment elsewhere had no factory jobs been available.

The reasons why these women reacted positively to information concerning employment opportunities in factories were both financial and social. When interviewees were asked why they started working, financial considerations predominated (see Table 7.5). Money for the family was by far the most frequent reason, even among single workers. The importance of this motivation among single workers is confirmed by the information they gave concerning the use made of their salary; on average, single workers gave about half of their earnings to their mothers. This behaviour reflects the strong family ties which exist in all religious groups in Mauritius and the strong feeling that children who work should contribute to the household budget.

However, the worker's salary was very rarely the main source of income for the household: only in 2 per cent of the households was the woman factory worker the only income earner. (Remember that most women factory workers are single and living with their family). On average, households included two other wage earners, and the earnings of women workers constituted about one-third of total household income. They were thus substantial enough to make a difference in the standard of living. Furthermore, the stability of these earnings and of the worker's contribution to the household probably made the factory worker's contribution more important than these overall figures would suggest. It should be pointed out that about 10 per cent of the other wage earners, particularly men, did not earn regularly. Also there were cases where the men contributed little or erratically depending on how much they spent on liquor.

Money for their own personal use was mentioned by about one-third of the workers as a reason for working, mainly those not currently married. If they did not work, they would have to ask their parents for money for clothes, make-up, etc. and would not be able to have many of the things they would like. A few specifically mentioned using the money they earned to prepare their trousseau for marriage.

Although money was given frequently as a reason for working, it was likely that this need would not have pushed the interviewees into domestic service, the main other type of employment available for them. When asked if they would accept a job as maid, with the same hours of work and pay as the factory, nearly all the workers said 'no'. In fact, workers were particularly talkative concerning their reasons for preferring the factory but only the main one was coded. Some clearly indicated that they felt domestic work was beneath them; in domestic work you are like a slave (12 per cent) and you do menial, dirty, less interesting tasks (24 per cent). Another 18 per cent suggested they had not gone to school and studied in order to end up as a servant. The regulated hours and conditions of work in the factory made it more attractive for 14 per cent. The status of domestic servant was clearly considered to be lower than that of factory worker, both because of the social situation involved and because of the nature of the work and working conditions.

Another important reason for preferring factory work over domestic service, even if the wages were the same, was the sociability of the factory. About one-fifth of the interviewees pointed out that as a servant, you do not have the same chance to meet new people and have your group of friends at work; you are all alone in the house with 'madame'. The importance of this social stimulation was also shown by the fact that one-quarter of all workers, in particular the single workers, gave 'something to do' as a reason for working (Table 7.5). Although the opinion of one manager who felt that workers came to his factory 'to have fun' is no doubt an exaggeration, escape from the boredom of staying at home was an important reason for working. They escaped not only boredom but also parental supervision. As mentioned earlier, families are generally quite strict about allowing young girls to go out unaccompanied. If they stayed at home, they would help their mother with household chores and be constantly under her supervision. Working provided these young women with a legitimate way of temporarily escaping parental control. The 'something to do' which was attracting these women to the factory was mainly the possibility for social interaction. Thus, although the principal attraction of the factory was economic, the possibilities for socialising and escaping the boredom at home added to this attraction.

7.3.3 Job satisfaction and dissatisfaction

Workers were asked whether they were satisfied, fairly satisfied or dissatisfied with their work, and were then asked to explain their reasons. This question was left completely open in order to minimise bias and find out which dimensions are important to them.

The highest proportion (56 per cent) said they were very satisfied while 25 per cent said that they were fairly satisfied and only 19 per cent said that they were dissatisfied. When satisfied workers were asked what they did not like about their work, 35 per cent said they had no complaints. It is clear that a considerable proportion of women factory workers were satisfied with their work.

Earning money was an important reason for satisfaction. The category 'earn money' in Table 7.6 does not mean that workers thought their salary was good (very few suggested this), but rather that they were pleased because they were earning money.

The social contacts at work are almost as important as earnings in workers' satisfaction. Indeed, if all reasons mentioned are considered, social contacts are more frequently given than earnings as a source of satisfaction. A typical comment classified in this category was 'I like my job because it's something good to do with my friends here and all

Catherine Hein   293

TABLE 7.6 *Reasons given for satisfaction by satisfied workers, percentages*

Reason for satisfaction	First reason	All reasons
Earn money	30	35
Relations with workers	26	42
Easiness of work	20	32
Job not tiring	12	22
Supervision	7	15
Job interest	2	3
Fringe benefits	2	5
Other reasons	1	3
Total	100	157[1]
N	306	306

[1] Total exceeds 100 per cent because of multiple replies.
   81 per cent of women workers reported that they were very or fairly satisfied.

SOURCE   1977 survey of women factory workers.

that'. Once they establish their group of friends, this becomes a great source of satisfaction at work. The social motive, which was seen earlier to be an important reason for joining the industrial labour force, can apparently find considerable satisfaction within the existing factory environment.

Despite the importance of social relations at the factory in worker satisfaction, the results of the survey indicate that social activities outside the factory are still mainly limited to family events such as weddings, first communions and the visiting of relatives. Cinema attendance was rare or non-existent for 87 per cent of the workers. Only 10 per cent met socially with new friends from the factory; for the majority of workers, friendships originating at the factory did not involve any contacts outside the work context. The continued control of workers' families over their activities outside the factory, contrasts with the pattern in Hong Kong for example, where Salaff and Wong (1977) report that workers spend a considerable amount of their leisure time with persons (often co-workers) in organised, non-familial settings. In Mauritius, the continuing social restrictiveness of the workers' family environment, despite their economic activity, probably enhanced the attraction of the factory for them.

Easiness of the work was another reason given for satisfaction. Some workers seem to have been worried about whether they could do a factory job, and were relieved to find that it was not all that difficult. For these workers, the semi-skilled nature of their work was a source of satisfaction.

TABLE 7.7 *Reasons for dissatisfaction, percentages*

Reasons for dissatisfaction	Main reason	All reasons
Tiring	37	58
Wages	28	39
Hours of work	16	47
Supervision	12	20
Travelling problems	3	12
Job difficulty	3	9
Other reasons	1	9
Total	100	194[1]
N	74	74

[1] Total exceeds 100 per cent because of multiple replies.
SOURCE   1977 survey of women factory workers

A remaining source of job satisfaction which was of some importance was lack of fatigue. As can be seen in Table 7.7, fatigue was a
major source of worker dissatisfaction and the fact that a number of
workers mentioned lack of fatigue as a reason for liking their work
underlines the importance of this dimension for them.

Given that fatigue was the most frequent reason for dissatisfaction,
it is essential to clarify the meaning of this category. Although it is
difficult to distinguish between fatigue caused by physical effort and
that caused by boredom, the content of the complaints classified in
this category suggests that, for the workers interviewed, the cause
was mainly physical in nature. They were tired from standing up and
from the effort of working long hours; some mentioned symptoms
such as feeling faint, backache and palpitations. It is quite likely that
malnutrition was partially responsible for the high frequency of
complaints about fatigue. A study of dietary habits of workers
(Peerbaye, 1979) concluded that their daily food intake was lacking
in calories, proteins, vitamins and minerals; the doctor who conducted this survey noted that a number of workers showed skin
changes, pallor, brittle hair and were underweight, and he thought
that a large proportion of women workers were suffering from
anaemia.

After fatigue, the other main complaints of dissatisfied workers
were their pay and hours of work (mainly compulsory overtime in
certain factories).[10] Some workers who were dissatisfied mentioned
fatigue, low pay and long working hours simultaneously in statements
such as: 'We exhaust ourselves working these long hours for such a
little bit of money'. Working hours were not frequently the main

reason for dissatisfaction but were an important secondary complaint often given in combination with fatigue.

The absense of complaints about boredom is rather unexpected given the routine nature of the workers' tasks. In England, studies of women textile workers (NEDO, 1972) and electronics workers (Wild, 1979) report that boredom is one of the main reasons for worker dissatisfaction. However, in Puerto Rico (Reynolds and Gregory, 1965) very few workers complained about boredom and women workers in particular expressed a preference for repetitive operations rather than a more varied work programme. It is likely that in developing countries, the expectation that one's task should be interesting is not as prevalent as in industrialised countries.

In summary, the majority of the workers were satisfied because they were earning money, had something to do outside the home and had a job which was not overly difficult. The main complaints were that the work was tiring and the hours long, particularly considering their wages.

To some extent this pattern of motivation must be understood in the context that for the majority of workers who were single, working was seen as a temporary phase in their lives. When asked if they intended to work after marriage, only 23 per cent said 'yes' and one-third said 'no'. The remaining 44 per cent either did not know or said it would depend on their husband. Commitment to working was thus, not very great and their expectations concerning their work were not very high.

7.4   EMPLOYERS' PREFERENCE FOR WOMEN

The results reported in this section are based on interviews with a sample of industrial employers. In total, over the period 1977–80, managers in 23 factories employing together about 9000 workers (about one-third of the Mauritian industrial labour force) were interviewed by the author (often a number of times). A special attempt was made to include factories with both male and female production workers as well as factories with male workers doing jobs comparable to those of women in other factories. The person interviewed was either the personnel manager, the chief executive or the production manager, depending on who was most directly involved in the personnel function.

Industrial employers in Mauritius are a very heterogeneous group and many factories are of mixed Mauritian-foreign ownership. It is generally estimated that over half of the capital invested in EPZ has been of Mauritian origin.[11] As regards factory management, the chief executive has tended to be an expatriate in cases where the foreign investor had full or majority ownership, and Mauritian in the opposite case. The foreign managers have come from such diverse places such as Hong Kong, India, North America and various European countries. The Mauritian managers are from different ethnic groups, although the Sino- and Franco-Mauritians are significantly over-represented in this category. The strict control of government on work permits, the availability of trainable Mauritians and the high cost of expatriates have tended to encourage a progressive Mauritianisation of factory staff.

The general operation of the female labour market during the 1970s illustrates convincingly the strength of the employers' preference for women workers. When the EPZ was first started in the early 1970s, the supply of female labour posed no problems. There were long lines of women in search of employment at factory gates; recommendations were solicited from influential people as a means of being selected. The main selection criteria, apart from recommendations, were usually physical robustness and years of formal schooling. Factories had long waiting lists of applicants, and could easily replace any worker who left.

By the latter half of the 1970s the situation had changed dramatically: the supply of women available and willing to work had disappeared, mainly as a result of the rapid expansion of female employment between 1971 and 1976 when many new factories had opened. Employers could no longer pick and choose their workers but had to accept almost any woman who presented herself. Employers reacted in various ways to this new situation, but almost none considered the possibility of using men instead of women. Although they were aware that men were more readily available, and had waiting lists of male candidates, employers went to considerable lengths to continue hiring women.

For example, some employers decentralised their production by putting smaller units in areas where there were fewer factories already established. As would be expected, this situation of scarce supply of labour put pressure on employers to improve working conditions and to increase salaries. Such measures as improved (in a few cases, subsidised) canteen facilities, piped-in music and better transportation facilities were taken as a means of attracting and retaining workers. Starting salaries above the basic minimum began to be offered, as well as more generous piece-rates.

In order to contact potential women recruits, women members of the personnel department in two of the sampled factories went from door to door in nearby areas trying to find new recruits. Another manager invited religious leaders and local dignitaries to the factory so that they could recommend it to appropriate women. In one case, the current employees were offered a bonus for each new woman recruit they brought who stayed more than two months. Another factory even provided some tutoring in arithmetic for new recruits who were not up to the level required but who had been hired for lack of better alternatives. The behaviour of employers demonstrates a strong bias in favour of women workers and in the present section the reasons of this bias, as revealed in employer interviews, will be discussed.

7.4.1 Type of industry

There is no doubt that the type of industry attracted to Mauritius is a factor which favoured the employment of women. Garment and electronics industries tend to be 'feminine' in many countries of Europe and Asia. However, in countries such as Egypt and Turkey, these industries use mainly male labour (Youssef, 1974). In Mauritius, most of the foreign managers and technical advisers came from Europe or Hong Kong and brought with them their belief that this sort of work was more suitable for women because it required manual dexterity rather than physical force. In the case of the garment industry, this belief did not necessarily correspond with the Mauritian traditional division of labour, as male tailors are common and the making of clothes is not considered to be women's work nor an activity which men cannot learn to perform with skill. Nevertheless, the type of industry, combined with employer *a priori* beliefs about the appropriateness of women for these industries, was an important factor in their original preference for women.

In fact, in 1977 women's share of employment in the garment industry (85 per cent) was even greater than the 69 per cent in 1977 in Hong Kong (Hong Kong Census and Statistics Department, 1978) or the 76 per cent in Britain in 1975 (British Department of Employment, 1977).

298   *Industrial Employment in Mauritius*

Clearly, other factors apart from the type of industry, were encouraging employers to use female labour, the most important being the lower minimum wage for women than for men.

7.4.2 Lower wages

Throughout the 1970s, the government has legislated different minimum wages for male and female industrial workers, with the male minimum wage being almost twice that of women (Mauritius has not ratified ILO's Equal Remuneration Convention No. 100 of 1951). The minimum wage legislation is such that a woman worker in her first year of service would have a minimum wage that was 57 per cent that of a male (if he is over 18 years old).[12] This ratio has been relatively stable throughout the 1970s since legislated increases are generally on a percentage basis.

Results of the 1977 survey of women factory workers provide an indication of actual earnings. The median weekly earnings for the week (or pay period) prior to interviewing were about Rs 65[13] as compared to the female minimum of about Rs 50 after the first year of service. These earnings were about equal to the minimum wage for a male under 18 years (which was Rs 66) and less than the minimum wage for a male over 18 (which was Rs 81). Earnings were strongly related to the type job: knitters, who were paid on a productivity basis, were much more likely to be earning above Rs 75 than unskilled workers who were often paid at a fixed rate (31 per cent compared to 8 per cent respectively).

In such a situation, an employer has every interest in maximising the use of female labour, even if women are somewhat less productive than men (which is not so in any case, as is shown below). Given that the government created the EPZ to alleviate the unemployment problem, which was perceived to be basically a male problem, it is interesting to consider the factors responsible for the setting of much lower minimum wages for women.

The practices of the sugar industry tend to dominate Mauritian thinking, and on the plantations there has traditionally been a high sex differential in wages. This differential may be at least partially explained by the tasks done by men on the plantations, where strength was important, and thus men were considered to be more productive than women. In setting the high sex differential in minimum wages for industrial workers, the government and the Wages

Councils were no doubt influenced by the tradition in the sugar industry.

As will be seen, the sex differential in minimum wages for factory workers did not reflect productivity differences, and it is likely that if market forces had been allowed to operate during the 1970s the male industrial wage would have been lower than that set by government and closer or equal to that women. The reasons for the continuation of this differential must be found in the institutional context of Mauritius.

Once a differential has been institutionalised, a positive pressure for change is necessary. No such pressure was forthcoming, as women were and still are considered to be secondary earners and not the breadwinners for the family. Trade unions have never suggested that women should be paid at the same rates as men. The greater financial needs of men are deemed to justify their higher salary. This sentiment that salary should be based on need and not just productivity is strong in Mauritian society. Furthermore, no strong organisation of women or women factory workers emerged to put pressure on government to reduce the sex differential in minimum wages. Because this difference in earnings has always existed, women expect and are prepared to earn less than men.

Employers, on their side, have little interest in taking steps to reduce the differential; any reduction could have been made only by raising women's wages, not by lowering men's. The availability of this less expensive labour force with perceived comparable productivity is an important incentive for investment, as many EPZ industries are based on a favourable wage/productivity ratio. By continuing to set lower minimum wages for women, the government is able to maintain this important incentive.

Although the lower minimum wages of women were an important factor in employer preference for women workers, this importance should not be exaggerated. With the scarcity of female labour during the late 1970s, some factories started offering women recruits initial salaries slightly more than the legal minimum. In one factory, for example, a considerable number of women on piece-rates were earnings more than the male minimum. By the late 1970s, women had developed a reputation among employers as more reliable workers than men, and hence more productive. In addition, women were considered to be more docile and easier to manage than men, and consequently involved lower supervisory costs. These other advantages of female labour will be examined below in more detail.

300   *Industrial Employment in Mauritius*

7.4.3 Lower absenteeism

Leave privileges of Mauritian workers as legislated by the government have always been generous by international standards, and
became even more so during the 1970s. As an illustration, in 1977 any
employee who had worked for 12 consecutive months was entitled
during the next year to the following leave on full pay: 23 public
holidays, 21 days of sick leave, 12 days of annual vacation leave and
two months of maternity leave. Untaken vacation leave must be
reimbursed in cash or can be carried over to the next year under
certain circumstances. For sick leave, a medical certificate is required
only after four consecutive days of absence. This system makes it
costless for workers to take a few days' sick leave, and does not
provide any incentive for not using all 21 days.

As concerns sex differentials in absenteeism, many factory employers have come to the conclusion that men are just as absent as, if
not more so than, women. This conclusion is based on early experiments with male labour in which absentee rates averaged 15–20 per
cent. One factory which used male labour and eventually closed
down claimed weekly rates of absenteeism as high as 50 per cent. The
belief of employers in the greater reliability of women was reinforced
by their perception that women were absent for legitimate reasons
such as illness or family responsibilities whereas men were absent for
'absolutely no good reason'. Mauritian employers would thus concur
with the following comment concerning a similar situation in Jamaica:

> As far as sickness schemes are concerned, they have tended to
> permit the type of absenteeism periodically required by women
> and at the same time encouraged a higher rate of male absenteeism
> than would otherwise have been the case (Standing, 1981, p. 117).

Data collected from sample factories concerning the average percentage of workers who were absent on each day during the month of July
1979 (see Table 7.8) did not support the general management
belief in higher absenteeism among men. The small number of
industries using male labour in jobs similar to those of women made
comparison difficult. Nevertheless, it can be noted that in factories
with a mixed labour force, two had higher rates of absenteeism
among women and one had higher rates for men, but the differences

Catherine Hein   301

TABLE 7.8 *Mean per cent absent[1] daily during the month of July 1979*

	Women		Men	
	% absent	No.	% absent	No.
Mixed labour force	9.3	604	9.6	208
Factor 1	9.3	188	8.6	36
Factor 2[2]	8.5	253	7.4	96
Factor 3	10.2	163	13.4	76
Male only labour force			3.7	360
Factor A			5.0	170
Factor B			2.3	190
Female only labour force	9.2	3579		
Factory M[5]	10.3	485		
Factory N[3]	11.5	200		
Factory O[3]	3.4	108		
Factory X	10.3	231		
Factory Z	7.4	1200		
Factory W	10.0	985		
Factory U	7.1	130		

[1] Workers on sick leave, local leave or who were absent without authorisation were all included as being absent.
[2] Data for women include only selected sections in this factory not entire female work force.
[3] Rural factories.

SOURCE   Factory records.

were small and insignificant. The absenteeism in two factories with only male workers was remarkably low and significantly less than in the factories with only female workers ($X^2 = 12.8$, $p < 0.01$). However, given differences in factory management and type, it cannot be concluded that worker sex is the main reason for this difference in absenteeism.

One leave benefit available to women but not to men is maternity leave, which is often mentioned as a disincentive to the employment of women. However, it does not appear that the two months on full pay at employer cost required by Mauritian law has resulted in any bias against women. First, despite this additional cost, female labour is still relatively cheap compared to men. Second, in any case, the majority of women workers are single and do not use this benefit: in fact they tend to resign at marriage. And third, the workers who are married tend to have few confinements (Hein 1982) and do not necessarily use the maternity benefit three times as permitted by the

302   *Industrial Employment in Mauritius*

law. One employer even thought that maternity leave was a good investment if the women returned subsequently, because women with children were more conscientious workers.

7.4.4 Difficulties with men on night shift

In Mauritius, women are allowed to work nights in EPZ factories but not in other factories[14] However, in practice, very few women have been willing to work nights and employers wishing to operate their factories continuously have been forced to recruit male labour for the night shift.

The initial experiences of employers who have operated a night shift with male workers have been generally negative. Of the five in the current sample, three had abandoned this shift and gave as one of the major reasons the high absenteeism and low productivity of workers on this shift. They also felt that their turnover had been high because of worker difficulties in adapting to a rotating shift schedule. In a fourth factory which employed men for the night shift and women during the day, the manager found that absenteeism and turnover among his male workers were much greater than among the women and concluded that women were more conscientious and reliable than men. In the fifth factory which employed some men on a rotating shift basis, the management was satisfied with their performance, although initially there had been discipline problems during the night shift. Another factory which employed men on rotating shifts, but which was not included in the sample because it had closed down, gave as one of the reasons for its closure high rates of absenteeism, particularly on the night shift.

The refusal of women to work at night and the resulting concentration of male workers in jobs involving night shift may thus be considered as reinforcing male workers' reputation of being less industrious than women. Although women's refusal to work at night has been to their short-term advantage, it is likely that in the longer term, with greater automatisation of factories, and the resulting necessity for 24-hour operation in order to utilise the more expensive equipment, this refusal will work to their disadvantage.

7.4.5   Turnover

The alleged lower turnover of men as compared to women is often cited as a reason for employer preference for men (for example, Chiplin and Sloane, 1974). It is often argued that as employers invest in training of workers, their eventual length of employment is an important determinant of the rate of return on this investment. If employers believe that turnover is likely to be greater among women than men, they will hire men, other things being equal.

Nearly all of the factory employers interviewed showed some concern about turnover of workers. They pointed out that although the initial training period was short (one–three months) and the basic skills acquired fairly quickly, worker productivity continued to improve, both in terms of quantity and quality, well beyond the initial training period. When all training costs were taken into account in terms of payment of wages, use of machines, wasted raw materials and supervisory time, they were substantial. Furthermore, recruitment of new workers involved certain costs, especially when female labour became scarce in the mid-1970s. Turnover of new recruits was notably high and in one factory where detailed figures were available, it was necessary to start with about four new recruits in order to have one trained worker by the end of six months. Thus although employer concern about turnover was admittedly less in the case of shop-floor workers than for skilled or supervisory workers, it was far from completely lacking.

Employers' impressions concerning sex differentials in turnover were less clear-cut than those concerning absenteeism. They thought that women left to get married, have babies, but men were more impulsive and more likely to be attracted to other employment (in particular, government 'relief' work with somewhat less pay but much shorter working hours).

Turnover data collected by the author tend to support the employer impression of little difference between women and men. Table 7.9 shows the total turnover during 1979 in 10 factories by the sex of the workers. If the two factories with only male workers are compared with those with only female workers, there is, overall, no significant difference in turnover. In factories with a mixed labour force, turnover is consistently less among men but differences are small and are significant only in Factory 3 ($X^2 = 4.4$, $p < 0.05$).

The variability in turnover among factories is very high, and much greater than any sex differential. Clearly other factors related to the

304   *Industrial Employment in Mauritius*

TABLE 7.9 *Turnover¹ of shop-floor workers during 1979*

	Women		Men	
	%	No.	%	No.
Mixed factories	95	633	81	238
Factory 1	35	190	25	40
Factory 2²	77	295	73	120
Factory 3	175	148	145	78
Male only factories			70	370
Factory A			65	170
Factory B			74	200
Female only factories	70	2370		
Factory M³	31	495		
Factory N³	58	200		
Factory X	85	230		
Factory Y	130	1200		

[1] Turnover was calculated by dividing the total number of workers who left the factory during the year by the average number of workers employed during the years. No distinction was made between voluntary and involuntary leavers, as employer figures do not usually make this distinction.

[2] Data for women includes only selected sections in the factory, not an entire female workforce.

[3] Rural factories.

SOURCE Factory records for 1979.

factory and its environment influence turnover to a much greater extent that the sex of the workers.

7.4.6 Relative docility of women

Employer's belief in the relative docility and submissiveness of women as compared to men is an important factor in their preference for women workers. The expressions used by employers to describe this characteristic were diverse: women are 'more serious', 'more conscientious', 'more hardworking', 'more submissive', 'more placid', 'less troublesome'. In all, eight of the 23 employers interviewed mentioned these sorts of qualities of women workers, particularly those who had first-hand experience of male workers. Whom would they get to supervise male workers? How would they deal with all the problems of discipline? Women, they felt, were so much easier to manage. They did not join unions and complain as men but quietly got on with their work. This belief in the relative docility of women was expressed in a local employers' journal where one author (Boullé, 1976) wrote: 'One cannot count on men for EPZ industries as they do not seem to be capable of submitting themselves to industrial discipline'.

Employers appreciate the quality of docility because it facilitates the supervision of the workforce. In nearly all the factories where women constitute the majority of workers, the first-line supervisor, often called 'lead girl' or 'forewoman', is a worker who has been promoted from the ranks. She is chosen because of her educational level and her skilfulness or 'personality'. She is given almost no training for her new role as most factories do not have staff with the time or the competence to conduct such training. Although women workers would accept the authority of a man, in a few factories which had male foremen there have been complaints from the women workers about coarse language and sexual harassment, which reinforced the employer belief in the merits of segregation. One of the advantages of female supervisors, mentioned by one manager, was the promotion of a 'moral' image of the factory which was particularly desirable in periods of female labour shortage.

Despite the obvious weakness of the current system for selection and training of forewomen, managers thought that it was adequate as long as they continued to employ women workers. On the other hand, male labour would require changes and additional costs, either because of the salaries they would have to pay for male foremen with appropriate supervisory experience, or because of the management time required to train male supervisors. It would be unthinkable to use the existing women supervisors, as men would not accept the authority of women. Most factories currently operating with a female labour force would thus probably continue to do so even if there were now no sex differential in minimum wages.

7.5 CONCLUSIONS AND POLICY IMPLICATIONS

This study had described the factors in Mauritius which are related to the high participation of women in industry in particular in labour-intensive export-processing industries. The Government of Mauritius set up the EPZ in the early 1970s as a means of reducing unemployment which was perceived as basically a male problem. Within the

Mauritian economy, this is the only sector where significant numbers of new jobs have been created since the mid-1970s, while employment has been shrinking in such key sectors as agriculture and construction.

Yet the operation of the labour market during the 1970s has been such that the employment created has gone mainly to women, and women's share of industrial employment and of formal sector employment as a whole has continually increased. Few women reported themselves as unemployed at the 1972 Population Census, but a considerable number were in fact available for work when the opportunity arose. This phenomenon shows the influence of employment opportunities on women's labour force participation rates, and the error in assuming that inactive women who are not officially looking for work are not available for work.

It is perhaps ironic that the starting point for understanding the operation of the industrial labour market in Mauritius must be the low status of women within the society and the general discounting of their economic role.[15] In terms of institutions, this is reflected in the lower minimum wages for women. This sex differential in minimum wages has been a key factor in employers' choice to hire women since industries attracted to EPZs are mainly labour-intensive ones with labour being an important part of their valued added in Mauritius.

In Mauritius, it is considered normal that women do not earn as much as men in comparable jobs because they are not the breadwinners for the family, and their needs are thus less. This mentality, which is also shared by women, means that they do not expect to earn as much as men and are willing to accept that women's jobs do not pay as well as men's. Also the fact that many women see working as a temporary phase in their lives means that they are less concerned than men about the intrinsic interest of their work and its long-term prospects.

Employer's appreciation of women workers for their docility can also be related to the position of women within the family. In all religious groups, the father is considered the main authority figure within the family and women are accordingly accustomed to being in a subordinate position. The greater restrictions on women's movements and social contacts are also a factor which has meant that they appreciate the factory as a place for meeting their peers, and this may facilitate their adaptation to factory work.

As a result of the low status of women within Mauritian society, the newly-created industrial sector has thus become a female preserve. If minimum wages for men and women had been the same as from the beginning of the industrial expansion of the 1970s, it is almost certain that more tasks would have been alloted to men from the beginning of industrialisation as compared to the number that actually were. Now that women have gained access to these jobs and proved their relative reliability and productivity, the important question is whether their earnings will become more comparable to those of men in similar work. There was some tendency in this direction, but not enough to make any firm conclusions.

The existence of minimum wages which are lower for women than for men is a case of sex discrimination and against the principle of equal pay for work of equal value. However, the only government action which might be politically acceptable would be to raise women's minimum wage rates to be closer to those of men.[16] But given the importance of labour costs for EPZ industries, such a measure might result in the closure of some factories and discourage future investment. In any case, since higher rates for men are generally accepted as fair within the society (even by the women) little political advantage would result from such action.

As concerns the process of occupational segregation by sex, the results suggest two remarks concerning employer behaviour:

(1) Employer beliefs on which their actions are based do not necessarily correspond with current facts as measured by economists or social scientists, and may be based on hearsay or past experiences which are out of date. This conclusion may appear to be obvious common sense, yet economists' models of employer behaviour tend to assume that employers have complete and accurate information on variables affecting worker productivity.

(2) Although employers are aware that their beliefs about the qualities of male and female workers do not apply to all men and to all women, there is a kind of 'statistical discrimination' which is occurring (i.e. hiring women because on average they are thought likely to be better workers than men).[17] However, this discrimination is not at the level of individual recruitment of particular candidates but rather in the decision concerning which sex will be hired for various sections and jobs with the factory. Mauritian employers tend to avoid mixing sexes within the factory environment, and so decisions concerning sex of workers are generally made before recruitment.

308   *Industrial Employment in Mauritius*

Sex segregation of occupations is often to the disadvantage of women because they are restricted to occupations with low wages and little opportunity for advancement. However, in the Mauritian context, where almost one-third of all employees work as agricultural labourers and male unemployment is high, industrial jobs are relatively good jobs. The result of the survey of women factory workers show that they consider their jobs as an improvement on the traditional female occupations of domestic servant or agricultural labourer, and (for single workers) as an improvement on staying at home and helping with household tasks. Men were also attracted to factory work, but few were actually hired by the factories.

Nevertheless, it should be noted that one important problem of Mauritian women in industrial employment is that of physical fatigue. This problem appears to be more important for Mauritian workers than for those in Europe and is probably related to their nutritional status. In developing countries, the diets of workers cannot be assumed to be reasonably adequate and poor nutrition of workers may increase absenteeism and turnover and reduce productivity. The employer has thus an interest in improving the nutrition of workers, although finding means which are both practical and acceptable to the workers can be difficult. Such measures as subsidised canteens and provision of milk drinks were being tried with varying success by some Mauritian factories and detailed examination of the problems encountered and the results of such attempts would be merited on the basis of the fatigue problem.

Furthermore, ways of reducing the physical effort required by workers in the garment and electronics industries should be investigated. One possible solution is automation but since this usually involves operating the factory 24 hours a day in order for the investment to be profitable, women tend to be excluded because of their difficulties in working at night. Also for work which involves mainly machine minding, employers tend to believe that men are more suitable than women. In any case, automation tends to reduce the number of jobs in industry and therefore, other intermediate solutions to the problem of fatigue need to be found.

Overall, it is difficult to make a judgement concerning the high female participation in industry in Mauritius. While foreigners may be quick to condemn the salaries and working conditions of Mauritian women in EPZ industries such as the Swiss politician Ziegler (1976, p. 37) who calls them 'scandalous', this opinion is not shared by the workers themselves. At the same time, the workers' opinion can be understood as emanating from the subordinate position of women within the society. The concentration of women in industry does involve the exploitation of a weaker socio-economic group, yet it has provided women with an opportunity to increase their participation in the modern formal sector of the economy.

NOTES

1. The reasearch reported in this chapter was conducted while the author was senior lecturer in Social Psychology at the University of Mauritius. the author thanks Margaret Peil and Richard Anker for comments on earlier drafts.
2. Mauritius is a small island in the Indian Ocean, with a population of just under 1 million and a population density of about 470 inhabitants per square kilometre.
3. There was no indigenous population on the island when French settlement started in 1722. About two-thirds of current inhabitants are descendants of indentured labourers who were brought from India by the plantation owners during the 19th century. The remaining third of the population includes descendants of French settlers and African slaves, mainly persons of mixed origin, as well as a small Chinese community. Currently the Mauritian population is composed of three main ethno-religious groups – Hindus (52 per cent), Muslims (17 per cent) and Christians (30 per cent).
4. The 1972 Population Census is the most recent published census as the result for the 1983 census are not yet available.
5. For comparison purposes, the figures for clerical workers in 1962 have been modified to include traffic controllers, postmen and telephone, operators, who were classified with 'workers in transport and communication' in 1962 but with clerical workers in 1972.
6. The EPZ does not correspond to a geographical area but refers to a collection of bonded factories which are declared 'export processing zones'.
7. The number of men employed declined between 1977 and 1982 particularly in government 'relief' work, where there were about 14 000 employees in 1977 and 6000 in 1982.
8. The field work was financed by the Ministry of Economic Planning Development of the Government of Mauritius.
9. The 57 factories which attained the criteria employed in total 15 270 women thus accounting for 90 per cent of the women in the manufacturing sector in 1977. Prior to selection, factories were stratified by location (three areas) and type of factory (knitting, sewing and other). One of the factories selected would not co-operate and was replaced by the next one on the list.
10. The work week in all but one of the factories sampled was 45 hours spread over five or six days. In the one factory which operated on two

310   *Industrial Employment in Mauritius*

shifts, a few workers complained that after the late shift they had difficulties returning to their home from where they were dropped by the company bus, and these complaints were also classified as 'hours of work'. The problem of women travelling after dark to homes some distance from main roads caused difficulties of recruitment and turnover for this factory.

11. The secretary-general of the Mauritius Chamber of Commerce and Industry estimated that 55 per cent of EPZ capital was Mauritian in a public lecture in 1978.

12. The Mauritian legislation on minimum wages for factory workers specifies the minimum wage for women by length of service and for men by age. For example, in 1977 when this survey was conducted, minimum wages in rupees per week were:

Women, first year of service	46.20
Thereafter	49.80
Men under 18 years	66.30
Over 18 years	81.00

13. In 1977, the Mauritian rupee was worth approximately US$0.15.

14. It can be noted that Mauritius has not ratified the ILO Night Work (Women) Convention (No. 89).

15. See Elson and Pearson (1981) for a more general discussion of the link between women's subordination and their employment in world market factories. They suggest (as in the current chapter) that this 'exploitation of women as wage workers is parasitic upon their subordination as a gender' (p. 157) and further argue that 'rather than ending subordination, entry into wage work tends to transform it' (p. 161).

16. Since this chapter was written, the Government of Mauritius has abolished the minimum wage for male workers in EPZ industries while continuing a minimum for women in an effort to encourage the employment of men.

17. This phenomenon is usually invoked to explain employer tendencies to favour male rather than female workers and to discriminate against racial minorities (see Phelps (1972)).

BIBLIOGRAPHY

Beckford, G. L. (1972) *Persistent poverty: Underdevelopment in plantation economies of the Third World* (New York: Oxford University Press).

Boserup. E. (1970) *Women's role in economic development* (New York: St Martin Press).

Boullé, P. L. (1976) 'La zone franche a-t-elle un avenir?', in *Bulletin of the Public Relations Office of the Sugar Industry* (Mauritius) no. 91.

British Department of Employment (1977) *British Labour Statistics Yearbook 1975* (London: HMSO).

Central Statistical Office (1971–1983) *Biannual Survey of Employment and Earnings in Large Establishments* (Port Louis: Government Printer).

Central Statistical Office (1975) *1972 Housing and Population Census of Mauritius* (Port Louis: Government Printer).

_____ (1978) *Biannual Survey of Employment by Occupation in Large Establishments (March–June 1977)* (Pout Louis: Government Printer).

Chiplin, B. and P. J. Sloane (1974) 'Sexual discrimination in the labor market', in *British Journal of Industrial Relations*, Nov, vol. XII, no. 3, pp. 371–402.

Elson, D. and R. Pearson (1981) 'The subordination of women and the internationalisation of factory production', in Young, K. C. Wolkowitz and R. McCullagh (eds) *Of marriage and the market* (London: CSE Books).

Government of Mauritius (1971) *Five-year plan 1971–75* (Port Louis: Government Printer).

Government of Mauritius, Ministry of Economic Planning and Development (1978) *Economic review 1975–77* (Port Louis: Government Printer).

Hein, C. (1982) *Factory employment, marriage and fertility: The case of Mauritian women* (Geneva: ILO) mimeographed World Employment Programme research working paper; restricted.

Hong Kong Census and Statistics Department (1978) *Hong Kong Annual Digest of Statistics* (Hong Kong).

National Economic Development Office (1972) *What the girls think* (London: NEDO, Millbank Tower).

Peerbaye, G. H. (1979) *A survey of the dietary intake of Export Processing Zone female workers* (Port Louis: Mauritius Institute of Management).

Peil, M. (1979) 'Urban women in the labour force', in *Sociology of Work and Occupation*, vol. 6, no. 4, pp. 482–502.

Phelps, E. S. (1972) 'The statistical theory of racism and sexism', in *American Economic Review*, Sept, vol. 62, pp. 659–61.

Reynolds, L. G. and P. Gregory, (1965) *Wages, productivity and industrialisation in Puerto Rico* (Homewood, Illinois: Richard D. Irwin).

Safa, H. I. (1980) *Export processing and female employment: The search for cheap labour* paper for Burg Wartenstein Symposium no. 85 (New York: Warner-Gren Foundation for Anthropological Research).

Salaff, J. W. and A. K. Wong (1977) 'Chinese women at work: Work commitment and fertility in the Asian setting', in Kupinsky, S. (ed.) *The fertility of working women* (New York, Praeger Publishers).

Standing, Guy (1981) *Unemployment and female labour: A study of labour supply in Kingston, Jamaica* (London: Macmillan).

Wild, R. (1979) 'Job needs, job satisfaction and job behaviour of women manual workers', in *Journal of Applied Psychology*, vol. 54, no. 2, pp. 157–62.

Youssef, N. H. (1974) *Women and work in developing societies* Population Monograph Series no. 15. Berkeley, Institute of International Studies (University of California Press).

_____ 1976–7. 'Education and female modernism in the Muslim world', in *Journal of International Affairs*, Fall/Winter, vol. 30, no. 2, pp. 191–210.

Ziegler, J. (1976) *Une Suisse au-dessus de tout soupcon* (Paris: Seuil).

[9]

Review of Radical Political Economics   Vol. 22(1)115-134(1990)

Transition to Export-Led Growth in Turkey: Is There a Feminization of Employment?

Nilüfer Çağatay and Günseli Berik

This paper uses the case of Turkey to examine the thesis that employment in manufacturing industry is feminized with the shift from import-substituting industrialization to export-led growth in the context of structural adjustment policies. Focusing on large-scale manufacturing industry, we find that in both public and private sectors and under both industrialization strategies the gender composition of manufacturing employment is explained by technological characteristics and the degree of export-orientation of establishments. Hence, the shift to export-led growth has been achieved without an accompanying or subsequent feminization of employment.

INTRODUCTION

There is growing evidence that economies that are implementing orthodox structural adjustment and stabilization policies are dismantling labor regulations, curtailing workers' rights and changing the conditions of employment. This process of labor reregulation enables employers to achieve lower unit labor costs necessary to enhance their international competitiveness by lowering real wages and by informalizing and decentralizing employment.[1] It is widely held that as such employment conditions traditionally associated with "women's work" become generalized, a feminization of employment, through the relative and absolute growth in the use of women's labor and the substitution of women for men workers is occurring (cf. Standing 1989). Indeed, many case studies of export-led industrialization (ELI) that reveal the association of growth of exports of manufactured goods and growth in female industrial employment on the basis of lower unit labor costs of women relative to men lend support to this argument (Joekes 1986, ILO 1985, Cho and Koo 1983, Hein 1984).

While one key component of the orthodox model is the attack on labor costs to achieve competitiveness, a feminization of employment, in the sense of an increase in the share of female employment, may not accompany this process. State policies may enhance the competitiveness and profitability of export-oriented manufacturing by providing incentives to export-oriented

We thank Lourdes Beneria, Ruth Pearson and Hugo Radice for comments on this paper and Korkut Ertürk for suggestions on an earlier draft. We also thank Mehmet Köymen and David Kucera for their skillful research assistance on this project. The usual disclaimers apply.

manufacturing enterprises, while at the same time setting an upper limit to the female share of employment in line with patriarchal imperatives (Pyle 1990); or, as we argue in this paper, competitiveness can be achieved by labor reregulation and repression.

The main objective of this paper is to examine the implications of the changes in industrialization strategy for the gender composition and segregation of employment by using Turkey as a case study.[2] For the Turkish economy, 1980 was marked by a shift from import-substituting industrialization (ISI) to ELI. This shift occurred in the context of structural adjustment policies which entailed a general lowering of labor standards, severe restrictions on union activity, significant deterioration of real wages, persistent unemployment and moves towards privatization of public manufacturing enterprises (Çağatay 1990, OECD 1990). Our investigation, focusing on large-scale manufacturing industry, shows that export-orientation has been achieved without a relative growth of women's employment, with a possible growth of women's employment occurring outside large establishments, through homeworking.

Our second objective is to develop a disaggregated and multivariate methodology for investigating changes in women's position relative to men in manufacturing employment during the industrialization process. We investigate econometrically a set of hypotheses concerning the gender composition of employment at the 3-digit manufacturing industry level through both the ISI and ELI periods. This analysis also distinguishes between private and public manufacturing sectors and examines the effect of the shift in industrialization strategy on the female share of employment in manufacturing industries.

In the following sections, first we discuss the literature on women and industrialization in the Third World and identify hypotheses concerning employment patterns by gender to be tested in the Turkish case. Secondly, we present an overview of the characteristics of Turkish industrialization, the shift in industrialization strategy and the adoption of structural adjustment policies in the post-1980 period. Thirdly, we examine the implications of each industrialization strategy and the shift in strategy for the gender composition and segregation of employment.

INDUSTRIALIZATION STRATEGIES AND GENDER COMPOSITION OF EMPLOYMENT IN THE THIRD WORLD

In the last two decades there have emerged two consecutive sets of literature which evaluate changes in women's relative position during the industrialization process, one focusing on the experience of ISI in Latin American economies and the other on ELI, especially in East Asian economies. Building upon Boserup's argument (1970), the earlier studies emphasize women's marginalization from modern manufacturing employment, while the more recent studies focus on the integration of women into manufacturing employment in the course of industrialization.

Case studies on the Latin American experience of post-World War II industrialization process document the slow growth of women's manufacturing employment, which is widely attributed to the strategy of ISI (Chinchilla 1977, Schmink 1978, Saffioti 1978, de Miranda 1977). The capital-intensive nature of the technology transferred by the multinational firms under ISI is claimed to absorb only a small proportion of the labor force and increase the availability of skilled jobs, which are filled by men (Chaney and Schmink 1976). The latter is implied to be the outcome of the lower skill levels possessed by women workers, as evidenced by their lower educational attainment relative to men.[3]

Studies of the last decade focus on the post-1960s East Asian industrial growth, which was fuelled primarily by the growth of export markets. ELI was partly accompanied by the relocation of labor-intensive manufacturing industry or processes from developed to developing economies. This trend was attributed to technological development, which has fragmented and standardized production processes and resulted in deskilling, which in turn results in increased female employment.

The high and growing proportion of women in export-oriented as well as labor-intensive sectors of manufacturing industry is attributed to the lower unit labor costs attained with female workers than with male workers. This cost advantage results from the lower wage rates of women and their reliability, stability and flexibility relative to male workers (cf. Anker and Hein 1986, Elson and Pearson 1981, Safa 1981, Joekes 1985, ILO 1985).[4] An additional reason for women's concentration in labor-intensive manufacturing is their exclusion from continuous production processes associated with capital-intensive techniques of production due to protective legislation or their reproductive responsibilities, which create disadvantages for women in shift/night work (Joekes 1986).

While the earlier studies emphasize the marginalization of women by exclusion from capitalist development and industrialization, this later vintage of studies emphasizes women's marginalization by inclusion and segregation into labor-intensive sectors with "low wages" and "low skills." We refer to these two approaches as the "Female Marginalization 1" (FM1) and "Female Marginalization 2" (FM2) theses[5] and identify two components of these theses. The first pertains to the direction of changes in gender composition of employment during the course of an industrialization strategy, on which the two theses differ. While the proponents of the FM1 thesis posit a defeminization of employment during ISI, the FM2 discussions posit a feminisation of employment during ELI. The second component pertains to the industrial characteristics of sectors in which women tend to be concentrated within each industrialization strategy, on which the two theses contain identical hypotheses.[6] First, the implicit connection between the type of technology and skill requirements of the labor force in the FM2 literature is identical to the one posited by the proponents of FM1: capital-intensive production processes require skilled labor and labor-intensive ones use unskilled labor. Secondly, the association between the skill requirement of the technology and the gender composition of the labor force is also identical: women constitute the unskilled and men the skilled labor force. Thirdly, country studies informed by either approach imply that women will be concentrated in the export-oriented as well as the relatively unskilled sectors of the manufacturing industry. Finally, both sets of literature assign multinational corporations (MNCs) a significant role in determining patterns of employment by sex, which gives the impression that the presence of MNCs is a sine qua non of the implementation of either industrialization strategy.[7]

There are studies contradicting these somewhat stylized arguments about women's manufacturing employment in the Third World. First, the association of increased female employment with export-oriented industrialization is not universal. Pyle (1990), for example, argues that in Ireland state policy attempted to limit the growth of female share of manufacturing in export-oriented enterprises by awarding financial incentives to those enterprises that proposed to employ fewer women workers. The policy was effective in achieving the target male proportion of employment (75 per cent), at least in the early part of the 1970s. Humphrey (1987) and Beneria and Roldan (1987) observe that the dramatic growth of women's share of manufacturing employment in the seventies in Brazil and Mexico City, respectively, is not limited to export-oriented industries and firms. Secondly, a few studies suggest that the growing proportion of women's employment in manufacturing may be associated with the upswing of the cycle and may not represent a trend, suggesting reversibility of the growth of women's employment in manufacturing under export-led industrialization (Joekes 1986, 26-27).[8] Thirdly, the experience of countries which have successfully implemented export-oriented industrialization (e.g. South Korea) suggests that as ELI proceeds there may be a reversal of the trend in increasing share of female employment accompanied by reskilling and greater mechanization (Joekes 1986, 42).

The FM1 and FM2 literatures leave a number of issues unexamined, which our investigation of the Turkish case will take into account.

1)While both sets of literature posit that women are employed in industries which have the same characteristics (such as low capital-intensity, high export-orientation or low skill-intensity of a sector), neither distinguishes between the separate effects of industrial characteristics and the macroeconomic shifts of policy on the gender composition of manufacturing employment. Is the impact of each of the industrial characteristics on gender composition of employment affected by the shift in industrialization strategy, and if so, is the change towards a feminization or defeminization of employment? These questions remain unexamined, partly because studies do not examine shifts per se but focus on trends within each type of strategy.[9]

There are a number of mechanisms through which macroeconomic shifts and structural adjustment policies could lead to feminization of employment. First, shifts in industrialization strategy imply changes in the incentive structures in an economy, which by their effects on relative profitability and costs across sectors might affect gender composition of employment. For example, giving incentives to export-oriented industries might spur the relative growth of such industries and bring about a rise in aggregate female share of manufacturing employment, to the extent that women are already concentrated in these industries. Secondly, shifts in industrialization strategy might be induced by a balance of payments crisis and a structural adjustment program. In this case, the incomes policies that accompany a structural adjustment program might again have implications for the gender composition of employment by inducing more women to enter paid employment. Thirdly, macroeconomic policy changes could also include changes in social policy that roll back protective legislation for women as part of the reduction in labor standards in the economy. This could make it more advantageous for employers to hire women, given their lower wages.[10] On the other hand, there are reasons why feminization of employment may not occur as a result of macroeconomic policy changes. For example, feminization of employment may not be forthcoming, if gender-typing of industries is resistant to changes in cost structure or other incentives, especially when the cost advantage of women over male workers is narrowed by repressive labor policies.

2) Both sets of FM literature tend to conflate the three characteristics of industries women tend to be concentrated in: low skill-intensity, high labor-intensity, and export-orientation. Sectors that have a high proportion of labor classified as unskilled are also thought to be labor-intensive and export-oriented, giving rise to the impression that women's over representation in export-oriented industries is due to the characteristics of Third World exports. However, export-orientation of a sector might play an independent role in the gender composition of employment of a sector. This independent effect may result from different pricing strategies associated with producing for the international versus the domestic market. Çağatay (1986) shows that in Turkey under ISI international competition had a disciplining effect on both the wages and the profitability of an industry. This implies that there may be greater incentives for export-oriented industries to employ more women workers who are generally paid lower wages to withstand the price competition in international markets.

3)Studies of gender composition of manufacturing employment do not distinguish between private and public manufacturing. Nor do the recent discussions of the global move toward privatization and cuts in public spending (for example, Standing 1989) sufficiently recognize the role of the public sector as an industrial employer. If the issue is addressed at all, by "public sector" authors usually refer to public service employment, or at most, to employment in government offices (i.e. civil servants). As defined, the public sector is observed to offer better wages and employment conditions for women and account for a larger female share of employment than the private sector (Anker and Hein 1986, 47, 84; Anker and Hein 1985, 77; Standing 1989, 1087). Given these favorable employment conditions for women workers, the implication of privatization and cuts in public spending is grim. The severity of adverse effects depends on the type of cuts put into effect (i.e. severe, if there are larger cuts in health and educational services, where women's share of employment tends to be high, Standing 1989, 1087).

Ibrahim (1989) is an exception in recognizing that in many developing countries the public sector is a significant employer in industry and agriculture, and not just in services. She observes that the public sector is superior to the private sector in terms of conditions of employment, wages and benefits for women workers, on grounds that the former enterprises are more closely supervised by labor ministries and are more responsive to social welfare concerns than the private sector (Ibrahim 1989, 1101). However, one could foresee circumstances under which the public sector may not be so favorable to women. In many cases, jobs in the public sector are allocated through patron-client relationships, which tend to be more advantageous to men than women since women are less integrated into political networks than men. Secondly, as Ibrahim implies, weakening government commitment to labor standards and a shrinking public sector may reverse the favorable conditions for women workers in public enterprises. For an adequate evaluation of the implications of the decline or outright privatization of public manufacturing enterprises (as distinct from public services) for gender inequalities in employment in many Third World economies, however, a systematic consideration of gender composition and segregation of employment and the relative conditions of pay and work in public versus private enterprises is essential.

4)Another issue that remains relatively unexplored in both sets of literature is the question of whether women tend to be concentrated in smaller manufacturing enterprises. Recent studies indicate employer resistance to hiring women workers where legislation requires that employers provide a child care facility in the workplace, if they employ more than a certain number of women employees (Anker and Hein 1985, 78). By increasing the costs of hiring over a certain number of women, such legislation may effectively set a limit on the number of women workers employed in large enterprises, hence leading to the association of female employment with smaller enterprises.

INDUSTRIALIZATION STRATEGIES AND
LABOR POLICIES IN TURKEY

The ISI period in the Turkish economy began in 1961 and was characterized by medium-term planning, protectionism, significant involvement of the state in the industrial sector and populist politics, which allowed trade unions to flourish and become an important factor in determining the distribution of urban income. The ISI strategy of the 1960s and 1970s resulted in rapid growth of manufacturing, which grew at an average annual rate of 10.2 per cent between 1963 and 1977. The share of manufactured goods in exports increased from an average of 20.6 per cent in 1963-65 to 31.2 per cent in 1978-1980. In spite of this, agriculture still accounted for 60.4 per cent of employment and 21.7 per cent of GDP in 1980, while for manufacturing the corresponding figures were 10.8 per cent and 22.3 per cent, respectively. At the same time, Turkey remained a relatively closed economy throughout this period, with exports and imports accounting for 5.2 per cent and 11.8 per cent of GDP, respectively, in 1980. During this period, public investment together with Turkish private investment in manufacturing built an industrial base without a significant presence of MNCs.

In 1977, Turkey started to experience an economic crisis which manifested itself in the form of a foreign exchange shortage, which led to negative growth rates in GDP in 1979 and 1980. The ISI era ended in January 1980 with the adoption of a stabilization package. The political crisis and political divisions accompanying the economic crisis since 1977 worsened, and in September 1980 the military removed the civilian government from power while keeping the architect of the stabilization program, Turgut Ozal, in charge of economic policy. The policies which have been implemented since 1980 contain the familiar elements of sharp devaluation of currency, import liberalization, encouragement of exports by heavy subsidies, tax rebates and credits, liberalization of financial markets, curtailment of domestic demand by an incomes policy, moves toward privatization and incentives (such as the establishment of export processing zones) to attract foreign direct investment.

These policies resulted in the restoration of positive growth rates in GDP, and an impressive growth in exports, initially during a period of sluggish world markets, despite trade barriers from industrialized countries and intense competition in the standardized labor-intensive commodity markets in which Turkey competes. Moreover, the composition of GDP and exports changed favorably toward manufactured goods which accounted for 25.1 per cent of GDP and 75.3 per cent of exports by 1985 (up from 22.3 and 36 per cent, respectively, in 1980). In the 1980s, Turkey became an outward-oriented economy with the share of exports in GDP increasing from 5.2 per cent in 1980 to 14.3 per cent in 1985 (OECD various years).[11]

In the early 1980s, Turkey was frequently cited as a "successful" case of structural adjustment by international agencies. The other side of the success story was the distributive consequences of liberalization policies, the cost of which was borne disproportionately by wage earners.[12] The fall in wages was achieved as a result of the repression of the labor movement in the aftermath of the military coup of 1980. Even though a civilian government took over in 1983, one result of the coup was the suspension of the rights to collective bargaining and strike between 1980 and 1983 and the suspension of the activities of several confederations of trade unions. During this period, an arbitration board oversaw wage increases which were consistently granted at a lower rate than the ensuing high rates of inflation. Legislation introduced in 1983 made it more difficult for workers to unionize, bargain collectively and strike compared to the pre-1980 period. As for unemployment rates, the restoration of GDP growth rate to positive levels after 1981, did not result in lower unemployment rates during the 1980s.[13]

Policies with regard to labor, in combination with export incentives and devaluation, played an important role in the achievement of the export drive since price competition was the basic competitive mechanism for Turkey's labor-intensive and standardized merchandise exports, such as apparel and textiles. The fall in wages also constituted a crucial link between the microeconomic and macroeconomic aspects of stabilization and structural adjustment. Domestic demand was kept in check to make goods available for external markets. The falling wages also kept unit labor costs low and countered the adverse effects of devaluation and increased interest rates on domestic costs. Reductions in the labor costs of public enterprises (and public sector wages in general) became one instrument for controlling public spending. Growth was thus restored at high social costs.

Even though structural adjustment policies included encouragement of foreign investment and eventual privatization of manufacturing industry, foreign investment did not register any remarkable increases in the first half of 1980s and the public sector has continued to have a significant presence (OECD, 1990).[14] During the 1980s, however, price controls on public sector establishments were partially abandoned while labor costs in such enterprises were lowered. Thus, their operation practices became similar to private establishments in terms of being subject to profitability criteria, i.e. the public enterprises were "rationalized."

The Turkish case of structural adjustment shows a general deterioration of labor standards for all workers in the 1980s. Whether or not this was accompanied by a feminization of employment in the economy as a whole or in large-scale manufacturing industry, is the question that we take up next.

TRENDS IN GENDER COMPOSITION
AND SEGREGATION OF EMPLOYMENT

In the course of both ISI and ELI, women constituted a relatively constant share of the economically active population in Turkey, their share declining by only 4 percentage points to 36.9 per cent between 1960 and 1985.[15] Between 1960 and 1985, close to 90 per cent of these women remained in the agricultural sector, and the overwhelming majority of the women in agriculture were unpaid family workers (93 per cent in 1985). In the same period, manufacturing's share of women's employment remained relatively constant at around 4.4 per cent.[16] Relative to the distribution of women across economic sectors, a lower proportion of men are in agriculture (43.2 per cent in 1985) and a higher proportion of men are in manufacturing (14.2 per cent in 1985).

In manufacturing industry, we observe a similar relative constancy of women's share of employment. According to population census data, during the ISI period, the female share of manufacturing employment initially increased, growing from 16.26 per cent in 1960 to 22.51 per cent in 1970, and subsequently declined to 15.36 per cent by 1980. In 1985 this share was 15.21 per cent.

Annual manufacturing survey data, which covers only large establishments (with 10 or more workers), also indicates a constancy of the female share in manufacturing employment around 18.5 per cent through both the ISI and ELI periods, albeit around a higher proportion than in the population census data due to differing coverage of the two data sources. Therefore, aggregate manufacturing employment statistics do not reveal an exclusion or marginalization in the sense of secular decline in the aggregate female share of employment as implied by the FM1 thesis, but a fluctuating behavior throughout the ISI period. Neither do they reveal a feminization of employment as implied by the FM2 thesis, at least in the early years of the shift.

However, with regard to trends in gender composition of employment, aggregate manufacturing industry data conceal more than they reveal. First, as in other countries, population census and manufacturing survey data in Turkey disguise the extent of female employment, since they underrecord much of homeworking and other informal activities, especially by women. Secondly, the aggregate data conceal differences between public and private components of manufacturing industry.

As regards the former, the 1988 Urban Household Labor Force Survey (SIS 1990) suggests that the underestimation of women's employment by population censuses and manufacturing surveys may be severe. The survey results indicate that the expected growth in women's labor force participation rates induced by the incomes policy of the 1980s has indeed occurred (with the urban female labor force participation rate increasing from 11.2 to 16.9

per cent between 1982 and 1988). However, during this period, the urban unemployment rate for women remained nearly three times as high as men's, reaching 28.4 per cent for women and 9.8 per cent for men in 1988 (SIS 1990, 12). In addition, according to this survey, in 1988, 30 per cent of women employed in manufacturing industry were homeworkers. The lack of comparable data on homeworkers for the late 1970s makes it impossible to assess the changes in the extent of homeworking with the outward-orientation of the economy. However, recent studies on Turkey suggest that working class households, which were hit hard by the decline in real wages in the post-1980 period, are striving to make ends meet through women's participation in homeworking geared to the export market (Çinar 1988). This was another consequence of the export drive and structural adjustment policies.

Secondly, the breakdown of the manufacturing survey data into their private and public components shows that large-scale private establishments during both industrialization strategies employed relatively more women than public establishments (Table 1). The female share of employment in the private sector remained relatively constant at a higher level than in the public sector during both the ISI and ELI periods, thereby giving rise to the constancy for all large manufacturing establishments. Except in 1966 (when women's share of public sector manufacturing employment was 18.4 per cent), this share did not exceed 14.9 per cent between 1964 and 1985, while in the private sector it remained around 20 per cent. Hence, in contrast to observations on the public sector elsewhere, in Turkey the public manufacturing establishments employed fewer women and the differences between the public and private establishments in this respect became slightly more pronounced during the ELI period.

According to the results of the 1985-1986 Manpower Training and Requirements Survey (SIS 1986), this divergence between the public and private sectors is likely to become more pronounced in the future. An interesting feature of this Survey is that, in addition to determining the actual gender composition of manufacturing employment, it has sought to determine employer preferences for the gender of workers in industrial subsectors (by occupation and educational level) in filling vacancies in 1985. Thus, inadvertently, the Survey serves to determine the gender-typing of jobs in manufacturing industry. According to the Survey results, in 1985-1986, on average, 23.44 per cent of marginal demand for labor in the manufacturing industry was for women. The public-private breakdown of this figure, however, indicates that while in private manufacturing 38.43 per cent of the demand for labor was for women, in public manufacturing this figure was only 8.18 per cent. These employer preferences are consistent — although in an exaggerated way — with the difference in the actual gender composition of employment between the two sectors (of 21.3 per cent in the private sector and 13.73 per cent in the public sector in 1985). For the

Transition to Export-led Growth in Turkey: ...   125

Table 1.
Gender Composition and Segregation in Large Establishments in Turkish Manufacturing
[3-digit SIC level]

	Female Employment	Male Employment	Female share in total employment	Dissimilarity Index
Total:				
1966	83,496	327,294	20.33	43.31
1982	151,949	684,304	18.17	42.70
1985	146,091	650,161	18.35	43.70
Private sector:				
1966	50,529	180,760	21.85	32.69
1982	117,570	456,891	20.47	38.64
1985	105,534	395,414	21.30	40.11
Public sector:				
1966	32,967	146,534	18.37	59.28
1982	34,379	227,413	13.13	55.92
1985	40,557	254,747	13.73	61.19

Sources: *Annual Survey of Manufacturing* for 1966 & 1982 (Preliminary Results), and *1985-1986 Manufacturing Industry: The Results of the Manpower Training and Requirements Survey* for 1985.

private sector, these figures either suggest a growing preference for women workers and may signal a future feminization of employment, or they may represent the ongoing preference of private employers for women which goes unfulfilled, as indicated by the lower actual relative to desired women's share of employment in private manufacturing. The opposite appears to be the case in public manufacturing, where the overall employer preference for women workers is much lower than the actual women's share of public manufacturing employment. In Turkey, therefore, one could talk of a defeminization of employment in public manufacturing and a feminization of employment in the private sector with the switch to ELI. The possible future defeminization of the public sector may be due to either "rationalization," whereby in the course of turning public enterprises into profitable establishments managers may be firing first those who were last hired, who might be women, or to changes in the technological characteristics of public industrial production towards more capital-intensity, or to changes in hiring practices. These trends need further investigation through detailed industry or enterprise level studies.

As for the patterns of gender segregation in Turkish manufacturing, the dissimilarity index (DI) for industries at the 3-digit level remained stable throughout both the ISI and ELI periods (Table 1).[17] This index slightly decreased from 43.31 in 1966 to 42.70 in 1982 and slightly increased to 43.70 in 1985. However, there were again marked differences between the private and public sectors. Throughout both periods, the public sector remained more segregated than the private sector, with the DI for this sector decreasing during the ISI period (from 59.28 to 55.92) and increasing (to 61.19) between 1982 and 1985. By contrast, the DI for the private sector increased (from 32.69 to 38.64) between 1966 and 1982, and continued to increase (to 40.11) in the ELI period. Thus, while gender segregation in the private sector establishments remained at a lower level, it registered a secular increase from 1966 to 1985. Moreover, assuming that employers were able to hire according to their preferences in 1985, the DIs in 1986 for the private and public sectors would have been 40.62 and 61.38, respectively, indicating a continued increase in segregation in both sectors in the 1980s.

Exploring the sources of these changes in the DIs reveals that in the public sector in both periods the change was predominantly due to changes in women's representation in industrial sectors of public manufacturing, rather than changes in the structure of output. While changes in gender composition also accounted for the increase in measured segregation in the private sector between 1966 and 1982, the interaction of compositional and structural effects accounted for the increase in the DI between 1982 and 1985.[18]

Despite these differences between the private and public sectors, there is a striking similarity in the ranking of manufacturing industries according to the share of women in total sector employment. In both public and private manufacturing, apparel, textiles, tobacco and pottery were the most "female-intensive" industries in 1966 and 1982. Over time, in both sectors the rankings of women's share of employment remained similar.[19] By 1985, apparel and tobacco were still the industries with the highest female shares of employment. In addition, from 1982 onwards women also exhibited a high share of employment in the scientific, measuring equipment industry in the private sector and the electrical machinery and appliances industry in the public sector. This pattern of overrepresentation of women in a limited number of sectors (relative to their overall share of manufacturing employment) conforms with patterns observed in other economies.

As for the relationship between earnings and gender composition of employment, in both 1966 and 1982 in the private sector women tended to be overrepresented in industries with lower average annual earnings per worker. There was no such relationship in the public sector.[20] The differences between the two sectors in this regard may reflect the greater cost-consciousness of the private sector relative to the public sector. T h e difference between the private and public manufacturing establishments in terms of gender composition and segregation of employment raises the question of whether this difference is due to differences in employment policies between the two sectors, or to the differences in technological characteristics and export-orientation of the two types of establishments. Indeed, in contrast to the private sector, the public sector consists of larger firms, has a higher degree of capital-intensity and greater representation in intermediate and capital goods industries, and is more oriented toward production for the domestic rather than the export market. We examine the relative effects of these characteristics of industries on women's share of manufacturing employment in the next section.

THE DETERMINANTS OF WOMEN'S SHARE OF EMPLOYMENT IN MANUFACTURING

In this section, employing regression analysis, we further investigate the effects of characteristics of manufacturing industry subsectors, the type of ownership of establishment (public or private) and the impact of the shift in industrialization strategy on the share of female employment in a manufacturing subsector.[21] Using pooled 3-digit sic level data provided separately for the public and private manufacturing establishments for 1966 and 1982, we tested the following specification by OLS:[22]

$$FEM_i = a_0 + a_1 SKILL_i + a_2 HP_i + a_3 EXP_i + a_3 SIZE_i + a_5 DPR_i + a_6 D82_i + a_7 EXPD82_i$$

where i = manufacturing industry subsector at the 3-digit SIC-level of disaggregation

FEM_i = female share of wage workers, which include administrative and clerical personnnel as well as production workers

SKILL = the ratio of skilled to non-skilled production workers

HP = total power of equipment installed per worker measured in horsepower

EXP = the ratio of exports to output

SIZE = average establishment size in terms of employment

DPR = dummy variable for type of ownership; 1 = private establishment component of subsector i, 0 = public establishment componenent of subsector i

D82 = dummy variable for year; 1 = 1982, 0 = 1966

EXPD82 = EXP*D82

The first three variables, skill, HP and EXP, are used to test the three hypotheses suggested by both sets of female marginalization literature about women's location in manufacturing employment, namely, that women are concentrated in sectors of low skill-intensity, high labor-intensity, and export-orientation. The variable size is used to examine whether women's share of employment is, on average, higher in larger workplaces than in smaller ones within large-scale manufacturing. The dummy variable DPR distinguishes private establishments from public ones, and tests whether private establishments indeed have a higher proportion of women workers compared to public ones when other characteristics of the two sectors are controlled for. Assessing the public sector's role with respect to the gender composition of employment is especially important in the context of the present move towards privatization in the Turkish economy. The dummy variable D82 is used to capture the effect of the switch in industrialization strategy to export-led industrialization and the changes in the macroeconomic policies, and the interaction variable EXPD82 is used to test whether or not the export-orientation of an industry has an even greater impact under the export-led regime than under a regime of import-substituting industrialization.

Table 2.
The Determinants of Share of Women in Manufacturing Industry Subsectors [3-digit SIC level]

(Dependent Variable: per cent female)

	(1)	(2)
Intercept	16.454	16.227
	(3.543)***	(3.527)***
SKILL	-16.309	-16.342
	(-1.845)*	(-1.856)*
HP	-0.411	-0.420
	(-2.440)**	(-2.526)**
EXP	0.365	0.427
	(2.149)**	(3.951)***
SIZE	-0.0005	-0.0005
	(-0.357)	(-0.352)
DPR	3.310	3.353
	(1.169)	(1.189)
D82	-1.553	-0.823
	(-0.433)	(-0.255)
EXPD82	0.103	
	(0.476)	
R^2 =	0.31	0.30
adjusted R^2 =	0.25	0.26
n =	102	102

Sources: *Annual Survey of Manufacturing* for 1966 and 1982 (Preliminary Results), Fifth Five Year Development Plan, 1985-1989.

Note: *t* - statistics are reported in parenthesis. *** ** and * indicate significance at the 1, 5 and 10% levels.

The results of the OLS regression are presented in Table 2. By and large, estimation results support the hypotheses distilled from the FM1 and FM2 literature: while the variables skill and HP each has a statistically significant negative effect on women's share of employment in an industry, EXP has a statistically significant positive effect. On the other hand, none of the other variables has a statistically significant effect on women's share of employment in an industry. Women, therefore, have higher representation when an industry is more export-oriented, more labor-intensive and has a high ratio of non-skilled to skilled production workers, and this pattern held during the ELI as well as the ISI period. Hence, the commonly observed presence of women in export-oriented industries in the Third World is not simply due to the labor-intensity and unskilled labor content of the exports of such countries. The degree of export-orientation per se also leads to a higher share of employment for women in an industry. This may be due to the greater disciplining effect of international competition on wage rates and profitability in the export-oriented industries and the greater need to employ a flexible and controllable labor force. Finally, the fact that type of ownership does not make any difference in terms of women's share of employment in an industry means that the differences between public and private establishments are solely due to differences in their industrial and market characteristics and not their employment policies. Because of the high degree of collinearity between EXP and EXPD82 (correlation coefficient = 0.79), we also estimated the model by leaving out the interaction term. These results, reported in the second column of Table 2, indicate that collinearity does not affect the first set results. EXP has an even stronger effect in explaining women's location in manufacturing industry compared to the model that includes the interaction term.

Since the year dummy (D82) and the interactive dummy (EXPD82) are not statistically significant, the macroeconomic policy change or the shift in industrialization strategy did not have a significant effect on gender composition of employment in manufacturing industry. This means that the determinants of women's share of employment have not been affected by the outward orientation of the economy. We should emphasize, however, that by 1982 the export-led growth strategy in Turkey was in effect for only two years, although significant growth in exports was already achieved by that time. Therefore, this result may reflect only the short-run effects of the implementation of this strategy. Specifically, it may reflect the effects of labor repression and reregulation that has ensured profitability of manufacturing establishments without a change in gender composition of employment. Unfortunately, 1982 is the last year for which comparable data on the independent variables used in the regression analysis are available, and this analysis needs to be updated as data becomes available. As discussed earlier, it is also likely that female employment growth associated with export-led industrialization may be occurring outside of large enterprises, particularly in homes under homeworking arrangements, in which case it is not reflected in large-scale manufacturing industry statistics.

CONCLUSION

Our investigation of the transition from import-substituting to export-led industrialization in Turkey shows that successful export-orientation of the economy has been achieved without a relative growth of women's employment in large-scale manufacturing enterprises. The lack of a feminization of employment in large-scale manufacturing in the 1980s could be due to the resistance of gender-typing of industries in the context of the labor repression which reduced the labor cost "advantage" of women workers vis-a-vis men. In the long-run, such gender-typing may change in response to changes in incentive structures or social policies associated with export-led industrialization.

Examination of trends in public and private manufacturing sectors suggests that such a feminization of employment may already be occurring in the private sector. Women's share of employment in private manufacturing establishments was consistently higher than in the public ones not only during the ELI but also in the ISI years. Moreover, the difference in the female shares in the two sectors became slightly more pronounced during the 1980s and is likely to become even more so, given different employer preferences in 1985 for the gender composition of prospective workers in the two sectors. Another difference between the public and private establishments was the incidence of consistently higher measured gender segregation in the former sector throughout the ISI and ELI periods.

A further investigation of the determinants of women's share of employment in manufacturing industry through regression analysis, has revealed that this share is more fundamentally explained by the technological characteristics and export-orientation of public and private establishments alike, during both periods of industrialization. Thus, the regression analysis does not support the argument that employment is feminized with the switch to ELI, at least through 1982. Nor does it support the argument that the public sector is more accessible to women, at least in the manufacturing industry. Since gender-focused studies comparing the public and private enterprises are rare, it is hard to conclude whether the Turkish case represents an anomaly or the more likely pattern in this regard.

While our study found no evidence for feminization of employment in large-scale manufacturing with the shift to ELI, we cannot rule out the possibility that gender composition of overall manufacturing employment may have changed in favor of women under the export-led regime through the use of flexible labor supplied by women outside of large manufacturing establishments. Yet, this trend towards feminization of employment cannot be substantiated due to lack of time series data on homeworking or other informal activities.

Our study points to the further need for similar country studies that would enable us to assess the varieties of experiences for women industrial workers during shifts in industrialization strategy. By revealing the conditions of men and women's incorporation into the labor force through disaggregated and multivariate investigation, such comparative studies would not only enhance our understanding of the ways of improving labor standards and working conditions globally but also contribute towards developing a gender-sensitive theory of employment in different phases of capitalist development in the Third World.

NOTES

1. We prefer the term "reregulation" over "deregulation," because the latter implies a reduction in regulation while reregulation leaves open the possibility that greater restrictions may be imposed on workers' ability to freely associate and negotiate over conditions of work, i.e. a reduction of labor standards.

2. We emphasize the distinction between "gender composition" and "gender segregation" of employment, which are often conflated in discussions of the relative employment position of women in the course of industrialization. While the former refers to the share (percentage) of women (or men) in an industrial sector, the latter refers to the dissimilarity of the distributions of men and women within manufacturing, measured by a single index of segregation (e.g. the

Transition to Export-led Growth in Turkey: ...   131

dissimilarity index used below). Many authors, however, inaccurately use the former as the sole measure of gender segregation. Even though the two are related, the dissimilarity index provides information about distributions of women and men across sectors which cannot be obtained from a mere share of employment figure.

3. Recent feminist literature, however, indicates that employer skill classifications tend to contain gender biases, which consistently type female labor as "unskilled" (Phillips and Taylor 1981, Elson and Pearson 1981).

4. Women's concentration in labor-intensive industries is widely noted and documented in the literature for the Western capitalist economies. Bridges (1980) establishes econometrically that in the U.S., capital-intensity of a subsector explains the underrepresentation of women in that sector. See also Dean (1988).

5. See Scott (1986) for a critique of the analytical issues in substantiating "marginalization." Scott's formulation of the "Female Marginalization Thesis" does not directly correspond to either of the FM1 and FM2 theses that we have distilled from the literature on women and industrialization. While Scott examines economy-wide marginalization theses on the basis of Latin American case studies, we concentrate on marginalization theses regarding manufacturing employment in the context of two industrialization strategies. Scott argues that the thesis that women are marginalised from/in employment in the course of dependent capitalist development is irrefutable, because various authors use different definitions of marginalization and measurement criteria. Women are marginalised along some of these dimensions, but not others, making it impossible to draw general conclusions. We agree with Scott's assessment of the need for micro level detailed analyses based on specification of definitions and measurement criteria as a precondition for constructing a general theory of women's employment under capitalism.

6. Here, we do not imply that there is a clear demarcation between ISI and ELI as ideal types in the actual industrialization experiences of countries, since countries may exhibit characteristics of both strategies in different phases of their industrialization.

7. While proponents of fm1 blame MNCs for the creation of a relatively small number of positions in modern manufacturing, from which women are excluded, proponents of FM2 blame MNCs for the appalling conditions of women's employment in export manufacturing. In addition, there is disagreement over the employment benefits to women workers employed by MNCs operating in export processing zones. Some document the poor wages and working conditions (e.g. Fuentes and Ehrenreich 1983), while others point out that, relative to the alternatives for women in these economies, the multinational export-oriented enterprise represents a superior employment opportunity (e.g. Lim 1990).

8. Ideally, studies on trends in female share of employment should be comparing figures from peaks of cycles. Data problems, however, make it extremely difficult to make comparisons using peak year figures. For a similar point regarding difficulties in substantiating marginalization see Scott (1986).

9. While these studies do not examine the shifts in strategy, given the commonly observed adoption of ELI strategies following ISI in the recent decades, one implication of the FM2 literature is an increase in the share of women's employment with the shift to ELI.

10. Indeed, Standing (1989) presents evidence that supports this view. Export-oriented economies have either never ratified ilo Conventions that protect the rights of women workers (e.g. Equal Remuneration Convention No.100 or Convention No.89 prohibiting night work for women) or denounced these Conventions (or made exemptions for EPZs). Employer practices such as the Brazilian practice of seeking certificates of sterilization from women of childbearing age, indicate the weakening of rights of women workers (Simons 1988).

11. The upward trend in these shares continued after 1985 (OECD, 1990).

12. In manufacturing industry real wages fell by about 24 per cent between 1977 and 1985, while the share of wages in manufacturing value added fell from 38.7 per cent in 1979 to 22.4 per cent in 1985. Other wage series that include non-manufacturing workers' wages registered an even more dramatic decline (Celasun and Rodrik 1990).

13. Throughout the 1980s the unemployment rate was around 15-16 per cent, increasing steadily from a low of 12 per cent in 1977 to 14.8 per cent in 1980 and 16.3 per cent in 1985. After the labor statistics were revised downward by the State Planning Organization in May 1989, however, the unemployment rates in 1980 and 1985 were 11.6 per cent and 11.7 per cent, respectively (OECD, various years).

14. While there occurred an impressive increase in foreign direct investment after 1980 compared to the isi period, this increase is not significant relative to the growth and stock of global foreign direct investment in this period. According to figures reported by the Foreign Investment Directorate, the cumulative foreign direct investment in Turkey which was U.S.$ 325 million until 1980 reached U.S.$ 1,438.2 million by 1985 (DPT 1987, 7)). As for the public sector, in 1985, it accounted for 37.6 and 39.4 per cent of manufacturing output and value added of large manufacturing establishments, respectively (Annual Manufacturing Survey 1985).

15. An overview of trends in women's labor force participation and occupational distribution in the Turkish economy from 1955 to 1975 is presented by Kazgan (1981).

16. The overwhelming participation of women in the agricultural labor force is partly a reflection of the Turkish Census method, which includes unpaid family workers in the labor force. Classifying women in agriculture as unpaid family workers, however, tends to obscure other economic activities that rural women engage in, and thereby underestimates their participation in industrial labor. In Turkey, a striking example of an invisible industrial activity is rural carpet weaving, which is carried out by women who often also participate in agricultural work. While the 1980 census figures place the number of carpet weavers at about 40,000, estimates based on annual carpet production and number of looms put that figure around 500,000 (Berik 1987).

17. DI is defined as:

$$\left(\frac{1}{2}\right)\sum_{i-1}^{k} \; \left| \; \frac{N_{fi}}{N_f} - \frac{N_{mi}}{N_m} \; \right| \; x \; 100$$

where n_{fi} = number of females in industry i,
N_f = total female employment
N_{mi} = number of males in industry i
N_m = total male employment

The value of DI ranges from 0 to 100, 0 corresponding to no sex segregation, 100 corresponding to total segregation by sex. For further discussion of this and other segregation indices see OECD (1985).

18. Decomposing the changes in the di makes possible to identify the sources of the change in (1) change in female representation within industries (compositional effect); (2) change in structure of output (i.e. the size of each industry) (structural effect); (3) the interaction between these two effects. The decomposition analysis figures are available from the authors. For the methodology of decomposition of the changes in the DI, see OECD (1985, 68).

19. The Spearman rank correlation coefficients indicate no significant changes in the rankings of 3-digit industries according to female-intensity in either sector between 1966 and 1982. The rank correlation coefficients are 0.81 and 0.68 for the private and public sectors, respectively. Both are statistically significant at the 1 per cent level.

20. While the Spearman rank correlation coefficients at the 3-digit level for the private sector are 0.34 in 1966 and 0.55 in 1982 (statistically significant at the 5 and 1 per cent levels, respectively), for the public sector the rank correlation coefficients are 0.16 in 1966 and 0.18 in 1982 (both are statistically insignificant). Due to the lack of earnings data broken down by gender for the manufacturing industry, we are unable to conduct a detailed analysis of wage differentials by gender.

21. This section is based on Berik and Çağatay (forthcoming).

22. The choice of years is partly dictated by data availability and partly by our attempt to compare peak years of cycles within each industrialization strategy. 1966 is a year in the ISI period and represents the highest growth rate in non-agricultural output over the 1954-1980 period. 1982 is a year during the ELI period, when the growth rate had recovered after the 1977-1980 crisis.

REFERENCES

Anker, Richard and Catherine Hein. 1985. Why Third World urban employers usually prefer men. *International Labor Review* 24(1): 73-90.

_____. 1986. Introduction and overview and sex inequalities in Third World employment: statistical evidence. In, *Sex Inequalities in Urban Employment in the Third World*, Richard Anker and Catherine Hein, (eds.). New York: St. Martin's Press.

Beneria, Lourdes and Martha Roldan. 1987. *The Crossroads of Class and Gender: Industrial Homework, Subcontracting and Household Dynamics in Mexico City*. Chicago and London: University of Chicago Press.

Berik, Günseli. 1987. Women Carpet Weavers in Rural Turkey. Geneva: International Labour Office.

Berik, Günseli and Nilüfer Çağatay. Forthcoming. Industrialisation strategies and gender composition of manufacturing employment in Turkey. In, *Women and Work in the World Economy*, B. Agarwal, B. Bergmann, S. Floro, and N. Folbre, (eds.). London: Macmillan.

Boserup, Ester. 1970. *Woman's Role in Economic Development*. New York: St. Martin's Press.

Bridges, William. 1980. Industry marginality and female employment: a new appraisal. *American Sociological Review* 45(1): 58-75.

Celasun, Melih and Dani Rodrik. 1990. Debt, adjustment and growth: Turkey. In, *Developing Country Debt and Economic Performance*. Vol. 3. J. Sachs and S. Collins, (eds.) Chicago and London: University of Chicago Press.

Çağatay, Nilüfer. 1990. Case study: Turkey. In, *Labour Standards and Development in the Global Economy*, Stephen Herzenberg and Jorge Perez-Lopez, (eds.). Washington, dc: us Department of Labour.

_____. 1986. The Interindustry Structure of Wages and Markups in Turkish Manufacturing. Unpublished PhD thesis, Stanford University, USA.

Chaney, Elsa and Marianne Schmink. 1976. Women and modernisation: access to tools, in *Sex and Class in Latin America*. New York: Praeger.

Chinchilla, Norma. 1977. Industrialisation, monopoly capitalism and women's work in Guatemala. In, *Women and National Development: The Complexities of Change*. Wellesley Editorial Committee, (eds.). Chicago, Ill: University of Chicago Press.

Cho, Uhn and Hagen Koo. 1983. Economic development and women's work in a newly Industrialising Country: The Case of Korea. *Development and Change* 14(4): 515-531.

Cinar, Mine E. 1988. Taking work at home: disguised female employment in urban Turkey. Loyola University of Chicago Working Paper No.8810, September.

de Miranda, Glaura Vasquez. 1977. Women's labour force participation in a developing country. In, *Women and National Development: The Complexities of Change*. Wellesley Editorial Committee, (eds.). Chicago, Ill: University of Chicago Press.

Dean, Jayne. 1988. Sex Segregation, Relative Wages and the Technical Conditions of Production: A Theoretical and Empirical Analysis. Unpublished PhD thesis, New School for Social Research, USA.

dpt. 1987. Yabanci Sermaye Raporu 1983-1986. Ankara: Yabanci Sermaye Baskanligi.

Elson, Diane and Ruth Pearson. 1981. The subordination of women and the internationalisation of factory production. In, *Of Marriage and the Market*, K. Young, C. Wolkowitz, and R. McCullagh, (eds.). London: Conference of Socialist Economists.

Fuentes, Annette and Barbara Ehrenreich. 1983. Women in the Global Factory. New York: Institute for New Communications, South End Press.

Hein, Catherine. 1984. Jobs for the girls: export manufacturing in Mauritius. *International Labour Review* 123(2): 251-265.

Humphrey, John. 1987. *Gender and Work in the Third World: Sexual Divisions in Brazilian Industry*. London and New York: Tavistock.

Ibrahim, Barbara. 1989. Policies affecting women's employment in the formal sector: strategies for change. *World Development* 17(7): 1097-1107.

ILO. 1985. Women Workers in Multinational Enterprises in Developing Countries. Geneva: ILO.

Joekes, Susan. 1985. Working for a lipstick? Male and female labour in the clothing industry in Morocco. In, *Women, Work and Ideology in the Third World*, H. Afshar, (ed.). London: Tavistock.

_____. 1986. *Industrialisation, Trade and Female Employment: Experiences of the 1970s and After*. Dominican Republic: instraw.

Kazgan, Gulten. 1981. Labour force participation, occupational distribution, educational attainment and socio-economic status of women in the Turkish economy. In, *Women in Turkish Society*, N. Abadan-Unat, (ed.). Leiden: E.J. Brill.

Lim, Linda. 1990. Women's work in export factories: the politics of a cause. In, *Persistent Inequalities: Women and World Development, I*. Tinker, (ed.). New York: Oxford University Press.

OECD. 1985. The Integration of Women into the Economy. Paris: OECD.

_____. Various years. Turkey. Paris: OECD Economic Surveys.

Phillips, Anne and Barbara Taylor. 1980. Sex and skill: notes towards a feminist economics. *Feminist Review* 6: 79-88.

Pyle, Jean. 1990. Export-led development and the underemployment of women: the impact of discriminatory development policy in the Republic of Ireland. In, *Women Workers and Global Restructuring*, K. Ward, (ed.). Ithaca: ILR Press.

Safa, Helen. 1981. Runaway shops and female employment: the search for cheap labour. *Signs* 7(2): 418-433.

Saffioti, Heleieth. 1978. *Women in a Class Society*. New York: Monthly Review.

Schmink, Marianne. 1977. Dependency, development and division of labour by sex: Venezuela. *Latin American Perspectives* (Winter-Spring): 153-179.

Scott, Alison. 1986. Women and industrialisation: examining the "female marginalisation" thesis. *Journal of Development Studies* 22(4): 649-680.

Simons, Marlise. 1988. Brazil women find fertility may cost jobs. *New York Times*. 7 December.

SIS. 1990. 1988 Urban Household Labour Force Survey, Ankara: State Institute of Statistics.

_____. 1986. 1985-1986 Manufacturing Industry: The Results of the Manpower Training and Requirements Survey. Publication No. 1220. Ankara: State Institute of Statistics.

Standing, Guy. 1989. Global feminisation through flexible labor. *World Development* 17(7): 1077-1095.

[10]

The Impact of Multinational Technological Transfer on Female Workforces in Asia

Jean Larson Pyle
Leslie Dawson

This article examines the technology transfer strategies of multinational firms as they have relocated labor-intensive manufacture to export processing zones in a succession of Asian nations. The production and managerial technologies transferred are intended to reduce costs, but their negative impact on the predominantly female workforces employed soon undermines this objective. Moreover, since women workers are also consumers, their alienation is counterproductive to marketing goals. As Asia becomes viewed not only as a low-cost production site, but also a dynamic growth market, strategies must be reassessed and reformulated if corporate goals are to be met.

MULTINATIONAL corporations (MNCs) have been a prominent component of the export-led development strategy adopted by successive tiers of Asian nations. This development strategy was implemented first in the late 1960s by what are now termed

Jean Larson Pyle is currently an Assistance Professor of Economics at the University of Lowell. She specializes in development economics and is the author of a forthcoming book examining the impact upon women of state policies in export-led economies.

Leslie M. Dawson is currently a Professor of Marketing at the University of Lowell. Dr. Lawson entered the academic field following a career in business management. He is the author of many articles and papers related to marketing and management, and has lectured in Europe, South America and Asia.

newly industrializing countries (NICs), Hong Kong, Singapore, South Korea (henceforth Korea), and Taiwan, and next in the 1970s by the ASEAN-4 nations of Indonesia, Malaysia, the Philippines, and Thailand. More recently, their ranks have been joined by third-tier, lower income countries such as Bangladesh, Sri Lanka, and some coastal provinces of China.

MNCs have contributed in key ways to the structural adjustments necessary for export-led development, especially expansion of manufacturing sectors. These global enterprises have provided capital, access to distribution and marketing channels, and political power to resist protectionist pressures in industrial economy mar-

kets. But perhaps their most important—and controversial—contribution has been the transfer of technology.

Technology is commonly understood to refer to the physical means whereby natural resources are transformed into produced resources through machinery, equipment, and manufacturing processes. However, development planners prefer a broader definition of technology that includes not only physical tools of production but also the many forms of knowledge and skill required to use them effectively. For example, the Technology Atlas Team (1987) defines technology to include not only "technoware" but also "humanware" (experience, skills, knowledge, and creativity of users); "orgaware" (management practices), and "infoware" (information systems). Madu (1989) observes that project failures in developing countries have often been caused by insufficient attention to such broader components of technology transfer packages, especially the management of human resources.

A wealth of literature has accumulated over the last three decades on the transfer of technology from industrial nations to the developing world.[1] The appropriateness of technologies transferred has been examined in various contexts: the balance between the domains of imported and domestic technology; labor versus capital intensiveness; large scale versus small scale; and most recently, the adverse environmental impact of technologies with respect to such issues as acid rain, destruction of the ozone layer, use and disposal of toxic substances, and the use of chemicals in agriculture. However, little attention has been paid to the appropriateness of technologies transferred by MNCs with respect to another critical resource of developing nations: their female labor forces.[2] Diehl (1989) suggests that a "management gap" of crisis proportions exists in the developing world due to insufficient study of the technologies for achieving results through organizations; i.e., management technology. Thus, the appropriateness of technologies transferred depends not only on the nature of production processes employed, but equally upon ways in which they are implemented; i.e., managerial strategies and policies concerning the use of workers.

This article examines the initial technological transfer strategies of multinational firms as they have located or relocated labor-intensive manufacture in the several tiers of Asian nations. The discussion focuses primarily on manufacturing operations that have been established in export processing zones (EPZs) and on the predominantly female workforces employed in them. The authors draw upon extensive research to demonstrate that in their pursuit of lower manufacturing costs, MNCs have consistently employed production processes that are hazardous to workers' health and safety, and managerial techniques that are in many respects exploitative. The belief has been that such technologies will reduce labor input costs while simultaneously achieving high levels of output. However, it is shown that transfer of these types of production and managerial technologies have a negative impact on the predominantly female labor force in EPZs, and soon generate countervailing forces that increase labor costs and reduce productivity.

The authors examine the adverse implications of a continuation of such strategies in an era when many MNCs are evolving into global rather than national entities, and in which they view the Asia-Pacific region not only as a low wage production site, but also a dynamically growing market. It is contended that inasmuch as corporate profitability depends on per unit costs of production and the existence of viable markets, profits can be diminished by transfers of technology which alienate workers who fulfill dual roles as producers and consumers. The authors argue that it is in the interest of multinationals to devise more appropriate strategies of technology transfer if they are to attain overall corporate goals in the next decade.

EXPORT-LED DEVELOPMENT IN ASIA

Over the past several decades an export-led strategy has become the new orthodoxy of developmental economics, due in no small measure to the exceptional growth performance of the Asian NICs and their ASEAN-4 neighbors. Between 1970 and 1980, the real GDP of the Asian NICs grew at an average annual rate of 8-10%, three times that of the US or the average of all industrial countries. In the same period the ASEAN-4 nations posted average annual increases of 6-8%, well above the average for developing countries as a whole. The global recession of the mid-1980s affected Asian countries and caused performance downturns, but the end of the decade has seen strong recoveries throughout the region and double-digit growth rates in some nations. Thus, current performance data testify to the capacity of nations committed to such a course to make necessary adjustments commensurate with changing global conditions.

In their initial drive to establish manufactured export industries, Asian countries have relied largely on the attraction of foreign corporations in labor-intensive industries. The enticements offered by Asian governments have included export and import tariff protection, tax exemptions, unrestricted ownership and profit repatriation, and direct subsidies. Most importantly, Asian governments have offered assurance of a large pool of low-cost, compliant, productive labor, relatively unhampered by unions or government regulations pertaining to wage levels, working conditions, safety, or health. This labor pool has been preponderantly female.

A cornerstone of implementing such policies has been the creation of the export processing zone, a modern trade enclave with prefabricated plant sites and self-contained infrastructure. Over 80 of these industrial estates are now in operation in Asia, with many more under construction or planned. Table 1 shows the locations of these facilities in 1986, and indicates that while the majority of operational facilities are in the NICs, most of those being developed are in ASEAN-4 and low-income countries.

Foreign enterprises have found these union-free, tax-free, unregulated manufacturing havens to be a solution to intense global competitive pressures to contain costs. The American semiconductor industry began transferring production to Singapore as early as the late 1960s, and other firms from the US, Europe, and Japan soon followed as offshore manufacturing spread through the region. In addition to well-known MNCs, many of the firms involved have been smaller enterprises for which overseas production was the first step in expanding into international operations. In recent times, an appreciable number of multinationals originating in NICs ("MENICS") have transferred some of their labor-intensive manufacture to second- or third-tier nations as labor costs have risen in home countries. Hong Kong firms, for example, now employ more workers in China than in the British colony itself.

While a broad spectrum of industry is now represented in Asian EPZs, the attraction has been greatest for products whose value is high relative to their weight and which have a large labor-intensive component in their manufacturing process. Both production and employment are heavily concentrated in two industries, garments/textiles and electronics. Other prominent industries include footwear, sporting goods, toys, and pharmaceuticals. When capital-intensive, high technology industries such as semiconductors first located operations in Asian countries, generally they transferred only labor-intensive production phases. In electronics the total production process has become international, involving complex transfers of raw materials, parts, and finished products between countries. Lately, as technological capability has deepened in some countries (e.g., Taiwan and Malaysia), there has been a trend toward transferring higher-end, capital-intensive phases of electronics manufacture to Asian EPZs.

THE CENTRAL ROLE OF WOMEN

With respect to the workers involved in EPZs, there have been numerous studies of the use of women in MNC industries.[3] However, full recognition has not been given to the central role women have played in the achievement of high growth rates in Asian countries, inasmuch as they constitute the dominant proportion of the MNC manufacturing workforce. Jones (1984) reveals, in his detailed study of female labor force participation in the NICs and ASEAN-4, that because of the selective nature of industrialization in these nations, the female share of their total manufacturing employment considerably exceeds that of Western countries. This has been influenced by relocation decisions of industries and the support of national governments as well as by the availability of female work-

Table 1
Number of Export Processing Zones In Selected Asian Nations, 1986

Country	In Operation	Under Construction	Proposed or planned
NICs			
Hong Kong	14	—	—
Korea	11	—	—
Singapore	22	—	—
Taiwan	4	1	1
ASEAN-4			
Indonesia	2	2	1
Malaysia	11	—	—
Philippines	3	2	—
Thailand	1	—	—
LOW-INCOME[a]			
Bangladesh	1	—	2
China	4	—	4[b]
India	2	4	1
Pakistan	1	—	4
Sri Lanka	3	—	1
TOTAL	79	9	14

[a]World Bank classification
[b]Based on 1990 proposal to create four new Special Economic Zones in coastal provinces.
Sources: International Labour Organization, *Economic and Social Effects of Multinational Enterprises in Export Processing Zones* (Geneva: International Labour Office, 1988), p. 164; Michael Osborne, *China's Special Economic Zones* (Paris: Development Centre of the Organization for Economic Co-operation and Development, 1986), pp. 82-83; *The Asian Wall Street Journal*, February 5, 1990, p. 2.

ers. For example, Wield and Rhodes (1988) note that the intensity of female employment in a developed-country industry has been a major determinant of its propensity to relocate production to the developing world. In addition, Lim (1985) concludes that the female labor supply has been viewed by Asian governments as their principal resource for industrial development.

Table 2 presents survey data from the International Labour Organization (1988) concerning employment in export processing zones and other offshore manufacturing in Asia in 1975 and 1986. These data illustrate the shift of manufacturing employment through successive tiers of Asian countries and the predominant use of women workers. Employment was heavily concentrated in NICs in 1975, while between 1975 and 1986 employment growth in the ASEAN-4 was three times that of the NICs. By 1986, low-income Asian nations had become established as significant offshore manufacturing employment centers. The proportion of women in EPZ industries ranged from 60% to 90% in the early 1980s, with the

highest shares occurring in second- and third-tier countries.

For several reasons, the data in Table 2 significantly understate the actual size of the workforce linked to multinationals in Asia, as well as the predominance of female workers. "Other offshore manufacturing" includes employment in non-EPZ plants operating under EPZ conditions, but not all countries reported such data. Moreover, the figures do not include workers in locally-owned firms producing under the direction of MNCs as subcontractors, nor the substantial and growing number of workers, virtually all female, who produce for MNCs or subcontractors as homeworkers.

Presently, the number of female workers in multinational-related manufacturing in Asia probably is well in excess of one million. While this constitutes a small fraction of women who receive income in the formal and informal sectors of Asian economies, such women are of particular significance to MNC management because of their dual roles as producers and income-earning consumers.

42

Table 2
Employment in Export Processing Zones and Other Offshore Manufacturing for Selected Asian Countries, 1975 and 1986

	Number employed 1975	Number employed 1986	Growth (percent) 1975-1986	Share of women in EPZ industries (percent) Early 1980s
NICs				
Hong Kong	59,607	89,000	33.0	60.0
Singapore	105,000	217,000	106.7	60.0
Korea	112,250	140,000	24.7	75.0
Taiwan	62,143	80,469	22.8	..
Total NICs	**339,000**	**526,469**	**55.0**	
ASEAN-4				
Indonesia	11,191	13,000	16.2	90.0
Malaysia	40,465	97,688	142.4	85.0
Philippines	9,827	89,000	805.7	74.0
Thailand	16,700	32,746	96.1	..
Total ASEAN-4	**78,183**	**232,434**	**197.1**	
LOW-INCOME[a]				
Bangladesh	—	4,515	n.a.	..
China	—	70,000	n.a.	..
India	—	77,000	n.a.	80.0
Pakistan	—	13,500	n.a.	
Sri Lanka	—	62,000	n.a.	88.0
Total Low Income		**227,015**	**n.a.**	

[a] World Bank Classification
— Negligible
.. Not available
n.a. Not applicable

Source: International Labour Organization, *Economic and Social Effects of Multinational Enterprises in Export Processing Zones* (Geneva: International Labour Organization 1988), pp. 18, 60, 162-163.

THE PREFERENCE FOR FEMALE WORKERS IN LABOR-INTENSIVE INDUSTRIES

Multinational firms transfer labor-intensive manufacture to Asian countries with the goal of lowering production cost. Two factors account for their decided preference for female workers. First, taking advantage of the gender-based wage differentials prevalent in Asian economies, women can be paid less than men for performing the same tasks. As Table 3 illustrates, women typically earn only 50% to 75% of men's wages in manufacturing in Asian nations.

Secondly, women are considered more productive for gender-related reasons. It is widely believed that women, due to their earlier socializa-tion, will acquiesce more readily to the lower wages, tedious jobs, and poor working conditions that accompany the production technologies transferred, as well as the long hours and high production norms that are part of the managerial approach utilized. In addition, it is assumed that they are naturally more adept and dexterous ("nimble fingers") than men at tasks such as garment making and electronics fabrication.

Given these factors, it has been concluded that women are not only cheaper workers, but also more productive and easily controlled, result-ing in lower per unit costs of produc-tion. It is interesting to note that this combination of low wages and high productivity runs counter to tradi-tional economic theory, which states that in a competitive society workers are paid according to marginal pro-ductivity; i.e., that a more productive workforce will be paid higher wage rates. Thus it is demonstrated that an economic principle can be counter-manded by discriminatory social and cultural forces within an economy.

In general, MNCs have shown a preference for young, single women, often migrants from rural areas, who tend to be unaware of their legal and trade union rights and who are more amenable to discipline and less likely to cause industrial strife. Rapid turn-over has been encouraged to keep wages depressed. Ong's study (1987) of the electronics industry in Malaysia suggests that corporations have at-tempted to limit the employment tenure of female workers to the short span of their working life cycle when they are most capable of intensive labor, and that rapid exhaustion of workers causes most to leave after three or four years. While this general profile prevails as multi-nationals enter a country, there may be change in the composition of EPZ workforces over time, both by country and industry, due to various social and economic factors. For example, a greater proportion of older, married women are now employed in Thai-land and the Philippines than in other countries, and they are more common in the garment industry than in electronics.

Second- and third-tier countries in Asia continue to promote their female labor supply to attract foreign invest-ment. For example, a 1987 investors' guide distributed by the government of Thailand states that:

> Those foreign companies locating in Thailand benefit through the use of Thai female labour. . . . Throughout Thailand females are found by many companies to be manually skilled, keen to work and have the patience to work for long hours at repetitive activities. (p. 38)

A similar promotional pamphlet from the Malaysian Industrial De-velopment Authority (1988) calls attention to the differential wage rates for males and females, while noting the high participation rates of females in the Malaysian labor force.

Some have argued that export-led development has been of benefit to the women employed by providing them with expanded outlooks and at least one more option to obtain income, albeit often at sub-subsistence wages, in their already constrained lives.[4] More predominant in the literature, however, is the view that it has simply served to add another dimension to the ways in which their lives are disadvantaged.[5] There now exists a substantial body of research that documents the ways in which the transfer of production and managerial technology has had a distinctly negative impact on these women.

NEGATIVE EFFECTS OF MNC TECHNOLOGY TRANSFER ON LABOR PRODUCTIVITY AND COST

The strategy of MNC technological transfer in labor-intensive industries originally implemented in the NICs, and now being extended to second- and third-tier Asian nations, has remained remarkably consistent over the past two decades. This strategy focuses on the goal of minimizing per unit labor cost, which is a function of wage rates and output per worker. Firms seek to accomplish this goal by paying the lowest possible wages (which means a predominantly female workforce), taking advantage of lax regulations pertaining to workplace health and safety, and employing managerial techniques such as high production quotas, assembly line speedups, and forced overtime to maximize output rates. Yet past and present experience in the NICs, and recently, some ASEAN-4 countries, demonstrates that this vision of low unit labor costs of production is soon undermined by negative effects on workers. These include impairment of workers' physical and mental health which diminishes productivity, and labor unrest which disrupts output and drives wages up.

Health and Safety

Workers' health has long been established as a major factor in productivity. The very fact that women workers in EPZ industries are often paid wages below (even by develop-

Table 3

Earnings of Women and Men in the Manufacturing Sector in Selected Asian Countries

Country	Year	Women's earnings as a percentage of men's earnings
NICs		
Hong Kong	1987	76
Singapore	1987	58
Korea	1987	50
Taiwan	. .	. .
ASEAN-4		
Indonesia	. .	. .
Malaysia	1980	73
Philippines	1980	62
Thailand	1983	70
LOW-INCOME[a]		
Sri Lanka	1987	71

[a]World Bank classification
. . Not available

Source: International Labour Organization, *Yearbook of Labor Statistics*, various years.

ing-country standards) poverty-line levels makes proper nutrition and health maintenance difficult. But adding to the difficulty of maintaining women's health are managerial practices that result in the high intensity and relentless pace of the work performed. The number of working hours in EPZ plants are higher than industrial country standards, and production quotas often require compulsory overtime until goals are met. A recent report on China's EPZs indicates that fourteen hour workdays are common, and that in one instance women workers were required to put in one or two 24-hour shifts per month.[6] Moreover, especially for women, EPZ jobs confer few social security benefits, and little job security or mobility.

Such stressful work conditions impact women's physical and emotional health in numerous ways. Ong (1987) reports that in Malaysian EPZ factories outbreaks of mass hysteria have occurred. Other results are high turnover due to exhaustion and burnout within a few years, low

levels of morale and motivation, and various manifestations of worker resistance—all of which may lower productivity or raise costs.

MNC employers in Asian EPZs are frequently not held accountable for job-related illnesses, and little statistical data is available on occupational disability rates. Nonetheless, there is substantial documentation of widespread health and safety hazards in the two most prominent EPZ industries, textiles and electronics.[7] These conditions are improving in the more advanced countries of the region, but hazards remain prevalent in second- and third-tier nations. The International Textile, Garment, and Leather Workers' Federation (ITGLWF) describes conditions in Asian textile/garment plants that rival those much vilified conditions present in nineteenth century US and British textile mills.[8] Closed, poorly lit rooms designed to preserve dampness in fibers cause arthritis and laryngitis, while excessive dust and fumes contribute to incidence of brown lung disease. Dermatitis and

44

allergies commonly occur as a result of contact with tissues and dyes. A study of women workers in Sri Lanka revealed that workers in EPZ plants had more health problems than those in non-EPZ plants, with 28% suffering chronic headaches and 20%, infectious diseases.[9] Hearing impairments caused by excessive noise levels are very prevalent (they remain the number-one cause of occupational disability in Singapore). Many injuries result from improperly guarded machinery.

In the electronics industry, which appears more modern and clean, the health hazards are often similarly serious, if less obvious. Assembly workers are exposed, with few controls, to acids, dangerous solvents, and carcinogenic chemicals. In a survey by Lin (1986) of 903 women workers in the semiconductor industry in Singapore and Malaysia, 50% reported some form of occupational illness in the previous six months, while 20% had at some time suffered an injury from work. Constant use of microscopes makes eye damage very common. A study of one Korean electronics plant revealed that 88% of its workers suffered chronic conjunctivitis caused by toxic fumes and dust,

while 47% suffered myopia and 19% astigmatism, likely to have been caused by microscope work.[10]

The documentation that does exist of deaths, injuries, and illnesses in EPZ plants no doubt understates the true dimensions of health and safety hazards. The ITGLWF points out that workers typically fear reprisals if they complain of unsafe conditions. There is much anecdotal evidence that workers often remain on the job after suffering illness or injury, out of fear of losing, permanently, their source of income.

Labor Unrest

Labor unrest can diminish productivity as workers develop strategies to resist practices they find oppressive, as well as raise costs when workers organize and demand higher wages. In many Asian nations, the alleged docility of women workers has proven to be short term at best. Women protesting poor working conditions have interrupted EPZ factory output by staging hunger strikes, demonstrations, and sit-ins. Women have frequently been at the forefront of labor movements in Asia. In Korea and the Philippines, it is women-led unions

that have been the most courageous and defiant, and some women have lost their lives in violent confrontations with the police and military. Labor insurgency in Korea and Taiwan forced both these countries to repudiate repressive anti-union laws in 1987. In that year alone, Korea recorded 3,500 strikes, while current labor unrest in Taiwan has been described as "alarmingly epidemic." [11] Union activism is on the rise in all ASEAN-4 nations, and is spreading to third-tier countries as well. China's constitution bars strikes, but in the Shekou EPZ alone there were 21 work stoppages or strikes in 1986 and 1987.[12]

Strikes and lockouts are measures of labor strife tracked by the International Labour Organization. Table 4 shows the number of workdays lost for these causes between 1978 and 1986 in Asian nations for which ILO data is available. These data show wide variation among countries in the same grouping, as well as sharp year-to-year fluctuations in each nation, reflecting both social diversities and the ebbs and flows of labor unrest over time. Data points from Korea and the Philippines, two countries with strong, volatile labor movements,

Table 4
Number of Workdays Lost to Strikes and Lockouts in Selected Asian Countries, 1978-1987 (Thousands)

Country	1978	1979	1980	1981	1982	1983	1984	1985	1986	1987
NICs										
Hong Kong	30.9	39.7	21.1	15.3	18.0	2.5	3.1	1.2	4.9	2.8
Korea	13.2	16.4	61.3	31.0	11.5	8.7	19.9	64.3	72.0	6,947.0
ASEAN-4										
Indonesia	5.2	19.7	33.8	65.5	72.6	13.7	1.7	557.0	109.4	48.6
Malaysia	..	..	24.6	20.2	10.0	8.0	11.5	36.0	18.6	11.0
Philippines	156.2	173.8	105.3	796.0	1,670.0	581.3	1,907.8	2,457.7	3,637.9	1,907.7
Thailand	8.6	33.8	5.4	173.4	116.8	54.5	183.7	13.1	157.9	89.3
LOW-INCOME[a]										
Bangladesh	662.3	647.6	1,160.4	1,198.5	238.7	392.6	1,022.9	284.9	2,079.7	
Sri Lanka	265.1	293.8	335.2	440.8	388.7	218.0	507.3	169.6	67.1	44.8
TOTALS	1,141.5	1,224.6	1,747.1	2,740.7	2,526.3	1,230.3	3,657.9	3,583.8	6,147.5	9,051.2

[a]World Bank classification

.. Not available

Source: International Labour Organization, *1988 Yearbook of Labor Statistics.*

may distort totals. Nonetheless, a pattern is evident of increasing work disruption over the decade, at a time when EPZ employment, predominantly female, was rising significantly.

Correspondingly, sharp increases in manufacturing labor costs have occurred in the region during the 1980s. Between 1984 and 1988, average industrial wage increases in Korea were 110%; in Taiwan, 84%; in Hong Kong, 50%; and in Singapore, 32%.[13] Significant wage increases are anticipated for 1990 in all of these countries, and in the ASEAN-4 group as well, with the exception of Thailand.[14]

STRUCTURAL CHANGE IN ASIAN ECONOMIES

The original success of the Asian NICs was based on exploitation of their abundant supply of largely female workers to attract labor-intensive industry. However, that very success has led to rising demands of workers and rapidly increasing real wages, thus eroding their comparative advantage in labor-intensive manufacture.

The response of many MNCs to these building cost pressures has been relocation to nations where there is a plentiful supply of low-cost female workers who, for a variety of reasons including socialization and state policies, remain compliant. EPZ plants often are potentially very mobile, inasmuch as they are relatively small, investment costs per workplace are low, equipment is simple and inexpensive, and there are few linkages with the host economy. MNCs moved first from the NICs to the next tier of ASEAN-4 countries. Lately, in the face of growing labor unrest and rising costs in some of these nations, the trend is for companies to move on to lower income, third-tier countries such as Bangladesh, Sri Lanka, and China. When firms relocate, they generally transfer the same production and managerial technologies, thus repeating the cycle of exploitation of females in a new labor pool.

At the same time that rising costs in the NIC nations are diminishing their attractiveness as sites for labor-intensive manufacture, technological

developments in computer applications and robotics are revolutionizing some production processes. In response to these forces of change, structural adjustments are well underway in each of the NICs. Taiwan and Korea are upgrading the skill level of their labor forces to attract higher technology industries. In Hong Kong, the share of GDP in industry is falling while that in services is rising. Singapore is committed to becoming a center for knowledge-intensive industry. As the NICs progress toward higher value-added manufactures and services, they are experiencing a new problem: a growing shortage of skilled workers.

The new technologies have led some MNCs to automate EPZ plants, particularly in high-end electronics. Indeed, it has been suggested that computer-aided automation may eventually cause offshore manufacturing to become obsolete and lead to "re-relocation" of factories back to industrial nations. Others argue that MNCs will continue to produce in developing countries, owing to their substantial investments there and the growing importance of being located in burgeoning new markets.[15] A 1987 United Nations report on the electronics industry concludes that while firms may begin to experiment with onshore automated factories for selected products, they are apt for many years to rely on offshore plants for the bulk of their assembly needs.[16] Automation involves both added costs and risks, and has not proceeded at the same pace in all phases of electronics manufacture. The shortening of product cycles in consumer electronics, for example, increases the risk of capital equipment becoming obsolete before investment costs are recovered, and this industry remains largely labor-intensive.

When automation does occur, workers are displaced, and a disproportionate burden falls upon females who predominate at low level jobs and who have acquired few transferable skills for obtaining alternate employment. Moreover, while blatantly harmful conditions and practices relative to workplace safety may be eliminated when factories modernize, taking their place are more subtle forms of worker exploitation. In the Malaysian high-end

electronics industry, for example, a trend toward automation has raised both skill and wage levels of workers, and safety condition in plants have been upgraded. But simultaneously, new methods of cutting back labor costs being employed. These include job enlargement at the same wage, added shifts to avoid overtime pay, and various schemes of labor shedding to match demand fluctuations. One government study showed that it has been common practice for firms to retrench experienced workers and then soon rehire many of them at entry-level wages.[17]

IMPACT ON CORPORATE GOALS AND THE NEED FOR STRATEGIC CHANGE

In summary, the vision MNCs have held of low and stable production costs in Asian manufacturing sites is being progressively undermined by rising wages and increasing labor unrest as the predominantly female workforce resists numerous aspects of the technology transferred, both production and managerial. The strategies of technology transfer that have been applied to successive tiers of Asian countries can now be seen to generate dysfunctional cost effects: costs associated with productivity decreases resulting from health impairment and worker resistance, costs associated with rising wages as labor organizes, and costs associated with either relocation to next-tier countries or automation of production processes. However, full realization of the magnitude of these costs and a subsequent reassessment of corporate strategies regarding transfer of productive and managerial technologies has yet to be made. On supply-side terms alone, corporate strategies need to be re-evaluated.

However, demand-side factors are also becoming important as firms locate in Asian countries not simply because of low production costs, but to gain more favorable access to growing markets. Structural changes involve markets as well as production. Already the Asia-Pacific region has surpassed Latin America as the largest market for US exports in the developing world. In the coming decade, market growth in Asian countries is predicted to be at an annual rate in excess of 5%, compared to 1-2% in industrial nations. In the 1990s, the Asia-Pacific market will be the most rapidly growing in the world for many industrial and high technology goods and services, as well as a wide range of consumer goods.

With the additional corporate goal of developing markets in Asia, it becomes even more urgent that the effect of corporate policies regarding the transfer of production technology and management techniques on the workforce be examined and policies reformulated for the 1990s. Achievement of broader corporate goals necessitates taking a different approach toward workers who are seen as potential consumers or members of a society of consumers. Robert H. Galvin, Chairman of Motorola, expressed such a vision while discussing his firm's production facilities in Malaysia:

> We need our Far Eastern customers, and we cannot alienate the Malaysians. We must treat our employees all over the world equally.[18]

Women have constituted a principal resource for Asian development to date, and their role will become even more important in the 1990s. Female employment in Asia is increasing more rapidly than that of men. The proportion of female-headed households is rising. Women are at the head of ruling or opposition parties in a number of Asian countries. For all these reasons, women will have more visibility and influence in Asian economies of the future. Women have successfully organized global boycotts of employers' products in the past, and this tactic may become increasingly widespread as women's international networks grow. The potential power of consumer protests and backlashes against firms is not to be underestimated. The global boycott of Nestle products prompted by the firm's marketing of infant formula in the Third World has, by one estimate, cost the company $5 billion to date.[19]

Thus, alienation of women workers is counterproductive to marketing goals. Both corporate and national interests make it vital to perceive the negative impact past transfers of productive and managerial technologies have had, and how they would affect such broader considerations if continued. Recognition of women workers not as a disposable resource, but as human capital to be developed can be to the distinct advantage of MNCs on the supply-side in reducing long run production costs and on the demand-side in cultivating new markets.

Rather than acquiescing to cultural traditions that subordinate and demean women, MNCs can and should demonstrate leadership in recognizing women's contributions and in ensuring equality of opportunity on a global basis. Some specific steps that firms can take include: applying minimum industrial-country standards to making workplaces safe; restructuring wage and benefit packages; revising production schedules to reduce shift lengths and forced overtime; providing for job mobility through training and upgrading of skills; increasing job security; incorporating women in management and supervisory positions; recognizing and supporting labor organizing rights.

Such improved treatment of women workers may adversely affect labor costs in the short run. However, so do work stoppages, labor shortages, and poorly motivated workforces. In evaluating the expense associated with a more equitable conception of human resource management, firms must also consider the productivity benefits that would ensue from reduced turnover, increased worker morale and loyalty, better trained workforces, and reduced incidence of labor strife. Lastly, better treatment of female employees would avoid the potential backlash of women as workers, citizens, and consumers, as the importance of Asian markets grows.

NOTES

1. The seminal study of the appropriateness of technology transfer to developing countries is E. F. Schumacher, *Small is Beautiful: Economics As If People Mattered*, Harper & Row, New York, 1974. Other representative sources include: A. Robinson (ed.), *Appropriate Technologies for Third World Development*, Macmillan Publishing Co., New York, 1979; Carl Dahlman and Larry Westphal, "The Transfer of Technology," *Finance and Development*, Vol. 20, No. 4, 1983, pp. 6-9; Martin Fransman, "Conceptualising Technical Change in the Third World in the 1980s: An Interpretive Survey," *Journal of Development Studies*, Vol. 21, July, 1985. pp. 572-652.

2. There is a literature on women and technolgy in the Third World, but it has yet to be fully integrated into the debate concerning the transfer of technology. For example, see: Susan C. Bourque and Kay B. Warren, *Access Is Not Enough: Gender Perspectives on Technology and Education*, in Irene Tinker (ed.) *Persistent Inequalities*, Oxford University Press, New York, 1990, pp. 83-100; Pamela M. D'Onofrio-Flores and Sheila M. Pfafflin, *Scientific-Technological Change and the Role of Women in Development*, Westview Press, Boulder, Colorado, 1982. This literature does not address the issues examined in this paper—the impact of the transfer of productive and managerial technologies by MNCs on their largely female labor forces.

See Noeleen Heyzer, "Asian Wage-Earners: Their Situation and Possibilities for Donor Intervention," *World Development*, Vol. 17, No. 7, 1989, pp. 1109-1123; Noeleen Heyzer (ed.) *Daughters in Industry: Work, Skills and Consciousness of Women Workers in Asia*, Asian and Pacific Development Centre, Kuala Lumpur, 1988; Gavin W. Jones, "Economic Growth and Changing Female Employment Structure in the Cities of Southeast and East Asia, in G. Jones (ed.) *Women in the Urban and Industrial Workforce, Southeast and East Asia*, The Australian National University, Canberra, 1984, pp. 17-59; Annette Fuentes and Barbara Ehrenreich, *Women in the Global Factory*, South End Press, Boston, 1983.

4. Perhaps the strongest advocate of this view is Linda Y. C. Lim. See "Women's Work in Export Factories: The Politics of a Cause," in Irene Tinker (ed.) *op. cit.*, pp. 101-119.

5. For a summary of this view, see Kathryn Ward, "Introduction and Overview," in K. Ward (ed.) *Women Workers and Global Restructuring*, Industrial and Labor Relations Press, Ithaca, 1990, pp. 1-22.

6. *Business Week*, October 31, 1988, p. 46.

7. See, for example, Gus Edgren, "Spearheads of Industrialization or Sweatshops in the Sun," in E. Lee (ed.) *Export Processing Zones and Industrial Employment in Asia: Papers and Proceeding of a Technical Workshop*, International Labour Office, Geneva, 1984, pp. 27-52; Rachael Kamel, *The Global Factory*, American Friends Service Committee, Philadelphia, 1990.

8. International Labour Office, *Social and Labour Practices of Multinational Enterprises in the Textiles, Clothing and Footwear Industries*, Geneva, 1984, p. 110.

9. Hema Goonatilake and Savitri Gooneseekere, "Industrialization and Women Workers in Sri Lanka: Working

Conditions Inside and Outside the Investment Protection Zone," in Noeleen Heyzer (ed.) *Daughters in Industry: Work, Skills and Consciousness of Women Workers in Asia, op. cit.*, pp. 184-208.

10. Lee, *op. cit.*

11. Walden Bello and Stephanie Rosenfeld, "Dragons in Distress: The End of an Era for South Korea and Taiwan," *Multinational Monitor*, Vol. 11, No. 11, November, 1989, p. 11.

12. *Business Week, op. cit.*

13. *Business Week*, May 15, 1989, p. 46.

14. *Business Asia*, January 1, 1990, pp. 6-7.

15. For a discussion of both points of view, see Manuel Castells and Laura D'Andrea Tyson, "High Technology and the Changing International Division of Production: Implications for the US Economy," in Randell B. Purcell (ed.) *The Newly Industrializing Countries in the World Economy: Challenges for US Policy*, Lynne Rienner Publishers, Boulder, 1989, pp. 13-50.

16. See "Transnational Corporations and the Electronics Industries of ASEAN Economies," (UNCTC Current Studies Series A, No. 5), United Nations Centre on Transnational Corporations, New York, 1987.

17. Kamal Salih and Mei Ling Young, "Changing Conditions of Labour in the Semiconductor Industry in Malaysia," *Labour and Society*, Vol. 14, Special Issue on High Tech and Labour, 1989, pp. 59-80.

18. *New York Times*, May 21, 1989, p. 1.

19. Carol-Linnea Salmon, "Milking Deadly Dollars from the Third World," *Business and Society Review*, No. 68, Winter 1989, pp. 43-48.

REFERENCES

Diehl, Lincoln W., "Transferability of Management Technology to Newly Industrializing Countries," in *1989 Papers and Proceedings of the Pan-Pacific Conference VI*, May 29-June 1, 1989, Sydney, Australia, pp. 214-216.

Economic and Social Effects of Multinational Enterprises in Export Processing Zones, International Labour Organization, International Labour Office, Geneva, 1988.

Jones, Gavin W., "Introduction," in G. Jones (ed.) *Women in the Urban and Industrial Workforce, Southeast and East Asia*, The Australian National University, Canberra, 1984, pp. 1-14.

Lim, Linda Y. C., *Women Workers in Multinational Enterprises in Developing Countries*, International Labour Office, Geneva, 1985.

Lin, Vivian, *Health, Women's Work, and Industrialization: Women Workers in the Semiconductor Industry in Singapore and Malaysia*, Women in International Development Working Paper No. 130, Michigan State University, 1986.

Madu, Christian N., "Transferring Technology to Developing Countries—Critical Factors for Success," *Long Range Planning*, Vol. 22, No. 4, August, 1989, pp. 115-124.

Malaysian Industrial Development Authority, *Malaysia: Manpower for Industry*, Kuala Lumpur, 1988.

Ong, Aihwa, *Spirits of Resistance and Capitalist Discipline: Factory Women in Malaysia*, State University of New York Press, Albany, 1987.

Technology Atlas Team, "Components of Technology for Resources Transformation, *Technological Forecasting and Social Change*, Vol. 32, 1987, pp. 19-35.

Thailand Board of Investment, *Thailand: Investor's Guide*, Bangkok, 1987.

Wield, David and Ed Rhodes, "Division of Labour or Labour Divided?" in Ben Crow *et. al.*, (eds.) *Survival and Change in the Third World*, Oxford University Press, New York, 1988, pp. 288-309.

[11]

Ruth Pearson

Male bias and women's work in Mexico's border industries

This chapter charts the trajectory of women's employment in Mexico's border industries and critically examines some interpretations of its significance. It argues that the female work-force should not be viewed as an undifferentiated mass of women all sharing the same characteristics, and highlights important differences between the female work-force in electronics and garment factories. It also shows how women in both sectors have largely been confined to low-paid jobs without prospects at the bottom of the production hierarchy. The growth in recent years of jobs requiring technical and administrative skills is shown to be associated with a fall in the female share of the labour force. Male bias has structured both the way in which women have been incorporated into the border industries, and the appraisal of the significance of this growth of industrial jobs for women.

The development of the border industries

Since the mid-1960s women have formed the major part of the industrial labour force in the border states of northern Mexico. The 'maquiladora'[1] or border industries are largely labour-intensive industries typical of the offshore manufacturing or 'export processing'[2] which has been the dominant feature of Third World industrialisation in the 1970s and early 1980s. Although there has been some diversification in the type of industries operating within the border areas, women continue to form the majority of those employed.

The preference for women workers for labour-intensive assembly operations in industries around the world is widely acknowledged.[3] However, it is interesting that in the early stages of the Border Industrialisation Programme (BIP), the employment of women was not anticipated. The programme was initiated by the Mexican government in 1965 as part of a series of measures to offset the adverse effects on the Mexican economy of immigration control and protectionist policies in the United States.

The economy of Mexico's northern states over the last hundred years has been more integrated with the economy of the southern states of the USA than with the rest of Mexico. Mexico's post-Second World War expansion of import-substituting industrialisation was not extended to the border states; and a large proportion of the consumption expenditure in this area goes directly on US goods (SIC, 1974).

The border between Mexico and the United States is of comparatively recent creation. It was not until 1851, with the annexation of Texas, that the USA finally halted its territorial expansion which had already forced Mexico to cede to its more powerful northern neighbour, the States of California, Arizona and New Mexico: thus losing more than fifty per cent of the territory which comprised the Republic of Mexico in 1821.

The border has remained a source of conflict between the two countries. In some senses it constitutes an artificial barrier which has been overridden when the dynamics of accumulation in the agricultural, industrial and service sectors in the USA have required access to the pool of cheap labour from Mexico. Migration from Mexico – often seasonal labour for agriculture and construction projects, as well as casual labour for the manufacturing sector and domestic and other low-paid service jobs – has been a constant feature of the economy of the south west of the USA throughout this century, in spite of periodic attempts to restrict immigration by the US government. The willingness and ability of Mexicans to migrate, often illegally, is partly a reflection of the fact that the population of the south-west of the USA is predominantly of Hispanoamerican origin (Flores Cabellero, 1982). It also reflects the high levels of unemployment in Mexico and the failure of the industrialisation programmes of the 1950s and 1960s to generate sufficient employment opportunities to absorb the growing population throughout Mexico.

The BIP was directly stimulated by a US Congress decision in 1964 to rescind the legislative basis of the 'Bracero' programme, by which a fixed number of Mexicans were permitted to migrate across the border for specified employment. This left the Mexican government with a serious crisis. Not only did the flow of potential migrants continue to head for the frontier cities in spite of the fact that there were no further legal opportunities to work in the USA; in addition, the Mexican economy stood to suffer from the drying-up of the flow of remittances from immigrants working in the USA, which in some years had contributed up to forty per cent of foreign exchange inflows. At the local level there was a rapid increase in population in the northern border cities, where officially estimated unemployment rates ran as high as forty to fifty per cent by 1966.

The Mexican government had made previous attempts to solve the chronic unemployment problem in the border towns, which acted both as a pole of attraction for rural migrants and those migrating from towns in the interior of Mexico, and as a stepping-stone and negotiating post for those intending to continue their journey north to seek work in the USA. In 1961 PRONAF (Programa Nacional Fronterizo) was launched with the aim of modernising northern cities, cleaning up their image as Rest and Recreation posts for troops serving in Panama and elsewhere in the region, and encouraging a higher participation of Mexican-produced goods in the commercial transactions of the areas (NACLA, 1975).

PRONAF resulted in the establishment of hotels, trailer camps and parks for North American tourists, and the construction of commercial complexes and shopping centres, but no significant industrial activity was inaugurated. The programme was ineffective in developing an industrial alternative to absorb the growing population of the urban areas, swelled by rural migrants displaced by the intensifying pace of mechanisation and concentration of ownership in agriculture, especially in the states of Baja California, Sonora and Chihuahua.

The BIP, which led to the development of the border industries, was thus intended as a substitute for emigration, as much to replace lost foreign exchange transfers as to provide employment opportunities. The basic idea of the programme was to encourage foreign (primarily American) firms to establish labour-intensive manufacturing activities in Mexico where they could profit from the differential between the cost of labour there and in the USA. Such a policy was seen as attractive both to the Mexican government, which stood to gain foreign exchange as US companies converted dollars to pay for Mexican workers and local inputs of goods and services, as well as employment creation within Mexico; and to the American companies which had been deprived of their legal access to cheap Mexican labour as the result of US labour union pressure. The initiative for the programme came from the Mexican government, following visits to East Asian countries where such labour-intensive manufacturing industries producing for the export market had been established for some years; and where such activity was frequently located in specially created Free Trade Zones.

For American firms, the possibility of taking advantage of the lower wage rates in Mexico (and in Asia), was enhanced by the introduction of certain special clauses in the US Tariff Schedule. These allowed American firms to export partially processed products or components for further processing and assembly abroad, and re-import them into the USA, with import duties only payable on the value added abroad – that is, primarily on the labour cost of the overseas operation.

Because of Mexico's proximity to the USA, it was argued that there were special advantages for American firms relocating part of their production process to the Mexican border areas rather than to more distant Third World countries, even though labour costs in Mexico were higher than those in South East Asia and Central America. First, the nearness to the US domestic market means that transportation costs are lower. This is particularly important for products which have a high weight to value ratio and accounts for the fact that there is a greater variety of goods produced by maquiladora industries than in many Free Trade Zones elsewhere. A second advantage is the possibility that firms can operate 'twin plants' – that is, a firm located in one of the US border towns can establish an assembly plant on the Mexican side of the border and run both plants as an integrated operation using a single management, technical and personnel structure.[4] Both the geographical proximity and the direct control available through twin plants make production in Mexico more flexible: for instance, when the dictates of fashion or unseasonal weather alter the predicted demand for certain lines in the apparel industry, it is easier to change the orders to a Mexican sub-contractor than to a plant located in Hong Kong or the Philippines.

Male bias and women's work in Mexico's border industries   137

In spite of these attractions, it took three or four years of official encouragement from the US government (NACLA, 1975), and considerable changes in the Mexican investment regulations for the area, before the maquiladora plants established themselves in Mexico in any significant numbers.[5] The Mexican government enacted a series of special measures which enabled foreign manufacturers to import components and export the finished goods incorporating them, under a bond system without incurring customs duties. In addition, machinery could be imported duty free on a temporary basis. Both the Federal government and individual states also introduced a number of fiscal incentives, including exemption from some local and national taxes, and some state governments initiated the construction of special industrial parks, complete with required utilities, telecommunications facilities and road networks (Carillo and Hernandez, 1985, pp. 94–89).

Mexico had to compete as a location for offshore processing with other Third World countries where wages were considerably lower. Whilst hourly wage rates in Mexico were less than twenty-five per cent of US unskilled wage rates, they were still considerably higher than those quoted for East and South-East Asian countries which were already exporting to the USA under items 807 and 806.30 of the US Tariff Schedule (USITC, 1975). However, the advantages of Mexico, in terms of the nearness to the final market, the reduction in transport costs both of materials and components and of assembled goods for re-export to the USA, together with the incentive package offered by Mexico and her long record of political stability, eventually proved sufficient inducements for US investments in the northern border area.

The BIP got off to a slow start as the administrative and infrastructural framework spread slowly across the major border towns. In December 1965 there were only twelve maquiladora plants, employing some 3,000 people; but by 1970 the official total was 120 plants, with a workforce of 20,000 (see Table 1). In the early 1970s the overall level of employment continued to increase until the sharp recession in the American economy led to employment cut-backs in 1975. A strong body of US entrepreneurial opinion, widely shared in Mexican government circles, held that escalating labour resistance in Mexico, as workers organised to demand better wages, fringe benefits and working conditions in many of the larger plants, was 'forcing' American firms to abandon production in

138   *Male bias in the development process*

Mexico for other locations where the work-force was more amenable to the conditions and remuneration they offered.

Table 1 *Growth of the maquiladora industry in Mexico 1968–88*

Year	Number of plants	Total labour force
1968	112	11,000
1969	108	15,900
1970	120	20,300
1971	251	29,200
1972	n.d.	48,100
1973	247	64,300
1974	455	76,000
1975	454	67,200
1976	448	74,500
1977	443	78,400
1978	457	90,700
1979	540	111,400
1980	620	119,500
1981	605	131,000
1982	585	127,000
1983	600	151,000
1984	672	199,700
1985	760	212,000
1986	987	268,400
1987	1055	290,579
1988	1450	330,579

Sources: Sklair, 1989, table 8–1; Carillo and Hernandez, 1985, fig 1, table III–I; SIC, 1974.

The Mexican government was sufficiently alarmed by the current and threatened scale of cut-backs in the maquiladora plants in the mid-1970s to offer an improved package of incentives to American firms, although there is little hard evidence that many of the companies withdrawing from Mexico actually did set up replacement operations in other Third World countries. New regulations increased the tax holidays enjoyed by the plants; reduced their obligations to pay social security quotas and other local taxes; extended the period during which workers could be legally kept on temporary contracts; and allowed a more liberal interpretation of the laws about 'justifiable dismissal of workers' (Carillo and Hernandez, 1985, p. 93). In 1976 the Mexican peso was substantially devalued, which reduced labour costs in dollar terms by approximately 100 per cent at a stroke. As the US economy started to recover from the recession, the maquiladora plants began to increase and expand employment again. The Mexican government was so convinced of the benefits of this type of industrial activity that the legal and administrative basis of the programme was extended to the interior and south-east of the country, though some ninety-five per cent of employment continued to be located in the northern border region.

Indeed, for some time after the 1976 currency devaluation, Mexico's competitive position *vis-à-vis* competing locations improved. The dollar cost of wages and salaries fell from US$215 million in 1976 to US$200 million in 1977, even though the total number employed rose by 4,000 in that year. One estimate indicates that the average savings per worker, compared with costs in the USA, increased from US$6,000 in 1972 to US$10–12,000 in 1978 (Fernandez-Kelly, 1978, cited in Carillo and Hernandez, 1985, p.100). In dollar terms the minimum wage paid to maquiladora workers had fallen to ten per cent of daily wage minimum rates in the USA by 1983, compared with a level of twenty per cent in 1969–78, (*ibid.*, p. 131). In spite of the fears of increased workers' militancy in 1975, Mexico regained a more stable political image with the ending of the Echeverria presidency in 1976, and with this the promise of a more stable economic and industrial relations environment. From 1979, the maquiladora regulations were extended beyond the border states to cover the whole country. Again in the early eighties, inflation and instability temporarily halted the expansion of the programme, but devaluation in 1982 again ensured a continuing growth of both employment and number of plants which continued unabated up to 1988 (see Table 1).

Gender composition of the labour force

In 1975, the overwhelming majority (78·3 per cent) of unskilled production workers ('operators') employed in the maquiladora plants were women (Table 2). No detailed breakdown of the gender composition of technical, administrative and managerial staff is available, but it is known that few women were employed at these levels. Women operators constituted 64·5 per cent of the total maquiladora labour force in 1975. Women's share of employment has been declining in the 1980s (see Table 2) for reasons that will be discussed later, but even in 1987, women constituted over two-thirds of operators, and female operators constituted over half of total employment in the maquiladora plants. Despite the declining share, the absolute level of women's employment has continued to rise, the number of women operators almost tripling in the decade 1975–85.

A study undertaken in 1975 by the Institute of Research on Labour (INET, 1975) gives more detailed information about the gender composition of the labour force in plants registered as maquiladoras in the municipalities of the six most important centres in northern Mexico. In these plants taken together, women comprised seventy-five per cent of the total labour force, but the proportion of women varied between plants in different industrial sectors.

Confirming the findings of other research, this study showed that women were concentrated in electronics, clothing, shrimp and other food processing, toymaking and coupon-sorting, where they comprised up to ninety per cent of the total labour force. Mexican government statistics indicate that in 1975, women comprised 81·6 per cent of the production workers in the electrical and electronics sector, 82·5 per cent in the shoes and garments sector, [6] and 73·5 per cent in the food products sector, but only 64·4 per cent in the miscellaneous sector, which includes metal processing and transportation equipment and components (SIC, 1974).

The INET study also indicated that men were the preferred labour force in maquiladora firms making transportation equipment, leather and synthetic goods including shoes, wood and metal furniture, photographic, sporting and paper goods. In two of these sectors – furniture, and transport and machinery – men comprised 96·5 per cent and 72·3 per cent of the labour force, although employment in these sectors was only 3·5 per cent of the total.

Thus in the sectors which accounted for the major part of employment, women made up eighty per cent of the total labour force. In those sectors which are untypical of export processing activities elsewhere in the world, and, until recent years, not extensive even in Mexico – that is, transportation equipment, wood and metal furniture – the percentage of men employed matched that

Table 2   Gender composition of Maquiladora labour force, 1975–87

	Total employment	Operator employment					Technical staff	Salaried (admin/manag)
		A Total	B Male	C Female	D Female as % of total operator employment	E Female operators as % of total employment		
1975 National (all Mexico)	65,318	53,771	11,653	42,118	78·3	64·5		
1979 National	111,365	95,818	21,981	73,837	77·0	66·3	9,569	5,978
Border industries	100,537	86,879	20,343	66,536	76·6	66·2	8,613	5,045
1980 National	119,546	102,020	23,140	78,880	77·3	65·0	10,828	6,698
Border industries	106,576	91,308	21,455	69,583	76·2	65·3	9,626	5,639
1981 National	130,973	110,634	24,993	85,691	77·4	65·4	12,545	7,744
Border industries	116,540	98,931	23,047	75,884	76·7	65·1	11,033	6,486
1982 National	127,048	105,383	23,990	81,393	77·2	64·1	13,377	8,288
Border industries	113,227	94,455	22,254	72,201	76·4	63·7	1,956	6,816
1983 National	150,867	125,278	32,004	93,274	74·4	61·8	16,332	9,267
Border industries	134,915	112,531	29,862	82,669	73·5	61·3	14,747	7,437
1984 National	199,684	165,505	48,215	117,290	70·9	58·7	22,381	11,798
Border industries	176,909	146,944	45,338	101,606	69·1	57·4	20,184	9,781
1985 National	211,968	173,874	53,832	120,042	69·0	56·6	25,042	13,052
Border industries	186,000	152,819	50,195	102,624	67·2	55·2	22,313	10,868
1986 National	242,234	197,836	62,492	135,346	68·4	55·9	29,615	14,881
1987 National	290,579	236,088	78,940	157,090	66·6	54·1	35,138	19,403

Source: Calculated from Table 8, INEGI (Instituto Nacional de Estadística, Geografía e Informática), Estadísticas de la Industria Maquiladora de Exportación, Mexico, Secretaría de Programación y Presupuesto.

of women in the other sectors (that is, up to ninety per cent). In paper clothing, there was apparently a more even division between men and women in the labour force. Though sewing in Mexico is a traditionally female occupation, the employment of men in manufacturing paper clothing was explained by less need for accurate and reliable sewing skills on a product that is designed for a very short life (INET, 1975, p. 6).

The sectoral variation in the proportion of women and men in the labour force corresponded to the variation in the ratio of labour costs to total production costs. Those sectors which employed a predominantly female labour force were those in which labour costs were the largest component of total manufacturing cost, but at the same time, unit labour costs (that is the ratio of value of total output to labour costs) were the lowest. Labour costs, which include wages plus legally enforceable labour-related payments such as social security payments, comprised between fifty-eight and sixty-eight per cent of total value of the products in the electronics, clothing and food maquiladoras. In other sectors, notably transport and electrical machinery, where a higher proportion of male labour was employed, the importance of labour costs in total costs fell to below fifty per cent (*ibid*).

The reasons for the preference for women in labour processes which rely on manual dexterity performed under closely supervised and/or speed-regulated conditions have been discussed elsewhere (Elson and Pearson, 1981). In the Mexican situation, it is clear that the availability of a potential pool of female labour was a major inducement for North American firms locating in the region, in spite of the Mexican government's expectation that the BIP would provide jobs for unemployed men. A report by Arthur D. Little Inc. in 1968 recommended that the availability of women workers could be increased rapidly by increasing women's participation in the work-force, recruiting workers from the commercial and agricultural sectors, and attracting additional migrants from the interior of Mexico (cited in Carillo and Hernandez, 1985, p. 88).

Appraisal of the implications of the growth in female employment: the problem of male bias

Appraisal of the implications of this growth in female employment has centred on two issues – has it increased rather than diminished

Male bias and women's work in Mexico's border industries   143

the problem of unemployment? Has it integrated women into development or led to their exploitation? Male bias can be seen in attempts to answer both questions.

The most crude form of male bias can be seen in the widely held view that maquiladoras have failed in their objective of employment creation because they have not provided enough jobs for male workers and may have actually deprived men of employment opportunities (Sklair, 1989, ch. 8). This argument is based on a number of gender-biased assumptions, the most common of which is that only male workers are considered to have an economic need to find employment. Yet Tiano's evidence (1987b), corroborated by the research carried out by Fernandez-Kelly (1983b), demonstrates that women's participation in the maquiladora industries is undertaken because of economic need, to support the households in which they are daughters, wives and/or mothers.

The second biased assumption is that before the establishment of the maquiladora factories women did not participate in Mexico's industrial labour force. In fact, it is well documented that since the initiation of industrialisation in Mexico in the 1950s, the participation of women has steadily grown (Noriega Verdugo, 1982). What has changed is the *visibility* of such employment; whilst women were employed in textile factories, food-processing factories and other traditional industries, they were part of a labour force that was not necessarily predominantly female, and were working in areas where men's industrial employment was very common, such as in the industrial areas around Mexico City, Monterey, Puebla and other centres of industrial growth. In the border regions, the situation is quite different. First, women are working in regions where no or few factories existed before; second, they are working in factories which employ a predominantly female labour force, so that they are a majority, not a minority, of the industrial labour force. And third, an enormous amount of government, academic and political attention has been focused on the maquiladora plants, which for some represented not only the opportunity to bring economic development to the Mexican border and increase its autonomy from the United States, but a new export-oriented development strategy that could have implications for the whole future of Mexico's development (see Sklair, 1988b).

However, there is a further question of whether the growth of the border industries has diminished the problem of *women's* unemployment. Some researchers argue that it has tended to increase the rate of female unemployment as conventionally measured. The logic of this position is that the demand for women in the maquiladora plants induced an increase in the level of women's labour force participation (that is, the proportion of women in any given age cohort who declare themselves in or seeking employment) in excess of the actual rate of employment creation, thus increasing women's unemployment rate (which is measured as the proportion of economically active women who are not in recognised employment). The findings of Tiano (1987b) that unemployment rates for women in the age groups from which the bulk of the maquiladora operatives are initially recruited are higher in the majority of the northern states than in Mexico as a whole, have been used to support this hypothesis, although statistically they are not conclusive.[7]

A UN-sponsored study suggests some reasons for the rising rate of measured unemployment. Konig (1975, p. 74) reports that 'much of the maquiladora manpower [*sic*], particularly at the operator level, is incorporated into the economically active population for the first time. In the case that the level of operations falls off, these people will not simply go back to their families, but rather join the ranks of those looking for work.' In addition, the numbers of unemployed are swelled by the many unsuccessful applicants for maquiladora jobs who prefer to wait for an opportunity for in-plant employment rather than take another job: '45 per cent of the total operators surveyed without previous work experience had not bothered to take up a job previously', and 'quite a few girls that had been suspended for some time in the past – three to eight months at a time because of the lack of work in maquiladoras . . . had not bothered to look for a job in the interim.' (*Ibid.*, p. 67).

However, the assumption that the women working in the maquiladora plants had become economically active for the first time is a further, more subtle, example of male bias. It is likely that women waiting for job opportunities in the maquiladora plants had not previously sought permanent, formal sector jobs, but had been involved in casual labour in the informal sector, though some may have been continuing their studies where economic circumstances permitted. This would be quite consistent with responses to a questionnaire, that earlier they had not been seeking or engaged in work, since, as is widely recognised, both interviewers and respondents to questions about work often adopt a conceptualisation of work which is restricted to formal sector employment, and excludes the range of other, informal, income-generating strategies which most women are constantly undertaking (see Beneria, 1981). Respondents were asked whether they had been in employment or had been seeking employment in the previous week. It is probable that the knowledge that formal sector factory work – 'employment' – now existed would have encouraged positive responses on 'seeking employment' from women who would previously have answered in the negative – either because they knew there were no possibilities of obtaining formal sector work, or to conceal informal sector casual work from the attention of the authorities. Konig's research techniques may thus have misidentified the reasons for an increase in measured unemployment.

There is a further argument that the labour supply has been increased because many of the maquiladora workers of non-local origin, who are successful in finding jobs, induce substantial migration of female relatives from elsewhere in Mexico to join them in order to seek similar employment. This would not only have the effect of increasing the available supply of appropriate labour for recruitment to the maquiladora plants, but also increase the economically active population by a larger amount than actual employment increases at any given time, thus again exerting an upward pressure on recorded rates of unemployment. Contrary to conventional assumptions, maquiladora workers were not necessarily recruited from the rural poor: Fernandez-Kelly's research indicates that, at least in the late 1970s , the majority of women workers in Cuidad Juarez's maquiladoras who were of migrant origin, came from smaller towns in the northern or neighbouring states – they were not the displaced rural migrants of the classical literature (Fernandez-Kelly, 1983a, p. 215).

Migration to the urban centres had been a continuing feature of the border regions for some years, and it is argued, would have continued even without the attraction of employment in the new manufacturing plants (Bustamente, 1983; Fernandez-Kelly, 1983b). What is new is the impact that the demand for female labour had on perceptions of women's labour force status. More women regarded themselves, and were regarded by labour force enumerators, as unemployed than would previously have been the case. Any discernible increase in measured unemployment rates is as likely to result from this change as from the migratory pull exercised by the growth of the maquiladora industry itself.

Another subtle form of male bias can be seen at work in the appraisal of whether women have been 'integrated' into national development by incorporating them into modern industry, or 'exploited' in the sense that maquiladora factories take advantage of and reinforce women's structural vulnerability within the labour market and the family (Sklair, 1989, ch. 8; Tiano, 1987a). The problem here is the treatment of women working in the border industries as an homogeneous category, so that 'women' are added on as a single category to a preconceived analytical framework. It is more helpful to use the concept of gender relations which permits a disaggregation of women by socio-economic class, age, education, marital status, etc., in order to understand the interaction between various sets of social relations within and between the labour market and the family (Pearson, 1986). This would modify Tiano's conclusion that the exploitation thesis cannot hold because the evidence indicates that 'companies do not appear to recruit their workers from the most vulnerable sections of the female labour force, as the exploitation thesis would predict' (Tiano, 1987b). However, evidence from Tiano's and others' research (Fernandez-Kelly, 1983a; Escamilla and Vigorito, 1977) indicates that different industrial sectors employ different women, and that conditions of employment and 'exploitation' also vary between sectors. In the electronics factories in Mexico, most of which are direct subsidiaries of MNCS, the work-force tends to be younger and better educated than those employed in the smaller garment factories, many of which are sub-contractors for US firms rather than direct subsidiaries. In the electronics factories, physical working conditions are superior and wages are more likely to comply with minimum wage legislation. Clearly, a greater disaggregation of both the maquiladora factories and the structure of the female labour force would modify the over-general conclusion cited above.

Whilst women's subordinate status in the abstract is often invoked as an explanation for the employment of women workers in labour-intensive assembly work, class, educational opportunities, age, marital status, domestic responsibilities and previous working experience all interact to determine the specific forms that women's employment takes. Moreover, different attributes are appropriate to different labour processes, and management uses a variety of strategies to try to ensure that the work-force recruited is optimal for the labour process in which it is being employed (see Pearson (1986) for an extended discussion on this point).

Characteristics of the female labour force in the border industries

In spite of the growth of other sectors within the border industries, clothing and electronics are still the largest, and comprise the sectors in which the bulk of women's employment continues to be concentrated. As demonstrated above, one of the consequences of the male bias in the discussion of employment in this, and other, export-oriented industrial locations is that an over-generalised analysis of the female labour force is produced. However, case study research reveals important differences between the characteristics of the women workers in each of these two sectors, differences which are related to the organisational structure of the industry, the technology of production, the organisation and control of labour in the production process, and the different contractual relationships between the maquiladora plants and their US partners.

The electronics plants in the Mexican northern border states tend to be larger (in terms of numbers of employees) than the clothing plants; are more often directly-owned subsidiaries of American companies; and are generally engaged in the production and assembly of components such as semiconductors or consumer products such as video recorders and colour television sets, which are re-exported and marketed in the US as the product of the parent company (Fernandez-Kelly, 1983a, pp. 102–7).

This association with the modern, American electronics industry is exploited by employers, who foster the impression that employment in electronics plants represents a superior option for the work-force. In part, this distinction reflects real factors, in that electronics workers are on average paid higher wage rates than those in clothing or comparable sectors. Moreover, the larger electronics plants have better and more modern working conditions. They are more likely to be located in specially constructed modern industrial parks, and to occupy newly built purpose-fitted factory buildings, which boast air-conditioning (to maintain the technical quality of the product rather than the comfort of the workers), piped music and company uniforms. Because of their more direct relationship with their US principals, and the larger scale of their investment, it is assumed – at least in normal (that is, non-recessionary) times – that these plants offer more stable employment, and that in general the wage level will approximate to the legal minimum wage, in addition to any fringe benefits such as health and social security insurance (Nurayama and Munoz, 1979, pp. 65–6).

In contrast, the clothing sector is characterised by smaller firms that generally operate under sub-contracting relationships with one or more US corporations, which are as likely to be marketing (retail or wholesale) companies (such as Sears Roebuck) as garment-production companies. These garment maquiladoras are very often owned, at least in name, by Mexican companies; and are distributed widely along the frontier region (and elsewhere) outside the special industrial parks. Partly because of their indirect relationship with their contracting partners in the United States, and also because of the volatility in the clothing market caused by fashion, the weather and intense competition, as well as fluctuations in consumers' disposable income, clothing maquiladoras have an unstable history. The composition of the garment sector fluctuates with continued closures of existing firms and establishment of new ones, or re-establishment of old firms with different legal identities (Escamilla and Vigorito, 1977).

The superiority of the electronics plants, at least up to the early 1980s, made them the preferred employment sector for women workers, and this allowed electronics employers to exercise a fair degree of control over whom they recruited. This is reflected in the disparity between the labour force in the electronics sector, compared to that in the clothing sector, over a wide range of characteristics. Fernandez-Kelly's study (1983a) in Ciudad Juarez confirms this view; of her sample, eighty-five per cent of women employed in the electronics plants were aged twenty-four or under, whilst seventy per cent were under twenty-one. On the other hand, only thirty-six per cent of those working for clothing maquiladoras were under twenty-four. At the youngest and oldest ends of the age range, the differences were even more extreme: only four per cent of workers in the clothing plants were under eighteen compared with thirty-two per cent in electronics – nearly a third of all electronics workers; but twenty-three per cent of clothing workers were over thirty-one, and a full sixty-four per cent were over twenty-five. None of the electronics workers surveyed was over thirty-one, and only fifteen per cent were between twenty-five and thirty. A later study confirmed this trend, showing that in 1978, 79·3 per cent of electronics workers were under twenty-four, whilst over thirty-eight per cent of clothing workers were over twenty-five.

There is a correlation between the different age profile of workers in these two sectors and their marital and maternal status. The electronics workers are more likely to conform to the 'young, single, childless' stereotype (see Pearson, 1986) than the older garment workers. Of Fernandez-Kelly's sample, sixty-one per cent were single, lower than what might have been expected from the literature, but higher than the fifty-four per cent of the garment-sector workers. While the younger age range of the electronics workers would tend to suggest a lower percentage of married women, there may be some discrepancy between the electronics firms' stated preference for single women and the actual situation.

The study by INET (1975, p. 12) reported that many women who were in fact married, declared themselves to be single because they knew that 'this increases their attraction to the firms'. Carrillo and Hernandez (1985, p. 115) reported that nearly ten per cent of all electronics workers were single parents; moreover, forty per cent of electronics workers were mothers, lower than the sixty per cent of clothing workers, but still a large deviation from the 'young, single, childless' stereotype. A study carried out by the authors in Cuidad Juarez in 1978 indicated that 57·5 per cent of electronics workers were single compared with thirty per cent of the clothing workers (*ibid*).

However, it was clear that the firms were concerned about whether the worker had children, responsibility for whom could detract from her productivity, availability for overtime and flexibility with regard to changing shift times and temporary shut-downs. Predictably, a higher proportion of the (older) women in the garment sector had children of their own, one in three of them being single parents. Electronics workers were more likely to live in households in which they were daughters, and to be one of two or more income providers in the household (sixty-eight per cent of total sample): whereas twenty-seven per cent of garment workers were the sole income earners in their households (Fernandez-Kelly, 1983a, pp. 54–7).

Comparison of educational qualifications also points up the differences between these two groups of workers. Women employed in the electronics factories had on average eight years' formal schooling compared to six in the clothing industry. It is interesting to note that nearly sixty per cent of electronics workers and thirty-three per cent of garment workers had over seven years' schooling compared to the average level for Mexican workers of just under four years. Many electronics managers demanded a high educational level from their workers, at least completion of primary school (six years' schooling); and many workers in the INET survey had commenced secondary school, whilst others had secondary school matriculation and even further educational experience in communal colleges, teacher training or even social work (INET, 1975, p. 27). This trend is confirmed by Carillo and Hernandez (1985, p. 120), who report that sixty per cent of women working in the electrical/electronics sector had some secondary education, and many had completed courses in commercial colleges or other professional training.

Male bias in selection procedures

The divergent characteristics of the women working in these two sectors and the superior status of the electronics sector indicate the freedom of the electronics sector management to target and recruit mainly those workers who meet their 'ideal' criteria. The higher educational qualifications demanded reflected not only employers' preference for a superior class background, which reinforced notions of the technological superiority of the sector, but also provided a guaranteed fluency in English, necessary not just for following the circuit diagrams and other working instructions from the American parent plant, but also the verbal commands and other communications from the predominantly US management and supervisory personnel employed at the plants.

Before the reported tightening of the labour market in the mid-1980s, the selection procedures of the electronics plants were extremely rigorous, and there was a low ratio of successful to total applicants. Konig (1975, p. 36) reported that the standard procedure 'usually involves a manual dexterity test, a check into vision and color perception (since deficient diet impairs color perception), a physical to check the applicant has no contagious diseases and is not pregnant, a check into hand-to-eye co-ordination and a general cultural test'.

However, the reasons given for rejection of unsuccessful applicants indicate the ability of management to use additional arbitrary and subjective criteria for the selection of what they consider a suitable labour force. Of 957 persons rejected, 241 had poor vision, 152 were physically incapable and lacked manual ability, 150 had too low an educational background and *130 lacked in appearance* (our emphasis) (*ibid.*). This was corroborated by two Mexican women researchers, who reported that women working in the smaller clothing plants believed that the large factories would not employ ugly workers (las feas). 'Since we considered it necessary to corroborate this view we interviewed all the owners of the larger plants who said, with no hesitation, that they preferred the prettier women, 'las bonitas', because the 'feas' caused a lot of problems and were always jealous. In order to double check we asked to be allowed to go into the plants and see for ourselves: in fact we could find no 'feas'.' (Escamilla and Vigorito, 1977, p. 24).

The selection of the ideal electronics worker, then, reflects a mixture of objective criteria (co-ordination and dexterity), social prejudice (against mothers, in spite of the existence of widespread evidence that women with children are more reliable workers because of both maturity and economic need), class prejudice (a preference for those with better schooling and a longer urban background) (Carrillo and Hernandez, 1985, p. 176), and sexist patriarchal fantasy (selection of only those considered good looking enough ('not lacking in appearance').

The rejection of older women with more obvious domestic responsibilities (children, husbands, etc.), who did not conform to the 'young, good looking' stereotype/fantasy of the managers, crowded such women into the lower-wage garment sector, where status, remuneration, benefits and security were inferior to those prevailing in the electronics sector (Fernandez-Kelly, 1983a).

Gender hierarchy in the maquiladora labour force

Whilst it is well documented that the majority of the workers at the maquiladora plants are women, little detailed research had been carried out regarding the sexual division of labour within the production process in the plants. The INET study contains an analysis of the production process, which indicates the manner in which male bias results in women being employed at the lowest levels of the hierarchy whilst supervisory positions are generally occupied by men (see fig.1). However, there is some contrast between the electronics and garment plants. Women are used in supervisory positions in garment plants where the dictates of the production process require that supervisors possess actual production skills. In contrast, where the supervisory functions are imbued with a technical mystique as in the electronics plants, women do not fill these positions.

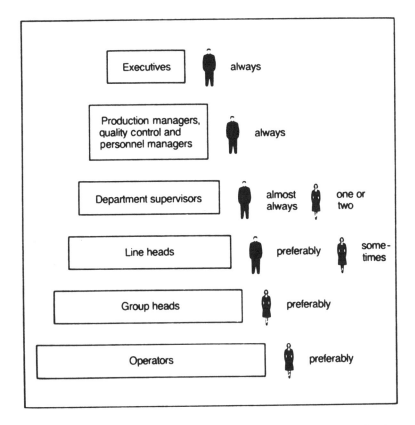

Fig.1 Schematic representation of the participation of women in the maquiladora workforce in Mexico.

Source: Translated and reproduced from INET, 1975, p.8.

Male bias and women's work in Mexico's border industries   153

The levels of work identified are operator, group head, line head, and supervisor (INET, 1975, p. 6). The high percentage of women in the maquiladora labour force as a whole reflects the concentration of women at operator level with the special exceptions described above. It is at this level that women's capacity to carry out boring and repetitive work is most appreciated by employers.

The next level in the hierarchy, the group head, refers to a person who is responsible for a group of five to ten operators. Her responsibility is to see that members of the group fulfil their work quotas, and to train new workers. Clearly, this job requires someone competent in the various tasks done by the workers in the group, and is consequently usually occupied by women recruited from the production line with the relevant work experience.

The line head occupies the next level in the hierarchy and undertakes a limited range of supervisory duties. Line heads have authority over five or ten groups (fifty to one hundred people). Their task is to distribute the materials amongst the different groups and to collect the processed articles and components, check that the required quality control norms have been met, and redistribute work for further processing. It is largely at this level that the differences between the sectors becomes most apparent. In the electronics sector line heads are always men, and it is reported that women are in fact reluctant to accept these jobs. There are two reasons for this: first, the production and quality control procedure is seen to be 'technical', in that the speed of production is controlled according to flow process procedures worked out by the management; and quality control is checked using machines rather than by the personal judgement of line heads. This creates the impression that the job is outside the capacity of women, who typically do not have technical qualifications. In addition, women are considered, and consider themselves, unsuitable for a position that demands authority and enforcement of discipline. The workers themselves identify these positions with management, causing the women who do occupy them to lose the solidarity and friendship of their work-mates. Since the companionship at work is one of the major reasons given by workers in electronics factories for job-satisfaction, women are reluctant to forego this, especially since the financial incentives are extremely small (*ibid.*, p. 7).

On the other hand, women are quite often found as line heads in the clothing factories where there is not such a distinction between groups and lines of production. In these plants, a production line will produce a complete garment. The person responsible for regulating the pace of the work and checking its quality must obviously be familiar with all the individual operations required. She must know how long it takes to insert a long zip rather than a short one, or to sew different kinds of sleeves or do different kinds of finishing or decorative operations, all of which vary with the type of garment produced and the efficiency of the sewing-machine being used. Quality control also rests on her judgement, which can only be reliable if she is fully experienced in all aspects of the production process. In this situation, line heads must obviously be recruited from experienced production workers, that is, from the female labour force.

The highest job amongst production workers is that of department supervisor, which is effectively a management position, demonstrated by the fact that no workers at this level are unionised. The department supervisor is responsible for the running of the whole production process. In the electronics sector, this job requires the ability to communicate the production targets and decisions of management to the workers in a manner which is both understood and acted upon; that is, it requires someone with both technical background and authority. Since women tend to lack technical education and, it is assumed, do not easily command obedience from other workers, whilst the reverse is true of men, companies usually appoint men to this position.

In fact, women do sometimes occupy supervisory positions in the clothing firms, especially the smaller firms which cannot afford to appoint a man, since he would not be able to work on the production line when necessary, as well as to supervise the operation. However, these women are both feared and reviled by the rest of the employees on the shop floor, which reduces women's willingness to accept this level of responsibility in a large plant.

The men employed on the factory floor who do not fall into the production and supervisory categories described above, carry out miscellaneous tasks peripheral to the main production process such as machine maintenance, materials handling and cleaning.

The gender hierarchy described here differs little from that prevailing in industry elsewhere in the world, where women form a major part of the unskilled labour force. Within this hierarchy, women are required to carry out jobs that are unskilled in the sense

Male bias and women's work in Mexico's border industries   155

that the worker has no control over the pace of the work, or responsibility for the total production process. Male bias is only overcome when supervisory positions require more than the transmission of authority and discipline but actually rest on the production experience of the person appointed, as in the garment industry.

Changes in the gender composition of the maquiladora work-force

As employment in the maquiladora industries has grown throughout the 1980s, the proportion of women operators, in relation to total employment and to total manual workers, has declined quite significantly as Table 2 indicates, so that by 1987, women operators comprised only 66·6 per cent of total manual workers, and just over fifty-four per cent of total employment.

Three explanations have been put forward for the fall in women's share of employment in the maquiladora industries. First, there is a sectoral explanation: those sectors which have traditionally employed more male workers – metal products, furniture and wood products, and transport equipment – have steadily increased, so that employment opportunities have grown much faster than the overall growth in women's employment. (This explanation is discussed at length in Sklair (1989) ch. 8).

Table 3 reveals the extent to which male-intensive employment sectors have grown during the 1980s. Whilst employment in the main female-intensive industries, textiles and clothing, assembly of electronic apparatus, and electronic components, grew only 5·6 per cent, 36·4 per cent and 46 per cent respectively, in the male-intensive industries such as furniture, footwear and leather, and transport equipment, the rates of growth were significantly higher, with the latter showing a more than 400 per cent increase between 1980 and 1985.

Second, there is the suggestion that there has been a certain amount of change in the nature and organisation of the labour processes in the previously female labour-intensive industries in northern Mexico, which have led to an increase in the proportions of technical and administrative employees, and hence a fall in the proportion of women employed. Whilst much of the Mexican evidence is indirect (*ibid.*), this would be consistent with changes in these industries in Europe and in other parts of the Third World

156   *Male bias in the development process*

(Pearson, 1986, 1989) where falls in the female intensity of the labour process can be partly attributed to changes in the technology and organisation of production leading to less reliance on manual production workers. Table 2 shows that in 1979 production workers accounted for eighty-six per cent of all maquiladora employment; by 1987, this had fallen to eighty-one per cent. On the other hand, the share of technical staff increased from 8·6 per cent to 12·1 per cent over the same period, while the share of salaried administrative and management employees rose from 5·4 per cent to 6·7 per cent.

The statistical evidence available indicates that the gender composition of employment *within* industries is changing as the proportion of operators falls. Table 3 indicates that women's manual employment as a percentage of total maquiladora employment fell from 65·5 per cent in 1980 to 55·2 per cent in 1985, and as a percentage of manual employment from 76·5 per cent to 67·2 per cent Since women are most heavily concentrated at the operator grade, it is instructive to look at the changes in the proportion of operator (manual) employment to total employment over this time period: overall, the proportion fell from 85·7 per cent to 82·2 per cent. However, in those sectors which are large employers of women, the decline is more significant; from 89·6 per cent to 85·0 per cent in textiles and clothing; from 84·0 per cent to 78·0 per cent in electronics assembly; and from 85·7 per cent to 79·5 per cent in the electronic components sector.

Since, as Sklair (1989, ch. 8) points out, 'it is safe to assume that most of the technicians are male, and that despite the growing numbers of women in administrative posts in the maquilas, men still had a clear majority of these posts', it would appear likely that the reduction in the proportion of operator labour in total employment is an important factor in leading to the declining proportion of women.

A third possible explanation is the direct substitution thesis: that as the pool of suitable female workers has dried up, managers are increasingly using men in tasks for which they would have preferred to recruit women. Certainly, there is evidence that the labour market in the northern states has tightened throughout the 1980s, and reports of labour shortages are frequent (*ibid.*). However, there is no clear evidence that this is because the maquiladora plants have already recruited all the available female labour; on the contrary, there is widespread evidence that women whom the firms would

Male bias and women's work in Mexico's border industries   157

have liked to recruit are preferring other employment opportunities – in the service sector as informal undocumented workers in the south-west of the USA – because the level of real wages in the maquiladora plants has been held at a low level. Sklair suggests that this is the result of an employers' cartel to keep wages down, in the face of falling profits, preferring a high turnover of labour to the potential increases in labour costs which would result from open competition for suitable labour.

Whilst there is clearly statistical evidence for the increase in male employment at all levels of the occupational structure in the maquilas , there is as yet no unequivocal evidence that men have been employed in a large-scale way specifically to substitute for women production workers. Moreover, it is plausible to assume that far from there being an unusual tendency to substitute men for women throughout the maquiladora industries, there may well be discernible and contrasting tendencies between the different sectors. Table 3 indicates that, for the maquiladora industries in the northern states, women operators' share of total employment fell from 65·5 per cent to 55·2 per cent between 1980 and 1985, and this is paralleled by a decline in women's share of operator (manual) employment from 76·5 per cent to 67·2 per cent. In the industries which have had the highest percentage of women workers, and those which have employed the largest number of women – that is clothing and textiles, and electronics assembly and components – women operators' share of total employment and women's share of operator employment have also fallen substantially; whereas in other smaller sectors – furniture and wood, transport equipment, and other manufactures – women operators' share of total employment has risen, and so has women's share of operator employment.

In the case of garments and textiles, it is likely that the product mix and the structure of the sector have changed significantly; a higher proportion of paper (disposable) garments, a larger share of more mechanised large sub-contracting firms and a change in the labour process itself would lead management to rely less heavily on the skills of the women operators. In the electronics assembly and components sector it is widely documented elsewhere that changes in the technology of production, including increased automation and integrated fabrication, not only reduce the share of operator employment, but also lead to a redefinition of operator jobs, some

Table 3 *Gender composition of maquiladora labour force, northern states, 1980 – 85; by industrial sector*

Industrial sector	Total employment	Employment growth 1980–85 (%)	Total operator employment	Total operator employment as % of all employment	Female operator employment	Female operators as % of	
						Total operator employment	Total employment
All industries							
1980	106,576	74·5	91,308	85·7	69,853	76·5	65·5
1985	186,000		152,819	82·2	102,624	67·2	55·2
Food production							
1980	1,393	33·2	1,260	90·5	926	73·5	66·5
1985	1,855		1,600	86·3	1,201	75·1	64·7
Clothing & textiles							
1980	14,256	5·6	12,771	89·6	10,588	82·9	74·3
1985	15,098		12,839	85·0	9,854	76·8	65·3
Footwear & leather							
1980	1,531	182·7	1,355	88·5	650	50·0	42·5
1985	4,328		3,803	87·9	2,103	55·3	48·6
Furniture							
1980	3,163	106·2	2,779	87·9	354	12·7	11·2
1985	6,522		5,519	84·6	1,174	21·3	18·0
Chemical products							
1980	83		66	79·5	20	30·3	24·1
1985	[n.d.]		[n.d.]		[n.d.]		
Transport equipment							
1980	7,100	420·8	5,981	84·2	2,006	33·5	28·3
1985	36,978		31,055	84·0	14,746	47·5	39·9

Table 3 contd.

Machines tools (non-electric)								
1980	1,834	30·1	1,541	84·0	495	32·1	30·0	
1985	2,386		2,010	84·2	679	33·8	28·5	
Assembly of electronic & electrical apparatus								
1980	28,580	36·4	24,000	84·0	20,456	85·2	71·6	
1985	38,994		30,430	78·1	23,089	75·9	59·2	
Electrical and electronic components								
1980	33,530	46·0	28,393	85·7	22,568	79·5	67·3	
1985	48,943		38,922	79·5	29,243	75·1	59·7	
Toys and sports goods								
1980	2,803	157·7	2,517	89·8	2,170	86·2	77·4	
1985	7,265		5,754	79·2	4,210	73·2	57·9	
Other manufactures								
1980	7,483	66·7	6,250	83·2	3,810	61·0	50·9	
1985	12,473		10,605	85·0	6,583	62·1	52·8	
Services								
1980	4,420	152.6	4,395	91·2	3,841	87·4	79·7	
1985	11,167		10,282	92·1	8,179	79·5	73·2	

Source: Calculated from Table 8, INEGI, 1988.

being reconstituted as technical or skilled jobs which are then redefined as male jobs. (See Pearson (1989) and Goldstein (1989) for a discussion of these processes in the electronics industry in Britain; and Cockburn (1985) for a more general discussion.)

Indeed, all previous studies of gender divisions in work have indicated that the organisation of the production process is itself gendered, and that jobs are created typically male or female. Where the gender composition of the work-force has been reconstructed in the same industry in the same location, this has been simultaneous with substantial changes in the technology of production, and the design and control of the labour process (see Cockburn, 1985); or it has involved the reorganisation of job specifications, albeit using similar technology, to 'create new female or male jobs' (Humphrey, 1987).

Sklair (1988b) indicates that over many of the industrial sectors there has been an attempt to upgrade the level of professional and managerial employment for Mexican nationals, and to increase the quality of technology transfer. The growth of new plants over time, together with the shake-out of marginal plants that occurs when the industry is in recession, would also be conducive to a continuing upgrading of technology of production. More research is needed on technological change in the maquiladora plants in the 1980s, and its relation to the changing gender composition of the work-force.

Conclusion

In addition to the changes in the relative demand for women and men to work in Mexico's border industry, one of the interesting issues to emerge during the 1980s is the difficulty encountered in recent years in recruiting women workers. Employers seem to have assumed that women constitute an inexhaustible supply of cheap labour, not requiring a higher wage because they are secondary workers rather than bread-winners.

But the main reason women gave for their reluctance to accept maquila employment at the going rate in 1985 was their inability to survive on the wages paid, given their role in supporting children and/or contributing to the survival of households in which they were daughters or spouses (Sklair, 1989, ch. 8). The opportunity (legal or not) of working on the other side of the Rio Grande in the USA was a better-paid option. In addition, the novelty and glamour of the maquiladoras has become somewhat tarnished by the experience of some fifteen to twenty years when the employment they provide for women has remained intense and exhausting, insecure, risky in terms of personal health and safety, and offering no prospects for long-term employment, promotion, training or skills enhancement. Whilst the Mexicanisation of salaried employment has proceeded alongside the increase in the share of technical, managerial and administrative jobs in the maquiladora industries, these opportunities have not been made available to women, from the ranks of the production operators or elsewhere. Any assumption that the maquiladoras provide an avenue for the incorporation of women into the industrial labour force on anything more than a short-term, low-paid, risky basis has been shown to be false. The possibility exists for intervention – by both the Mexican authorities and the US companies – to enhance the prospects, conditions and rewards of the women employed in the maquila industries; there is as yet little evidence that any such policies are even under consideration.

Notes

1 'Maquiladora' is a term used solely in Mexico to describe manufacturing plants, both subsidiaries of MNCS or nationally owned, whose main activity is the assembly or processing of products to be exported primarily to the USA. It is believed to derive from the word 'maquilar' – to make up.

2 Export processing is the assembly or processing of goods from imported or other components for export markets.

3 A full discussion of the employment of women workers in export processing can be found in Elson and Pearson (1981).

4 This is only one organisational structure amongst a variety of ways in which the maquiladora plants are integrated into the USA economy. For a full guide to the literature on this and other issues see Sklair (1988a).

5 See Bettwy (1985) for an extensive discussion on the legal and administrative infrastructure of the maquiladora industry.

6 If it were possible to exclude shoe and leather products, which use a substantial proportion of male labour, the figure for female employment in the clothing sector would be higher.

7 To fully test the hypothesis it would be necessary to use longitutional time series data to establish the comparative unemployment rates before the inauguration of the maquiladora plants, and the extent to which these had changed since the mid-1960s.

162   *Male bias in the development process*

References

Beneria, L. (1981), 'Conceptualizing the labour force: the underestimation of women's economic activities', *Signs*, vol. 7, no. 2.

Bettwy, S. (1985), 'Mexico's development: foreign trade zones and direct foreign investment', *Comparative Judicial Review*, no. 122, pp. 49–66.

Bustamente, J. (1983), 'Maquiladoras: a new face of international capitalism on Mexico's northern frontier', in J. Nash and M. P. Fernandez-Kelly (eds) (1983), *op. cit.*

Carillo, J., and Hernandez, A. (1985), *Mujeres fronterizas en la industria maquiladora*, SEP/CEFNOMEY, Coleccion Frontera, Mexico City.

Cockburn, C. (1985), *Machinery of Dominance: Women, Men and Technical Know How*, Pluto Press, London.

Elson, D., and Pearson, R. (1981), ' "Nimble fingers make cheap workers": an analysis of women's employment in Third World export manufacturing', *Feminist Review*, spring, no. 7, pp. 87–107.

——(eds) (1989), *Women's Employment and Multinationals in Europe*, Macmillan, London.

Escamilla, N., and Vigorito, M. A. (1977), 'El trabajo feminino en las maquiladoras fronterizas', *Nueva Antropologia*, vol. 8, April.

Fernandez-Kelly, M. P. (1978), 'Mexican border industry: female labour force participation and migration', Paper presented at annual meeting of American Sociological Association, California.

——(1983a), *For We Are Sold, I and My people: Women and Industry in Mexico's Frontier*, SUNY Press, Albany.

——(1983b), 'Mexican border industrialisation, female labour force participation and migration', in J. Nash and M. P. Fernandez-Kelly (eds) (1983), *op. cit.*

Flores Cabellero, R. (1982), *Evolucion de de frontera norte*, Centro de Investigaciones Economicas, Monterrey.

Goldstein, N. (1989), 'Silicon Glen: women and semiconductor multinationals', in D. Elson and R. Pearson (eds) (1989), *op. cit.*

Humphrey, J. (1987), *Gender and Work in the Third World: Sexual Divisions in Brazilian Industry*, Tavistock, London.

INEGI (Instituto Nacional de Estadistica, Geografia e Informatica) (1988), *Estadisticas de la Industria Maquiladora de Exportacion*, Secretaria de Programacion y Presupuesto, Mexico City.

INET (Instituto Nacional de Estudios Sobre El Trabajo) (1975), *Incorporacion de la mano des obra Feminina a la industria maquiladora de Exportacion*, Informe Preliminar, Investigacion de Campo, Mexico City.

Konig, W. (1975), *Towards an Evaluation of International Sub-contracting Activities in Developing Countries: Report on 'Maquiladoras' in Mexico*, UNECLA, Mexico City.

NACLA (North American Congress on Latin America) (1975), 'Hit and run: US runaway shops on the Mexican border', *Latin America and Empire Report*, vol. 9, no. 5, July–August.

Nash, J., and Fernandez-Kelly, M. P. (eds) (1983), *Women, Men and the International Division of Labour*, SUNY Press, Albany.

Male bias and women's work in Mexico's border industries   163

Noriega Verdugo, S. (1982), *La Mujer trabajadora en Baja California: Una apreciacion estadistica*, Cuadernos de Ciencias Sociales Series, Universidad Autonoma de Baja California, Tijuana.

Nurayama, G., and Munoz, C. (1979), 'Empleo de la mano de obra feminina en la industria maquiladora de exportacion', *Cuadernos Agrarios*, ano 4, no. 9, September.

Pahl, R. (ed.) (1988), *On Work*, Blackwell, Oxford.

Pearson, R. (1986), 'Female workers in the First and Third Worlds: the greening of women's labour', in K. Purcell *et al.* (eds) (1986), *op. cit.*, Reprinted in R. Pahl (ed.) (1988), *op. cit.*

——(1989), 'Women's employment and multinationals in the UK: restructuring and flexibility', in D. Elson and R. Pearson (eds) (1989), *op. cit.*

Philip, G. (ed.) (1988), *The Mexican Economy*, Routledge, London.

Purcell, K. *et al.* (eds) (1986), *The Changing Experience of Employment*, Macmillan, London.

Ruiz, V., and Tiano, S. (eds) (1987), *Women on the US-Mexico Border: Responses to Change*, Allen & Unwin, Boston.

SIC (Secreteria de Industria y Comercio) (1974), *Zonas fronterizas de Mexico: perfil socio-economico*, Mexico City.

Sklair, L. (1988a), *Maquiladoras: Annotated Bibliography and Research Guide to Mexico's In Bond Industry 1980–88*, Monograph Series No. 24, Centre for US Mexican Studies, University of California, San Diego.

——(1988b), 'Mexico's maquiladora programme: a critical evaluation', in G. Philip (ed.) (1988), *op. cit.*

——(1989), *Assembling for Development: The Maquila Industry in Mexico and the USA*, Unwin Hyman, Boston.

Tiano, S (1987a), 'Women's work and unemployment in northern Mexico', in V. Ruiz and S. Tiano (eds) (1987), *op. cit.*

——(1987b), 'Maquiladoras in Mexicali: integration or exploitation', in *ibid.*

USITC (United States International Trade Commission) (1975), *US Imports for Consumption: Tariff Items 807·00 and 806·30*, Washington DC.

[12]

North–South Trade and Female Labour in Manufacturing: An Asymmetry

by Adrian Wood*

A simple method of measuring the impact of North–South trade on the female intensity of manufacturing is applied to data for developed and developing countries. The results confirm that growth of exports has increased the relative demand for female labour in the South. However, there does not appear to have been a general counterpart reduction in the relative demand for female labour in Northern manufacturing, even among blue-collar workers. There are several possible reasons for the apparent conflict between these findings and other evidence that in Northern manufacturing females have been disproportionately displaced by trade with the South.

I. INTRODUCTION

It is widely believed that female workers have been affected much more than male workers by the rapid expansion of developing country manufactured exports to developed countries over the past three decades. Women constitute a high proportion of the labour force in some conspicuous parts of developing-country export-oriented manufacturing (clothing and electronic products, and export processing zones). In developed countries, women are over-represented in the sectors on which manufactured imports from developing countries have been concentrated, and under-represented in the manufacturing sectors which export to developing countries [*Schumacher, 1984: Table 1; 1989: Tables A.8, A.10*]. Similarly, in developed countries women are overrepresented among trade-displaced workers [*Baldwin, 1984:593*].

There is much less agreement and evidence on the causes, and on the magnitude and nature of the consequences, of these trade-induced shifts in the female intensity of manufacturing in developed and developing countries. Why have manufactured exports from the South to the North been concentrated on female-intensive sectors? How beneficial have these exports been to female workers in developing countries, and how harmful to those in developed countries?

Of considerable interest in this connection is an incongruity in developed

*Institute of Development Studies at the University of Sussex. The calculations were carried out by Trevor King, Rachel Lambert and Terence Moll. Valuable comments and suggestions were also provided by Christopher Colclough, in his capacity as JDS editor, and by Jamie Galbraith and an anonymous referee. Financial support from the Overseas Development Administration (ESCOR) and the Economic and Social Research Council (ESRC) is gratefully acknowledged.

NORTH–SOUTH TRADE AND FEMALE LABOUR IN MANUFACTURING   169

countries. Trade appears to have disproportionately *reduced* the demand for female manufacturing workers. Yet the relative demand for female labour in general has apparently *increased* in developed countries over the past two or three decades – as evidenced by rises both in the ratio of female to male employment and in the ratio of female to male pay.[1] Was it just a fortunate coincidence that demand expansion in other sectors absorbed manufacturing workers displaced by autonomous increases in imports? Or were female workers perhaps sucked out of manufacturing by increased demand in other sectors, thus creating the opportunity for developing countries to export female-intensive manufactures? Or are the facts not quite what they seem?

The objective of the present study is to re-examine the facts about North–South trade and female labour, as a prelude to further investigation of causes and consequences. The approach taken to these facts is different from that of the studies mentioned above, which started from information on exports and imports, and used this to identify particular parts of manufacturing (sub-sectors, or firms, or localities), in which the gender composition of employment or redundancies was then examined. By contrast, the present paper looks at manufacturing as a whole. Moreover, it starts from information on changes in the gender composition of employment, and then attempts to measure the extent to which these have been caused by trade.

The next section explains the method used. Section III presents the results for developing countries, while section IV examines the results for developed countries. A final section draws together the conclusions, and suggests possible avenues for further research.

II. METHOD

The method is simply to calculate for each country the change in the female intensity of manufacturing between the early 1960s and the mid 1980s, relative to the change in the female intensity of non-traded sectors. The logic of the procedure is straightforward. The South's manufactured exports to the North, which have financed a roughly commensurate increase in the North's manufactured exports to the South, grew from virtually nothing in 1960 to about $120 billion in 1985.[2] If the expansion of North–South trade in manufactures has boosted the demand for female labour in developing countries, then, other things being equal, one would expect to observe an increase over this period in the female intensity of developing country manufacturing. Similarly, if this trade has disproportionately displaced women workers in the North, there should have been a decline in the female intensity of manufacturing in developed countries.

Needless to say, other things affecting female labour supply and demand have not in fact been equal. Economic, social, legal and cultural changes have altered the availability of women for paid work and the willingness of employers to hire them. Moreover, these changes have occurred at varying speeds and to varying extents in different countries. As a rough control for these broader changes and differences, the present calculations compare the trend in the female intensity of manufacturing in each country with that in its non-traded sectors (using a fixed-weighted average of the female intensities of all sectors other than agriculture, mining and manufacturing).[3] The underlying assumption is that most of the changes in these domestic influences on the female labour market are economy-wide, and in a given country affect all sectors in similar ways and to a similar extent. Divergent movements in female intensity as between traded sectors (such as manufacturing) and non-traded sectors are thus assumed to reflect the effects of foreign trade on the former.

This procedure has various limitations and weaknesses. (1) It cannot distinguish the effects of North–South trade from those of North–North or South–South trade. For developed countries, however, this limitation is unlikely to be serious, since North–North trade in manufactures, unlike North–South trade, appears to be gender-neutral.[4] Moreover, most of the South's manufactured exports go to the North. (2) The sectors defined as nontraded in the present calculations unavoidably include some traded services, which could cause the effects of trade on manufacturing to be underestimated. (3) If the domestic forces which have altered the female intensity of either manufacturing or non-traded activities are sector-specific rather than economy-wide, then the present procedure will not accurately measure the effects of trade on female intensity.

The data used to measure female intensity in the various sectors come from published tabulations of population censuses and labour force surveys, in most cases using the summaries provided in various issues of the ILO *Yearbook of Labour Statistics*, but in some cases going back to national sources. The coverage of developed countries is more or less complete. The developing country sample was constrained by data availability and includes only 35 countries, but there is no reason to suppose that a more comprehensive sample would yield substantially different results.

III. RESULTS: DEVELOPING COUNTRIES

The results for developing countries are set out in Table 1. The first two columns show the female intensity of manufacturing relative to that of the nontraded sectors, in 1960 and 1985 (or as close to these years as the data permit). The third column shows the change in this relativity over the period, measured by dividing the recent value by the early value.[5] The next three columns show the early and recent levels of, and the change in, the *absolute* female intensity of manufacturing. The last two columns show the early and recent absolute levels of female intensity in the nontraded sectors. (In all the tables in this study, 'female intensity' is defined as the number of female employees per 100 male employees, rather than as the percentage of female workers in the labour force, which is why some of the numbers are above 100.)[6]

An obvious feature of the numbers in Table 1 is their wide variation across countries. The level of manufacturing female intensity ranges in absolute terms from below 10 to over 100, and relative to the non-traded sectors from less than 0.2 to more than 8. The changes over the period in

NORTH–SOUTH TRADE AND FEMALE LABOUR IN MANUFACTURING   171

the female intensity of manufacturing likewise vary widely – the recent/early ratios ranging from 0.6 to 8.0 for the absolute measure, and from 0.4 to 11.6 for the relative measure. Part of this variation undoubtedly arises from errors in the data – especially inconsistencies over time and across countries in definitions and coverage. But most of it is probably genuine, reflecting the economic and social heterogeneity of developing countries and their diverse developmental experiences over the past three decades.

In most of these developing countries, the female intensity of manufacturing increased between the early 1960s and the mid-1980s. The increases are generally larger for the absolute than for the relative measure, since in most of the countries there were also increases in the female intensity of the nontraded sectors. But in 21 of the 35 countries, the relative female intensity of manufacturing rose, in accordance with the expected effects of increased North–South trade. Some of the results for individual countries, however, appear odd. In particular, the 14 countries in which the relative measure declined include two of the leading East Asian exporters of manufactures – Korea and Singapore.

To investigate further, these cross-developing-country variations in manufacturing female intensity were compared with cross-country variations in export performance. Export performance was measured by the ratio of manufactured exports (to developed countries) to manufacturing value added, using data from the Indicators tables of the World Bank's *World Development Report*. This measure of export performance has certain shortcomings, including two sorts of inconsistency between its numerator and its denominator. Exports are gross of non-manufactured and imported intermediate inputs (and include re-exports), whereas manufacturing value added excludes these.[7] Moreover, the numerator excludes processed primary products such as canned food and refined oil, while the denominator includes them – as do the manufacturing employment data used to calculate female intensity. The ratio of exports to manufacturing value added is also sensitive to exchange rate alterations. But for the present purpose, this measure of export performance is an adequate approximation.

The results were mixed. There is a clear and strong positive relationship (described in more detail below) between changes in export performance and changes in the absolute measure of female intensity. In other words, developing countries which exported a rising proportion of their manufactured output to the North tended to employ a rising proportion of females in their manufacturing sectors. There is also a positive but weaker relationship between the level of the export performance variable at the end of the period and the level of the absolute measure of manufacturing female intensity. In other words, countries with export-oriented manufacturing sectors tend to have female-intensive manufacturing sectors.

It is not surprising that the relationship with export performance is weaker in levels than in changes, since absolute levels of manufacturing female intensity are more likely than changes in female intensity to vary across countries for country-specific reasons. It was more surprising to discover that the relative (to non-traded sectors) measure of manufacturing

TABLE 1
FEMALE/MALE RATIO IN MANUFACTURING EMPLOYMENT 1960-85:
DEVELOPING COUNTRIES

| Country | Data Period | As Ratio of Nontraded Sectors | | | Absolute Levels (x100) | | | | |
| | | Early Level | Later Level | Later/Early | Manufacturing | | | Nontraded Sectors | |
					Early	Later	Late/Early	Early	Later
Argentina	1960-80	0.47	0.43	0.91	26	28	1.06	56	64
Chile	1960-85	0.38	0.47	1.24	31	32	1.04	82	69
Costa Rica	1963-84	0.37	0.76	2.05	31	41	1.33	85	54
Dominican R	1960-81	0.26	0.44	1.69	21	35	1.63	82	79
Ecuador	1962-82	0.72	0.78	1.08	46	34	0.74	63	43
Egypt	1960-83	0.27	0.80	2.96	4	18	4.88	13	22
Ghana	1960-84	0.45	0.58	1.29	73	197	2.71	161	336
Greece	1961-86	1.69	0.79	0.47	47	40	0.86	28	51
Hong Kong a	1961-85	0.99	1.15	1.16	40	65	1.62	41	56
India	1961-81	1.99	1.57	0.79	37	22	0.59	19	14
Indonesia	1961-85	1.50	1.32	0.88	60	83	1.38	40	63
Israel b	1961-86	0.38	0.39	1.03	20	33	1.61	54	84
Jamaica	1960-86	0.55	0.33	0.60	96	44	0.46	175	132
Korea	1960-85	1.03	0.90	0.87	36	63	1.72	35	70
Liberia	1962-84	0.38	0.14	0.37	10	7	0.68	25	46
Malaysia	1957-80	1.35	1.48	1.10	20	65	3.27	15	44
Mauritius	1962-83	0.23	2.67	11.61	9	73	7.99	40	27
Mexico	1960-80	0.34	0.60	1.76	19	36	1.88	56	60
Morocco	1960-82	2.19	2.83	1.29	43	57	1.32	20	20

(Continued overleaf)

	Data Period								
Pakistan	1961–81	1.53	1.30	0.85	9	0.71	6	6	5
Panama	1960–85	0.46	0.43	0.93	34	1.22	42	74	98
Paraguay	1962–82	1.11	0.94	0.85	77	0.70	54	70	58
Peru	1961–81	0.65	0.70	1.08	39	0.82	32	61	46
Philippines	1960–85	1.48	0.77	0.52	117	0.81	95	79	123
Portugal	1960–86	0.57	0.91	1.60	33	1.93	64	58	70
Singapore	1957–86	1.60	1.43	0.89	32	2.67	85	20	60
South Africa	1960–85	0.21	0.39	1.86	18	2.26	40	83	103
Sri Lanka	1963–85	1.41	2.22	1.57	25	3.16	80	18	36
Taiwan	1956–80	1.17	1.78	1.52	20	2.93	58	17	33
Thailand	1960–84	0.93	0.95	1.02	60	1.34	81	65	86
Trin & Tobago	1960–80	0.57	0.71	1.25	31	1.36	42	54	59
Tunisia	1966–84	5.00	8.41	1.68	31	4.10	125	6	15
Turkey	1965–85	0.94	1.44	1.53	9	2.08	18	9	12
Uruguay	1963–85	0.62	0.60	0.97	37	1.37	50	59	84
Venezuela	1961–86	0.72	0.57	0.79	39	0.89	35	54	61

General Notes:
1. The first two columns of data show the female intensity of manufacturing as a ratio of the average female intensity of nontraded sectors in the first and last years available (see 'Data Period' column). The third column shows the change in this relativity. The fourth, fifth and sixth columns show the absolute female intensity levels (×100), and the change, in manufacturing.
2. The seventh and eighth columns show the absolute average female intensity levels (×100) of nontraded sectors. The average female intensity of nontraded sectors is calculated as a fixed-weighted average of all sectors other than manufacturing, agriculture and mining, using as weights mid-data-period shares of all nontraded sector employment.
3. All calculations omit workers with sector 'not adequately described'. Arithmetic discrepancies are due to rounding.

Specific Notes:
a. Manufacturing includes construction. In manufacturing alone in 1985, the absolute female/male ratio was 86.9. In 1961, in non-engineering manufacturing, it was 48.9.
b. Manufacturing includes mining.

Sources: ILO Yearbooks, national population censuses and labour force surveys. Further details available from author.

female intensity, which is intended to control for these country-specific influences, failed to do so. Indeed, there is no discernible cross-country association, either in levels or in changes, between manufactured export performance and the relative female intensity of manufacturing. This was instantly apparent from visual inspection of scatter diagrams, and none of the alternative specifications of the variables and relationships that were tried altered the outcome.

So, for developing countries, the methodological conclusion must be that comparisons with female intensity in non-traded sectors are a poor way of isolating the effects of trade on the female intensity of manufacturing. This relative measure of female intensity is in fact worse than useless, since it conceals and distorts the effects of exporting, which emerge readily from simple calculations of absolute manufacturing female intensity. The measured changes in the female intensity of non-traded sectors thus cannot be reflecting economy-wide influences, but must instead be dominated by sector-specific influences. With hindsight, this is not surprising. The content and mixture of non-traded activities change fundamentally in the course of development, perhaps more so than for manufacturing, and in ways which are not adequately controlled for by the present method of calculating fixed-weighted averages across a few coarsely defined sectors. Moreover, employment in non-traded activities in developing countries tends to be particularly inaccurately measured, with inter-country and intertemporal inconsistencies of definition and coverage [*Blades, 1974*].

However, the substantive conclusions for developing countries are not in doubt. Figure 1 is a scatter diagram of the cross-country relationship between changes in manufactured export performance and changes in absolute manufacturing female intensity between the early 1960s and the mid-1980s. Female intensity is measured for this purpose by the percentage of females in the total manufacturing labour force (rather than by the female/male ratio), since this specification seems more congruent with that of the trade performance variable (exports to the North as a ratio of total manufacturing value added). The change in both variables over the period is measured as the arithmetic difference between the recent and the early levels (rather than as the ratio of the recent to the early level, whose numerical value is more sensitive to errors in the data). And a rough adjustment has been made for the re-exports of Hong Kong and Singapore.[8] These particular specifications seem most defensible a priori, and yield the strongest statistical relationship, but the obvious positive association between the two variables remains significant regardless of how they are specified.

It can be seen from the figure that there are several countries in the sample with large increases in both the export orientation and the female intensity of manufacturing. These include all four of the East Asian little tigers, as well as Malaysia, Mauritius, Portugal, Sri Lanka and Tunisia. There is also one country (Jamaica) in which both the export orientation and the female intensity of manufacturing have fallen substantially. In most of the other countries the changes in the two variables are smaller, with less evidence of a positive relationship. (Their bunched points have

FIGURE 1
CHANGES IN FEMALE INTENSITY AND EXPORT
ORIENTATION OF SOUTHERN MANUFACTURING 1960–85

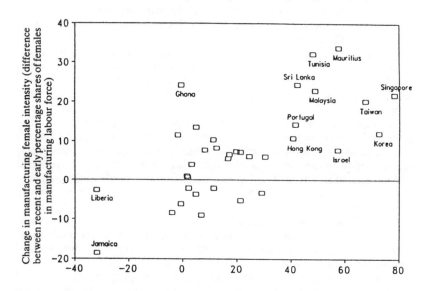

Change in manufacturing export ratio (difference between recent and early levels of
Northbound export/value added percentage)

Sources: See text and Table 1.

been left unlabelled for clarity.) And two countries in sub-Saharan Africa
are conspicuous and conflicting outliers – Liberia, with a large decline in
exports but little decline in female intensity, and Ghana, with no change
in export-orientation and a large increase in female intensity.[9]

The simple coefficient of correlation (R) between the two variables is
+0.67, which differs from zero at any conventional level of statistical
significance. If Ghana and Liberia are excluded, R increases to 0.74. So
R^2 is around one half, which means that about half the cross-country
variance of female intensity change is not explained by changes in export
performance. However, to be able to explain this much variance in a
single-variable cross-section regression is highly satisfactory, especially
in view of the many weaknesses of the underlying data (which include
differences between the lengths of the data periods over which changes in
export performance and female intensity are calculated).[10]

A regression line fitted to the data in Figure 1 passes virtually through
the origin, implying that, apart from the influence of changes in export
performance, there has been no general tendency for the female intensity
of manufacturing in developing countries either to rise or to fall.[11] The
slope of the regression line implies that a ten percentage point increase

176   THE JOURNAL OF DEVELOPMENT STUDIES

in the ratio of North-bound manufactured exports to manufacturing value added is associated on average with an increase of between three and four percentage points in the share of females in the manufacturing labour force. This may seem low, since earlier studies suggest that females typically constitute 70–90 per cent of the workforce in developing-country export-oriented manufacturing.[12] But if the export performance variable could be calculated more consistently, with the value added content of exports rather than their gross value in the numerator, the slope of the regression line would be steeper.[13] The present results thus confirm that expansion of manufactured exports to the North has been strongly associated with increases in the female intensity of manufacturing employment in the South.

IV. RESULTS: DEVELOPED COUNTRIES

Table 2 presents the results of the female intensity calculations for developed countries, laid out in the same way as the developing-country table. Surprisingly, given the expected effects of expanded North–South trade, they show that there was not a general decline in the female intensity of developed-country manufacturing during 1960–85. This is clear from the employment-weighted averages for the whole group at the bottom of the table (weighting is necessary because of the wide disparities of country size).[14] The absolute female intensity of manufacturing rose over the period by about one fifth. There was a proportionately similar increase in the nontraded sectors, and hence no change in the relative female intensity of manufacturing.

Examination of the results for individual developed countries reveals widely varying movements in the absolute female intensity of manufacturing, though some of the variation may be due to weaknesses in the data. The absolute female intensity of manufacturing rose unusually rapidly (from an initially low level) in the US, and increased somewhat more than average in Japan (to an exceptionally high level). By contrast, the absolute female intensity of manufacturing increased in only one of the four large European economies (Italy). It declined slightly in France, and fell by about ten per cent in Germany and about 15 per cent in the UK. The eleven smaller countries experienced a mixture of increases and decreases. For the developed group as a whole, these varying movements in individual countries reduced the cross-country dispersion of absolute female intensity in manufacturing (the unweighted coefficient of variation declines from 0.30 to 0.22), though Japan in particular moved further away from the average.

Some of these inter-country differences in absolute manufacturing female intensity movements were paralleled by changes in the female intensity of non-traded sectors. For example, the large increase in the female intensity of US manufacturing was matched by a large increase in non-traded sectors, and in Germany there were declines in the female intensity of both manufacturing and the non-traded sectors. In consequence, there was somewhat more cross-country uniformity as regards changes in the

TABLE 2

FEMALE/MALE RATIO IN MANUFACTURING EMPLOYMENT 1960–85:
DEVELOPED COUNTRIES

Country	Data Period	As Ratio of Nontraded Sectors			Manufacturing			Absolute Levels (x100) Nontraded Sectors	
		Early Level	Later Level	Later/Early	Early	Later	Late/Early	Early	Later
Australia	1961–85	0.48	0.46	0.96	29	37	1.29	59	80
Austria	1961–85.	0.59	0.41	0.69	52	38	0.73	89	92
Belgium	1961–85	0.48	0.38	0.79	30	30	0.99	63	79
Canada	1961–85	0.39	0.40	1.03	27	40	1.45	71	100
Denmark	1960–85	0.31	0.39	1.26	35	46	1.33	112	119
Finland	1960–85	0.38	0.45	1.18	59	58	0.99	156	129
France	1962–87	0.54	0.45	0.83	45	43	0.97	82	95
Germany	1961–84	0.53	0.53	1.00	48	43	0.90	89	82
Ireland	1961–85	0.71	0.57	0.60	50	39	0.77	71	69
Italy	1961–85	0.83	0.95	1.14	39	47	1.23	46	50
Japan	1960–85	0.84	0.89	1.06	48	60	1.26	57	68
Netherlands	1960–85	0.38	0.31	0.82	19	21	1.07	51	68
New Zealand	1961–86	0.55	0.47	0.85	31	43	1.40	56	91
Norway	1960–86	0.35	0.34	0.97	23	37	1.59	67	108
Sweden a	1960–86	0.25	0.27	1.08	28	36	1.32	109	136
U.K.	1961–86	0.59	0.41	0.69	48	41	0.86	82	100
U.S.	1960–86	0.44	0.46	1.05	34	47	1.41	75	103
Weighted Averages		0.57	0.57	1.00	40	47	1.18	73	89

General Notes: See general notes to Table 1; weighted averages across countries use mid-period economy-wide labour force weights.
Specific Note a: manufacturing includes mining and electricity.
Sources: as for Table 1.

178   THE JOURNAL OF DEVELOPMENT STUDIES

relative female intensity of manufacturing (the unweighted coefficient of variation is 0.17 for column 3 of the table, as compared to 0.22 for column 6). Among the six large developed countries, only France and the UK deviate noticeably from the group average experience of no relative change – in both cases with a relative decline in manufacturing female intensity. The relative changes in the smaller countries are more dispersed around the group average.

The greater cross-country uniformity of relative than of absolute movements in manufacturing female intensity is consistent with the view that movements in nontraded sectors can be used to control for influences other than trade. In other words, these results go some way towards redeeming the poor performance of the present method with the developing country sample. However, the greater diversity of relative movements among the smaller than among the larger developed countries suggests the need for cautious interpretation, especially where a country's manufacturing sector is based heavily on particular subsectors or materials (such as food processing).

Although for the developed-country group as a whole, neither the relative nor the absolute calculation gives any support to the view that expansion of North–South trade has reduced the female intensity of manufacturing, some of the inter-country variations could be due to variations in exposure to North–South trade. For example, the marked relative reduction of female intensity in the UK might reflect an initial concentration of manufacturing on simple labour-intensive products that was particularly vulnerable to competition from developing countries. We therefore examined the cross-country correlation between changes in (a) manufacturing female intensity and (b) developing country import penetration – measured as the ratio of manufactured imports from developing countries to manufacturing value added.[15]

No significant association could be discovered. Both absolute and relative measures of female intensity were experimented with, as were alternative measures of the import penetration ratio (including and excluding processed primary products in the numerator, and using gross apparent consumption rather than value added in the denominator). We also tried using the manufactured trade balance with developing countries instead of imports, and excluding the smaller developed countries. Figure 2 shows the results based on relative female intensity and narrow manufactured imports. This specification came closest to exhibiting a negative relationship, but is still far from statistically significant. For example (considering only the six largest countries), Japan, Germany and the US all experienced little change in manufacturing female intensity, but with widely varying changes in import penetration, while Italy, Germany, France and the UK all experienced similar changes in import penetration but with widely varying changes in relative female intensity.

The lack of correlation could be because these measures of exposure to trade with the South are inadequate. For example, they do not capture the loss of markets for labour-intensive products in other developed countries which a country such as the UK might have experienced as a result of

NORTH–SOUTH TRADE AND FEMALE LABOUR IN MANUFACTURING   179

FIGURE 2
CHANGES IN FEMALE INTENSITY AND SOUTHERN
IMPORT PENETRATION OF NORTHERN MANUFACTURING 1960–85

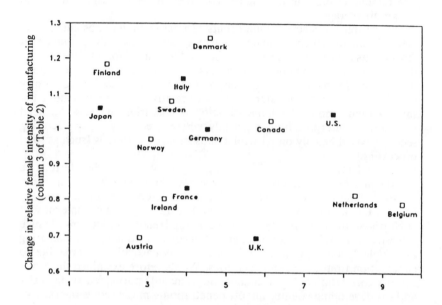

Change in Southern import penetration (difference between recent and early levels
of manufactured import/value added percentage)

Sources: See text and Table 2.
     ■large country

increased competition with the South. Nor do they capture the effects
of labour-saving innovations introduced by Northern firms in response to
competitive pressures from the South, variations in which across countries
may be unrelated to import penetration ratios. Another possibility is that
differences in labour market institutions and policies have caused the
consequences of similar increases in trade with the South to vary among
developed countries.

The results for the developed-country group as a whole in Table 2 could
also be misleading because they refer only to the period during which the
South's manufactured exports have been expanding rapidly. In particular,
it is possible that prior to 1960 the relative female intensity of developed-
country manufacturing was rising (due to sector-specific trends either in
manufacturing or in the nontraded sectors), and hence that its constancy
during 1960–85 might represent a decline relative to the earlier trend,

which could be attributable to the growth of North–South trade.

To investigate this possibility, the calculations were repeated with data for the 1950s. The results, reported in Table 3, suggest if anything the opposite interpretation. In the 1950s, the relative female intensity of manufacturing declined on (weighted) average in the developed-country group, and increased only in four of the smaller countries. Moreover, country-by-country comparisons between the 1950s and 1960–85 (standardised in column 3 to allow for the different lengths of these periods) reveal that only in four of the smaller countries is the change in the trend of relative female intensity such as to suggest that trade had a negative effect in the latter period. The absolute female intensity of manufacturing increased faster in the 1950s than during 1960–85 in five countries, including Germany, Japan and the UK, but on average for the group at the same (standardised) rate in both periods.

Another possibility is that the true effects of trade since 1960 are concealed in the sort of data used in Tables 2 and 3 by lumping together white-collar (or non-manual) and blue-collar (or manual) employment. In particular, it seems likely that the adverse effects of North–South trade on the demand for female labour in developed-country manufacturing would have been concentrated on blue-collar workers. It is also possible that such a reduction in female blue-collar employment might have been offset by an autonomous increase in female white-collar employment, due to a rise in the white-collar share of total manufacturing employment, or to an increase in the female share of white-collar employment.

To investigate these possibilities requires data on employment broken down by industry, occupation and sex, which are less readily available than the industry-by-sex data used in Tables 2 and 3, especially for the early 1960s.[16] The results reported in Table 4 are therefore limited to the six largest countries (which accounted between them for about 85 per cent of the developed group's total manufacturing employment throughout the period), and in three of these cover slightly shorter periods than in Table 2. The calculations were done separately for white and blue-collar workers, but in other respects Table 4 is laid out in the same way as the earlier tables.

The numbers in Table 4 actually cast further doubt on the hypothesis that North–South trade has reduced the demand for female labour in developed-country manufacturing. The relative female intensity of white-collar manufacturing employment declined during 1960–85 in five of the six countries – with absolute increases in most of them, but larger increases in the non-traded sectors. However, among blue-collar workers, where trade would be expected to have had more of an adverse impact, the trend was the opposite. On average, and in five of the six countries (the exception being the UK), the relative female intensity of blue-collar manufacturing employment increased. There was a particularly marked relative increase in Japan, which is the only country in the sample where blue-collar employment is more female intensive in manufacturing than in the non-traded sectors (and also the only one where the female intensity of blue-collar manufacturing employment exceeds that of white-collar

TABLE 3
FEMALE/MALE RATIO IN MANUFACTURING EMPLOYMENT 1950–60:
DEVELOPED COUNTRIES

Country	Data Period	As Ratio of Nontraded Sectors			Absolute Levels (x100)				
		Early Level	Later Level	Standardised Change	Manufacturing			Nontraded Sectors	
					Early	Later	Std'd Change	Early	Later
Australia	1954-61	0.52	0.48	0.76	28	29	1.02	55	59
Austria	1951-61	0.55	0.59	1.18	42	52	1.66	77	89
Belgium	1947-61	0.57	0.48	0.74	31	30	0.95	55	63
Canada	1951-61	0.39	0.39	1.00	25	27	1.21	65	71
Denmark	1950-60	0.29	0.31	1.18	38	35	0.80	129	112
Finland	1950-60	0.51	0.38	0.48	64	59	0.80	127	156
France	1954-62	0.68	0.54	0.49	47	45	0.83	70	82
Germany	1950-61	0.58	0.53	0.83	40	48	1.48	68	89
Ireland	1951-61	0.62	0.71	1.38	48	50	1.12	77	71
Italy a	1951-61	1.11	0.80	0.46	40	37	0.82	37	46
Japan	1950-60	0.85	0.84	0.97	40	48	1.52	47	57
Netherlands	1947-60	0.40	0.38	0.91	22	19	0.81	54	51
New Zealand	1951-61	0.54	0.55	1.05	30	31	1.07	56	56
Norway	1950-60	0.36	0.35	0.93	30	23	0.52	84	67
Sweden b	1952-60	0.39	0.25	0.24	38	28	0.35	98	109
U.K.	1951-61	0.69	0.59	0.68	45	48	1.18	65	82
U.S.	1950-60	0.45	0.44	0.94	32	34	1.14	71	75
Weighted Averages		0.63	0.57	0.83	37	40	1.18	63	73

General Notes: see general notes to Tables 1 and 2; weighted averages use same weights as in Table 2; changes in columns 3 and 6 are standardised for comparability with the corresponding columns in Table 2 (for each country, the actual recent/early change during the 1950s is extrapolated to allow for the greater length of the data period in Table 2).

Specific Notes: (a) Manufacturing includes mining, which is why the 1961 numbers are inconsistent with those in Table 2.
(b) Manufacturing includes mining and electricity.

Sources: as for Table 1.

TABLE 4

FEMALE/MALE RATIO IN WHITE COLLAR AND BLUE COLLAR MANUFACTURING EMPLOYMENT 1960-85: SIX LARGEST DEVELOPED COUNTRIES

		Data Period	As Ratio of Non-traded Sectors			Absolute Levels (×100)				
			Early Level	Later Level	Later/Early	Manufacturing			Non-traded Sectors	
						Early	Later	Late/Early	Early	Later
White Collar										
France	a	1962–82	0.72	0.57	0.79	62	63	1.02	86	110
Germany	b	1961–84	0.68	0.63	0.93	58	66	1.14	85	105
Italy	c	1961–81	0.80	0.80	1.00	38	53	1.38	48	66
Japan		1960–85	0.62	0.33	0.53	38	48	1.27	61	144
UK		1961–81	0.62	0.41	0.66	63	50	0.80	100	123
US	d	1960–86	0.35	0.31	0.89	43	60	1.40	121	194
Weighted Averages			0.55	0.43	0.78	47	56	1.21	91	146
Blue Collar										
France	a	1962–82	0.51	0.62	1.22	41	37	0.91	80	60
Germany	b	1961–84	0.41	0.48	1.17	40	32	0.80	97	67
Italy	c	1961–81	0.67	0.79	1.18	37	43	1.15	55	54
Japan		1960–85	0.81	1.20	1.48	51	66	1.28	63	55
UK		1961–81	0.55	0.38	0.69	44	38	0.86	80	99
US	d	1960–86	0.48	0.55	1.15	30	41	1.34	63	74
Weighted Averages			0.57	0.70	1.22	39	45	1.14	70	69

General Notes:

1. See general notes to Tables 1 and 2.
2. White-collar workers are defined (in relation to the International Standard Classification of Occupations) as professional and technical, managerial and administrative, clerical and sales workers, except in commerce, where managerial and sales workers are excluded, the former because of inconsistencies of definition among countries and time periods, the latter because shop assistants are more comparable in education and training to manual than to other white collar workers. Blue collar workers are all other workers, apart from those whose occupation is 'not adequately described', who are excluded. For countries whose data are not classified according to the ISCO (see specific notes below), the closest possible approximations to these definitions are used, subject to the need for consistency between the early and the recent year.

Specific Notes:

a. Non-ISCO classifications of occupations in both years, and imperfect comparability between the early and the recent year.
b. Non-ISCO classification of occupations in early year. In both years all sales workers classed as blue collar and commerce managers as white collar.
c. Manufacturing includes mining. Commerce managers included in white collar category.
d. Based on data which classify employees as nonmanual (white collar) or manual (blue collar).

Sources: Population census or labour force survey data, from national sources and ILO Yearbooks.

manufacturing employment).

These relative measures should be interpreted cautiously, since the nature of manual work and the composition of manual occupations differ between manufacturing and the non-traded sectors. However, the *absolute* female intensity of blue-collar manufacturing employment also increased on (weighted) average for the group, which is again inconsistent with the expected effects of more trade with the South. There is considerable inter-country variation around this average, with absolute increases in Italy, Japan and the US, and absolute declines in France, Germany and the UK. In four of the countries these deviations from the group average are more pronounced than with the relative measure, supporting the view that comparisons with nontraded sectors can control for economy-wide influences on the female intensity of manufacturing. But in Japan and the UK, and for all six countries taken together, the relative deviations are larger than the absolute deviations, which contradicts this view.

These changes in the absolute female intensity of blue-collar manufacturing employment are strongly correlated across the six countries with changes in the level of (male plus female) blue-collar manufacturing employment – as shown in Figure 3. In France, Germany and the UK, there have been declines in both the female intensity and the overall level of manufacturing employment. By contrast, in Italy, Japan and the US, where blue-collar employment in manufacturing has remained constant or increased, the female intensity of blue-collar manufacturing employment has also increased. Moreover, much the same correlation exists for total (blue plus white) manufacturing employment, both for these six countries and (with more dispersion) for the smaller countries.

This correlation implies that changes in manufacturing employment in developed countries, whether increases or decreases, have been concentrated on females. In Japanese manufacturing, for example, male blue-collar employment increased by one-fifth, while female blue-collar employment increased by three-fifths. In Germany, by contrast, there was a decline of one-fifth for males, and a decline of two-fifths for females. A more detailed industrial disaggregation of this pattern might shed some light on its causes. But there is no immediately obvious explanation, whether connected with North–South trade or otherwise. The hypothesis that it represents general convergence to a norm appears to be refuted by the case of Japan. And the contrary hypothesis that it represents increasing intra-North specialisation of manufacturing according to female intensity appears inconsistent with the evidence mentioned earlier that North–North trade is gender-neutral.[17]

V. CONCLUSIONS AND EXPLANATIONS

The results presented in the previous two sections are in combination rather paradoxical. Those for developing countries add support to the accepted view that expansion of exports to the North has boosted the demand for female (relative to male) labour in manufacturing. Yet the results for developed countries suggest, contrary to other evidence, that this expansion of trade has not caused a general counterpart reduction in the demand for female workers in Northern manufacturing. There have been declines in the female intensity of manufacturing, absolute and relative, in some European countries, but these have been offset by increases in the US and in Japan (whose manufacturing sector remains remarkably female-intensive). Moreover, these variations among developed countries do not seem to be correlated with their exposure to trade with the South.

How might one explain this asymmetry between the present results for the North and the South, as well as the apparent inconsistency between the present results for the North and earlier studies of the effects of trade with the South on female workers in developed countries? There are various possibilities:

(i) One is that the overall effect of North–South trade on the demand for manufacturing labour of both sexes in developed countries is so small that its impact on female intensity is undetectable. The effects on developing countries are observable, in this view, because the South's manufactured exports are concentrated on a few countries. But in the North the effects on employment are both smaller (because higher wages cause less labour-intensive techniques to be used) and more thinly diffused among countries. Hence they are noticeable only in specific manufacturing subsectors. This explanation would be in accordance with the conclusions of most formal studies of the effects of trade with the South on employment in the North, but is at variance with the results of recent work by the present author (Wood [*1990b; 1990c*] which also survey the earlier studies).

(ii) Another possibility is that the present method of measuring the impact of trade on female intensity is seriously inaccurate, especially in assuming that other influences can be controlled for by a simple comparison with nontraded sectors. This assumption is clearly wrong for the developing country sample, in which the control conceals rather than reveals the effects of trade on manufacturing. The assumption is not obviously wrong for the developed country sample. Moreover, comparisons between trends before and after 1960 give no support to the view that the effects of expanding North–South trade in 1960–85 have been masked by offsetting sector-specific influences on female intensity. But it remains possible that since 1960 there has been either an autonomous increase in the demand for female labour in manufacturing or an autonomous reduction in the demand for female labour specific to the non-traded sectors.[18] It is also possible that the lack of correlation across developed countries between changes in manufacturing female intensity and changes in their exposure to trade with the South is due to inadequate measurement of trade exposure.

(iii) Part of the explanation may also be exaggeration of the female intensity of developing-country competition with developed-country manufacturing. Earlier studies and the present results make clear that export-oriented manufacturing in developing countries is unusually female-intensive. However, even in Hong Kong and Singapore in the mid-1980s there were

NORTH–SOUTH TRADE AND FEMALE LABOUR IN MANUFACTURING   185

FIGURE 3
CHANGES IN FEMALE INTENSITY AND OVERALL LEVEL
OF BLUE COLLAR MANUFACTURING EMPLOYMENT 1960–85

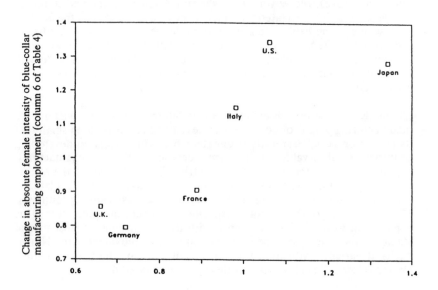

Change in blue-collar manufacturing employment (recent/early number of workers)

Sources: See text and Table 4.

more male than female blue-collar manufacturing workers, while in Korea and Taiwan females were only about 40 per cent of the blue-collar manufacturing labour force.[19] The proportion of males is high perhaps partly because sectors which supply intermediate inputs are less female-intensive than those which export directly. Moreover, although the South's manufactured exports are still concentrated on female-intensive sectors, their growth has for some time been fastest in male-intensive sectors such as steel, ships and automobiles. Finally, developing-country import substitution, which also tends to reduce developed-country exports and production, has generally been spread across a wide range of sectors.

(iv) Another part of the explanation for the apparent lack of effect in developed countries may well be that female workers, though (as earlier studies have documented) more extensively displaced by trade than males from particular manufacturing activities, have also been more readily

186   THE JOURNAL OF DEVELOPMENT STUDIES

reabsorbed into other manufacturing activities. This could be because males tend through longer and more continuous labour force participation to acquire higher levels of sector-specific skills, and hence find it more difficult and costly to transfer from one sector to another. Evidence to support this interpretation includes the comparative experience of displaced textile and steel workers in the US [*Summers, 1989: 290*].

(v) A final possibility is that the effect of increased trade with the South on the demand for female labour in Northern manufacturing may itself have been mixed. Many female workers have been forced out of particular jobs by imports. At the same time, however, and perhaps in a broader range of manufacturing sectors, price competition from developing countries may have stimulated developed-country manufacturing firms to replace male with cheaper female labour, sometimes on a casual or part-time basis, and especially where (as in the US and in small firms in other countries) there are fewer institutional obstacles to doing so.[20]

These five possible explanations of the paradoxical results of the present study are not mutually exclusive. There may be more than one reason why expansion of North–South trade in manufactures appears to have benefited women in developing countries without harming women in developed countries. It would evidently be hard to determine conclusively which, or what mixture, of these explanations is correct, or whether or how the answer has varied among developed countries. But further research on the issue appears both feasible and worthwhile.

final version received July 1990

NOTES

1. On the trend increase in female (relative to male) labour force participation rates in most developed countries, see, for example, Pencavel [*1986*] and Killingsworth and Heckman [*1986*]. On increases in the female/male pay ratio in developed countries, see Chiplin and Sloane [*1988: 833*] and Cain [*1986: 708*].
2. This figure, which is taken from Wood [*1990a*], excludes exports of processed primary products.
3. Averaging is used to increase the chances of accurately capturing economy-wide influences. Fixed (employment) weights are used in calculating the average to reduce the risk of the results being distorted by changes in the relative sizes of non-traded sectors of differing female intensity, rather than the more relevant changes within each sector. This effort to avoid distortion is limited by the coarseness of the sectoral classification of non-traded activities. It is also somewhat undercut by the 1968 revision of the international standard industrial classification.
4. More precisely, in most developed countries there is little difference between the female intensity of the sectors which export manufactures to other developed countries and those which compete with manufactured imports from other developed countries [*Schumacher, 1989: Table A. 10*]. The North's trade with Eastern Europe is not gender-neutral, but the difference in female intensity between exports and imports is smaller than for trade with the South. Moreover, North–East trade in manufactures is much smaller than North–South trade.
5. The unequal lengths of the data series reduce the comparability of these changes across countries. Adjustment to a uniform 25-year basis was experimented with, but made little difference to the results.

NORTH–SOUTH TRADE AND FEMALE LABOUR IN MANUFACTURING   187

6. Female intensity is defined in this way (a) because the female/male employment ratio corresponds to the commonly calculated ratio of female to male pay, and (b) because it facilitates interpretation of the manufacturing/nontraded female intensity relativity. However, in Figure 1 below, female intensity is measured in percentage terms.

7. The value added share of all developing-country manufactured exports is estimated in Wood [*1990a*], which also summarises earlier estimates of the imported intermediate input content of exports.

8. Though there are data for the total re-exports of these countries [*e.g. GATT, 1989: Table III.56*], they are not broken down by commodity or destination. Hence it was not possible to determine accurately what proportions of their exports of narrowly defined manufactures to the North (the numerator of the trade performance variable) consist of re-exports. But to make no adjustment would be misleading. So for both countries the trade performance change variable (the arithmetic difference between the recent and early levels of the manufacturing exports-to-value-added ratio) was simply halved. The effect of this adjustment on Figure 1 was to shift the two points concerned substantially leftwards, making the estimated regression line steeper (see note 11 below).

9. The data in Table 1 imply that Ghana in 1984 had by far the most female-intensive manufacturing sector in the world. Whether manufacturing in Ghana really is unusually female intensive, and if so why, or whether the data are misleading, could not be determined.

10. In principle, the early and recent years for the trade variable are 1965 (the earliest available) and 1985, though in some countries the underlying data refer to other nearby years. The early and recent years for the female intensity variable are in principle 1960 and 1985, but as can be seen in Table 1 the data periods vary somewhat among countries.

11. Applying ordinary least squares to all the observations in Figure 1, the estimated regression equation (with standard errors in parentheses) is

$$Y = \begin{array}{c} 1.051 \\ (8.935) \end{array} + \begin{array}{c} 0.301X \\ (0.058) \end{array} \qquad R^2 = 0.45$$

With 33 degrees of freedom, the intercept is insignificantly different from zero, and the slope coefficient significantly different from zero, at any conventional significance level. If Ghana and Liberia are excluded, the equation is

$$Y = \begin{array}{c} -0.831 \\ (8.014) \end{array} + \begin{array}{c} 0.344X \\ (0.056) \end{array} \qquad R^2 = 0.55$$

If no adjustment had been made for the re-exports of Hong Kong and Singapore, the equation would have been

$$Y = \begin{array}{c} 2.431 \\ (9.673) \end{array} + \begin{array}{c} 0.202X \\ (0.047) \end{array} \qquad R^2 = 0.36$$

12. For example, Lim [*1980: 6*] records that in Mexico women constituted 85 per cent of the workers in the border export industries, in Korea three-quarters of the workers in export industries, and in Malaysia and Mauritius more than 80 per cent of all workers in export processing zones. In export processing zones in the Philippines and Sri Lanka, the proportions of female workers were 74 per cent and 88 per cent respectively [*Lee, 1984: 173, 220*].

13. Value added in domestic manufacturing is estimated to have accounted for 37 per cent of the gross value of all developing-country manufactured exports in 1985 [*Wood, 1990a: Table 2*], though this ratio varies among products, countries and time periods [*ibid.: Table 4*]. If the value added content of manufactured exports were substituted for their gross value in the numerator of the export performance variable, the arithmetic difference between the recent and early levels of this variable would generally be substantially reduced. The points in Figure 1 would shift horizontally towards the y-axis, and the slope of the regression line would become steeper.

14. The weights for the averages in the table are based on total economy-wide employment. The averages are virtually the same with weights (fixed or current) based on manufacturing employment.

15. The data used in calculating the import penetration ratios (including the variants mentioned in the following paragraph) are from OECD sources. Broadly defined manufactured imports and exports, and gross apparent consumption of manufactures (gross production plus imports minus exports), are from Berthet–Bondet and others [*1988*]. Manufacturing value added is from the OECD national accounts, and the data on narrow manufactured imports from OECD trade statistics. The period covered by the import penetration ratios is 1970–85, which is shorter than the 1960–85 period of the female intensity data, but it is unlikely that this affects the results much, since most of the increase in manufactured imports from developing countries occurred after 1970. In these calculations, developing countries are defined as non-OECD non-COMECON plus Greece, Portugal, Turkey and Yugoslavia. Further details are available from the author on request

16. The ILO *Yearbook* started publishing this sort of data only in 1983. The retrospective edition of the *Yearbook* on population censuses published in 1990 contains some information for earlier years, but for many countries it is necessary to use national sources, which are often hard to find.

17. However, the strength of this evidence should not be overstated. The calculations concerned relate only to European countries (though including their trade with other parts of the North), and thus leave some doubts about the US and Japan. Moreover, there is clearly some variation even among European countries: for example, Italy appears to specialise in female-intensive and Germany in male-intensive manufactures [*Sapir and Schumacher, 1985: Table 1; Schumacher, 1989: Table A.10*]. Factor content studies of this type also have methodological shortcomings, though more so for the analysis of North–South than of North–North trade [*Wood, 1990b*].

18. Possible 'sector-specific' influences (both on manufacturing and on the nontraded sectors) include changes in the sub-sectoral composition of the domestic demand for output. For example, within manufacturing there may have been a relative increase in the demand for (female-intensive) processed food. Likewise, although the nontraded sector averages used in the present calculations are fixed-weighted in order to control for compositional shifts, such shifts may have occurred within the broader non-traded sectors. The effects of changes in industrial structure on the demand for female labour in the UK are examined by Borooah and Lee [*1988*].

19. These numbers are derived from section 2C of the 1987 ILO *Yearbook*, except for Taiwan (Table 21 of the 1980 *Census Extract Report*). The definition of blue collar is as in Table 4 above.

20. Professor Jamie Galbraith has argued in a personal communication to the present author that this is actually not a plausible interpretation of US experience. If it were true, the female intensity of manufacturing sub-sectors exposed to strong competition from the South should have increased relative to the female intensity of other manufacturing sub-sectors. The data on sectoral female intensity changes in Galbraith and Calmon [*1990*] seem inconsistent with this hypothesis, though the paper does not explicitly test for correlation with measures of exposure to competition with the South.

REFERENCES

Baldwin, R.E., 1984, 'Trade Policies in Developed Countries', in R.W. Jones and P.B. Kenen (eds.), *Handbook of International Economics*, Vol.1, Amsterdam: North Holland.
Berthet–Bondet, C., Blades, D. and A. Pin, 1988, 'The OECD Compatible Trade and Production Data Base 1970–1985', *OECD Department of Economics and Statistics Working Paper* No.60, Paris.
Blades, D and others, 1974, *Service Activities in Developing Countries*, Paris: OECD.
Borooah, V.K. and K.C. Lee, 1988, 'The Effect of Changes in Britain's Industrial Structure on Female Relative Pay and Employment', *Economic Journal*, Vol.98, No.392, Sept., pp.818–32.

NORTH–SOUTH TRADE AND FEMALE LABOUR IN MANUFACTURING   189

Cain, G.G., 1986, 'The Economic Analysis of Labor Market Discrimination: A Survey', in O. Ashenfelter and R. Layard (eds.), *Handbook of Labor Economics*, Vol.1, Amsterdam: North Holland, pp.693–785.

Chiplin, B. and P.J. Sloane, 1988, 'The Effect of Britain's Anti-Discrimination Legislation on Relative Pay and Employment: A Comment', *Economic Journal*, Vol.98, No.392, Sept., pp.833–43.

Galbraith, J.K. and P.D.P. Calmon, 1990, 'Relative Wages and International Competitiveness in US Industry', *Working Paper* No 56, LBJ School of Public Affairs, University of Texas at Austin.

GATT, 1989, *International Trade 1988–9*, General Agreement on Tariffs and Trade, Geneva.

Killingsworth, M.R. and J.J. Heckman, 1986, 'Female Labor Supply: A Survey', in O. Ashenfelter and R. Layard (eds.), *Handbook of Labor Economics*, Vol.1, Amsterdam: North Holland, pp.103–204.

Lee, E., 1984, *Export Processing Zones and Industrial Employment in Asia*, International Labour Organisation Asian Employment Programme (ARTEP), Bangkok.

Lim, L., 1980, 'Women in the Redeployment of Manufacturing Industry to Developing Countries', *UNIDO Working Papers on Structural Change*, No.18.

Pencavel, J., 1986, 'Labour Supply of Men: A Survey', in O. Ashenfelter and R. Layard (eds.), *Handbook of Labor Economics*, Vol.1, North Amsterdam: Holland, pp.3–102.

Sapir, A. and D. Schumacher, 1985, 'The Employment Impact of Shifts in the Composition of Commodity and Services Trade', in OECD, *Employment Growth and Structural Change*, Paris, pp.115–27.

Schumacher, D., 1984, 'North–South Trade and Shifts in Employment', *International Labour Review*, Vol.123, No.3, May–June, pp.333–48.

Schumacher, D. 1989, 'Employment Impact in the European Community Countries of East–West Trade Flows', *International Employment Policies Working Paper* 24, World Employment Programme, ILO, Geneva.

Summers, L.H. 1989, Remarks in discussion reported in *Brookings Papers on Economic Activity: Microeconomics*, pp.209–90.

Wood, A., 1990a, 'What Do Developing-Country Manufactured Exports Consist Of?', *Development Policy Review*, forthcoming.

Wood, A., 1990b, 'The Factor Content of North–South Trade in Manufactures Reconsidered', unpublished paper, IDS, University of Sussex.

Wood, A., 1990c, 'How Much Does Trade with the South Affect Workers in the North?', *World Bank Research Observer*, forthcoming (Jan. 1991).

[13]

Changes in the
urban female
labour market

Irma Arriagada

Social Affairs Officer,
Social Development Division,
ECLAC.

This article seeks to make an orderly summary of the information on urban female labour in Latin America in the 1990s and thus make a contribution to an updated diagnosis of the female labour market to help serve in the formulation of policies for women. It looks at the past evolution of female labour, analyses the effects of the crisis of the early 1980s on this sector of labour, and reviews the changes that have taken place in it, which have undermined the validity of some myths on this subject. It also looks at some critical aspects of female labour, such as income, occupational segmentation, the segregated incorporation of women into jobs involving new technology, and the reduction of the stability of female employment, as reflected in the increase in homeworkers and own-account workers. Finally, the author analyses the situation of domestic workers, who have traditionally enjoyed little stability or social protection. The statistical information presented comes from the 1980 and 1990 household surveys for thirteen countries which account for over 80% of the population of Latin America. On the basis of the analyses, policy guidelines are proposed regarding the labour market, the educational system and the family and society, with a view to improving the situation of working women and making better use of female human resources against the background of a new regional setting which assigns increasing importance to technical change, innovation, intellectual added value, and flexibility in adapting to this new situation which will permit really effective participation in development.

I

Introduction

Social policies are formulated on the basis of the knowledge and hypotheses of real social conditions which are obtained from research. Policy design is tested in real conditions, or rather, the hypotheses concerning those conditions are verified, while at the same time it influences and modifies them. These changes must be recorded if it is desired to develop effective and efficient public policies. An up-to-date diagnosis of the real conditions is therefore of fundamental importance for the formulation of economic and social policies, and moreover public policies must be formulated from the standpoint of societies made up of men and women who behave in different ways in different stages of their life-cycle, taking into account the needs arising from such conditions.

On the basis of special tabulations of household surveys, this article gives an ordered compilation of the information on urban female labour in Latin America in the 1990s. It seeks to prepare an updated diagnosis of the situation as regards female labour and the main changes observed in it between the 1980s and 1990s, as a contribution to the formulation of policies for women.

Section II looks at the evolution of female labour and analyses the effects of the crisis of the early 1980s. Section III reviews the changes which have taken place in the female labour sector and which have shown many of the assertions hitherto in vogue in this area to be pure myths. Section IV reviews the aspects of female labour which give rise to the greatest concern, namely, income, occupational segmen-

tation, the segregated incorporation of women into jobs involving new technology, the reduction of the stability of female employment, as reflected in the increase in homeworkers and own-account workers, and the situation of domestic servants, who have traditionally enjoyed little stability or social protection.

The statistical information presented is based on household surveys carried out in 1980 and 1990 in thirteen countries which account for over 80% of the population of Latin America. These surveys were processed and standardized by the ECLAC Division of Statistics and Economic Projections. The author was responsible for the design of the special tabulations and their final preparation. As most of the surveys did not have national coverage, in order to make them comparable with each other only the urban areas of the countries were taken into account. For the same reason, the economically active population considered is that consisting of persons of 15 or more years of age.

The analysis of this information suggests various policy lines regarding the labour market, the educational system, the family and society. It is not only a question of improving the situation of working women, but also of achieving more efficient use of female human resources. This aspect is of central importance in a new regional setting in which technical change, innovation and intellectual added value will increasingly affect the labour market and flexibility to adapt to these new conditions will make possible really effective participation in development.

□ The author wishes to express her gratitude for the comments made by Thelma Gálvez (INE), Virginia Guzmán and Rosalba Todaro (CEM) and Petra Ulshoeser (ILO), as well as colleagues in ECLAC. They bear no responsibility, of course, for any shortcomings observed in this study.

CEPAL REVIEW 53 • AUGUST 1994   **93**

II

Changes in women's employment:
the crisis and its effects

Gender-based relationships are strongly affected by the State and the market, in accordance with the various movements of the existing cultural substrata. These institutions create the material bases which organize people's daily life. In the region, deregulation and the greater role played by the market in resource allocation are having a pronounced effect on the functioning of the labour market and labour relations, as well as on the lines of employment, wages and social security policies. Here, we shall look at some aspects of the labour market and its effects on women during the period of crisis and structural adjustment.

The main changes due to the crisis and the adjustment policies took place at the household and the production levels and affected men and women differently. At the production level, there was an increase in the participation of women in the labour market and in the number of hours they devoted to paid work. In spite of the crisis –or, indeed, because of it– more women entered the labour market (with an anti-cyclical form of behaviour). The female participation rate rose and so did female unemployment, especially among the younger women. Moreover, as much of the female labour force works in sectors which are not clearly structured and have low levels of productivity, women are affected not only by actions aimed specifically at women workers but also by those aimed at the sectors in which they work. In this respect, the reduction in the size of the State meant a decline in State employment for women, so that not only was the pre-existing inequality a cause of the differential effects of the crisis on men and women, but at the same time the most far-reaching consequence of the crisis was the perpetuation of that inequality.

The subsistence needs of the lower-class sectors had various effects within the family. The need for the reproduction of the family unit strengthened the interdependence of its members, while the family structure underwent some quite complex changes which do not display any clear trends, since in some cases the family shrank, while in others it expanded with the arrival of "allegados" who contributed to the subsistence of the family group. Observations in various Latin American countries indicate that women increased their participation in the labour force, as did children and young people.

A study on Mexico shows that the restructuring of the Mexican economy after the debt crisis, with the consequent adjustment policies, also forced the restructuring of daily life. Most families survived the crisis by making an enormous effort in which all their members participated through new combinations of work for home consumption and work to earn an income. There was thus an increase in the participation of the family members in work for the market, but at the same time there was an increase in work on reproductive activities, the result being an unequal distribution of responsibilities within the household, where the women had to bear most of the burden. The paradoxical aspect of this strategy is that it made possible the continuation of adjustment policies involving great social costs (Benería, 1992).

Another of the most obvious effects of the crisis was the growing unemployment among the population in general, but especially among women, and above all among young women. Although female unemployment in the region is in line with a longstanding trend, the effects of the crisis sharply accentuated it. The greater female unemployment in Latin America is due to the following structural factors: insufficient economic growth to absorb the increasing labour supply, further accentuated by the crisis; the difficulty of finding jobs for women because of the occupational segmentation of the labour market, which limits the number of jobs for which women are eligible; the generalized view of employers that female labour suffers more interruptions because of pregnancy and child-rearing, and the mistaken idea that the contribution made by women is not vitally important in the family income. The data for the 1990s indicate that in 12 countries of the region rates of unemployment among young people were almost double the overall unemployment rates, while the rates among young women were higher than those of young men, except in Chile and Paraguay, whose economies were in a growth phase (ECLAC, 1993). Even so, however, the information for 1992 indicates that in Chile female unemployment rates for the 15 to 24 age group were higher than those for men (SERNAM, 1993).

With regard to the effects of the crisis on non-wage-earning domestic work, studies made in various countries of the region indicate that female work increased in order to make up for the absence or reduction of family income and to cope with the rise in the prices of foodstuffs and vitally needed goods and the reduction in social service budgets, which was reflected in the deterioration of health, education and housing services. A world study based on information for 17 countries –among them Argentina, Brazil, Chile, Colombia, Jamaica, Mexico and Peru– shows that the application of structural adjustment policies has caused a marked deterioration in the male/female ratio at all levels of education, but especially in secondary education, and above all among girls from rural and marginal urban families; it also reveals, on the basis of some case studies, that there has been a bigger increase in the incidence of malnutrition among girls than among boys (United Nations, 1989).

An aspect which has not been analysed much is that of the changes caused by the crisis within Latin American societies in the dividing lines between the areas of action of the State, society at large and the family. For many years, there was a tendency to transfer functions from the private to the public area: a good example of this is the care of small children, which has tended to be transferred from the mother to a kindergarten attendant. With the crisis, however, many activities formerly carried out by the public authorities were "privatized", so that with the cuts in such areas as the education and health budgets the responsibility for this care was given back to the family and hence to women in their homes. Likewise –to continue with the same example– the decline in family income and the chronic insufficiency of public resources for free preschool care has obliged families, and especially mothers, to look after small children themselves once again or to seek community or individual solutions for the problem of child care. As a result of the shortcomings of the State in looking after preschool children, some interesting initiatives have emerged, [1] which have also had some unexpected side effects: women's need to organize themselves to deal with these problems has meant that they have broken out of their isolation and there is a new-found awareness of their potential, while their work is now more visible. These changes in the borders between the public and private spheres, which vary from one country to another, are a little-explored area of the relations between the sexes. An integrated approach would be needed to gain a clearer view of these movements.

III

Women in the 1990s:

myths and concrete facts

Along with the great changes that have taken place in the macroeconomic indicators and the effects of the crisis and the adjustment, structural trends have also changed the life of Latin American women through their longer life expectancy, their higher level of education, and the tendency to have fewer children. These aspects have affected their participation in the labour force, which has steadily increased and has been reflected in an increase in the number of years of economically active life of the female population. Thus, between 1970 and 1990 the life expectancy of women in the region increased by seven years, their global fertility rate went down from 5.0 to 3.1, and their economically active life increased by rather more than five years (CELADE, 1989 and 1993). At the same time, many women migrated to the cities in search of paid employment, thus joining an urban population which rose from 58% of the total population in 1970 to 73% in 1990 (CELADE, 1991).

---

[1] For example, the Association of Community Mothers in Colombia (AMColombia). For more details, see Mujer/Fempress, 1994.

CEPAL REVIEW 53 • AUGUST 1994   95

Although these data do point to a substantial process of change over these twenty years, they do not express the full magnitude and nature of the changes to which women have been exposed. Perhaps there are grounds for maintaining –as has been done in the case of Spain (Garrido, 1992)– that there are two different social biographies for the region, covering two very different worlds: that of the population over 50, and that of the people who have not yet reached that age. The distance between two generations of women –mothers and daughters– is seen to be very great even if only two indicators are considered: level of education and participation in the labour force. The cut-off point between these two worlds would appear to be in the 1970s. Methodologically, in this context the age variable and still more the generational dimension take on enormous importance as explanatory factors. The cut-off point in question raises some uncertainties about labour trends, however, for if the structural trends towards increasing female participation continue, this generational dimension will lose importance.

Among the most evident of the new phenomena in Latin American societies is the growing presence of women in the labour market. This tendency is particularly marked among young women, whose rates of participation (and also of unemployment) are among the highest. The participation of middle-aged women also increased appreciably during the 1980-1990 period. Nevertheless, despite the generalized increase in female participation (except in urban areas of Panama), and although male participation has gone down or remained unchanged, the gap between the sexes continues to be very considerable. Information from household surveys (table 1) shows that rates of female activity in urban areas range from 34% in Chile to 50% in Paraguay, whereas male participation rates range from 73% in Bolivia to 84% in Paraguay and Guatemala. Panama registers declines in both female and male participation in the labour market, probably due to discouragement at the very high rates of unemployment: around 22% for women and 17.2% for men.

Information for urban areas shows that the highest rates of female economic activity are between the ages of 20 and 54. In the group of women between 25 and 29 (the group with the highest proportion of economically active members), participation rates ranged from 45% in Mexico to 71% in Uruguay. Women over 55, and especially women between 60 and 64 (who reflect a historical tendency towards non-participation), and very young women under 20 (who may still be in the educational system and have difficulty in finding jobs) are those who have the lowest rates of participation in the labour market. In other words, rather than trying to establish a direct link between participation and age, a distinction should be made between the activity of two generations of women.

Conventional wisdom and some studies for the 1970s in other regions or in Latin America have given rise to various assertions on female labour participation which, according to the information collected for urban areas of the region in the 1990s, are now mere myths (that is to say, beliefs which serve as the basis for prejudices although they have no foundation in reality).

These myths have arisen as the result of two gaps: a time-gap between the knowledge of a fact and the occurrence of changes in that fact, and a context gap due to the application to one context of an empirical observation made in another. Some of these myths are examined below.

Myth No. 1. Female participation has the shape of a "U"

A very common belief –based on the experience of the developed world– is that female participation has the shape of a "U", with two points when it is at its maximum: thus, participation is allegedly greatest before the birth of the first child, and after the youngest child starts school.[2] An analysis of female participation by age groups which makes it possible to gain an idea, through the age cohorts, of the labour participation trends of different groups of women shows that in the 1990s, in 13 urban areas of Latin America, female participation has risen steadily in the 15 to 54 age group but has fallen sharply among older women. This indicates that urban women who enter the labour market do not withdraw from it when they have children, but remain economically active throughout the period of greatest reproductive work. This tendency became more marked between the 1980s and the 1990s (table 2), with the biggest increases in female participation taking place in the 25-34 and 35-44 age groups.

[2] See in this connection the stylized curves for the industrialized countries and for Latin America prepared by Psacharopoulos and Tzannatos (1992, p. 17).

96   CEPAL REVIEW 53 • AUGUST 1994

TABLE 1

Latin America: Participation rates, by sex, 1980 and 1990 [a]
(Percentage)

Country	Female economically active population		Male economically active population	
	1980	1990	1980	1990
Argentina	32.4	38.2	75.6	75.7
Bolivia	...	46.6	...	73.3
Brazil	37.2	45.1	81.5	82.5
Colombia	41.8	45.7	79.3	79.2
Costa Rica	33.6	39.1	77.6	77.6
Chile	...	34.0	...	73.2
Guatemala	...	42.9	...	84.4
Honduras	...	43.4	...	80.2
Mexico	...	35.9	...	77.3
Panama	44.5	42.8	76.2	75.6
Paraguay	...	49.7	...	84.2
Uruguay	37.3	43.8	74.6	74.7
Venezuela	31.2	37.5	78.4	77.9

Source: ECLAC, Social Development Division and Division of Statistics and Economic Projections, on the basis of special tabulations of household surveys for the respective countries.
[a] Urban population aged 15 or more.

TABLE 2

Latin America: Rates of female economic activity of selected age groups in urban areas, 1980 and 1990
(Percentage)

Country	15-24 years		25-34 years		35-44 years	
	1980	1990	1980	1990	1980	1990
Argentina	44.9	41.1	45.4	52.5	42.7	52.9
Bolivia	...	33.8	...	56.7	...	62.0
Brazil	42.9	48.1	43.9	55.7	42.3	55.3
Colombia	42.4	41.2	52.1	61.2	49.2	56.8
Costa Rica	33.2	39.2	45.6	52.6	44.4	51.8
Chile	...	26.4	...	46.1	...	46.8
Guatemala	...	42.1	...	50.1	...	50.0
Honduras	...	34.5	...	53.8	...	57.2
Mexico	...	36.4	...	44.6	...	42.3
Panama	40.0	35.5	63.3	58.7	58.3	60.6
Paraguay	...	50.6	...	62.8	...	61.4
Uruguay	43.2	46.5	56.6	69.3	54.5	65.7
Venezuela	25.7	24.8	42.6	50.8	42.0	53.7

Source: ECLAC, Social Development Division and Division of Statistics and Economic Projections, on the basis of special tabulations of household surveys for the respective countries.

A recent study carried out in Argentina tends to confirm this trend, since it shows greater growth in the labour participation of married women than in that of single women (Montoya, 1993). The same phenomenon is to be seen in Mexico: there, on the basis of fertility surveys, it is concluded that labour force participation by married women or common-law wives between 20 and 49 increased by 62% between 1976 and 1987 (García and Oliveira, 1993). In Uruguay, the category of women which most increased its share was that of married women and common-law wives, followed by divorcees, separated women and widows, with single women coming in last place (Filgueira, 1992). These changes also entail substantial modifications in the organization of the daily life of households and in the amount of work needed inside and outside the home.

Myth No. 2. Female workers are a secondary labour force

According to another very widespread myth, female workers are a secondary labour force, subject to the cyclical fluctuations of the labour market, to which they only resort at times of crisis, in order to supplement the family budget.

Since the 1980s, the percentage of households headed by women who are the sole breadwinner has reached very substantial levels: between a quarter and a third of all households. [3] There are also households –not detected in population censuses or household surveys because of the definition of "head of household" used– where the woman's contribution is equal to or greater than that of the male head. A study carried out in the metropolitan Buenos Aires area which went into this matter in detail found that the proportion of households where a woman was the main breadwinner had risen from 19% in 1980 to 25% in 1989 (Geldstein, 1992). Moreover, in the countries where the stabilization process is beginning to take hold more strongly and employment conditions have improved for men, there is no evidence of any withdrawal by women from the labour market, as would occur if women really were a secondary labour force.

Myth No. 3. Women earn less because they have a lower level of education

There is a widespread belief that women earn less than men because they have a lower level of education or less experience. Some qualitative studies which have analysed career paths show that men and women with similar levels of qualifications start off at similar income levels, but as their careers progress the paths of men and women tend to

diverge, as men quickly rise to positions of greater income, prestige and power, while women remain at the levels where they started. Recent studies show that even for the same number of hours worked and the same level of education and training, there are very substantial differences of income between men and women for which there is no valid explanation (Psacharopoulos and Tzannatos, 1992).

Statistical data show that on average, women in the labour market have a higher level of education than men. Both in the 1980s and now, women's wages are markedly lower than those of men for all levels of education. In the 1980s, the income gap between men and women tended to improve in four countries and got worse in two (Costa Rica and Uruguay), but if the educational variable is introduced the situation changes. At the lowest level of education (less than three years' schooling) the gap narrowed in all cases, but at the highest level of education (over 13 years) the gap between women's wages and those of men widened again in urban areas of Costa Rica, Uruguay and Venezuela. Thus, when the 1980 data are compared with those for 1990, the biggest income difference corresponds to the highest levels of education (table 3).

It is a surprising fact that even when women with high levels of education earn wages far below those of men, female participation in the labour force still remains almost the same as that of men for the highest educational level (over 13 years). This finding raises doubts about the neoclassical analyses of cost and benefits as determining factors regarding women's "option" to work. It would be very interesting, in this respect, to study women's labour behaviour by economic and social groups and household characteristics, as it is only in the highest income-groups that women can view work as an "option". Perhaps a more detailed analysis should be made of the segregation of the labour market, which restricts women to a limited number of kinds of jobs: a situation which some authors interpret as a "preference" of women for certain types of work.

Myth No. 4. Most Latin American women are housewives with a large number of children

Among the stereotypes of the region is the myth that Latin American women are mostly housewives and, as they have a large number of children to look after, they cannot work outside the home. The

---

[3] In 1980, the percentages of households headed by women were as follows: Barbados 44%, Chile 22%, Cuba 26%, Dominica 38%, El Salvador 22%, Grenada 45%, Guadeloupe 34%, Guyana 24%, Honduras 22%, Jamaica 34%, Martinique 35%, Netherlands Antilles 30%, Panama 22%, Peru 23%, St. Kitts & Nevis 46%, St. Lucia 39%, St. Vincent and the Grenadines 42%, Trinidad and Tobago 25%, Uruguay 21% and Venezuela 22% (United Nations, 1991). The information from the 1990 household surveys gave the following values for urban areas: Argentina 21%, Bolivia 16.7%, Brazil 20.1%, Chile 23.2%, Colombia 22.6%, Costa Rica 22.6%, Guatemala 20.8%, Honduras 26.6%, Mexico 17.7%, Panama 24.7%, Paraguay 19.7%, Uruguay 25.2% and Venezuela 22.1%.

98   C E P A L   R E V I E W   5 3   •   A U G U S T   1 9 9 4

TABLE 3

Latin America: Income differences, by sex, for selected levels of education, [a] 1980 and 1990
(Percentage)

Country	Total		0.3 years education		13 or more years education	
	1980	1990	1980	1990	1980	1990
Argentina	63.5	68.8	...	...	...	...
Bolivia	...	57.4	...	58.4	...	46.0
Brazil	46.3	56.0	41.0	45.8	38.8	50.7
Colombia	56.1	66.7	51.0	58.8	55.0	60.4
Costa Rica	80.6	71.0	48.2	51.3	86.4	64.2
Chile	...	59.2	...	67.7	...	41.9
Guatemala	...	65.8	...	45.4	...	64.2
Honduras	...	57.9	...	49.9	...	51.5
Mexico	...	68.2	...	63.8	...	61.2
Panama	...	77.0	...	46.1	...	68.4
Paraguay	...	56.7	...	64.0	...	47.1
Uruguay	53.9	44.3	46.6	50.1	44.0	37.3
Venezuela	67.8	72.7	56.3	64.0	71.1	68.0

Source: ECLAC, Social Development Division and Division of Statistics and Economic Projections, on the basis of special tabulations of household surveys for the respective countries.
[a] Average female income as a percentage of average male income for urban population aged 15 or more.

information from the household surveys of the 1990s, however, gives quite a different picture. First of all, the proportion of women in 13 cities and urban areas of the region who describe themselves as housewives varies widely, ranging from 20% in Montevideo to 49% in Santiago, Chile. [4] Only from the age of 45 onwards do the majority of women describe themselves as housewives. Moreover, the fertility rate (for both urban and rural areas) has gone down in the region, and the estimated fertility rate for the five-year period 1990-1995 is 3.1 (CELADE, 1993). The decline in urban fertility is greater than this, as this estimate covers the countries of the region as a whole and hence also covers rural areas, where fertility rates are much higher.

Myth No. 5. Latin American working women mostly have domestic servants

A myth which is complementary to the preceding one is that the growing female participation in the labour force has been made possible by the existence of domestic servants. Although it is true that, compared with developed regions, the proportion of Latin American women who are domestic servants is much

higher –between one-tenth and a quarter of total female employment, depending on the country–,[5] the total proportion of working women is much greater still. Furthermore, many domestic servants are employed by housewives who do not work outside the home. Finally, the proportion of women working as domestic servants is going down, while women's participation in the labour market is increasing, especially in the case of married women with children. Thus, although there is indeed a certain proportion of households where the housewife works outside the home but has a domestic servant or servants to look after the family, there are more and more women who are not in this position and have to play the dual role of worker and housewife. This has important consequences which should be taken into account in the design of policies for working women.

To sum up, then, the statistical information for the 1990s shows that most Latin American women, and especially those between 20 and 45, participate in the labour market, and that they have high levels of education but are paid much less than men, whatever the educational level in question. It also shows that the changes which have taken place in the female labour market are doing away with some myths regarding working women.

---

[4] The figures for urban areas are as follows: Argentina 37%, Bolivia 29%, Brazil 41%, Chile 49%, Colombia 39%, Costa Rica 42%, Guatemala 46%, Honduras 40%, Mexico 48%, Panama 36%, Paraguay 36%, Uruguay 20%, and Venezuela 46%.

[5] With regard to domestic servants, see section IV, subsection 4 a).

There are still many other similar beliefs, however, which the information from household surveys cannot prove or disprove, so that it would be interesting to investigate them by other means in order to see whether they are true or not: for example, the beliefs that absenteeism among women workers is more frequent because they need to look after their children; that women work fewer hours than men, and that the cost per woman worker is higher than for men because of the cost of day nurseries and pre- and post-natal leave. This latter belief does not appear to take account of the fact that the wages of female workers –married or single, with or without children– are much lower than those of men. The dynamism of the situation of female workers makes it more and more necessary to verify this and many other assertions empirically.

Most of the quantitative studies of women's labour participation determine the effects that such participation has on their lives, but little research has been done on the new feelings of women entering the world of work and the changes to which women give rise when they enter it. It has been suggested that women's abrupt transition from the home to the outside world means moving from a family-oriented, domestic outlook to a new commercial rationale. The most interesting point, however, is that when women enter the world of work they also bring with them some criteria from the private, domestic world, along with values such as affective attitudes, which they display in line with the degree of labour satisfaction they derive from the treatment and recognition given to them. This attitude that women have towards their work, and their conscious or unconscious attempts to modify some of its rules by bringing in concepts from their private, domestic life, reflects a criticism of the separation between life and work which offers considerable political potential for change (Aranda, 1991; Darcy de Oliveira, 1989). This general assessment must be tested, of course, in the light of the different positions that women occupy in the world of work (the degree of power they attain), the type of jobs they work in (more or less traditionally feminine, more or less modern) and the form of work chosen. In the latter respect, a more detailed analysis of own-account work –which has increased in recent years– would make it possible to confirm whether they choose this kind of work because of the more flexible working hours it offers or because it is the option most similar to

the kind of work women do as housewives, thus facilitating their transition from the home to paid work.

Some elements derived from qualitative studies made in business firms show that when women begin to work in previously male workplaces there is a change in the workers' language, although in the modernization process the "culture" of the firm is maintained, and the only things changed in it are the forms of reproduction of discrimination against women. This phenomenon takes place in particular through the firms' practices of selecting, hiring, evaluating and promoting staff (Hola and Todaro, 1992). The male stamp is so strong that if a woman who enters the firm wants to be listened to and understood, she has to make a special effort to express herself in a language that fits in with the model prevailing in that social environment, rather than in her own normal way of thinking and feeling. In modern firms, however, proposals are being made for the recovery and enhancement of "feminine" elements which could lead to more efficient organization of the firm, such as negotiating capacity, better personal relations, greater commitment and fulfillment of tasks, etc., although in other contexts these same elements have been used to justify the exclusion of women from certain posts.

Through in-depth studies it could be possible to find out if the concentration of women in "female" sectors is determined only on the side of the demand for female labour or if, on the contrary, part of this concentration represents a choice by women themselves because of the obstacles they face in seeking to enter jobs that are not seen as "women's work". Among these obstacles are firms' recruitment practices, their rank and salary structures, the way they evaluate job performance, and the access they provide to training and upgrading (Rico, 1994). In order to break with sex-based occupational segregation and move towards unbiased labour participation it is necessary above all to clearly identify the obstacles women face in their working life, but also to identify elements that favour greater female participation. On the one hand, increased female participation has been favoured by the increase in the number of jobs in the tertiary sector, where women have traditionally worked on a large scale. It remains to be seen if the growing demand for versatile human resources may become a positive factor for well-educated women entering the labour market.

100   CEPAL REVIEW 53 • AUGUST 1994

IV

Critical aspects: income, occupational segregation, new technologies, and the growing precariousness of some female jobs

1. Income

The greatest inequalities between men and women in the labour market are in income. Of the difference in income between men and women, the percentage attributable to sex discrimination varies, depending on the country, from 10% to 85%, and it tends to be greater than 50% in the developing countries. Some studies suggest that occupational segregation and the resulting differences in income are much more extreme in the region than in developed countries (Barbezat, 1993). Estimates of the effects that occupational segregation has on women's income likewise vary greatly. With growing female participation in the labour force, both the income disparities and the percentage of them attributed to discrimination tend to go down with the passage of time. This latter trend, which it has only been possible to measure in the developed countries, is linked with government policy initiatives or trade union efforts through collective bargaining, but these have been less successful in countries with highly decentralized labour markets, such as the United States (González, 1992).

In the region, the income differences between men and women confirm the existence of wage discrimination against women. In no country do men and women with the same level of education receive identical wages. The wages of young or adult women are usually less than those of men, whatever the level of education in question, and discrimination is present in all occupational groups. The relative disadvantage in terms of hourly pay between adult women and men is equivalent to some four years' formal education (ECLAC, 1993). If we look at what happened in the 1980s, the statistical data show that in the five countries for which information is available, the wage difference between men and women improved between 1980 and 1990 in the case of the lowest levels of education, but at the higher levels the disparity increased in three cases and went down in

only two (table 3). A probable explanation of the smaller wage difference between men and women at the lowest educational levels is that the wages received by women with this level of education are so low that it is impossible to reduce them further.

More precise information on Costa Rica shows that the wage difference increased during the crisis and stabilization period (1980-1983) but went down somewhat with the recovery (1983-1986). The increase in the disparity between male and female wages during the recession (1980-1982) was due mainly to the increase in the labour participation of less educated women who entered the labour market in response to the drop in the real income of heads of families. These women mainly entered sectors of the economy which paid the lowest wages (Gindling, 1992).

A study recently published by the World Bank concludes, on the basis of information on 15 countries of the region for the period from 1950 to 1985, that only 20% of the differences in income between men and women can be explained by differences in their human capital: the rest is due to factors of discrimination. After correcting this estimate to take account of the selection that women make themselves with regard to the labour market (their work options), it is estimated that a further 20% is due to women's smaller capacity to generate income, so that finally the unexplained portion of the income disparity between men and women amounts to 60%: much more than the level determined for more advanced countries (Psacharopoulos and Tzannatos, 1992). This unexplained 60% corresponds mainly to cultural aspects which segregate the labour market and establish a limited number of jobs considered to be suitable for women.

The information available for the 1990s on 13 urban areas of the region shows that the average income of women is only between 44% and 77% that of men. This disparity is even more marked in the

TABLE 4

Latin America: Differences in average income, by sex and household status, [a] 1980 and 1990
(Percentage) [b]

Country	Wome/Men		Heads of household	
	1980	1990	1980	1990
Argentina	63.5	68.8	70.5	69.6
Bolivia	...	57.4	...	56.0
Brazil	46.3	56.0	40.2	53.2
Colombia	56.1	66.7	59.2	62.1
Costa Rica	80.6	71.0	63.3	64.7
Chile	...	59.2	...	56.4
Guatemala	...	65.8	...	62.6
Honduras	...	57.9	...	51.3
Mexico	...	68.2	...	65.9
Panama	...	77.0	...	64.2
Paraguay	...	56.7	...	54.7
Uruguay	53.9	44.3	52.5	45.0
Venezuela	67.8	72.7	59.2	65.6

Source: ECLAC, Social Development Division and Division of Statistics and Economic Projections, on the basis of special tabulations of household surveys for the respective countries.
[a] Urban population aged 15 or more.
[b] Average female income as a percentage of average male income for all employed persons and for those who are also heads of households.

case of heads of households: the average income of female heads of households is only between 45% and 69% that of their male counterparts (table 4). This information points once more to the need for special social and employment policies for such women, who suffer from the highest levels of poverty.

2. Occupational segmentation

Sex-based occupational segmentation is a common denominator of the labour markets of both industrialized and developing countries, and it has persisted through the decades and across international frontiers. In a number of countries the indexes of segregation increased in the 1980s, and in some cases there was even resegregation of occupations, with marked vertical segregation within occupations and firms (Barbezat, 1993).

In the region, sex-based occupational segregation in the labour market is reflected in the concentration of women in a small number of jobs culturally defined as suitable for women (horizontal segregation). On top of this, there is vertical segregation, since women are concentrated in the lowest ranks of each occupation, meaning that their jobs are the worst-paid and the most unstable (Abramo, 1993). A study made in Peru revealed that each industry

followed an organizational principle involving strict division of labour into male and female jobs, although there was a wide variety of different situations among the firms studied (Guzmán and Portocarrero, 1992).

The information available on 13 urban areas of the region reflects a process of growing tertiarization, since women continue to be concentrated mainly in the services sector. Between 1980 and 1990 this sector grew steadily and absorbed between 42% and 65% of the female labour force. [6]

The occupations with the largest numbers of women are professional and technical posts, saleswomen and domestic servants. The information for 1990 also shows that a higher proportion of women than of men work as professionals and technicians, while a higher proportion of men work as managers and manual workers. Among workers in the services sector, there are two or three times as many women as men, depending on the country. In Venezuela, one out of every four employed women is a professional or technician (table 5).

[6] The values for the various urban areas are as follows: Argentina 66%; Bolivia 43%; Brazil 64%; Chile 57%; Colombia 47%; Costa Rica 53%; Guatemala 42%; Honduras 44%; Mexico 52%; Panama 65%; Paraguay 55%; Uruguay 61% and Venezuela 61%.

102   CEPAL REVIEW 53 • AUGUST 1994

TABLE 5

Latin America: Distribution of economically active population [a] among selected types of occupations, 1990
(Percentage) [b]

Country	Professionals and technicians		Managers		Service worker		Manual workers	
	Women	Men	Women	Men	Women	Men	Women	Men
Argentina	...	...	...	...	...	...	...	...
Bolivia	13.8	13.5	1.8	4.7	23.3	6.3	12.4	52.9
Brazil	15.9	6.2	5.0	10.2	33.2	16.6	14.6	38.2
Colombia	13.6	13.3	...	...	30.8	8.7	17.6	47.0
Costa Rica	20.2	14.6	3.4	6.2	26.1	9.9	18.8	39.9
Chile	14.7	7.1	2.6	5.5	32.1	7.8	11.6	46.1
Guatemala	13.9	10.1	4.8	5.9	25.1	5.5	19.1	41.1
Honduras	13.9	9.4	1.9	4.3	30.3	8.5	18.9	47.0
Mexico	17.7	11.7	1.7	4.5	23.5	7.9	13.6	48.3
Panama	20.2	10.8	4.0	7.8	31.4	12.0	7.8	34.8
Paraguay	13.7	8.9	1.3	4.6	36.3	9.9	12.3	44.5
Uruguay	17.7	6.9	1.6	4.7	31.0	9.8	16.2	47.5
Venezuela	24.5	10.0	2.2	5.3	26.6	10.0	10.1	43.2

Source: ECLAC, Social Development Division and Division of Statistics and Economic Projections, on the basis of special tabulations of household surveys for the respective countries.
[a] Urban population aged 15 or more.
[b] Percentages of total number of employed persons of each sex in each category.
[c] "Professionals and technicians" also includes "Managers".

It has been noted that in Venezuela the rapid growth in the number of workers with university education has not been accompanied by a similar increase in the demand for such workers, thus leading to greater unemployment, a deterioration in real wages, greater internal differentiation, and growing frustration among professionals. Female university professionals have suffered most from this situation, as they tried to enter a market in which they had not been able to consolidate their position earlier when it was expanding slowly. Women gained access to education in similar numbers to men, but the credentials they obtained were not enough to ensure them jobs (Bonilla, 1992).

Generally speaking, women work in a smaller number of occupations than men. A study made in Chile shows that women are more concentrated in certain types of jobs and certain economic sectors than men. Thus, a single occupational category (personal services) absorbs over 70% of all the women working in the financial sector, while for all sectors taken together it accounts for 31.3% of the female employees (Hola and Todaro, 1992). When an index of occupational segregation by sex was constructed for the manufacturing, commerce and services sectors in Mexico, it was found that the greatest degree of segregation was in manufacturing plants, followed by services and finally commerce (Rendón, 1993). In Greater Santiago (Chile), it has been confirmed that in the manufacturing sector women are segregated from three angles: i) by size of firm: as the size of the firm increases the participation of women is lower; ii) by industrial branch: women are concentrated in the textile, clothing and leatherware, and foodstuffs, beverages and tobacco industries; and iii) by occupational category: women are concentrated in the areas of administration, sales and services (Abramo, 1993).

3. The new technologies

Various studies have found that no systematic effects of the new technologies are to be observed as regards the definition of jobs and the divisions between them, since these technologies have given rise to movements of male and female workers both into and out of the labour market and between different types of jobs. Their short- and long-term effects therefore need to be analysed.

The effects observed in some countries of the region show that there has been an increase in women's participation in banks, insurance and financial establishments, in which substantial technological changes

CEPAL REVIEW 53 • AUGUST 1994   103

have taken place. This process of incorporation of women into "modern" high-technology occupations has not meant any decrease in occupational segmentation, however, for it would appear that the modern jobs into which women move are promptly redefined as "women's jobs", and although they involve the use of complex technology the wages paid to women are lower than those earned by men in the same branches. It is therefore necessary to make an in-depth study of the changes due to the incorporation of new technologies in production processes and the trends towards greater or lesser occupational segregation brought about by such incorporation.

In financial establishments, banks and insurance companies, modernization has been an ongoing feature in recent years. In the 13 urban areas of the region already referred to, female participation in this branch varies from 28% of the total number of employees in Guatemala to 40% in Venezuela and has been increasing since the 1960s. [7] In Brazil, a study of technological change and its effects on the division of labour by sex reveals various ways in which female qualifications are not properly recognized in the microelectronics sector. They include the payment to women of wages far below those warranted by their educational level; failure to recognize the skills acquired by female workers in terms of socialization and domestic matters; failure to give proper credit to the greater discipline and obedience of women, and finally, failure to acknowledge the experience acquired in previous jobs (Hirata and Humphrey, 1986, quoted in Rangel de Paiva Abreu, 1993).

A study carried out in Chile shows that female employment has increased considerably in the financial sector. In 1990 the proportion of women in this sector (33%) was higher than in all sectors taken together (31%), but men nevertheless monopolized the posts of managers and directors to an even greater extent than in the economy as a whole (Hola and Todaro, 1992).

A study made in Brazil in the printing industry reveals that the labour force associated with the new technologies is younger and better educated than the

employees of the industry as a whole, but here too there is a marked difference between the sexes. Thus, the average income of scanner operators (who have a lower level of education and are mostly men) is equivalent to 14.1 minimum wages; for photocomposition operators (who have a higher level of education and include a substantial number of women) it is 5.22 minimum wages, and for keyboard operators (who have the highest level of education and are largely women) it is only 4.7 minimum wages (Rangel de Paiva Abreu, 1993).

4. The growing precariousness of women's jobs

During the crisis of the early 1980s the growth of the informal sector was the main variable in the adjustment of the Latin American labour market. The increase in unemployment and informal sector activities was accompanied by sharp drops in labour income and rapidly growing instability of employment; temporary and part-time work increased, and at the same time its quality went down. In 1989 over 50% of non-agricultural employment corresponded to micro-enterprises or informal activities (compared with 38% in 1980), to say nothing of precarious work (García, 1993).

One of the trends in the region which has already been referred to is the increase in non-wage-earning work. The crisis and the new pattern of restructuring of production has led to an increase in jobs –a great many of them done by women– which may be defined as precarious in terms of their discontinuity in time and the lack of regulation regarding labour laws (failure to sign proper contracts), wages (failure to comply with the minimum wage), working hours, social security, and health protection. Among these jobs are traditionally precarious occupations such as domestic service, but also new forms of home work, own-account work and work in micro-enterprises, some of which are virtually clandestine activities. We thus see how three factors: the crisis, which caused medium-sized and large firms to reorganize their activities and reduce the number of workers; the restructuring process, which led to the replacement of permanent staff with subcontracted small enterprises; and the various survival strategies of the sectors most affected by the crisis, all converged to foster the emergence of small production units. In view of the growing heterogeneity of production units, their various degrees of precariousness need to be investigated

---

[7] The 1990 values for the 13 urban areas are as follows: Argentina 38%; Bolivia 29%; Brazil 35%; Chile 32%; Colombia 36%; Costa Rica 20%; Guatemala 27%; Honduras 35%; Panama 36%; Paraguay 30%; Uruguay 36% and Venezuela 40%.

in greater depth. In general, however, it can be said that in Latin America there is widespread deregulation of labour and loss of the labour advances won by the workers in the past.

In measuring women's participation in the informal and precarious sector, the general problems encountered in measuring female labour are greatly aggravated. Many of the activities carried out by women which could be classified under this sector are not recorded in any way, as they are considered a normal part of women's domestic duties. Nevertheless, it can be confidently stated that the poorest working women are in the urban informal sector, and if those employed in domestic service are added to them, then women's share in total employment in the sector exceeds 70% in most cases. In some countries of the region, according to data from household surveys, women make up between 8% (Panama) and 64% (Cochabamba, Bolivia) of the informal sector (Pollack, 1993).

The characteristic difficulties in measuring informal activities are compounded by the wide variety of definitions and indicators used in such measurement, which partly explains the differences in the estimated size of the informal sector. The visibility or invisibility of this type of work is a very important feature, since the labour activities of a substantial proportion of women are not registered. A study of the informal sector made in Guatemala City shows that in this sector there is a greater relative presence of women, old people (it is seen as a suitable place for prolonging a person's working life), migrants, Indians, and above all people with low levels of education (Pérez Sáinz, 1992).

We shall now take a brief look at the situation of female workers in some types of new and traditional occupations where there is a high proportion of women. The main feature of these occupations is their unstable, precarious nature. They comprise domestic servants (on whom most information is available), home workers, and own-account workers (on whom there is less information, and such information as is available is more patchy). This list is not exclusive, since broadly speaking all these workers can be included in the informal sector, but in fact not all belong to it, as in the case of some own-account or home workers.

a) *Domestic servants*

According to the United Nations, if housework were taken into account it would make up as much as 40% of the gross national product of the industrialized countries. In spite of the great technological advances made in order to lighten this work, women in industrial countries still work an average of 56 hours per week (United Nations, 1991).

With regard to paid housework, or domestic service, and especially that carried out on a live-in basis, the following characteristics have been identified: workplace identical with dwelling, in the case of live-in maids; labour relations which are close to servitude and in which labour relations proper are mingled with affective and personal elements; and elasticity of supply in the case of live-out maids (ECLAC, 1990). Domestic service is a dead-end job, since a rise in status can only take place by changing jobs or, in a few cases, by changing from live-in to live-out status. Because of the solitary nature of this work, domestic servants are out of the circuit where other employment opportunities may be found (Montero, 1992).

Up to the 1980s, domestic service was one of the occupations which absorbed most female labour, but in 1990 women working as paid domestic servants in the urban areas of 13 countries of the region represented between 7% (Venezuela) and 24% (Paraguay) of total female employment. Among the countries where information is available for 1980 and 1990, domestic service has tended to decline as a women's occupation in Brazil, Colombia, Costa Rica and Uruguay, while it has increased slightly in Argentina, Panama and Venezuela. In the latter country, however, although the proportion of women working as domestic servants went up between 1980 and 1990, it is still less than in the other countries. This tendency towards the decline of paid domestic work in general terms and as a women's occupation has been noted in several studies, although it has been suggested that the impact of the crisis and of the adjustment programmes may have tended to reverse it.

Although there may be some under-recording of the number of domestic servants, as this is a job which is looked down on and is of low status, the figures indicate that it is still very important for women as a way into the labour market.

According to some special tabulations of household surveys for the years 1989 and 1990, most domestic servants are young, single, have a low level of education, and work on a live-in basis. There is a tendency, however, towards a move to live-out employment, especially in the countries with a higher

CEPAL REVIEW 53 • AUGUST 1994   105

level of development. At the same time, there are big differences depending on the country in question and the type of work: live-in or live-out. The vast majority of live-in maids are single, under 30, and have a somewhat lower level of education than live-out maids. Live-out maids have a rather higher level of education, receive lower average wages, are older, and are mostly married or common-law wives (table 6).

One of the most serious problems faced by domestic servants is the isolation in which they work, which makes it difficult to organize them and engage in a joint struggle to improve their labour conditions. They also suffer from the fact that they are not covered by the regular labour laws, on the grounds that they do not share a common workplace, do not

produce tangible goods, and receive part of their wages in the form of board and lodging. In countries (such as Peru) where legislation has been passed ensuring them eight hours' rest, this has had the opposite effect to that desired, since employers have interpreted it as a licence to demand 16 hours' work per day (Chaney and Castro, 1993). Nevertheless, a substantial change is taking place, since domestic servants have managed to organize themselves into a regional confederation covering 11 Latin American countries (the Latin American and Caribbean Confederation of Household Employees). Although this enormous organizational effort does not include all those working in the sector, it nevertheless represents an important awareness of their position as workers.

TABLE 6

Latin America (seven countries): Characteristics of live-in and live-out domestic servants, 1990 [a]
(Percentage)

Characteristics	Bolivia [b]	Brazil	Colombia	Chile	Guatemala	Uruguay	Venezuela
Unmarried	89.8	...	88.6	87.7	76.2	77.4	85.8
10-29 years of age	87.7	78.5	76.4	55.2	77.2	52.8	69.9
No education	9.7	41.2	6.1	...	...	3.8	6.1
Primary education	51.9	12.8	69.5	...	...	67.0	67.1
Average income [c]	47.4	38.0	91.1	...	48.7	84.1	44.7
Unmarried	52.8	...	40.5	40.1	28.8	33.8	39.1
10-29 years of age	63.0	58.0	46.2	33.9	48.8	37.2	61.3
No education	8.8	33.1	10.5	...	58.2	3.8	13.0
Primary education	52.1	27.7	64.6	...	7.9	63.6	67.2
Average income [c]	...	35.7	...	...	27.4	29.5	22.1

Source: ECLAC, Special tabulations of the 1989 and 1990 household employment and unemproyment surveys carried out by Rosa Bravo for the Second Meeting of the Latin American and Caribbean Confederation of Domestic Workers.

[a] Urban population aged 10 or more.
[b] Urban population aged 15 or more.
[c] Average income of live-in and live-out domestic servants, as a percentage of the average income of all employed persons.

b) *Home workers*

The existence of home workers stems from the quest for cheaper production arrangements, especially in the case of labour-intensive tasks. Home work helps to increase the flexibility of the labour supply to meet a demand which is not subject to regulations on working hours or time worked (Benería and Roldán, 1992). This work does not involve much use of tools or machines, but instead makes intensive use of labour; it requires very little investment and can easily be carried out at home. It generally represents a phase or step in the production process involving simple, repetitive, monotonous tasks. The increased geographical flexibility made

possible by the adoption of new technologies offers potential for reorganization which can have a considerable impact on women's labour participation.

Home work forms part of a modern flexible production strategy which can permit greater accumulation for capital and an income generation strategy for workers (Benería and Roldán, 1992). It is a possible alternative to traditional forms of work for people who have family responsibilities (as is the case of most of the women who work in this way), suffer from some physical incapacity, or simply need greater independence. When the unemployment rate rises, it is also a way in which those who cannot get a steady job can obtain some income. Women who

106   C E P A L   R E V I E W   5 3   •   A U G U S T   1 9 9 4

work at home represent the cheapest form of labour, and at times of crisis and adjustment this also makes it possible to solve the dilemma of increasing the family income while doing more housework. The activities in which home work is mostly concentrated are of a traditional nature: clothing, textiles, leather, footwear, tobacco products, etc.

There are not enough regional-scope studies to show how this sector of workers has evolved, but it is obvious that their labour conditions, like those of informal-sector workers and domestic servants, are either not subject to any regulations, or if they are, then those regulations are not complied with. There is extreme dependence in the case of home workers who are subcontracted, since the negotiations on prices and continuity of deliveries are carried out through third parties who act as intermediaries between the workers and the enterprise. As this is a form of activity in which the technical and production decisions are taken by the employer, however, it could well be considered as a wage-earning job and thus be subject to the relevant regulations, the only differences being that the work is carried out outside the firm, at the worker's home, that there is no stability over time, and that payment is on a piece-work basis.

One of the general conclusions reached after a comparative analysis of home work in developed and developing countries is that this activity appears to be "regulated" by an extensive collection of laws in the various countries. The fundamental problem, then, would appear to be the lack of real application of those laws. Thus, "...home work is seen to be a dispersed and isolated phenomenon, subject to little or no control: the truth is that if there is an appropriate term for describing this phenomenon in general, it is undoubtedly the word 'precarious'" (Vega, 1992, p. 19).

c) *Own-account workers*

The sector of own-account workers is a category that displays great diversity in censuses and household surveys, as the occupations it covers may range from independent professionals such as doctors or dentists to street vendors whose activities may even be of a semi-clandestine nature. What distinguishes own-account work from wage-earning employment is the form of payment, which does not come from an employer but is the result of the operation of an enterprise or the independent practice of a profession or trade. For women who are not independent professionals, the precarious character of this category

takes the form of the absence of social security, paid holidays, maternity or sick leave, and other benefits received by wage-earners. Information from household surveys shows that the category of own-account workers grew between 1980 and 1990. The numbers of men and women who engage in own-account work are fairly similar, except in Bolivia, where over half the working women do so in this category. [8]

In the 1980s, both men and women increased their participation in this form of work in all the countries of the region. It has been noted, however, that women participate as own-account workers to a larger extent in countries with a large Indian population: Bolivia, Guatemala, Honduras and Paraguay. Another occupational category which is very small in numbers but receives very small incomes is that of family workers (paid or unpaid). Consequently, in order to make a really thorough evaluation of the precariousness of own-account work in the informal sector it is necessary to make a more detailed analysis than that permitted by household surveys, that is to say, one which also covers the number of hours worked, the income received, and the past labour background.

A study carried out in Buenos Aires reveals that own-account workers have increased in recent decades. When compared with wage workers, it is noted that own-account workers are older, especially in the case of women, more of whom had migrated and who also display a greater degree of informality in terms of the type of work they do (Gallart, Moreno and Cerrutti, 1990). The same conclusion has been reached regarding female informal-sector workers in Chile, who are less educated and older, both in comparison with the rest of the labour force and with men working in the urban informal sector.

Attempts have been made to favour own-account workers through various measures, such as special systems of credit, training with a view to the development of entrepreneurial capacity, support for the creation of small enterprises, etc. It is also necessary, however, to consider the adoption of special measures for female own-account workers, who have both special skills and also special difficulties due to the gender-based system prevailing in the region.

---

[8] According to data from the 1990 surveys, the percentages of urban women who are own-account workers or unpaid family workers are as follows: Argentina 26%; Bolivia 55%; Brazil 24%; Chile 22%; Colombia 24%; Costa Rica 18%; Guatemala 37%; Honduras 39%; Mexico 21%; Panama 14%; Paraguay 30%; Uruguay 21% and Venezuela 20%.

IV

Final comments

1. Summary

Latin America has partly overcome the short-term
adjustment stage following the external debt crisis of
the early 1980s and is now in a stage of restructuring
marked by opening up to external markets, in which
it is trying to incorporate itself into international
trade on competitive terms. This process has brought
great dynamism to the labour market, expressed in
changes in the role of the State, in the regulation of
labour relations and, more generally, in employment,
wage and training policies.

These changes, which have included the reorganization of production processes, with the incorporation of new technologies, have altered the
composition of the labour market, and they have had
strong effects on women's labour participation.
Among these effects, the most noticeable has been
the so-called "feminization of the labour force" or the
"silent revolution". This phenomenon has been taking place since the 1960s, and although its pace has
been slackening in recent years, it still continues.

Although the increase in female participation is
tending to bring it close to male levels, the patterns
by gender are different, and there continues to be a
wide gulf between the two. On the labour supply
side, there are differences in terms of age and civil
status (which are tending to diminish), and in terms
of the educational level of women. On the side of the
demand for labour, women are employed in a smaller
number of occupations, they are paid far less than
men, and there is majority female participation in the
informal (and more precarious) sector. There can be
no doubt that in the 1980s substantial changes took
place in the situation of female workers which involve a change in the perceptions regarding female
labour held in the past. The trends which have been
observed in this respect display both continuities and
breaks which tend to make many past or existing
assertions obsolete.

The information from household surveys on the
urban areas of 13 Latin American countries shows
–as do many studies made in the region– the growing
female participation in the labour market, especially

by middle-aged (25-45) and married women.
Together with this feminization of the labour force
there has been a process of tertiarization of the active
population (new employment opportunities have opened up for women in the services sector) and growth
of small-scale economic activities. This increase in
the economic participation of women in the region
shows the ambivalence of the change, since at the
same time there is still a highly segmented labour
market and women's employment is increasingly unstable and precarious, as reflected in income levels
markedly below those of men, unemployment rates
which are generally higher, and an increase in own-
account and informal-sector work by women.

2. Methodological suggestions

Some methodological comments are called for here
with regard to the analysis of the labour situation.
Above all, it is important to analyse gender-related
aspects of the labour market. Failure to do so tends to
bias analysis of the labour sector, since opposing
trends for men and women cancel each other out
when considered as a whole.

It is also important to maintain some degree of
continuity in evaluating the changes which are taking
place, in view of the speed at which the labour sector
evolves, especially with regard to such sensitive variables as activity rates, employment and unemployment, average income, etc.: assertions which were
valid at the beginning of the crisis no longer hold
good in phases of economic recovery.

Analysis of the situation indicates that in order
to fully understand the processes of change in the
countries, it is necessary to have a clear knowledge
of the context in which the crisis occurred and in
which the adjustment policies were applied, since
this is of enormous importance for understanding the
different reactions of the labour market and of the
social actors, both men and women.

Such processes back up the idea that the effects
of external changes and social actions should be continually evaluated. The undesirable effects of the
legislation on domestic servants' rest periods

(referred to earlier), or what happened when legislation was adopted on the need for day nurseries in firms, are a warning on the need for continuous monitoring, not only to check the application of legal measures but also to avoid evasion of the spirit of the rules.

Finally, it may be concluded from an analysis of the features of female employment that the growing labour participation of women should not be viewed as the only key dimension: at the present time there are also other aspects which are important for evaluating the labour situation of women, such as working conditions, the expansion of work options, and the elimination of occupational segmentation.

3. Significance of the changes

A challenge which still remains to be faced is that of elucidating the mutual relations between the dimensions of female participation in the economy and the effects that may be observed in other areas, such as the family, social, political and cultural spheres. It is well known that the evolution of these dimensions takes place at uneven rates, but it is also known that their interrelation means that when changes take place in one dimension, the others will necessarily be affected too: consequently, the magnitude and direction of these changes should be closely analysed. A query also arises in this connection: does female labour participation, which is a basic requisite for women's independence, lead to independence on other levels too, or does it merely mean an increase in their responsibilities and an overload of work?

In the new development proposals, especially the ECLAC proposal for changing production patterns with social equity, improving the skills and qualifications of human resources is one of the key elements. There can be no doubt that highly qualified female labour is a resource which is currently misused in the labour market: women are not paid in keeping with their level of education, and they are segregated in a limited number of occupations. The labour market could make better use of women's qualifications, however, if their work opportunities were expanded and the rigid vertical and horizontal segmentation of occupations were eliminated. Changes in the organization of the system of production offer women opportunities of which they must take advantage. Whether these potentials strengthen or weaken occupational segregation, for example, will depend on the

bargaining power that working women achieve. From the standpoint of the labour market, the greater flexibility of highly educated female labour could become a highly attractive feature within the new development pattern.

From the point of view of their social background, the labour situation of women is more complex and heterogeneous than that of their male counterparts. In the future, they will have greater potential and possibilities for following working careers different from those of their own age-groups and generations, in accordance with their greater flexibility as human resources.

The fact that a third of the region's labour force consists of women has a new and different significance in the cultural image of the region. Firstly, in sheer numbers working women represent a factor that cannot be ignored or denied. Secondly, it has a major demonstration effect on society as a whole, since now there is no longer any doubt that paid work is a valid option for women. What remains to be cleared up is whether the future new context will tackle the "ambiguity" that prevails as regards the recognition of women's right to work, not in the legislation itself, but in unwritten social practices (Aguirre, 1990). This ambiguity is reflected in the lack of social support services, lack of family backing, and a feeling of guilt among women themselves for not fulfilling their "natural" duties. The acceptance in the received social image of the idea that women with small children may work outside the home should be reflected in more support services, especially for the care of pre-school children (creches and day nurseries) and children who are attending school (extension of school hours to coincide with the working day).

With regard to the relationship between work and the family, the changes in female employment undoubtedly have effects on the family. A woman naturally has more influence within the family when she has an income of her own, but it is well known that the distribution of labour by gender within the home remains largely unchanged. If, as the data show, the greatest increase in female participation is among married women with children, while at the same time the proportion of domestic servants is going down, then the consequences in terms of an overload of work for women are beyond doubt. This fact further heightens the need for policies designed to provide much-needed aid in child care.

With regard to the labour market, on the other hand, there is ample scope for improvements in such areas as regulating the working hours and pay of home workers, whether own-account workers or subcontractors, and raising the status of female labour in the eyes of employers. Society still needs to recognize the domestic work, and especially the child-raising duties carried out by women, as socially vital tasks that could well be carried out by both sexes.

(Original: Spanish)

Bibliography

Abramo, Lais (1993): Reconversión productiva, cambio tecnológico y empleo femenino en América Latina, paper presented at the Latin American seminar on the effects of changing production patterns and technological change on women's employment and working conditions in Latin America, Santiago, Chile, International Labour Organisation (ILO)/Servicio Nacional de la Mujer (SERNAM), 8-12 March.

Aguirre, Rosario (1990): *Los efectos de la crisis sobre la mujer en el Uruguay*, Documentos de trabajo, No. 60, Montevideo, Centro Interdisciplinario de Estudios sobre el Desarrollo (CIEDUR).

Aranda, Ximena (1991): *Tejenderas de Putaendo. Para no mirar la cerca en redondo*, Joint project, La Edición Pepa Foncea/Ibero-American Co-operation Institute, (ICI), Santiago, Chile.

Barbezat, Debra (1993): *Occupational Segmentation by Sex in the World*, Women/WP-13, Geneva, ILO/IDP.

Benería, Lourdes (1992): The Mexican debt crisis: Restructuring the economy and the household, in L. Benería and S. Feldman (eds.), *Unequal Burden: Economic Crisis, Persistent Poverty, and Women's Work*, Oxford, Westview Press.

Benería, Lourdes and Martha Roldán (1992): *Las encrucijadas de clase y género. Trabajo a domicilio, subcontratación y dinámica de la unidad doméstica en la Ciudad de México*, Mexico City, Colegio de México/Fondo de Cultura Económica/Economía Latinoamericana.

Bonilla, Elssy (1992): La mujer colombiana en la universidad y en el mundo del trabajo, Boletín No. 29, Proyecto principal de educación en América Latina, United Nations Educational, Scientific and Cultural Organization (UNESCO), UNESCO Regional Office for Education in Latin America and the Caribbean (OREALC).

CELADE (Latin American Demographic Centre) (1989): *Demographic Bulletin*, vol. XXII, No. 44 (LC/DEM/G.80), Santiago, Chile.

——(1991): *Demographic Bulletin*, vol. XXIV, No. 47 (LC/DEM/G.97), Santiago, Chile.

——(1993): *Demographic Bulletin*, vol. XXVI, No. 52 (LC/DEM/G.135), Santiago, Chile.

Chaney, Elsa and Mary García Castro (eds.) (1993): *Muchacha, cachifa, empleada, empregadinha, sirvienta y...más nada*, Venezuela, Editorial Nueva Sociedad.

Darcy de Oliveira, Rosyska (1989): Femme et travail: sens, nonsens et ambigüité, paper presented at the seminar L'accès des femmes au travail salarié comme source de changement social et ses effets sur la socialisation des femmes et des autres membres de la collectivité, Ankara, Turkey, UNESCO.

ECLAC (Economic Commission for Latin America and the Caribbean) (1990): *Los grandes cambios y la crisis. Impacto sobre la mujer en América Latina y el Caribe* (LC/G.1592-P), Santiago, Chile. United Nations publication, Sales No. S.90.II.G.13.

——(1993): *Panorama social de América Latina* (LC/G.1768), Santiago, Chile.

——(1994): *The Social Summit: A View from Latin America and the Caribbean (Note by the Secretariat)* (LC/G.1802(SES.25/5), Santiago, Chile.

Filgueira, Nea (1992): *Mujeres uruguayas: un futuro incierto*, Serie Lila, No. 28, Montevideo, Study Group on the Status of Women in Uruguay (GRECMU).

Gallart, Antonia, Martín Moreno and Marcela Cerrutti (1990): Estrategias laborales de los trabajadores por cuenta propia del Area Metropolitana de Buenos Aires, in P. Galin and M. Novick (eds.), *La precarización del empleo en la Argentina*, Buenos Aires, International Centre for Tropical Agriculture (CIAT)/Latin American Social Sciences Council (CLACSO)/Bibliotecas Universitarias/Centro Editor de América Latina (CEAL).

García, Brígida and Orlandina de Oliveira (1993): *Trabajo femenino y vida familiar en México*, Mexico City, El Colegio de México.

García, Norberto (1993): Reestructuración económica y mercados de trabajo, in Instituto Internacional de Estudios Laborales (IIEL), *Reestructuración y regulación institucional del mercado de trabajo en América Latina*, Research Series, No. 98, Geneva.

Garrido, Luis (1992): *Las dos biografías de la mujer en España*, Madrid, Ministry of Social Affairs, Institute for Women's Studies (IM).

Geldstein, Rosa (1992): Aumentan los hogares sostenidos por las mujeres, *Boletín del SIDEMA*, No. 5, Argentina, Servicio de Información Documental y Estadística sobre la Mujer en la Argentina (SIDEMA), December.

Gindling, T. H. (1992): La mujer y la crisis económica en Costa Rica, *Ciencias económicas*, vol. XII, No. 2, San José, Costa Rica, Editorial de la Universidad de Costa Rica.

González, Pablo (1992): El diferencial de ingresos entre hombres y mujeres: teoría, evidencia e implicaciones de política, *Colección estudios CIEPLAN*, No. 34, Santiago, Chile, Economic Research Corporation for Latin America (CIEPLAN).

Guzmán, Virginia and Patricia Portocarrero (1992): *Construyendo diferencias*, Lima, Flora Tristán Ediciones.

Hola, Eugenia and Rosalba Todaro (1992): *Los mecanismos del poder: hombres y mujeres en la empresa moderna*, Santiago, Chile, Centre for Women's Studies (CEM).

Montero, Cecilia (1992): Los problemas de integración social: el caso de los empleos femeninos y masculinos de fácil acceso, *Proposiciones: Género, mujer y sociedad*, N°21, Santiago, Chile, Sur Ediciones.

Montoya, Silvia (1993): Implicancias distributivas del trabajo femenino, *Estudios*, vol. XVI, No. 67, Córdoba, Argentina, Instituto de Estudios Económicos sobre la Realidad Argentina y Latinoamericana (IEERAL).

Mujer/Fempress (1994): No. 148/149, Santiago, Chile, ILET, February-March.

Pérez Sáinz, Juan Pablo (1992): Empleo informal en la ciudad de Guatemala, *Mujer y sector informal*, Guatemala City, Latin American Faculty of Social Sciences (FLACSO)/Oficina Nacional de la Mujer (ONAM)/United Nations Children's Fund (UNICEF).

Pollack, Molly (1993): *¿Feminization of the Informal Sector in Latin America and the Caribbean?*, "Mujer y Desarrollo" series, No. 11 (LC/L.731), Santiago, Chile, ECLAC.

Psacharopoulos, George and Zafiris Tzannatos (1992): *Women's Employment and Pay in Latin America. Overview and Methodology* (regional and sectoral studies), Washington, D.C., World Bank.

Rangel de Paiva Abreu, Alice (1993): Mudança tecnológica e gênero no Brasil, *Novos Estudos*, No. 35, São Paulo, Brazil, Brazilian Centre for Analysis and Planning.

Rendón, Teresa (1993): *El trabajo femenino en México en el marco de la transformación productiva con equidad* (LC/MEX/R.407), Mexico City, ECLAC Subregional Headquarters in Mexico.

Rico, Nieves (1994): *Formación y desarrollo de los recursos humanos femeninos: un desafío para la equidad* (LC/L.829), Santiago, Chile, ECLAC.

SERNAM (National Women's Service) (1993): *Situación de las mujeres en el mercado de trabajo en 1992, Informe de coyuntura*, Santiago, Chile, Programme for Labour Economics (PET)/National Women's Service (SERNAM), May.

United Nations (1989): *1989 World Survey on the Role of Women in Development* (ST/CSDHA/6), New York. United Nations publication, Sales No. E.89.IV.2.

———(1991): *Women. Challenges to the year 2000*, New York. United Nations publication, Sales No. E.91.I.21.

———(1992): *Situación de la mujer en el mundo. Tendencias y estadísticas 1970-1990*, Series K, No. 8 (ST/ESA/STAT/SER.K/8), New York.

Vega, Luz (1992): El trabajo a domicilio: ¿Hacia una nueva regulación?, *Revista internacional del trabajo*, vol. III, No. 1, Geneva, ILO.

[14]

Pergamon

World Development Vol. 27, No. 3, pp. 583–602, 1999
© 1999 Elsevier Science Ltd

PII: S0305-750X(98)00151-X

Global Feminization Through Flexible Labor: A Theme Revisited

GUY STANDING
International Labour Organisation, Geneva, Switzerland

"Women taught me how to do the unskilled work."[1]

1. INTRODUCTION

Since the 1970s the global economy has been in an era of market regulation and growing labor market flexibility, in which new technologies, new labor control systems and reformed forms of work organization have transformed patterns of labor force participation throughout the world. In the process, the turn of the century will mark the end of the century of the laboring man in a literal and real sense, in that women will account for almost as many of the "jobs" as men.

This paper is a "revisit" to ideas and data presented in a paper written in 1988.[2] The main hypothesis of that paper was that the changing character of labor markets around the world had been leading to a rise in female labor force participation and a relative if not absolute fall in men's employment, as well as a "feminization" of many jobs traditionally held by men.

The term "feminization" was intentionally ambiguous. Perhaps a better term could have been used. It was intended, however to capture the double meaning and the sense of irony that, after generations of efforts to integrate women into regular wage labor as equals, the convergence that was the essence of the original hypothesis has been toward the type of employment and labor force participation patterns associated with women. The era of flexibility is also an era of more generalized insecurity and precariousness, in which many more men as well as women have been pushed into precarious forms of labor.

Feminization arises because available employment and labor options tend increasingly to characterize activities associated, rightly or wrongly, with women and because the pattern of employment tends to result in an increasing proportion of women occupying the jobs. The term could be decomposed into its constituents. A type of job could be feminized, or men could find themselves in feminized positions. More women could find themselves in jobs traditionally taken by men, or certain jobs could be changed to have characteristics associated with women's historical pattern of labor force participation. The characteristics include the type of contract, the form of remuneration, the extent and forms of security provided, and the access to skill.

A further difficulty arises from the connotations. Most observers think that work patterns that are intermittent, casual and partial are bad, while those that are stable, continuous and full are good. If the surrounding conditions are appropriate, however there is nothing intrinsically bad about a pattern of work involving multiple statuses, multiple activities and varying intensity of involvement in different forms of work.

Gender outcomes in labor markets do not reflect natural or objective differences between men and women, but rather reflect the outcome of discrimination and disadvantage, and the behavioural reactions by workers and employers. This means that even if the thesis of feminization were supported empirically, a reversal of trend could still be possible. That stated, the following does no more than bring the original hypothesis up to date with a decade more of data used in the original paper, bearing in mind all the difficulties of making crossnational comparisons.

To reiterate, the contextual developments that have shaped the growing feminization of the labor market include:

(a) International trade in goods and services has grown enormously as a share of national incomes, as has the share of foreign or multinational investment in total investment in most countries.

(b) Trade and investment have been directed increasingly to economies in which labor costs have been relatively low (or where they have been expected to be relatively low), putting a premium on the level of wages, nonwage labor costs and labor productivity.

(c) In the postwar era up to the 1970s, trade between countries was predominantly in complementary goods (e.g., primary for nonprimary) or between countries with similar labor rights, and therefore roughly equivalent labor costs (balanced by differences between wages and productivity). From the 1970s onward, partly as a consequence of actual and incipient industrialization of some parts of the developing world, labor rights in industrialized countries became increasingly perceived as *costs* of production to be avoided in the interest of enhancing or maintaining "national competitiveness."

(d) In the past few years, there has been a "technological revolution," based on micro-electronics, which *inter alia* has permitted a wider range of technological-managerial *options* in working arrangements, which again means that cost considerations of alternatives have become more significant determinants of allocations and divisions of labor. This has affected patterns of employment in industrialized and industrializing economies, and the international division of labor, accentuating tendencies to allocate to where labor costs are lowest (which depends on wages, nonwage labor costs, productivity and supporting infrastructure).[3] There is also the possibility that we have been in a phase of what some analysts have described as "technological stalemate," in which process (cost-cutting) innovations predominate over product innovations.

(e) There has been a crystallization of a global economic strategy, under the banner of "structural adjustment," "shock therapy" and other supply-side economic policies. This strategy has been associated with radical changes in labor market relations, involving erosion of protective and pro-collective labor regulations, decentralization of wage determination, erosion of employment security and a trend to market regulation rather than statutory regulation of the labor market.

(f) There has been an erosion in the legitimacy of the welfare systems of industrialized countries. In the era following WWII, for much of the world universal social protection within a "redistributive welfare state" was regarded as a long-term development goal and as the basis of well-functioning labor markets. The erosion of that model has been due to many factors, including the rising costs of achieving social protection in the context of high unemployment, the rejection of Keynesianism and its replacement by faith in supply-side economics, by which public spending is perceived (or presented) as "crowding out" private, productive investment, and a loss of faith among welfare state defenders in its ability to be redistributive. There has been growing privatization of social protection and an individualization of social security, whereby more workers have to depend on their own contributions and entitlements.

These contextual developments have both shaped the gender division of labor and have been influenced by the labor market developments themselves. In particular, they have increased the emphasis placed on labor costs. That has led to greater use of alternative forms of employment to the conventional one of regular, full-time wage labor, which has weakened the dualistic segmentation of employment in which men have been relatively protected "insiders".

2. GENDER IMPLICATIONS OF LABOR MARKET FLEXIBILITY

Among the labor market implications of the supply-side, structural adjustment agenda pursued around the world in recent years, several are relevant to our general hypothesis.

First, in industrialized countries in particular, the increasing selectivity or "targeting" of state benefits has meant fewer people having entitlements. This has boosted "additional worker" effects — pushing more women into the labor market in recessions and inducing more women to remain in the labor market because of the growth of *income insecurity*. The trend to means tests and tighter conditionality has also encouraged the growth of the "black economy" and precarious forms of work, since those without entitlements have been obliged to do whatever income-earning work they can. This phenomenon has been strong in industrialized economies, although it has affected many industrializing countries as well.

Second, the erosion of neocorporatist labor relations and the promotion of market regulation have eroded the strength of labor market "insiders," notably unionized (male) workers in stable full-time jobs.[4] That has weakened the defence of *employment security* regulations and customary practices preserving *job security*. Governments in all types of economy have made it easier to dismiss workers and to "downsize." In doing so they have also made it easier for firms to alter job boundaries, reducing the rights of existing workers and encouraging resort to *external* labor markets, enabling employers to substitute lower-cost labor for "core" workers.

Third, the *income security* of the employed has been reduced in many countries, in part by the removal or weakening of *minimum wage* legislation, or by the non-enforcement of existing laws. Among the consequences has been a growth of very low-wage employment, including jobs paying "individual" rather than "family" wages. This has encouraged a substitution of women for men and induced labor force entry by women.

Fourth, in low-income countries in particular, the emphasis put on trade liberalization and export-led industrialization has had implications for women's economic activity. The *direct* effect has been documented by several analyses.[5] Indeed, all countries that have successfully industrialized have done so only by mobilizing large numbers of (low-paid) women workers. *Indirectly*, the industrialization strategy has meant that subsidies for domestic "non-tradables" have been cut, often including staple food items typically produced by women, and structural adjustment programes have involved deflationary stabilization plans that, in reducing domestic consumption so as to shift resources to export industries, have also had adverse effects on the living standards of women producing basic consumer goods. But, as noted earlier, through an increasing emphasis on cost-cutting competitiveness, globalization has also meant a search for ways of lowering labor costs, meaning that firms have put a greater premium on workers prepared or forced to take low-wage jobs. In industrialized and industrializing countries, firms have turned to forms of labor offering the prospect of minimizing fixed non-wage costs. As a result, they have turned increasingly to casual labor, contract labor, outsourcing, home-working and other forms of subcontracting.

As part of this flexibilization, there has been an "informalization" of employment across the world. Although the dichotomy of "formal" and "informal" *sectors* has always been misleading, a growing proportion of jobs possess what may be called informal characteristics, i.e., without regular wages, benefits, employment protection, and so on. Such forms of employment have been compatible with characteristics *presumed* to be associated with women workers — irregular labor force participation, willingness to work for low wages, static jobs requiring no accumulation of technical skills and status, etc. The informalization could thus be expected to be a major factor stimulating the growth of female employment across the world.

Fifth, in this process enterprises around the world have been introducing production techniques that have been changing skill and job structures in particular ways. Whether there has been "deskilling" or "upgrading" overall, two trends seem widespread. First, there has been a decline in the proportion of jobs requiring "craft" skills learned through apprenticeship or prolonged on-the-job learning. Such crafts have traditionally been *mainly* the domain of men, so that their decline and the changing character of "skill" are likely to have influenced the gender division of labor. Second, there has been a trend to skill "polarization," with a minority of workers required to possess specialist skills and a majority required to possess minor training, typically imparted through "modules of employable skill," in which docility, application, rote learning and related "capacities" figure prominently.

This polarization places greater reliance on external rather than internal labor markets, since fewer workers are in "progressive" jobs while more are in "static" jobs involving little upward mobility or returns to on-the-job continuity. This has weakened one reason for discrimination against women, that (whether true or not) women have a higher labor turnover. If there were less benefit to enterprises from workers' on-the-job experience, that reason for discrimination would be removed. Indeed, for many monotonous jobs *high* labor turnover may have a positive value for employers, since maximum efficiency may be reached after only a few months, thereafter plateauing or declining.[6]

This diminishing return to on-the-job continuity has been one reason for resorting to casual or temporary labor, or for job-rotating, and has been a determinant of the tendency to collapse job classifications into more broadly based job clusters, such that workers can be shifted from one set of tasks to another from time to time. This has been a trend in many labor markets, and has represented a growth of *job insecurity* that has accompanied the growth of income and employment insecurity marking the shift to more flexible labor markets.

So, the primary hypothesis is that the growing labor market flexibility and the diverse forms of insecurity have encouraged greater female labor force participation and employment. The evidence presented in the earlier paper seemed to support this hypothesis. The question is whether the trends continued in the succeeding decade.

3. GLOBAL FEMINIZATION?

Let us start by considering the changing levels of female participation in officially recognized labor force activities. There has been a long debate on the gender bias in official statistics and concepts of labor force participation. The recorded rates of participation have been seriously affected by conceptual and statistical practices that have made much of women's work "invisible" and undervalued. Besides these issues (which should always be borne in mind), female labor force participation is determined by a mix of economic, demographic, cultural and labor market factors.[7]

Table 1. *Trends in adult male and female activity rates during 1975–95* [a]

	Women rose	Women fell	Women no change
Men rose			
Developing	Chile, Guatemala, Jamaica, Mexico, Panama, Korea Rep., Thailand 20.0% [b]	Cameroon (−), Ecuador (0) 5.7%	
Developed	Switzerland 5.0%		
Men fell			
Developing	Argentina (+), Bolivia (−), Costa Rica (−), Peru (+), Puerto Rico (−), Netherlands Antilles (−), Trinidad and Tobago (−), Venezuela (+), Uruguay (+), Algeria (−), Egypt (+), Mauritius (+), Bahrain (+), Israel (−), Kuwait (+), Pakistan (−), Singapore (+), Sri Lanka (+) 51.4%	Barbados, Haiti, Hong Kong, Zimbabwe 11.4%	Indonesia 2.9%
Developed	Denmark (−), Germany (+), Iceland (+), Italy (−), Netherlands (0), Portugal (+), Spain (−), Sweden (0), United States (0), Canada (+), New Zealand (+), Japan (+), South Africa (0) 65.0%	Austria, Finland, France 15.0%	Australia, Greece, Norway 15.0%
Men no change			
Developing	Honduras 2.9%		Philippines, Syrian Arab Rep. 5.7%
Developed			

[a] Age coverage is 15–64 except as follows: 15–69: Cameroon (1985), Syrian Arab Republic (1984); 15–59: Costa Rica, Honduras, Panama, Seychelles (1985), Sri Lanka (1981), Thailand, Zambia; 16–59: Puerto Rico, Norway, Spain, Sweden; 18–64: Israel (1989); 20–59: Algeria; 20-64: Finland (1980), Italy, Jamaica, South Africa. Symbols in parentheses indicate net direction of change, male and female combined: (+) Net increase; (−) Net decrease; (0) Zero net change.
[b] Percentage of countries in the category.
Source: ILO (various years).

It might be useful to reiterate a few stylized interpretations:

(a) As initially shown by Ester Boserup, women's participation in predominantly rural economies has been linked to the *type* of agriculture, and as a result urbanization and industrialization have not always been associated with a rise or a fall in the rate of participation.[8]

(b) Marriage, child-bearing and child-raising have been barriers to labor force entry and to retention of employment, and these "barriers" have been linked to the availability of wage employment, the costs for women of labor force entry, the type of employment and type of social transfers available.

(c) Cultural determinants of participation have been widely cited, notably religion and patriarchal ideology, and these too have been stronger in economies in which work away from the home has predominated. As with the fertility determinant, most analysts would now be more skeptical than used to be the case of the strength of cultural barriers to women's economic activity, since modifications in working patterns seem remarkably rapid in the face of alterations in incentives, economic needs and opportunities.

(d) With industrialization based on textiles, garments, electronics and other "light" industry, female participation and employment has tended to rise very sharply.

(e) Traditionally, with growing or high unemployment, discriminatory barriers and discouragement have probably had a greater negative effect on women's labor force participation, and this has tended to dominate the "additional worker" effect of recessions.

According to most analyses, in recent years the negative determinants have been weakened and the positive factors have been strengthened. Among the changes have been rising divorce rates, declining fertility rates and the passage in many countries of anti-discrimination legislation. The main factor, however has been the changing nature of the labor market. The concept of regular, full-time wage labor as the growing type of employment has been giving way to a more diverse pattern, characterized by "informalization" of employment, through more outworking, contract labor, casual labor, part-time labor, homework and other forms of labor unprotected by labor regulations. Whereas traditionally informal economic activities were mainly the means of survival by the rural and urban poor, in recent years in both industrialized and industrializing countries there has been a trend in which even larger-scale enterprises have been informalizing their labor process.

In that context, having done so for the early 1970s and 1980s for the first article, we have

Table 2. *Trends in adult activity rates, during 1975–95, by percentage of countries with each type of change, total and by gender* [a]

Gender	Type of change	Developing countries	Developed countries
Women	Increased	74	70
	Decreased	17	15
	No change	9	15
	Total	100	100
Men	Increased	26	5
	Decreased	66	95
	No change	9	0
	Total	100	100
Total	Increased	52	35
	Decreased	40	45
	Compensated [b]	3	20
	No change	6	0
	Total	100	100

[a] For national definitions of activity rates and labor force participation, refer to the ILO *Yearbook of Labour Statistics*. For a critique of this concept in developing countries, see Standing (1981). Figures have been rounded.
[b] Activity rates of men and women changed in the opposite directions, involving a fall in male and a rise in female activity rates, so that they approximately offset each other.

assembled national-level official data for as many countries as possible having information from the early 1980s and from the 1990s.[9] Often the concepts used and the measurement vary, and one should be wary about making detailed comparisons. At best, one can paint an impressionistic picture. Fortunately, the trends do seem strong enough for us to have reasonable confidence in their validity.

For the past 30 years or so, the trend across the world has been for female labor force participation to rise, while the male participation rate has been falling.[10] Tables 1 and 2 show that in 51% of so-called developing countries with available data female labor force participation rose while the male participation rate fell, and in no less than 74% of those countries the female rate rose, while in 66% of countries the male rate fell. In industrialized countries the divergence was even greater, with male participation falling in 95% of all cases. Within countries, differences between male and female labor force participation rates have shrunk considerably. But at least between industrialized countries, there has been no convergence between activity rates for women. Within the European Union, for example, the substantial differences between countries have been virtually unchanged over recent years.[11] In countries of Central and Eastern Europe, despite the upheavals and economic decline, the levels of female participation have remained high, although they have dropped as if converging to the (rising) levels of Western Europe. Most significantly, in much of Eastern Europe and the former Soviet Union male labor force participation rates have dropped to a greater extent so that the female share of the labor force has risen.

A trend brought out by Tables 1 and 2 is that in a majority of countries in which male participation fell, *total* labor force participation rose, suggesting a strong change in the gender division of labor and suggesting that female labor force entry was more than substituting for men.[12] With many more women continuously in the labor force or finding it easier to move in and out of it, or combining labor force and other work, more women are remaining in the labor force until a later age. Another interesting point is that the net increase in overall participation seemed to be greater than over the previous decade *even though the drop in male participation was much stronger in the later period.*[13]

Among other points emanating from Tables 1 and 2 is that, as observed in the earlier

data summarized in the 1989 article, in those countries that have pursued an export-led industrialization strategy as part of a structural adjustment program, the female labor force participation has been high and has risen. This leads to a second series of considerations.

Table 3 shows that in all three regions of developing countries there has been a tendency for the female share of non-agricultural employment to rise, even though women still comprise a minority of such employment. Table 4 gives the patchy time-series data that exist on the female shares of manufacturing wage employment in industrializing countries. Although there are relatively few countries with such data, they do suggest that the trend has been upward, even though the slight slippage in the Republic of Korea and Hong Kong may have something to do with the changing character of industrial growth in such countries.

In Western Europe and in other industrialized countries the female share of non-agricultural employment has risen everywhere (except in Denmark, where the level has long been high). In Eastern Europe and the former Soviet Union, despite claims to the contrary, women's share of industrial employment has remained very high and at least in the largest two (the Russian Federation and Ukraine), as well as in Slovakia and Slovenia, women's *relative* employment position actually improved after 1990, largely because the sectors and jobs held by men shrunk even more than other sectors.[14]

Table 5 shows a rather more mixed picture of trends in women's share of production workers in industry, although definitional differences become even greater with data on what is a smaller category of workers, making such comparisons hazardous, as exemplified by the case of Botswana. There is also doubt about whether all countries include unpaid and own-account workers in this category. With these caveats, the main finding is that the female share of such jobs remains low. It seems that in low-income countries barriers to *formal* forms of wage labor have remained strong, even though it is *possible* that women have not been seeking such jobs. In rapidly industrializing countries their share has been higher, as in Thailand and Malaysia.

Table 5 is consistent with the hypothesis that it is the spread of more flexible and informal employment that accounts for much of the upward trend in the female share of the labor force. One possible reason for the implied substitution of women for men is the lower

Table 3. *Percentage share of women in non-agricultural employment* [a]

Country	[b]	1975	1980	1983	1984	1985	1986	1987	1988	1989	1990	1991	1992	1993	1994
Africa															
Botswana	(3)	19	24	18	17	30	31	29	31	31	33	34	36	n.	n.
Egypt	(1)	10	11	17	16	16	n.	n.	n.	18	19	19	17	n.	n.
Gambia	(3)	10	12	15	15	15	15	18	n.	n.	n.	n.	n.	n.	n.
Kenya	(3)	n.	17	19	19	20	21	21	21	21	21	22	n.	n.	n.
Malawi	(3)	7	9	12	14	16	14	n.	10	10	11	11	n.	n.	n.
Mauritius	(3)	20	26	28	31	35	36	36	37	37	37	38	38	37	37
Niger	(2)	4	4	14	8	7	7	8	8	9	11	9	n.	n.	n.
Swaziland	(3)	22	26	28	29	31	31	n.	n.	n.	n.	n	n	n	n.
Tanzania	(3)	12	17	15	15	17	n.	n.	n.	n.	n.	n.	n.	n.	n.
Zimbabwe	(3)	13	13	14	15	16	15	16	15	15	15	16	14	16	17
Latin America and the Caribbean															
Barbados	(1)	42	43	43	43	44	45	45	46	45	46	45	48	47	47
Bermuda	(3)	n.	43	46	46	46	47	47	48	48	49	49	50	50	50
Brazil	(1)	33	35	37	38	38	39	39	39	39	40	n.	n.	n.	n.
Colombia	(1)	37	39	n.	n.	38	39	40	40	40	40	41	42	n.	n.
Costa Rica	(1)	n.	30	33	35	34	34	35	36	36	36	37	37	36	36
Cuba	(3)	n.	36	39	40	41	41	42	42	n.	n.	n.	n.	n.	n.
Chile	(1)	n.	34	36	34	36	36	35	35	35	36	35	36	36	37
Haiti	(4)	66	71	59	n.	n.	n.	n.	56	n.	n.	n.	n.	n.	n.
Jamaica	(1)	46	48	46	48	48	48	n.	49	48	49	49	50	n.	n.
Mexico	(1)	n.	n.	n.	n.	n.	n.	n.	n.	n.	n.	37	n.	37	n.
Netherlands Antilles	(4)	35	n.	37	37	37	37	n.	n.	n.	n.	45	39	n.	n.
Panama	(1)	38	39	42	40	40	40	n.	44	46	n.	45	39	n.	n.
Paraguay	(4)	39	35	42	44	44	46	46	44	45	42	41	44	43	43
Peru	(1)	n.	n.	n.	n.	n.	n.	40	n.	n.	n.	39	38	38	39
Puerto Rico	(1)	35	38	39	39	39	40	40	41	41	40	40	41	42	42
Trinidad and Tobago	(1)	28	31	32	33	34	34	34	35	35	34	36	38	39	n.
Venezuela	(1)	32	32	32	32	32	32	32	32	34	35	36	36	35	n.
Asia and the Pacific															
Bahrain	(4)	n.	10	n.	n.	11	n.	7	7	7	8	9	9	10	10
Cyprus	(4)	30	33	34	35	35	35	36	37	38	38	38	36	39	n.
Hong Kong	(3)	40	39	37	37	40	40	41	37	36	38	38	37	42	42
India	(3)	10	11	11	11	11	12	12	12	13	n.	n.	n.	n.	n.
Indonesia	(1)	37	34	n.	n.	37	39	39	39	39	38	38	38	n.	n.
Israel	(1)	33	37	38	39	39	39	40	40	41	41	40	41	42	42
Jordan	(3)	14	17	21	23	23	23	22	22	23	23	24	23	23	n.
Korea Rep.	(1)	33	35	38	37	38	38	39	39	40	40	40	39	38	n.
Malaysia	(1)	n.	30	32	32	33	34	35	35	35	36	n.	36	35	n.
Philippines	(1)	47	46	48	47	48	48	47	46	46	46	46	46	46	46
Singapore	(1)	30	35	36	36	36	38	38	42	40	39	40	40	40	40
Sri Lanka	(3)	18	18	22	23	25	28	n.	35	45	39	39	n.	29	29
Syrian Arab Rep.	(1)	8	9	10	9	9	n.	n.	n.	11	n.	11	n.	n.	n.
Thailand	(1)	42	42	43	42	44	44	46	45	45	45	45	n.	n.	n.

[a] Coverage refers to total employed except as follows: Employees — Botswana, Gambia, Kenya, Mauritius, Niger, Swaziland, Tanzania, Zimbabwe, Cuba, India, Jordan, Sri Lanka; All persons engaged — Malawi, Bermuda, Hong Kong. Figures have been rounded.

[b] Source: (1) Labour Force Survey; (2) Social insurance statistics; (3) Establishment surveys; (4) Official estimates. Figures were not available for the years specified, and those of the closest years were given as follows: Botrwana, Niger, Barbadas, Cyprus: 1975 = 1976; Egypt, Tanzania, Syrian Arab Rep. 1985 = 1984; Gambia, Panama Bahrain: 1980 = 1979; Barbados 1980 = 1981; Brazil 1975 = 1977; Bahrain, Indonesia 1985 = 1982.

Source: ILO, Yearbook of Labour Statistics, Table 4 (various years).

Table 4. *Percentage of women among manufacturing workers, developing countries, 1975–94* [a]

Country	b	1975	1980	1983	1984	1985	1986	1987	1988	1989	1990	1991	1992	1993	1994
Africa															
Botswana	(3)	n.a.	17	22	20	27	24	27	29	n.a.	32	37	37	n.a	n.a.
Kenya	(3)	n.a.	9	9	10	10	10	10	11	11	11	12	n.a	n.a	n.a.
Mauritius	(3)	49	56	59	63	62	59	57	58	58	58	60	60	61	60
Swaziland	(3)	16	26	25	24	27	31	n.a.	n.a.	n.a.	n.a.	n.a	n.a	n.a	n.a.
Tanzania	(3)	10	9	11	10	n.a.	n.a.	n.a.	n.a.	n.a.	n.a.	n.a	n.a	n.a.	n.a.
Zimbabwe	(3)	8	7	7	8	7	7	7	7	7	7	71	10	7	9
Latin America and the Caribbean															
Bermuda	(3)	n.a.	n.a.	n.a.	n.a.	35	35	36	36	37	36	36	36	36	34
Costa Rica	(1)	n.a.	27	33	31	30	30	31 [c]	39	39	37	40	37	35	35
Cuba	(3)	n.a.	26	30	30	31	31 [d]	32	34	n.a.	n.a.	n.a.	n.a.	n.a.	n.a.
Ecuador	(3)	n.a.	n.a.	n.a.	n.a.	n.a.	n.a.	n.a.	n.a.	n.a.	32	35	38	35	35
El Salvador	(1)	n.a.	n.a.	n.a.	n.a.	42	44	n.a.	39	43	44	46	46	n.a.	n.a.
Mexico	(2)	n.a.	21	24	24	25	26	n.a.	n.a.	n.a.	n.a.	35	n.a.	34	n.a.
Panama	(1)	25	n.a.	26	29	28	30	30	28	29	n.a.	31	28	n.a	n.a.
Puerto Rico	(3)	48	48	47	46	49	48	48	48	46	45	43	43	44	43
Venezuela	(3)	21	24	25	26	26	26	27	26	27	26	28	28	27	n.a.
Asia and the Pacific															
China	(4)	n.a.	40	n.a.	n.a.	40	41	41	41	41	44	45	44	n.a	45
Hong Kong	(3)	52	50	50	50	50	50	50	49	48	47	47	45	45	44
India	(3)	9	10	10	9	10	9	9	9	9	n.a.	n.a	n.a	n.a	n.a.
Jordan	(3)	12	10	10	11	11	11	10	10	12	11	11	11	11	n.a.
Korea, Rep.	(3)	n.a.	45	43	43	42	42	42	41	39	38	42	41	39	38
Singapore	(1)	41	47	50	52	51	53	55	55	54	53	44	44	44	n.a.
Sri Lanka	(3)	32	31	35	38	39	45	n.a.	47	n.a.	53	58	61	n.a.	n.a.
Thailand	(1)	41	42	45	49	45	45	48	50	48	50	50	n.a.	n.a.	n.a.

[a] Figures have been rounded.
[b] Source: (1) Labour force survey; (2) Social insurance statistics; (3) Establishment surveys; (4) Official estimates.
[c] Prior to 1987: including mining
[d] Prior to 1986: including water
Source: ILO *Year Book of Labour Statistics* Table 3B (various years).

wage earnings received by women. International comparisons of wage data are probably even more problematical than for other aspects of labor force participation. But a basic hypothesis here is that the increasing globalization and the more systematic pursuit of international competitiveness have made wage and labor costs more important in determining the geographical changes in production and employment and thus in determining which groups are employed.

In this regard, one should be wary about interpretations of the available data on wage differentials. Women's wages may be lower than men's because of job or training discrimination, because of occupational segregation, because of direct wage discrimination or because women are prepared to labor for less, having lower "aspiration wages." The erosion of minimum wage legislation — and the institutional machinery needed to make it meaningful — coupled with the sanctioning under structural adjustment programs of real wage cuts, are likely to induce substitution of women for men, partly because men are less willing to work for sub-family wage rates and partly because they would be expected to respond to lower wages by a lower "effort bargain." So, employers would be inclined to hire women more readily. While the promotion of female employment is desirable, this is surely not the way to achieve it.

The national statistical evidence on *wage differentials* in developing countries is again deplorably patchy, and one would be foolhardy to state from what is available that there has been an international trend one way or the other.[15] As shown in Table 6, however, in most countries where there are time-series data the gender wage earnings' differential has remained substantial.

Table 5. *Proportion of women among production workers (all statuses, percentage, from early 1970s to mid-1990s)* [a]

Africa					
Botswana	C	1981	1984	1986	n.a.
	LFSS	7	23	9	
Cameroon	C	1976	1982	n.a.	n.a.
	OE	12	8		
Egypt	LFSS	1975	1984	1989	1992
	LFSS	2	6	9	8
Ghana	C	1970	1984	n.a.	n.a.
	C	35	45		
Morocco	C 10%	1971	1982	n.a.	1992
	C 5%	16	23		22
Mauritius	C	1972	1983	n.a.	n.a.
	C	6	21		
Seychelles	C	1971	1981	n.a.	n.a.
	OE	10	15		
South Africa	Cs	1970	1985	n.a.	n.a.
	C	7	13		
Tunisia	C	1975	1980	n.a.	n.a.
	LFSS	24	22		
Latin America and the Caribbean					
Bahamas	HS	1970	1980	n.a.	n.a.
	C	11	12		
Barbados	HS	1977	1987	n.a.	1993
	LFSS	22	26		19
Belize	C	1970	1980	n.a.	1994
	C	10	13		13
Bermuda	HS		1985	n.a.	1994
	C		8		10
Costa Rica	C	1973	1987	1992	1994
	HS	12	20	22	19
Chile	C	1970	1986	1991	1994
	LFSS	12	15	12	13
Dominican Republic	C	1970	1981	n.a.	n.a.
Ecuador					
	C	22	14		
	C 10%	1974	1982	1990	1994
	C	15	12	16	15
El Salvador	C	1971	1986	n.a.	1992
	HS	19	26		30
Honduras	LFSS		1986	n.a.	1992
	C		22		31
Guatemala	C	1973	1981	n.a.	n.a.
	C	14	12		
Guyana	LFSS	1977	1980	n.a.	n.a.
	C	15	9		
Haiti	C	1971	1982	n.a.	n.a.
	Cs	43	32		
Jamaica	LFSS	1976	1986	1990	n.a.
	LFSS	26	23	21	
Mexico	C	1970	1980	1991	1993
	C	24	17	18	21
Panama	C	1970	1986	1992	1994
	LFSS	11	12	14	10
Paraguay	C 10%	1972	1985	1989	1993
	C	28	22	23	15
Peru	C	1972	1981	1987	1994
	C	14	11	19	14
Puerto Rico	LFSS	1975	1988	1992	1994
	LFSS	20	24	20	19
St. Pierre and Miquelon	C	1974	1982	n.a.	n.a.

Continued overleaf

Table 5 — *Continued*

	C	7	5		
Trinidad and Tobago	LFSS	1978	1986	1989	1990
	LFSS	13	12	11	12
Uruguay	C 12%	1975	1985	1989	1993
	C	20	18	21	19
Venezuela	C 25%	197 1	1987	1990	1993
	HS	10	10	10	10
Virgin Islands (UK)	Cs	1970	1980	n.a.	n.a.
	C	2	5		
Asia and the Pacific					
Bahrain	C	1971	1981	1989	1994
	C	0	1	1	5
Bangladesh	C	1974	1984	n.a.	n.a.
	C	5	17		
Brunei	C	1971	1981	n.a.	n.a.
	C	3	4		
Hong Kong	C	1976	n.a.	1986	1993
	C	37		31	16
India	C	1971	1981	n.a.	n.a.
	C	12	13		
Indonesia	C	1971	1985	n.a.	n.a.
	HS	27	26		
Israel	Cs	1972	1987	1990	1994
	LFSS	12	13	13	13
Jordan	OE	1976	1979	n.a.	n.a.
	C	3	1		
Korea, Rep.	C	1975	1985	1989	1993
	LFSS	28	27	31	26
Malaysia	C	1970	1980	1988	1993
	C	17	22	25	27
Pakistan	C		1985	1992	1994
	LFSS		5	9	9
Philippines	C	1970	1985	1990	1994
	HS	33	24	20	20
Singapore	C	1970	1985	1989	1992
	LFSS	19	25	30	37
Sri Lanka	C	1971	1981	n.a.	n.a.
	C	15	13		
Syrian Arab Republic	LFSS	1970	1984	1989	1991
	LFSS	5	4	5	3
Thailand	LFSS	1970	1985	1988	1991
	LFSS	29	30	32	34
Oceania					
Cook Islands	C	1976	1981	n.a.	n.a.
	C	22	15		
Fiji	C	1976	1985	1988	1990
	C	4	8	14	22
French Polynesia	C	1977	1983	n.a.	n.a
	C	8	17		
Samoa	C	1976	1981	n.a.	n.a
	C	6	9		
Tonga	C	1976	1986	n.a.	n.a.
	C	5	13		

[a] Includes conventional categories: own-account workers, employees, employers, and unpaid family workers.
Figures have been rounded. C = Census; C...% = Census: sample tabulation, size specified; Cs = Census: sample tabulation, size not specified; HS = Household survey; LFSS = Labor force sample survey; OE = Official estimates.
Source: ILO, *Year Book of Labour Statistics* Table 3C (various years).

Table 6. *Female earnings as a percentage of male earnings in manufacturing, selected developing countries, 1975–94* [a]

Country	1975	1980	1981	1982	1983	1984	1985	1986	1987	1988	1989	1990	1991	1992	1993	1994
Africa																
Egypt	68	n.	n.	66	n.	n.	73	74	72	72	71	68	72	75	n.	n.
Kenya	66	63	59	76	80	77	76	73	65	68	69	73	73	n.	n.	n.
Tanzania	71	79	78	n.	n.	n.	n.	n.	n.	n.	n.	n.	n.	n.	n.	n.
Swaziland	n.a.	81	82	81	61	55	72	73	82	78	81	88	90	82	n.	n.
Latin America																
Costa Rica	n.a.	n.	n.	n.	n.	73	74	75	78	67	73	74	72	72	72	72
El Salvador	90	81	86	89	77	84	82	85	90	90	91	94	n.	n.	n.	n.
Netherlands Antilles	n.a	n.	51	66	65	67	68	64	n.	65	n.	n.	n.	n.	n.	n.
Paraguay	n.a.	n.	n	n.	79	79	87	91	n.	89	72	66	67	52	73	77
Asia																
Burma	89	86	89	91	92	94	99	86	n.	59	58	58	60	61	n.	n.
Cyprus	47	50	54	56	55	56	56	56	58	59	58	58	60	60	57	n.
Hong Kong	n.a.	n.	n.	78	79	81	79	78	76	74	73	69	69	69	66	68
Jordan	n.a.	58	64	n.	n.	n.	n.	n.	n.	n.	n.	n.	n.	n.	n.	n.
Korea Rep.	47	45	45	45	46	47	47	49	50	51	50	50	51	52	52	n.
Malaysia	n.a	n.	n.	n.	n.	n.	49	47	48	46	49	50	52	54	n.	n.
Singapore	n.a.	62	62	63	64	65	63	56	58	n.	54	55	56	56	57	57
Sri Lanka	n.a.	81	87	82	71	69	72	78	71	71	69	66	75	85	88	86

[a] n.a. indicates no available data. Figures have been rounded
Source: ILO, *Yearbook of Labour Statistics*, Table 17A (various years).

Intriguingly, it is in rapidly industrializing countries in which the female share of employment has risen most that show *greater* wage differentials, although recently it may have narrowed marginally in the Republic of Korea. Although data differences and deficiencies might explain some of the observed pattern, one hypothesis is that if women's relative wages are typically lower in Southeast Asia than in other developing regions of the world the differential may have been both a primary factor in the rapid industrialization of that region and have been perpetuated in part by the character of that industrialization.[16]

Although this is not the place to try to document such interpretations, one hypothesis to explain the combination of wide gender differentials, low wages and rapid industrial growth in the region is that the average *social wage* is lower in much of Southeast Asia than elsewhere. By this is meant that the individual money wage needed to meet a socially acceptable subsistence is lower, both in absolute terms and as a proportion of any person's social income. If one conceives the wage as one part (perhaps none, perhaps all) of a person's income, with other parts coming from family or community transfers, state transfers and enterprise benefits, the contribution of the various components is likely to vary according to the type of economy and society. In Southeast Asian economies, a woman wage worker has been typically young, single and highly exploitable in part because to a certain extent her wage labor income has been supplemented by transfers from her (village) community, both at the time of her wage labor and subsequently when returns to their village.[17] Although this practice exists everywhere, it may be much more systematic in these countries.[18] One should also recall that women in Southeast Asian factories (as in many other parts of the world) have typically worked very long work weeks, little or no different from those worked by men.

As for industrialized and Eastern European countries, in the latter gender-based wage differentials may have been growing, while in Western Europe they have probably shrunk in recent years, although in some countries they may have widened after many years of improvement.[19] There and elsewhere, a research issue is whether the feminization of employment and the lower wages received by women have contributed to the growth of income inequality that has occurred in many parts of the world.

Another facet of the flexibilization of labor markets has been the rolling back of the *public*

Table 7. *Female share of public service employment, selected developing countries, 1975–94 (percentages)* [a]

Country	1975	1980	1981	1982	1983	1984	1985	1986	1987	1988	1989	1990	1991	1992	1993	1994
Africa																
Benin			15													
Botswana		20		35	37		36	36	36	36	39	39				
Burkina Faso	16					20			21	22						
Burundi			41						38			42				
Ethiopia					20		22		23							
Kenya	18	18	19													
Malawi			12	12	11	12	12	13	12							
Morocco						29	28	28	29		29	29	30	31		
Nigeria		13														
Rwanda					32		33									
Swaziland			25	31	30	32	33	34								
Latin America and the Caribbean																
Barbados			43	45	42											
Bolivia		24	24	24												
Brazil		21	23			24										
Cuba	30	33	33	37	38	39	39	37	38	38						
Jamaica		50	48	48												
Mexico													30		33	
Panama			41	43	43	43	45	45	45	45	46	47				
Trinidad and Tobago				32		37	37	37								
Venezuela		41	42	43		43	44	45	45			49	49	52	52	
Asia and the Pacific																
Bahrain						32	31	31	32							
Cyprus		31	32	32	32	32	33	33	33	34	35	35	36	36		
Hong Kong	20	23	25	28	28	28	28	29	29	30	31	31	32	31	31	31
India			10		11											
Indonesia		23	24		27	27	29	29	30	31	32	31	33	34		
Kuwait				31			34		35		33	33	33		38	39
Qatar		11	12		16			9	9	9						
Syrian Arab Rep.			20				24			26	27	24	25	26		

[a] Public service employment in the total public sector except: Central government- Burundi, Ethiopia, Mali, Rwanda, Kuwait, Bahrain; Government- Botswana, Morocco, Mexico, Trinidad and Tobago; Federal government- Nigeria; Public administration- Brazil. Blank spaces indicate no available data. Figures have been rounded.

Sources: Bahrain: "Statistical Abstract," 1985–87; Barbados: "Labour Force Report," 1975–83 Benin "Revue de Statistique et de Legislation du Travail," July 1984; Bolivia: "Anuario de Estadísticas del Trabajo," 1982 ; Botswana: "Labour Statistics Bulletin," 1977, 1987–90 regular publication; Employment Survey 1982; Brazil: "Anuario Estatistico do Brasil," regular publication. 1986: Government reply; Burkina Faso: "Annuaire Statistique du Burkina Faso," 1984, 1987; Burundi: "Revue de Statistiques du Travail," 1986–90. Government reply to ILO General Report, JCPS, 3rd Session, 1983; Cuba: "Anuario Estadístico de Cuba," 1986–89; Cyprus: 1977–82: "Statistical Abstract," 1985, 1986, 1991, 1992; 1983–86: "Labour Statistics Bulletin," Dec. 1986; Ethiopia: Government reply; Hong Kong: "Monthly Digest of Statistics," 1987–94 regular publication; India: "Pocket book of labour statistics," regular publication. Data supplied to ILO; Government reply; Indonesia: "Statistical Yearbook of Indonesia" 1987, 1992 regular publication; Jamaica: "The Labour Force," regular publication; Kenya: "Statistical Abstract," regular publication; Panama: "Situación Social; Estadísticas del Trabajo," 1987–91 regular publication; Qatar: "Annual Statistical Abstract," 1987–90 regular publication; Rwanda: Government reply; Swaziland: "Annual Statistical Bulletin," 1987, "Employment and Wages," regular publication; Syrian Arab Rep.: "Statistical Abstract," 1987–93 regular publication; Trinidad and Tobago: "Quarterly Economic Report," 1986 regular publication; Venezuela: "Indicadores de la Fuerza de Trabajo", 1987–93, "Encuesta de Hogares por Muestreo," regular publication.

GLOBAL FEMINIZATION THROUGH FLEXIBLE LABOR   595

Table 8. *Share of women in non-agricultural self-employment, selected developing countries, early 1970s to the mid-1990s (percentages of total)*

Africa					
Egypt	C	n.a.	1986	1990	1992
	LFSS		3	8	8
Ghana	C	1970	1984	n.a.	n.a.
	C	73	77		
Mauritius	C	n.a.	1987	1990	n.a.
	C		34	11	
Seychelles	C	1971	1981	n.a.	n.a.
	OE	23	19		
Latin America and the Caribbean					
Costa Rica	C	1973	1987	1992	1994
	HS	13	27	30	32
Chile	C	1970	1986	1992	1994
	LFSS	28	28	29	30
Dominican Republic	C	1970	1981	n.a.	n.a.
Ecuador					
	C	23	27		
	C	1974	1982	1990	n.a.
	C	25	22	28	
El Salvador	C	1971	1980	1991	n.a.
	HS	48	65	62	
Guatemala	C	1973	1981	1989	1991
	C	29	25	52	44
Mexico	C	1970	1980	1990	1993
	C	28	33	31	37
Panama	C	n.a.	n.a.	1990	1993
	LFSS			26	24
Paraguay	C	n.a.	1989	1991	1994
	LFSS		43	44	44
Peru	C	1972	1981	1991	1994
	C	31	29	40	42
Puerto Rico	C	1975	1988	1992	1995
	LFSS	16	15	16	19
Trinidad and Tobago	C	n.a.	1987	1991	1993
	LFSS		29	30	29
Venezuela	C	1971	1987	1991	1993
	HS	17	23	30	27
Asia and the Pacific					
Bangladesh	C	1974	1984	1991	n.a.
	C	3	8	15	
Hong Kong	C	1976	1986	1993	1994
	C	16	20	12	13
India	C	1971	1981	n.a.	n.a.
	C	9	8		
Indonesia [b]	C	1971	1985	1992	n.a.
	HS	24	41	38	
Iran	C	1976	1986	n.a.	n.a.
	C	9	5		
Korea, Rep.	C	1975	1987	1992	1993
	LFSS	29	35	30	29
Kuwait	C	1975	1985	n.a.	n.a.
	C	1	1		
Malaysia	C	n.a.	1987	1990	1993
	LFSS		31	29	26
Pakistan	C	n.a.	1989	n.a.	1993
	OE		5		5
Philippines	C	n.a.	1987	1992	1994

Continued overleaf

Table 8 — *Continued*

	HS		56	53	55
Singapore	C	1970	1987	1992	1993
	LFSS	13	19	18	17
Sri Lanka	C	1971	1981	1992	1994
	C	12	9	16	21
Thailand	LFSS	1970	1985	1990	1994
	LFSS	40	44	45	44
United Arab Emirates	C	1975	1980	n.a.	n.a.
	C	1	1		
Oceania					
Fiji	C	1976	1986	n.a.	n.a.
	C	15	23		
French	C	1977	1983	1988	n.a.
Polynesia	C	31	33	41	
Samoa	C	1976	1981	n.a.	n.a.
	C	30	27		

[a] Figures have been rounded. C = Census; Cs = Census: sample tabulation, size not specified; HS = Household survey; LFSS = Labour Force sample survey; OE = Official estimates.
[b] Includes agriculture.
Source: ILO, *Yearbook of Labour Statistics* Table 2A (various years).

sector, most notably as part of structural adjustment programes, as part of "privatization" initiatives and as a result of the growing practice of outsourcing public service functions. In many parts of the world, the public sector had been a leading source of employment growth in the 1960s, 1970s and early 1980s, and in many countries (particularly industrialized and Eastern European countries) women have comprised a higher share of total public sector employment than private sector employment.

The reversal or slow-down of public sector growth in the late 1980s and 1990s would in itself have been expected to lower the female share of total employment, *if* the average ratios had remained the same as in the earlier era. As far as developing countries are concerned, however, although our data base is not very representative, Table 7 suggests that the female share of public sector employment has tended to *rise*. This continued the trend observed for the 1980s.[20]

Almost definitionally, a key feature of labor market flexibilization has been a relative and absolute growth of *non-regular* and non-wage forms of employment. There is considerable national, anecdotal and sub-national data to testify to this trend.[21] Most statistical offices, however have either not collected information on casual and other forms of non-regular wage labor or have started only recently. As far as so-called 'self-employment' is concerned (which might be taken as a proxy indicator), it is not surprising that internationally comparative data for developing countries are poor.[22] The available statistics mostly suggest an upward trend, notably in Latin America and the Caribbean, as indicated in Table 8.

In industrialized economies, numerous statistics show that the relative and absolute growth of temporary, casual, contract and part-time labor have been widespread, substantial and sustained over the past two decades, so that in some countries, such as Spain, a majority of all jobs are non-regular.[23]

Some of the most rapidly growing forms of flexible labor are increasing feminization in both senses of the term — they are absorbing more women than men and involve less secure working conditions. An example is *teleworking*. Many women have been employed in this way,

Table 9. *Change in ratio of adult female to male unemployment rates, from mid-1970s to mid-1990s (percentage of countries with each type of change)*

	Country type	
Type of change	Developing	Developed
Increase	13.7	26.8
No change	3.4	0.0
Decrease	82.5	72.8

Source: ILO, *Yearbook of Labour Statistics*, Table 9A (various years).

GLOBAL FEMINIZATION THROUGH FLEXIBLE LABOR   597

Table 10. *Ratio of adult female/male unemployment rates (from the mid-1970s to the mid-1990s)* [a]

Initial level	Overall change					
	Increase		No change	Decrease		
				Became < 1	Became = 1	Remained > 1
>1						
Developing	Seychelles			Costa Rica, Chile, Egypt, Guyana Fr., Philippines, Trinidad and Tobago	Panama, Bahamas	Barbados, China, Cyprus, Israel, Jamaica, Uruguay
	3.4%			20.6%	6.9%	20.6%
Developed	Saint Marin			Austria, Australia, Canada, Germany, Luxembourg, Netherlands, New Zealand, Norway, Sweden, United States	Italy, Spain	Belgium, France, Greece, Iceland, Portugal
	3.8%			38.4%	7.7%	19.0%
= 1 or < 1	Became > 1	Remained < 1		Became < 1		Remained < 1
Developing	Thailand, Mauritius	Singapore	Korea	Syrian Arab Rep.		Burkina Faso, Ethiopia, Ghana, Hong Kong, Mexico, Netherlands Antilles, Puerto Rico, Senegal, Venezuela
	6.9%	3.4%	3.4%	3.4%		31.0%
Developed	Denmark	Finland, Isle of Man, Japan, Malta, Switzerland				Ireland, United Kingdom
	3.8%	19.2%				7.7%

[a] 15 years and older.
Source: ILO, *Yearbook of Labour Statistics*, Table 9A (various years).

and have been doing so far more systematically than men. Several empirical studies have shown that men who have done this sort of work have been working at home only for part of the time, whereas women have usually been working full-time at home and in an informal way, leaving them with only "second-class citizenship."[24]

Relocation of flexible forms of labor have also been linked not just to feminization but to a certain form of subordinated flexibility. For instance, a study of suburbanization of employment in the United States reported that the decision to relocate was linked to the employers' preference for married, white women as clerical workers.[25] Teleworking promises to be one of the fastest growing forms of employment and a major source of female employment in the next decade.

Finally, in both the 1980s and 1990s women's rate of *unemployment* relative to men's fell in a considerable majority of industrialized and developing countries. Table 9 shows that in 83% of the developing countries covered women's relative unemployment fell, and that this was the case in 73% of industrialized countries. The table also shows that in a substantial majority of industrialized countries the female unemployment rate was less than the male equivalent. Although comparable statistics were not given in the earlier article, a longer version of that paper did present this information. A comparison those figures with Table 10 indicates that in the 1970s female unemployment relative to male rose in a majority of industrialized countries (78%) and in the same number of developing countries as it fell (45%), whereas in the 1980s it fell in 63% of industrialized countries and 59% of developing countries. In other words, the drop in women's relative unemployment has been a fairly recent phenomenon but the deterioration of men's position has been accelerating.

Given that women's labor force participation rates and employment have been rising and women's unemployment rates have fallen, this change cannot be explained by reference to withdrawal from the labor force in times of high overall unemployment. It seems to reflect a considerable erosion in the position of men in labor markets throughout the world (see Tables 11 and 12). For an example, consider the case of the United Kingdom. Between the early 1960s and the mid-1990s, UK male employment dropped by about four million (excluding a rise in self-employment), so that by the mid-1990s about 4.2 million men aged 16–64 were either unemployed or inactive. Meanwhile, female employment rose by nearly three million. These developments could not be explained by demographic factors. The developments in other countries might not have been so dramatic, but throughout the industrialized world the trend seems to have continued. For instance, in Belgium in 1990 the female–male

Table 11. *Ratio of female/male unemployment rates, developing countries, from mid-1970s to mid-1990s*

Latin America and the Caribbean				
Bahamas	1979: 2.5	1986: 1.5	1991: 0.9	1994: 1.0
Barbados	1976: 1.7	1987: 1.7	1990: 1.8	1994: 1.3
Chile	1976: 1.4	1986: 1.2	1990: 0.5	1994: 0.6
Costa Rica	1976: 2.0	1987: 1.7	1990: 0.6	1994: 0.7
Guyana Fr.	1977: 2.4	1987: 1.8	1990: 0.9	1994: 0.7
Jamaica	1976: 2.5	1986: 2.3	1990: 2.2	1992: 2.1
Mexico		1988: 0.8	1991: 0.9	1993: 0.7
Netherlands Antilles	1983: 1.9	1985: 2.0	1990: 1.0	1991: 1.2
Panama	1979: 2.0	1987: 1.8	1991: 0.9	1994: 1.0
Puerto Rico	1975: 0.9	1985: 0.4	1990: 0.4	1994: 0.4
Trinidad and Tobago	1978: 1.8	1985: 0.6	1990: 0.7	1993: 0.8
Uruguay	1979: 2.4	1984: 2.0	1990: 1.1	1993: 1.2
Venezuela	1975: 1.0	1984: 0.7	1990: 0.4	1993: 0.3
Africa				
Burkina Faso		1985: 0.1	1990: 0.1	1994: 0.1
Ethiopia		1985: 0.7	1990: 0.7	1993: 0.6
Egypt	1979: 4.9	1984: 4.8	1989: 0.8	1992: 0.8
Ghana	1975: 0.3	1986: 0.1	1990: 0.1	1992: 0.1
Mauritius		1985: 0.3	1990: 0.4	1994: 1.6
Senegal		1985: 0.2	1990: 0.2	1993: 0.1
Seychelles	1980: 1.1	1985: 2.0		
Asia				
China	1983: 1.6	1985: 1.5	1990: 1.4	1994: 1.4
Cyprus	1974: 1.6	1987: 0.9	1990: 1.1	1994: 1.2
Hong Kong	1976: 1.0	1985: 0.4	1990: 0.6	1994: 0.5
Israel	1974: 1.7	1985: 0.7	1990: 0.9	1994: 1.2
Korea, Rep.	1974: 0.5	1985: 0.3	1990: 0.4	1994: 0.5
Philippines	1975: 1.6	1985: 1.0	1990: 0.8	1994: 0.7
Singapore	1976: 0.7	1985: 0.6	1990: 0.5	1994: 0.8
Syrian Arab Rep.	1979: 1.0	1984: 2.0	1989: 0.4	1991: 0.6
Thailand	1976: 0.8	1985: 1.3	1990: 1.0	1991: 1.5

Source: ILO, *Yearbook of Labour Statistics* Table 9A (various years).

GLOBAL FEMINIZATION THROUGH FLEXIBLE LABOR   599

Table 12. *Ratio of female/male unemployment rates, developed countries, from mid-1970s to mid-1990s*

Europe				
Austria	1979: 1.4	1985: 0.6	1990: 0.8	1993: 0.8
Belgium	1976: 2.4	1985: 1.5	1990: 1.6	1994: 1.2
Denmark	1976: 0.9	1985: 1.3	1990: 1.0	1994: 1.1
Finland	1975: 0.5	1985: 0.8	1990: 0.6	1994: 0.8
France	1980: 2.3	1985: 1.1	1990: 1.3	1994: 1.1
Germany	1978: 1.6	1985: 0.8	1990: 0.9	1994: 0.7
Greece	1981: 1.7	1985: 1.1	1990: 1.6	1993: 1.4
Iceland	1975: 1.5	1985: 1.4	1990: 1.1	1993: 1.1
Ireland	1981: 0.8	1985: 0.4	1990: 0.5	1993: 0.5
Italy	1980: 2.7	1985: 1.3	1990: 1.4	1994: 1.0
Luxembourg	1980: 2.4	1985: 0.9	1990: 0.7	1993: 0.8
Netherlands	1980: 1.2	1985: 0.7	1990: 1.3	1994: 0.9
Norway	1979: 1.8	1985: 1.1	1990: 0.7	1994: 0.7
Portugal	1978: 1.8	1985: 1.3	1990: 1.2	1993: 1.1
Saint Marin	1980: 1.2	1985: 2.9	1990: 3.1	1993: 2.5
Spain	1980: 1.2	1985: 0.5	1990: 1.1	1994: 1.0
Sweden	1980: 1.5	1985: 0.9	1990: 0.9	1994: 0.7
Switzerland	1975: 0.5	1985: 0.8	1990: 0.8	1994: 0.7
United Kingdom	1980: 0.6	1985: 0.5	1990: 0.4	1993: 0.3
Oceania				
Australia	1980: 1.5	1985: 0.7	1990: 0.8	1994: 0.7
New Zealand	1980: 1.3	1985: 0.6	1990: 2.2	1993: 0.5
Isle of Man	1977: 0.6	1987: 0.8		
Malta	1980: 0.1	1987: 0.6		
America				
Canada	1979: 1.2	1985: 0.8	1990: 0.8	1994: 0.7
United States	1980: 1.1	1985: 0.8	1990: 0.8	1994: 0.8
Asia				
Japan	1975: 0.8	1985: 0.7	1990: 0.7	1993: 0.7

Source: ILO, *Yearbook of Labour Statistics*, Table 9A (various years).

unemployment ratio was 2.5; by 1993, it was 1.8; in Germany in the same period, the ratio fell from 1.5 to 1.1; in Canada, it fell from 1.0 to 0.9. Women can no longer be regarded as the primary "labor reserve," since their labor force participation rates have risen, their share of employment has risen and their relative unemployment rates have fallen. The rising relative and absolute levels of male unemployment are creating a crisis for social and labor market policy, since the welfare state was based on the presumption of the full employment of men in regular full-time jobs.

This long-term trend should not be interpreted as implying that women's position is "good." The reality is that men's position has become more like that of women, and this is especially the case with respect to entitlement to a modicum of income security once unemployed. Even in the European Union, known to

have the most developed of state transfer mechanisms, by the mid-1990s only about one-third of all unemployed were receiving unemployment benefits, and in this regard (as in so many others) women's position remains worse than men's.[26] But men's position has deteriorated. What should be most worrying is that the income security for the unemployed has been declining, due in part to the chronic character of mass unemployment and in part to the explicit and implicit disentitlement to benefits.

4. CONCLUDING REMARKS

There are some who take exception to the notion of "feminization" of the labor market. The three trends identified in the earlier article have however remained powerful and have possibly accelerated over the past decade or so. The types of employment and labor force involvement traditionally associated with women — insecure, low-paid, irregular, etc. — have been spreading relative to the type of employment traditionally associated with men — regular, unionized, stable, manual or craft-based, etc. In addition, women have been entering, reentering and remaining in the labor force to a growing extent. A third trend is that more men have been forced into the margins of the labor market, if not out of it altogether. In effect, there has been a convergence of male and female patterns of labor force participation. While there has been an overall trend toward more flexible, informal forms of labor, women's situation has probably become *less* informal, while men's has become more so.

A welcome development is that, according to a recent exhaustive assessment, there has been some decline in the extent of sex-based occupational segregation in most parts of the world.[27] However, this too may largely reflect the weakening position of men rather than any dramatic improvement in the occupational opportunities of women.

The trends of flexibility and feminization combine to pose an historical challenge to social and labor market policy. It is not possible to presume (as too often has been the case) that the "family wage," "breadwinner" model of labor force behavior is anything like the norm, either currently or likely to arise in the near future. Social insurance predicated on regular, stable full-time wage labor with "temporary interruptions in earning power" does not provide women, or increasingly men, with social protection. Means-tested "social safety nets" do not do so either.

So, among the challenges are the need to reform systems of social protection. There is a corresponding need to promote alternative forms of collective institution to protect and enhance the status of vulnerable groups in labor markets, and a need to combine flexibility with steadily improving economic security. Women's growing involvement in labor force activities is to be welcomed as facilitating a trend toward gender equality, and should be strengthened. But the conditions in which women and men are typically in the labor market do not seem to have been improving. The trend is toward greater insecurity and inequality. Reversing that trend, which is associated with labor flexibility, is the most important labor market and social policy challenge of all.

NOTES

1. Construction laborer in India. van der Loop (1996), p. 390. There was no suggestion that either the laborer or the author appreciated the irony of the statement.

2. Standing (1989), pp. 1077–1095.

3. Some claim that globalization has not had much effect on labor markets (IMF April). But, not only is there evidence of export-oriented industrialization in many developing countries as well as "de-industrialization" in industrialized countries, but there is evidence of "whipsaw bargaining" by managements, along the lines that unless workers accept lower wages and less employment security, etc., the firm would relocate or channel new investment elsewhere.

4. For a perspective on issues raised in this paragraph, see Standing (1997).

5. See, for instance, Wood (1991). Wood concluded that "developing countries which exported a rising proportion of their manufacturing output to the north (sic) tended to employ a rising proportion of females in their manufacturing sectors" (p. 171).

6. In visits to electronics factories in Malaysia in the 1980s, it was interesting to find that many managers expected and even wanted the young women workers to remain in their jobs for only two or three years. They knew that after a short time their physical productivity declined, often as a result of illness or spinal or optical injuries.

7. The determinants of female work patterns around the world were synthesized some time ago (Standing, 1978, 1981). There are strong grounds for radically overhauling conventional labor force statistics.

8. Boserup (1970).

9. Of course, there has been a vast amount of other data and analysis in recent years. This is an attempt to see what one can tell from official national data.

10. For trends in the post-1945 era, see Standing (1981), chapter 1. For more recent years, for industrialized countries, see, for example, Meulders *et al.* (1993).

11. Rubery *et al.* (1995), p. 5.

12.   One cannot say anything conclusive from such data about the overall rate of labor absorption, let alone the elasticity of employment with respect to growth, etc., simply because the quantity of labor and rate of employment relative to unemployment are not captured by participation rate data.

13.   Standing (1989), Tables 1 and 2, pp. 1081–1082.

14.   This has been documented through the Russian Labor Flexibility Survey and the Ukrainian equivalent, which have been the biggest surveys of industrial enterprises conducted in those countries, covering hundreds of thousands of workers. See, for instance, Standing (1996a, b); Standing and Zsoldos (1995).

15.   Case studies have suggested that in the 1970s and 1980s gender-based wage differentials did decline. Anker and Hein (1986).

16.   Some analysts have asked why, in the light of the large wage differentials, did the workforces not become entirely female. Feminist (and Marxisant) interpretations would postulate that disciplinary and other divide-and-rule tactics would induce a mixed-gender strategy in the workplace. See, for instance, Elson and Pearson (1981): Joekes (1993), p. 17

17.   This does not rule out cash remittances from workers in urban areas, but the *two-way* process has long characterized labor circulation in the region. Too often studies of remittances only consider the flow from urban to rural areas.

18.   One could argue that families are exploited through the superexploitation of young women workers, meaning that they could scarcely survive on their wage earnings alone. Another way of putting the argument of the text is that the wage is less than the cost of reproducing their labor power in part because the young

woman's family has a rural production base or is working in periurban informal economic activities. In southern Africa, by contrast, the urban wage has been higher in part because that has been needed to secure a stable and productive supply of wage labor because urban-industrial workers have rarely received much in the form of community transfers and have been expected to support rural households through remittances.

19.   Gonzalez (1995).

20.   Standing (1989), p. 1087. The trend suggests a teasing question: Since in some countries the female share of the public sector has been lower than in the private economy, would a cut in the public sector have boosted the female share of total employment? Would the reverse have applied in countries where the female public sector share has been higher than in the private economy?

21.   See, for instance, Bettio *et al.* (1996).

22.   There is good reason to believe that commonly and indefinsibly women working for an income other than a wage are classified as "unpaid family worker" whereas a man in similar work would be classified as "self-employed" or "own account." This is one of the many reasons for not collecting labor force participation data on the basis of *a priori* categories if possible.

23.   Standing (1997), Table 3.

24.   Lie (1985).

25.   Moss (1984).

26.   Meulders (1996), p. 24. This remarkable fact is documented in more detail in Standing (forthcoming).

27.   Anker (1998).

REFERENCES

Ankerf, R., *Gender and Jobs: Sex Segregation of Occupations in the World* (Geneva: ILO; 1998).

Anker, R., and C. Hein, *Sex Inequalities in Urban Employment in the Third World* (Basingstoke: Macmillan, 1986).

Bettio, F., Rubery, J., and M. Smith, "Gender, flexibility and new employment relations," Mimeo (Manchester: University of Sienna and UMIST, 1996).

Boserup, E., *Women's Role in Economic Development* (New York: St.Martin's Press, 1970).

Elson, D., and R. Pearson, "The subordination of women and the internationalisation of factory production and of marriage and the market," in K. Young, C. Wolkowitz, and O.R. McCullogh (Eds.),

Of Marriage and the Market: Women's subordination in International Perspective (London: CSE Books, 1981).

Gonzalez, P., "Indicators of the relative performance of women in the labour market," Mimeo (Cambridge: University of Cambridge, 1995).

International Labor Organization, *Year Book of Labour Statistics* (Geneva: ILO, various years).

International Monetary Fund, *World Economic Outlook* (Washington, DC: IMF, 1997).

Joekes, S., "The influence of international trade expansion on women's work," Paper prepared for ILO Project on Equality for Women in Employment (Geneva: ILO, 1993).

Lie, M., "Is remote work the way to" "the Good Life" "for women as well as men?" (Trondheim, Norway: Institute for Industrial Research, 1985).

Meulders, D., "Women and the Five Essen Priorities" (Brussels: Universite Libre de Bruxelles, 1996).

Meulders, D., R. Plasman, and V. Vander Stricht, *Position of Women on the Labour Market in the European Community* (Aldershot: Dartmouth Publishing, 1993).

Moss, M.L., *New Telecommunications, Technologies and Regional Development* (New York: New York University, 1984).

Rubery, J., M. Smith and C. Fagan, *Changing Patterns of Work and Working Time in the European Union and the Impact on Gender Divisions.* Report for the Equal Opportunities Unit, European Commission Directorate General V, V/6203/95-EN (Brussels: European Directorate General, April 1995).

Standing, G., *Shadow of the Future: Global Flexibility and Distributive Justice* (Harmondsworth: Macmillan, forthcoming).

Standing, G. "Globalisation, labour flexibility and insecurity: The era of market regulation," *European Journal of Industrial Relations*, Vol.3, No.1 (March 1997), pp. 7–38.

Standing, G., *Russian Unemployment and Enterprise Restructuring: Reviving Dead Souls* (Basingstoke: Macmillan, 1996a).

Standing, G., "The "shake out" in Russian factories: The RLFS fifth round, 1995" (Geneva: ILO, 1996b).

Standing, G., and L. Zsoldos, "Labour market crisis in Ukrainian industry: The 1995 ULFS" (Geneva: ILO, 1995).

Standing, G., "Global feminisation through flexible labour," *World Development*, Vol. 17, No.7 (1989).

Standing, G., *Labour Force Participation and Development* (Geneva: ILO, 1978).

Standing, G., *Labour Force Participation and Development* (Geneva: ILO, 1981).

Van der Loop, Theo, *Industrial Dynamics and Fragmented Labour Markets: Construction Firms and Labourers in India* (New Delhi: Sage Publications, 1996).

Wood, A., "North-South trade and female labour in manufacturing: An asymmetry," *Journal of Development Studies*, Vol.27, No.2 (January 1991).

Part III
Structural Adjustment and Economic Restructuring

Part III

Structural Adjustment and Economic Restructuring

[15]

Pergamon

World Development, Vol. 23, No. 6, pp. 881–896, 1995
Copyright © 1995 Elsevier Science Ltd
Printed in Great Britain. All rights reserved
0305–750X/95 $9.50 + 0.00

0305–750X(95)00022–4

The Gender Dimensions of Economic Adjustment Policies: Potential Interactions and Evidence to Date

LAWRENCE HADDAD
LYNN R. BROWN
International Food Policy Research Institute, Washington, DC, U.S.A.
ANDREA RICHTER
University of Oxford, U.K.
and
LISA SMITH*
University of Wisconsin, Madison, U.S.A.

Summary. — Many developing countries have implemented stabilization and structural adjustment programs over the last 20 years. The success of these programs depends critically on individual-level responses to changing economic incentives. Access to, control of, and an ability to move productive economic resources between sectors is determined, in part, by gender. If an individual's gender impedes their ability to fully participate in the economic adjustment process by inhibiting resource access, control or movement adjustment will be impaired. This paper discusses the potential gender dimensions of structural adjustment policies and examines the evidence to date.

1. INTRODUCTION

Throughout the last decade, the World Bank/International Monetary Fund (IMF) prescription for developing countries with severe debt service problems has been to pursue:

> domestic policies oriented toward enhancing productive investment. These would include in general, macroeconomic policies designed to raise domestic savings, reduce inflation and foster capital formation and long term growth, as well as structural policies to allocate resources more efficiently and to nourish sustainable growth over the medium term. A reduction of external debt with strong adjustment would assist these countries in resuming growth (IMF, 1989).

Exactly what constitutes the most appropriate type of adjustment remains controversial.[1] The debate has centered on two questions:
(a) In the long run, which adjustment measures are most effective in generating sustainable improvements in living standards?
(b) In the short run, what are the social costs of different adjustment measures, and who bears them?

Answers to the above questions will have a gender dimension because an individual's sex is an important determinant of his or her economic and social roles. Precisely how useful that gender dimension is in generating answers to the above questions is not clear. For instance, an assessment of the impact of structural adjustment measures on the individual might be better informed by analysis based on stratifiers such as occupation, age, or region.

If, however, adjustment measures ignore the host of nonprice mechanisms that hinder the response of women relative to men, adjustment will be impaired. Likewise, if the costs of adjustment measures are expected to be borne disproportionately by women when they are less able than men to bear them, adjustment will ultimately fail. Consequently, this paper addresses two questions: which aspects of adjustment

---

* The authors would like to thank Graham Pyatt, Jeffrey Round, and three anonymous referees for their comments on earlier versions of this paper. Any remaining errors are the responsibility of the authors. Final revision accepted: December 28, 1994.

may have gender-differentiated determinants and impacts; and does the evidence at hand provide any support for the hypothesized gender-specific effects?

An overview of some of the main components of adjustment policies and the potential gender dimensions of adjustment is presented in section 2. Methodological and data problems associated with the evaluation of adjustment policies are presented in section 3, and section 4 presents the empirical evidence organized around a set of 10 key questions. Conclusions are provided in section 5.

2. ADJUSTMENT, THE POOR, AND GENDER

(a) *The nature of economic adjustment policy packages*

Adjustment lending programs were launched by the IMF and the World Bank in the late 1970s and early 1980s with the intention of promoting long-run economic growth; this has remained their focal concern (Faini *et al.*, 1991). By early 1992, 78 countries worldwide had accepted structural adjustment loans (Mosley and Weeks, 1993). In 1980, only four nations in sub-Saharan Africa (Kenya, Malawi, Senegal, and Sudan) received adjustment loans but, by 1989, the number of African nations involved in adjustment programs had risen to 31.

Economic adjustment is comprised of two phases: stabilization, generally the domain of the IMF, designed to put a floor under the downward spiral in key economic indicators such as budget deficits; and structural adjustment, generally the domain of the World Bank, designed to restructure the economy and secure longer term economic efficiency (World Bank, 1994).

Stabilization, through the removal of internal (domestic budget) and external (balance of payments) financial disequilibria, aims to provide a stable environment for resource reallocation, a crucial part of structural adjustment.

The stabilization phase of adjustment focuses on demand restraint policies, usually effected by large reductions in government expenditure — via measures such as subsidy removals, public sector employment cuts, and the introduction of user fees. Accompanying expenditure-switching policies, focused on "structural adjustment," involve a realignment of the real exchange rate (through devaluation), privatization, liberalization of interest rates, and tax reform, including reductions in import/export barriers (removal/reduction of tariffs, quotas, and taxes) in order to improve the economy's relative trading position. These policies effect a shift in relative prices and, thus, a transfer of resources from the nontraded sector to the traded goods sector.

(b) *Economic adjustment and poverty: potential impacts*

Towards the middle to late 1980s, the realization that the welfare impacts of adjustment on the poor may be negative "trickled up" to those designing and implementing adjustment programs. Positive action to counter possible negative effects began to be considered. Eighteen of 32 and six of 17 adjustment operations in 1992 and 1993, respectively, included specific measures to protect the poor (World Bank, 1993a).

The potential for negative welfare impacts of adjustment remains, however, irrespective of the poverty-sensitive content of adjustment policies. These impacts are likely to be differentiated by several factors, including the structure of the economy, the extent of urbanization, and individual-level characteristics. In many countries, for instance, both the incidence and depth of poverty is greater in rural areas (World Bank, 1990a). This is true of predominantly rural economies, as in Africa, and the more urbanized economies of Latin America. Nevertheless, poor rural areas that already lack both primary health and education provision are typically less affected by government social sector spending cutbacks. For example, in a predominantly rural economy such as Mali (20% urban), 42% of physicians, 40% of registered nurses, 51% of midwives, 35% of nurses' aides, and 37% of sanitation workers are employed in the capital city, but just 8.5% of the total population reside there (World Bank, 1991). More than 55% of the population live further than 15 kilometers from a health facility.

Case studies by Glewwe and de Tray (1988, 1991) from Côte d'Ivoire and Peru illustrate the potential impact of structural adjustment on the poor. Data from these studies illustrate the rural nature of poverty, even in the more urbanized Peru (70% urban). The vast majority of the poorest 10% of households reside in rural areas (96% in Côte d'Ivoire and 83% in Peru). Moreover, the utilization rates of medical care of the poorest 10% of households are low (33.5% in Côte d'Ivoire and 20.8% in Peru), as is the primary school enrollment rate (8% in Côte d'Ivoire and 14.2% in Peru). Low utilization rates of these services make the poor potentially less vulnerable to the social sector spending cutbacks likely to accompany stabilization.

On the other hand, agricultural reforms, part of most structural adjustment policies, are likely to have positive impacts on the poor, due to the predominance of the poor in this sector. In the Côte d'Ivoire, agricultural policy promoted cash crops (cocoa, cotton, coffee). Of the poorest 30% of households, 52% grow at least one of these three cash crops. While the production cost of cotton increased due to the removal of subsidies on inputs, the reduction in export taxes (i.e. through the liberalization program) increased revenue by enough to offset increased input costs (Glewwe and de Tray, 1988).

Due to complicated tax and subsidy policies on various crops, the design of agricultural reforms to benefit the poor can be extremely difficult. In Peru, for example, farmers growing white maize, cotton, and coffee stand to benefit from the removal of price controls and subsidies, whereas those growing yellow maize, sorghum, and barley would be hurt substantially (Glewwe and de Tray, 1989). For this example, a gender disaggregation of crop-growing responsibilities would shed light on whether women would benefit or lose under these reforms relative to men.

The importance of regional and household resource endowments in determining the impact of adjustment policies on labor supply is illustrated by a comparison of agricultural commercialization case studies from Kenya and the Philippines (Kennedy and Bouis, 1989). In both cases, a production switch from semi-subsistence crops such as corn to a commercial crop such as sugarcane raised household incomes. In the Philippines, relative labor abundance allowed the hiring of additional labor with the income gains, relaxing female time constraints; women were able to do less work during periods of pregnancy and nursing. In labor-constrained Kenya, however, cash crop production tightened female time constraints by increasing own-farm demand for their labor without the guarantee of commensurate remuneration.

(c) Gender and adjustment: potential interactions

Given that societal norms tend to delineate different economic and social roles for men and women, it is perhaps inevitable that the study of adjustment has a gender dimension. Elson (1992) argues that while macroeconomic policies are presented in a language of gender neutrality, they are gender blind and, hence, embody an inherent bias against women; that is, macroeconomic analysis and consequent policy formulation are grounded in an economy defined on marketed goods and services, with some allowance for subsistence crop production in developing countries. Macroeconomic policies may, then, appear gender neutral but they are, in essence, gender blind. Women's additional roles in the "unrecognized" economy, such as household management, reproduction, and child care, impose additional constraints on women's ability to respond to changes within the "recognized" economy initiated by macroeconomic policy.

In order to assess the expected degree of success of adjustment policies as well as the expected distribution of its costs between men and women, one needs to consider the individual's ability to cope and to reallocate his/her resources. For successful adjustment, the need of the individual to bear the cost of adjustment and reallocate resources bears some resemblance to their ability to do so. Adjustment is unlikely to be successful when those individuals expected to bear the burdens of adjustment and to acquire additional resources and move them into new sectors are unable to do so. This approach, focused as it is on the individual, gender-differentiates the ability to respond and/or bear the costs of the potential employment, income, and consumption effects of adjustment.

Many of the arguments for gender-differentiated impacts of adjustment may be explained in terms of gender-differentiated initial conditions. Where these favor males, policies with a gender-neutral intent will likely have a pro-male effect. The danger of obfuscating intent and impact of adjustment programs when studying gender issues has been outlined by Mukhopadhyay (1992):

> The problem as I perceive it lies in investing the macro-concepts and the macro policies per se with a gender bias, whereas in reality the bias lies in the socioeconomic environment within which such policies are applied. It is important to clearly demarcate the two, not merely for the sake of conceptual clarity but also to be able to design effective policy interventions to counter such bias (p. 1).

Addressing such a bias is important, given that adverse conditions are reinforced by gender-specific role model formation (Collier, 1988).[2]

Adjustment policies have direct and indirect impacts and it is necessary to consider both when examining the distribution of costs and benefits between men and women. While it is relatively straightforward to identify individuals likely to be directly affected by an adjustment policy — the cash crop farmer facing higher input and output prices and the public sector worker in an urban area who loses a job — it is less easy to identify adjustment's indirect effects. In rural areas of many African economies, for example, men both grow cash crops and control the incomes from them. Cash crop farmers are, as noted above, likely to benefit from structural adjustment. Women, however, are generally responsible for subsistence food crops, which may not be tradable, and thus adjustment-induced relative price shifts will have a negative direct impact. Cutbacks in public sector employment may also reduce the demand for ancillary services, e.g., cleaning services, generally provided by women.

Due to their roles in the "unrecognized" economy, it is the indirect effects of adjustment that women may be most vulnerable to. Indirect impacts are felt through changes in household resource allocation. In urban areas, when the male worker loses a public sector job, female labor force participation may increase. While this increases women's time burdens, it may, through the increasing share of household income earned by women, increase women's influence in other resource allocation decisions. This happens through an improvement in the fallback positions of women relative to men. Indirect effects may not, however, always favor women. For example, in cash crop production, women are often obliged to supply unremunerated labor to household production (Schoepf and Engundu, 1991). This obligation increases with increased incentives for cash crop production induced by structural adjustment. Women's ability to generate an independent income decreases due to more binding time constraints, while male income-generating ability increases due to the increased prices for cash crops. This shift in relative income-earning ability in favor of males may have a negative impact on women and children in terms of decreased female influence in other areas of household resource allocation.

Indirect effects are also associated with the rising prices and falling incomes brought about by stabilization policies that affect women through their household management roles. This may be manifest in traveling longer hours to obtain lower prices, the production of more household goods "in house," and the purchase of less prepared, more time-intensive foods, all of which further tighten women's time constraints. Given that economic decline precipitated stabilization, however, it is unclear whether these responses are exacerbated or mitigated by stabilization policies.

The previous discussion related to the more immediate impacts of adjustment, direct and indirect. The new incentives that economic adjustment policies bring about will also cause the rate and pattern of agricultural commercialization to alter dramatically in the future. This, in turn, will alter the rate and pattern of growth of family labor demand, especially in areas where the labor market is underdeveloped, and the hiring of labor is difficult.

In the absence of hired labor, families are forced to choose between sending a child to school or having the child work long hours on-farm. When the household judges the private returns to education to be lower than the private returns from child labor, the rational choice for the household is not to send the child to school. In many cases, the private return to male education is higher than that of females due to higher labor market returns, resulting in lower female school attendance.

Two common components of structural adjustment policy, the introduction of user fees in education and the commercialization of agriculture, both serve to lower the private rate of return to education relative to the private rate of return to child labor. Where this ratio is already low for girls, even more girls are likely to be withdrawn from school. This is particularly true where adult female labor is in high demand to increase cash crop production, requiring older girls to care for siblings. This has future consequences in that more (and better) education for girls has been shown to be strongly associated with increased female wages, improved household nutrition and health, and, importantly, reductions in fertility (Subbarao and Raney, 1993). These returns are achieved by raising the value of women's time and by improving women's decision-making power and status within the household and within society.

Much of the previous discussion can be summarized in the conceptual framework as presented in Figure 1. The figure centers on individual-level constraints, such as time, which can ratchet up or down according to the ability of the individual to cope and thrive in an adjustment climate. The recurring question is whether these abilities and constraints are gender-differentiated. The eight key questions in Table 1 underpin the analytical framework in Figure 1 and will serve as guideposts for the empirical review in section 4. Questions 1 and 2 explore the initial gender-differentiated conditions upon which adjustment programs operate; are women more vulnerable than men to falling incomes, higher prices, and reduced social services; and is sectoral mobility gender differentiated? Question 3 asks whether adjustment programs are achieving macroeconomic goals. Answers to Question 4 explore the magnitude and pattern of social service expenditure cutbacks. Question 5 asks whether the prices of tradables to nontradables are changing, and Question 6 asks from which sectors do resources need to be drawn in response to relative price changes. Question 7 looks at evidence linking the effects of these policy changes with the welfare of the poor. Question 8 asks whether the impacts of stabilization and adjustment on women have been negative

Table 1. *Key questions for a gender-disaggregated analysis of adjustment*

(1) Initial Conditions 1: Are women more vulnerable to reductions in provision of social sector services, public sector employment, and price increases?

(2) Initial Conditions 2: Sectoral resource reallocation — Are needs and abilities gender-differentiated?

(3) What has happened to macro indicators during adjustment?

(4) Has there been a postadjustment reduction in government services and/or employment?

(5) Has a nominal exchange rate devaluation led to a real devaluation (i.e., a change in the price of tradables to nontradables)?

(6) Preadjustment, which sectors are classified as protected/unprotected?

(7) What has happened to the poor under adjustment?

(8) What can be inferred about the impact of stabilization and adjustment on women and women on adjustment?

and to what extent were women able to participate in the adjustment process.

Before presenting evidence related to these questions, we make a brief presentation of methodological and data problems encountered in the interpretation of said evidence.

3. METHODOLOGICAL AND DATA PROBLEMS IN EVALUATING ECONOMIC ADJUSTMENT POLICIES

Policy evaluations face the fundamental methodological problem of not knowing what would have happened in the absence of the policies in question.

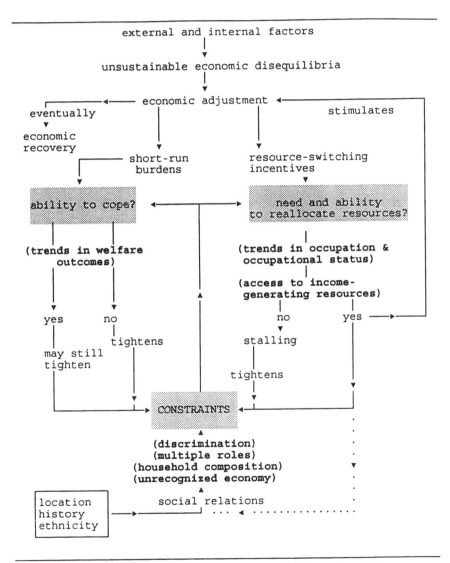

■ Are the shadowed areas gender-differentiated?

Figure 1. Economic adjustment, individual living standards, and gender.

The evaluation of adjustment policies is especially complex, however, for a number of additional reasons.

First, one needs to determine whether what was promised is actually delivered. As noted by Johnson (1994):

> one observes that adjustment programs are rarely, if ever, implemented (in scope, sequencing, and speed) as initially designed and hardly any program has been a complete failure in the sense that in scope, sequencing, and speed, no element of it was implemented. What one normally observes is partial implementation of a program.

Second, it is difficult to distinguish between the effects of the economic crisis, of the adjustment policies themselves, and of the massive inflow of foreign resources that follow their adoption. Third, it is difficult to control for other external effects such as war and climate, as well as changing terms of trade in the international arena. Fourth, the policies have not been in effect for very long; we thus have only a limited time series to analyze. Fifth, the combination and sequence of specific policies is complex.

Attempts to overcome the "with and without" problem include explicitly pairing adjusting countries with "comparable" nonadjusting countries (Harrigan, Mosley, and Toye, 1991), and implicitly doing so using regression analysis (Faini *et al.*, 1991). As the next section will show, the "before and after approach" has been used widely, although it should be noted that determining what did happen during the adjustment program is also controversial. Two further problems with this approach are: conclusions are very sensitive to the two time periods chosen for comparison, and the preadjustment time-trend of indicators chosen in the comparison is usually not taken into account (Behrman and Deolalikar, 1991).

In general, data problems confronted in evaluating economic adjustment policies are more mundane but no less constraining than the conceptual problems (Squire, 1991; Elson, 1991; MayaTech, 1991; Quisumbing, 1991). It is an unusual household-level data set that is nationally representative and contains gender-disaggregated information in key sections such as credit, farm labor, time allocation, farm extension contacts, origins of female headship, and fuel and water collection.

In the absence of gender-disaggregated information, the classification of households by gender of household head is one option. While data exist upon which to account for and describe the heterogeneity of these female-headed households, this classification bypasses much information about poor women in male-headed households.

Connected with data limitations, one of the biggest gaps in the literature is the lack of studies that examine the net effects on the welfare of the poor of a range of adjustment policies. Too often, the direct effects of a particular policy are held forth as evidence that the poor are suffering disproportionately under structural adjustment. When both the direct and indirect effects of a policy are considered, results may be very different. Finally, country specificity of initial conditions — sector structure, taxes, tariffs, culture — and of the applied policy package itself make it difficult to generalize as to the impacts on the poor in other countries undergoing adjustment. This is summarized by Dorosh and Sahn in their four country study of Cameroon, The Gambia, Madagascar, and Niger (1993):

> the magnitude of the effects and the differential impact of policies on various income groups in the four countries illustrate the importance of proper country-specific policy analysis. Likewise, the indirect effects of certain policies often outweigh the direct, or expected, effects, further increasing the importance of examining policies in a general equilibrium framework (p. 31).

4. EVIDENCE

(a) *Initial Conditions 1: are women more vulnerable to reductions in social sector services, public sector employment, and price increases?*

The vulnerability of women to social service sector cuts depends on who in the household assumes responsibility for provision of the services cut, and whether their use is essential. In examining changing gender roles in agriculture, Lado (1992) notes:

> Although women have taken over some of the tasks that were traditionally outside their domain, most men are reported unwilling or unable to share women's work. Whenever someone has to assume someone else's role, it is the women who automatically assume men's roles and not vice versa (p. 791).

Country and regional differences as to what constitutes "social services," and in the sectors in which those service reductions take place, make it difficult to generalize as to whether men or women are hit harder by decreases in social service expenditure. If the cutbacks are on health expenditures, Elson (1988) argues that "the result [...] has been to shift more of the burden of health care to the community and household — which in practice means women" (p. 20). This has further implications for women's already tight time constraints.

Reviews of formal time-allocation studies confirm that, on average, women in developing countries put in more hours per day in nonleisure activities than do men (Juster and Stafford, 1991). Not only are women actively engaged in agriculture and wage-generating activities, but a substantial amount of a woman's day is devoted to home production activities such as getting water and fuelwood, preparing meals, and child care. For example, Haddad's (1991) gender-disaggregated analysis of Ghanaian data shows that in terms of time burdens, women are consistently worse off than men. Reported female nonleisure time loads are 15–25% higher than those of males. The main source of the discrepancy is the much heavier commitment of women to household work. The general tendency is for women to spend 20 hours per week in this activity compared to the male contribution of five hours per week. Only one-third of this discrepancy is compensated for by a reduction in female time spent in employment outside the home, as women work about 27 hours to men's 31 hours for single jobholders, and 42 compared to 47 hours for multiple jobholders.

For the formal sector, UNDP (1992) figures for 1988–90 showed that while 38.8% of the total less-developed country (LDC) population is active in the formal labor force, women represent just 29.8% of this group. As 49% of the LDC population are women, the participation rate for women in the formal sector is 23.6%. Given the lower number of women involved in formal sector employment and the traditionally low participation rate of women in the public sector, if adjustment-necessitated retrenchment is gender blind, women should not be directly affected as adversely as men, at least in absolute terms.

With regard to the removal of consumer price subsidies, many of the rural poor may benefit because they produce the commodity in question. Food price subsidies are rarely effectively targeted at poor consumers and often the greatest benefits of subsidized food preadjustment accrue primarily to upper income urban households (World Bank, 1994). When subsidized food is consumed by the poor, subsidy reductions may have little effect on the overall welfare of the poor, as the subsidized goods often represent a small share of the poorest of the poor's consumption bundle.[3] For many subsidized goods, demand probably exceeds supply, resulting in rationing and the likely creation of a parallel market. Parallel market prices often diverge substantially from official prices. Economic adjustment can result in a convergence of the official and parallel market prices such that the final market price is higher than the previous official price but below that of the parallel market — a direct benefit to the rationed urban poor. Finally, it is far from clear that women are unable to rely on compensating changes in the intrahousehold transfer of income when the cost of the good actually increases.

(b) Initial Conditions 2: sectoral resource reallocation — are needs and abilities gender-differentiated?

A necessary condition for successful adjustment is the mobility of factors of production, including labor, between sectors. Following Addison and Demery (1990) and Collier (1988), a simple framework composed of the following three sectors can be used to describe the impact of various government policies on the preadjustment disequilibrium: (i) nontradables (both consumer and capital goods); (ii) exports and unprotected import substitutes; (iii) protected import substitutes. Adjustment policy seeks to lower the return to factors of production used in the formerly protected and nontradable sector and raise the returns to factors of production in the unprotected and tradables sector.

Does women's labor need to be sectorally mobile for adjustment to succeed? In order to answer this question, an economy's protected and unprotected sectors have to be identified and potentially mapped into the International Labour Organization's (ILO) country-level breakdowns of the economically active population by industry, status in employment, and sex. One can then use these ILO statistics (1990) to anticipate the effects of structural adjustment on women. To the best of our knowledge, this has not yet been attempted.

If women are required to be sectorally mobile for successful adjustment, adjustment is likely to be impeded. This is because women are, in general, constrained in their attempts to respond to changing price signals (Gladwin and McMillan, 1989; Gladwin, 1991; Mehra, 1991; Joekes *et al.*, 1988; Lele, 1991; Collier, 1988; Commonwealth Secretariat, 1989). Unfortunately, many of these studies do not provide comparable evidence on the ability of men to respond to the same price signals; this makes it difficult to tell whether gender is a key constraint.

Evidence on the ability of women to reallocate their primary resource, namely their own labor, is available from Horsnell (1990). This study presents results for wage employment participation based on a sample of the 1986 Living Standards Survey data for the Côte d'Ivoire. The sample is restricted to urban clusters and includes all individuals of 16–65 years of age who have left school. Horsnell finds that men exhibit a higher probability of labor market participation than women. This could be due to differential access/barriers to female entry or to women having higher reservation wages. Further analysis shows that the assumption of no barriers to female labor market entry would imply estimates of female reservation wages three times as high as a male with identical characteristics. This strongly suggests that women face barriers to wage employment in the Côte d'Ivoire. Education was found to be a significant factor in female labor force participation, but for males, it was found to exert no influence on participation. There are two possible explanations: either education reduces female reservation wages or it overcomes the discriminatory barriers to labor market entry. If we again assumed no barriers to labor market entry, we would have to accept that primary and secondary education combine to lower female reservation wages by 78%. This is also unlikely. Far more likely is that education overcomes the barriers females face in access to the labor market. Once females have gained access to the labor market, however, results indicate that there is little wage discrimination.

More generally, other studies show that women are less able to reallocate their time between different activities. This relative immobility can be related to two main factors that stem from the asymmetry in men's and women's obligations, rights, and bargaining positions within the household (Collier, 1988; Elson, 1991; Haddad, Hoddinott, and Alderman, 1994).

First, the gender-based delineation of household roles restricts the substitution of male and female labor time. Maintenance of a minimal level of welfare requires that women spend a given amount of time in the "unrecognized" economy. Therefore, women's ability to reallocate their time to other activities in response to changes in market opportunities (e.g., increased producer prices or job openings) and non-market opportunities (e.g., new land opening up for home production of food) is lower than that of men (Elson, 1991; Palmer, 1988).

Gender-based delineation of economic roles also has efficiency costs. A study by Tibaijuka (1994) in Tanzania suggests that by liberalizing gender roles in a smallholder agricultural community growing coffee and bananas, cash incomes could increase by 10%. In addition, the productivity of labor and capital would increase by 15 and 44%, respectively.

A second factor explaining women's labor immobility is the failure of the household economy to transmit changing price incentives to women. Koopman (1990) provides two case studies showing that in situations where women do have access to resources, they will tend to increase both their labor supply and labor productivity if they expect to receive the profits from their production activities. The asymmetry of household-level control over income decreases the incentive for women to reallocate labor; generally, women do not command a share of the proceeds that is commensurate with the effort exerted in the activity. This suggests that the constraint on women's engagement in new income-generating opportunities in agriculture could be due more to low expected benefits rather than time limits imposed by reproductive and household maintenance responsibilities.

(c) What has happened to macroeconomic indicators during adjustment?

A World Bank study of 26 African countries, comparing 1981–86 and 1987–91, concluded that six[4] of the adjusting countries had a "large" improvement in macro indicators, nine[5] had a "small" improvement, and 11[6] had a deterioration[7] (World Bank, 1994). The median increase in GDP per capita growth was two percentage points between 1981–86 and 1987–91 for large-improvement countries and 1.5 percentage points for small-improvement countries. For deteriorating countries, there was a 2.6 percentage point decline. The median increase in export growth was almost eight percentage points for the large-improvement countries, three percentage points for countries with small improvement, and a decline of 0.7 percentage point for countries with deteriorating indicators. While the deteriorating indicator countries managed a 1.7 percentage point increase in industrial output the best performing countries achieved a 6% growth in industrial output. Countries that recorded the largest declines in agricultural export crop taxation had median agricultural growth of two percentage points compared to a 1.7 percentage point decline for countries that actually increased taxation of export crops (World Bank, 1994).

The same World Bank study argues that the declines recorded in total public expenditure, particularly current expenditure, were not due to adjustment programs *per se* but were due to the preadjustment crises (World Bank, 1994, p. 169).

It remains to be seen how sensitive the results in the World Bank study are to choice of time periods and to the classification of countries. An earlier report by the World Bank and UNDP[8] that claimed success for structural adjustment based on 1985 as a watershed year provoked considerable controversy. Indeed, Mosley and Weeks (1993) conclude:

> With the evidence indicating that recovery did not begin in the mid 1980s and that there was no significant difference between "adjusters" and "nonadjusters" (or among adjusters, "strong," "weak," "early intensive," etc.) One is left in somewhat of a quandary: a substantial amount of multilateral money went to Africa in the 1980s and surely it must have made some difference (p. 1589).

Is the evidence any more conclusive for adjustment in Latin America? Morley (1993) states:

> The 1980s were a development disaster for Latin America. Only 2 countries (Chile and Columbia) managed to increase their per capita incomes. Rising poverty and inequality were widespread. Now, however, at the conclusion of this difficult adjustment one can see encouraging signs. Many countries are now on the road to sustained recovery, with good growth, rising exports and stable prices (p. 25).

Morley (1993) concludes that when the traded goods sector is large and is a heavy employer of the poor, as in Costa Rica, Paraguay, and Colombia, the impact of adjustment is both more progressive and rapid.

It is interesting to note that Peru, rather than implementing orthodox stabilization and structural adjustment policies in 1985, followed an expansionary policy (raising minimum wages, reducing taxes, postponing external debt repayments) designed to stimulate consumer demand. After an initial growth spurt, it is estimated that during 1985–90, average consumption dropped by 55%, with a fall of 60% for the poorest 20% of households. The incidence of poverty increased from less than 1% of the population to more than 17% (Glewwe and Hall, 1992).

(d) Have there been postadjustment reductions/increases in government services, public sector employment, and food prices?

(i) Government services

It is important to realize that despite the prominent place that public sector expenditure reductions take among IMF/World Bank conditionalities, governments are not obliged to reduce expenditures on health and education. For example, Pakistan's adjustment program contains provisions for maintaining expenditure growth in education and health care (MayaTech, 1991, pp. 23, 114). Further, a World Bank study (1990b) shows that growth in real expenditure per capita on health and education slowed for the early intensive adjustment-lending countries, whereas the growth rate was maintained or increased in the other adjustment-lending and nonadjustment-lending countries. Finally, Sahn (1990) shows that although spending on health and education in sub-Saharan countries increased at a faster rate (in percentage terms) than GDP, per capita spending in these sectors declined after adjustment.

Even if government per capita expenditures were to decline under structural adjustment, intrasectoral reallocation of health and education spending in favor of primary provision can benefit the poor. In the Philippines, for example, government expenditure in support of four modern specialist hospitals is five times as high as expenditure on primary health care (Cornia, Jolly, and Stewart, 1987). In Indonesia, despite reductions in poverty and concerted efforts in the 1980s to improve health services for the poor, government subsidies to health for the richest 10% of households in 1990 were still almost three times the level of subsidies received by the poorest 10% of households (World Bank, 1993b, p. 4). In Chile, however, despite lower overall public spending during the period 1974 to 1986, the percentage of education expenditure targeted to the poorest 30% increased, while that of the richest 40%

declined (World Bank, 1990a, p. 117). During adjustment in Zimbabwe in the 1980s, the shares of primary education and primary health care in total education and health sector expenditures increased (Davies and Saunders, 1987).

(ii) Employment

Public sector retrenchment policies, undertaken as part of stabilization, resulted in reductions in the number of civil servants of 27% in Guinea during 1985–90, of 12% in Ghana during 1987–90, of 25% (including parastatals reduction) in Bolivia during 1985–87, and of approximately 65% of the lower levels of the civil service in Tanzania. In Guinea, 70% of state-owned enterprises were also liquidated or privatized during 1985–90.[9]

(iii) Food prices

Due to the removal of subsidies and the devaluation-induced increase in the price of imported food, one would expect food prices in general to rise under adjustment. Sahn (1990) cites evidence that "runs contrary to the customary notion that the structural adjustment process will necessarily raise real prices of cereals in urban areas" (p. 79). In Ghana, Mali, Somalia, and Tanzania, the real price of major cereals fell after adjustment.

(e) Has a nominal exchange rate devaluation led to a real exchange rate devaluation?

In flexible exchange rate regimes, nominal devaluations have led to real devaluations in most of the countries studied (World Bank, 1994; Sahn, 1990; Alderman, 1990; Harvey, 1988). One indicator of the degree of real depreciation and alignment of the real exchange rate is the parallel market premium for foreign exchange. The average exchange rate premium in Africa fell from 300% in 1981–86 to 46% in 1990–91 (World Bank, 1994). Blundell, Heady, and Medhora (1990), however, show for the Côte d'Ivoire that real exchange rate devaluations do not necessarily lead to an increase in the relative traded/nontraded goods price faced by farmers.

(f) Preadjustment: which sectors are classified as protected/unprotected?

Much of the discussion of the potential impact of structural adjustment on household welfare has centered on groupings such as female-headed households, urban poor, rural poor, or the landless (see next section). In order to fully understand the impact of adjustment on households and individuals, however, these groupings need to be mapped into the sectors of activity described in section 4(b), namely nontradables, exports and unprotected import substitutes, and protected import substitutes. This crossclassification will, of course, vary on a country-by-country basis. Unfortunately, crossclassification exercises of this sort are extremely rare (Gonzalez-Soriano, 1990).

(g) *What has happened to the poor under adjustment?*

Despite extensive surveys and analysis, the World Bank, as yet, can offer no stronger statement on the impact of structural adjustment on poverty in Africa than: "In summary, the increase in growth from stronger adjustment programs has probably helped many of the rural poor" (World Bank, 1994, p. 169).

This echoes the conclusion from the May 1991 edition of the *World Bank Economic Review* dedicated to "Poverty and Adjustment." The editorial from that edition acknowledged that "the articles in this issue cannot conclusively answer how adjustment policies have affected the poor" (p. 185). On the one hand, the lack of conclusive results, while disappointing, is understandable given the methodological and data problems outlined in section 3. On the other hand, there is a growing body of evidence offering a wide divergence of views on the poverty impacts of adjustment. A review of this literature is useful, particularly given the mounting evidence that women are over-represented among the poor (Haddad, Peña, and Slack, 1994).

Inferential analyses of the effects of adjustment on the poor include those of Glewwe and de Tray for Peru (1991) and Côte d'Ivoire (1988), and Sahn and Sarris (1991) for five sub-Saharan countries. These analyses are based on the sectors of employment, income sources, and expenditure patterns of the poor. Outcomes are then inferred by modeling the outcomes of real or simulated price and wage changes. Sahn and Sarris (1991) summarize results from their extensive study as follows:

> Thus although the search for generalizations will continue, at this juncture, it is safe to conclude that there is little evidence of large welfare gains or losses accruing to [rural] smallholders in the wake of policy reforms that have been initiated in the countries studied [Côte d'Ivoire, Ghana, Malawi, Madagascar, and Tanzania] (p. 282).

A time-trended before-and-after analysis for Jamaica by Behrman and Deolalikar (1991), is particularly interesting because they are able to contrast their analysis with the untrended results of Body (1987) and Cornia and Stewart (1987). Behrman and Deolalikar state:

> Focusing on deviations from secular trends to see if the situation worsened significantly in 1984–85 relative to

the underlying movements (rather than just whether it was bad) leads to a much less negative assessment of the situation in these years than by some previous analysts (p. 309).

They find that in 1984–85, macro indicators differ significantly from the trend: total per capita government expenditure declines and the exchange rate is devalued. No deviations from trend are found for any of the indicators of employment (either male or female), real wages (either male or female), agricultural employment of the poor, or government transfers to the poor. None of the education indicators deviated either. Average real expenditure on food deviated positively and significantly from trend in 1984–85, although the quality of the diet probably declined (more root crops, cereals, sugar products, less meat). These results paint a less negative picture than those of other analysts with access to the same data. Behrman and Deolalikar summarized their results as follows: "Although we find evidence of substantial cuts in government expenditures on social services, there is little confirmation of significant short-run deterioration in human capital indicators during the adjustment period" (p. 291).

Some studies have, however, cast considerable doubt on the ability of human capital indicators such as infant mortality rate (IMR), life expectancy at birth, and primary school enrollment ratios to track poverty during times of economic transition (Fields, 1990; Sahn, 1994; Osmani, 1994; Cornia, 1994). For example, in only one of the three case studies cited by Fields, Costa Rica, did these indicators worsen during the economic crisis of the 1980s. For Brazil and Mexico, the indicators improved despite rising poverty as measured using income and consumption data.

Studies on Indonesian household consumption data (Huppi and Ravallion, 1991) indicate reductions in poverty during 1984–87 following structural adjustment initiated in 1983. Three income-based poverty measures, the head count ratio, the poverty gap, and a distributionally sensitive measure, all support this result. A more robust first order dominance test[10] was also used, which confirmed that poverty, in terms of both income and consumption per person had unambiguously fallen. Moreover, for Indonesia, Thorbecke (1991) concludes that

> the adjustment strategy... helped to restore internal and external equilibrium. Even though it entailed a slowdown in economic growth during the adjustment period, this strategy reinforced some of the desirable distributional trends that had begun before the adjustment period (p. 1611).

A question remains as to whether the apparent improvement in poverty measures was a result of the adjustment program or the lagged effect of preadjustment policies designed to address poverty.

Given the dominance of food in poor households' consumption expenditures, movements in food prices as a result of structural adjustment programs can have a major impact on the welfare of the poor. While nominal food prices probably rise due to adjustment, it is necessary to look at real food price changes, as well as previously parallel food market prices, the tradability of a given food prior to adjustment, and the shares of particular foods within household budgets, in order to assess the impact of food price changes on the welfare of the poor. In Mali, for example, prior to adjustment cereal prices in the parallel market were up to four times higher than those in official markets (Sahn, 1990).

When food is a tradable good its price can be expected to rise under adjustment. Cereals in Ghana and Somalia are largely classified as tradables but because the diets of the poor consist largely of non-traded staples, they were unlikely to have witnessed major falls in real income due to cereal price increases. In the Côte d'Ivoire, however, rice is a tradable good and is the primary staple of even low-income households, making them vulnerable to price increases. In Tanzania, the official nominal price of maize increased by 160%, but a 35% increase in nominal wages compensated the increase as purchases of maize meal represented no more than 20% of the expenditures of low income households.

Further, a removal of food subsidies leading to a rise in the nominal price of food does not necessarily translate into a deterioration of nutritional status. In Morocco, a 50% increase in the price of soft wheat following subsidy removal resulted in a 12% decline in its consumption. Substitution favored the relatively inferior, but nutritionally richer hard wheat.

If the above evidence reveals the possibility that adjustment may hurt the poor, how effective have emergency social funds (ESF), a component of more recent adjustment packages, been in mitigating potential negative impacts? The most detailed economic evaluation of the effectiveness of an emergency social fund (ESF) "safety net" designed to at least maintain the poor's standard of living in the short-run adjustment climate has been undertaken by Newman, Jorgensen, and Pradhan (1991) for Bolivia's ESF. Their results indicate that the ESF, through the provision of temporary employment, did indeed help the poor.

(h) *What can be inferred about the impact of stabilization and adjustment on women and of women on adjustment?*

Given the lack of data, it is difficult to be conclusive about the impacts of stabilization on women's welfare. We are fairly certain that the poorest of the poor are women (but not necessarily vice versa), and that women bear responsibility for the food and nutrition security of their households (Haddad, Peña, and Slack, 1994; Haddad, 1993). We are less certain about the extent, composition and impact of the cutbacks in government services and subsidies. Even if we were certain, it is unclear which household members derive the greatest benefit from these services. The major impact of the removal of food price subsidies is potentially on net food-purchasing households. No extensive work has yet been done on the representation or potential overrepresentation of women in these households.

The limitations of current nationally representative data sets have prohibited intrahousehold analyses of the impacts of structural adjustment. We know of no time-series data which would permit an analysis of changing time allocations as a result of structural adjustment impacts. Consequently, the initial assertion that adjustment was bad for women relied heavily on community based case studies (Onimode, 1989; Gladwin, 1991; Afshar and Dennis, 1992; Beneria and Feldman, 1992). It should, however, be noted that these are not typically purposive case studies — they are either attempts to look at secondary data with an eye to the effects of adjustment, or they are primary data sets, collected to assess the impacts of economic recession/crises on women. Of the studies that have some "before and after" information on women (Moser, 1992; Guyer and Idowu, 1991; Safa and Antrobus, 1992; Ensminger, 1991), only three show declines in female welfare.

Moser's studies of low-income women in Guayaquil, Ecuador, showed that women had been forced to allocate more time to the provision of community services due to social expenditure cutbacks called for by adjustment and stabilization programs. Moser's data do not, however, permit separation of the effects of economic crisis and of economic adjustment.

Recent survey evidence from the Dominican Republic sheds further light on the impact of adjustment on women but is limited to a household-level analysis disaggregated by gender of household head. During 1986–92, a period of adjustment, the number of female-headed households living below the poverty line decreased by 7%, from 23% to 16%, and the number of male-headed households below the poverty line increased from 15% to 17%. Overall caloric adequacy increased over the same period although, for lower income groups, there was still a problem of caloric inadequacy. For households in the lowest overall income quintile, however, caloric intake increased marginally for male-headed households but deteriorated significantly for female-headed households. Thus the 1986 caloric adequacy differential between male- and female-headed households widened during

1986–92 in the lowest income quintile (Dauhajre, Achecar, and Swindale, 1994).

Part of the adjustment strategy in the Dominican Republic involved the expansion of labor-intensive, export-orientated manufacturing located in Export Processing Zones (EPZ) (Free Trade). This strategy resulted in the number of companies in the Free Trade Zone rising from 103 in 1983 to 224 in 1988. In the same period, the number of employees quadrupled, reaching some 85,000 in 1988, of whom 84% were women (Moser, Herbert, and Makonnen, 1993). During 1986–92, a further 63,300 jobs were created. For women employed in the EPZ, their EPZ salary is the most important source of income for their household. The expansion of EPZ employment opportunities is believed to be a partial explanation of why the number of female-headed households living below the poverty line fell during this period. Similarly, a Jamaican case study conducted by Boyd (1987) reported that "this particular [EPZ] program... has no doubt benefited women at the base of the economy in terms of increasing skill and experience levels and providing them with some income" (p. 18). Wages in EPZs tend to be higher than for comparable work outside the zones (ILO, 1988), but workers, on the whole, enjoy fewer rights than their counterparts outside the zones (Heyzer, 1989).

In Nicaragua, the role of the export-oriented Free Trade Zone, Zona Franca, in structural adjustment has resulted in a somewhat mixed impact on women. Textile and garment factories, the main source of female industrial employment in Managua, shut down in terms of domestic production, and relocated operations in Zona Franca. This relocation proved a problem for many women with no transportation for the cross-city trip to new factories. At the same time, the state-owned garment and textile factories inside the zone were privatized. This resulted in layoffs for many older female workers, changed employment conditions, and the hiring of younger workers (Wiegersma, forthcoming). At one shoe factory inside Zona Franca, 70% of employees were female prereform at the beginning of 1990. By November of the same year, most employees were male (Wiegersma, forthcoming).

In terms of employment, the most direct impact of adjustment is in the public sector. In regard to public sector retrenchment policies, household survey work conducted in Guinea by Sahn (1992) concludes that the male-female ratio of those who had a public sector job and then lost it is identical to the male-female ratio of those who currently hold a job. In Ghana, however, women fared worse than men. A study by Alderman, Canagarajah, and Younger (forthcoming) showed that while women represented 21% of civil service employees, they constituted 35% of those "redeployed" in public sector retrenchment policies. This was due in large part to the "last in, first out" rule —

widespread hiring of women in the civil service having been a relatively recent phenomena in Ghana — rather than discrimination *per se*.

Evidence on the direct impact on women of food price subsidy removal is scant. Our evidence is limited to a case study in Lusaka, which shows that women may benefit from the removal of consumer price subsidies. Faced with the need to secure income from selling roasted groundnuts and cigarettes for long hours as street traders, poor women were forced to buy food through the black market to avoid valuable time queuing for subsidized food (Muntemba, 1989). The removal of subsidies thus benefited these women.

We saw in the previous section that ESF programs, at least for Bolivia, had some success in mitigating the impacts of adjustment on the poor. Did they, however, achieve this by reinforcing or mitigating existing gender inequities? In the case of Bolivian ESF-generated employment, women were not the direct beneficiaries, in that 99% of participants were male. This predominance of men reflects extant cultural attitudes to the gender division of labor. Of those employed by the ESF, however, 93% were household heads, and 71% were married. Given that ESF employment significantly boosted household income, we can infer that women benefited indirectly, although this is not necessarily the case. The knock-on effects of unemployment of the male household head were not passed on to women in these families due to the ESF. It remains an open question whether ESF-type mechanisms can be designed so as to compensate for initial pro-male conditions.

Taken together, the studies in this section provide a rather ambiguous message about the gender-differentiated effects of economic adjustment. Few of the methodological problems outlined in section 3 are resolved by the studies.

5. CONCLUSIONS

Based on the evidence at hand, how important are the potential interactions between gender roles and economic adjustment policies? Put another way, to what extent can women proactively participate in the adjustment process as players; to what extent are women caught up in the adjustment process as spectators — adjusting where they can to deflect the potentially negative effects of adjustment; and finally, to what extent are women innocent victims, incapable of mitigating the negative impacts of the adjustment process?

Providing incontrovertible answers to these questions is no mean feat. Adjustment policies are implemented at the macro level in order to affect macroeconomic aggregates. As the evidence presented in section 4 (c) indicates, the jury is still out as to whether adjustment policies have achieved their

GENDER DIMENSIONS OF ECONOMIC ADJUSTMENT   893

macroeconomic goals. If impact is hard to measure at the macro level, it is much more difficult at the micro level. Evidence of the impact of adjustment on poverty at the micro level is uneven, contentious, and somewhat polarized. The evidence presented by the key proponents of adjustment argues that, when implemented without slippage, adjustment will mitigate poverty by stimulating broad-based economic growth. Counter to this view is that adjustment programs, even if implemented with no slippage, should themselves be adjusted in order to provide a framework within which all can benefit from economic growth.

Analysis of the individual and intrahousehold impacts of adjustment provides yet more challenges. Virtually no panel data, gender-disaggregated in key areas, have been collected for the expressed purpose of disentangling the interactions between gender roles and adjustment policies. This lack of data inhibits our ability to assess the impact of adjustment on male and female time allocation and time burdens. In particular, household survey evidence as to whether poor women increase their time to services formerly provided by the state is scarce.

The absence of good data is, however, a poor excuse for not attempting to contribute to the debate on this important subject. In this spirit, and by using the evidence presented in this paper, we venture a few observations.

First, our review of the initial conditions on vulnerability and sectoral mobility indicates that, compared to men, women are at a distinct disadvantage. In order to participate in the adjustment process, an individual or household must own factors of production, or have access to them, and must be able to reallocate them in line with the new economic incentives that adjustment precipitates. Women are less likely to own or have access to resources, and they are less able to reallocate the few resources they do command. This makes women more likely to be "innocent victims" and "spectators" of, rather than "players" in, the adjust-

ment process. Whether adjustment reinforces, mitigates, or has a neutral impact on the asymmetries of resource ownership and access remains a subject of some controversy. *Ceteris paribus*, if women are to be full players in the adjustment process, the adjustment process itself needs to mitigate these asymmetries.

Our second observation is that many women are simply spectators rather than innocent victims. We suggest three types of spectators: (a) those women who have access to factors of production used in the traded sector, and do not have to switch them in order to benefit from increased incentives to produce traded goods; (b) women who have access to factors of production, but are constrained in their ability to switch them, in order to benefit from an increase in the production of traded goods; and (c) women who do not have access to factors of production, but are linked to individuals who can benefit from an increase in the production of traded goods, and are thus increasingly dependent on intrahousehold income transfers.

Our third observation is that some women are innocent victims of the adjustment process, as indeed are some men. These women tend to be in households where no one can respond to the new economic incentives, but, nevertheless, may have to shoulder the associated burdens (female-headed households with high dependency ratios, for example).

What are the relative sizes of these groups and do they differ by gender? Is it the initial gender-differentiated socioeconomic structures, poverty, or both, that consign some individuals to be victims or spectators of the adjustment process? How important a brake on the adjustment process is the neglect of these structures? The literature reviewed here suggests that answers to these questions are not on the horizon. In conclusion, it is crucial that the impact of structural adjustment on the poorest segments of society continue to be assessed. The conclusion from this paper is that those assessments should be neither gender-blinded nor gender-blind.

NOTES

1. Stewart (1991). Please (1992). Zattler (1993). Mosley and Weeks (1993).

2. A more optimistic school of thought counters the preceding view by noting that the traditionally lower economic and social status of women relative to men may, in any case, prohibit them from collecting preadjustment. distortion-enhanced economic rents. Adjustment and reform will therefore necessarily improve the lot of women. Once the distortions are removed, those previously collecting economic rent, assumed to be predominantly male, can no longer do so. Despite the fact. however. that adjustment policies may be geared toward weakening the links between gender and economic welfare. many of the initial inequities will surely remain in the "postreform" environment.

3. For Peru and Côte d'Ivoire, Glewwe and de Tray (1991, 1988 respectively); for Ghana and Somalia, Sahn (1990).

4. Ghana. Tanzania. The Gambia, Burkina Faso, Nigeria. Zimbabwe.

5. Madagascar. Malawi, Burundi. Kenya. Mali. Mauritania, Senegal, Niger, Uganda.

6. Benin. Central African Republic, Rwanda, Sierra Leone, Togo, Zambia, Mozambique, Congo, Côte d'Ivoire, Cameroon. Gabon.

7. These improvements/deteriorations were based on an index which captured changes in three policy indicators —

fiscal (budget deficit, domestic tax revenue), monetary (average of changes in seignorage and inflation), and exchange rate (for fixed rate countries — changes in the real exchange rate, REER, and for flexible — average of movements in REER and parallel market exchange rate premium) policies during 1981–86 and 1987–91. Numerical scores ranging for –3 to +3 were assigned, depending on the size of change of each indicator, higher scores indicating greater improvements. Countries achieving aggregate scores above 1 were classified as showing large improvements in macroeconomic policies; between 0 and 1, small improvement; and those less than 1 were considered to have deteriorated.

8. *Africa's Adjustment and Growth in the 1980s.*

9. However severe these public sector reductions were in some countries, employment cuts did not necessarily secure comparable reductions in government expenditure. In Guinea, increases in real government wages of 152% during 1986–90, designed to improve morale and productivity, resulted in government expenditure, which never fell below its 1986 level, and in 1990 was 22% higher.

10. If the cumulative distribution of income, for the entire interval up to the poverty line, for 1987 lies nowhere above the cumulative distribution of income for 1984, then poverty has unambiguously fallen. Every percentile of the distribution was better off in 1987 than 1984. For further discussion of first order dominance tests, see Ravallion (1992).

REFERENCES

Addison, T. and L. Demery, "The poverty effects of adjustment with labor market imperfections," Mimeo (Coventry: DERC, Economics Department, University of Warwick, 1990).

Afshar, H. and C. Dennis (Eds.), *Women and Adjustment Policies in the Third World* (London: Macmillan Academic and Professional Ltd., 1992).

Alderman, H., "Downturn and economic recovery in Ghana: Impacts on the poor" (Washington, DC: Cornell University Food and Nutrition Policy Program, 1990).

Alderman H., S. Canagarajah and S. Younger, "Consequences of permanent lay-off from civil service: Results from a survey of retrenched workers in Ghana," in D. Lindauer and B. Nunberg (Eds.), *Rehabilitating Government: Pay and Employment Reform in Developing Countries* (Washington, DC: World Bank, forthcoming).

Behrman, J. and A. Deolalikar, "The poor and the social sectors during a period of macroeconomic adjustment: Empirical evidence from Jamaica," *World Bank Economic Review*, Vol. 5, No. 2 (1991), pp. 291–314.

Beneria, L. and S. Feldman, *Economic Crises, Persistent Poverty, and Women's Work* (Boulder, CO: Westview Press, 1992).

Blundell, R., C. Heady and E. Medhora, "Labor markets in an era of adjustment: The case of Côte d'Ivoire," Mimeo (London: Department of Economics, University College London, 1990).

Boyd, D., "The impact of adjustment policies on vulnerable groups: The case of Jamaica 1973–85," in A. Cornia, R. Jolly and F. Stewart (Eds.), *Adjustment with a Human Face, Vol 1: Protecting the Vulnerable and Promoting Growth* (Oxford: Clarendon Press, 1987).

Buvinic, M. "The feminization of poverty," in *Women and Nutrition*, ACC/SCN Symposium Report, Nutrition Policy Discussion Paper 6 (New York: United Nations, 1990).

Colcough, C. and R. Green, "Do stabilization policies stabilize?," *Institute of Development Studies Bulletin*, University of Sussex, Vol. 19, No. 1 (1988).

Collier, P., "The impact of adjustment on women," in L. Demery, M. Ferroni, C. Grootaert with J. Worg-Valle (Eds.), *Understanding the Social Effect of Policy Reform* (Washington, DC: World Bank, 1993).

Collier, P., "Women in development. Defining the issues." Policy, Planning, and Research Working Paper WPS 129 (Washington, DC: World Bank, 1988).

Commonwealth Secretariat, *Engendering Adjustment for the 1990s* (London: Marlborough House, 1989).

Cornia, A., "On nutritional changes during economic transition in Eastern Europe and CIS," Paper presented at Welfare Changes During Periods of Economic Transition: The Case of Nutrition, American Economic Association Meetings (Boston, MA: 1994).

Cornia, A. and F. Stewart, "Country experience with adjustment," in A. Cornia, R. Jolly and F. Stewart (Eds.), *Adjustment with a Human Face, Vol. 1: Protecting the Vulnerable and Promoting Growth* (Oxford: Clarendon Press, 1987).

Cornia, A., R. Jolly and F. Stewart, *Adjustment with a Human Face, Vol. 1: Protecting the Vulnerable and Promoting Growth* (Oxford: Clarendon Press, 1987).

Dauhajre, Jr., A., J. Achecar and A. Swindale, *Stabilization, Liberalization, and the Dynamic of Poverty in the Dominican Republic, 1986–1992* (Santa Domingo: Fundacion Economica Ey Desarrollo Inc., 1994).

Davies, O. and D. Saunders, "Adjustment policies and the welfare of children: Zimbabwe, 1980–1985," in A. Cornia, R. Jolly and F. Stewart (Eds.), *Adjustment with a Human Face. Vol. 1: Protecting the Vulnerable and Promoting Growth* (Oxford: Clarendon Press, 1987).

Dorosh, P. and D. Sahn, *A General Equilibrium Analysis of the Effect of Macroeconomic Adjustment on Poverty in Africa*, Cornell Food and Nutrition Policy Program Working Paper 39 (Ithaca, NY: Cornell University, 1993).

Due, J., "Policies to overcome the negative effects of structural adjustment programs on African female-headed households," in C. Gladwin (Ed.), *Structural Adjustment and African Women Farmers* (Gainesville, FL: University of Florida Press, 1991).

Elson, D., "Male bias in structural adjustment," in H. Afshar and C. Dennis (Eds.), *Women and Adjustment Policies in the Third World* (London: Macmillan Academic and Professional Ltd., 1992).

Elson, D., "Gender and adjustment in the 1990s: An update on evidence and strategies," Mimeo (Manchester: Economics Department, University of Manchester, 1991).

Elson, D., "From survival strategies to transformation strategies: Women's needs and structural adjustment," Paper prepared for Cornell University Workshop on Economic Crises and Household Survival (Ithaca, NY: September, 1988).

Ensminger, J., "Structural transformation and its conse-quences for Orma women pastoralists," in C. Gladwin (Ed.), *Structural Adjustment and African Women Farmers* (Gainesville, FL: University of Florida Press, 1991).

Faini, R., J. de Melo, A. Senhadji and J. Stanton, "Growth-oriented adjustment programs: A statistical analysis," *World Development*, Vol. 19, No. 8 (1991), pp. 957–967.

Fields, G., "Poverty and inequality in Latin America: Some new evidence," Mimeo (Ithaca, NY: Cornell University, 1990).

Gladwin, C. (Ed.), *Structural Adjustment and African Women Farmers* (Gainesville, FL: University of Florida Press, 1991).

Galdwin, C. and D. McMillan, "Is a turnaround in Africa possible without helping African women to farm?," *Economic Development and Cultural Change*, Vol. 37, No. 2 (1989), pp. 345–369.

Glewwe, P. and D. de Tray, "The poor in Latin America dur-ing adjustment: A case study of Peru," *Economic Development and Cultural Change*, Vol. 40, No. 1 (1991), pp. 27–54.

Glewwe, P. and D. de Tray, *The Poor in Latin America during Adjustment: A case study of Peru*, LSMS Working Paper No. 56 (Washington, DC: World Bank, 1989).

Glewwe P. and D. de Tray, *The Poor During Adjustment: A Case Study of the Côte d'Ivoire*, LSMS Working Paper 47 (Washington, DC: World Bank, 1988).

Glewwe, P. and G. Hall, *Poverty and Inequality during Unorthodox Adjustment: The Case of Peru, 1985–90*, World Bank Working Paper 86 (Washington, DC: World Bank, 1992).

Gonzalez-Soriano, C., "Classifying the economy into traded or nontraded sectors," *Journal of Philippine Development*, Vol. XVII, No. 2 (1990).

Guyer, J. and O. Idowu, "Women's agricultural work in a multimodal rural economy: Ibarapa District, Oyo State, Nigeria," in C. Gladwin (Ed.), *Structural Adjustment and African Women Farmers* (Gainesville, FL: University of Florida Press, 1991).

Haddad, L., "Promoting household food security: Women as gatekeepers, shock absorbers, and a focal point for policy," Paper presented at the Second World Health Organization Symposium titled Lessons for the 21st Century (Kobe, Japan: November, 1993).

Haddad, L., "Gender and poverty in Ghana: A descriptive analysis of selected outcomes and processes," *IDS Bulletin*, Vol. 22, No. 1 (1991), pp. 5–16.

Haddad, L., J. Hoddinott and H. Alderman, *Intrahousehold Resource Allocation: An Overview*, Policy Research Working Paper 1255 (Washington, DC: Policy Research Department, World Bank, 1994).

Haddad, L., C. Peña and A. Slack, "Poverty and nutrition within households: Review and new evidence," Report prepared for the Nutrition Unit, World Health Organization, Geneva (Washington, DC: International Food Policy Research Institute, 1994).

Harrigan, J. and P. Mosley, "Evaluating the impact of World Bank structural adjustment lending: 1980–87," *Journal of Development Studies*, Vol. 27, No. 3 (1991), pp. 63–94.

Harrigan, J., P. Mosley and J. Toye, *Aid and Power: The World Bank and Policy Based Lending in the 1990s* (London: Routledge, 1991).

Harvey, C., "Nonmarginal price changes: Conditions for the success of floating exchange rate systems in Sub-Saharan

Africa," *IDS Bulletin*, Vol. 19, No. 1 (1988).

Heyzer, N., "Asian women wage-earners: Their situation and possibilities for donor intervention," *World Development*, Vol. 17, No. 7 (1989), pp. 1109–1124.

Horsnell, P., "Gender inequalities in the labour market: Evidence from the Côte d'Ivoire," Mimeo (Oxford: Unit for the Study of African Economies, 1990)

Huppi, M. and M. Ravallion, "The sectoral structure of poverty during an adjustment period. Evidence for Indonesia in the mid-1980s," *World Development*, Vol. 19, No. 12 (1991), pp. 1653–1678.

International Labour Organization (ILO), *Yearbook of Labour Statistics* (Geneva: International Labour Organization, 1990).

International Labour Organization (ILO), *Economic and Social Effects of Multinational Enterprises in Export Processing Zones* (Geneva: International Labour Organization, 1988).

International Monetary Fund (IMF), *Annual Report 1989* (Washington, DC: International Monetary Fund, 1989).

Jaycox, E., "The benefits of adjustment," *CERES*, No. 143 (1993), pp. 21–23.

Joekes, S., M. Lycette, L. McGowan and K. Searle, *Women and Structural Adjustment: Part II Technical Document* (Washington, DC: International Center for Research on Women, 1988).

Johnson, O. E. G., "Managing adjustment costs, political authority, and the implementation of adjustment pro-grams, with special reference to African countries," *World Development*, Vol. 22, No. 3 (1994), pp. 399–411.

Juster, F. T. and F. P. Stafford, "The allocation of time: Empirical findings, behavioral models, and problems of measurement," *Journal of Economic Literature XXIX*, June (1991), pp. 471–522.

Kennedy, E. and H. Bouis, "Traditional cash crop schemes' effects on production, consumption, and nutrition: Sugarcane in the Philippines and Kenya," Mimeo (Washington, DC: International Food Policy Research Institute, 1989).

Koopman, J., *Women and Rural Poverty*, State of the World Rural Poverty Working Paper 7 (Rome: International Fund for Agricultural Development, 1990).

Lado, C., "Female labour participation in agricultural pro-duction and the implications for nutrition and health in rural Africa," *Social Science and Medicine*, Vol. 34, No. 7 (1992), pp. 789–807.

Lele, U., "Women, structural adjustment, and transforma-tion: Some lessons and questions from the African experi-ence," in C. Gladwin (Ed.), *Structural Adjustment and African Women Farmers* (Gainesville, FL: University of Florida Press, 1991).

Lindauer, D. and B. Nunberg, (Eds.), *Rehabilitating Government: Pay and Employment Reform in Developing Countries* (Washington, DC: World Bank, forthcoming).

MayaTech, *Gender and Adjustment*, Series TR 91–1026–02 (Silver Spring, MD: The MayaTech Corporation, 1991).

Mehra, R., "Can structural adjustment work for women farm-ers?," Mimeo (Washington, DC: International Center for Research on Women, 1991).

Morley, S. A., "Structural adjustment and the determinants of poverty and inequality in Latin America," Revised ver-sion of paper presented at Brookings Conference on Poverty and Inequality in Latin America (Washington, DC: July, 1993).

Moser, C., "Adjustment from below: Low-income women, time, and the triple role in Guayaquil, Ecuador," in H. Afshar and C. Dennis (Eds.), *Women and Adjustment Policies in the Third World* (London: Macmillan Academic and Professional Ltd., 1992)

Moser, C., A. Herbert and R. Makonnen, "Urban poverty in the context of structural adjustment: Recent evidence and policy responses," Transportation, Water, and Urban Development Discussion Paper 4 (Washington, DC: World Bank, 1993).

Mosley, P. and J. Weeks, "Has recovery begun? Africa's adjustment in the 1980s revisited," *World Development*, Vol. 21, No. 10 (1993), pp. 1583–1606.

Mukhopadhyay, S., "Impact of structural adjustment policies on women: Some general observations," Note prepared for the workshop on The Impact of Macro Policies on Women in the Period of Liberalization and Adjustment: Comparative Perspectives from Canada and India, North-South Institute (Ottawa, Ontario, Canada: June 19–21, 1992).

Muntemba, D., "The impact of IMF-World Bank programs on women and children in Zambia," in B. Onimode (Ed.), *The IMF, The World Bank, and African Debt. The Social and Political Impact* (London and New Jersey: Zed Books Ltd. for the Institute for African Alternatives, 1989).

Newman, J., S. Jorgensen and M. Pradhan, "How did workers benefit form Bolivia's Emergency Social Fund?," *World Bank Economic Review*, Vol. 5, No. 2 (1991), pp. 367–393.

Onimode, B. (Ed.), *The IMF, The World Bank, and African Debt. The Social and Political Impact* (London and New Jersey: Zed Books Ltd. for the Institute for African Alternatives, 1989).

Osmani, S. R., "On economic reforms and nutritional capability in South Asia," Paper presented at Welfare Changes During periods of Economic Transition: The Case of Nutrition (Boston, MA: American Economic Association Meetings, 1994).

Palmer, I., "Gender issues in structural adjustment of sub-Saharan agriculture," Working Paper, World Employment Programme (Geneva: International Labour Organization, 1988).

Please, S., "Beyond structural adjustment in Africa," *Development Policy Review*, Vol. 10 (1992), pp. 289–307.

Pinstrup-Andersen, P., "Economic crises and policy reforms during the 1980s and their impact on the poor, in *Macroeconomic Environment and Health: With Case Studies for Countries in Greatest Need* (Geneva: World Health Organization, 1993).

Quisumbing, A., "Structural adjustment and women in agriculture: What do we know?," Women in Development, Mimeo (Washington, DC: World Bank, 1991).

Ravallion, M., "Poverty comparisons: A guide to concepts and methods," LSMS Working Paper 88 (Washington, DC: World Bank 1992).

Safa, H. I. and P. Antrobus, "Women and economic crisis in the Caribbean, in *Economic Crises, Persistent Poverty and Women's Work* (Boulder, CO: Westview Press, 1992).

Sahn, D., "On economic reforms and change in nutritional status in Sub-Saharan Africa during the 1980s," Paper presented at Welfare Changes During periods of Economic Transition: The Case of Nutrition, American Economic Association Meetings (Boston, MA: 1994).

Sahn, D., *Labor Markets in Conkaray, Guinea* (Washington, DC: Cornell Food and Nutrition Policy Program, Cornell University, 1992).

Sahn, D., "Fiscal and exchange rate reforms in Africa: Considering the impact upon the poor," Monograph 4 (Washington, DC: Cornell Food and Nutrition Policy Program, Cornell University, 1990).

Sahn, D. and A. Sarris, "Structural adjustment and the welfare of rural smallholders: A comparative analysis from Sub-Saharan Africa," *World Bank Economic Review*, Vol. 5, No. 2 (1991), pp. 259–290.

Schoepf, B. and W. Engundu, "Women and structural adjustment in Zaire," in C. Gladwin (Ed.), *Structural Adjustment and African Women Farmers* (Gainesville, FL: University of Florida Press, 1991).

Squire, L., "Introduction: Poverty and adjustment in the 1980s," *World Bank Economic Review*, Vol. 5, No. 2 (1991), pp. 177–186.

Stewart, F., "Are adjustment policies in Africa consistent with long-run development needs?," *Development Policy Review*, Vol. 9, No. 4 (1991).

Subbarao, K. and L. Raney, "Social gains from female education: A cross national study," World Bank Discussion Paper 194 (Washington, DC: World Bank, 1993).

Thorbecke, E., "Adjustment, growth, and income distribution in Indonesia," *World Development*, Vol. 19, No. 11 (1991), pp. 1595–1614.

Tibaijuka, A., "The cost of differential gender roles in African agriculture: A case study of smallholder banana-coffee farms in the Kagera Region, Tanzania," *Journal of Agricultural Economics*, Vol. 45, No. 1 (1994), pp. 69–81.

UNDP (United Nations Development Program), *Human Development Report* (Oxford: Oxford University Press, 1992).

Wiegersma, N., "State Policy and the Restructuring of Women's Industries in Nicaragua," in N. Aslanbeigui, S. Pressman and F. Summerfield (Eds.), *Women in the Age of Economic Transformation* (London: Routledge, forthcoming).

World Bank, *Adjustment in Africa. Reforms, Results, and the Road Ahead* (New York: Oxford University Press, 1994).

World Bank, *Annual Report, 1993* (Washington, DC: The World Bank, 1993a).

World Bank, *World Development Report* (New York: Oxford University Press, 1993b).

World Bank, *Second Health, Population, and Rural Water Supply Project* (Washington, DC: The World Bank, 1991).

World Bank, *World Development Report 1990* (New York: Oxford University Press, 1990a).

World Bank, *Adjustment Lending Policies for Sustainable Growth* (Washington, DC: The World Bank, 1990b).

World Bank/UNDP (United Nations Development Program), *Africa's Adjustment and Growth in the 1980s* (Washington, DC and New York: World Bank and United Nations Development Program, 1989).

Zattler, J., "Adjusting adjustment — Supply response and the sequencing of reform policies," *Intereconomics* Vol. 28, No. 6 (1993), pp. 293–301.

[16]

World Development, Vol. 23, No. 11, pp. 1851–1868, 1995
Elsevier Science Ltd
Printed in Great Britain
0305–750X/95 $9.50 + 0.00

 Pergamon

0305–750X(95)00087–9

Gender Awareness in Modeling Structural Adjustment

DIANE ELSON*
University of Manchester, U.K.

Summary. — The macroeconomic models underpinning the design of structural adjustment programs are gender-blind. This paper discusses strategies for introducing gender analysis into these models and evaluates the strengths and weaknesses of the models from a gender perspective. It concludes that besides being blind to gender, the models are also blind to the waste of resources and impoverishment that stems from deficient aggregate demand, undemocratic decision making and directly unproductive expenditures that buttress male power. This waste is, however, likely to be diminished by moves to more egalitarian systems of gender relations, entailing changes in the structure of entitlements and the social matrix in which macroeconomic processes are embedded.

1. INTRODUCTION

More than 100 structural adjustment programs have been introduced since 1980 in the developing countries of the South at the instigation of the World Bank. The objective of such programs according to numerous World Bank documents is to introduce policy changes which permit a reduction of balance-of-payments deficits and budget deficits while at the same time boosting growth rates through policy changes which are supposed to improve the efficiency of resource use and liberate resources for private sector business investment. Structural adjustment programs (SAPs) have two components: a package of aid finance from the World Bank and other multilateral and bilateral donors, and a package of economic reforms, introduction of which is specified as a condition for release of the aid. The macroeconomic analysis underpinning SAPs also has two components: a relatively simple one-good model — the Revised Minimum Standard Model (RMSM), derived from the Harrod-Domar model — is used for attempting to quantify how much aid a country needs; in addition, a two-good (tradables and non-tradables) model, based on the Swan-Salter model of the small dependent economy, is used to analyze the restructuring of expenditure and production. This paper considers strategies for introducing gender into these models; and evaluates both the strengths and weaknesses of these models from a gender perspective.

Section 1 discusses strategies for making macro models gender-aware. Section 2 considers just which structures are adjusting. The key features of the RMSM are introduced in section 3; followed in section 4 by an analysis of how gender can be introduced

into the RMSM, and a critique of the RMSM from a gender perspective. Section 5 introduces the tradables-nontradables model of adjustment, while section 6 appraises Collier's gender-disaggregated version of the model. Section 7 puts forward some theses about gender and aggregation processes. Section 8 offers some brief conclusions.

2. GENDER AWARENESS: PERSPECTIVES AND PARAMETERS

The most obvious way of introducing gender into a macroeconomic model is to disaggregate at least one of the variables by gender. This procedure would fit very well into the gender analysis framework proposed by the World Bank, which emphasizes the socially and culturally constructed gender differentiation of economic agents (World Bank, 1994). Its use to analyze gender and adjustment by Professor Paul Collier, of the Centre for the Study of African Economies, University of Oxford is discussed in section 6. This strategy emphasizes the discontinuities of gender but tends not to call into question the basic vision of the model itself.

A second strategy is to look at the economy from women's viewpoint and to identify missing variables which have a particular gender significance and bring

_____
*The author acknowledges the financial support of the Economic and Social Research Council (UK) and of the Swedish International Development Authority.
© Crown Copyright (1995).

them into the model. Thus a nonmonetized "social reproduction"[1] sector may be added as a constraint or resource to a model which initially focuses only on the market economy (see Walters, this issue). This strategy implies a critique and extension of the vision implicit in the preexisting model, with an emphasis on the bounds that the missing variables may place upon those variables that are included.

A third strategy is to conceptualize the economy as a gendered structure (see Elson and McGee, this issue). This entails recognizing that the matrix of gender relations[2] is an intervening variable in all economic activities: economic institutions which are not themselves intrinsically gendered, are nevertheless bearers of gender (Whitehead, 1979; Elson, 1993). That is, although relations between buyer and seller, lender and borrower, employer and employee, and provider and user of public services, are not gender ascriptive in the way that kin relations are, they are nevertheless permeated by gender via the norms and networks that are essential for the functioning of incomplete contracts; via the constitution of property rights; and via the endogenous constitution of the behavioral characteristics of economic agents. If the economy is seen as a gendered structure, then the parameters of a model may be seen as reflecting that structure. A different institutional configuration of gender relations will tend to result in a different set of parameters. This approach modifies the preexisting vision of any model through introducing the idea that gender relations, like class relations, affect the functioning of the market economy from within. It goes beyond the idea (explored by Taylor, this issue) that the domains of macroeconomics and gender relations are two separate and interacting domains, to suggest that the macroeconomy is itself gendered via the institutions through which economic agents operate. But it does not necessarily entail a critique of the ways in which a model depicts the interaction of financial relations and real resource utilization based on its treatment of the aggregation of millions of separate transactions into processes of growth or stagnation, boom or bust.

To deal with this point, a fourth strategy is needed that looks at the process of aggregation itself as a gendered process; and asks questions about how priorities are established, and who gives way when agents' decisions do not add-up to a coherent whole. This implies looking at the "closure" of the model, and the coordination process implicit in it, from a gender perspective.

There are clearly parallels with ways in which class relations can be introduced into macroeconomic models, as distributional variables or as dimensions of the "social matrix" which comprises "politically relevant groups, the major economic variables which affect them, and those variables over which they have some control" (Taylor, 1988, p. 21). In the following

analysis we sometimes refer to these parallels. The main focus is gender, however, because this dimension has remained largely unexplored.

Gender relations are understood as dynamic and historical rather than as static; that is as relations which are continually subject to decomposition and recomposition (Elson and Pearson, 1981) in planned and unplanned interactions between people (as individuals and collectives) and institutions.[3] They will also be understood as policy variables in the sense that they can be reshaped by deliberate public action to change institutions, albeit policy variables that are much more complex than the exchange rate or the rate of income tax. Gender inequality will be understood as stemming from women's lack of independent entitlements, which is closely linked to ways in which caring for people is articulated with getting a living (Elson, 1991a). From this point of view, more equal gender relations are associated with women having greater control over resources (associated with a new articulation of production and social reproduction), not simply with women participating more in the labor and goods markets, or being more often targeted by policy makers.

3. WHICH STRUCTURES ARE ADJUSTING?

The processes set in motion by SAPs may be seen as fundamentally matters of changes in the structure of entitlements. The implementation of SAPs implies reconfiguration of social, political and economic power in favor of the rights of owners of large-scale money capital, from International Financial Institutions in Washington to merchants in newly liberalized markets in developing countries (Beneria and Feldman, 1992; Elson, 1992, 1994b, 1995; Mbilinyi, 1990; Standing, 1989; Ruccio, 1991). In effect, adjustment programs attempt to recreate the privatized production of "classical capitalism"[4]; and also to privatize the costs of social reproduction. In some circumstances this may lead to new patterns of increased investment in real assets, and restructuring takes place with growth, especially at locations favored by internationally mobile capital. In less favored locations it leads to the run down of public investment, with no compensating increase in real private sector investment, and restructuring takes place with stagnation and increases burdens on most women, through extension and intensification of their work (see Floro, this issue). The former has been more characteristic of Asia[5]; and the latter of sub-Saharan Africa and Latin America.[6] To suggest that this is due to purely internal factors would be to commit the fallacy of composition — international competition implies uneven development.

Restructuring with growth is preferable in that it

leads to higher levels of employment and consumption than restructuring with stagnation; but in both cases the restructuring entails the subordination of more and more activities and people to a calculus of financial profit and loss and to the vagaries of market forces with the attendant risks of entitlement failure. This may be efficient in the short run in extracting the resources réquired to service the debt burden and keep repayments flowing to the World Bank and the International Monetary Fund (IMF), but it is by no means self-evidently efficient from the perspective of improving social productivity so as to meet long-run human development objectives. This is because it may lead to a variety of forms of human resource depletion, either through enforced overwork or enforced idleness, both of which are conducive to the deterioration of human mental and physical capabilities (Elson, 1994a); and because it fails to mobilize human resources in the most creative and productive ways to meet human needs.

The World Bank puts forward the idea that deregulated markets will generate the "right prices" and thus promote a labor-intensive growth pattern that will meet the needs of those who own little or no capital (World Bank, 1990b). But a detailed analysis of the externalities associated with the reproduction and use of labor power undermines confidence in this strategy. Dasgupta, examining the issue from a physical efficiency wage point of view concludes that "in a poor economy markets on their own are incapable of empowering all people with the opportunity to convert their potential labour power into actual labour power" (Dasgupta, 1993, p. 477). Pagano, (1991), emphasizing the asset-specificity of labor power and incompleteness of property rights over this asset in "deregulated"[7] labor markets concludes that a greater incentive to invest in machines rather than in workers stems from the property rights of "classical capitalism."

In such an entitlement structure, most people do not so much choose how to allocate their labor, as move hither and thither, propelled and repulsed by a now swelling, now falling tide of capital accumulation. Rather than a symmetrical interaction of interdependent supply and demand, there is a one-sided dependency of the owners of labor power upon the owners of large scale capital. No matter how low the wages, capital accumulation tends to destroy jobs by replacing people with machines, as well as create jobs by expanding output. As Marx puts it, in his discussion of capital accumulation in the nineteenth century:

> It is not a case of two independent forces working on each other. Les dés sont pipés.[8] Capital acts on both sides at once (Marx, 1976, p. 793).

One can see capital acting "on both sides at once" in the local and global processes that have propelled many young women into the tradable manufacturing sector in Asia and the Caribbean and which underlie the increased feminization of the labor force associated with SAPs (see Çağatay and Özler, this issue). Those processes begin with destruction of alternative renumerative job opportunities for the women, and for their fathers, brothers and husbands. This is followed by the offer of a new kind of "women's work," often with higher wages than those offered elsewhere, but with long hours of stressful work. Once alternative livelihoods have been weakened or destroyed, existing gender relations prove malleable. Even in countries such as Bangladesh with a tradition of seclusion of young women, ways are found to reconcile the employment of young women in factories with social and religious restrictions on "respectable" behavior (Feldman, 1992). Wives and daughters become a more economically valuable asset. But the subordination of women is reinscribed into the organization of the factory, with women concentrated at the bottom of the occupational hierarchy in dead-end jobs with little security (Pearson, 1992; Elson and Pearson, 1981). Research on Taiwan and South Korea shows that high rates of export-orientated industrial growth are quite compatible with the maintenance of a high degree of gender inequality in earnings and employment conditions and opportunities (Berik, 1995; Seguino, 1994).

The women who are propelled into work in export-oriented factories do, however, have the advantage in working in an expanding sector where their earnings are likely to rise absolutely, even if not relatively to those of men. The same is not true of the many women impelled to work as domestic servants and petty traders for falling earnings in a stagnating sector; nor of the men made redundant from construction sites and factories producing import substitutes for whom the main "masculine" alternative opportunity is all too often petty crime (for further discussion of evidence see Elson, 1995; Moser, 1992). Moreover, high levels of unemployment and marginalization from the process of capital accumulation is not merely a transitional phenomenon. It is built into the internal structure of "classical capitalism," providing a means of disciplining workers in an unequal labor market and providing the flexibility for rapid responses to new opportunities on the part of a mass of uncoordinated individual firms (Sawyer, 1989; Green, 1988). But unemployment and marginalization also reduces demand for the output of the private business sector and thereby increase risks. This can create a vicious circle of stagnation, holding back the commitment of investment in real assets (Sawyer, 1989). The attempt to recreate the conditions of classical capitalism in Africa and Latin America has not so far unleashed a dynamic private sector enthusiastic to make long-term investment. Stable growth with full employment on a general scale is likely to require a different reconfiguration of entitlements to produce a more inclusive process of aggregation of myriads of individual decisions, capable of internalizing dynamic external economies and creating better macro synthesis of micro-level decisions (see Howes and Singh, this issue, for a discussion of this point in terms of a national corporatatist compact; Elson, 1988, considers this issue in terms of socialization of the market).

The World Bank view of which entitlement structures need to adjust and are adjusting is rather different. Emphasis placed on the reduction of the role of the state (including cuts in public expenditure) and the removal of policy-induced distortions in prices, wages and interest rates. This is seen as strengthening the independent position of owners of small and medium-scale enterprises (especially farmers and manufacturers) and is frequently accompanied by á rhetoric of "empowering the people." The fate of owners of small and medium-scale productive capital, however, is generally related in practice to the buoyancy of aggregate demand and the plans of owners of large-scale capital (both financial and productive) on whom small firms are often dependent for inputs and for markets. The self-employed owners of small enterprises, no less than those who possess only their own labor power, also find themselves in markets in which the dice are loaded against them. In the real world, there is plenty of evidence to suggest that micro-level efficiency is no guarantee of macro-level sustainability, but World Bank models are built in ways that eliminate this disturbing possibility.

4. THE REVISED MINIMUM STANDARD MODEL

Let us now turn to the first of the models we shall be considering. The Revised Minimum Standard Model (RMSM) is said to be the most widely used macro model in the World Bank (Tarp, 1993). It is a multisector variant of the two-gap (savings and foreign exchange) growth model developed by Chenery and Strout (1966) on the basis of a full-capacity utilization version of the Harrod-Domar model. It is used to derive estimates of the foreign aid required to achieve a specified real output growth target on the basis of estimated, or assumed, values of savings ratios, import ratios and Incremental Capital-Output Ratios (ICORs).[9]

As a set of equations depicting an equilibrium, this model specifies no particular pattern of entitlements. It is silent on the issues of who owns the capital stock and how labor is reproduced and mobilized to use that stock. It does not specify how savings are generated; and or how foreign exchange flows into the economy and by whom its patterns of use are determined. It contains no explicit statements about the relation of patterns of entitlements to the parameters of the model and to the processes through which aggregation takes

place and equilibrium is established. In applying the model, however, implicit assumptions are made about entitlement structures and about how they affect the working of the model.

It is apparently common practice to iterate the model introducing a series of changes in the parameters; and to assume that the level of consumption is residually determined, so that the savings gap is suppressed and foreign exchange for the import of physical capital is left as the binding constraint (Tarp, 1993).

A rationale for expecting parameter changes during the course of adjustment programs can be found in the policy conditions attached to structural adjustment loans, which are expected to reduce capital-output and import coefficients and increase savings propensities, through exogenously introduced reductions in price distortions, leading to a lower level of rent-seeking behavior and less engagement in directly unproductive activities.

This is premised on a particular kind of entitlement structure, that of a "mixed economy" with a large self-interested profit-driven private business sector and a public sector also driven by self-interest, but in pursuit of political power as well as financial gain (Kreuger, 1974). Structural adjustment programs change the public/private balance of this pattern of entitlements in the short run through changing exchange entitlements, through market liberalization and cutbacks in state expenditure; in the longer run through changing resource endowments, by privatization of public assets.

The presence of this kind of entitlements structure, however, may be thought to call into question the assumption of full-capacity utilization. In Harrod's original application of the model, the whole economy was assumed to consist of privately owned, profit-seeking businesses and in Harrod's view this raised important problems about the incentive to invest — private businesses would only invest if they believed this to be warranted by their expectations about demand. Steady growth with full capacity utilization was a happy accident, but there were no systematic forces operating to bring this about (see Walters, this issue). The assumption of full-capacity utilization is more plausible in an economy in which those making investment decisions do not have to worry too much about the rate of return to investment because there are soft budget constraints and a state which will always act as buyer of last resort. These conditions are much more characteristic of centrally planned or highly *dirigiste* economies with very small private sectors — just the opposite of what structural adjustment programs are designed to create.

There is thus a degree of incoherence between the assumption that the model can be applied iteratively with improvements in the parameters resulting from liberalization and privatization and the assumption that the full-capacity utilization rule can be left unchanged.

Moreover, no attention appears to be paid to possibility of SAPs leading to deterioration of the parameters. But a variety of scenarios can be constructed in which this may happen owing to interdependence of variables and parameters which the RMSM takes as independent. For instance, the level and productivity of private sector investment may depend positively on the level of public sector infrastructural investment, ("crowding in" rather than "crowding out") so that cutbacks in the latter may lead to declines in the former. The productivity of public and private sector investment may depend positively on the level of wages and job security and other welfare benefits, so that if labor market liberalization leads to a drop in wages and in job security, productivity declines. The propensity of households to save may depend negatively on the availability of imported consumer durables, so that import liberalization leads to a drop in the savings parameter. The propensity of governments to save may depend negatively on the availability of quick-disbursing aid for import support. *A priori*, it is difficult to say which would be likely to be stronger, the positive or negative impacts of SAPs on the parameters. But some acknowledgement of potential negative impacts would help to temper what appears to have often been considerable overoptimism about the positive impacts.

A comparable insouciance is displayed in the assumption that consumption may be taken to be the residual variable without considering that decline in aggregate consumption may entail entitlement failure for many poor people; and may have negative feedbacks (through both supply side and demand side effects) on aggregate output. It may also lead to civil disorder and violent resistance to SAPs. As Tarp, 1993, comments, this assumption may make neither economic nor political sense.

Certainly, it makes no sense to assume that all consumption is discretionary (Dasgupta, 1993); and it is highly risky to assume that any required compression of consumption can be achieved without jeopardizing the necessary (or productive) consumption of some groups, as studies of poverty and structural adjustment have clearly shown (Cornia, Jolly and Stewart, 1987).

The role of income distribution in the determination of aggregate output has been stressed in structuralist macroeconomics.[10] The behavior of the economy is held to depend critically upon the distribution of income between different social classes which are assumed to have different consumption and savings behavior. Reactions to policy changes will generally involve redistribution of income and frequently entail conflict between competing claims on output. The "closure" of structuralist models can take a variety of forms, the two most common being variations in the level of output (via a Keynesian multiplier effect) in

which the necessary changes in savings to close any *ex-ante* gap is generated primarily through increased incomes; and variations in the level of consumption through "forced savings" brought about by price increases which crowd some social groups out of the market. Which social groups bear the brunt of "forced savings" depends on the social matrix (Taylor, 1988, p. 21). If the groups affected by forced savings have sufficient power to try to counteract forced savings by raising their money incomes, then the scene is set for a stagflationary response, rather than a convergence to a stable level of output and prices. Structuralist macroeconomics has not, however, emphasized class differentiation as a factor in the production, as distinct from the distribution, of aggregate output.

In general, there are some strong arguments suggesting that all types of undemocratic and nonparticipatory processes of decision making about the volume, allocation and use of investment in both public and private sectors lead to a loss in social productivity compared with what would be likely to prevail under more democratic and egalitarian economic, political and social relations (Bowles, Gintis and Gustafsson, 1993; Pagano, 1985, 1991; Hodgson, 1988). On the other hand, it may also be the case that given an undemocratic and nonparticipatory structure of control over investment, maximum short-run private profit for owners of capital is achieved through undemocratic and nonegalitarian labor markets and labor processes that serve to extract more effort from people rather than improve the productivity of a given amount of effort. As Pagano (1991) demonstrates, however, though such a system may be good for private profits, it is less socially efficient than more egalitarian and democratic forms of capitalism (for instance, forms that give workers more rights), once the individual skills, initiative and commitment of workers become important. Socially inefficient forms of organization may persist owing to a vicious circle of mutually supportive property rights, technologies and values. But at the same time there are processes which operate to disrupt the stability of that nexus, dislocations caused by technological innovation (as argued by Pagano, 1991) and mismatches between the real and monetary aspects of a private property, market economy (as argued by Lebowitz, 1994). These provide a space for public action with a transformatory potential (Elson, 1992; Young, 1993) which may be able to propel the society into a new trajectory with a new structure of more democratic, egalitarian and socially efficient control and use of investment, which both leads to higher productivity[11] and is also valuable in itself for its contribution to humanizing development.

The conceptual framework of the RMSM does not allow for the analysis of endogenously generated transformation. It is stronger on the analysis of existing constraints, than on the analysis of new possibili-

1856   WORLD DEVELOPMENT

ties. The only way to consider alternative worlds in the framework of this model is to make exogenous changes to the parameters.

5. GENDER RELATIONS AND THE RMSM

The RMSM, like all two-gap models, is gender-blind. The lack of explicit consideration of gender relations does not mean, however, that they play no part in determining the level and rate of growth of aggregate output as depicted in the model. Here it will be argued that gender relations may be introduced into the RMSM via their role in determining the values of parameters, the composition of spending and the form of closure through which inconsistencies in agents' plans tend to be eliminated. The RMSM may also be criticized from a gender perspective for failing to take into account the important complementarities between public sector investment which supports social reproduction and the productivity of private sector investment.

Let us first consider the role that gender relations may play in the determination of the productivity of investment (represented in the model by the value of ICORs). The first point to note is that the invisibility of women's unpaid work in reproduction may give a false impression of the effectiveness of SAPs with respect to improving ICORs. Typically ICORs are calculated from statistics that take no account of non-monetized investment and output in social reproduction. The policy reforms introduced in structural adjustment programs may appear to be having success in reducing the value of ICORs, whereas what they are actually doing is transferring some of the costs of the market economy to the reproductive sector where they are met through unpaid labor (Elson, 1991a). A typical example would be changes in the organization of the health sector which lead to shorter stays by patients in hospitals and appear to be thereby leading to great output per unit of investment. On closer examination it may be revealed that shorter stays in hospital are matched by longer periods of convalescence at home and greater expenditure of nonmonetized resources in patient care. Here the productivity gain is illusory — the output is the same, but there is a transfer of the costs from the monetized public or private sector hospital to the nonmonetized reproductive sector.

The second point is that gender inequality is likely to raise the potential value of ICORs above the level that would prevail with more egalitarian gender relations. There is a wealth of evidence which demonstrates male bias in entitlements to productive resources. Male bias disadvantages women in access to and control of credit and land; in the creation and dissemination of new technologies; and in the acquisition of health, strength and skills. Male bias disadvantages women in labor and product markets and intrafirm labor processes, marginalizing women from decision-making processes; in access to and control of infrastructural services (energy, water, transport, buildings) and in intrahousehold arrangements for the organization of both production of commodities and the social reproduction of people. Male bias excludes women's voices from the policy processes in which public expenditure patterns are determined. There is a large literature on all these forms of male bias which leaves no doubt that they are widespread and have a significant impact on women's well-being[12] (Young, 1993; Kabeer, 1994; Agarwal, 1988; Tinker, 1990; Collier *et al.*, 1991; Birdsall and Sabot, 1991). But in addition, gender inequality just like class inequality, is likely to be a barrier to the most effective and productive use of human resources to meet human needs.

Quantitative evidence can be cited to illustrate this point with respect to control over the use of resources by small-scale producers in particular parts of the private sector. For example, Ongaro (1988) looked at the adoption of new farming technology in maize production in Kenya in the 1980s and investigated the impact of gender relations on the use of technology by comparing the effect of weeding on yields in female-headed households and male-headed households. It was found that in female-headed households the weeding undertaken raised yields by 56%, whereas in male-headed households the increase in yield was only 15%. After controlling for other differences between the two types of household, the study concluded that the most likely explanation was a systematic difference in effort due to differential entitlement structures, with women in female-headed household having more incentive to weed more effectively because they controlled the proceeds of their own work whereas the women in male-headed households did not. Collier (1990) comments that

> if Ongaro's sample is representative of rural Kenya, the national maize loss from this disincentive effect is about equal to the maize gain from the application of phosphate and nitrogen fertilisers (p. 7).

Output is also lost because women small-scale producers do not have the same entitlements as men to productive inputs, including education. For instance, another study located in Kenya, Moock's (1976) investigation of the efficiency of women as farm managers, which found that their performance compared very well with that of men, but that their access to resources was more restricted. On the basis of the coefficients in Moocks's study, it has been calculated that if the women farmers had the same access to inputs and education as the men farmers in the sample, yields could be increased by 9%. Another study covering beans and cowpeas as well as maize suggests even bigger increases in yields, of around 22%, would be possible if women farmers had the same access to inputs and education as men farmers (Quisumbing, 1993).

Similar findings are reported in a study of small-scale urban retailers in Peru (Smith and Stelcner, 1990). This established that women were as effective managers of resources as men. Firms with a smaller amount of capital, however, tended to have much higher returns to capital, and a much higher proportion of female-owned firms than male-owned firms had low amounts of capital. Directing increments of capital (via reforms of credit) to female-owned firms would therefore tend to raise the overall rate of return to capital (and *ipso facto* reduce the ICOR).

Similar arguments can be made with respect to eliminating discrimination against women in labor markets. Such discrimination has been treated in economic analysis mainly as an equity issue, but can also be seen as socially inefficient. A pioneering study by Tzannatos (1992) has demonstrated that if gender discrimination in patterns of occupation and pay were eliminated, total output, as well as women's income, could increase considerably.

In counterpoint to this, it is certainly possible to construct scenarios in which greater gender inequality might lead to increased output through extracting more effort from women, prodded by diminishing entitlements and increasing responsibilities. It is also possible to view male-biased institutional norms and practices as conducive to the creation of bonds of solidarity and trust between men that help to fill the gaps in incomplete contracts and increase output by promoting better teamwork among men (Cockburn, 1985). Such effects would also help to explain the persistence of employer discrimination, even though simple models based on preferences that are biased against women predict that there will be a conflict between maximizing profits and discriminating against women. Before concluding that there is therefore a tradeoff between gender equality and productivity, however, we need to consider how far such tradeoffs are globally and intertemporally stable and how far they are the result of localized and time-bound "vicious circles" which can be broken given appropriate interventions. People may be temporarily locked into a particular path-dependent set of unequal gender relations which are conducive to the persistence of behavior patterns that create adverse tradeoffs between equality and productivity. There are clearly parallels here with the debates on productivity and democratic or participatory economic institutions (see for instance Bowles, Gintis and Gustafsson, 1993). Much depends on whether agents' preferences are believed to be exogenous or endogenous. Insofar as agents' preferences are endogenous then there is much more scope for dynamic institutional transformations which can move societies out of vicious circles and into virtuous circles in which equality and efficiency are mutually reinforcing rather than at odds. The key

issue then is how such dynamic transformations can be accomplished. The view taken here is that what is required is not "investment *in* women,"[13] but investment *with* women in institutional changes which change preferences, perceptions, norms, and rights. In considering the costs of this investment it must be remembered that perpetuating gender inequality is also costly, requiring expenditures that buttress male power without enhancing productivity, a point we return to below.

What is missing are macro-level studies which gather and review available micro evidence on gender inequality and productivity for a particular country and attempt to synthesize their findings to produce some estimate of the implications of failure to reduce male bias for the country's sectoral and aggregate ICORs; and to indicate which forms of male bias have greatest quantitative significance for the value of the ICORs. This is likely to depend on economic structure, with male bias in labor markets being a more significant factor in reducing the return to investment in countries whose production is largely organized through wage employment in private and public sector corporations; and male bias in credit and product markets being more significant in countries where self-employment and small businesses account for a larger share of output. The World Bank is ideally placed to undertake a set of studies of this kind and relate them to the detailed specification of the RMSM for the countries in question. But so far its work on gender has remained largely at the micro level.

Besides the ICORs, the other important parameters in the RMSM are savings and import propensities. Direct evidence linking the degree of gender inequality with the values of these parameters is hard to find. But there is plenty of evidence suggesting that a more equal gender distribution of income would be conducive to spending patterns that contribute to long-term development as well as satisfy immediate needs.

Given the prevailing structures of gender relations, household investment in nutrition, health and education of children tends to be more the responsibility of women than of men. There is a great deal of evidence from all over the world to suggest that there is incomplete pooling of income within households, and that there are significant differences between expenditure from female-controlled income and expenditure from male-controlled income. Women attach a higher priority to expenditure on family nutrition, health and education-related goods (e.g., such as school uniforms) than do men. Men are much more likely than women to spend part of their income on purely personal consumption of commodities such as alcohol, cigarettes, gambling, higher status consumer durables, and female companionship.

Among the important sociological and anthropological studies to have established this are Kumar (1979), Guyer (1980), Tripp (1981), Pahl (1983),

Dwyer and Bruce (1988) and articles in special issues of *Development and Change* (1987) and *World Development* (1989). More recently their findings have been corroborated by econometric studies based on a new class of household models which do not assume a single household utility function. For instance, a positive relationship was found between the proportion of cereals produced under women's control and household consumption of calories in Gambian households by von Braun (1988). Similarly a study in the Philippines found that raising the share of income accruing to wives increased household acquisition of calories and proteins (Garcia, 1990). Particularly revealing is a study of households in the Côte d'Ivoire which found that doubling women's share of cash income raised the budget share of food and lowered the budget share of alcohol and cigarettes (Hoddinott and Haddad, 1992).

Within the context of an extension of the RMSM framework to include human resources as determinants of growth, this evidence could be interpreted as indicating a greater propensity on the part of women than on the part of men to save, and invest the savings in maintenance and enhancement of human capacities. This gendered difference in expenditure patterns may be partly the result of a greater incidence of maternal than paternal altruism. It may be partly the result of information asymmetries — since men are not so involved in the day-to-day care of children, they are not so well informed about the needs of children. It is also likely to be determined by efforts to preserve existing sources of power and advantage. One of the few sources of power and advantage to women in many countries is privileged access to their children, especially sons. Women save and invest in their children to gain and maintain access to this resource. A source of power and advantage to men in many countries is privileged access to an autonomous public sphere of life outside the family. Much of their "leisure" expenditure may be interpreted as expenditure to gain and maintain their access to this sphere, and the alternative to family life that it offers. (Among poor men this public sphere, in which they have "free time," may also serve to reconcile them to their lack of power in relation to richer men.) In both cases an analogy may be made with rent-seeking behavior, understood as expenditure to create and retain some position of advantage; but in the case of women's expenditure on their children, much of the expenditure is directly productive; whereas in the case of men's expenditure on leisure commodities, a considerable proportion of it is directly unproductive (e.g., excessive consumption of alcohol, tobacco, gambling) leading to a depletion rather than an enhancement of human capacities, particularly since it is often associated with violence against women (Elson, 1992). It would be interesting to explore the possibilities of estimating the scale of loss of productive output in

relation to GDP that arises from diversion of resources to these forms of activity that serve to buttress male power and at the same time deplete human resources.

Let us finally turn to the issue of gender and the "closure" of the RMSM. As mentioned above, the problem of *ex-ante* incompatibility of savings and investment is apparently dealt with by assuming that consumption is residually determined to generate whatever level of savings is required to match the investment requirements of the growth target.

In evaluating this assumption, a gender-aware analysis will bring into the picture the role of women's unpaid work in the organization of consumption in the reproductive sector. It is true that a squeeze on consumption of marketed goods can be met to some extent by an increase in output of nonmarketed goods for own-consumption. Clothes can be sewn at home rather than bought ready-made; bread can be baked at home rather than bought from the bakery; grain can be processed by hand rather than taken to the mill; kitchen gardens can be cultivated; "voluntary" labor can be mobilized in community self-help schemes to substitute for public sector provision. It may even be possible for increases and decreases in the amount of time spent in unpaid labor to stabilize total real consumption, even though aggregate consumption as conventionally measured in the national income accounts is changing. There are good reasons not to be complacent, however, for there is a limit to the time that can be made available for increasing production of nonmarketed consumption goods without jeopardizing the supply of exports and the level of investment in human capacities (see Elson, 1995, for a review of some relevant evidence).

In the short run, the most significant feedback loop may be production of export goods, where there is a tradeoff between the allocation of womens' time to activities in the reproductive sector and to the production of cash crops or light manufactures. (See Darity, this issue, for a model exploring this tradeoff.) This possible constraint is likely to be more significant the greater the required drop in consumption, the greater the female intensity of export production, the greater the female intensity of production in the reproductive sector, and the lower the level of existing female leisure time.

In the longer run another feedback loop may be of greater significance: that between increasing the extent of the participation of girls in housework, childcare, collecting of fuel and water, cooking, etc., and the education of girls. There is some micro-level evidence to suggest this is an important cause for concern (see Elson, 1995), corroborated by macro-level evidence of setbacks to the education of girls (Rose, this issue). Such setbacks are likely to have adverse effects on productivity, as well as upon the degree of gender inequality and the overall well being of women. Thus, although women's unpaid labor may operate to cushion the effects of cuts in consumption of marketed goods, and provide some rationale for the treatment of aggregate consumption as residual, it is not available in limitless supply; and placing too great a burden on it will tend to have negative implications for other components of output and investment, some in the medium term and others in the longer run. It will obviously also have negative implications on women's well-being, through loss of time for rest and recuperation.

Drops in consumption may also act as a closure mechanism in structuralist models. In the presence of supply-side constraints, equilibrium is achieved in structuralist models through "forced saving" induced by changes in the distribution of income brought about by price changes (Taylor, 1988, p. 28). Typically it is assumed that savings out of wages are lower than out of profits, and that a savings gap induces price changes that redistribute income to profits, forcing wage-based households to reduce their consumption, and generating a higher level of aggregate savings. The role of "forced labor" (i.e. increases in the amount of unpaid work done in the reproductive sector) in permitting forced savings to be extracted has, however, been ignored.

Let us now summarize this argument. We have suggested that the RMSM could be made gender-aware by relating the values of some key parameters, and the form of "closure" of the model, to the degree of gender inequality. The model could be iterated with parameter changes representing a move to more egalitarian gender relations. We must, however, end on a note of caution. The RMSM is structured in ways that may lead us to be overoptimistic about the impact on total output and of human well-being of greater gender equality in processes of production and spending. This is because it assumes away the possibility of mismatches between aggregate supply and aggregate demand, and hence neglects the possibility of underutilization of capacity and unemployment. It may well be, however, that institutionalizing a gender perspective in macroeconomic policy processes would help to diminish such mismatches. This argument is discussed in the final section of the paper.

6. THE SMALL DEPENDENT ECONOMY MODEL OF STRUCTURAL ADJUSTMENT

The macro changes in the structure of resource allocation required to achieve macroeconomic balance without sacrificing growth have been analyzed by economists[14] inside and outside the Bank on the basis of the Swan-Salter model of a small open economy. This model divides the economy into two sectors, the tradable and the nontradable.[15] The combinations of tradable and nontradable output which a given set of resources can produce is assumed to take the

form of a well-behaved production possibility curve. Macroeconomic imbalance is depicted in terms of the demand for tradables exceeding supply, the causes for which may be internal (such as an overexpansion of government expenditure) or external (such as an unfavorable trade shock). Structural adjustment implies a switch of resources to the production of tradables and a switch in expenditure away from the consumption of tradables through a combination of policies designed to raise the domestic price of tradables relative to nontradables, and reduce the domestic absorption of tradables. In addition, deregulation is expected to have an additional effect of increasing the size of the production possibility set by eliminating rent-seeking and directly unproductive activities (comparable to the effect of reducing ICORs in the RMSM). The net result is then expected to be restoration of internal and external balance with an expansion of output, achieved through a change in the structure of the economy in terms of the division of resources between tradables and nontradables.

The small dependent economy model offers an almost complete contrast to the RMSM. There are just two important similarities — the assumption that adjustment takes place with a given set of fully utilized resources, and the lack of formal specification of the structure of entitlements. But otherwise, this model offers flexibility, whereas the RMSM offers rigidity; this model shows a balance-of-payments deficit being eliminated, with growth of output and full employment during a process of costless resource reallocation (typically depicted in terms of sliding along a smooth production possibility frontier), whereas the RMSM shows a balance-of-payments deficit persisting and constraining growth, so that foreign aid is required for an expansion of output. The small dependent economy model does not provide a justification for aid, since the economy is depicted as capable of growth-lead adjustment provided the right combination of policy instruments is used. One can think of possible justifications in terms of political economy, e.g., the aid is needed to "persuade" reluctant policy makers to "get the prices right"; or to compensate dispossessed rent-seekers.[16] But these lie outside the model. Within the model, as normally presented, the only clue that aid might have a role to play lies in the idea that the prices of nontradables might be subject to downward stickiness. This opens up a space for the possibility of micro-level rigidities which slow down the speed of response to the policy measures[17]; and aid may be introduced into the framework as a way of promoting a faster response. Although no particular entitlement structure is specified, the model is often applied in ways that suggest that the agents whose response is in question are independent farmers, traders and artisans, free to choose whether transfer from production of nontradables to production of tradables. Supply constraints, rather

1860 WORLD DEVELOPMENT

than demand constraints, are identified as the possible problem; whereas SAPs are likely to increase the likelihood of deficient demand by reducing the role of the state as buyer of last resort.

The small dependent economy model is not operationalizable in the same way as the RMSM since the aggregates it uses do not directly correspond to national accounting categories, and the functional relations it postulates cannot easily be expressed in terms of simple coefficients. It is a heuristic model designed to provide an argument for the use of a particular combination of policy instruments rather than to quantify their effects in an operational way. It is open to criticism on the grounds that it misspecifies the relation between the production of tradables and nontradables by posing them as substitutes, whereas in many instances they are complementary. The model also is open to criticism for neglecting the issue of risk. It takes the world market prices facing a particular country as "given" but fails to emphasize that although, in many cases, these prices can plausibly be taken as given in the sense of being exogenously determined, they are not "given" in the sense of being constant or certain. Very many adjusting economies, especially in sub-Saharan Africa, have faced fluctuating and deteriorating terms of trade during their adjustment programs. Attempts to increase the production of tradables may jeopardize the security of people's livelihoods. A third weakness of the model is that it leaves out of account the way in which restructuring tends to change the nature and composition of the labor force itself (rather than simply transferring it from one sector to another), making some existing elements redundant, while calling into being new categories of paid workers and calling into play new types of skills and ways of using them.

The basic model makes no reference to gender. The lack of explicit reference does not mean that gender relations play no role in determining how resources are transferred and reallocated in the process of structural adjustment. Both feminist and neoclassical economists have discussed gender in this context (Elson, 1989 and 1992; Collier, 1990, 1994). In the next section we discuss the neoclassical account.[18]

7. GENDER IN THE SMALL DEPENDENT ECONOMY: A NEOCLASSICAL ANALYSIS

Collier's neoclassical analysis of gender and adjustment focuses in particular on the theme of "gender aspects of labour allocation during structural adjustment" (Collier, 1994). Gender analysis, for Collier, is fundamentally a matter of disaggregation. It is worth quoting his account of his method at some length.

Gender is one of many ways in which data can be disaggregated and the rationale for doing this is twofold. First, in earning income, women often face different constraints from men. Since structural adjustment is largely about changing constraints, if those facing women and men are sufficiently different, it is illuminating to treat the genders as distinct groups rather than studying gender-undifferentiated averages. Second, women and men often have radically different propensities to consume particular public services and so budgetary changes can have powerfully gender-differentiated effects . . . It should be stressed that gender is not a topic in itself but rather a possible disaggregation to be borne in mind when studying a topic . . . Sometimes gender disaggregation will not add enough to be worthwhile. However, for some topics it will be useful and for others essential . . . A corollary of this rationale for an analysis which distinguishes between women and men is that, generally, there is not a small, self-contained set of "women's issues" which can be appended to an otherwise unaltered analysis. Rather, the claim is that many standard issues in resource allocation became better illuminated when the analysis is disaggregated by gender (Collier, 1990, pp. 149–150).

There is much to agree with here, but there is a danger that in treating gender simply as a form of disaggregation of agents, gender inequality is located outside the economy in social norms and personal psychology and the issue of women's lack of independent economic entitlements is not made central to the analysis. Thus it is with Collier's analysis which identifies the constraints that women face in deciding how to use their labor in terms of the following four distinct processes (1990, p. 159):

(a) discrimination against women outside the household;

(b) copying of gender-specific role models;

(c) asymmetric rights and obligations within households leading to weak incentives for women to undertake tasks in male-controlled cash crop production;

(d) the burden of [biological] reproduction,[19] leading to confinement to a restricted range of economic activities that are more easily compatible with motherhood.

A more extensive discussion of the nature of these processes is to be found in Collier (1988) and Collier *et al.* (1991) which makes more explicit the assumption that the constraints stem from outside the economy in biological processes ("the physiological asymmetry of reproduction"); in social conventions and traditions about appropriate gender roles; and in individual preferences, whether preferences that discriminate against women or women's own lack of aspiration to achieve higher income or status. Key to the perpetuation of these four processes is the tendency of boys to copy men and girls to copy women: all of which points in the direction of women choosing to be unequal and disadvantaged. There is no counteracting focus on coercion; and the pressures stemming from women's lack of control over resources which confine them to a limited range of activities. But nor is there any allowance for women challenging and changing gender norms. The potential idiosyncrasy of preference is paradoxically constrained by a kind of "iron law" of imitation.[20]

Collier combines disaggregation of economic agents by gender with a sectoral disaggregation of activities which distinguishes between protected and unprotected tradables; and between marketed and nonmarketed output. This latter is identified, however, purely in terms of public sector services.[21] There is no attempt to look at the economy through women's eyes, and to include domestic care and maintenance of human beings as a significant economic activity. The process of adjustment is specified in terms of the need to move labor from nontradables and protected tradables, to tradables. It is argued that gender is a significant disaggregation in this context if men and women are initially allocated differentially between the sectors and have differing capacities for mobility because of facing differing constraints.

> For example, women might be disproportionately located in sectors which need to contract and at the same time have less capacity than men to reallocate resources to sectors which should expand (Collier, 1990, p. 152).[22]

To answer this question requires an analysis of "the various processes by which female-controlled resources (primarily their own labour) are allocated" (Collier, 1994, p. 279). The presence of constraints to the mobility of women's labor, it is argued, will both have an adverse impact on women and an adverse impact on the achievement of an expansionary adjustment. Collier focuses particular attention on barriers to women shifting to export crop production in sub-Saharan Africa. In this context, it is argued that constraints (b) and (c) are likely to be important. Gender-specific role model imitation (constraint (b)) is held to be a factor constraining the adoption of export crops by female-headed households in situations where export crops have typically been grown under male control and are identified as "male" crops. In support of this, reference is made to a study of the adoption of tea in Kenya[23] (Bevan, Collier and Gunning, 1989) which suggests that female-headed households had only half the propensity to adopt tea as male-headed households (the implication being that this is connected to women having fewer women tea producers as role models to copy).

There are reasons to be skeptical about the identification of gender-specific imitation as a key factor. For instance, it may be that farmers do not so much copy what their neighbors do as learn from what their neighbors do. Learning probably requires interaction

(e.g., asking questions) as well as observation, and there may well be gender barriers to those kinds of interactions between male farmers and female farmers unless they are members of the same household. Furthermore, it may be that female heads of households do not adopt export crops to the same degree as men because of unidentified differences between themselves and male heads of households (such as greater risk aversion because of greater direct responsibilities for well-being of children). In addition, marketing boards may operate out-grower schemes in ways that disbar many women farmers from obtaining licenses to grow tree crops even if they wish to do so.

The other constraint that is emphasized by Collier is constraint (c), asymmetric rights and obligations within households which result in a weak incentive for women in male-headed households to spend more time and effort on export crop production. This occurs because the receipts from export crop sales tend to accrue to the male household heads, even though the bulk of the work may have been done by their wives. Collier sees this as an instance of the "principal-agent" problem; but although there is frequently a gender-differentiated incentive problem in cash-crop production in sub-Saharan Africa, one may question whether it is best characterized as a "principal-agent" problem. For it arises most acutely precisely in circumstances in which women are not in a "principal-agent" relation with their husbands; that is, there is more of a problem when women are not empowered to act on behalf of their husbands in export cash-crop production, exercising authority delegated to them by him.[24] When women do enjoy such delegated authority, perhaps in the supervision of a jointly run family business, there is likely to be far less of an incentive problem and more propensity for team work. But the situation of many women farmers in sub-Saharan Africa is much more akin to that of a taxpayer[25]: their husbands possess the authority to attempt to exact from their wives some payment of labor services in cash-crop production in return for which there will be provision of services similar to those provided by the state — such as protection against predators, a degree of social insurance, and some transfer of income in cash or kind, bearing no particular relation to work done. Just like many taxpayers, many women farmers tend to try to minimize their tax burden by finding loopholes in existing tax structures; and they tend to contest the legitimacy of new tax demands, unless they are convinced that sufficient benefits will flow (or penalties be avoided). Other things being equal many women seem to prefer to spend additional working time on activities from which all the proceeds accrue directly to them and which are under their authority, such as (in many cases) food-crops production in fields assigned to them by their husbands for this purpose.[26] In some circumstances women have sufficient autonomy to assert this preference, and then gender relations do indeed constitute a barrier to the transfer of women's labor from nontradables to tradables. In other circumstances men are powerful enough to override women's preferences, or women feel that they have to cooperate with husbands to secure their children's future and women do transfer labor to export cash crop production. Studies in Zaire have come up with examples of both situations. In southeastern Shaba where high-yielding maize varieties were introduced women continued to cultivate manioc (which was indispensable to the family food supply) rather than switch their labor to their husbands' maize fields. However, in north and central Shaba, women proved to be insufficiently autonomous to refuse their husbands' demands on their labor, and ceased to grow a second peanut crop and cultivate their family food gardens (Schoepf and Engundu, 1991, p. 160).

It is not necessarily a cause for celebration when women do transfer their labor to export cash-crop production, for such a transfer may jeopardize other important objectives such as household food security. Nor does such a transfer indicate only weak gender constraints on women's economic activities. Rather it may signify the presence of much more profound constraints than those identified by Collier — constraints placed by the exercise of male power on the ability of women to decide how to allocate their own labor, and to treat it as their own asset, rather than an asset belonging in the first instance to their husband or father or a senior male relative. The weakness of women's entitlements is illustrated by the fact that women's labor is not generally a fully female-controlled resource. As Jones found in her studies of rice cultivation in north Cameroon "married women are expected to work in their husbands' fields if they are not working in their own. If they refuse to work in their husbands' fields, they risk a beating!" (Jones, 1986, p. 11). This is one graphic instance of the fact that women frequently face not just constraints on the content of their decisions about how to use their own labor owing to their precommitment of their time to motherhood and household duties and subsistence production; but also constraints on the extent to which they are free to be autonomous decision makers, as a result of their confinement within a set of parameters laid down by men and policed by nonmarket mechanisms. The problem for many women farmers in sub-Saharan Africa is conflict of expectations and obligations.[27] They are expected and obliged to produce food crops to supply household food needs and to supply labor for production of export crops controlled by their husbands. The conflict is exacerbated by low productivity in household food-crop production and low cash returns to export crops. The latter frequently persist in spite of the fact that structural adjustment programs are supposed to improve incentives for small farmers, because of rising costs of farm inputs,

lack of credit to support timely payments to farmers, and falling international prices. It is likely that many women are being required to work more in their own fields and their husbands' fields. Rather than being encouraged to transfer labor from one activity to another they are being pushed and prodded (both metaphorically and literally) to supply more labor to both activities.

One reason for this conflict is that gender relations also affect the mobility of men's labor and the mobilization of men's time, constraining the transfer of men's time and effort into tasks regarded as "women's work," whether they be agricultural tasks such as weeding, transplanting, plucking or social reproduction tasks such as gathering fuel and water, and cooking. The sanction here is not domestic violence but loss of masculine identity through performance of "unmanly tasks" with all this implies for recognition of both social and sexual potency. Interestingly, Collier does not address this kind of constraint in the transfer of male labor between different activities. Although he talks about gender, it is women's activities, not men's, which are seen as the problem. This is symptomatic of the fact that the economy is not viewed from women's perspective, even though the labor variable is disaggregated by gender. The male angle of vision is reflected in the failure to integrate social reproduction into the model as a set of activities which are fundamental to the future growth of the economy. Insofar as time spent in the social reproduction sector is mentioned, it is only as a constraint upon the mobility of women to the tradables sector, not as a necessary activity which underpins both the production of tradables and the promotion of human well-being. Much more attention is paid to the issue of social reproduction by Palmer (1991) in an analysis which in some other respects is comparable to that of Collier.[28]

The kind of gender analysis proposed by Collier makes little difference to the basic vision of the small dependent economy model. It simply implies that gender differentiation will increase the time it takes to transfer resources from nontradables to tradables, so that the economy will be in disequilibrium for longer than it would be with more equitable gender relations. The policy implication is that structural adjustment programs should target women with measures to reduce barriers to their incorporation into the tradable sector, and provide more aid to cushion the economy while these measures take time to work.

It is, moreover, an analysis developed with the economic and social structure of rural sub-Saharan African in mind, with limited applicability to other locations in which small-holder cash crops are not the main tradable. It is predicated on a structure of entitlements in which women have not yet been dispossessed of nonmarket access to land but have weak entitlements to complementary inputs. For women, that is both a source of strength and a source of weakness. They have a fallback position which may often be stronger than that of women who have no land. But their disconnection from the circuits of capital means there is little interest in investing to increase the productivity of their farming. The key gender issue in the reallocation of resources during structural adjustment is not the immobility of women's labor, but women's weak and unbalanced entitlements, and lack of voice in the determination of economic priorities.

Measures to improve women's mobility from nontradables to tradables are in any case of little use if there is insufficient demand for their labor in the tradable goods sector. Urban women in many parts of sub-Saharan Africa do not seem to be faced with expanding opportunities for employment in the production of tradables, while rural women who move to producing cash crops for export have seen falling international terms of trade erode their return. The problems lie not only in gender-differentiated responses to market-led adjustment, but also in the reliance on markets as currently constructed to mobilize resources for production. But the institutionalization of a gender perspective may also have a role to play in improving the systems through which millions of individual decisions are aggregated to create a macroeconomy.

8. GENDER AND THE POLITICAL ECONOMY OF AGGREGATION

The creation of macroeconomic aggregates such as consumption, savings, investment, and gross national product is not simply the work of government statisticians. The figures in the national accounts represent real processes of aggregation in which the plans of millions of decision makers are synthesized via the operation of a variety of monetized transactions in the private and public sectors. If these plans do not "add up" (i.e., are not compatible), some will have to be changed; and the way these plans are changed depends, among other things, on the patterns of command over resources (or structure of entitlements). Macro models reflect this in the way they depict the closure of the model. Those with fewer entitlements will count for less and the process of aggregation will reflect the priorities of those with strongest control of resources.

The process of aggregation is more likely to result in a sustainable macroeconomy producing patterns of employment and output that meet peoples needs if it is a socially inclusive process which encourages a degree of mutuality and reciprocity, capable of internalizing externalities, and looking beyond short term profits (see Elson, 1988; Howes and Singh, this issue).

Thus macroeconomic analysis needs to be concerned with the social matrix within which macroeconomic processes unfold (Taylor, 1988). All over the world, women and women's organizations tend to be relatively excluded from an independent role in the social matrix. Their inclusion on an autonomous basis might well make an important difference in institutionalizing a perspective that recognizes interdependencies which neither market nor bureaucratic transactions reveal, and puts more emphasis on reciprocity and consensus-building — not because women are essentially more attuned to these insights and values, but because their life experiences have tended to foster such views. As Gita Sen puts it:

> A gender perspective means recognizing that women stand at the crossroads between production and reproduction, between economic activity and the care of human beings, and therefore between economic growth and human development. They are workers in both spheres — those most responsible and therefore with most at stake, those who suffer the most when the two spheres meet at cross purposes, and those most sensitive to the need to better integration between the two (Sen, 1995, p. 12).

Such a belief in the transformatory potential of institutionalizing a gender perspective in the social matrix in which macroeconomic processes are embedded is central to the strategy of the DAWN network of women activists in the South (see DAWN, this issue). Such institutionalization requires more than women's access to the policy-making process. It requires a change in the structure of entitlements so that the dice are no longer loaded against those who are not large-scale owners of money capital. To access the potential prospects for the gains from institutionalizing a gender perspective, formal model building has to be complemented with comparative institutional analysis at national and international level, which considers gender as an intervening variable in all the parts of the system from which macroeconomic results emerge.

9. CONCLUSIONS

Gender-awareness in macroeconomic analysis requires that we look at economic models from the standpoint of women's lives, in which much time is devoted to unpaid work in social reproduction as well as to paid work in production; and that we recognize unequal gender relations as an intervening variable that structures economic processes at macro, meso and micro levels. The models that inform the design of structural adjustment programs are gender-blind. Nevertheless, we have shown that gender is likely to have a significant role in determining the parameters and processes of closure of the model used to examine growth prospects and aid requirements; and that this significance is enhanced when the framework is extended to cover investment in human capacities and social reproduction. We have also considered the model used to analyze resource reallocation from non-

1864   WORLD DEVELOPMENT

tradables to tradables; and the introduction of gender into this framework via the gender disaggregation of economic agents, and the postulate of differential gender mobility. Our conclusion was that this approach to gender awareness is limited by a lack of appreciation for the role that women's work in social reproduction plays in producing a vital input for the production of both tradables and nontradables, namely, the labor force. Sustainable structural adjustment requires investment in social reproduction, not merely the transfer of labor from nontradables. In addition, more significant than differential gender mobility with respect to labor, is the persistence of gender segregation in social reproduction activities, and in the production of both nontradables and tradables; together with the persistence of male-biased entitlement structures which limit the control that women have over resources, even their own labor.

A limitation of both the models we have discussed is their neglect of the waste of resources and impoverishment that stems from deficient aggregate demand, from undemocratic decision making, and from directly unproductive expenditures that serve to buttress male power. We have argued that these kinds of waste of resources, are likely to be diminished by moves to more egalitarian systems of gender relations. Though maintaining gender inequality may sometimes lead to higher profits in the short run, it also tends to generate negative feedbacks which hamper the process of restructuring to a development path which is sustainable in the long run. The outcome of macroeconomic policies depends upon the gendered social matrix in which they are introduced. But that gendered social matrix could in principle be changed in ways that promote both more effective macroeconomic policies and greater gender equality.

NOTES

1. The term social reproduction is widely used in feminist economics (Humphries and Rubery, 1984; Folbre, 1994; Picchio, 1992) to refer to the social and material processes through which the labor force, or the human population as a whole, is maintained and renewed on a daily and intergenerational basis.

2. Gender relations are helpfully defined by Young (1993) as follows: "gender relations are those socially constituted relations between men and women which are shaped and sanctioned by norms and values held by members of a given society (but not necessarily held with same degree of firmness)" (p. 138).

3. For a thoughtful discussion of the interplay between agency and structure in the perpetuation and restructuring of gender relations, see Young (1993), p. 139.

4. "Classical capitalism" is the term used by Pagano (1991) to refer to a system based on labor markets in which workers hold few rights in contrast to "company workers' capitalism" and "unionised capitalism." We may observe that women's paid employment has predominantly been "classically capitalist" even in economies in which many male workers have become stakeholders in the company employing them (e.g., Japan) or have obtained job rights through trade union organization (e.g., Germany).

5. There is a fierce debate about the factors leading to the East Asian miracle and the relatively successful adjustment of newly industrialized countries (NICs), such as Indonesia (see, for instance, Amsden, 1994). The argument focuses on state intervention vs. "getting the prices right" in industrial strategy. Far less attention has been paid to the labor market and labor process dimensions of this performance, and the balance of entitlements as between labor and capital.

6. For studies which illuminate the class and gender dimensions of restructuring with stagnation in Latin America, see Ruccio (1991) and Tanski (1994).

7. "Deregulated" labor markets are more properly seen as labor markets in which owners of labor power have few rights in comparison with owners of other assets.

8. "The dice are loaded."

9. There is not a great deal of material published on the details of the model and how it has been used in conjunction with the introduction of structural adjustment programs; here we shall rely primarily on the accounts provided by Addison (1989) and Tarp (1993).

10. Structuralist economics does not form one consolidated body of theory, but comprises a variety of ideas and concepts, united by a common agreement on the restricted usefulness of assumptions such as perfect competition, well-functioning markets and free mobility of resources. Tarp (1993) distinguishes at one end of the spectrum "neoclassical structuralism" which recognizes a series of supply-side constraints at the micro level; and "macro structuralism" which emphasizes demand-side constraints whose causes are embedded in the underlying economic, social and political characteristics of society. "Macro structuralism" is exemplified by Bacha (1984), Fitzgerald (1988) and Taylor (1989) among others.

11. And to more adequate definitions of productivity, which take into account the need for conservation of human and natural resources and measure productivity in terms of effectiveness in meeting human needs.

12. Where there is debate in this literature is on the processes through which male bias is produced and reproduced: there is disagreement about how far this is due to individual preferences (such as men's prejudice and women's low aspirations); and how far due to social structures and institutional norms. Discrimination and discouragement can be the result of either or both, and conventional of forms empirical testing are frequently inconclusive (Humphries, 1994).

13. "Investing in women" is the official slogan of the World Bank (see World Bank, 1994). It reflects a point of view in which women are seen more as resources for the achievement of development, than as people whose control over resources should be strengthened.

14. See for instance, Lal (1984) and (1989); Demery and Addison (1987); Gillis *et al.* (1992); World Bank (1990a).

15. Tradable goods and services are those whose prices within the country are determined by supply and demand in world markets. It is assumed that world market prices are exogenously determined (and this is the sense in which the economy is small and dependent). Nontradables are goods and services that are not easily or usually traded across the country's borders, owing to very high transport costs, or impossibility of separating production and consumption. Examples usually given are activities such as transportation, construction, retail trade and household services (Gillis *et al.*, 1992, p. 581). Prices of these nontradable goods are determined by supply and demand within each country.

16. Further discussion of this point is beyond the scope of this paper. For extensive discussion see Mosley, Harrigan, and Toye (1991).

17. Lal (1984 and 1989), for instance, focuses on immobility of labor and capital.

18. Though the approach is fundamentally neoclassical, it may be seen as having elements of an institutional analysis in the way it treats gender roles (Lockwood, 1992) and elements of a "neoclassical structuralist" perspective in the way that it treats micro-rigidities (Tarp, 1993).

19. Collier does not distinguish biological and social reproduction but it is evident from the examples given — "the physical demands of child-bearing and breast feeding" that "reproduction" here means a biological process.

20. ". . . a universal feature of human behaviour: the tendency to imitate or copy role models" (Collier, 1994, p. 286).

21. Though increasing introduction of user charges means that more and more public sector output is marketed.

22. Collier attempts to operationalize this conceptual framework by matching his sectoral disaggregation of activities with the activity categories to be found in conventional statistics of national output. In the case of sub-Saharan Africa, he argues, manufacturing is the protected tradable sector; nonfood export crop agriculture the unprotected tradable; and marketed services, trade and construction the nontradable sector. Food crop production can potentially be in any of those three sectors, depending on the circumstances of

the particular country, and can only be assigned after investigating those circumstances. On the basis of this kind of rough approximation, it is possible to match the sectors with employment data, and make some estimates of the percentage of the female labor force engaged in each sector, and of the female percentage of the total labor force engaged in each sector (or female intensity of the sector). This analysis assumes that tradability of a product and the female intensity of its production are independent variables. That may not be the case, however. While "the designation as between tradable and non-tradable depends upon transport costs" (Collier, 1990, p. 153), transport costs are themselves gendered. Women frequently lack transport entitlements (Calvo, 1994), so that food crops grown by women are more likely to be nontradable than food crops grown by men.

23. This study controlled for age and gender of household head, male and female labor endowment of the household, the proportion of households growing tea, and whether the household is already growing coffee.

24. The modern principal-agent literature, in contrast with an earlier literature, does tend to elide the difference between the two circumstances. (Compare the old and new entries on principal and agent in the *New Palgrave Dictionary of Economics*, p. 966.) Much is thereby lost, such as the importance of the distinction between those employees who are engaged to act on the owners behalf, exercising authority delegated to them ("managers") and those employees who are not engaged to exercise authority but rather be subject to it ("workers").

25. Palmer (1991) has also drawn an analogy between the situation of women farmers in sub-Saharan Africa and tax-payers, but she argues that it is the obligation to undertake the work of social reproduction which is akin to a tax. The problem here is that the process through which that obligation is enforced and met are not directly comparable to paying tax, since women undertake a great deal of the work of social reproduction for those who are weaker and have less authority, especially for children.

26. For further discussion on this issue see Roberts (1979), Guyer (1980); Gladwin and McMillan (1989); Whitehead (1990); Kabeer (1991); and Dey (1993).

27. Whitehead (1990) refers to "the growing evidence (in rural Africa) of struggles over new rights and obligations between household members: these are about the use of household labour, especially the labour input to cash crop supply, about the sexual designation of tasks and about the distribution of household income and how it is spent" (p. 58).

28. Further discussion of Palmer is outside the scope of this paper, but see Elson (1994).

REFERENCES

Addison, D., "The World Bank Revised Minimum Standard Model: Concepts and Issues," Policy, Planning and Research Paper WPS231 (Washington, DC: The World Bank, 1989).

Agarwal, Bina (Ed.), *Structures of Patriarchy* (New Delhi: Kali for Women; London: Zed Books, 1988).

Amsden, A. (Ed.), "The World Bank's The East Asian Miracle: Economic Growth and Public Policy," Special

Section, *World Development*, Vol. 22, No. 4 (1994), pp. 615–670.

Bacha, E.L., "Growth with limited supplies of foreign exchange: A reappraisal of the two-gap model," in M. Syrquin, L. Taylor and L. E. Westphal (Eds.), *Economic Structure and Performance: Essays in Honour of Hollis B. Chenery* (New York: Academic Press, 1984).

Beneria, L. and S. Feldman (Eds.), *Unequal Burden: Economic Crises, Persistent Poverty, and Women's Work* (Boulder, CO: Westview Press, 1992).

Berik, G., "Growth with gender inequity: Manufacturing employment in Taiwan," Mimeo (Salt Lake City, UT: Department of Economics, University of Utah, 1995).

Bevan, D. L., P. Collier and P. Gunning, *Peasants and Governments: an Economic Analysis* (Oxford: Oxford University Press, 1989).

Birdsall, N. and R. Sabot (Eds.), *Unfair Advantage: Labour Market Discrimination in Developing Countries* (Washington, DC: World Bank, 1991).

Bowles, S., "The production process in a competitive economy: Walrasian, neo-Hobbesian and Marxian models," *American Economic Review*, Vol. 75 (March, 1985).

Bowles, S., H. Gintis and B. Gustafsson, *Markets and Democracy* (Cambridge: Cambridge University Press, 1993).

Braun, J. von, "Effects of technological change in agriculture on food consumption and nutrition: Rice in a West African setting," *World Development*, Vol. 16, No. 9 (1988), pp. 1083–1098.

Braun, J. von and P. Webb, "The impact of new crop technology on the agricultural division of labour in a West African setting," *Economic Development and Cultural Change*, Vol. 37, No. 3 (1989), pp. 513–534.

Çağatay, N. and S. Ozler, "Feminization and structural adjustment: A cross country analysis," *World Development* (1995), this issue.

Calvo, Christina Malmberg, "Case study on intermediate means of transport: Bicycles and rural women in Uganda," SSATP Working Paper No. 12, Technical Department, Africa Region (Washington, DC: The World Bank, 1994).

Chenery, H. B. and A. M. Strout, "Foreign assistance and economic development," *American Economic Review*, Vol. 56, No. 4 (1966), pp. 679–733.

Cockburn, C., *Machinery of Dominance: Women, Men and Technical Knowhow* (London: Pluto Press, 1985).

Collier, Paul, "Gender aspects of labor allocation during structural adjustment — A theoretical framework and the Africa experience" in Susan Horton, Ravi Kanbar and Dipak Mazumdar (Eds.), *Labor Markets in an Era of Adjustment*, Vol. 1 (Washington, DC: The World Bank, 1994).

Collier, Paul, "The impact of adjustment of women," in L. Demery, M. Ferroni and C. Grootaert (Eds.), *Understanding the Effects of Policy Reform* (Washington, DC: The World Bank, 1993).

Collier, Paul, "The impact of adjustment on women," in World Bank, *Analysis Plan for Understanding the Social Dimensions of Adjustment*, SDA Unit, Africa Region (Washington, DC: World Bank, 1990).

Collier, Paul, "Women in development — Defining the issues", Policy, Planning and Research Working Paper No. 129 (Washington, DC: The World Bank, 1988).

Collier, Paul *et al.*, "Public services and household allocation

in Africa: Does gender matter?," Mimeo (Oxford: Centre for Study of African Economies, 1991).

Cornia, G. A., R. Jolly and F. Stewart, *Adjustment with a Human Face* (Oxford: Clarendon Press, 1987).

Darity, William, "The formal structure of a gender-segregated low income economy," *World Development* (1995), this issue.

Dasgupta, Partha, *An Inquiry into Well-Being and Destitution* (Oxford: Clarendon Press, 1993).

Demery, L. and T. Addison, "Stabilization and income distribution in developing countries," *World Development*, Vol. 15, No. 12 (1987), pp. 1483–1498.

Dey, J., "Gender asymmetries in intra household resource allocation in sub-Saharan Africa: some policy implications for land and labor productivity," Mimeo (Washington, DC: IFPRI, 1993).

Dwyer, D. and J. Bruce (Eds.), *A Home Divided: Women and Income in the Third World* (Stanford, CA: Stanford University Press, 1988).

Eatwell, J., M. Milgate and P. Newman (Eds.), *The New Palgrave: A Dictionary of Economics* (London: Macmillan, 1987).

Elson, Diane, "Household responses to stabilisation and structural adjustment: Male bias at the micro level," in Diane Elson (Ed.), *Male Bias in the Development Process* (Second Edition) (Manchester: Manchester University Press, 1995).

Elson, Diane, "Economic paradigms and their implications for models of development: The case of human development," Paper presented to Colloquium on Global Development 50 Years After Bretton Woods (Ottawa: North–South Institute, June 22–24, 1994a).

Elson, Diane, "People, development and international financial institutions: An interpretation of the Bretton Woods System", *Review of African Political Economy*, Vol. 21, No. 62 (1994b), pp. 511–524.

Elson, Diane, "Structural adjustment with gender awareness?," *Indian Journal of Gender Studies*, Vol. 1, No. 2 (1994c), pp. 149–167.

Elson, Diane, "Gender-aware analysis and development economics," *Journal of International Development*, Vol. 5, No. 2 (1993), pp. 237–247.

Elson, Diane, "From survival strategies to transformation strategies: Women's needs and structural adjustment," in L. Beneria and S. Feldman (Eds.), *Economic Crises, Persistent Poverty and Women's Work* (Boulder, CO: Westview Press, 1992).

Elson, Diane, "Male bias: An overview," in Diane Elson (Ed.), *Male Bias in the Development Process* (Manchester: Manchester University Press, 1991a).

Elson, Diane, "Male bias in macro-economics: The case of structural adjustment," in Diane Elson (Ed.), *Male Bias in the Development Process* (Manchester: Manchester University Press, 1991b).

Elson, Diane, "The impact of structural adjustment on women: Concepts and issues," in B. Onimode (Ed.), *The IMF, the World Bank and the African Debt*, Vol. 2, The Social and Political Impact (London: Zed Books, 1989).

Elson, Diane, "Market socialism or socialization of the market," *New Left Review*, No. 172 (November/December, 1988), pp. 3–44.

Elson, Diane and Rosemary McGee, "Gender equality, bilateral programme assistance and structural adjustment:

Policy and procedures," *World Development* (1995), this issue.

Elson, Diane and Ruth Pearson, "'Nimble fingers make cheap work': An analysis of women's employment in Third World export manufacturing," *Feminist Review*, No. 7 (Spring, 1981), pp. 87–107.

Feldman, S., "Crisis, Islam and gender in Bangladesh: The social construction of a female labour force," in L. Beneria and S. Feldman (Eds.), *Unequal Burden — Economic Crises, Persistent Poverty, and Women's Work* (Boulder, CO: Westview Press, 1992).

Fitzgerald, E. V. K., "The analytics of stabilization policy in the small-semi-industrialized economy," Development Economics Seminar Paper No. 7 (The Hague: Institute for Social Studies, 1988).

Folbre, Nancy, *Who Pays for the Kids? Gender and the Structures of Constraint* (London: Routledge, 1994).

Garcia, M., "Resource allocation and household welfare: A study of the impact of personal sources of income on food consumption, nutrition and health in the Philippines," Ph.D. thesis (The Hague: Institute of Social Studies, 1990).

Gillis, M., D. Perkins, M. Roemer and D. Snodgrass, *Economics of Development*, Fourth edition (New York: Norton, 1992).

Gladwin, C. and D. McMillan, "Is a turnaround in Africa possible without helping African women to farm?," *Economic Development and Cultural Change*, Vol. 37, No. 2 (1989), pp. 345–369.

Green, F., "Neoclassical and Marxian conceptions of production," *Cambridge Journal of Economics*, Vol. 12, No. 3 (1988).

Guyer, J., "Household budgets and women's incomes," African Studies Centre Working Paper 28 (Boston, MA: Boston University, 1980).

Haddad, L., J. Hoddinott and H. Alderman, "Intrahousehold resource allocation: An overview," Policy Research Working Paper No. 1255 (Washington, DC: World Bank, 1994).

Hoddinott, J. and L. Haddad, "Does female income share influence household expenditure patterns?," Mimeo (Oxford: Trinity College, Oxford University, 1992).

Hodgson, G., *Economics and Institutions* (Cambridge: Polity Press, 1988).

Howes, C. and A. Singh, "Long term trends in the world economy: The gender dimension," *World Development* (1995), this issue.

Humphries, Jane, "Economics, gender and equal opportunities'" Paper presented at the Conference on the Economics of Equal Opportunity (Manchester: Equal Opportunities Commission, October 10–11, 1994).

Humphries, Jane and Jill Rubery, "The reconstruction of the supply side of the labour market: The relative autonomy of social reproduction," *Cambridge Journal of Economics*, Vol. 8, No. 4 (1984), pp. 331–346.

Jones, C., "Intrahousehold bargaining in response to the introduction of new crops: A case study from North Cameroon," in J. L. Moock (Ed.), *Understanding Africa's Rural Households and Farming Systems* (Boulder, CO: Westview Press, 1986).

Kabeer, Naila, *Reversed Realities — Gender Hierarchies in Development Thought* (London: Verso, 1994).

Kabeer, N., "Gender, production and well-being: Rethinking

the household economy," Discussion Paper No. 228 (Brighton: Institute of Development Studies, 1991).

Kreuger, A., "The political economy of the rent-seeking society," *American Economic Review*, Vol. 64 (1974), pp. 291–303.

Kumar, S., "Impact of subsidised rice on food consumption and nutrition in Kerala," Research Report 5 (Washington, DC: IFPRI, 1979).

Lal, Deepak, "A simple framework for analysing various real aspects of stabilisation and structural adjustment policies," *Journal of Development Studies*, Vol. 25, No. 3 (1989).

Lal, Deepak, "The real effects of stabilization and structural adjustment policies," World Bank Staff Working Papers No. 636 (Washington, DC: World Bank, 1984).

Lebowitz, M., "Analytical Marxism and the Marxian theory of crisis," *Cambridge Journal of Economics*, Vol. 18, No. 2 (1994), pp. 163–179.

Lockwood, Matthew, "Engendering adjustment or adjusting gender? Some new approaches to women and development in Africa," Discussion Paper No. 315 (Brighton: Institute of Development Studies, 1992).

Marx, K., *Capital*, Vol. I (Harmondsworth: Penguin Books, 1976).

Mbilinyi, M., "Structural adjustment, agribusiness and rural women in Tanzania," in H. Bernstein et al. (Eds.), *The Food Question* (London: Earthscan Publications, 1990).

Moock, P., "The efficiency of women as farm managers: Kenya," *American Journal of Agricultural Economics*, Vol. 58 (1976), pp. 831–835.

Moser, C., "Adjustment from below: Low-income women, time and the triple role in Guayaquil, Ecuador," in H. Afshar and C. Dennis (Eds.), *Women and Adjustment Policies in the Third World* (London: Macmillan, 1992).

Moser, C., "The impact of recession and structural adjustment policies at the micro-level: Low income women and their households in Guayquil, Ecuador," in *Poor Women and Economic Crises: The Invisible Adjustment* (Santiago: UNICEF, 1989).

Mosley, Paul, Jane Harrigan and John Toye, *Aid and Power: The World Bank and Policy Based Lending* (London: Routledge, 1991).

Ongaro, W. A., "Adoption of new farming technology: A case study of maize production in Western Kenya," Ph.D. thesis (Gothenberg: University of Gothenberg, 1988).

Pagano, Ugo, "Property rights, asset specificity, and the division of labour under alternative capitalist relations," *Cambridge Journal of Economics*, Vol. 15, No. 3 (1991), pp. 315–342.

Pagano, U., *Work and Welfare in Economic Theory* (Oxford: Basil Blackwell, 1985).

Pahl, J., "The allocation of money within marriage," *Sociological Review*, Vol. 32 (1983), pp. 237–264.

Palmer, Ingrid, *Gender and Population in the Adjustment of African Economies: Planning for Change* (Geneva: ILO, 1991).

Pearson, Ruth, "Gender issues in industrialization," in T. Hewitt, H. Johnson and D. Weld (Eds.), *Industrialization and Development* (Oxford: Oxford University Press, 1992).

Picchio, Antonella, *Social Reproduction — The Political Economy of the Labour Market* (Cambridge: Cambridge University Press, 1992).

1868   WORLD DEVELOPMENT

Quisumbing, A., "Women in agriculture" (Washington, DC: World Bank Education and Social Policy Department, 1993).

Roberts, P., "The integration of women into the development process: Some conceptual problems," *IDS Bulletin*, Vol. 10, No. 3 (1979), pp. 60–67.

Rodriguez, L., "Housing and household survival strategies in urban areas: A case study of the Solandes settlement: Quito, Ecuador," in F. Meer (Ed.), *Poverty in the 1990s — the Responses of Urban Women* (Paris: UNESCO, 1994).

Rose, P., "Female education and adjustment programs: A crosscountry statistical analysis," *World Development* (1995), this issue.

Ruccio, D.F., "When failure becomes success: Class and the debate over stabilization and adjustment," *World Development*, Vol. 19, No. 10 (1991), pp. 1315–1334.

Sawyer, M., *The Challenge of Radical Political Economy* (Hemel Hempstead: Harvester Wheatsheaf, 1989).

Schoepf, B. and W. Engundu, "Women and structural adjustment in Zaire," in Christina Gladwin (Ed.), *Structural Adjustment and African Women Farmers* (Gainesville, FL: University of Florida Press, 1991).

Seguino, S., "Gender wage discrimination and export-led growth in South Korea," Paper presented at Meeting of Allied Social Science Association (Boston, MA: January 2–5, 1994).

Sen, G., "Alternative economics from a gender perspective," *Development* (1995), pp. 10–13.

Smith, J. B. and M. Stelcner, "Modelling economic behaviour in Peru's informal urban retail sector," PHRD Working Paper No. 469 (Washington, DC: World Bank, 1990).

Standing, G., "Global feminization through flexible labor," *World Development*, Vol. 17, No. 7 (1989), pp. 1077–1096.

Tanski, J. M., "The impact of crisis, stabilization and structural adjustment on women in Lima, Peru," *World Development*, Vol. 22, No. 11 (1994), pp. 1627–1642.

Tarp, Finn, *Stabilization and Structural Adjustment* (London: Routledge, 1993).

Taylor, L., "Environmental and gender feedbacks in macroeconomics," *World Development* (1995), this issue.

Taylor, L., "Stabilization and growth in developing countries: A structuralist approach," Fundamentals of Pure and Applied Economics, Vol. 29, Economic Develop-ment Studies Section (New York: Harwood Academic, 1989).

Taylor, L., *Varieties of Stabilization Experience: Towards Sensible Macroeconomics in the Third World* (Oxford, Clarendon Press, 1988).

Tinker, I. (Ed.), *Persistent Inequalities: Women and World Development* (Oxford: Oxford University Press, 1990).

Tripp, R., "Farmers and traders — some economic determinants of nutritional status in northern Ghana," *Journal of Tropical Pediactrics*, Vol. 27 (1981), pp. 15–22.

Tzannatos, Zafiris, "Potential gains from the elimination of labor market differentials," in "Women's Employment and Pay in Latin America Part 1 Overview and Methodology," Regional Studies Program Report No. 10 (Washington, DC: World Bank, 1992).

Walters, Bernard, "Engendering macroeconomics: A reconsideration of growth theory," *World Development* (1995), this issue.

Whitehead, Ann, "Food crisis and gender conflict in the African countryside," in Henry Bernstein *et al.* (Eds.), *The Food Question* (London: Earthscan Publications, 1990).

Whitehead, A., "Some preliminary notes on the subordination of women," *IDS Bulletin*, Vol. 10, No. 3 (1979).

World Bank, *Enhancing Women's Participation in Economic Development* (Washington, DC: World Bank, 1994).

World Bank, *Making Adjustment Work for the Poor* (Washington, DC: World Bank, 1990a).

World Bank, *World Development Report 1990* (Oxford: Oxford University Press, 1990b).

Young, Kate, *Planning Development with Women* (London: Macmillan, 1993).

[17]

 Pergamon

World Development, Vol. 23, No. 11, pp. 1883–1894, 1995
Elsevier Science Ltd
Printed in Great Britain
0305–750X/95 $9.50 + 0.00

0305–750X(95)00086–0

Feminization of the Labor Force: The Effects of Long-Term Development and Structural Adjustment

NILÜFER ÇAĞATAY
University of Utah, Salt Lake City, U.S.A.

and

ŞULE ÖZLER
University of California, Los Angeles, U.S.A.

Summary. — Using crosscountry data pooled for 1985 and 1990, we analyze the relationship between women's share of the labor force and the processes of long-term economic development, and macroeconomic changes associated with structural adjustment. We find that the relationship between long-term development and women's share of the labor force is U-shaped. Controlling for the feminization U, we also find that structural adjustment policies have led to an increase in feminization of the labor force via worsening income distribution and increased openness.

1. INTRODUCTION

Evidence suggests that gender composition of the labor force exhibits a systematic change through long-term economic development. During initial stages of commercialization and transition to capitalist development, women's labor force participation rate (LFPR) declines and at a more advanced stage of development it increases. Underlying this U-shaped pattern is increased commercialization, increasing significance of nonagricultural sectors, urbanization and the accompanying changes in education and fertility behavior. These long-term changes interact with women's responsibility as reproducers and producers, resulting in the U-shaped pattern of women's LFPR. In contrast, men's LFPR has been observed to fall slowly with economic development.

Women's share of the labor force also varies with macroeconomic fluctuations and shifts in macroeconomic policies. Standing (1989) has attributed the global feminization of the labor force since the early 1980s, to supply-side macroeconomic policies and structural adjustment. Feminist economists also have been theoretically and empirically investigating the relationship between cycles and feminization of the labor force especially in the case of industrialized economies.[1]

Changes in the feminization of the labor force, in turn, have been argued to have macroeconomic consequences. For example, United Nations (1994) explains the mass unemployment of the 1980s and 1990s in industrialized economies by the rise in women's labor force participation rates.[2] Ertürk and Çağatay (this issue) consider the macroeconomic consequences of cyclical and secular changes in feminization.

In this paper we empirically analyze the relationship between women's share of the labor force and the processes of long-term economic development, and short-term macroeconomic changes. We focus on short-term changes in macroeconomic indicators that are associated with structural adjustment policies. We investigate if and how adjustment policies have led to a feminization of the labor force, controlling for the U pattern associated with long-term development processes. In particular, we ask if changes in income distribution and outward orientation of the economy operate as the transmission mechanisms for feminization. For our analysis we pool crosscountry data for 1985 and 1990.

The main findings of our paper are that structural adjustment policies lead to a feminization of the labor force, through changes in income distribution as reflected in a reduction of the share of wages in manufacturing value added; and through shifts in the outward orientation of the economy as measured by the increase in the ratio of exports to GNP.

The paper is organized as follows: in section 2, we

1884   WORLD DEVELOPMENT

review the literature on development and women's LFPR, and structural adjustment and feminization. Section 3 contains our empirical results. In section 4 we conclude with a discussion of further research questions.

2. FEMINIZATION OF THE LABOR FORCE

(a) *Economic development and feminization of the labor force*

Traditional development economists and modernization theorists have viewed economic development as a process in which economic growth and women's incorporation to the labor force would go hand in hand.[3] This view was challenged by Boserup (1970) who argued that women were "marginalized" during economic development. She pointed out that men's privileged access to new technologies and education leads to growing productivity differences between men and women, and hence a decline in women's share of the labor force. In the agricultural sector, the growing productivity differences would cause women to withdraw from agricultural sector.[4] In nonagricultural sectors, based in urban areas, women, would again be disadvantaged for two reasons. First, productivity differences would lead employers to prefer men. Second, it would be more difficult for women to combine reproduction and production activities in urban work settings in contrast to rural settings, where women's activities of production are more compatible with their activities of reproduction.[5] With urbanization and industrialization, female-dominated home-based production would be replaced by male-dominated factory production.[6] Hence, urbanization and the emergence of the factory system is associated with the downward portion of the U pattern.

Women's labor force participation is likely to increase, however, with further economic development. Industrialization, more education for women, commodification of domestic labor, and falling fertility rates give rise to the U-pattern both over time for individual countries and also cross-sectionally at any moment in time (Oppenheimer, 1970; Boserup, 1990).

Overall, empirical evidence supports the existence of the feminization U. Some studies have found no relationship or have found a linear relationship between economic development and women's LFPR.[7] More recent studies suggest, however, the presence of the feminization U. Using 1965 and 1970 data for 70 countries, Pampel and Tanaka (1986) have found that women's LFPR falls and then rises with economic development. Using cross-section data for more than 100 countries, Goldin (1994) also finds that women's LFPR exhibits a quadratic relationship with respect to the log of per capita income.[8]

Historical studies of what are now advanced capitalist countries suggest a similar feminization U. Studying the evolution of organization of production in France and England between 1700 and the present, Tilly and Scott (1987) also find evidence for the feminization U.[9] Hartmann (1979) analyzes the transition from the family industry system to the factory system in the United States and England, and emphasizes the role of men workers in restricting women's roles in the labor market, thus providing an explanation of the downward portion of the U as well as the origin of gender segregation in wage labor.[10] Goldin (1994) discusses the U-shaped female labor force function for the US economy.[11]

Between 1950 and 1980, most advanced industrialized countries experienced feminization along with most Eastern European, East Asian, Caribbean, Latin American, Middle Eastern and North African economies. Sub-Saharan economies mostly underwent a process of defeminization (Blau and Ferber, 1992). Within and across regions, however, significant variations remained. In 1980 sub-Saharan economies as a whole remained more feminized compared with all the other regions with the exception of Eastern Europe. Economies with similar levels of industrialization or per capita income exhibited vastly different gender compositions of employment.

Besides the level of economic development, industrialization and demographic factors such as fertility and education patterns, cultural and ideological factors also have an influence on women's LFPR. For example, the economies of Eastern Europe represent cases of highly feminized labor forces as a result of the socialist commitment to and imperative for women's economic mobilization. On the other hand, Islam and Catholicism are often discussed as impediments to women's participation in the labor force. Cultural and ideological factors may play a role in the reduction of measured LFPR of women in several ways. First, "the male breadwinner" or "family wage" ideologies, stronger in particular cultural settings than in others, may lower women's LFPR. Second, male breadwinner ideologies may continue to have a life even when they do not accurately reflect the conditions of economic life leading to underreporting of women's production activities.[12]

(b) *Structural adjustment and feminization of the labor force*

Adjustment programs typically are constituted of macroeconomic stabilization policies in conjunction with trade reforms. One consequence of these programs is the expansion of the export-oriented sector. Export-oriented industries in developing countries tend to be feminized. These industries are also labor-intensive, and use "unskilled" labor. Women's "comparative advantage" as workers in export-oriented industries or export-processing zones with especially labor-intensive production requiring little or no formal training has been widely documented through case studies.[13] Wood (1991) shows that the growth of exports has increased the relative demand for female labor in manufacturing industries of developing countries between the 1960s and the mid-1980s. With the advent of structural adjustment policies, under the pressure of global competition, employers could be favoring women workers since women receive lower wages, leading to a process of substitution of women for men (Standing, 1989). Trade reforms, then, "pull women into the labor market" because they are "cheap" and more "flexible" workers.[14]

Evidence also shows, however, that feminization need not follow adjustment policies or that feminization associated with export-orientation can be reversible (Çağatay and Berik, 1991, 1994; Benería, 1994; Pearson, 1991). A process of defeminization can result from adoption of techniques that require more "skilled" labor or greater mechanization.

Another impact of adjustment policies is to push women into the labor force. It is well known that adjustment policies lead to a worsened income distribution. Because of this effect, more family members among low-income groups are forced to seek paid employment to compensate for declining family incomes. Hence women are pushed into the labor market.

3. EMPIRICAL INVESTIGATION

Our empirical investigation is aimed at analyzing whether adjustment programs have led to feminization of the labor force. In particular, we ask whether in countries where trade openness has increased as well as in those where the income share of workers in manufacturing industries has declined, female share of employment has increased. Prior to a more detailed discussion of our results in section (c), we describe our estimation model in section (a), the empirical construction of the variables we use and the data we employ in section (b). We present alternative specifications in section (d) to demonstrate the robustness of our findings.

(a) An empirical model

The model estimated here builds upon existing crosscountry studies of Pampel and Tanaka (1986) and Goldin (1994). The primary empirical result established in those studies is that the hypothesis of the feminization U (FEMU) cannot be rejected. In other words, women's LFPR is a quadratic function of the log of gross national product (GNP) per capita or

some other indicator of economic development. We are concerned with asking a somewhat different question, namely whether structural adjustment has led to feminization U is taken into account. We use a panel data set to conduct our analysis.

The following equation describes the basic structure of the model we estimate in this paper:

$$FEMINIZATION = C + LGNP + LGNP^2 +$$
$$DEMOGRAPHIC + OTHER ECONOMIC +$$
$$ADJUSTMENT + U \qquad (1)$$

where FEMINIZATION is a measure of feminization of the labor force. C represents the constant term. LGNP, log of GNP per capita, and $LGNP^2$, the square of LGNP, capture the feminization U. We incorporate OTHER ECONOMIC and DEMOGRAPHIC variables to capture the observable characteristics of countries that are theoretically relevant for feminization of the labor force. ADJUSTMENT is our measure of structural adjustment programs. U is the random error term distributed normally with mean zero.

We incorporate various DEMOGRAPHIC characteristics that have been discussed in the theoretical and empirical literature. The most important are levels of fertility, urbanization and female education. We incorporate variables in order to control for their influence on the gender composition of the labor force.

We include OTHER ECONOMIC variables to capture economic characteristics other than GNP variables that might be relevant for feminization. The theoretical literature suggests that the degree of feminization of the labor force could be influenced by trade openness, as well as changes in income distribution. We also include the degree of expansion as another relevant variable. Sustained economic expansion could create tight labor markets and in general allow greater employment opportunities for women. Hence we incorporate average values of the variables in these three categories.

We take two approaches to constructing an empirical measure of the ADJUSTMENT variable. The first approach is to construct a dummy variable indicating the countries that have undertaken adjustment programs. As we discuss in the data section, there are several methods of construction, such as using a simple versus weighted dummy variable.

The second approach is an attempt to identify the economic impact of adjustment programs. The three economic categories incorporated under OTHER ECONOMIC (degree of expansion, trade openness, income distribution) are also precisely those that are known to have been affected by adjustment programs in a number of countries. Our second approach then is to construct measures of the degree of change stemming from adjustment programs in these three categories. Employing the changes of the variables along with their long-term averages allows us to separate the impact of the two.

We estimate the model by ordinary least squares. We attempt to control for unobservable characteristics cross-sectionally or over time by using a fixed effects model. A standard problem in using panel (or cross-section) data for countries is that the sample size is usually not large enough to allow use of individual country indicators. Hence, following convention, we use geographic region indicators, which capture the ideological and cultural characteristics that might influence the degree of feminization.[15] We incorporate year indicators to control for unobservable changes over time.

(b) *Measurement and data discussion*

(i) *Measurement*

We constructed the data from several World Bank data bases (World Bank 1993a, 1993b, 1993c, 1990). We pool data for 165 countries and for the years 1985 and 1990. We pool data only for two years because the degree of feminization of the labor force changes slowly over time. In addition, most of the adjustment programs have been undertaken since the early 1980s. The number of countries that enter our sample is reduced to 96 because of missing variables (the sample size varies somewhat in alternative specifications). The empirical construction of the variables in equation (1) is as follows:

FEMINIZATION is measured by the female share of the labor force (*FSH*).

LGNP is the log of GNP per capita measured by the real dollar value of gross national product in 1987 dollars and as we indicated above, $LGNP^2$ is the square of *LGNP*.

OTHER ECONOMIC variables contain three categories of variables: expansion, openness and income distribution. For each of these categories, we use long-term average values. Specifically, for 1985 we use averages of yearly data for 1975–85 and for 1990 we use averages for 1975–90.

Expansion: *INGP*, constructed as investment share of GNP is one approach to measuring expansion. Alternatively, we use GRGD, growth rate of GDP.

Openness: We use exports to GNP ratio, referred to as XGP from here on.

Income distribution: Inflation is one plausible measure of distributional changes. We construct the inflation variable *INFLAT* using consumer price indices. Though it has been suggested that high inflation worsens income distribution, it is an indirect measure of it. As an alternative, labor's share of manufacturing value added, *LSMVA*, is used. This alternative has two potential weaknesses in comparison to inflation rate. It only captures distribution with respect to

manufacturing sector workers, and it is more prone to measurement error than the inflation rate.[16]

DEMOGRAPHIC is measured in three alternative ways. These are: share of urban population, *URB*; total fertility rate, *FER*; and percentage of school-age females enrolled in secondary schools, the secondary enrollment ratio for women, *SECED*.

ADJUSTMENT is measured in five alternative ways:

— All adjusters, *ALA*: This variable takes the value of one for countries that have undertaken either a World Bank adjustment program or International Monetary Fund agreements during 1978–90.

— Early intensive adjusters, *EIA*: This is a dummy variable based on the World Bank's (1990) classification of adjusting economies. It takes the value of one for those countries that have received two structural adjustment loans (SALs) or three Adjustment Operations or more, with the first adjustment operation in 1985 or before.

— World Bank adjusters, *WBA*: This variable takes the value of one for any country that has undertaken a World Bank adjustment program up to two years prior to the year in the sample (i.e. during 1978–83 for 1985 and during 1978–88 for 1990). The reason for the two-year lag is to allow time for the adjustment programs to have an impact on the economy.

— Intensity of World Bank adjusters, *WBA#*: This is a weighted dummy variable version of *WBA*. The weights we use are the number of adjustments undertaken during the period as specified above.

— Economic impact of World Bank adjusters: This again is a weighted dummy variable. We construct these variables to take into account the impact of adjustment programs on expansion, openness and income distribution variables. Let us take XGP as an example and describe our procedure in detail. Suppose a country has undertaken its first World Bank agreement in 1986.

The adjustment variable for 1985 is zero. The adjustment variable for 1990 is:

$$WXGP\# = (AXGP\ 1988{-}90 - AXGP\ 1975{-}85)/ \atop (AXGP\ 1975{-}85) \times WBA\# \qquad (2)$$

where, *AXGP* year 1–year *N* stands for average *XGP* for the period between years specified, and *WBA#* is as described above. We leave out the year of the adjustment and the year following it in computing the percentage change in *AXGP* to allow time for the programs to have an impact on the economy. This variable is an attempt to capture the impact of adjustment programs on the variable of concern by taking into account the intensity of the program undertaken. Here, consistent with World Bank interpretations, intensity is measured with the number of adjustment programs undertaken during the period. Using the same method we also computed *WINGP#*, *WGRGD#*, *WINFLAT#*, and *WLSMVA#*, corresponding to *INGP*, *GRGD*, *INFLAT*, and *LSMVA*, respectively. Alternatively, we recalculated these variables without the weights (*WBA#*). The unweighted variables, corresponding to *WXGP#*, *WINGP#*, *WGRGD#*, *WIN-FLAT#* and *WLSMVA#* are *WXGP*, *WINGP*, *WGRGD*, *WINFLAT* and *WLSMVA*.

The region dummies we use in the regression are based on the following classification of regions: sub-Saharan Africa (*AFRICA*), South Asia (*SOUTHA*), Middle East and North Africa (*MEAST*), Caribbean (*CARAIB*), Latin America (*LATIN*), East Asia and the Pacific (*ASIA*), Former Socialist Economies (*XSOC*), industrialized economies (*INDUST*).

(ii) *Data description*

To describe the salient features of our data, we present the means and standard deviations of the variables that enter into the estimations in Table 1. This table presents the summary statistics for adjusters and nonadjusters separately, allowing us to compare these two groups. The adjuster indicator we used to separate the sample in this table is *WBA*. In other words, adjusters are those countries that have taken an adjustment loan from the World Bank during the period. It is important to recall that these comparisons do not yield any information on the impact of adjustment programs. They are only descriptions of long-term characteristics of adjuster and nonadjuster countries.

Overall, Table 1 indicates that the mean values of the variables differ when we compare the adjusters and the nonadjusters. An inspection of the standard

deviations, however, indicates that these differences are not statistically significant. Nevertheless, a comparison of the means of the variables indicates that the sample of adjusters on average have higher values for *FSH*, *INFLAT*, and *FER*. In contrast the adjusters have lower means for the variables *LGNP*, $LGNP^2$, *XGP*, *INGP*, *LSMVA*, *SECED*, and *URB*.

To ensure that the results of the comparisons between adjusters and nonadjusters are not a consequence of the presence of industrialized countries in the sample, all of which are nonadjusters, we computed the summary statistics excluding them. The qualitative results of the comparisons continue to hold.

We also inspected the comparisons by region. Regional comparisons do not follow the same pattern. For example, in Asia adjusters have lower levels of *GNP*, *FER* and *XGP* as well as a higher level of *SECED* in comparison to nonadjusters.

Finally, a note of caution on the quality of the data is in order. As we discussed in section 2, female share of labor force or female labor force participation levels are subject to measurement error. This error can be a consequence of undercounting or reporting errors in compiling the statistics for formal labor markets. Undercounting is a particular problem for those countries where the agricultural sector or the informal sector is large in the economy. This error would not be a particular concern when the error of measurement in the explained variable, *FSH*, is not correlated with the errors of measurement in the explanatory variables.

(c) *Results*

In this section we will be discussing two alternative empirical specifications of equation (1). These two alternatives, which we refer to as Model I and Model II, differ only in terms of whether the income distribution is measured using *INFLAT* or *LSMVA*. The expansion variable is *INGP* and the demographic variable is *URB* in both specifications. We will discuss other alternative specifications in section (d) in the context of addressing the robustness of our primary results.

We should first note that the results we present below are obtained from the pooled data that contain information for both 1985 and 1990. The "F" tests we computed indicated that we cannot reject the null hypothesis that the two years are from the same sample at high levels of significance. Hence, we discuss only the estimations using the pooled data.

Table 2, based on Model I, presents the results of estimations that use the adjustment variables which do not incorporate the economic impact of adjustment programs, i.e., adjustment variables *ALA*, *EIA*, *WBA*, *WBA#*. In the first column of Table 2 is the basic specification of Model I without the incorporation of any

Table 1. *Sample statistics*

Variable	Adjusters (WBA = 1) Number = 66		Nonadjusters (WBA = 0) Number = 125	
	Mean	St. Dev.	Mean	St. Dev.
FSH	34.15	8.87	30.62	11.19
LGNP	42.45	12.17	56.90	22.59
XGP	0.30	0.19	0.34	0.26
INGP	23.17	6.89	28.58	11.88
INFLAT	70.89	213.10	31.39	113.57
LSMVA	30.50	8.82	36.42	13.57
WXGP#	0.79	3.55	0	0
WINGP#	0.023	1.32	0	0
WINFLAT#	12.76	66.85	0	0
WLSMVA#	-0.42	0.87	0	0
URB	44.62	21.22	49.88	23.97
FER	4.33	1.95	4.24	1.94
SECED	38.93	28.29	52.15	31.53
EIA	0.76	0.43	0.07	0.25
WBA#	2.65	1.81	0	0
ALA	1.0	1.0	0.09	0.29

of the measures of adjustment. An inspection of column one indicates that the *FEMU* hypothesis cannot be rejected at high levels of confidence in our sample, as indicated by the "t" values of the positive *LGNP* parameter and the negative *LGNP²* parameter. On the other hand, the long-term averages of the economic variables do not have any statistically significant impact on the female share of employment. This can be seen by inspecting the rows corresponding to *XGP*, *INGP* and *INFLAT*. The demographic variable *URB* has a negative parameter value and is statistically significant at high levels of confidence. An increase in the urban share of population leads to a defeminiza-

tion of the labor force, consistent with the theoretical arguments. The intercept terms for African, Caribbean and Former Socialist economies are statistically significantly higher than the omitted group, industrialized economies. The Middle East and North Africa, and South Asia intercept terms, on the other hand, are lower than the industrialized country intercept term. Finally, Latin American, Asian and the year indicators are not statistically significant.

The remaining columns of Table 2 incorporate alternative measures of the adjustment variable. All the adjustment variables have a positive and statistically significant impact on *FSH*. This can be seen by

Table 2. *Model I — Adjustment variables without economic variables**

LGNP	1.30†	1.38†	1.42†	1.38†	1.50†
	(0.32)	(0.32)	(0.33)	(0.32)	(0.31)
LGNP²	−16.25†	−17.12†	−17.83†	−17.12†	−18.71†
	(4.74)	(6.47)	(4.75)	(4.67)	(4.58)
AFRICA	8.77†	7.83†	7.91‡	7.82†	8.21†
	(3.15)	(3.12)	(3.15)	(3.12)	(3.02)
ASIA	4.84	3.88	3.93	3.88	4.18†
	(3.22)	(3.19)	(3.22)	(3.19)	(3.10)
CARAIB	7.96‡	7.91‡	7.57‡	7.91‡	7.29‡
	(3.41)	(3.35)	(3.38)	(3.35)	(3.27)
LATIN	−1.43	−1.62	−1.52	−1.62	−0.90
	(3.17)	(3.12)	(3.14)	(3.12)	(3.04)
MEAST	−10.04†	−10.09†	−10.04†	−10.09†	−10.55†
	(2.97)	(2.92)	(2.94)	(2.92)	(2.85)
SOUTHA	−9.39†	−9.58†	−9.85†	−9.58‡	−9.33†
	(3.80)	(3.73)	(3.76)	(3.73)	(3.64)
XSOC	17.89†	17.47†	18.58†	17.47†	18.55†
	(3.52)	(3.47)	(3.50)	(3.47)	(3.38)
DUM85	0.39	0.57	−0.40	0.57	1.21
	(1.07)	(1.11)	(1.05)	(1.11)	(1.09)
XGP	−3.53	−3.18	−2.59	−3.18	−2.63
	(2.43)	(2.40)	(2.45)	(2.40)	(2.34)
INGP	−0.004	0.006	−0.003	0.006	0.001
	(0.07)	(0.07)	(0.07)	(0.07)	(0.07)
INFLAT	0.003	0.002	0.003	0.002	0.003
	(0.003)	(0.003)	(0.003)	(0.003)	(0.003)
URB	−0.13†	−0.14†	−0.15†	−0.14†	−0.16†
	(0.04)	(0.04)	(0.04)	(0.04)	(0.04)
ALA		2.13§			
		(1.17)			
EIA			2.68‡		
			(1.24)		
WBA				3.15†	
				(1.19)	
WBA#					1.42†
					(0.34)
CONSTANT	83.91	85.01	89.21	84.99	89.55
	(16.36)	(16.27)	(16.38)	(16.10)	(15.75)
R²	.60	.61	.61	.62	.64
Adj R²	.57	.58	.58	.59	.61
Number of observations	193	193	193	193	193

*Numbers in parentheses are standard errors.
†Significant at 99% level of confidence.
‡Significant at 95% level of confidence.
§Significant at 90% level of confidence.

inspecting the rows corresponding to *ALA, EIA, WBA,* and *WBA#.* In other words, countries that have undertaken adjustment programs have experienced feminization of their labor force. This result is robust to all alternative measures of adjustment indicators.

The next step we undertake is an attempt to identify the channels through which adjustment programs lead to feminization of the labor force. In Table 3, we present results from estimations that use *WXGP#, WINFLAT#,* and *WINGP#* one at a time. Finally in column four we present results from an estimation that employs all three simultaneously. The primary result here is that the coefficient of *WXGP#* is positive and

statistically significant at high levels of confidence. This result suggests that in intensively adjusting countries that have experienced an improved performance of exports share of GNP, there has been a feminization of the labor force. Other performance variables for adjusting countries, *WINGP#, WLSMVA#,* do not have a statistically significant impact on feminization.

We next turn to Model II. The results in Tables 4 and 5 are based on an estimation which employs labor share of manufacturing value added (*LSMVA*) instead of the inflation rate (*INFLAT*). Again we first focus on simple adjustment dummy variables, and later focus on the adjustment dummy variables with economic

Table 3. *Model I — Adjustment variables with economic variables**

LGNP	1.43†	1.27†	1.27†	1.38†
	(0.32)	(0.33)	(0.33)	(0.33)
LGNP²	−18.15†	−15.94†	−15.93†	−17.59†
	(4.64)	(4.77)	(4.86)	(4.78)
AFRICA	8.99†	8.84†	8.64†	8.91†
	(3.08)	(3.16)	(3.19)	(3.11)
ASIA	5.00	4.89	4.63	4.83
	(3.13)	(3.23)	(3.25)	(3.15)
CARAIB	7.87‡	7.82‡	7.77‡	7.57‡
	(3.31)	(3.42)	(3.43)	(3.33)
LATIN	−0.88	−1.39	−1.78	−1.20
	(3.08)	(3.18)	(3.20)	(3.10)
MEAST	−11.38†	−10.03†	−10.27†	−11.62†
	(2.91)	(2.98)	(3.00)	(2.92)
SOUTHA	−9.23†	−9.28†	−9.53†	−9.27†
	(3.71)	(3.80)	(3.84)	(3.74)
XSOC	18.83†	17.83†	17.64†	18.55†
	(3.56)	(3.53)	(3.61)	(3.59)
DUM85	−0.01	−0.36	−0.46	−0.04
	(1.04)	(1.07)	(1.09)	(1.06)
XGP	−2.78	−3.47	−3.31	−2.55
	(2.36)	(2.44)	(2.46)	(2.39)
INGP	0.007	0.006	0.006	0.01
	(0.07)	(0.07)	(0.07)	(0.07)
INFLAT	0.003	0.003	0.005	0.005
	(0.003)	(0.003)	(0.005)	(0.004)
URB	−0.14†	−0.13†	−0.13†	−0.14†
	(0.04)	(0.04)	(0.04)	(0.04)
WXGP#	0.92†			0.93†
	(0.24)			(0.24)
WINGP#		0.48		0.34
		(0.67)		(0.69)
WINFLAT#			−0.01	−0.01
			(0.01)	(0.01)
CONSTANT	89.86	82.55	83.04	87.93
	(16.09)	(16.69)	(16.86)	(16.67)
R²	.63	.60	.60	.63
Adj R²	.60	.57	.57	.60
Number of observations	191	193	188	187

*Numbers in parentheses are standard errors.
†Significant at 99% level of confidence.
‡Significant at 95% level of confidence.

Table 4. *Model II — Adjustment variables without economic variables**

LGNP	0.63§	0.67§	0.70	0.72‡	0.84‡
	(0.34)	(0.35)	(0.35)	(0.34)	(0.34)
LGNP²	−7.74	−8.25	−8.80§	−8.92§	−10.37‡
	(5.16)	(5.18)	(5.17)	(5.12)	(5.02)
AFRICA	7.95‡	7.33‡	7.14‡	6.78‡	7.44‡
	(3.43)	(3.49)	(3.46)	(3.44)	(3.29)
ASIA	2.94	2.41	2.06	1.73	2.29
	(3.56)	(3.59)	(3.58)	(3.55)	(3.43)
CARAIB	4.63	4.59	4.35	4.43	3.40
	(3.85)	(3.85)	(3.83)	(3.8)	(3.72)
LATIN	−4.72	−5.11	−5.08	−5.14	−4.25
	(3.37)	(3.39)	(3.36)	(3.33)	(3.25)
MEAST	−15.08†	−15.10†	−15.19†	−15.17†	−15.62†
	(2.94)	(2.94)	(2.93)	(2.91)	(2.84)
SOUTHA	−10.38†	−10.66†	−10.75†	−10.80†	−10.23†
	(4.15)	(4.16)	(4.13)	(4.10)	(4.00)
XSOC	13.54†	13.30†	13.96†	12.94†	14.20†
	(3.80)	(3.81)	(3.79)	(3.76)	(3.67)
DUM85	0.01	0.43	0.01	1.06	1.70
	(1.20)	(1.27)	(1.20)	(1.27)	(1.24)
XGP	−5.83‡	−5.54‡	−4.98‡	−5.15‡	−4.80‡
	(2.75)	(2.76)	(2.79)	(2.74)	(2.67)
INGP	0.08	0.09	0.08	0.09	0.09
	(0.09)	(0.09)	(0.09)	(0.09)	(0.08)
LSMVA	−0.01	−0.022	−0.02	−0.02	−0.01
	(0.06)	(0.06)	(0.06)	(0.06)	(0.06)
URB	−0.044	−0.053	−0.058	−0.05	−0.06
	(0.044)	(0.04)	(0.04)	(0.04)	(0.04)
ALA	1.46				
	(1.35)				
EIA			2.30‡		
			(1.39)		
WBA				3.15‡	
				(1.37)	
WBA#					1.46†
					(0.38)
CONSTANT	55.5	56.55	59.06	58.16	61.51
	(18.22)	(18.24)	(18.26)	(18.04)	(17.63)
R²	.58	.59	.59	.57	.62
Adj R²	.55	.55	.55	.56	.58
Number of observations	184	184	184	184	184

*Numbers in parentheses are standard errors.
†Significant at 99% level of confidence.
‡Significant at 95% level of confidence.
§Significant at 90% level of confidence.

variables. In the first column of Table 4, the estimated model does not contain any adjustment dummy variables. Comparing Model II to Model I, we observe some changes. First, we find *FEMU* to be much weaker in the current specification.

Second, the coefficient for *XGP* in Model II is negative and statistically significant at 96% level of significance. An overview of partial correlation coefficients among the explanatory variables sheds some light on the reasons for this change. *LSMVA* is highly correlated with both *XGP* and *INGP* as indicated with correlation coefficient values of .22 and .53, respec-

tively, whereas, the correlation coefficient values between *INFLAT* and *XGP*, and between *INFLAT* and *INGP* are −.13 and −.16, respectively.

In addition, the region dummy variables differ somewhat from those we found for Model I. In particular, we find that East Asian and Caribbean countries have intercept terms that are not statistically significantly different from those of industrialized countries.

The results pertaining to the primary focus of our investigation are in columns 2–5 of Table 4. Overall the coefficients of the adjustment variables are positive and statistically significant as indicated in the

Table 5. *Model II — Adjustment variables with economic variables**

LGNP	0.80‡	0.62§	0.78‡	0.80‡	0.87†
	(0.34)	(0.35)	(0.35)	(0.35)	(0.35)
LGNP²	−10.38†	−7.78	−9.47§	−9.59§	−9.43§
	(5.08)	(5.17)	(5.23)	(5.29)	(5.33)
AFRICA	8.32‡	8.01‡	10.01†	10.37†	16.25†
	(3.39)	(3.46)	(3.44)	(3.47)	(2.25)
ASIA	3.44	3.00	4.50	4.41	9.03§
	(3.47)	(3.57)	(3.47)	(3.47)	(2.83)
CARAIB	4.25	4.43	1.43	1.58	5.24
	(3.74)	(3.89)	(3.91)	(3.90)	(3.60)
LATIN	−3.74	−4.62	−3.34	−3.20	−0.91
	(3.29)	(3.39)	(3.29)	(3.31)	(2.66)
MEAST	−16.28†	−14.99†	−15.54†	−16.14†	−12.02†
	(2.88)	(2.95)	(2.87)	(2.87)	(2.39)
SOUTHA	−10.09†	−10.37†	−9.84†	−9.56‡	−9.84†
	(4.07)	(4.16)	(4.13)	(4.15)	(4.12)
XSOC	15.06†	13.58†	15.54†	15.73†	19.51†
	(3.85)	(3.81)	(3.74)	(3.82)	(3.34)
DUM85	0.33	0.006	0.96	0.83	1.34
	(1.18)	(1.21)	(1.28)	(1.29)	(1.30)
XGP	−5.05§	−5.80‡	−5.53‡	−5.37‡	−5.53‡
	(2.68)	(2.76)	(2.70)	(2.70)	(2.70)
INGP	0.07	0.08	0.08	0.08	0.09
	(0.09)	(0.09)	(0.09)	(0.09)	(0.09)
LSMVA	−0.01	−0.01	−0.006	−0.01	−0.008
	(0.06)	(0.06)	(0.06)	(0.06)	(0.069)
URB	−0.05	−0.05	−0.05	−0.05	−0.04
	(0.04)	(0.04)	(0.04)	(0.04)	(0.04)
WXGP#	0.97†			0.65	
	(0.26)			(0.42)	
WINGP#		0.39		−1.01	−1.70
		(1.08)		(1.33)	(1.31)
WLSMVA#			−4.06†	−1.66	−4.21†
			(1.35)	(2.11)	(1.37)
CONSTANT	63.54	55.54	57.12	57.80	47.07
	(18.00)	(18.27)	(18.72)	(19.06)	(18.84)
R²	.61	.58	.64	.65	.63
Adj R²	.57	.55	.60	.60	.60
Number of observations	182	184	161	160	161

*Numbers in parentheses are standard errors.
†Significant at 99% level of confidence.
‡Significant at 95% level of confidence.
§Significant at 90% level of confidence.

rows corresponding to *EIA, WBA, WBA#*. In contrast, the adjustment variable that incorporates information on International Monetary Fund (IMF) programs in addition to the World Bank programs is not statistically significant as indicated with the "t" value of *ALA*.

In the estimations we present in Table 5, we construct the adjustment variables using changes in economic performance. These are *WXGP#, WINGP#*, and *WLSMVA#*. Again we first employ these variables one at a time. In column 2 we observe that improved export performance leads to feminization of the labor force, as indicated with parameter and "t" values estimated for *WXGP#*. Consistent with the earlier specifi-

cation, adjustment variable *WINGP#* does not have any impact on *FSH*. The adjustment variable *WLSMVA#* has a negative and statistically significant impact on *FSH*. In other words, as the income distribution worsens for labor, among intense adjusters, the labor force is feminized. In column 4 we employ all these three adjustment variables simultaneously. In this case none of the adjustment variables appear to have any impact.

The fact that we do not find any statistically significant impact of adjustment when all adjustment variables are employed simultaneously is a consequence of the very high correlation between *WXGP#* and *WLSMVA#*. This is evident in column 5 where

WXGP# is eliminated from the estimated equation. We find that worsening income distribution for intense adjusters again leads to feminization of the labor force. The partial correlation coefficient between *WXGP#* and *WLSMVA#* is –0.76. This observation, interesting in itself, suggests that increased export orientation is accompanied by a decline in the labor share of manufacturing value added. Not surprisingly, when both these variables are incorporated in a specification, they are both estimated with low "t" values. Experiences of many adjusting countries suggest that the decline of labor share is a consequence of reforms undertaken to increase export orientation, an issue beyond the scope of this paper.

(d) *Sensitivity*

To see if our primary results pertaining to the impact of adjustment are robust to alternative specifications, we considered various other alternative estimations. First, we used *WGRGD#* instead of *WINGP#* as a measure of the impact of adjustment on economic expansion. The results we described above are robust to this alternative. Second, we used alternative demographic variables in place of *URB*. Unfortunately, it is not possible to investigate independent effects of these alternative demographic variables by employing them jointly. The partial correlations among these variables are extremely high. For example, the partial correlation coefficient between *URB* and *SECED* is .75, between *URB* and *FER* it is –.65, between *FER* and *SECED* it is –.85.

SECED does not have a statistically significant parameter when employed in Model I. It is estimated however, with 92% significance in Model II. The qualitative results pertaining to other variables in Model I and II continue to be robust to this change. In particular, *FEMU* holds, and findings concerning the *ADJUSTMENT* variables are as discussed in the results section.

Fertility (*FER*) does not have a statistically significant impact on *FSH* either in Model I or Model II. The results pertaining to other variables in Model I are not influenced with this modification. In Model II, the results with respect to the *ADJUSTMENT* variables 1–4 continue to hold. The findings concerning the *WLSMVA#* variable is also consistent with those in the results section as it has a negative impact on *FSH*. This

variable, however, is now statistically significant only at lower levels of confidence.

Third, we consider the impact of being a fuel exporter because the oil industry is male-intensive. The fuel exporter dummy (*FUEL*) is based on the World Bank (1993c) classification of economies by major export category. *FUEL* takes the value of one for those countries in which fuel accounts for 50% or more of exports between 1987–89. In fact, when we incorporate the fuel exporter dummy variable (*FUEL*) in Model I and Model II, it has a negative and statistically significant coefficient. Incorporation of this variable does not have a qualitative impact on the results.

Finally, all the results for both models continue to hold with *WXGP, WINGP, WINFLAT,* and *WLSMVA,* which are the adjustment variables that use changes in economic conditions without *WBA#* weights. The only exception is that this version of *WLSMVA* is statistically significant only at low levels of confidence.

4. CONCLUSION

Our empirical investigation points to a robust relationship between women's share of the labor force and the level of economic development or what we have called the feminization U. At the same time, we have found that demographic as well as cultural/ideological factors play a role in determining the degree of feminization of the labor force. Our second finding is that, controlling for the feminization U, structural adjustment policies have led to an increase in feminization via worsening income distribution and increased openness. These findings raise further questions for investigation.

It would be important to investigate the impact of such feminization patterns on gender segregation and the gender gap in wages. How does feminization of the labor force affect women's well-being and health? Does feminization take place through the substitution of women for men workers during structural adjustment or does it take place through compositional changes in the economy without influencing the patterns of gender segregation? What are the income distributive effects of feminization? Empirical investigation of these questions, which are beyond the scope of this paper, would help us further think about feminization as a macroeconomic variable.

NOTES

1.   See Rubery (1988) and Ertürk and Çağatay (this issue).

2.   See Howes and Singh (this issue) for an evaluation and critique of this argument and an alternative analysis.

3.   For example. see Lewis (1955). p. 116.

4.   "With the introduction of improved agricultural equipment, there is less need for male muscular strength; nevertheless, the productivity gap tends to widen because men monopolize the use of new equipment and the modern agricultural methods. . . . The corollary of this relative decline in women's labor productivity is a decline in their relative sta-

tus within agriculture, and as a further result, women will want either to abandon cultivation and retire to domestic life, or to leave for the town" (Boserup, 1970, p. 53).

5.   For an example of the literature that has emphasized the relationship between production and reproduction activities of women and how they influence each other, see Beneria (1979).

6.   "Economic progress benefits men as wage earners in the modern sector, while the position of women is left unchanged, and even deteriorates when competition from the growing modern sectors eliminates the traditional enterprises carried on by women" (Boserup, 1970, p. 139).

7.   For example, Semyonov (1980) finds that women's participation, controlling for industrialization, fertility and divorce rates, is negatively related to income inequality. Comparing Latin America and the Middle East, Youssef (1974) concludes that fertility and family structure are the factors that explain women's participation and not the level of economic development.

8.   For other examples of studies on the relationship between development and women's *LFPR*, see Ward and Pampel (1985), Nuss and Majka (1983), Psacharopoulos and Tzannatos (1989), Ferber and Berg (1991), Schultz (1990).

9.   "The historical record shows a U-shaped pattern of female productive activity from relatively high in preindustrial household economy, to a lower level with the development of the modern tertiary sector. Married women's productive work contributed to this pattern" (Tilly and Scott, 1987, pp. 229–230). Also see Tilly (1993) for a comparative account of industrialization and women's work experience in England, Germany, France, the United States, Japan and China.

10.   Hartmann argues that men workers restricted women's access to wage labor through denying skills to women and through the actions of unions which supported protective legislation for women. The rise of the "male breadwinner"

ideology, in her view, accompanies this exclusion of women from wage labor. She also argues that women's relative disadvantage was due to the fact that they were less well organized in England (Hartmann, 1979). For a different interpretation of the limiting of women's work in early industrialization, see Humphries (1977) who sees such limiting of women's work as a working class strategy to obtain higher wages than would otherwise be possible. For an examination of the U hypothesis for the Greek economy during the 1970s and early 1980s, see Kottis (1990).

11.   Goldin's explanation of the underlying reasons for the feminization U is somewhat different in that she uses a choice-theoretic framework.

12.   For example, examining the agricultural sector, Dixon (1982) reports that the greatest underrecording of agricultural work occurred in the Middle East and Latin America where the male breadwinner ideologies might be stronger than in other regions. Also see Dixon (1983) and Çağatay (1990).

13.   See Çağatay and Berik (1991).

14.   Standing (1989) also provides evidence of feminization for a limited number of developing and developed economies between the mid-1970s and mid-1980s. He attributes the evidence for feminization patterns to the economic policies of the 1980s, without separating the impact of the long-term feminization U from the impacts of the particular policies of the 1980s. For critiques, see Berik and Çağatay (1992), Elson (1995). For examples of other studies which examine women's work under structural adjustment policies, see Beneria (1992), Beneria and Roldan (1987), and Perez-Aleman (1992).

15.   Region dummies, of course, do not capture the variations within a region.

16.   Other measures of income distribution, such as the Gini coefficients were not used because they would have reduced the number of observations considerably.

REFERENCES

Benería, L., "Gender, technology and the feminization of the labor force," Unpublished paper (Cornell University, Department of City and Regional Planning, 1994).
Benería, L., "The Mexican debt crisis: Restructuring the economy and the household," in L. Beneria and S. Feldman (Eds.), *Unequal Burden: Economic Crises, Persistent Poverty, and Women's Work* (Oxford: Westview Press, 1992), pp. 83–104.
Benería, L., and M. Roldan, *The Crossroads of Class and Gender: Industrial Homework, Subcontracting and Household Dynamics in Mexico City* (Chicago: University of Chicago Press, 1987).
Benería, L., "Reproduction, production and the sexual division of labor," *Cambridge Journal of Economics*, Vol. 3, No. 3 (September 1979).
Berik, G., and N. Çağatay, "How global is 'global feminization through flexible labor'?," Paper presented at the

Tenth International Economic Association Congress (Moscow: August 1992).
Blau, F. D., and M. A. Ferber, *The Economics of Women, Men, and Work* (Englewood Cliffs, NJ: Prentice-Hall 1992).
Boserup, E., "Economic changes and the roles of women," in I. Tinker (Ed.), *Persistent Inequalities: Women and World Development* (New York: Oxford University Press, 1990).
Boserup, E., *Woman's Role in Economic Development* (New York: St. Martin's Press, 1970).
Çağatay, N., "Women's labor force participation in the Middle East: Some comparative observations," Unpublished paper (University of Utah, Department of Economics, December 1990).
Çağatay, N., and G. Berik, "What has export-oriented manufacturing meant for Turkish women?," in P. Sparr (Ed.),

1894   WORLD DEVELOPMENT

Mortgaging Women's Lives: Feminist Critiques of Structural Adjustment (London: Zed Press for the United Nations, 1994).

Çağatay, N., and G. Berik, "Transition to export-led growth in Turkey: Is there a feminization of employment?," *Capital and Class*, No. 43 (Spring 1991).

Dixon, R., "Women in agriculture: Counting the labor force in developing countries," *Population and Development Review*, Vol. 8 (1982).

Dixon, R., "Land, labour and sex composition of the agricultural labour force: An international comparison," *Development and Change*, Vol. 14 (1983).

Elson, D., "Appraising recent developments in the world market for nimble fingers: Accumulation, regulation, organization," forthcoming in A. Chhachhi and R. Pittin (Eds.), *Confronting State, Capital and Patriarchy: Women Organizing in the Process of Industrialization* (New York: Macmillan, 1995).

Ertürk, K., and N. Çağatay, "The macroeconomic implications of cyclical and secular changes in feminization: An experiment at gendered macromodeling," *World Development*, Vol. 23 (1995), this issue.

Ferber, M., and H. Berg, "Labor force participation and the sex ratio: A cross-country analysis," *Review of Social Economy*, Vol. 48, No. 1 (1991).

Goldin, C., "The U-shaped female labor force function in economic development and economic history," NBER Working Paper Series, No. 4707 (Cambridge: National Bureau of Economic Research, April 1994).

Hartmann, H., "Capitalism, patriarchy and job segregation by sex," in Z. Eisenstein (Ed.), *Capitalist Patriarchy and the Case for Socialist Feminism* (New York: Monthly Review, 1979).

Howes, C., and A. Singh, "Long-term trends in the world economy: The gender dimension," *World Development*, Vol. 23 (1995), this issue.

Humphries, J., "Class struggle and the persistence of the working-class family," *Cambridge Journal of Economics*, Vol. 1 (September, 1977).

Kottis, A. P., "Shifts over time and regional variation in women's labor force participation rates in a developing economy: The case of Greece," *Journal of Development Economics*, Vol. 33 (1990).

Lewis, A. W., *The Theory of Economic Growth* (London: Allen and Unwin, 1955).

Nuss, S., and L. Majka, "The economic integration of women: A cross-national investigation," *Work and Occupations*, Vol. 10, No. 1 (February, 1983).

Oppenheimer, V., *The Female Labor Force in the United States* (Berkeley, CA: Institute for International Studies, 1970).

Pampel, F. C., and K. Tanaka, "Economic development and female labor force participation: A reconsideration," *Social Forces*, Vol. 64, No. 3 (March, 1986).

Pearson, R., "Male bias and women's work in Mexico's border industries," in D. Elson (Ed.), *Male Bias in the Development Process* (Manchester: Manchester University Press, 1991).

Perez-Aleman, P., "Economic crisis and women in Nicaragua," in L. Benería and S. Feldman (Eds.), *Unequal Burden: Economic Crises, Persistent Poverty, and Women's Work* (Oxford: Westview Press, 1992), pp. 239–258.

Psacharopoulos, G., and Z. Tzannatos, "Female labor force participation: An international perspective," *The World Bank Research Observer*, Vol. 4, No. 2 (July 1989).

Rubery, J. (Ed.), *Women and Recession* (London: Routledge, 1988).

Schultz, T. P., "Women's changing participation in the labor force: A world perspective," *Economic Development and Cultural Change*, Vol. 38 (1990), pp. 457–488.

Semyonov, M., "The social context of women's labor force participation: A comparative analysis," *American Journal of Sociology*, Vol. 86, No. 3 (1980).

Standing, G., "Global feminization through flexible labor," *World Development*, Vol. 17, No. 7 (1989), pp. 1077–1096.

Tilly, L. A., "Industrialization and Gender Inequality," in M. Adas (Ed.), *Islamic and European Expansion: The Forging of A Global Order* (Philadelphia, PA: Temple University Press, 1993).

Tilly, L. A., and J. W. Scott, *Women, Work and Family*, Second edition (New York: Routledge, 1987)..

United Nations, *World Economic and Social Survey* (New York: United Nations, 1994).

Ward, K., and F. C. Pampel, "Structural determinants of female labor force participation in developed nations, 1955–1975," *Social Science Quarterly*, Vol. 66 (1985).

Wood, A., "North-South trade and female labour in manufacturing: An asymmetry," *The Journal of Development Studies*, Vol. 27, No. 2 (January 1991).

World Bank, *Social Indicators of Development 1993* (Washington, DC: The World Bank, 1993a).

World Bank, *World Development Report 1993* (New York: Oxford University Press, 1993b).

World Bank, *World Tables 1993* (Washington, DC: The World Bank, 1993c).

World Bank, *Adjustment Lending Policies for Sustainable Growth*, Policy and Research Series, No. 14 (Washington, DC: World Bank, 1990).

Youssef, N., *Women and Work in Developing Societies* (Berkeley, CA: University of California Press, 1974).

[18]

Pergamon

World Development, Vol. 23, No. 11, pp. 1963–1968, 1995
Copyright © 1995 Elsevier Science Ltd
Printed in Great Britain. All rights reserved
0305–750X/95 $9.50 + 0.00

0305–750X(95)00082–8

The Formal Structure of A Gender-Segregated Low-Income Economy

WILLIAM DARITY, JR.*
University of North Carolina at Chapel Hill, North Carolina, U.S.A.

Summary. — Based upon insights drawn from research concerning the nature of the gender-based division of labor in agrarian regions of developing countries, a formal model is advanced of the interactions that take place in such a setting. Males are characterized as seeking to maximize their income from production of an exportable cash crop by drawing women out of household/social maintenance activities, by dint of coercion, cooperation and compensation. The paper also explores repercussions on the efficiency and output of the social maintenance or "subsistence" sector due to the loss of female labor-power to the male-controlled export sector. Finally, the impact of an International Monetary Fund mandated currency devaluation on an economy of this type is considered as well.

1. INTRODUCTION

This paper presents a compact formal framework for the analysis of interactions that take place in a low-income developing country characterized by a high level of gender segregation with respect to economic activity. The model is based directly upon the observations and insights advanced by researchers whose focus has been on the roles performed by women in developing countries, particularly the work of Elson (1991, 1993), Mbilinyi (1988), Lado (1992), Kennedy and Bouis (1989), and Tibaijuka (1994). Their findings are especially applicable to economic systems with a pronounced sexual division of labor in agrarian regions of sub-Saharan Africa.

This body of work was prompted, in part, by interest in exploring dimensions of structural adjustment typically ignored by development economists and by multilateral institutions such as the International Monetary Fund (IMF). While addressing the effects of structural adjustment, however, this body of work (and the model advanced here) goes beyond the ramifications of specific policy initiatives to suggest that there is a unique economic structure at play in these low-income regions.

The degree of gender segregation in tasks is, perhaps, more sharply drawn here than in many actual conditions where the model has applicability, but it is hoped the model will provide a basis for further investigations into the nature of economies of this type when modified appropriately. In this aggregative framework the community in question has two sectors of economic activity, a sector producing a cash crop

that can be exported and a sector producing household goods or social maintenance resources, or what otherwise might be called "subsistence." The cash crop could be rice, tea, groundnuts, bananas or tobacco in various parts of sub-Saharan Africa.

The gender division of labor operates at two levels. First, women are the sole workers in the social maintenance or "subsistence" sector. Men remain idle rather than assist with household chores. Women's output in the household sector is a composite commodity that includes growing and preparation of food for their families, childrearing, and the upkeep of the home.

Second, although both men and women work in smallholder export production, there is a partition between men's and women's tasks in the cash-crop sector. For example, males engage in "land preparation" which is identified as "men's work" while women engage in "other tasks such as transplanting and weeding" which is identified as "women's work" (Elson, 1991, p. 173). While there is no intrinsic difference in men's and women's abilities to perform one set of tasks or the other in the cash-crop sector, different efficiencies are associated with their efforts because the tasks are gender-typed.

---

*The author is grateful to Nilüfer Çağatay, Diane Elson, David Gordon, Caren Grown, Charles Kahn and an anonymous referee for extremely helpful suggestions. A preliminary version of this paper was presented at an URPE session on Gender and Development at the January 1995 Allied Social Science Association meetings in Washington, D.C.

1964   WORLD DEVELOPMENT

Moreover, men control the income generated in smallholder export production. Correspondingly, they seek to determine the level of female participation in cash crop production consistent with maximization of male incomes from the export activity. To the extent that they can exercise male power over a wife's and/or older, unmarried daughter's labor time, the scale of female labor available to cash-crop production will be higher.

Women also may willingly supply some effort *gratis*, as their husband or father increases his time devoted to the export sector's output, due to a spirit of interfamilial cooperation. On the other hand, women also may require some compensation to induce them to reduce their time devoted to household work and to increase the time devoted to export good production. Men pull women out of social maintenance activities; they can do so by dint of male authority, by dint of women's cooperativeness with spouse or father, by dint of wage payments, or, more generally, by the combined effect of all three factors (see the essays in Gladwin, 1991; see Collier, 1990).

In this model, a nearby village offers a market where consumer or investment goods can be purchased. Male investment activity over time can augment the stock of tools, equipment, and animal power available to enhance production in the export sector. In the abstract time period of the model, the flow of new additions to this stock of labor-augmenting goods, called "capital" if one prefers, is so small that the stock is treated as fixed.

Males also may invest in the household sector, using a portion of their income to buy goods from the village market that ease women's tasks in subsistence production. Again, of course, the men do not deign to lend a hand directly. Finally, male income will be devoted to purchases of pure luxury items from the village market.

Women use their incomes for two types of purchases. Either they buy luxury goods or they invest in the household sector. In either case as long as all categories of expenditure increase with rising incomes, i.e. all three categories represent "normal" goods, we can ignore luxury consumption altogether in what follows.

The efficiency of female production in the subsistence sector is endogenous for three reasons. Female efficiency in the provision of social maintenance resources can suffer as women devote more and more hours to cash crop production. They must extend the overall length of their workday because they must still produce a threshold minimum of household output, sufficient to meet the customary provisions the men expect as well as enough to at least sustain themselves and their families physiologically. Moreover, fewer hours devoted to household production mean less task specialization among women and also lower efficiency. The contrasting two effects arise from the pos-

sible efficiency-enhancing effects of village market purchases of goods for the household sector out of both women's and men's incomes.

For simplicity, it is assumed that the total number of male and female hours of awake time is fixed. Awake time is divided between work and leisure. The model also abstracts from any direct role for government. This may not be unrealistic because of the comparative spatial distance between a community of this type and an urban-based national government. Still, it is not difficult to indicate how the model can be modified to introduce the effects of policies pursued by the national government. The effects of a devaluation as part of a national structural adjustment package that has the expected effect of raising export demand will be considered in detail.

2. THE SMALLHOLDER EXPORT SECTOR

Equation (1) is the Cobb-Douglas technology representing the production function for the smallholder export sector. This constitutes the output of the cash crop. X_c is the quantity of the cash crop, M_c represents male labor in cash crop production, F_c represents female labor in the same sector, and K_c represents the stock of labor-augmenting resources, treated as fixed in the period of analysis:

$$X_c = M_c^{\alpha} F_c^{\beta} K_c^{\gamma}. \tag{1}$$

It is assumed that the sum of the exponents α and β is less than unity.

Equation (2) indicates that total female awake time, $\bar{F}$, is divided between cash crop production, F_c, social maintenance or subsistence production, F_s, and leisure, L:

$$\bar{F} = F_c + F_s + L. \tag{2}$$

Women's leisure time is squeezed as participation in cash crop production expands. Any male time not devoted to cash crop production is devoted exclusively to leisure.

The next equation of the model depicts the special nature of the female labor supply process to the export sector:

$$F_c = CM_c^{\sigma}(w/p_v)^{\rho} \tag{3}$$

$$C \geq 1, \sigma \geq 0, \rho \geq 0.$$

The term C is a scale factor that represents the prevailing level of male control over female labor time in this community. When $C = 1$, males exercise no coercive power over the allocation of women's time; when $C > 1$, male power becomes operative in dictating the split of women's time between the export sector and household work. Interpret C, then, as the male social coercion parameter *vis-à-vis* women,

The sensitivity of female labor supply to male employment in the cash crop sector represents an opposite effect, the extent of female cooperation with a husband or a father's efforts to raise output in the sector. If σ, the elasticity of female employment in cash crop production with respect to male employment, is zero, females offer no uncompensated, uncoerced labor to export production. The higher the value of σ the easier it is for men to get women to work the fields without asserting male authority or paying higher compensation to women.

The variable w is the money wage rate and P_v is the given price of goods available in the village. Women's labor supply in cash crop production responds positively to a higher real wage calculated in terms of village goods. Thus, equation (3) captures all three factors: coercion, cooperation, and compensation. As we will see below, such a framework is amenable to old-fashioned marginalist techniques but provides some interesting results, nonetheless.

3. MALE AND FEMALE INCOMES

The objective men have is to maximize male income, Y_M. Male income is the difference between the money value of the cash crop and the compensation paid to women:

$$Y_M = P_c X_c - w F_c \qquad (4)$$

where P_c is the money price of the cash crop, also given from the perspective of the farmers. Men will seek to maximize (4) by selecting the level of their own activity in the export sector, M_c, and the money wage paid to women, w.

Substituting equations (1) and (3) into (4) and differentiating Y_M with respect to M_c and w yields:

$$Y_M = P_c M_c^{\alpha} [CM_c^{\sigma}(w/p_v)^{\rho}]^{\beta} K_c^{\gamma} - w_c M_c^{\sigma}(w/p_v)^{\rho} \qquad (5)$$

$$\frac{\partial Y_M}{\partial M_c} = (\alpha + \beta\sigma) \, P_c \, \frac{X_c}{M_c} - \sigma w \, \frac{F_c}{M_c} \qquad (6)$$

$$\frac{\partial Y_M}{\partial w} = \beta\rho \, P_c \, X_c W - (\rho + 1) \, F_c. \qquad (7)$$

Each of the expressions has a straightforward interpretation. In (6) the marginal contribution of male employment to male incomes is determined by the difference between the total effect of increased male employment on the money value of cash-crop production and the money cost of the additional female labor.

The bracketed expression $(\alpha + \beta\sigma)$ weights the money value of the average product of male labor in the first component of (6). It consists of the sum of the elasticity of export output with respect to male labor and the product of the elasticity of export output with respect to female labor and the elasticity of female labor supply with respect to male employment (the cooperation effect). The latter elasticity also weights the female wage multiplied by the female-male employment ratio in cash crops as the second component of (6).

In (7) the marginal effect of an increase in the female wage on male incomes can be viewed as the difference between the gain in output value prompted by the increased female employment (the compensation effect) net of the direct cost associated with increased female employment. Here the elasticity of female cash-crop employment with respect to the real wage figures prominently. In both (6) and (7) the coercion effect, C, is embedded in both the output variable, X_c, and the female labor supply variable, F_c.

Setting (6) and (7) equal to zero for a maximum permits solutions to be derived for the equilibrium levels of male employment, M_c^*, and the female wage, w^*:

$$w^* = \left\{ \frac{(\rho+1)}{\rho} \, D^{-(\alpha + \sigma\beta - \sigma)} \, (\beta P_c C^{\beta} K_c^{\gamma})^{-1} P_v^{\rho(1-\beta)} \right\}^R \qquad (8)$$

$$M_c^* = D \left\{ \frac{(\rho+1)}{\rho} \, D^{-(\alpha + \sigma\beta - \sigma)} \, (\beta P_c C^{\beta} K_c^{\gamma})^{-1} P_v^{\rho(1-\beta)} \right\}^{RQ} \qquad (9)$$

$$D \equiv \left[\frac{1}{J P_c C^{\beta} (1/p_v)^{\rho\beta} K_c^{\gamma}} \right]^{[1/(\alpha + \sigma\beta)]}$$

$$J = \left(\frac{\sigma}{\alpha + \sigma\beta} \right)$$

$$Q \equiv \frac{1 - \rho\beta}{\alpha + \sigma\beta}$$

$$R \equiv \frac{1}{Q(\alpha + \sigma\beta - \sigma) + (\rho\beta - 1 - \rho)}.$$

With the equilibrium values of w^* and M_c^* in hand, given the prevailing level of male control over female labor time and the prevailing price of goods in the village, the equilibrium amount of women's work time in cash crop production is determined:

$$F_c^* = C M_c^{*c} (w^*/P_v)\rho. \qquad (10)$$

1966   WORLD DEVELOPMENT

Female income from smallholder export production, Y_F, also is determined:

$$Y_F^* = w^* F_c^* \tag{11}$$

4. THE SUBSISTENCE SECTOR

The production conditions in the household sector are depicted as follows:

$$S = E \cdot F_s. \tag{12}$$

"Subsistence" output, S, is the product of an efficiency factor, E, and the amount of women's work time devoted to subsistence production.

The efficiency factor is endogenized as follows:

$$E = E(F_c, Y_F/P_v, Y_M/P_v) \tag{13}$$

$$E_1 < 0, E_2 > 0, E_3 < 0.$$

The efficiency of housework declines as more hours of women's awake time is devoted to export sector production, rises as female incomes increase and rises as male incomes increase, the latter two measured in terms of command over village goods.

Using (2), equation (12) can be rewritten as follows:

$$S = E(F_c, Y_F/P_v, Y_M/P_v) \cdot (\bar{F} - F_c - L). \tag{14}$$

Note that as female work time is reallocated toward cash-crop production, the squeeze must take place on women's leisure (recreation, rest and recuperation). This is because a threshold amount of household goods must be provided to reproduce the community according to customary standards. Men must be "fed" what men expect to be "fed" as first claimants on subsistence. Women receive a residual after the men's needs are met:

$$S_F = S - \bar{q}\bar{M}. \tag{15}$$

Equation (15) indicates that female subsistence consumption is dictated by what is left after men take their share. $\bar{M}$ represents total male awake time, and $\bar{q}$ is the community norm for male consumption of subsistence per waking hour. If $\bar{z}$ represents the minimum amount of female consumption of social maintenance resources per waking hour to maintain normal physiological existence, then the following condition must be true:

$$S_F \geq \bar{z}\bar{F}. \tag{16}$$

The presumption here is generally $\bar{z} < \bar{q}$.

Condition (15) means, in turn:

$$E(F_c, Y_F/P_v) \cdot (\bar{F} - F_c - L) \geq \bar{q}\bar{M} + \bar{z}\bar{F}. \tag{17}$$

Again, depending upon community norms, this constraint need not be absolutely binding. It will be relaxed, first, by women receiving less than $\bar{z}$ in average subsistence consumption, thereby facing health dangers. Under encroaching famine conditions, male priority would lead to women suffering first.

If women devote more hours to cash-crop production there is one unambiguous adverse effect on subsistence production: the adverse effect on scale associated with the negative efficiency effect attributable to the increased length of the female workday (and the accompanying loss of leisure) along with the decreased specialization. Whether this adverse effect dominates the efficiency gains associated with the household investment goods from the village market provided by the women themselves or by the men is the critical question. The range of village goods that can raise efficiency in the social maintenance sector will be wider the greater is infrastructural development. Obviously, many appliances common to U.S. or British kitchens cannot be used without electricity.

Absolute hours devoted to household production will not decline as long as there is still "free" or leisure awake time that can be squeezed downward. But women must continue to maintain sufficient hours in social maintenance work to meet the threshold requirements. As cash-crop production expands, women necessarily have a longer and longer workday. If the scale effect captured by the partial derivative E is dominant, efficiency will decline. With female hours in household production relatively unchanged, there will be a drop in subsistence output. Since men have the initial claim on subsistence output, there could be circumstances in which women are pulled so sharply into cash-crop production that women's average consumption of subsistence is driven perilously close to $\bar{z}$ or even below $\bar{z}$. Gender-specific nutritional deficiencies can arise despite an export boom in a community of this type if the pressure on female labor time in the household sector cannot be offset by village resources purchased with incomes generated in the export sector.

5. EFFECTS OF A CURRENCY DEVALUATION

What, then, are the potential effects of an IMF-mandated structural adjustment package in this type of an economy? Consider specifically the effects of a devaluation of the domestic currency. The standard justification for such a policy is to promote foreign export demand. If the policy does prompt such a response, it will be manifest in the economy modeled here by a rise in P_c, the money price of cash crops.

Under reasonable parameterizations (i.e., technological and labor supply parameters stay within empirically plausible bounds), a higher price of cash crops will lead men simultaneously to raise their own hours devoted to the export sector and the wage paid to women. Tedious differentiation of (8) and (9) with respect to P_c demonstrates this result. The effect will be a movement of women's work hours toward the export sector. The greater the success of domestic currency devaluation in raising the relative price of cash crops, the greater the pressure on female labor time in the subsistence sector. Once more, if the higher income for both males and females associated with the rise in P_c does not result in an offsetting gain in efficiency through greater access to village resources, efficiency and output will fall in the household sector. Women will bear a disproportionate brunt of the drop in subsistence output. It is precisely when there is a highly successful effort to promote exports through a devaluation that gender-specific health disadvantages are more likely to rise.

It also can be shown easily that a rise in the price of village goods under similar parameterizations will have exactly the opposite effects. After all, the parameter P_v enters both (8) and (9) in an inverse fashion with P_c. Both w^* and M_c^* will fall in response to an increase in P_v, leading to a reverse pattern: a decline in output in the export sector but greater efficiency and output in the subsistence sector.

If there is a high foreign import content of goods available in the village market, the currency devaluation will have precisely this effect on P_v. A rise in P_v coincident with a rise in P_c could mitigate the upward pressure on women's total labor time driven by their shift toward cash-crop production. The shift would be muted by the higher price of village goods. Of course, both female and male command over village goods also would be reduced. Underlying gender relations certainly have profound implications for the effects of at least this prong of a structural adjustment program.

6. CONCLUSIONS

Thus far the model has been analyzed under the premise of maintenance of a stable regime of gender relations. But there are avenues for exploration of the comparative statics of changes in gender relations. The most obvious is a change in the degree of male control over female labor which can be considered by a variation in C, the scale parameter that captures the level of coercive influence men exercise over women's work time.

Suppose the coercive influence becomes greater. If men have a relatively strong preference for leisure

they not only could reduce the money wage they pay women but they also could reduce their own labor time, particularly if the increased coercive effect dominates the cooperation effect. Regardless of whether men reduce or increase their own labor time, the ratio F_c/M_c will rise as a consequence of a rise in C.

But C is more likely to trend downward over time as gender relations move toward greater equality. In this case, men would find their incomes maximized by working longer hours and by paying women a higher money wage. In a community where C is trending downward, male priority over subsistence consumption should diminish also. The likelihood of women being subjected to nutritional deprivation during an export boom would be lowered as well. Three effects would come into play that would benefit female health status: (a) women are less readily drawn into cash-crop production, thereby having less of an adverse efficiency effect on subsistence production; (b) the higher wage per female in cash-crop production can provide greater access to village goods that may substitute for the lost hours; and (c) the diminution of male priority over subsistence means women need not wait until male requirements are met fully before partaking in consumption.

In this model women have no alternative source of money income aside from working in the fields with their fathers or husbands. But the money income they obtain from cash-crop production is discretionary and a source of female independence. Women could accumulate resources to develop other options to facilitate migration to the village or city to attempt to take up other employment, to provide schooling opportunities for daughters, or to gain access to additional land and tools to grow their own cash-crops and have direct control over the income from cash crop production. Gender-specific government policies such as subsidies and cheap credit arrangements for women's farming enterprises could aid women in developing their own nonsubsistence farming activities. But these programs are unlikely to be adopted or maintained if a structural adjustment package mandates a sharp deficit reduction accompanied by cuts in social programs.

Such changes would raise the money wage men would have to pay to their female relatives. Indeed, if women move into their own smallholder export activity en masse, the strict gender separation in farming tasks would have to break down. The time/work burden in a gender-segregated, low-income economy falls disproportionately on women. A prevailing structure of gender rules concerning work, consumption and authority makes this the case. The breakdown of that structure opens the door to other possibilities, even the possibility that men might contribute significantly to household production. But that is a yet to be realized revolution in high income countries with considerably lower levels of gender-segregation in employment.

REFERENCES

Collier, P., "Gender aspects of labor allocation during structural adjustment," Unpublished manuscript (Oxford: Unit for the Study of African Economics, Oxford University, 1990).

Elson, Diane, "Gender-aware analysis and development economics," *Journal of International Development*, Vol. 5, No. 2 (1993), pp. 237–247.

Elson, Diane, "Male bias in macro-economics: The case of structural adjustment," in Diane Elson (Ed.), *Male Bias in the Development Process* (Manchester: Manchester University Press, 1991), pp. 164–190.

Gladwin, C. (Ed.), *Structural Adjustment and African Women Farmers* (Gainesville, FL: University of Florida Press, 1991).

Kennedy, E. and H. Bouis, "Traditional cash crop schemes effects on production, consumption and nutrition: sugar-

cane in the Philippines and Kenya," Unpublished manuscript (Washington, DC: International Food Policy Research Institute, 1989).

Lado, C., "Female labor participation in agricultural production and the implications for nutrition and health in rural Africa," *Social Science and Medicine*, Vol. 34, No. 2 (1992), pp. 787–807.

Mbilinyi, M., "The invention of female farming systems in Africa: Structural adjustment in Tanzania," Workshop on Economic Crisis, Household Strategies and Women's Work (Ithaca, NY: Cornell University, 1988).

Tibaijuka, A., "The cost of differential gender roles in African agriculture: A case study of smallholder banana-coffee farms in the Kagera Region, Tanzania," *Journal of Agricultural Economics*, Vol. 45, No. 1 (1994), pp. 69–81.

[19]

The Journal of Developing Areas 33 (Fall1998) 73–98

Restructuring of Labor Markets in the Philippines and Zambia: The Gender Dimension

MARIA SAGRARIO FLORO and KENDALL SCHAEFER

This paper critically examines labor market changes accompanying the process of structural adjustment and, in particular, the resulting impact on women's economic participation. In doing so, the paper explores the manner in which structural adjustment programs (SAPs) can alter overall levels of employment as well as conditions in the organization of production so as to significantly affect women's participation and bargaining power within a market economy and within the household. The analysis makes use of the experience of two countries that have undergone structural adjustment in the 1980s, namely, Zambia and the Philippines, to illustrate how gender permeates the functioning of labor markets and how economic reforms create differential impacts on women and men *vis-à-vis* the use of their labor time.

World Bank SAP reforms implemented in the 1980s were designed to remove market regulations, liberalize prices, and achieve optimal market outcomes. Their design was heavily shaped by a neoliberal ideology which argues that market interventions adversely affect employment because they lead to inefficient sectoral compositions of output and distorted input and factor prices.[1] Structural reforms that aim to remove market distortions, as in the case of SAPs, are expected to improve employment, at least after initial reallocations have taken place.

During the 1980s, the World Bank began to take a formal "proactive" stance toward gender issues. According to a 1995 World Bank study, a program of countrywide assessments of gender issues for some 50 countries was undertaken

---

Maria Sagrario Floro is Associate Professor, and Kendall Schaefer is a doctoral student, Department of Economics, The American University, Washington, DC 20016-8029.

during the 1985–93 period.[2] Specific Women in Development (WID) programs were advocated to address preexisting gender inequalities, improve access to the market economy, and strengthen overall economic efficiency.[3] A careful examination of these programs shows that they were mainly investment projects focusing on agriculture, health and nutrition, education, and credit.[4] Moreover, the quality of gender analysis in the Country Assistance Strategy (CAS) and the Economic and Sector Work (ESW) varies considerably. In some cases, discussions of gender issues in the reports are limited to mentioning "women" and "gender" a few times.

The World Bank formally maintains that SAPs be accompanied by policies that integrate women into the development process. Yet bank projects submitted for approval frequently ignore WID issues, and any gender analysis in ESW documents has yet to be integrated into sectoral studies, poverty assessments, and country economic memorandums.[5] The absence of a clear conceptual framework—including a rationale for why gender equity is important to poverty reduction and sustainable development—continues to undermine any progress toward "mainstreaming" gender concerns in bank lending operations. It is striking to note that the bank's most comprehensive evaluation on mainstreaming gender, which was produced in March 1997, gives no mention of structural adjustment lending and the extent to which this lending has taken women's needs into account.[6]

The slow progress of the World Bank in integrating gender concerns into its macroeconomic and sectoral reforms is hardly surprising. The bank has selectively recognized market failure existing as a result of socially defined gender norms and has argued that the persistence of gender inequality within households represents a challenge to the full integration of women into labor markets.[7] Hence, the bank has called heavily upon governments to increase investments in women's and girls' education and health in order to expand their options in the labor market. Interestingly, although markets have failed when gender concerns are at issue, the bank implicitly assumes that drawing women into the market will inevitably empower them. In the simplest and most powerful market model, gender inequalities will at least be minimized by market forces.

Our study challenges this bank-predicted outcome in the context of the Philippine and Zambian experiences. We hypothesize that the gender-based patterns of labor force participation and employment patterns continue to permeate the Philippine and Zambian economies despite expansion and liberalization of markets. The specific process of economic restructuring adopted in these countries under SAPs, combined with an institutional environment characterized by skewed distribution of resources and unequal gender norms, has altered the form of women's subordinate status in the market economy, but does not necessarily redress it. The current mobilization of human resources by evolving labor markets has produced a different set of outcomes for men versus women as well as among women themselves.

Before further examining this claim, however, it is important to remember that economic reform designed to enhance labor market development is neither good nor bad by definition. Its effects on individuals depend primarily on the specific form and structure of the developing labor market and on the institutional and sociopolitical context within which the market evolves. What our analysis aims to show is that the process of structural adjustment brings about changes in the configurations of the labor market without necessarily challenging the prevailing distribution of power and unequal gender relations. As a result, the evolving structure tends to replicate these institutional characteristics. Moreover, the globalization of labor markets, while enhancing the mobility of labor across national boundaries and allowing for new employment opportunities, tends to subject migrant workers to both cyclical fluctuations in the market and disruptions in prevailing gender patterns within the household.

Our paper begins with a brief summary of SAP performance in Zambia and the Philippines. We use these two countries as case studies to illustrate common gendered patterns of reform in countries with significant differences in structure and initial conditions.[8] We show that in Zambia reform was accompanied by persistent economic stagnation, while in the Philippines it was eventually followed by a gradual and uneven pattern of economic recovery. Labor market reconfiguration during and as a result of the process of structural adjustment is then discussed.

In Zambia, unemployment has been growing and is increasingly characterized by a female dimension. In the Philippines, employment growth has been sporadic, and female labor force participation follows the fall and rise of output growth. Sectorally, in both countries agricultural- and urban-sector reforms have had a significant bearing on the conditions of production and on the demand for female labor and have resulted in a general increased reliance on informal-sector activity. The role of the global labor market in the case of the Philippines is particularly noteworthy inasmuch as it extends the gender character of the labor market beyond the confines of the domestic economy. Finally, labor supply decisions in the face of economic restructuring are discussed to emphasize the importance of gendered bargaining processes and decision making within Philippine and Zambian households.

Nature of Economic Restructuring in Zambia and the Philippines

Level and Pattern of Economic Growth. In response to economic crisis triggered by mounting debt and recession, both the Philippines and Zambia underwent structural adjustment in the early 1980s after negotiating with the International Monetary Fund (IMF) and the World Bank for structural adjustment loans (SALs).[9] Several measures were adopted by each government to move its economy toward more liberalized markets. The success of these measures differed between the two, however, and this differing success has ultimately affected their respective labor market situations. We shall consider the details of the Zambian reform experience first.

Zambia has been undergoing structural adjustment for 15 years with programs consistently designed to address perceived excessive and distortionary government involvement in the economy. Since the first program in 1983, SAPs in Zambia have directed the government to move toward liberalized prices and the elimination

76   Maria Sagrario Floro and Kendall Schaefer

TABLE 1
MACROECONOMIC INDICATORS FOR ZAMBIA

Indicator	1980–87	1988	1989	1990	1991	1992	1993	1994	1995	1996	1997
Growth rates (% change)											
Real GDP	1.1	6.3	– 1.1	– 0.5	– 0.1	– 1.7	6.8	– 3.4	– 2.3	6.5	3.5
Consumption per capita	– 0.4	– 0.7	– 13.4	– 8.6	– 5.9	10.2	– 35.7	4.7	– 2.0	– 4.4	9.0
Consumer prices	26.3	55.4	127.7	117.4	93.2	169.1	188.1	53.6	34.2	46.3	24.8
Investment	-7.2	11.5	– 29.0	– 37.6	– 15.8	12.0	4.8	9.4	5.1	9.6	16.2
Growth rate (as % of GDP)											
Agriculture	22.1	26.5	26.1	23.9	25.1	17.1	26.9	13.5	18.4	17.2	16.0
Mining and other industry	20.1	14.9	15.6	14.8	13.8	15.2	12.7	24.9	20.5	18.8	20.1
Manufacturing	20.5	24.9	25.0	27.1	27.1	30.9	26.6	9.8	10.0	9.9	10.3
Services	27.4	28.1	24.0	22.6	24.7	26.2	23.1	38.9	39.1	42.3	42.3
Current account balance (before official transfers) (%)	– 14.9	– 7.1	– 5.6	– 10.4	– 15.2	– 22.8	– 14.4	– 11.9	– 13.3	– 12.9	– 10.8
External debt (%)	170.9	183.4	168.0	193.5	215.8	209.9	207.4	194.1	193.6	217.8	174.8
Government deficit (including current grants) (%)	– 14.2	– 10.8	– 6.6	– 12.7	– 15.9	– 12.6	– 13.6	– 11.8	– 9.5	– 8.7	– 10.2
Government current expenditures (%)	32.8	25.9	23.0	26.7	29.3	27.2	26.3	27.9	24.2	18.5	22.5
On education	–	–	–	2.2	2.9	2.4	1.9	2.1	1.5	2.6	3.6
On health	–	–	–	2.5	1.6	1.7	1.7	1.8	1.3	1.8	2.6

SOURCES: World Bank, *World Development Indicators* (Baltimore, MD: Johns Hopkins University for the World Bank, 1997); and Central Statistical Office (CSO), *National Income Statistics* (Lusaka: CSO, 1998).

of tariffs, and to sharply cut back spending, largely through privatization, restructuring of parastatals, and significant reductions in the civil service. The macroeconomic performance of the Zambian economy is illustrated in table 1.[10]

As in much of sub-Saharan Africa, the performance of Zambia's economy throughout the period of structural adjustment has remained weak. According to a World Bank study, real gross national product (GNP) per capita steadily declined from 1981 to 1987 and now rests at approximately its 1971 value.[11] Current account balances have continued unfailingly to display deficits since the year 1980. Rising interest rates have failed to reduce inflation or attract savings while negatively affecting production, because firms have found it too costly to borrow for needed inputs.[12] Intended investment and export growth needed to make up for fiscal restraint and falling private consumption have yet to be realized. Meanwhile, Zambia's external position has become more and more tenuous, and by 1996 external debt accounted for over 200 percent of gross domestic product (GDP). The resulting level of debt service payments has used up most of donor balance-of-payments support, thus preventing this aid from adding to public investment. The declining level of public-sector production and employment has shifted workers into the informal sector, and the share of GDP allocated to compensation of employees has declined.[13]

In comparison to Zambia, the Philippine reform experience bears some similarities as well as distinct differences. While the standard reform formula was the same in both, implementation was case specific. In the Philippines, major economic reforms took the form of liberalization of interest rates, removal of certain trade restrictions, price decontrols on agricultural outputs and inputs, and the adoption of a market-oriented exchange rate. The path of reform was one of initial economic hardship (1983–87), followed by an eventual increase in output (1988–90), which was disrupted by a period of recession (1991–92). The unsteady growth of the Philippine economy is reflected in table 2 in the growth rates of its GDP and GNP from 1981 to 1996.

The economic performance of the Philippines during the early period of structural adjustment (1980–84) paralleled that of Zambia's economic crisis. Implementation of SAP reforms coincided with the most serious political crisis faced by the country up to that time, as growing social unrest undermined Marcos's authoritarian rule. Despite the increase in political instability, growing evidence of large-scale corruption, and rising concentration of power and wealth, the World Bank proceeded with SAP-loan negotiations in 1980 and sought implementation of policy reforms consisting of import liberalization initially and financial liberalization soon thereafter.[14] As these programs were being implemented, important sectors such as sugar and coconut trading, construction, fertilizers, and tobacco, became more and more monopolized by Marcos cronies. By 1983, a massive capital flight that contributed strongly to the depletion of foreign exchange took place following the assassination of Marcos's leading opponent, Benigno Aquino, and a loss of confidence in the government.[15]

The sharp increase in current account and balance-of-payments deficits during this time brought about the imposition of a new stabilization program, spearheaded by the Central Bank of the Philippines (CBP) in collaboration with the IMF.

78   Maria Sagrario Floro and Kendall Schaefer

TABLE 2
MACROECONOMIC INDICATORS FOR THE PHILIPPINES

Indicator	1980–84	1985–87	1988	1989	1990	1991	1992	1993	1994	1995	1996
Growth rates (% change)											
Real GDP	1.3	0.2	6.8	6.2	2.7	-0.2	0.3	2.1	4.4	1.4	9.6
Consumption per capita	-0.1	-0.7	3.3	2.2	2.7	-0.1	0.9	0.7	1.3	8.1	8.4
Consumer prices	20.9	9.2	8.7	12.2	14.1	18.7	8.9	7.6	9.1	8.1	8.4
Growth rate (as % of GDP)											
Agriculture	19.8	24.2	23.0	22.7	21.9	21.0	21.8	21.6	22.1	21.6	21.4
Industry	28.4	34.7	35.2	34.9	34.5	34.0	32.8	32.7	35.5	32.1	31.8
Of which manufacturing	25.0	24.9	25.6	24.8	24.8	25.3	24.2	23.7	23.3	23.0	22.6
Services	37.1	41.1	41.9	42.4	43.6	45.0	45.3	45.7	45.5	46.3	46.9
Current account balance (%)	-6.5	0.6	-1.1	-3.4	-6.1	-2.3	-1.9	-5.5	-4.6	-2.7	
Balance of payments											
surplus/deficit (%)	0.0	4.2	1.6	1.1	-0.4	3.1	0.7	-0.9	2.3	5.6	4.3
Portfolio investment (%)	0.1	0.1	0.1	0.9	0.4	0.5	1.1	4.2	4.7		
External Debt (%)	6.6	9.0	76.4	37.2	69.0	71.5	62.3	66.0	62.3	53.2	49.1
Government deficit											
(including grants)(%)	-2.8	-3.1	-2.9	-2.1	-3.5	-2.1	-1.2	-1.5	1.0	0.6	0.3
Government current											
expenditures (%)	9.3	11.8	11.9	12.1	13.3	14.3	14.5	14.6	13.4	13.8	13.2

SOURCE: World Bank, *World Development Indicators.*

Drastic cutbacks in the fiscal sector and contractionary monetary policies led to a reduction in aggregate demand and current account deficits. There was a sharp contraction in manufacturing sector growth and in the market economy as a whole, with an overall decline in GDP growth between 1980 and 1985 as table 2 reveals. In real terms, gross investment fell by more than 50 percent between 1983 and 1985.[16] Likewise, the government reduced all expenditures except for interest payments for debt service, which increased. Corresponding to the severe contraction of the economy were steep declines in incomes and in domestic savings, which fell from 17.3 percent of GDP in 1982 to 6.5 percent in 1985.[17]

Unlike Zambia, however, the Philippine economy began to recover after 1986. With the end of the authoritarian Marcos regime, confidence slowly returned, and the economy embarked on its path to recovery. Inflation declined, consumption and investment increased, and GDP grew, although somewhat unsteadily. By 1994, the rate of real GDP growth was a moderate 4.4 percent.[18] This expansion was largely fueled by external sources such as the increase in direct foreign investment, foreign loans, and remittances from overseas contract workers (nonmerchandise trade), as shown in the current account and balance-of-payments balances in table 2. At the same time, import liberalization and the continued appreciation of the Philippine peso fueled an increase in the import content of investment and production as well as a rise in the level of capital intensity in medium- and large-scale business enterprises.[19] By the early 1990s, with the lifting of most restrictions on foreign capital and with the ease of foreign bank entry, globalization was well underway in the Philippines. These reforms brought about a massive surge of portfolio capital flows that further intensified an import-dependent, relatively capital intensive pattern of growth.[20] As illustrated later in the paper, much of the growth in employment is taking place in the informal and service sectors where, as in Zambia, activity is outpacing that of the formal economy.[21]

Labor Market Reconfiguration under the Process of Structural Adjustment. The level and pattern of economic growth in each country bears primary importance on our understanding of labor market dynamics. Despite the flow of foreign loans in the case of Zambia and the increase in both foreign loans, foreign capital, and labor remittances (from overseas employment) in the Philippines, economic restructuring has failed to establish sustained growth in employment in either country. On the contrary, employment growth has been sporadic and accompanied by trends that signal distinct forms of gender inequality in access to labor market opportunities and in the nature of employment. This inequality is exemplified in Zambia by the disproportionate rise in female unemployment, and in the Philippines by the cyclical movement in female labor force participation rates. We shall examine first the relationship between structural adjustment, employment growth, and gender inequality in labor markets through overall employment trends. In the next section we shall then take a closer look at sectoral-level changes.

Implementation of structural adjustment in Zambia, which severely dampened aggregate demand, has combined with a deterioration in the purchasing power of Zambians to create a rather glum labor market picture.[22] First, as shown in table 3, lagging aggregate demand has led to a decline in the level of overall and formal-sector employment. Second, worsening income distribution and falling real

80   Maria Sagrario Floro and Kendall Schaefer

TABLE 3
EMPLOYMENT TRENDS IN ZAMBIA
(In Percentages)

Trend	1980	1982	1984	1986	1988	1990	1994
Total labor force (%)							
Formally employed	23.90	21.40	19.80	13.40	9.80	9.80	13.00
Of which primary	6.90	6.18	5.59	3.69	2.72	2.66	3.40
Of which secondary	6.55	5.43	5.02	3.32	2.32	2.28	2.10
Of which services	10.45	9.79	9.19	6.39	4.75	4.86	7.50
Unemployed (%)	21.00					30.00	
Male	8.70					18.90	
Female	17.80					24.90	
Employed (%)							
Nonwage employment	78.50	80.50	88.30	89.30	90.10		
Unemployed (%)							
Female	49.83			65.96			
Female (share of urban							
unemployed)	49.78			62.77			
Male	50.17			34.04			
Male (share of urban							
unemployed)	50.22			37.23			
Economically active by							
sector (%)							
Women in agriculture	84.70					82.80	
Men in agriculture	69.00					67.90	
Women in industry	2.80					3.20	
Men in industry	12.50					12.80	
Women in services	12.50					14.10	
Men in services	18.50					19.30	
Female economic activity							
rate (%)	30.00						35.00
Male economic activity							
rate (%)	88.00						86.00

SOURCES: Formal employment figures and sectoral economic activity are from World Bank, *Zambia: Prospects for Sustainable Growth 1995–2005* (Washington, DC: World Bank, 1996); and idem, *World Development Indicators* (Washington, DC: World Bank, 1997); Unemployment statistics are from Central Statistical Office (CSO), "Employment Trends 1985 to 1993" (CSO, Lusaka, 1994).

incomes have led to an increasing number of nonwage earners attempting to enter the labor force.[23] As a result, new labor market entrants, many of whom are women, cannot find jobs and are forced either to create their own employment in the informal sector or to contribute instead to the growing pool of unemployed and discouraged workers.[24]

This gender dimension to Zambian open unemployment is partially illustrated in table 3 by recent labor force data that show a distinct increase in the female share of the unemployed between 1980 and 1990. Both the unemployment rate of women and the absolute number of women unemployed greatly outweighed the corresponding figures for men. In 1980, women's unemployment rate was roughly 17.8 percent while men's unemployment rate was only 8.7 percent with the gender gap slightly more pronounced in rural areas. By 1990, women's unemployment rate had risen to 24.9 percent while that of men rose to 18.9 percent.[25] Although data on wage earnings differentials between men and women tend to be sparse, the 1986 figures show that women's earnings are persistently lower than those of men, particularly in the agricultural sector and in sales and administrative/managerial positions, as figure 1 shows. While it is important to recognize the limitations of data in Zambia due to the quality of the statistics and the difficulty in measuring informal employment, these figures do suggest an increase in the open unemployment rate as well as a widening of the gender gap during structural adjustment.

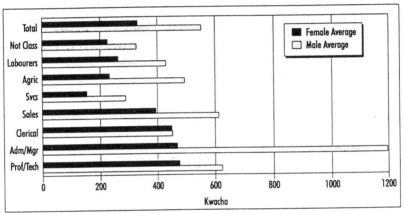

Fig. 1. Zambia: Earnings by Occupation and Gender (1986)
SOURCE: Central Statistical Office (hereafter CSO), "Labor Force Survey 1986" (CSO, Lusaka, 1989).

In comparison to Zambia, Philippine labor market change in response to the implementation of structural adjustment has been somewhat more complex. Specifically, the cyclical pattern of economic growth, characterized by a sharp contraction of the economy followed by a gradual period of economic recovery beginning in 1986, has led to a similar pattern of decline and rise in overall employment levels. Labor force participation rates, however, steadily rose from 60 percent in 1980 to 66 percent in 1992 and then remained fairly constant in the 1990s, as shown in table 4. In absolute terms, the total labor force increased from 16.8 million in 1980 to 27.5 million in 1994. In contrast to these trends, female labor force participation rates in the Philippines followed a cyclical pattern, first declining from 50 percent in 1983 to 41 percent in 1990 and then increasing to 48 percent in 1993. Men's labor force participation rates, on the other hand, remained somewhat constant, averaging about 78 percent during the same period.

Another salient feature of the Philippine labor force is the increasing share of workers with partial and completed secondary education. Between 1976 and

82   Maria Sagrario Floro and Kendall Schaefer

TABLE 4
EMPLOYMENT TRENDS IN THE PHILIPPINES
(In Percentages)

Trend	1980	1983	1985	1990	1992	1993	1994
Unemployed							
Labor force							
participation rate	59.6	63.5	63.1	64.5	66.1	65.6	65.5
Unemployment rate	7.9	10.4	12.6	8.4	9.9	9.3	9.5
Underemployment rate	22.0	32.8	23.8	22.4	20.5	21.7	20.9
Economically active							
Women		50.0	48.3	41.2		47.8	
Men		78.9	79.5	70.0		81.8	
Employed							
Agriculture	51.4		49.0	44.9		45.7	
Industry	15.0		14.2	15.4		15.6	
Of which							
manufacturing	11.0		9.7	10.1		10.1	
Services	33.0		36.8	39.6		38.7	

SOURCES: Activity rates are from International Labor Office (ILO), *Yearbook of Labor Statistics* (Geneva: ILO, various years). Unemployment Statistics are from ILO, *Yearbook of Labor Statistics* (for the years 1980–94); and Institute of Labor Studies as cited by Emmanuel Esguerra, "Employment, Competitiveness, and Growth: 1980–94, in *Towards Sustained Growth,* ed. Raul Fabella and Hideyoshi Saki (Tokyo: Institute of Developing Economies, 1995), pp. 193–222. Sectoral employment is from E. Reyes and T. Sanchez, "Employment Strategies for Accelerated Economic Growth: The Philippine Experience,", Working Paper Series 89-08 (Philippine Institute for Development Studies, Makati, Philippines, 1989) for 1970–85; and from Bureau of Labor and Employment Statistics (BLES), "Current Labor Statistics for 1990–93," as cited by Esguerra, in "Employment, Competitiveness, and Growth," p. 197.

1987, this share increased from 21.9 percent to 29.9 percent.[26] Moreover, employed women exhibit higher educational backgrounds compared to their male counterparts as reflected in the 1988 and 1994 Labor Force Survey results given in figure 2. The proportion of employed Filipino women who have completed higher education is 43 percent whereas the comparable figure for employed men is only 37.6 percent. In 1994, the proportion of employed women who graduated from college is 16.5 percent or more than twice the proportion of employed who are college graduates (7.2 percent).[27] The rise in the educational level of employed workers is partly attributed to increased competition for jobs, particularly during the period of high unemployment and underemployment that peaked in 1985 and 1986 at 12.5 percent and 26.9 percent respectively.[28] Rising educational levels also result from stringent requirements on the part of employers that compel workers to acquire training and education.

High levels of education and skills are also characteristic of the unemployed in the Philippines. Table 5 shows that a growing proportion of unemployed in the Philippines have secondary and tertiary levels of education. In fact, the share of unemployed with a college education rose from 10 percent in 1980 to 14 percent in 1993. Moreover, the highest unemployment levels seem to afflict those who have reached tertiary schooling, a fact pointing to the lack of growth in skilled and semiskilled jobs in the country.

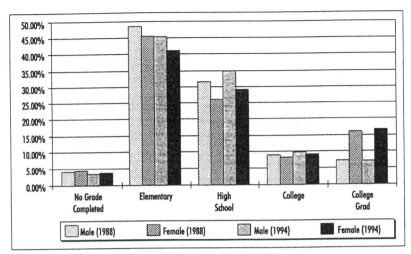

Fig. 2. Percentage of Philippine Employed by Highest Grade Completed
SOURCES: 1988 and 1994 Labor Force Surveys, National Statistical Office (NSO), cited in *Filipino Women: Issues and Trends*, National Commission on the Role of Filipino Women and Asian Development Bank (hereafter NCRFW and ADB) (Manila: NCRFW and ADB, 1995).

TABLE 5
EDUCATIONAL CHARACTERISTICS OF UNEMPLOYED PERSONS: PHILIPPINES
(In Percentages)

Unemployed	1980	1985	1992	1993	1994
No grade completed	3.7	1.0	2.1	2.0	1.9
Elementary	34.9	21.7	22.9	23.4	24.2
High school	34.3	40.9	42.1	42.4	41.3
Some college	27.1	36.4	32.9	32.2	32.3
College degree	10.3	16.8	14.0	14.1	14.5

SOURCE: National Statistical Office (NSO), "Labor Force Surveys," various years, as cited in Esguerra, "Employment, Competitiveness, and Growth," p. 205.

Thus, despite the growth in Philippine GDP per capita (at an average of 2.1 percent during 1986–92 period), there seems to be a persistent lag between the increase in aggregate output and the increase in employment. In fact, recent studies point to a disturbing trend of so-called "jobless growth" in the case of the Philippines, and they question the sustainability of employment generation under SAPs based on the lack of improvement in employment during the latest growth period (1993–present).[29] The jobless growth trend is also reflected in the employment patterns as revealed by the 1991 and 1994 Labor Force Survey results. Although total employment grew on average by 5.1 percent annually, that of the formal sector grew by only 1.8 percent, while the number of informal-sector workers grew by much more: 9.6 percent for those that are self-employed, and 6.5 percent for those that are unpaid, family workers.[30]

Economic Reform and Changes in the Organization of Production

Given the preceding picture of overall labor market conditions, we now examine the sectoral changes in the organization of production in order to generate some insight into the sectoral-level and firm-level adjustments affecting the terms of labor contracts and hiring. Such an analysis can enhance understanding of the reasons for persistent gender inequality, as these sectoral changes have important gender implications for both labor force participation rates and the respective bargaining power of men and women.

Labor Use Patterns in the Agricultural Sector. One important area where both Zambian and Philippine economic reforms have influenced labor market conditions is in agriculture. This sector still accounts for at least 75 percent of the Zambian labor force and 35 percent of total formal-sector employment in the Philippines. In both countries, economic reforms in the agricultural sector have rested on general price liberalization, promotion of modern technology to raise productivity, and commercialization of agricultural production. In Zambia, however, agricultural reform has unfortunately been accompanied by a decline in cultivated land, maize production, and the proportion of households selling to the market as well as a concentration of services in central areas.[31] In the case of the Philippines, agricultural reform has generally entailed agricultural commercialization, consolidation of land for commercial and agribusiness use, and promotion of export crops to meet balance-of-payment deficits.

To begin the analysis, we note that price liberalization necessarily has varied impacts on agricultural workers and farmers. The particular mix of benefits and costs depends to a large extent on the individual's access to resources, the scale of production and type of crop, and the gender pattern of labor use on the farm. For example, in Zambia, SAP-based agricultural reforms have acted through several channels, such as affecting credit and support services to the disadvantage of small-scale farmers, especially those in outlying areas. When price decontrols on maize led to a tripling of its consumer price, this increase was insufficient to compensate for the sevenfold increase of the fertilizer (input) price.[32] As a result, small maize farms, a large portion of which are cultivated by women, were marginalized or pressured out of existence.[33] In fact, between 1985 and 1995, marketed maize output fell by 46 percent, and the proportion of land in maize production fell from 68 percent to 56 percent.[34]

Second, for small farmers in remote areas or for those who were not participating in cash-crop production, privatization has increased the disparities in available support services for marketing, distribution, and transportation. In Zambia, privatization of agricultural production began with the liberalization of the National Agricultural Marketing Board (NAMBOARD) in 1986 and the transfer of marketing responsibilities to cooperatives that focused on export production. Much of the vegetable and other minor produce grown by small-scale women farmers did not qualify for export, and women were thus restricted from using such services. Small and subsistence farmers were further disadvantaged by the fact that, once privatized, most cooperatives lacked the resources to provide the traditional services of transportation and distribution.[35] When private trading networks emerged in the early 1990s, outlying provinces with weaker infrastructure had limited access, and large numbers of small-scale farmers had to revert to subsistence production.[36]

The manner in which these Zambian agricultural reforms affected labor market conditions is neither completely clear nor straightforward. From 1986 to 1991, the unemployment rate for men in rural areas doubled from 7 percent to 14 percent.[37] The rural unemployment rate for women remained consistent, but at 15 percent it was higher than that for men, as was women's percentage of the rural labor force throughout the period. In addition, from 1986 to 1993, the number of rural participants in the informal sector rose, and the proportion of paid employment provided by the agricultural sector declined.[38] Indeed, the data is insufficient to warrant any definite conclusions, but it is possible that wage labor in agriculture and the gender gap in rural employment may have fallen. Consistent with this possibility is the dynamic of a growing informal labor force in agriculture and a growing dependence on agricultural piecework, an area where women comprise the majority.[39] Concerning remuneration, women's growing dependence on agricultural piecework has reinforced the gender gap in earnings.[40] The gender wage differential of roughly 47 percent is in fact the second largest among the occupation data given in figure 1.

In the Philippines, agricultural reforms accompanying structural adjustment involved a somewhat different set of dynamics and outcomes than in Zambia. Specifically, promotion of modern technology and agricultural commercialization at first appears to have created increased employment opportunities that should benefit both men and women.[41] A few studies that have examined longitudinal data, however, have raised concerns regarding the longer-term effects on employment.[42] A study on technological change and labor use in Central Luzon, Philippines, reveals that while total labor per hectare increased in the 1970s by about 20 percent as a result of the introduction of new rice technologies, this figure later declined steadily until 1986.[43]

These policy reforms are also important bearers of gender relations, and their effects on women's and men's roles and the level of both paid and unpaid work are often complex. In a study of the impact of the mechanical reaper in the Philippines during the mid-1980s, findings show that landless workers, particularly women, protested against its use since it would displace labor, and several farmers and manufacturers decided not to adopt it.[44] The same study also indicates that with the introduction of minithreshers, men took over what had been considered to be a woman's job, leading to women's underemployment or partial displacement. As a result, women have resorted to gleaning, a development indicative of the marginalization of women's status.[45] The findings of another study on the impact of agricultural commercialization and export promotion in Mindanao, Philippines, during the late 1980s show that effects on women are not uniform either.[46] The shift from maize (a subsistence crop) to sugar (an export crop) in the area has brought about an overall reduction in the time spent by women as unpaid family workers in farming. This has led to increased time for women in landowning households to engage in their own income-generating activities such as running a store or dressmaking. Women in landless households, however, have found it more difficult to seek employment, and many have stopped looking for work altogether since male hired workers are given preference by export crop (sugar) growers. For those women whose entry into the labor market is driven by economic necessity, their responsibility as income providers has become even harder to fulfill.

Examination of the Urban-Sector Employment Pattern. Structural adjustment reforms in Zambia and the Philippines have also significantly affected conditions of production in the urban sector. SAP reform of the Zambian public sector, which dominates the urban labor market, has entailed vast civil service retrenchment and the dissolution of large publicly owned enterprises. At the early stage of SAP reform in the Philippines, there was an initial boost in labor-intensive, export-oriented industries like those producing electronics and garments. But policy reforms such as financial liberalization and trade liberalization, together with currency appreciation, began to hurt the export market in the early 1990s, except for semiconductor exports, and fueled the growth of an import-dependent, low-labor-absorptive manufacturing sector that did not help reduce unemployment and underemployment. Moreover, there was an influx of the so-called "butterfly" or portfolio type of foreign investment that is short term and speculative in nature and takes advantage of profitable stock market movements and rising real interest rates.[47]

Public-sector reform is particularly important for employment in Zambia since traditionally there has been heavy government involvement in most key economic activities. According to the Central Statistical Office (CSO), by the late 1970s, the public sector accounted for approximately 70 percent of formal-sector employment. By 1995, this ratio had fallen to 55 percent.[48] Between 1985 and 1997, close to 60,000 public employees had been retrenched with another 50,000 retrenchments required in the following two years by the current SAP program. As such, retrenchment has been a primary source of unemployment for formal-sector workers, because there has been no dynamic private sector to fill the gap in labor demand.[49]

As a result of the shrinking civil service and declining levels of domestic investment, it is likely that many Zambians have been pushed into the informal sector. The 1986 Labor Force Survey estimates that there were 1.8 million participants in the informal sector, twice the number in 1980.[50] Of this 1.8 million participants, those located in the urban sector accounted for 77.2 percent of total urban employment.[51] By 1996, approximately 3.4 million Zambians were reported to be employed in the informal sector, almost double the figure for 1986.[52] Of this 3.4 million participants, over two-thirds were women.

Sectorally, employment data in table 3 show that for both men and women, the share of economically active in services has increased from 1980 to 1990, but that the total share of those formally employed in services has declined. As in many African countries, much of service-sector employment is increasingly likely to be located in the informal sector and likely to be done by women. Table 6 shows that in 1986, only 31 percent of men's service work was informal compared to 71 percent of women's service work. Data is not available for this sectoral breakdown in the 1990s. In 1986, however, the majority of urban informal production was in sales (57.9%), the majority of women's employment in services was informal (65%), and the majority of informal participants were women (59%).[53] As such, it is indeed likely that in Zambia, as in much of sub-Saharan Africa, informal-sector participation is becoming increasingly feminized.[54]

TABLE 6
A Snapshot of the Informal Sector in Zambia in 1986
(In Percentages)

	Women	Men
Informal labor force	72.0	29.0
Manufacturing	81.0	31.0
Transport	0.0	8.0
Services	71.0	31.0
Distribution of informal-		
sector labor force	59.0	41.0
Manufacturing	41.0	59.0
Transport	11.0	89.0
Services	65.0	35.0
Distribution of urban informal		
activity by occupation		
Professional/technical/administrative/		
managerial	1.1	3.1
Clerical	0.5	0.8
Sales	57.9	28.1
Services	4.9	10.6
Agriculture	1.1	2.8
Subsistence farming	28.1	30.1
Laborers	7.1	24.5

SOURCES: For informal-sector employment by occupation for Chawama Region, see Caroline Moser, "Poverty and Vulnerability in Chawama, Lusaka, Zambia," Final Draft (Urban Development Division, World Bank, Washington, DC, 1994); other data are from United Nations (UN), *The World's Women 1995: Trends and Statistics*, Social Statistics and Indicators, Series K, No. 12 (New York: UN, 1995).

Another gender dimension to urban employment trends is the fact that wages in the informal sector have remained less than 50 percent of those in the formal sector, despite falling formal-sector wages.[55] Figure 2 reveals a disaggregation of earnings by gender that implies a skewed distribution toward higher average male earnings. Wage differentials in sales, where studies have shown women's informal-sector participation to be concentrated (table 6), are among the highest. In fact, it has been argued that gender income differentials grew during the 1980s and that most of the disparity was due to informal-sector activity.[56]

Structural adjustment in the Philippines has also brought little improvement to urban employment, which has been shaped by the outward-oriented industrialization strategy of the late 1980s. As revealed in table 4, overall industrial employment accounts for 14 to 16 percent of total employment since 1980, but the growth was largely in construction and not in manufacturing. In fact, recent studies reveal that the share of manufacturing employment in total employment has declined from 11 percent in 1980 to 8.55 percent in 1996.[57] The share of women workers in total manufacturing employment (including electronics and garments) was roughly 11.64 percent for the 1987–96 period.[58] A few studies argue that the increased investment per worker, which has raised labor productivity, suggests that the incentive structure of the system continues to retain its strong capital bias.[59] The type of policy reform pursued during structural adjustment seems to have failed to correct the structural problem of production in the Philippines that favored bigness and capital-intensive methods. Moreover, the policy reforms under SAPs and stabilization have encouraged foreign capital investment that is short term in nature as the increasing proportion of portfolio investment during the 1990s in the balance-of-payment capital accounts indicates (see table 2). This has created speculative bubbles in the Philippine stock market as elsewhere in East Asia. As the grave lessons from the recent financial crisis in the region demonstrate, this type of growth, to say the least, has neither made any substantial contribution to the production capacity of the economy, nor has it helped promote sustainable growth and employment. In fact, prior to 1996 there were serious concerns raised by some economists and policymakers over the worrisome trend whereby much of this short-term portfolio investment has been channeled toward real estate and financial speculation that does not create jobs on a sustained basis.

Not surprisingly, gender permeates the functioning of the urban labor market in the Philippines as it does in Zambia. Women make up 39 percent of the total employed in the urban areas. Available evidence shows that the type of industrialization promoted in the Philippines during the 1970s and under SAP has contributed to the increase in female employment, mostly for young women, and particularly in the so-called export processing zones (EPZs).[60] There has also been an increase in industrial subcontracting where women workers perform labor-intensive tasks on a piecerate basis in their own homes.

With the exception of the export-oriented garment and electronic industries, however, the manufacturing sector has been limited in its capacity for generating female employment. Occupational segregation tends to characterize the Philippine labor market, as revealed in a study using the 1988 and 1994 Labor Force Survey data.[61] Figure 3 illustrates some of the data from these studies. It indicates that women constitute the majority of those employed in wholesale and retail trade (66.3%) and in community, social, and personal services (56.3%). In the manufacturing sector, 59.3 percent of total women employed are production workers in the textile, wearing apparel, and leather industries alone. The share of women in those industries or sectors that are considered to be traditionally male dominated (e.g., construction) has not increased. The same study also illustrates the implications of occupational segregation on the conditions of employment facing men and women. For instance, in the textile/apparel industries, flexible labor arrangements have begun to replace regular labor contracts. Since women make up the bulk of those who work as tailors, dressmakers, and sewers (81%)

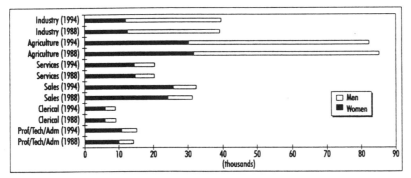

Fig. 3. Philippine Employed Persons by Occupation

SOURCES: See fig. 2.

and as spinners, weavers, knitters, and dyers (79.3%), the majority of work is performed under low-paid subcontracting arrangements. Furthermore, the study reveals that there has been no compositional change in the types of jobs available that are occupied by women within the different sectors.

Stylized notions of "feminine" and "masculine" jobs continue to permeate the hiring and promotion practices in most business enterprises. A study on recruitment practices and preferences of Philippine industrial establishments reveals several interesting findings in this regard.[62] Based on the 1990 Philippine Labor Flexibility Survey (PLFS), over 56 percent of the 1,311 industrial establishments in the survey sample said they prefer men as production workers, while 12 percent said they prefer women, and a little over 31 percent said they were indifferent.[63] The same study also reveals that, in most industrial sectors, a slight majority of firms have only 10 percent or less of their total employment not working under a regular labor contract.[64]

Given the stagnancy in manufacturing employment and sparse industrial deepening, the jobs that seem to be growing rapidly in the Philippines are those in low-productivity types of production, menial work, and sales and services. Among the service occupations employing women, one major activity is sex work (the provision of sexual services, e.g., as entertainers, massage parlor attendants, etc.), which has been spurred on by the growth in tourism.[65] Other more conventional service jobs for women include domestic service, petty and retail trading, home-based manufacturing and craft production, and laundry work. Available evidence also indicates that the informal sector has grown substantially in the late 1980s and early 1990s, particularly in low-productivity, low-paying jobs.[66]

International Labor Migration as a Labor Safety Net. International labor migration has been a particularly distinct feature of the Philippine labor market. Since 1974, when the Marcos government unveiled its overseas employment program, overseas contract employment has served as a major foreign exchange earner. It has also been an important coping mechanism for the rapid expansion of the labor force and the growing inability of the economy to generate a corresponding level of labor demand. In contrast to the economic stagnation and recession experienced by the Philippines in the mid-1980s and early 1990s, its Asian neighbors and the Middle East countries were experiencing an economic boom and increased demand for both skilled and menial-job workers. Initially, international labor migration has tended to be associated with men who assume jobs overseas that require male-stereotype skills, for example, those calling for technical, construction, and production-related education and training. In recent years, the changing nature of the demand for Filipino workers has resulted in a gradual shift toward female migrant workers. By 1992 women represented over 51 percent of the newly hired contract workers and by mid-1995, 60 percent, as table 7 reveals. Employment opportunities for Filipino women dramatically expanded particularly as domestic helpers, even though nearly 50 percent of them have finished tertiary education.

TABLE 7
OVERSEAS WORK IN THE PHILIPPINES

	Women	Men
Newly hired overseas workers		
1992	132,131	128,457
1993	140,664	115,533
1994	155,319	103,665
1st half of 1995	69,433	45,191
	Percentages	Percentages
Overseas workers–highest grade completed		
Elementary–1992	9	10
High school–1992	41	34
College–1992	51	57
Elementary–1994	11	8
High school–1994	38	32
College–1994	50	60
	1990 Total	1990 Percentage Distribution
Employed women overseas contract workers (OCWs) by skill		
Professional/technical/administrative/ managerial	9,539	8.2
Clerical	950	0.8
Sales	597	0.5
Service	58,522	50.6
Prod/transport	3,800	3.3
Agriculture	24	0.0
Entertainers	31,113	26.9
No data	11,174	9.7
Total	115,719	100.0

SOURCES: Carolyn Medel Anonuevo, "Confronting Feminization of Migration" (School of Economics, University of the Philippines, Quezon City, 1996); and National Commission on the Role of Filipino Women and Asian Development Bank (NCRFW and ADB), *Filipino Women Migrants: A Statistical Factbook* (Manila: NCRFW and ADB, 1996).

As within the Philippine economy, occupational segregation characterizes the employment patterns in international labor markets. Filipino female workers tend to occupy jobs that are service oriented and fit the gender-based functions assigned to women. The story of Filipino women taking over the domestic and childcare chores of other women is repeated in many parts of the world, where, in addition, women are in demand as nurses and entertainers.[67] In fact, domestic help is the most highly demanded occupation for women in 69 countries, and domestic work is perhaps the most common job for Filipinos working overseas.[68] A study on the feminization of migration shows that in 1990, 51 percent of the women employed can be found in the service sector while 27 percent are entertainers.[69] Only 8 percent of migrant women take on jobs that require professional and technical skills while, by contrast, there is a concentration of professional, construction, and transportation jobs among male contract workers.

Effects of Structural Adjustment on Intrahousehold Dynamics

Economic restructuring also shapes the decision of household members to participate in the labor market by altering their incentives and constraints as well as the process of decision making within households. Numerous studies have examined the variety of determinants affecting labor force participation decisions. Determinants include such factors as the wage, access to resources and credit, skills and education, access to information, and the extent and nature of reproductive work. Recently, some feminist economists have raised the importance of bargaining processes and intrahousehold dynamics on labor market decisions as well.[70] Given the interaction between economic and intrahousehold change, a comprehensive approach to understanding labor force participation decisions is warranted.[71] This comprehensive approach must explicitly address bargaining.

In this study, the paucity of longitudinal data for the Philippines and Zambia does not allow for a detailed study of the various mechanisms by which structural adjustment affects the intrahousehold division of labor, the manner of negotiation between men and women, and the size and structure of the household. However, one must note that these institutional changes influence the range of options and constraints faced by men and women for participating in the labor market. Following are a few examples illustrating interactions between intrahousehold structure changes, decision processes, labor supply, and economic change. The examples suggest the need for further research into these issues.

One study has made use of a longitudinal community panel survey of Chawama, Zambia, between 1978 and 1992 in order to identify the constraints limiting the poor's capacity to respond to macroeconomic change.[72] Relying on a random sample survey of 200 households, a subsample survey of 30 women, and a community-level survey of basic services and infrastructure, the study illustrates that economic reform in Zambia has led to household restructuring in such a manner as to increase women's participation in the labor force due to economic distress. Extending the household in Zambia is often done to act as a safety net for young unemployed men, decreasing the vulnerability of the individual, but resulting in increased vulnerability of the household.[73] The proportion of extended households in the Chamawa study increased from 7 percent to 36 percent during the period from 1978 to 1992. Increasing household vulnerability then translates into increased labor market participation of young and old female household members, in both the rural and the urban areas. The ability to increase labor market participation is, in turn, enhanced by the addition of female members to the extended household who can aid in household work and childcare.

In the Philippines, the labor force participation story at first appears to be the opposite. Labor force growth rates diminished from 1985 to 1986, with open unemployment and underemployment rates reaching 12 percent and 26 percent respectively. Moreover, as table 4 shows, the participation of females dropped slightly between 1983 and 1993. Some studies suggest that this may be due to the prevailing cultural norms in Philippine society that women's preferred status is to be a "homemaker" and that the material and psychological needs of their husbands and families assume greater importance than their own.[74]

In examining our data however, and in taking into account some in-depth studies of household dynamics in the Philippines, it is not exactly clear whether these norms were strong enough in the 1980s to constrain women from seeking employment. Even if one bears in mind the difficulties of making strong generalizations about gender in a society as diverse as the Philippines, there is strong evidence indicating that women in the Philippines have a prominent role both within the household as well as in the labor market, particularly during periods of economic crises.[75] But the burden of coping during periods of economic downturn falls disproportionately on women as shown in a recent study of urban Philippine household responses to vulnerability. While women average 13 to 16 hours a week in reproductive activities, men average 5 or fewer hours a week on these tasks. At the same time, women have increasingly taken on paid work, although in many cases, as in informal-sector employment, such a contribution is often underestimated or overlooked. Moreover, the difficulties in finding employment in the formal sector may have discouraged some women altogether.

Undoubtedly, economic motivations play a primary role in determining female labor supply in both Zambia and the Philippines. Economic incentives are important for bargaining processes, given that female-male interpersonal relationships are often contractual and dynamic in nature. In fact, not only does the division of labor change as a result of changing economic conditions, but the spheres of control and authority are also likely to be altered.

The importance of employment and wage income for intrahousehold bargaining power has been supported by several household studies in Zambia and the Philippines.[76] Unpaid labor in production activities under the control of men can play a significant role in undermining women's bargaining position within the household. Women themselves may perceive their labor as merely "assisting men" and as not directly value producing. Bargaining power is shaped by the nature of the work and by each member's accompanying perception of that work's contribution.

There are several gender-based constraints in regard to which access to employment and income-earning ability can shift power relationships within the household. Men still retain legal ownership of most land in the Philippines and Zambia and maintain decision-making powers over resource allocation and output disposal. Moreover, despite the autonomy that women exercise in certain economic domains, the ultimate orientation of women in both societies is that of domestic matters.[77] As a result, women's work hours may lengthen considerably as their primary "duty" for the reproduction and maintenance of the household remains. The fact that many women tend to be found in lower-paid occupations and/or jobs with more flexible hours such as in industrial subcontracting or home-based piecework in the Philippines relates very much to the practical constraints imposed by the household division of labor as well as to the fact that employers tend to regard women as secondary workers whose earnings are merely supplementary to those of their husbands. Moreover, several studies in Zambia have revealed that men control women's additional income, so that increased informal-sector activity simply reinforces the subordination of women and the degree to which female access to resources is mediated through men.[78]

The constraints facing women in making labor supply decisions and in acting as decisionmakers are therefore not simply independent of male interests but are "policed" by nonmarket mechanisms that operate within the context of the household institution.[79] Hence, the response to increasing or diminishing employment opportunities resulting from economic restructuring can vary not only with education, age, and resources, but also with the specific sociocultural norms that prevail.

When one is examining reform, it is important to remember that the governing pattern of the household division of labor and, consequently, the pattern of decision making within the household may be changing as well. This is true, for example, when there is a reconfiguration of the household owing to either the migration or abandonment of its male household head, or the migration of female household members. In the Philippines, the rapid growth in the number of female overseas workers seems to influence household dynamics and has challenged the traditional notions of sex roles. With the household highly dependent on the worker's remittances for its needs, the remitter acquires an important status and becomes a major decisionmaker, particularly in expenditures allocation.[80] He or she is seen as a "role model" and a conduit for other household members and friends to locate work elsewhere. Hence, the altered labor-use pattern and individual earning capacity may create tension between prevailing gender norms and the sources of bargaining power; on the other hand, they may reinforce existing social constraints and gender inequalities not only in the market economy but also within the household.

Summary and Conclusions

Labor market changes during the process of economic restructuring in Zambia and the Philippines have been similar in some respects and very different in others. Economic performance in Zambia has not been sufficient to generate wide-based employment and has been characterized by rising unemployment. Gradual recovery leading to modest steady growth in the Philippines has unfortunately been characterized by a growth in joblessness, specifically with regard to skilled and semiskilled employment. Global integration of labor markets has afforded some employment opportunity to workers like those in the Philippines who are willing and able to seek jobs overseas, but not to those in Zambia, where many factors constrain labor mobility. The gender dimension of these labor market trends as shown in the preceding discussion is quite significant and, at the same time, quite complex.

Sectorally, in both the Philippines and Zambia, agricultural reform has shifted female labor toward agricultural wage work (which is seasonal and low paid) or the informal sector. In urban areas, certain export-oriented industries in the Philippines have created some jobs, predominantly for young women, but this number constitutes only a small proportion of total females employed. Much of the growth in female jobs has occurred in sales and service sectors, including sex work, domestic service, and petty trade. Employment patterns throughout many establishments continue to be characterized by a high degree of occupational segregation.

International labor migration in the Philippines has been an important labor safety net. Since the mid-1980s, international labor migration has become more feminized, with women constituting the majority of overseas contract workers. Occupational segregation extends to the international level, with the majority of women employed in the service sector as entertainers and domestic helpers.

Access to paid work in some cases may empower women, yet in other cases their power may be diminished. The specific character of the labor market development and the nature of the accompanying economic reform, both of which alter the ability of women and men to take advantage of opportunity, is important in this regard. Reform shifts patterns of production organization and location of employment and, as such, can either reinforce the prevailing distribution of power or provide tension, thereby challenging the governing pattern of income control and decision making.

This study reveals that the economic restructuring undertaken by the Philippines and Zambia during the 1980s did not necessarily bring about significant changes in the configurations of the labor market such that gender equality would be promoted. Continuing gender inequalities were illustrated by higher female unemployment in Zambia, the persistence of occupational segregation among domestic and overseas Filipino contract workers, and the increasing job insecurity among female informal-sector participants and homeworkers. Within the household, such labor market developments have created an intensification of women's work, particularly in the low-income households, and, in many cases, have simply allowed the traditional division of labor and decision-making processes.

NOTES

1.   See World Bank, *Labor and the Growth Crisis in Sub-Saharan Africa* (Washington, DC: World Bank, 1995).

2.   See World Bank, *Gender Issues in World Bank Lending* (Washington, DC: World Bank, 1995). In Zambia and the Philippines, the World Bank undertook in the early 1990s a Women in Development (WID) assessment, community surveys, and research in intrahousehold decision making in the urban areas (Caroline Moser, "Poverty and Vulnerability in Chawama, Lusaka, Zambia," Final Draft [Urban Development Division, World Bank, Washington, DC, 1994]; idem, *Household Responses to Poverty and Vulnerability,* vol. 3: *Confronting Crisis in Commonwealth, Metro Manila, Philippines* [Washington, DC: World Bank, 1997]).

3.   See World Bank, "Towards Gender Equality: The Role of Public Policy" (Education and Social Policy Department, World Bank, Washington, DC, 1995).

4.   Those that involved formal wage labor market-related programs were primarily done for the regions of Europe and Central Asia (ECA) and Latin America and the Caribbean (LAC).

5.   See World Bank, *World Tables* (Baltimore, MD: Johns Hopkins University Press for the World Bank, 1995); idem, *Gender Issues in World Bank Lending.*

6.   In recent years, under the leadership of President James Wolfensohn, the World Bank has broadened its set of gender-based initiatives, including the introduction of Gender Action Plans for each region and the creation of a Gender Sector Board.

7.   See World Bank, "Advancing Gender Equality: From Concepts to Action" (Gender Analysis and Policy Division, Poverty and Social Policy Department, World Bank, Washington, DC, 1995).

8.   Both the Philippines and Zambia have recently experienced very rapid urban growth in the last three decades. Nonetheless, agriculture remains the primary source of livelihood for about three-fourths of the Zambian population and more than a third of the population in the Philippines. See Beatrice Kalinda and Maria Floro, "Zambia in the 1980's: A Review of National and Urban Level Economic Reforms," Working Paper (Urban Development Division, World Bank, Washington, DC, 1992); and Orville Solon and Maria Floro, "The Philippines in the 1980's: A Review of National and Urban Level Economic Reforms," Working Paper (Urban Development Division, World Bank, Washington, DC, 1993), for a more thorough discussion of the economic structures of the two countries and their pattern of sectoral growth over the last two decades.

9.   For a discussion of the economic reforms implemented under the Structural Adjustment Programs, see Solon and Floro, "Philippines in the 1980's "; and Kalinda and Floro, "Zambia in the 1980's."

10.   The early 1980s in Zambia were characterized by no real growth in gross domestic product (GDP), declining consumption per capita, and a sixfold rise in inflation. By 1987, maize prices had risen so substantially that riots broke out and the government was forced to restore subsidization. At that time, liberalization policies were abandoned, and the government initiated its own reform program that included lowering interest rates and establishing a debt payment cap. These reforms failed, however, largely as a result of the suspension of foreign credit, and the government resumed negotiations with the International Monetary Fund (IMF) in 1988 (Kalinda and Floro, "Zambia in the 1980's").

11.   See World Bank, *World Tables 1995.*

12.   See Caleb Fundaga, "Interest Rate Policy in Zambia," *Southern Africa Political and Economic Monthly* (Harare), July 1988, p. 10.

13.   A study by William J. House, "Priorities for Urban Labor Market Research in Anglophone Africa," *Journal of Developing Areas* 27 (October 1992): 49–68, discusses the rapid growth of informal-sector activity across Anglophone Africa. The author states that the growth of urban wage employment in this region has fallen and has forced increased reliance on informal-sector activity.

14.   See Robin Broad, *Unequal Alliance: The World Bank, the International Monetary Fund, and the Philippines* (Berkeley: University of California Press, 1988).

15.   James Boyce, "The Political Economy of External Indebtedness: A Case Study of the Philippines," Monograph Series No. 12 (Philippine Institute for Development Studies, Metro Manila, Philippines, 1990).

16.   See Joseph Lim, *Philippine Macroeconomic Developments 1970–1993* (Quezon City, Philippines: Philippine Center for Policy Studies, University of the Philippines, 1996).

17.   See Joseph Lim, "Structural Shifts in Key Macro Parameters: Implications on the Sustainability of Growth," in *Towards Sustained Growth,* ed. Raul Fabella and Hideyoshi Sakai

(Tokyo: Institute of Developing Economies, 1995), pp. 1–32; and Lim, *Philippine Macroeconomic Developments 1970–1993*.

   18.   The economic recovery of the Philippines has been attributed to several factors including expansion of domestic consumption fueled by an increase in real wages and low inflation as well as by steady government spending. See Solon and Floro, "Philippines in the 1980's"; Lim, *Philippine Macroeconomic Developments 1970–1993*; and Emmanuel Esguerra, "Employment, Competitiveness, and Growth: 1980–94," in *Towards Sustained Growth*, ed. Fabella and Sakai, pp. 193–222.

   19.   See Joseph Lim, "Employment Effect of Globalization and the East Asian Crisis on Women: The Philippine Case," Working Paper (School of Economics, University of the Philippines, Quezon City, Philippines, 1998); and Esguerra, "Employment, Competitiveness, and Growth: 1980–94."

   20.   See Lim, "Employment Effect of Globalization."

   21.   See Esguerra, "Employment, Competitiveness, and Growth: 1980–94."

   22.   The deterioration in real purchasing power is revealed through the increase in the consumer price index (CPI) by 153 percent from 1980 to 1985 and by 1,522 percent from 1985 to 1990. Though nominal salaries also rose, their increase was well below that of the CPI, indicating a significant erosion of real income. Several government subsidization programs were attempted in order to restrain the rise in living costs, but these have all since been abandoned. Such programs included the 1987–88 urban consumer subsidy, the 1989–91 maize meal subsidy coupon scheme, and the 85 percent basic wage and salary adjustment of 1990 (Kalinda and Floro, "Zambia in the 1980's," p. 29).

   23.   See ibid.

   24.   Over 60 percent of those in extreme poverty reported engaging in piecework as a central survival strategy (Central Statistical Office [hereafter, CSO], "The Evolution of Poverty in Zambia 1991–1996" [Lusaka, Zambia: CSO, 1997]).

   25.   See CSO, "Employment Trends 1985 to 1993" (Lusaka, Zambia: CSO, 1994).

   26.   See Solon and Floro, "Philippines in the 1980's. "

   27.   See National Commission on the Role of Filipino Women and the Asian Development Bank (NCRFW and ADB), *Filipino Women: Issues and Trends* (Manila: NCRFW and ADB, 1995).

   28.   See Esguerra, "Employment, Competitiveness, and Growth: 1980–94."

   29.   See Lim, *Philippine Macroeconomic Developments 1970–1993*; and Esguerra, "Employment, Competitiveness, and Growth: 1980–94."

   30.   See Esguerra, Employment, Competitiveness, and Growth: 1980–94."

   31.   See World Bank, *Zambia: Prospects for Sustainable Growth 1995–2005* (Washington, DC: World Bank, 1996).

   32.   Note that much of the fertilizer used in maize production has high import content so that its price was heavily affected by the currency's devaluation. See Gisela Geisler and Karen Tranberg Hanson, "Structural Adjustment, the Rural-Urban Interface, and Gender Relations in Zambia," in *Women in the Age of Economic Transformation: Gender Impact of Reforms in Post-Socialist and Developing Countries*, ed. Nahid Aslanbeigui, Steven Pressman, and Gale Summerfield (London and New York: Routledge, 1994), pp. 95–112.

   33.   Maize production was discouraged in several outlying provinces in the 1990s once the fertilizer subsidy was removed and farmers could not cover fertilizer costs (p. 166). This displacement of production had both equity and efficiency repercussions since outlying areas are less prone to drought. Nonetheless, the World Bank viewed price liberalization as necessary for competition (Kalinda and Floro, "Zambia in the 1980's," p. 17).

   34.   See World Bank, *Zambia: Prospects for Sustainable and Equitable Growth* (Washington, DC: World Bank, 1993).

   35.   Kathryn H. Larson and Joyce Kanyangwa, "Women in Market-Oriented Agriculture," in *The Dynamics of Agricultural Policy and Reform in Zambia*, ed. Adrian P. Wood, Stuart A. Kean, John T. Milimo, and Dennis Michael Warren (Ames: Iowa State University Press, 1990), pp. 473–94.

   36.   See World Bank, *Zambia: Prospects for Sustainable and Equitable Growth*.

   37.   See CSO, "Employment Trends 1985 to 1993."

   38.   See ibid.

   39.   See Geisler and Hanson, "Structural Adjustment, the Rural-Urban Interface."

40. Sisisra Jayasuriya and R. T. Shand, "Technical Change in Labor Absorption in Asian Agriculture: Some Emerging Trends," *World Development* 14, no. 3 (1986): 415–28; and Violeta Cordova, Keiko Otsuka, and Fe Gascon, "Technological Change and Labor Use in Rice Farming" (paper presented at the Fourth Meeting of the Federation of Crop Social Society of the Philippines, Davao City, 26–30 April 1988).

41. For example, Randolph Barker, Robert Herdt, and Beth Rose, *The Rice Economy of Asia* (Washington, DC: Resources for the Future, 1985), reviewed about 20 village studies of labor use both before and after the adoption of modern rice varieties and showed gains in labor productivity as well as labor use. Most of these studies were done in the1970s.

42. See for example, Jayasuriya and Shand, "Technical Change in Labor Absorption."

43. See Cordova, Otsuka, and Gascon, "Technological Change and Labor Use in Rice Farming."

44. See F. Juarez et al., "The Development and Impact of Mechanical Reapers in the Philippines," Agricultural Economics Paper No. 88–23 (International Rice Research Institute [IRRI], Los Banos, Philippines, 1988); and Thelma Paris, "Technology and Policy Needs of Poor Women in Asian Rice Farming," *Gender, Technology, and Development* 2, no. 2 (1998): 188–217.

45. See Paris, "Technology and Policy Needs of Poor Women."

46. Maria Sagrario Floro, "Women, Work, and Agricultural Commercialization in the Philippines," in *Women's Work in the World Economy*, ed. Nancy Folbre et al. (New York: New York University Press, 1991), pp. 3–40.

47. See Lim, "Structural Shifts in Key Macro Parameters"; idem, "Employment Effect of Globalization and the East Asian Crisis"; and Esguerra, "Employment, Competitiveness, and Growth: 1980–94." The share of women workers in total manufacturing employment (including electronics and garments) was roughly 11.74 percent for the 1987–96 period.

48. See CSO, "Living Conditions Monitoring Survey Report" (CSO, Lusaka, 1997).

49. See Moser, "Poverty and Vulnerability in Chawama, Lusaka, Zambia."

50. See CSO, "Labor Force Survey 1986" (CSO, Lusaka, 1989).

51. See Kalinda and Floro, "Zambia in the 1980's."

52. See CSO, "Living Conditions Monitoring Survey Report."

53. See CSO, "Living Conditions Monitoring Survey Report."

54. Kate Meagher, in "Crisis, Informalization, and the Urban Informal Sector in Sub-Saharan Africa," *Development and Change* 26 (1995): 259–84, discusses the trend of feminization in the informal sector for Africa.

55. See Kalinda and Floro, "Zambia in the 1980's."

56. See Venkatish Seshamani, "The Economic Policies of Zambia in the 1980's: Towards Structural Transformation with a Human Focus," in *Africa's Recovery in the 1990's: From Stagnation and Adjustment to Human Development*, ed. Giovanni Andrea Cornia, Rolph Vander Hoeven, and P. Thandika Mkandawire (New York: St. Martin's, 1992), pp. 116–34.

57. See Lim, "Employment Effect of Globalization and the East Asian Crisis"; and NCRFW and ADB, *Filipino Women: Issues and Trends*; and idem, *Trends in Women's Employment in the Regions 1991–94* (Manila: NCRFW and ADB, 1995).

58. See Lim, "Employment Effect of Globalization and the East Asian Crisis."

59. See Esguerra, "Employment, Competitiveness, and Growth: 1980–94."

60. See Sylvia Chant and Cathy McIlwaine, *Women of a Lesser Cost: Female Labour, Foreign Exchange, and Philippine Development* (Quezon City, Philippines: Ateneo de Manila University Press, 1995); NCRFW and ADB, *Filipino Women: Issues and Trends*; idem, *Trends in Women's Employment in the Regions 1991–94*; and Moser, *Confronting Crisis in Commonwealth, Metro Manila, Philippines*.

61. See Marina Fe Durano, "Hazards in Women's Workplace," Working Paper (Philippine Center for Policy Studies, University of the Philippines, Diliman, Quezon City, 1996); and NCRFW and ADB, *Filipino Women: Issues and Trends*.

62. See Guy Standing, "Identifying the Human Resource Enterprise: A South-east Asian Example," *International Labor Review* 131, no. 3 (1992): 281–93.

63.   One of the questions in the Philippine Labor Flexibility Survey (PLFS) examines the extent to which firms have a non-sex-discriminatory hiring policy. There are well-known problems with such indicators as discussed in the study. Given such drawbacks, the preceding results were based on the response of the establishments to the question on whether in recruiting production workers, they had a preference for men or women (p. 287).

64.   The exceptions are the construction, wood products, and food-processing industries. Nonregular labor contracts involve the use of casual or temporary labor, contract labor, unpaid labor, and subcontracting.

65.   See Chant and McIlwaine, *Women of a Lesser Cost.*

66.   See Esguerra, "Employment, Competitiveness, and Growth: 1980–94."

67.   In Hong Kong and Singapore, 98–99 percent of Filipino workers are household helpers.

68.   See Carolyn Medel Anonuevo, "Confronting Feminization of Migration" (University of the Philippines, School of Economics, Quezon City, 1996).

69.   See ibid.

70.   See Bina Agarwal, *A Field of One's Own: Gender and Land Rights in South Asia* (Cambridge: Cambridge University Press, 1994); and Gillian Hart, "Gender and Household Dynamics: Recent Theories and Their Implications," in *Critical Issues in Asian Development: Theories, Experiences, and Policies,* ed. M. G. Quibria (Hong Kong: Oxford University Press for the Asian Development Bank, 1995).

71.   A detailed study on women's time use was conducted for Bangladesh by Habiba Zaman, "Patterns of Activity and Use of Time in Rural Bangladesh: Class, Gender, and Seasonal Variation," *Journal of Developing Areas* 29 (April 1995): 371–88. This study is an illuminating example of the methodology here recommended. Using time-use surveys, the author discusses how a deterioration in socioeconomic conditions affects women's time allocation decisions within the framework of gender and class structures.

72.   See Moser, "Poverty and Vulnerability in Chawama, Lusaka, Zambia."

73.   According to CSO, "The Evolution of Poverty in Zambia 1991–1996" (CSO, Lusaka, 1997), the incidence of extreme poverty increases exponentially with household size in Zambia. Between 1991 and 1996, the largest increase in poverty was accounted for by households with more than nine members.

74.   See Judy Sevilla, "The Filipino Woman and the Family," in *The Filipino Woman in Focus: A Book of Readings,* ed. Amaryllis Torres (Quezon City, Philippines: University of the Philippines Press, 1989).

75.   See Moser, *Confronting Crisis in Commonwealth, Metro Manila, Philippines.*

76.   See Nancy Folbre, "Household Production in the Philippines: A Non-neoclassical Approach,"*Economic Development and Cultural Change* 32 (January 1984): 303–33; Shubh Kumar, *Adoption of Hybrid Maize in Zambia: Effects on Gender Roles, Food Consumption, and Nutrition,* Research Paper 100 (Washington, DC: International Food Policy Research Institute, 1994); and Sevilla, "Filipino Woman and the Family."

77.   This does not mean that women's employment is frowned upon or disapproved in society, however.

78.   See Geisler and Hanson, "Structural Adjustment, the Rural-Urban Interface"; and Jane Guyer, "Intra-household Processes and Farming Systems Research: Perspectives from Anthropology," in *Understanding Africa's Rural Households and Farming Systems,* ed. Joyce Moock (Boulder, CO: Westview, 1986), pp. 92–104.

79.   See Diane Elson, "Gender Awareness in Modeling Structural Adjustment," *World Development* 23 (November 1995): 1862.

80.   See Anonuevo, "Confronting Feminization of Migration."

[20]

Structural Adjustment Policies

Structural adjustment policies (SAPs) refer to high-powered austerity pro-grammes implemented in many countries across the globe since the early 1980s and propelled by international financial loans tied to International Monetary Fund (IMF) and World Bank conditionalities. From Africa to Asia, Latin America and Eastern Europe, over 100 countries have applied similar packages, despite significant differences in their economies. Earlier versions

688   Structural Adjustment Policies

of these types of policies had been part of stabilization plans imposed by the IMF during the post-World War II period on countries with chronic balance of payments problems. What was new with SAPs was their wider scope and their connection with the foreign debt problem that developed in the late 1970s and early 1980s. The accumulated debt was the result of a variety of factors – from the oil crisis of the 1970s to the very lax lending policies that resulted from the accumulation of petrodollars in international banks, and from the rise in interest rates in the United States in the late 1970s to the withdrawal of large amounts of funds from indebted countries resulting from fears of devaluation and the growing trade and balance of payments deficits. In addition, falling prices of commodities exported from Third World countries further intensified these external economic shocks.

Two of the first SAPs packages were adopted by the Philippines in September 1980 and Mexico in August 1982, both under the close guidance of the IMF and the World Bank. The public announcement by the Mexican government that it could no longer meet its debt payments and the importance of Mexico as one of the largest Latin American countries made this case particularly significant. Hence, the Mexican package was viewed as the response of the international financial community to the prevailing fear of the global crisis that could have developed if many governments defaulted. The package consisted of a set of tough policy measures adopted as a condition for the new loans, amounting to $5.3 billion and put together with help from the IMF, the World Bank, the US government and international commercial banks. The goal was to return Mexico to economic health and generate resources that would help pay its debt. Additionally, the standard set of policies which would have tremendous consequences for the lives of millions of people was adopted without public discussion, setting the model followed by other countries across the globe during the 1980s and 1990s.

Since their inception, SAPs were inspired by the neoliberal model associated with the 'Washington Consensus', that is, an emphasis on the market as the main allocator of economic resources and a corresponding decrease in the role of government. Although some details might have varied from country to country, the basic characteristics can be summarized as falling in four major policy areas. First, a common starting point is the adjustment in the area of foreign exchange, beginning with currency devaluation in order to deal with normally overvalued currencies. This leads to an automatic increase in the price of imports, followed by that of domestic prices and inflationary trends.

Second, drastic cuts in government spending are used not only to reduce deficits in the public sector but also to shift resources and economic activity from the public to the private sector. They are also used to decrease aggregate demand in order to stem inflation. These cuts reduce or eliminate government services and subsidies, such as in education, health and other sectors, that contribute to the social wage, particularly of low income groups. Another aspect of the reduction of the government's role in the economy is the process of privatization of public firms. Although privatization might serve the important function of reducing the domestic deficit and eliminating inefficient and even corrupt activities in the public sector, it has also played a significant role in the imposition of the market over welfare and human development criteria in the functioning of the economy.

Third, SAPs have been used to stimulate deep economic restructuring through market deregulation, including labour and capital markets. This in turn creates strong pressures to restructure production, which leads to the introduction of new technologies, reorganization of labour processes and an emphasis on efficiency and 'modernization'. Fourth, this process is reinforced by trade liberalization and the easing of rules regulating foreign investment, increasing the degree of globalization of the economy and emphasizing the production of tradables over non-tradables. This reinforces the need to strive for more efficient production so as to be able to compete in international markets and reverse the external debt problem.

To sum up, orthodox SAPs represent deep economic and social changes aimed at a variety of objectives: increasing productivity levels even though, at least during the initial stages, at lower real wages; eliminating waste and inefficiency while 'rationalizing' the economy according to the signals dictated by an expanding market; achieving a higher degree of openness to foreign competition and integration in the global economy through trade and financial liberalization; altering economic and social relations and shifting the distribution of resources, rights and privileges towards social groups benefiting from the market; responding to the needs and interests of international capital and powerful global and domestic interests, including the large financial institutions, transnational corporations and international organizations such as the World Bank and the IMF; and reaching the final objective of returning to acceptable levels of economic growth and stability.

Almost two decades after the initial SAPs were adopted, have these goals been achieved? In the short run, the impact of SAPs is felt strongly throughout the economy and among all social groups. Higher import prices affect producers and consumers although trade liberalization may result in cheaper prices for some imports. At the same time, those linked to exports and the financial sector see their fortunes grow. Government budget cuts and foreign competition generate unemployment in some sectors and often force many domestic producers out of the market, with subsequent multiplier effects. All of these can result in negative rates of growth, as in the case of the 'lost decade' in Latin America during the 1980s. The average per capita GNP for the region as a whole was 8 per cent less in 1989 than in 1980 – equivalent, in real terms, to its 1977 level (ECLAC 1990). The fall in per capita income

690   Structural Adjustment Policies

under SAPs is accompanied by shrinking household budgets for a large proportion of the population, downward social mobility, increasing poverty rates and other social ills (Taylor 1988; ECA 1989; ECLAC 1995). At the same time, higher unemployment rates place downward pressure on wages which, together with inflationary pressures, contribute to the deteriorating position of labour. This is justified with the expectation that it will reverse the initial economic conditions and therefore return the economy to rising employment and living standards.

In the long run, however, the rationale behind SAPs is that they will result in a more efficient economy with positive growth. The record shows that in many ways this has been the case – at least in the short run – although at high social costs. In such cases, macroeconomic indicators have led to optimistic evaluations, with renewed economic activity and positive growth rates, inflationary tendencies under control, high levels of net foreign investment, significant increases in trade and buoyant stock markets (World Bank 1992–94; ECLAC 1995). At the same time, case studies at the micro level and reports on people's daily lives portray a more negative view, documenting hardships of survival, social tensions and increasing economic and social inequalities – implying that even optimistic macroeconomic results do not trickle down easily to the population at large (Cornia et al. 1987; Elson 1991; Benería and Feldman 1992; Floro 1995).

Thus, two major critiques of SAPs have emerged. The first emphasizes the social costs of adjustment and their gender dimensions. The second calls attention to the ineffectiveness of SAPs in the long run. One of the initial critiques of SAPs was published by UNICEF (Cornia et al. 1987). It included empirical studies documenting different aspects of the harder and longer-than-expected social costs of adjustment and argued in favour of an 'adjustment with a human face'. Although it did not underline any specific gender bias, subsequent research showed the extent to which SAPs have not been gender-neutral. Feminist critiques emerged, pointing out ways in which the hardships of adjustment were unequally distributed, displaying not only a bias against specific groups of people – mostly a class bias – but also a gender bias. Empirical research has shown that gender biases are due to several different reasons. First, given the division of labour and women's role in the household economy, austerity programmes and shrinking household budgets intensify women's domestic and reproductive work (Moser 1989; Floro 1995). In this sense, greater efficiency and lower costs of production might in fact represent a transfer of costs from the market to the sphere of the household (Elson 1991). Second, budget cuts in essential services such as health, education and housing tend to affect especially the poor and to increase women's responsibilities in family care (Benería and Feldman 1992; Lind 1992; Barrig 1996). Third, lower real incomes force new household members to participate in the paid labour force – particularly women and the young, given their historically lower participation rates – often under the precarious conditions of the informal sector (Tripp 1992; Moser 1989; Manuh 1994). Fourth, low wages in the export sector, particularly women's wages in labour-intensive industries, is a significant factor in keeping exports competitive (Standing 1989; Çagatay et al. 1995b).

All of this implies that macroeconomic policies are not socially and gender-neutral as normally assumed. As Elson (1991) has argued, apparently neutral concepts such as productivity increases and resource-switching assume that human resources are free and can be 'costlessly transferable between different activities' and that 'households and people will not fall apart under the stress of the decisions that adjustment requires' (p. 168). To be sure, these critiques of SAPs have been subject to debate on the basis that they have been made from case studies that could not be generalized. In addition, the critiques are more conclusive for some countries and regions, such as Latin America, than for others (Sahn et al. 1994; ECLAC 1995). However, the accumulated evidence of many studies makes a strong case for the feminist critiques, which even sceptics have admitted.

In addition to analysing the gender dimensions of the impact, feminists have also emphasized that existing gender inequalities might be an obstacle to efficient allocation of resources and the success of SAPs. For example, empirical work on sub-Saharan Africa has shown that farmers might not respond to policy incentives as a result of constraints set up by the traditional gender division of labour (Palmer 1991; Çagatay et al. 1995b; Elson 1995). Likewise, some of the social investment funds set up in many countries to deal with the most urgent problems of adjustment have missed the opportunity of tapping women's skills and providing sources of livelihood for them due to the dubious assumption that funds going to men will benefit women and their families (Benería and Mendoza 1995).

SAPs have also been critiqued on the basis of their mixed results and impact on sustainability. Structural adjustment has succeeded in solving the debt problem for the international financial community, keeping debt payments flowing. At the country and regional level, however, the debt continues to represent a burden for its citizens (Benería 1996). It has been argued that many countries and regions have moved from a debt crisis to a crisis of development, with low or unstable growth rates and vulnerable economic and social conditions (ECLAC 1995). The Mexican crisis of 1994 typified this problem. Despite several years of optimistic trends in the early 1990s, Mexico had to be rescued again by the international community, with a financial package that surpassed the $50 billion mark, ten times larger than the 1992 package (Benería 1996). Likewise, the 1997 South-East Asian economic crisis raised similar issues, particularly the dependency on unregulated external capital, this time in economies viewed as having provided a successful development model (Bello 1997; Kohr 1998).

Likewise, these critiques point to the precariousness of the economic and social model promoted by SAPs, underlining the growing evidence of economic and social inequalities which feed social tensions and contribute to growing crime rates, urban squalor and environmental degradation. This has led some authors to view these trends as leading to a 'socially unsustainable' development model, not only in countries in which SAPs were originally implemented but also in cases of more recent implementation, such as in Eastern Europe (ECA 1989; ECLAC 1995; Slomczynski and Shabad 1997).

One of the common responses to critiques of SAPs is that there was no alternative given the economic conditions of many countries. Thus, the 1980s and 1990s witnessed a standardization of adjustment policies despite the different conditions prevailing in their economies. The implementation of similar packages in the Eastern European countries since 1989 and in South-East Asia since the outburst of the 1997 crisis illustrates this trend. Hence, for the most part, alternative paths to adjustment were not given an opportunity. In Mexico, for example, the IMF-inspired package adopted in 1982 prevailed over the more structuralist 'managed adjustment' policies promoted by a different team of economists working with the Ministry of Industry (Singh 1991). The alternative package included a series of trade and exchange rate controls, bank nationalization and direct negotiations with international commercial banks; its aim was to deal with the crisis without creating shocks and painful adjustments. It also included the formation of a common front of Latin American countries to negotiate the debt collectively so as to increase their bargaining power (Benería 1996). Thus, the historical opportunity to try an alternative path was missed.

An alternative strategy would include policies to induce growth and efficiency as well as equity, including a more equal distribution of the debt burden. In this sense, feminist economics has made an important contribution to a discussion of alternatives, suggesting, for example, how the more prevalent gender analysis at the micro level has macroeconomic implications along the following lines (Benería 1995; Çagatay et al. 1995a; Elson 1995).

First, alternative policies should not assume that people have an infinite capacity to bear the costs of adjustment. The literature has illustrated the tremendous endurance of people, but at the high costs of suffering and depletion of human resources. Second, the hidden costs of adjustment should be taken into consideration, including health-related problems, discontinuities in children's schooling due to women's work intensification, infrastructure and ecological deterioration, and increased crime and violence. Third, alternative packages should include two types of policy: short-run compensatory measures to deal with the most urgent needs resulting from SAPs, and longer-

Structural Adjustment Policies 693

term transformative measures – such as distributive policies focusing on property rights and income – generating changes in the division of labour between paid and unpaid work, educational and retraining programmes and productivity increases in agriculture and other sectors. Fourth, there should be a clear recognition of the links between the paid and unpaid sectors of the economy and between productive and reproductive work. This is crucial if we are to view macroeconomic models as a tool to design policies for the provisioning of needs and maximization of social welfare and not just as a way of maximizing efficiency and economic growth. Fifth, gender equality can contribute to achieving macroeconomic objectives. Thus, anti-discriminatory policies might result in a more efficient allocation of resources. For example, given the empirical evidence showing that women's control of income contributes more than men's to household welfare and family nutrition (Dwyer and Bruce 1988; Elson 1991), income schemes addressed to women can meet both efficiency and anti-discriminatory goals.

These contributions of feminist economics have also resulted from an effort at engendering macroeconomics at the conceptual and practical levels (Çagatay et al. 1995a). With an emphasis on understanding gender relations and addressing gender inequalities, different authors have demonstrated the usefulness of such an approach for growth theory, resource allocation and distribution, labour market analysis, public finance, time allocation and policy initiatives, among others. Still at an incipient stage, a similar effort at engendering international trade is also a recent contribution of feminist economics to our understanding of the effects of SAPs (Joekes and Weston 1994). Although originated among gender and development circles, this body of work has wide relevance for feminist economics in general.

LOURDES BENERIA

See also

Development Policies; Development, Theories of; Economic Restructuring; Globalization; Growth Theory (Macro Models); International Economics.

Bibliography
Barrig, Maruja (1996), 'Women's Collective Kitchens and the Crisis of the State in Peru', in J. Friedmann, R. Albers and L. Autler (eds), *Emergences: Women's Struggles for Livelihood in Latin America*, Los Angeles: UCLA Latin American Studies Center, pp. 59–77.
Bello, Walden (1997), 'Addicted to capital. The ten-year high and present day withdrawal frame of South East Asia's economies', University of the Philippines, Center for Political Studies Issues and Letters, **6** (9–10).
Benería, Lourdes (1995), 'Towards a Greater Integration of Gender in Economics', in Çagatay et al. (eds), Special issue on 'Gender, Adjustment and Macroeconomics', *World Development*, **23** (11), pp. 1839–950.
Benería, Lourdes (1996), 'The Legacy of Structural Adjustment in Latin America', in L. Benería and M.J. Dudley (eds), *Economic Restructuring in the Americas*, Ithaca, New York: Latin American Studies Program, Cornell University, pp. 3–30.

694   Structural Adjustment Policies

Benería, Lourdes and Shelley Feldman (1992), *Unequal Burden; Economic Crises, Persistent Poverty and Women's Work*, Boulder: Westview Press.

Benería, Lourdes and Breny Mendoza (1995), 'Structural adjustment and social investment funds: the case of Honduras, Mexico and Nicaragua', *The European Journal of Development Research*, **7** (1), (June), 53–76.

Çagatay, Nilufer, Caren Grown and Diane Elson (eds) (1995a), Special issue on 'Gender, Adjustment and Macroeconomics', *World Development*, **23** (11).

Çagatay, Nilufer, Caren Grown and Diane Elson (1995b), 'Introduction', Special issue on 'Gender, Adjustment and Macroeconomics', *World Development*, **23** (11), 1827–38.

Cornia, Giovanni, Richard Jolly and Frances Stewart (eds) (1987), *Adjustment with a Human Face*, Vol. 1, New York: UNICEF/Clarendon Press.

Dwyer, Daisy and Judith Bruce (eds) (1988), *A Home Divided: Women and Income in Third World Countries*, Stanford: Stanford University Press.

ECA (Economic Commission for Africa) (1989), *Adjustment with Transformation, ECA/CM 15/6/Rev. 3*, Addis Ababa: United Nations.

ECLAC (Economic Commission for Latin America and the Caribbean) (1990), *Transformación Productiva con Equidad*, Santiago de Chile.

ECLAC (1995), *Social Panorama of Latin America*, Santiago de Chile.

Elson, Diane (1991), *Male Bias in the Development Process*, Manchester: Manchester University Press.

Elson, Diane (1995), 'Gender Awareness in Modeling Structural Adjustment', in Çagatay et al. (eds), Special issue on 'Gender, Adjustment and Macroeconomics', *World Development*, **23** (11), pp. 1851–68.

Floro, M. Sagrario (1995), 'Economic Restructuring, Gender and the Allocation of Time', in Çagatay et al. (eds), Special issue on 'Gender, Adjustment and Macroeconomics', *World Development*, **23** (11), pp. 1913–30.

Joekes, Susan and Ann Weston (1994), *Women and the New Trade Agenda*, New York: UNIFEM.

Kohr, Martin (1998), 'IMF policies in Asia come under fire', *Third World Economics*, No. 176, 1–15 January.

Lind, Amy (1992), 'Power, Gender and Development: Popular Women's Organizations and the Politics of Needs in Ecuador', in Arturo Escobar and Sonia Alvarez (eds), *The Making of Social Movements in Latin America*, Boulder: Westview Press, pp. 134–49.

Manuh, Takyiwaa (1994), 'Ghana: Women in the Public and the Informal Sectors Under the Economic Recovery Programme', in Pamela Sparr (ed.), *Mortgaging Women's Lives. Feminist Critiques of Structural Adjustment*, London: Zed Books, pp. 61–77.

Moser, Caroline (1989), 'The impact of recession and adjustment at the micro level: low income women and their households in Guayaquil, Ecuador', *The Invisible Adjustment: Poor Women and the Economic Crisis*, New York: UNICEF.

Palmer, Ingrid (1991), *Gender and Population in the Adjustment of African Economies: Planning for Change*, Geneva: ILO.

Sahn, David, Paul Rorosh and Stephen Younger (1994), 'Economic Reform in Africa: A Foundation for Poverty Alleviation', Cornell University Food and International Nutrition Program, Working Paper No. 72.

Singh, Ajit (1991), 'Employment and output in a semi-industrial economy: modeling alternative policy options in Mexico', in A. Dutt and K. Jameson (eds), *New Directions in Development Economics*, Aldershot: Edward Elgar.

Slomczynski, Kazimierz and Goldy Shabad (1997), 'Systemic transformation and the salience of class structure in Central Europe', *European Politics and Societies*, **II** (1), (Winter).

Sparr, Pamela (ed.) (1994), *Mortgaging Women's Lives. Feminist Critiques of Structural Adjustment*, London: Zed Books.

Standing, Guy (1989), 'Global feminization through flexible labour', *World Development*, **17** (7), 1077–96.

Taylor, Lance (1988), *Varieties of Stabilization Experience. Towards Sensible Macroeconomics in the Third World*, New York: Clarendon Press. Oxford.

Tripp, Aili Mari (1992), 'The Impact of Crisis and Economic Reform on Women in Urban

Tanzania', in L. Benería and S. Feldman (eds), *Unequal Burden; Economic Crises, Persistent Poverty and Women's Work*, Boulder: Westview Press, pp. 159–80.

UNDP (United Nations Development Programme) (1995), *The Human Development Report*, Oxford University Press.

World Bank, *World Development Report (1992–94)*, Oxford University Press.

Part IV
Gender and Markets

[21]

 Pergamon

World Development, Vol. 24, No. 5, pp. 821–829, 1996
Copyright © 1996 Elsevier Science Ltd
Printed in Great Britain. All rights reserved
0305-750X/96 $15.00 + 0.00

0305-750X(96)00003-4

Gender, Markets and States: A Selective Review and Research Agenda

GITA SEN*

Indian Institute of Management, Bangalore, India

Summary. — This paper attempts to define a research agenda that will explore the relationships among gender, markets and states, taking account of the recent and continuing processes of market liberalization, regionalization, and transformation of the relations between states and societies. It argues that, in order to understand what market liberalization or the formation of regional economic blocs might mean for women, one needs to look beyond market activity *per se* to nonmarket activity and to women's well-being more generally. It selectively reviews some of the literature on structural adjustment and regional trading blocs in order to clarify underlying concepts, and point to new directions for empirical research. In the penultimate section it raises a set of policy and research questions on the role that women's non-governmental organizations can play in shaping the emerging relationships between governments and the private sector. Copyright © 1996 Elsevier Science Ltd

1. INTRODUCTION

Women have always had an ambivalent relation to markets. In their liberating aspect, markets create new opportunities for exchange and accumulation, break through existing social barriers and transform relationships that impede their expansion. But commercialization often also takes the path of least resistance. Faced with intransigent social structures and rigid hierarchies such as those based on gender, race or caste, the expansion of commerce builds on these hierarchies, altering and reshaping them in the process, and transforming the life experiences of those involved. Sometimes such processes lay the bases for transforming hierarchies over the longer run; at other times they deepen the hold of existing authority structures; and at still others they create new forms of authority and control, more subtle and difficult to identify precisely because they work through the market.

Research on gender and development recognized the dual potential of markets fairly early in its evolution. Much of the social science literature of the first decade, the 1970s, pointed out just how mixed a blessing the market has been for women. Breaking with earlier traditions of sociological writing on the transforming impacts of modernization on the family, feminist research uncovered the structures of oppressive gender relations, new and old, that shape women's experience of markets. Much of the debate from this period did not focus on whether markets are good or bad for women. Rather, it questioned whether women

were marginalized and excluded from the beneficent possibilities of market expansion through capitalist development (Boserup, 1970), or whether they are in fact integrated into such processes but near the bottom of the hierarchy, with little prospect for changing that status (Beneria and Sen, 1981). The first view focused on the discriminatory formulation of government policies and operation of labor and commodity markets. The second pointed, in addition, to the rigidity of the domestic division of labor and women's continuing and lop-sided burdens in familial and biological reproduction.[1]

Underpinning this debate were widely divergent perceptions about capitalist development itself: as an inherently beneficial process expanding human wealth and welfare, or as a process that reproduces inequality, social disparities and poverty at the same time. If inherently beneficial, then what was needed was state policy directed to remove the sources of discrimination against women, through changes in laws and education, and in development planning and its practice. If not, then more fundamental and systemic changes would be needed that would generate development processes inherently less hierarchical and inequitable, and specifically addressing the area of reproduction and domestic relations. Prominent among proponents of the second view were socialist-feminists of many stripes.[2]

---

*Final revision accepted: November 27, 1995.

Socialist-feminists were not, however, only critical of capitalist development. They also criticized the theories and practices of socialist states that premised their approaches to "the woman question" on the belief that women's oppression is rooted in their exclusion from productive participation in economic activity. While socialist development can ease many pressures on the poor and on women through its emphasis on equity and on social development (health, education, the provision of basic needs), it has rarely acknowledged the role of domestic work and relations of reproduction within the home in reinforcing hierarchies outside the home, and in structuring women's and men's experiences of work and family differently.[3] But despite their critique of socialism, socialist-feminists have held a vision of a more feminist *socialist* theory and practice as the goal to be achieved, rather than some variant of capitalist development.[4]

Explicit discussion of markets formed only a small part of these debates among socialist-feminists and between them and liberal feminists. But the socialist-feminist critique is important for the purposes of this paper precisely because it was more than a critique of markets per se. It looked behind markets in two directions — one, the structures of property that determine the endowments with which people enter markets, and two, the structures of reproduction that govern domestic divisions of property and labor, and thereby shape women's particular relationships to markets.

These debates between socialists and nonsocialists have been overtaken by the transformations that the global political economy has been undergoing in the last decade. The conversion of Eastern Europe and the Soviet Union into would-be capitalist states, together with the globalization of production processes and distribution channels, necessitate a fresh look at the relationship between women and markets. National-level policies have become so bound up with international economic processes in both real and financial spheres that their gender implications can no longer be examined purely at the national level. At the same time, countervailing pressures for the formation of regional production and trading blocs and spheres of influence have potential effects on the gender division of labor and on women's well-being that requires analysis.[5]

These changes are altering the relationship between states and markets in a variety of ways, with new forms of regulation, coordination, and economic management beginning to take shape. Fundamental to these altered relationships is the opening up of new political spaces for the institutions of civil society, and the transformation of their role, both internationally and at the national level. Nongovernmental organizations (NGOs) have begun to intervene in new ways to reshape the relationships between states and markets, and this again has significant implications for

women's organizations concerned with gender justice and equitable development.

This paper attempts selectively to review the literature and to define a research agenda that will explore the relationships between gender, markets and states, taking account of the recent and continuing processes of market liberalization, regionalization, and transformation of the relations between states and societies. It argues that, in order to understand what market liberalization or the formation of regional economic blocs might mean for women, one needs to look beyond market activity *per se* to nonmarket activity and to women's well-being more generally. It selectively reviews some of the literature on structural adjustment and regional trading blocs in order to clarify underlying concepts, and point to new directions for empirical research. In the penultimate section it raises a set of policy and research questions on the role that women's NGOs can play in shaping the emerging relationships between governments and the private sector.

2. MARKET LIBERALIZATION AND GENDER

Few analysts of the market liberalization programs that gained momentum and ideological strength during the 1980s have seen many positive effects for women. Almost everyone agrees that, given the nature of the crisis and deeper structural transformation in the global economy (deep recession up to 1982 followed by halting growth, continuing inflation and unemployment in high-income countries, continued high interest rates, and declining primary product prices, continuing globalization and transformation of production processes and technologies), some type of "adjustment" is necessary. But who should adjust? And what should be the nature of adjustment?

The Bretton Woods and related regional lending institutions have provided a particular answer, which has gained dominance partly through the sheer power of financial muscle. But many have challenged the conceptual basis of the neoliberal ideology of the market, as well as noted its harmful effects on national economic performance and on livelihoods and well-being.

Feminist research has been an important part of this critique from very early on even though the wave of market liberalization and structural reforms that began to sweep through the Third World during the 1980s caught researchers working on women and development on somewhat the wrong foot. The field was still new and much of its research up until then had consisted of particular case studies of the expansion of markets and commerce, or of the impact of policy and program interventions on the ground. As such it did not provide many guidelines to address the gender implications of macroeconomic policies.

Despite this, the field as it had developed had two strengths. Strong interactions between research, program intervention, and social activism alerted researchers early to the changing pressures on women and the poor more generally.[6] Much of this writing has been empirical, focusing on particular regional or sectoral implications of structural adjustment and economic crisis. But the field had also developed a useful conceptual basis through its attention to reproduction, domestic divisions of labor and the structure of the household.

This conceptual framework rests on the argument that production and reproduction, market and nonmarket activity are intrinsically linked and organized by relations of power. Factors affecting one tend to affect the other. The labor of women is critical to both, but women have relatively little autonomy to make decisions about either. Thus it is women's work-day that is most elastic, stretching or shrinking to meet the needs of both income earning and the maintenance of the household. Increased involvement in income-earning rarely means that women are freed from the tasks of reproduction, although tasks may alter and be performed to different rhythms. Major economic processes such as market liberalization and structural adjustment reforms alter the demand for women in markets, but also affect the resources available for household maintenance.

In order to organize empirical research, three sets of queries can be posed: First, does liberalization remove or reinforce prior barriers to women's participation in markets (product, labor, credit, other inputs) on equal terms with men, or is it neutral to such barriers? Second, does liberalization make it easier or more difficult for women to perform reproductive work in terms of their labor time, time management, access to (both physically and financially) and availability of inputs for domestic work and consumption of public services and goods? Does it alter the household division of labor and resources, and the structures of authority and control within the household and community, i.e. transform an important aspect of gender relations? Third, what are the impacts of liberalization on women's own well-being — their health, nutritional status, access to basic needs such as food, water, fuel, childcare, sanitation, housing, education? How does liberalization affect the security of women's livelihoods, access to and control over income and food? How does it affect the threat of violence (domestic, community or state level) through which gender relations are usually maintained and enforced?

While these three areas of inquiry can be separated for purposes of conceptual clarity, there are likely to be a number of complex linkages among them. For example, market liberalization, may expand women's potential to earn incomes through trade and encourage a switch of labor time away from food self-provisioning toward trading; but involvement in trade, while holding out a promise of higher income, may be more risky and less secure. Higher income earning by women may also increase the threats of domestic violence from men who feel their authority is being undermined. Thus, even if women's situation improves along some dimensions, it may worsen along others, and a look at the full picture becomes necessary as argued below. The importance of not looking at a single aspect in isolation from others is reinforced by the fact that patriarchal authority and gender relations expressed in one area often have impacts in other areas as well.

Among researchers who have explored the conceptual underpinnings of such issues, Elson (1992) argues, that structural adjustment programs are not simply gender-blind, but gender-biased by virtue of that blindness. By failing to take into account the asymmetry of gender relations and the fact of women's subordination in economy and society, neoliberal policies are guilty of three types of bias. First, they ignore the implications of the gender division of labor. Second, they ignore women's unpaid work in reproduction. Third, they ignore intrahousehold gender relations by focusing on the household as the micro unit of economic decision making. These biases mean that the policies restructure economic incentives and disincentives so as to constrain women's ability to access economic resources including paid employment, and reduce state provisioning of public services on the assumption that the slack can be picked up by households without examining exactly who within households picks up the burden. The result of these biases is that policies shift the costs of adjustment from the paid to the unpaid economy, and, as a result, disproportionately on to women who are the primary workers in the unpaid economy, and subordinated by gender relations within the household.

Gender blindness can also affect the allocative efficiency of the macro and meso policies themselves. For markets to allocate resources efficiently, agents need information, the absence of barriers to the mobility of resources, and the absence of monopoly (monopsony) or oligopoly (oligopsony). Palmer (1992) argues that there are two major gender-based distortions in markets. Women and men participate on unequal terms in markets because of the social constraints on women's participation which distort the allocation of labor and other productive resources. Important among such constraints are traditions and customs that limit women's physical mobility in public spaces outside the home, dictate rigid codes that exclude women from certain types of work, and give men (or older women) the right to decide about women's participation in income-earning work.[7]

Second, the rigid and socially sanctioned (and sanctified) sexual division of labor that allocates primary responsibility for the care of human beings to women functions like a tax. This "reproduction tax" which levies women's unpaid labor to reproduce human resources for society misallocates resources since the price of women's labor is set at zero through extraeconomic mechanisms. Paying women below the marginal return from their labor means that labor is expended beyond its efficiency level, and also that capital-labor ratios are lower than they ought to be.

According to Palmer, structural adjustment policies worsen this gender-based misallocation of resources in at least the following ways. They crowd the informal sector; they increase women's domestic work burdens by reducing social sector expenditures; levying user charges in health and education aggravates discrimination against girls and women; and they work against the access of women farmers to resources other than their own labor. Socializing the costs of reproduction is one clear way to avoid the misallocation of resources that results from the hidden "reproduction tax" that women bear.

The empirical evidence that has accumulated over the last decade on the effect of neoliberal policies on women is complex and varied, but the cumulative picture is bleak. Stewart (1992) interprets the crosscountry evidence of the impact of adjustment as being largely negative in terms of laying the basis for growth, of macroeconomic indicators, of poverty and basic needs. For women, this has meant that they have suffered both absolutely and relative to men on a number of fronts such as employment, social services, prices, and trade regimes.

Such generalizations have to be qualified by the specific experiences of women in different countries. For instance, women's employment in a range of labor-intensive export-based manufacturing activities (especially garments) increased dramatically in both Sri Lanka and Bangladesh in the 1980s (Jayaweera, 1994; Feldman, 1992). Working conditions however, were poor in these jobs, including health and safety hazards, overcrowding, and overt or tacit exemptions for the employers from a range of labor laws providing limits on hours of work, childcare and maternity benefits, or guaranteeing rights of association and formation of workers' organizations. Women also lost large numbers of jobs as a result of the collapse of the traditional handloom weaving industry in Sri Lanka in this same period due to competition from cheaper imports. The pressure to generate incomes for families led to a significant increase in the numbers of women working as unpaid family labor or self-employed in petty trade and services (Jayaweera, 1994). In Ghana, another country considered a neoliberal policy success, structural reforms led to job increases in mining, transportation, and timber logging, but none of these traditionally hired women workers. On the other hand, incentives for cash cropping led to an increased demand for and use of unpaid female family labor at the expense of labor for food crop cultivation (Manuh, 1994). The migration of

female workers in domestic service or the entertainment industry under difficult and sometimes dangerous conditions, has seen considerable increases in the Philippines and a number of other countries in the last decade.

Other aspects of neoliberal policy regimes such as credit liberalization, privatization of state enterprises and parastatals, and general administrative reforms have had relatively little positive impact on women, since there has been little attempt to gear these changes to the needs of women (or the poor more generally) (Stewart, 1992). Indeed, country-level experiences provide evidence of a number of negative effects. In Egypt the scaling back of public sector employment, and the growing attempt by public sector firms to become competitive by flouting established public sector labor laws and standards has worsened both employment and working conditions for women workers in a sector that had traditionally been hospitable to women (Hatem, 1994). In Ghana too, the scaling back of production and investment in state farms has reduced women's access to jobs as casual laborers on these farms (Manuh, 1994).[8]

While most of the research along the lines exemplified above is critical of neoliberal policies, it is not necessarily critical of markets *per se*. Elson (1992), for instance, argues in favor of focusing on the possible complimentarity between markets and states, since neither is automatically better for women. For women to gain access to markets, they need support for their unpaid work and the redressing of other biases. This implies a need to restructure both the public and private sectors; since bias cannot be redressed purely through the instrument of the market, ignoring the public sector's role will lead to bias.

Similarly, Palmer (1992) argues that a crucial requirement for more efficient resource use is to reduce the "reproduction tax" on women. This ought to be done by supporting the tasks involved in reproduction through general taxes and expenditures; specific taxes on employers run the risk of repeating the experience with most protective legislation (e.g., maternity leave, prohibition on night work, hours legislation), namely, employers simply reduce their hiring of women.[9] Action by the state will encourage the free movement of women's labor and bring the labor involved in reproduction as much as possible into the sphere of market exchange.

In both the sets of recommendations cited above, the state has not only a strong regulatory role but also a fiscal one. Markets however, are the linchpin of productive economic activity.[10] Stewart argues the need to complement (or modify) neoliberal domestic policies along three dimensions if women's needs are to be served. First, redesign *meso* policies (affecting distribution and sectoral allocations) so as to include women, e.g., through structured markets providing them greater access to credit or foreign exchange.

Second, promote institutional change especially through education in order to reduce social barriers to their participation in markets. Third, strengthen specific support policies such as employment schemes, and nutrition programs to mitigate the costs of adjustment. Again, the role of the state is key to these recommendations as well, but they cannot be accused of being market-unfriendly.

Although the bulk of research in this area suggests that neoliberal policies have been inimical to women, a few skeptics remain. Haddad (1991) argues, for example, that the problem lies not with the policies themselves, which he believes are not promale in intent, but with preexisting gender relations. Most critics argue, however, that the policies are biased precisely because they ignore preexisting gender relations. Haddad also argues that much of the research does not differentiate the impact of adjustment from the effects of the underlying crisis, and may well be wrongly assigning the blame on adjustment.[11]

The problem of finding the appropriate counterfactual evidence for a complex macro policy shift is formidable, particularly given the paucity of baseline data broken down by gender; detrending the data (assuming reliable time-series data exist) is unlikely to resolve the problem. Looking at the disaggregated impacts of specific policies may be more illuminating, and here the point is well taken that data analysis needs to be careful. It also needs to be emphasized that policy makers need both to design structural reforms that are more gender-sensitive, and to directly tackle traditional gender biases, e.g., through providing land rights to women.[12] In the end, however, independent of the question of whether to blame the crisis or adjustment policies, women seem to be doing poorly and their situation seems to have worsened during the last decade.

Another argument, and one that is worth taking seriously, is that the poor and women do not have access to many social services anyway, so the cuts in services under structural adjustment are unlikely to have affected them. Sahn (1990) argues that liberalizing food markets might raise the price of food but not necessarily for the poor, who might have had to rely on higher priced black-market food supplies in the past. These arguments merit serious consideration and further research. They may have greater validity in rural South Asia and sub-Saharan Africa than in Latin America whose highly urbanized populations typically have had greater access to both social services and food supplies, however inequitable or poor. But while such arguments enrich the empirical discussion, and point to the need to distinguish between classes of women (and the poor), they do not alter, in my opinion, the core of either the conceptual argument or the empirical findings.

Returning to the queries detailed earlier in this section, it appears from this brief review of some of the key literature that, although much has been clarified conceptually, a number of questions remain as yet unanswered. The empirical literature has focused on the effects of fiscal cutbacks on the availability of public services, and hence on women's work-burdens in reproduction. The impact on women's employment in wage-labor or in trade provides more mixed empirical evidence, but the overall balance is negative. There has not been enough research focus however, on the set of queries about women's overall well-being detailed earlier in this section, in part because of the absence of adequate baseline data for many of the variables. New and innovative ways of expanding the knowledge base on these questions is essential. One problem is that national statistical systems are not set up to elicit information regarding the deployment of domestic work. Intrahousehold data on work, consumption, control of economic resources, or access to public services such as healthcare are rarely collected, if ever. Even when collected, the original data are rarely analyzed.[13] Clearly a systematic attempt to make data systems more gender-sensitive at the national level is needed. Along with this, communities could be drawn into the process of data collection as part of a process of self-empowerment discussed in the penultimate section of this paper.

3. REGIONAL TRADE AGREEMENTS AND GENDER

The implications of trade agreements for gender relations have received less attention thus far than the impact of stabilization and structural adjustment. Regional trade agreements and the formation of market blocs are far from new in the global economy; however, from the 1980s on we have been witnessing a new spurt in them as national economies attempt to cope with the transformation of production structures, technology and the globalization of capital markets. The fact that gender has not been a major issue in the debates around trade agreements partly reflects their weak concern with social issues more generally.[14] Traditional economic discussion of the impact of regional trade agreements has usually focused on the issues of trade creation and trade diversion among member countries in an agreement. Concern over employment effects has been newer (although not among labor organizations, obviously); over issues of health, social services, the environment or gender even more recent.

A conceptual framework similar to that outlined above for the analysis of structural adjustment, i.e., distinguishing between women's market activity, nonmarket activity, and general well-being might also be appropriate to the analysis of trade deals. The experience of Canada in its Free Trade Agreement with the United States shows that such agreements can affect employment by reducing trade barriers as well as barriers to capital mobility, alter the bargaining position of workers with respect to both wages and social benefits, and change the capacity of governments to finance social sector expenditures by altering their revenue base. Which direction these changes will take depends on whether capital and employment flow into or out of a country consequent on the agreement.

The general expectation is that countries with lower direct and indirect wage costs will, *ceteris paribus*, attract capital and thereby jobs. Thus, the Mexican government hopes that the North American Free Trade Agreement (NAFTA) will lead to inflows of capital that will generate a new burst of economic growth and labor-intensive exports with rising employment and incomes. On the other side, Canadian labor organizations fear that they will lose both jobs and social services as the revenue base of provincial governments is eroded. The ability of higher wage (direct and indirect) countries to benefit from such agreements depends on the countervailing strength of economies of scale in established industries, and their ability to break into new, higher technology industries.

Economic theory predicts that, when there is free trade in commodities, the prices of their factors of production will be equalized between countries. But will this be a race up or a race down? Moreover, the factor price equalization theorem is based on an assumption of perfect competition which is not generally valid. The reality that most female workers (and those from subordinate ethnic, racial, caste or other groups) face is of segmented labor markets where employers take advantage of existing gender and other hierarchies. For example, in fruit and vegetable production, the same ethnic group of Mixtecs do field labor on both sides of the border in California and Baja California. But the Northern workforce is largely male migrants (who are not members of the farmworkers' union), while the Southern workforce is largely females recruited by their Mexican employers from the poorest villages. The women cannot afford to or are afraid to go North, and their wages are considerably lower than those of their male counterparts (Zabin, 1992). The extent of labor mobility written into an agreement is clearly a key to this issue, but most agreements are unlikely to allow much mobility.

As can be seen, the gender implications of agreements are likely to be both complex and varied, and warrant careful examination. Will women in Southern newly industrialized countries (NICs) (such as Mexico) that are included in Northern trade agreements gain increased employment in labor-intensive industries? Is this likely to further segment the labor market along gender or other lines? Is it likely to improve wages or working conditions if labor mobility continues to be restricted? What will happen to the employment of women in the economically weaker

Northern countries such as Canada? Are they likely to have their nonmarket burdens increased due to greater pressure on social services? Will women in Southern countries outside the agreement (e.g., the Caribbean in the case of NAFTA) lose jobs as firms find it cheaper to produce within the trading zone?

An important set of questions is contingent on the actual macroeconomic growth effects of an agreement. In countries where investment and incomes grow, will the tax base become stronger?[15] Will this improve the scope for public services, and thereby reduce the burdens of women's reproductive tasks? What will be the impact on women's well being generally, bearing in mind the queries in the previous section? Since most regional agreements are relatively new, this may indeed be the time to generate a few statistically sound data baselines on specific aspects of women's well-being in panels that can be followed over a number of years.

4. GENDER, MARKETS AND STATES

The political economy of the relations between states and markets raises issues of a different order from those of the previous two sections. The dominant mainstream debate focuses on the relative efficiency of states versus markets in mobilizing and allocating resources, and shaping development strategies responsive to people's needs. The neoliberal argument that "government failure" is worse economically than "market failure" has been challenged on both theoretical and empirical grounds. Feminists have in the past criticized both processes of commercialization and the state. The former involves the expansion and consolidation of markets, and often devalues and destroys the bases of livelihoods, and increases women's burdens. But while market expansion in many instances builds on and reinforces preexisting gender relations, it may also destabilize such relations, and open up new spaces for feminist action. States, on the other hand, are more often than not patriarchal and authoritarian; whatever their ideological hue, they tend to control and instrumentalize women and the sphere of human reproduction in various ways.

The feminist critique of structural adjustment programs has mainly drawn from one strand of the earlier socialist feminist critique, *viz.*, the structures of reproduction that shape women's relationships to markets. The other strand which examines the structures of property undergirding markets, and related analysis of the political economy of the state has received less than adequate attention. Practical experiences derived from women's development experiments point to two ways in which a consideration of gender might enrich the ongoing debate about the role of the state.

First, the efficiency of the state might be enhanced not by wholesale privatization (meaning profit orientation) but by devolving the implementation of a range of development activities to community-level organizations (public or private) working mainly on a nonprofit basis. Such activities might include basic needs such as health, education, sanitation, housing, as well as employment generation and anti-poverty programs. Decentralizing the responsibility for implementation does not absolve the central government from responsibility for assisting in strategic planning, ongoing monitoring or finance. But it relieves central (and often rigid and top-heavy) bureaucratic appartuses of the day-to-day management of programs for which they are often ill-suited. Community development organizations (local government bodies, grassroots organizations) on the other hand can be more flexible, responsive to people's needs, and adaptive to lessons learned from experience. Their weaknesses are usually the result of small scale and poor finance. Complementarity between the central state and local organizations might work better than exclusive reliance on one or the other.

While community organizations generally share, to a greater or lesser extent, in the features outlined above, organizations working with women have been particularly innovative and experimental in certain areas. For instance, the growing acknowledgement among development practitioners that formal credit an be extended to the poorest with low default risk rests largely on the experience of organizations such as the Self-Employed Women's Association in India or the Grameen Bank in Bangladesh, the bulk of whose lending goes to the poorest women in a community. In other areas, typically poorly handled by both states and markets, women's organizations have been highly successful, e.g., community kitchens in Peru and the environmental movement in Kenya. Typically governments have been highly ambivalent about such experiences. But the opportunities provided by a time of crisis need more positive assessment of potential complementarity and hence greater efficiency of resource use.

Individual cases such as those identified above have sometimes been studied in considerable depth on dimensions such as the possibility of scaling-up and replicability. But there is growing evidence of the dangers of overextension, and the problems of accountability within the nongovernmental sector itself (DAWN, 1995; Edwards and Hulme, 1992). There has been some discussion on the potential for complementarity rather than substitution of state or market by an NGO. In specific sectors, is there is a division of labor possible between the government, private producers, and NGOs which builds on the strengths of each, but retains both fiscal soundness and accountability?

Another set of issues arises from the fact that most innovative NGOs are heavily dependent on the qualities and charisma of their founders. What types of

structures can help strengthen organizations and reduce personality dependence without destroying flexibility and capacity for innovation?

A second area where gender might enrich the discussion of the state is on questions of accountability. Recent debates on the political economy of the state have revolved around questions of governance and accountability. Most protagonists are not convinced that wholesale privatization is the answer to the perceived problems of the state to manage the nation's economic affairs and promote development. Instead they would argue that the problem of the state's institutional capacity ought to be solved by building up both the capacity for governance and the institutions of civil society rather than by destroying the developmental agency of the state (DAWN, 1995).

SIDA (1992) argues, for instance, that three key features of the functioning developmental state are autonomy (defined as the ability to set strategic goals independent of particularistic interests), capacity (as embodied in an efficient bureaucracy protected by a strong political elite) and statecraft (defined as the ability to shape the economic and other environments to its advantage). But the notion of governance is more than technocratic. The institutional capacity of the state is crucially dependent on its legitimacy, which depends in turn on the existence of clear and generally accepted rules of conduct for all agents, and on accountability.

The latter depends critically on the strength of the institutions of civil society. Building up these institutions is critical to the enterprise of development, and it is here again that women's organizations have played a key role in the recent past. Whether in opposing state violence, challenging legal frameworks, organizing against ethnic or religious bigotry and fundamentalism, or in goading the state to make good its promises of development, such organizations, along with other voluntary organizations have been central. More recently, newer levels of engagement which link national and local organizations to exercise leverage in global policy debates are becoming apparent.[16] How might these efforts be strengthened so as to ensure gender-sensitive policy implementation at multiple levels? There is potential for much rich analysis here. Much of the discussion of the empowering role of women's community organizations has been in terms of its effect on women. It is perhaps time to reverse the question to ask how the presence of empowered women and their oganizations in the public sphere strengthens the capacity of civil society and its institutions.

5. CONCLUSION

This paper has attempted a selective review of the ways in which research on gender and development

has met the challenges posed by recent transformations in global and national political economies.
Moving beyond its early preoccupation with the
pluses and minuses of capitalist and socialist development, research has become more nuanced in its assessments, and more aware of the potential for mixed
effects whether one is concerned with the individual
woman, or looking across women located differently
in national and global economies.

While the basic conceptual framework is in place,
however, it needs amplification, and much empirical

work still remains to be done. Gender as a conceptual
category has a great deal to offer that can enrich the
debate about liberalization and the "new" political
economy. By consistently focusing on the links
between production and reproduction, by pointing to
the important influence of noncompetitive structures,
and by drawing on a rich tradition of nongovernmental program implementation and activism, a gendered
analysis can direct research and policy analysis in
directions where it would not otherwise go.

NOTES

1.   The concept of reproduction has now been used extensively in feminist research. It includes both the physical
processes involved in "reproducing" human beings over time
(daily and over generations), and the social relations (of
power, control over and access to resources, division of
labor, based on gender, age, race or other basis) within which
these physical processes are embedded. Since women have
historically had considerable responsibilities for the labor of
reproduction, a consideration of reproduction is critical to
understanding how different sets of policies affect them.

2.   The socialist-feminism of the time had as many variants as there were of socialism, from democratic-socialism to
Maoism.

3.   Cuba's Family Code of 1974 was an exception that
proved the difficulty of the task.

4.   These differences in vision did not influence the practical discussions of women's projects, programs, "mainstreaming," or gender-sensitive planning, largely because the
links between current policies and long-term goals was
insufficiently addressed.

5.   See the case studies in Edwards and Hulme (1992a) for
evidence of the range of nongovernmental activities in working with government, increasing their own impact through
organizational growth, and linking grassroots actions
through lobbying and advocacy.

6.   An example is the effort of the South-based feminist
network, Development Alternatives with Women for a New
Era (DAWN). The DAWN effort stemmed from a meeting in
mid-1984 which brought together a number of researchers
and activists from different parts of the Third World who
were concerned about the growing impoverishment of
women and its links to the misdirection of policy, and the
interlocking crises of development.

7.   It is important to remember that "traditions" are sometimes invented to justify such control over women's autonomy.

8.   It is worth noting that cutbacks in public sector
employment do not only reduce highly paid, unionized jobs
as neoliberals appear to believe, but also large numbers of
nonunionized casual and low-paid work which farms a tradi-

tional second tier of public sector workers. Women are often
heavily represented in this second tier even if they are not in
the first tier.

9.   Detailed empirical analysis of the effect of protective
legislation actually tells a more complex story. Breen (1988)
shows that while protective legislation in parts of the United
States pushed women out of occupations and industries
where they were in a minority to begin with, it did improve
working conditions in situations where women workers were
numerically dominant.

10.   Elson argues, as have others, that a key policy issue for
production is who will control investment and accumulation;
shifting this from the public to the private sector might make
a great deal of sense provided it is recognized that the private
sector includes not only firms but also cooperatives, community associations, unions, and research/action groups to name
a few.

11.   Haddad cites Behrman and Deolalikar's (1991) work
on Jamaica which detrends the macroeconomic data to argue
that much of the worsening of macroeconomic indicators in
the 1980s is due to the underlying crisis in the economy and
not due to adjustment policies *per se*. This procedure can,
however, be challenged on a number of grounds, including
the possibility that the real "adjustment" in Jamaica's economy began long before the formal adjustment, i.e., when the
International Monetary Fund (IMF) began to pressure the
Jamaican government in the 1970s over its attempt to control
a greater share of the rents from bauxite production.

12.   For an extensive discussion of the problem of land
rights for women in South Asia, see Agarwal (1994).

13.   The National Sample Survey collects a range of interesting information in India but a great deal of these data
remain in the original questionnaire schedules and is not analyzed.

14.   For a discussion of the implications of the
GATT/WTO negotiations for women, see Joekes (1995).

15.   The Mexican experience was of a regionally highly
skewed industrialization pattern under the neoliberal
reforms. The bulk of manufacturing output increase was in
the *maquilas* on the northern border with the United States;

not much of this could be taxed and transferred to the impoverished states, one of the causes perhaps of the rebellion in Chiapas.

16.   At both the International Conference on Human Rights

in Vienna in 1993, and at the International Conference on Population and Development in Cairo in 1994, women's organizations emerged as key actors who were able by their political maturity and crossnational links to significantly shape the policy agenda.

REFERENCES

Agarwal, Bina, *A Field of One's Own: Gender and Land Rights in South Asia* (Cambridge: Cambridge University Press, 1994).

Behrman, Jere and Anil Deolalikar, "The poor and the social sectors during a period of macroeconomic adjustment: empirical evidence from Jamaica," *World Bank Economic Review*, Vol. 5, No. 2 (1991), pp. 291–314.

Beneria, Lourdes and Gita Sen, "Accumulation, reproduction and women's role in economic development: Boserup revisited," *Signs: Journal of Women in Culture and Society*, Vol. 7, No. 2 (Winter 1981), pp. 279–298.

Boserup, Ester, *Woman's Role in Economic Development* (New York: St. Martin's Press, 1970).

Breen, Nancy, "Shedding light on women's work and wages: Consequences of protective legislation," Ph.D. dissertation (New York: New School for Social Research, 1988).

DAWN, *Markers on the Way: the DAWN Debates on Alternative Development* (Barbados: DAWN, 1995).

Edwards, Michael, and David Hulme (Eds.), *Making a Difference: NGO's and Development in a Changing World* (London: Earthscan Publications, 1992a).

Edwards, Michael, and David Hulme, "Scaling up the developmental impact of ngo's: concepts and experiences'" in M. Edwards and D. Hulme (Eds.), *Making a Difference: NGO's and Development in a Changing World* (London: Earthscan Publications, 1992b), pp. 13–27.

Elson, Diane, "Male bias in structural adjustment," in H. Afshar and C. Dennis (Eds.), *Women and Adjustment Policies in the Third World* (New York: St. Martin's Press, 1992), pp. 46–68.

Feldman, Shelley, "Crisis, Islam and gender in Bangladesh: the social construction of a female labor force," in Lourdes Beneria and Shelley Feldman (Eds.), *Unequal Burden: Economic Crises, Persistent Poverty, and Women's Work* (Boulder: Westview Press, 1992), pp. 105–130.

Haddad, Lawrence, "Gender and adjustment: Theory and evidence to date," Paper presented at the Workshop on

Effects of Policies and Programs on Women (Washington, DC: International Food Policy Research Institute, 1991).

Hatem, Mervat, F., "Privatization and the demise of state feminism in Egypt" in Pamela Sparr (Ed.), *Mortgaging Women's Lives: Feminist Critiques of Structural Adjustment* (London: Zed Books, 1994), pp. 40–60.

Jayaweera, Swarna, "Structural adjustment policies, industrial development and women in Sri Lanka," in Pamela Sparr (Ed.), *Mortgaging Women's Lives: Feminist Critiques of Structural Adjustment* (London: Zed Books, 1994), pp. 96–115.

Joekes, Susan, and Ann Weston, *Women and the New Trade Agenda* (New York: UNIFEM, 1995).

Manuh, Takyiwaa, "Ghana: Women in the public and informal sectors under the Economic Recovery Programme," in Pamela Sparr (Ed.), *Mortgaging Women's Lives: Feminist Critiques of Structural Adjustment* (London: Zed Books, 1994), pp. 61–77.

Palmer, Ingrid, "Gender equity and economic efficiency in adjustment programmes," in Haleh Afshar and Carolyne Dennis (Eds.), *Women and Adjustment Policies in the Third World*, (New York: St. Martin's Press, 1992), pp. 69–86.

Sahn, David, "Fiscal and exchange rate reforms in Africa: considering the impact upon the poor," Monograph 4 (Ithaca: Cornell Food and Nutrition Policy Program, 1990).

SIDA, *Redefining the Role of the State and the Market* (Stockholm: Swedish International Development Agency, 1992).

Stewart, Frances, "Can adjustment programmes incorporate the interests of women?" in Haleh Afshar and Carolyne Dennis (Eds.), *Women and Adjustment Policies in the Third World* (New York: St. Martin's Press, 1992).

Zabin, Carol, "Binational labor markets and segmentation by gender: agriculture and the North American Free Trade Agreement," Mimeo (1992).

[22]

Review of Radical Political Economics   Vol. 28(3)92-101(1996)

Gender and International
Labor Standards in the World Economy

Nilufer Cagatay

ABSTRACT: This paper examines the debate on labor standards between neoclassicals and institutionalists from a feminist perspective and elaborates on some key elements of a feminist approach to labor standards. It argues that both neoclassical and institutionalists share a gender-based definition of labor. Rejecting the notion that upward harmonization can be achieved by reliance on deregulated markets or labor standard regulation alone, the feminist perspective calls for new approaches to policy and politics.

1. INTRODUCTION

Several trends have recently stimulated a renewed interest in discussions of international labor standards or worker's rights Among these are the transition from a "mass-production for mass-consumption" economy to the "flexible production" system, rising globalization of production, and increasing global mobility of capital. These tendencies are all the more enhanced by the neo-liberal structural adjustment policies carried out in developing countries where governments compete to attract capital by lowering labor standards, thereby also threatening labor standards for workers in the industrialized countries.

There are two frequently mentioned positions with respect to discussions of labor standards: the "neoclassical" and the "institutionalist" perspectives. These two schools disagree on whether labor standards help or hurt the constituencies that they are intended to empower as well as whether labor

Department of Economics, BUC 308, University of Utah, Salt Lake City. UT 84112. cagatay@econ.sbs.utah.edu.

Published by Blackwell Publishers, 238 Main St., Cambridge, MA 02142, USA, and 108 Cowley Rd., Oxford, OX4 1JF, UK.

Gender and International Labor Standards in the World   93

standards help or hinder growth and trade. Recent discussions have also generated disagreements between these schools of thought in terms of whether there should be a linkage between labor standards and trade agreements, as in the context of discussions of the Uruguay Round and the WTO. Another point of disagreement is about whether greater globalization will lead to downward harmonization of labor standards. Institutionalists tend to argue that without regulation, there will be downward harmonization. They advocate regulation, and some among them propose trade-linked schemes such as "social tariffs" to ensure "upward harmonization," while neoclassicals argue that labor conditions can best be improved in the long run by deregulating labor markets.[1]

The purpose of this paper is to briefly examine these two approaches from a feminist perspective and elaborate on what that perspective might be. Even though the institutionalist and neoclassical perspectives disagree on a number of important questions, as I argue below they tend to share a common gender-biased definition of labor.[2]

---

[1]See Herzenberg and Perez-Lopez (1990), and Schoepfle and Swinnerton (1994) for examples of such debates. Needless to say, the neoclassical and neoinstitutionalist schools are not monolithic. A third approach, the Marxist one, as discussed by Dorman (1995), argues that worker rights are an aspect of the struggle of workers against capital via the state apparatus. Some Marxists support trade-linked schemes, while some oppose them.

[2]In these discussions, there is generally a distinction between "core standards" which include freedom from forced labor and slavery and the freedom to associate freely, which are seen to be more human rights related and expected as absolute conditions by everyone, versus those standards which are viewed as being linked to the level of economic development and therefore as relative conditions. The most frequently cited and ratified standards include the above standards, minimum age laws, collective bargaining laws, and freedom from discrimination.

2. ALTERNATIVE PERSPECTIVES ON LABOR STANDARDS

1) The neoclassicals generally view labor standards as impediments to labor market clearing.[3] "Excessive labor standards" increase labor costs, cause unemployment and allocative inefficiency, jeopardize growth, and drive a wedge between "protected" and "unprotected" workers benefiting protected workers at the expense of the unprotected. In this view, there is a trade-off between labor standards and employment. The major income distributive concern is the distribution of income among workers or wage structures.

Neoclassicals advocate relying on market forces to bring about improvements in labor conditions. They argue that such improvements follow from growth or come about as a result of increased demand for labor standards by consumers. The industrializing economies' comparative advantage lies in their relatively abundant labor. Thus comparative advantage can be made use of only if wages reflect the forces of supply and demand without interference from the government or other "market distorting" entities like labor unions. In the long-run, outward orientation and the resulting high growth rates translate into increasing wages and better labor conditions. Neoclassicals, therefore, advocate delinking trade agreements and labor standards. They also fear that labor standards might be used for protectionist purposes by industrialized countries.

While there is no or little discussion of *gender* as such, neoclassicals discuss women workers generally in terms of the negative impact of market distortions and regulations on women. Protective legislation is seen as an impediment to women's full participation in labor markets. Likewise maternity benefits and child care provisions are usually seen as disadvantaging and limiting women's employment. Deregulation is beneficial to women since they are seen as the "main victims" of regulation.

2) According to the alternative view, usually referred to as institutionalist, the causal link between standards and outcomes runs contrary to the neoclassical arguments.[4] In

---

[3]See Bhagwati (1994), Srinivasan (1994), Fields (1990) as examples.
[4]See Wilkinson (1994), Singh (1991), Piore (1990).

this view, standards encourage the adoption of new technologies that enhance productivity. According to Piore (1990), for example, the original development of labor standards was based on the rationale for getting rid of sweatshops and a switch to a higher productivity regime under mass production systems. In an example from the industrializing economies, Standing (1992) has found that in Malaysia unions both contributed to productivity enhancement and a narrowing of the gender gap in wages.

Institutionalists, therefore, advocate the adoption and observation of labor standards. There are also variants of this approach which argue that corporatist bargaining systems (such as in Sweden) were more successful in both protecting workers rights and leading to better macroeconomic outcomes. Singh (1991) argues that a new expansionist macroeconomic regime can be founded on the basis of a new social consensus reached by corporate institutional arrangements between employers, governments, and workers. Given the erosion of standards within more flexible production systems, Standing (1991) advocates new forms of organizing which are more appropriate in the context of flexible production.

Some institutionalist writers have addressed gender issues in the context of discussions of feminization as well as in discussions on standards with regard to discrimination. For example, Standing (1989) views global feminization and flexibility (in the context of supply-side macroeconomic policies) as interlinked phenomena which undermine labor standards. Within this framework, women are sometimes viewed as a "vulnerable" segment of workers who are recruited by capital in ways that undermine existing labor standards. In contrast to the neoclassicals, the institutionalists locate the central power relations in the capital-labor relationship. More recently Howes and Singh (1995) have argued that the new social consensus generated by a corporatist regime referred to above must include specifically "women's voice" as distinct from having only unions represent women workers' interests. Institutionalists also advocate upholding anti-discrimination laws and other regulations such as minimum wage laws and maternity benefits, whose costs, they argue, must be socialized.

3. TOWARD A FEMINIST APPROACH
TO LABOR STANDARDS

Feminist views on workers' rights are more complicated than the neoclassical or institutionalist approaches, which share the commonality of defining labor primarily as "paid labor" and, therefore, focus on paid labor.[5] While both approaches tend to view women as a vulnerable segment of workers, the bases of vulnerability, which need to be located in gender as well as class relations, are not systematically addressed. A feminist approach to labor standards would start with the introduction of the concept of gender as an analytical tool in understanding both the rise and evolution of labor standards.[6]

Feminist economists view the basic gender division of labor as that division between productive/reproductive labor activities.[7] Further, women's responsibilities for social reproduction performed in the form of unpaid domestic labor influence their position in labor markets as paid laborers. Women's labor force participation rate is lower than men's. However, women tend to have a greater combined labor burden consisting of paid and unpaid activities in the world economy. Occupations and industries tend to be gender-typed, and those that are associated with the female gender tend to be lower paying and of lower social status. Women also often receive lower wages for the same work. They tend to engage more frequently in part-time, casual, flexible, or informal labor activities as a result of their unpaid domestic labor responsibilities. These gender-based inequalities in markets, in turn, reinforce men's power vis-a-vis women

---

[5]Although I cannot elaborate within the limits of this paper, the institutionalist perspective has much more in common with the feminist perspective than the neoclassical one.

[6]Gender refers to the social meanings constructed around sex differences, and is an important social stratifier. Feminist economists would start with uncovering gender based divisions of labor, and try to understand how such divisions (together with race, class, ethnicity, sexual orientation) contribute to the perpetuation of (mostly gender related but not exclusively so) asymmetries and inequalities in social and economic relations. Given the diversity among feminist economists, it should be added that not all of them would necessarily agree with my characterizations.

[7]See, for example, Picchio (1992) .

within households and other institutions. For feminists, therefore, a fundamental goal is the elimination of the "traditional" gender division of labor within households, since this division reinforces the gender inequalities within labor markets and vice versa. Focusing on a narrow definition of labor as "paid labor" is insufficient.

Given the gender based division of labor and the patterns of gender segregation and differentiation in labor markets, a feminist question is what have labor standards meant for women and men historically (as opposed to an ungendered category of workers)?

a) Feminist scholars have argued that in industrialized economies, various forms of protective legislation, restrictions of child labor, and the demands of unions concerning the "family wage" in the nineteenth century helped create the gender-based division of labor between (women's) unpaid domestic labor and (largely men's) paid laboring activities. Thus, traditional union strategies which have been predicated upon a "male breadwinner ideology" must change and take into account both the breakdown of this ideology and the reality of feminization of the labor force in the post-war period in most regions of the world economy.

b) Furthermore, the *conditions associated with flexible production* had defined the conditions of women's paid labor activities before the arrival of flexible production for male workers. Hence, historically and at present, women tend to engage more frequently in unpaid family labor, casual, part-time, homeworking work arrangements and are overrepresented in the informal sector compared to men. For example, women frequently work for subminimum wages in many informal or homeworking types of activities because such forms of work allow them to care for their children as they engage in paid work. This has meant that they are in sectors or in types of activity that are more difficult to organize. There may be no employer to negotiate with, or those who employ them may be male family members as in the case of women who perform unpaid family labor. Under such conditions, what is at issue is not only the unequal power relation between capitalists and workers, but also the unequal power relations based on gender (within and outside the family). These mean that women have not benefited from some labor standards such as collective bargaining to the same degree as men.

c) Even for women who work in "organizable" sectors such as manufacturing, problems persist. Feminists have argued that the freedom to associate and bargain over the conditions of work has a gender-bias in that women, due to their (unpaid) domestic labor responsibility, cannot fully participate in collective bargaining or unionizing activities. Hence the degree of unionization of women is generally lower compared to that of men. The fact that unions are dominated by men, especially at the higher ranks, has meant that unions historically have not been as concerned with work conditions that affect women more, *given the present state of gender relations*. For example, they have not been as sensitive to harassment issues or childcare provisions at the workplace.

d) However, feminists and others have shown that in industries or firms that are unionized the gender gap in wages is narrower compared to nonunionized sectors.[8] This is because unions are effective in enforcing equal pay for equal work provisions and other labor standards for their members. Moreover, it is evident from cross-country studies of industrialized economies that in countries with more centralized bargaining systems the gender earnings gap is lower compared to those with more decentralized bargaining systems (Blau and Kahn 1992, Howes and Singh 1995). Feminists also view minimum wage laws as a possible way of alleviating (especially but not exclusively) women's poverty. They see maternity benefits and child care facilities as mechanisms that offset "pre-existing distortions that arise because the costs of women's unpaid work in having and rearing children are not taken account of by markets" (Elson 1991). They also see pay equity schemes as important policy tools. Thus feminists advocate regulation of labor markets, notwithstanding the historical gender-biases embedded in the formation of labor standards in the age of "male breadwinner" ideology.

e) In spite of all the gender-bias against women's ability to benefit from labor standards as discussed above, recently women have been organizing themselves in new and

---

[8]See Hartmann et al. 1994, and Standing 1992.

innovative ways that have proven to be empowering (Martens
and Mitter 1994). Such new innovative forms of organizing
entail various types of national and international networks,
credit unions, and other types of associations such as SEWA
(self employed women's association in India). These networks
tend to be organized less vertically and more horizontally.
They entail training, provisioning of credit, and acquiring of
empowering knowledge as well as the formation of
international solidarity networks. Such forms of organizing are
important and crucial for all workers, especially in the
changing conditions of work toward greater flexibility.

f) Feminists have been pursuing their goals of gender equity
in a wide variety of international fora such as the UN
conferences on women. Such conferences have led to CEDAW
(Convention on the Elimination of All Forms of Discrimination
Againsts Women), and various platforms for action geared
toward empowerment of women. Such international
conferences have encouraged rethinking the concept of labor
from women's perspectives. One such important step was
taken at the recent Beijing conference on women with the
recognition of unpaid domestic labor as work.

4. CONCLUSION

The neoclassical and institutionalist approaches rely on a
gender-biased definition of labor, since the debates generally
take market-related work as the appropriate definition of
labor, leaving out unpaid domestic labor. Redefining labor
along feminist lines means that we also need to rethink the
nexus of productivity, wages, trade, and labor standards. The
nonfeminist approaches either ignore the gender-biases
historically embedded in *some* standards (the
neoinstitutionalists) or the gender-biases that are produced or
reproduced by markets (the neoclassicals).

It is the contention of this paper that neither a simple
reliance on "deregulated markets," nor on labor standard
regulations defined in terms of "market related work," or
mechanical trade-linked schemes can bring about an
improvement in the conditions of work. A feminist perspective
fundamentally challenges the meaning of labor and worker
assumed by both schools of thought, helps us rethink the

100   Nilufer Cagatay

theoretical parameters of the debate and come up with *new* policies and politics that can be more conducive to attaining "upward harmonization" for both genders across the development divide in the context of the changing world economy.

REFERENCES

Bhagwati, Jagdish. 1994. Policy Perspectives and Future Directions: A View from Academia. In, *International Labor Standards and Global Economic Integration: Proceedings of a Symposium.* Gregory K. Schoepfle and Kenneth A. Swinnerton (eds.), Washington D.C.: U.S. Department of Labor.

Blau, Francine and Lawrence Kahn. 1992. The Gender Earnings Gap: Learning from International Comparisons. *American Economic Review* 82(2): 533-528.

Dorman, Peter. 1995. Policies to Promote Labor Rights: An Analytical Review. James Madison College, Michigan State University, East Lansing.

Elson, Diane. 1991. Appraising Recent Developments in the World Market for Nimble Fingers: Accumulation, Regulation, Organization. University of Manchester, Department of Economics.

Fields, Gary. 1990. Labor Standards, Economic Development and International Trade. In, *Labor Standards and Development in the Global Economy.* Stephen Herzenberg and Jorge Perez-Lopez (eds.) Washington: U.S. Department of Labor.

Hartmann, Heidi, Roberta Spalter Roth and Nancy Collins. 1994. What Do Unions Do For Women? *Challenge,* July/August.

Herzenberg, Stephen and Jorge Perez-Lopez (eds.). 1990. *Labor Standards and Development in the Global Economy.* Washington: U.S. Department of Labor.

Howes, Candace and Ajit Singh. 1995. Long-Trends in the World Economy: The Gender Dimension. *World Development* 23(11).

Martens, Margaret Hosmer and Swasti Mitter (eds.). 1994. *Women in Trade Unions: Organizing the Unorganized,* Geneva: ILO.

Picchio, Antonella. 1992. *Social Reproduction: The Political Economy of the Labour Market.* Cambridge: Cambridge University Press.

Piore, Michael. Labor Standards and Business Strategies. In, *Labor Standards and Development in the Global Economy.* Stephen Herzenberg and Jorge Perez-Lopez (eds.) Washington: U.S. Department of Labor.

Schoepfle, Gregory and Kenneth A. Swinnerton (eds.) 1994. *International Labor Standards and Global Economic Integration: Proceedings of a Symposium.* Washington, D.C.: U.S. Department of Labor.

Gender and International Labor Standards in the World   101

Singh, Ajit. 1991. Labor Markets and Structural Adjustments. In, *Towards Social Adjustment*. Guy Standing and Victor Tokman (eds.), Geneva: ILO.

Srinivasan. T.N. 1994. International Labor Standards and International Trade: International Labor Standards Once Again!. In, *International Labor Standards and Global Economic Integration: Proceedings of a Symposium* Gregory K. Schoepfle and Kenneth A. Swinnerton (eds.), Washington, D.C.: U.S. Department of Labor.

Standing, Guy. 1989. Global Feminization Through Flexible Labor. *World Development* 17(7).

Standing, Guy. 1991. Structural Adjustment and Labour Market Policies: Towards Social Adjustment? In, *Towards Social Adjustment*. Guy Standing and Victor Tokman (eds.), Geneva: ILO.

————. 1992. Do Unions Impede or Accelerate Structural Adjustment? Industrial Versus Company Unions in an Industrializing Labour Market. *Cambridge Journal of Economics* 16: 327-354.

Wilkinson, Frank. 1994. Equality, Efficiency and Economic Progress: The Case for Universally Applied Equitable Standards for Wages and Conditions of Work. In, *Creating Economic Opportunities: The Role of Labour Standards in Industrial Restructuring.* Werner Sengenberger and Duncan Campbell (eds.), Geneva: ILO.

[23]

FEMALE AND MALE GRAIN MARKETING SYSTEMS

Analytical and policy issues for West Africa and India

Barbara Harriss-White

The study of markets cannot be scientific unless studied in the context of their relevant institutions.
(Penny, 1985: 101)

Gender is constructed by a plurality of oppressions.
(Bardhan, 1993: 147)

This chapter concerns gender and one aspect of micro-economic relations which seems understood as being endowed with many adverse implications for gender-political change.[1] The material subordination of women has been most richly researched in two institutional sites. The first is within the household where gender divisions of task have been explained in relation to the opportunity costs of male and female labour on stylised markets outside the household (as developed in the new home economics: see Haddad *et al.*, 1997). Implicit in this market driven theory of intrahousehold divisions of labour is a social process of decision making. While some have seen patriarchal authority at work (whether despotic or benign: Folbre, 1986), others have stylised the process as one of bargaining (Kandiyoti, 1988; Sen, 1990). The consequences of gender differentials in fall-back positions and unequal conjugal contracts have been invoked to explain gender asymmetries in command not only over decision making but also over resources, autonomy and welfare. Further, the operation of rules of property ownership and control and its transfer at inheritance and marriage have been found to deprive women of resources and thereby of access qualifications for many aspects of public participation (Agarwal, 1995). The second well researched institutional site of material subordination is the process of production. This is almost invariably analysed in terms of the operation of labour markets and labour relations since so little property is controlled by women. Here, life cycle vulnerabilities, employment probabilities, skill acquisition and differentials in remuneration, income

189

FEMINIST VISIONS OF DEVELOPMENT

and their security (differentials not justified by productivity or by demand and supply) are stacked against women.[2] In this chapter, the gendering of a third area, markets in commodities other than labour, will be explored in a preliminary way, taking staple foods as examples, since almost everywhere they form the basis of social reproduction and are thus a useful 'prism'. Such markets have been comparatively less researched than other gendered interfaces (as is the fate of market behaviour more generally despite its centrality to a wide range of economic theory).[3] Three analytical issues suggest themselves:

1   the gender construction of non-labour, commodity markets;
2   market relations as ambivalent processes of gender emancipation and subordination;
3   the impact of women's participation in marketplace exchange on economic relations within the household.

From these, four 'policy issues' appear to follow:

1   technical change in rural marketing and its impact on livelihoods;
2   liberalisation, the expansion and integration of national markets and the masculinisation of control over trade;
3   the efficiency of gender divisions;
4   political organisation within marketing systems.

First, however, it is necessary to clarify the nature of markets.

Markets as institutions

The 'market' is conventionally seen as an atomistic realm of impersonal economic exchange of homogeneous goods carried out by means of voluntary transactions. These are mediated on an equal basis by large numbers of autonomous, fully informed entities with profit maximising behavioural motivations able to enter and leave freely. The market is thus the supreme medium for the expression of individual choice (Hodgson, 1988: 178). Much more often than not it is assumed to be perfectly competitive. Models of other stylised market structures (monopoly, oligopoly) alter certain criteria, retain others and predict the consequences for prices and quantities.

The abstractions leave us shorn of means whereby to understand not only how supply is supplied and demand is demanded, but also the structure and behaviour of real market systems which relate demand and supply. For exactly the reason that real markets are highly diverse and complex socio-economic phenomena, real markets have indeed proved awkward to define.

A restrictive definition of market exchange in which voluntarism, egalitarianism and informational availability are stressed has been offered by Pandya and Dholakia: 'the simultaneous transaction of valued goods and services between

190

FEMALE AND MALE GRAIN MARKETING SYSTEMS

two parties [who are] capable of accepting or rejecting the value offered . . . and [who are] uncoerced . . . and capable of communication and delivery' (1992: 24). Markets are then efficient mechanisms of resource allocation, resulting in an expansion of productivity.

By contrast, Fourie sees a real market as 'an economically qualified, purposeful interchange of commodities on the basis of *quid pro quo* obligations at a mutually agreed upon exchange rate . . . in a cluster of exchange and rivalry relations' (1991: 43, 48). Here, the social relations unique to market exchange require the combination of 'horizontal' and adversarial competition between populations of buyers (and populations of sellers) on the one hand and a mass of 'vertical', exclusive, mutualistic, bilateral transactions between one buyer and one seller on the other. The implications of this definition (*pace* the voluntarist definition) are that exchange rates mutually agreed on may not always be mutually beneficial, that vertical contractual arrangements may prevail over horizontal competition and that purposeful bargaining and the obligations resulting from it may rest on and reinforce a highly unequal base or fall-back position. Without wishing to be reductionist, it would seem that market exchange will be a site of exploitation as well as of allocation. It has the capacity to be a site of ethnic and/or gender subordination as well as of liberation.

Much exchange which would fall within Fourie's definition of market would fall outside that of Pandya and Dholakia – repeated, relational contracting, the socially consensual determination of prices (Jorion, 1994; Guerrien, 1994) coercive inter-locked contracts (Bhaduri, 1986). The extent of such non-market marketing will affect the pace at which markets react to deregulation and other policy levers normally considered to provide incentives.

Systems of non-market exchange have been recognised to comprise two principal sorts: redistribution and reciprocity. Polanyi contrasted such non-market exchange with that of a stylised modern society where commercial logic rules and an unembedded pricemaking market dominates economic life (Polanyi, 1957/1985). But, as Braudel has observed, it is too easy to reduce one phenomenon to sociology and another to economics (1985: 227). John Davis is the most recent of many to argue against Polanyi's dualistic schema on the empirical grounds *not* that reciprocity and redistribution did or do not characterise under-developed exchange, but that they are deeply pervasive in what he calls OECD economies (Davis, 1992) where he has identified over 50 different types of exchange. Market and non-market exchange jostle together. With reference to markets for agricultural products with which we shall be principally concerned here, it is likely that both redistribution and reciprocity are of quantitative importance themselves. Further, when market relations are entered into in order to acquire an input to a relation of reciprocity (e.g. grain for gifting; procurement for a state-administered public distribution system), it is the logics of reciprocity or redistribution not the profit or utility maximising market logic that is the motivation for marketing.

Fourie's kind of market is conventionally distinguished from other types of

FEMINIST VISIONS OF DEVELOPMENT

economic activity, for example that within firms. Although some theorists have depicted firms as clusters of individual market-like contractual relationships, firms can also be seen as 'a command economy in microcosm' (Folbre, 1994: 45). Their internal structure of authority is understood by some primarily to minimise transactions costs and by others primarily as a coercive mechanism. Upon empirical scrutiny, it is apparent that firms cannot be reduced to bundles of micro-markets. Firms are a distinct type of economic institution. A conventional characterisation contrasts institutions/firms with markets. If that contrast is accepted, then markets would have to be understood as '*not-institutions*' (see Folbre, 1994: 24 for one example).

But markets cannot exist in a deinstitutionalised form: no economic phenomena do. It is only possible to construct supply and demand schedules on the assumption that buyers and sellers react as though any price could be the equilibrium price. Prices are thus formed in logical time as if expectations had vanished and memories were eliminated but as if complete information existed about other prices at the moment of price formation. This is a necessary condition for perfect competition. But perfect competition not only does not exist, it would not be viable for long if it did exist because entry, exit, investment and disinvestment depend in the actual world upon the belief or the fact that information regarding opportunities is restricted. Two central tenets of the neoclassical project are incompatible: the 'methodological individualism' involving voluntarist, individualist subjective preference; and instrumental rationality on the one hand, and the market (as an actually existing bundle of 'legal, customary, political and other social arrangements': Hodgson, 1988: 174) on the other. Markets are institutions.

'Institution' is a notion used in at least three rather loose ways. The first is sociological. Any behavioural regularity is the manifestation of an institution (Fourie, 1991: 52). Thus a conference is an institution, but so also is the way in which biological sex becomes social gender, or norms of justice and other aspects of ideology and social rules are developed and reproduce. Exchange processes are constituted by, and constitute in turn, a wide set of social institutions: state, locality, class, ethnic group, age and gender. It is one thing to state this but quite another to examine these complex relationships empirically. Yet, since all social institutions are specific to time and place, since they change over time and place, and since the social configurations of markets vary in significant ways, there can be no escape from empirical enquiry. The further two senses in which the idea of 'institution' is understood also involve behavioural regularities. Thus the first sociological usage can be argued to be all encompassing. Economists, however, distance their use of the concept from that of sociologists by carving out two further distinct territories for 'institution'. Thus the second is micro-economic. Institutions are understood in 'special case' terms. North (1990) would have us recognise organisations as distinct from (social normative) institutions and examine the tensions between them. Organisations are groups of individuals bound by some common purpose to achieve objectives (North 1990: 5). The organisations or micro-economic institutions of interest to economists are those concerned with

FEMALE AND MALE GRAIN MARKETING SYSTEMS

production: firms and contracts. The third sense of institution is macro-economic and legal, encompassing the definition of rights, the scope of economic behaviour, the mechanisms to protect exchange, penalise miscreants and through taxation ensure state legitimacy (Giddens, 1992; Shaffer, 1979).

In her recent book, Folbre (1994) has convincingly sustained her hypothesis that production and reproduction are shaped by a variety of types of institution of collective action. These institutions can be ascribed (e.g. caste), acquired (e.g. 'Lionesses'), multiple, not coordinated (patriarchal behaviour, for instance, may be in direct conflict with egalitarian developmental beliefs; families are sites of both cooperation and conflict) and not monitored. *Pace* the new home economics, returns to participation in such social institutions are not consciously calculated, nor is it likely that they are calculable with a precision making economic sense.

Social institutions can be of two types: first, social groups (e.g. family, caste and ethnic group in all of which patriarchy may tilt the distribution of resource control in male favour); second, social norms, ideologies and conventions (e.g. patriarchy as a cultural construct). These are Kalpana Bardhan's 'plurality of oppressions' (1993). We will look here principally (though not exclusively) at the intersection of two social institutions: gender and class in which markets for staple foods are embedded.

The gender construction of staple food markets

Marketplaces and staple food markets are highly gendered complexes of social institutions. But (although there are no textual religious proscriptions of women from trading) gender works in these markets in ways differing radically from society to society. The central questions concern institutional autonomy: whether the social institutions of production, household reproduction and the reproduction of gender ideologies 'enable' certain kinds of female participation in such markets and 'constrain' others, and if so how and why.

For Boserup, gender divisions of labour in production were related straightforwardly to those in markets (1970: 87–92). The gendering of property ownership or usufructuary rights over land was reflected in those over products. Female farming systems had female traders. Male farming systems, male traders. Empirical analysis shows that this is not, nor was it at the time, an accurate generalisation.

In West Africa, for instance, while agricultural production may be controlled by women as well as by men, local trade in basic consumption goods has been widely observed to be a public domain for women in which not only can competition be fierce, but also accumulation not entirely unknown.[4] Even so, women are portrayed as tending to occupy particular niches in female grain marketing systems,[5] more often than not defined by:

- commodity (staple food, cooked food, beer) perhaps because access to, or production of, these goods can be carried out domestically; these goods may

FEMINIST VISIONS OF DEVELOPMENT

also be a female gendered subset where commodities are gendered according to notions of rank, status and purity (where female goods are inferior);

- points in the market system (small-scale processing and retailing perhaps because of highly gendered concepts of the 'strenuous work' required by other marketing activities or because of the prior requirements of the reproductive burden);

- organisational forms (individuated) and forms of reproduction of the firm (simple/oriented to subsistence, perhaps the result of gendered inheritance customs and access to capital and of gendered constraints on spatial mobility);

- motivation (household subsistence/target incomes, perhaps because of the gendered division of intrahousehold expenditure responsibilities and gender-specific norms of ostentation in private consumption, savings and investment);

- territoriality and spatial mobility (local, non-mobile because of male gendered transport ownership and gendered notions of propriety in the public territories of marketplaces);

- season (most active in, if not fully confined to, the post-harvest months with a rapid turnover time and lower capital requirements). The irresistible implication is that other forms of local trade will tend not to be controlled by women, even in 'female' marketing systems.

Pujo has thoughtfully reviewed speculation about the female gendering of West African trade (1997: 41–4). All the explanations put forward are problematical. One materialist hypothesis – of 'residualisation' – stresses the role of land scarcity under conditions of rapid commercialisation which results in production's becoming increasingly dominated by men. Women then turn to the control of commercialisation and the sphere of distribution, giving them a domain independent of men.[6] But for this there is little empirical support. In particular, the division by gender of male production and female distribution is not rigid in any society and trade is far from a residual activity, being capable of generating comparatively great wealth. A second hypothesis – that of 'compatibility' – rehearses the idea that trade is easy to combine with household activities (which are understood as prior claims on female labour). Where social reproduction requires market exchange as well as labour within the household, then women are found in markets. Again, this is toppled by empirical evidence. A third 'cultural' argument sees female identity as involving both fertility and independence. Thus trading and the separate budget associated with it are just as much required of women as a large number of children. But not all women trade and marketplaces and processes are not so simply arranged.[7] A general explanation has not proved possible. As with so many social phenomena (the regional patterns of the sex ratio spring to mind) the explanations for patterns of gendering will be both specific and complex. To reveal how social institutions and economic behaviour interact it is useful to be able to examine gender ideologies and then the contrariness of their outcomes in the 'actual' observable gendering of tasks, control over technologies and capital in markets, and their impact on structural aspects of

FEMALE AND MALE GRAIN MARKETING SYSTEMS

markets: entry, concentration, competition and information and thus on performance. To my knowledge, Pujo's work in the forest interior of Guinee in 1992 is the only study that has succeeded in looking systematically at the rice market anywhere in this way. Performance has even been specified in gendered industrial organisation terms:[8] the gendered distribution of returns to trade, employment and comparative productive efficiency (Pujo, 1997: 239–74).

While the labour process in rice production in Guinee Forestière is mostly gender-sequential, that of marketing is gender-segregated. 'The idea that processing transforms "male" paddy into "female" rice is used by many peasant women to obtain access to the output' (Pujo, 1997: 182) . But from then onwards the rice market is segmented by gender, operational scale and technology. The vast bulk of trading firms are individuated. In 1992, 80 per cent of firms in Guinee Forestière were run by women and all of them were individuated. The classification of activity in the marketing system therefore corresponds with types of firm (which is not the case in India). The gender division of labour is summarised in Figure 9.1. In practice it coincides closely with the ideologies of appropriate activity. Marketplace trade is indeed female. These women traders are relatively younger than male traders (average age 37 versus 50) and their firms are smaller (average 32 tonnes versus 134). Female traders tend to operate through personalised 'network' trading contracts and are price takers. By contrast, shop-based trade is controlled by men. Men control all derived markets (e.g. the rental markets for transport and storage) and all materially productive activity (mechanical milling). They are price makers and can and do practise collusive price formation. Quite exclusive proscriptions prevent women from being mill mechanics. Trading capital and skills result from gender-specific social relations. While young men acquire capital and skill by labouring (seasonally) in the firms of relatives and/or by commercial loans, young women (when released from reproductive chores) watch female relatives in the marketplace but their access to trading capital depends entirely on loans from parents, siblings or husbands. These loans are more restricted in size than those to men. Further, they carry with them the obligation to share the returns from trade – on average half of their earnings.

Thus the gender construction of trade limits the access of women to capital and causes an unequal distribution of costs, returns and obligations. Gender intersects with other social institutions:

- class: found to be particularly awkward. Though the commoditisation of labour is at an incipient stage, males dominate capital accumulation; the household is a site of exploitation through exchange; dependent women traders can also be exploited by means of usurious interest on credit from male wholesalers. Indeed, in these circumstances gender has been argued to be *the* class division (Pujo, 1997: 291–4);
- locality (information and access to capital is heavily urban biased);
- ethnic group (the historically trading *ethnies* put up barriers to entry to interregional trade);

FEMINIST VISIONS OF DEVELOPMENT

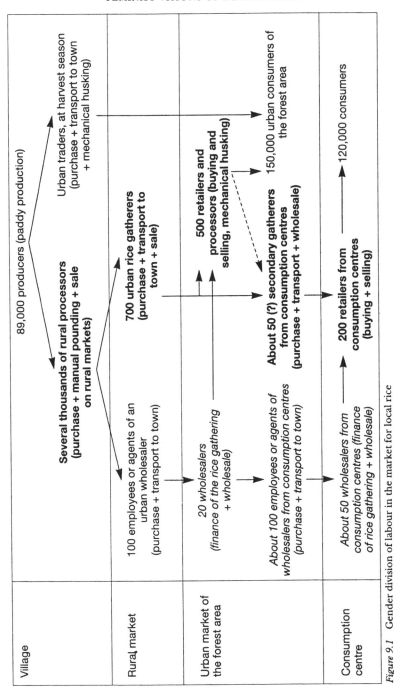

Figure 9.1 Gender division of labour in the market for local rice

Source: Pujo, 1997: 191.
Note: Bold letters represent women, italics represent men and roman type represents both men and women.

196

FEMALE AND MALE GRAIN MARKETING SYSTEMS

- religion (allegiance to which consolidates network transactions and may also lead to forms of contract which mask interest payments);
- family (marriage patterns affect entry to marketing systems);
- age (women gain independence with age and can accumulate at a faster pace; however, the great majority of women stop trading altogether when their dependants leave the households);
- the state (whose political oppression provoked the emigration of (male) traders and encouraged accumulation through smuggling and where current new entrants to the large-scale wholesale trade in rice are male officials who have often derived their starting capital from bribery) (Pujo, 1997: 291–301).

So not only can certain men be far poorer than certain women (in the Kissi region, male peasants are universally poorer than female bulkers of rice), but female traders are themselves far from being a homogeneous category. In Guinee, the returns to female traders are more highly unequal than those to men (differing by a factor of four between female retailers and wholesalers in Gueckedou: 253). At the other extremity in Hausa Nigeria, though the grain trade is dominated by men, and women are generally secluded, there is very considerable economic differentiation among female traders (Robson, forthcoming).

In South Asia, by contrast, local staple food markets would appear to be much more highly commercialised and economically differentiated. Depending on location, private wholesaling forms are up to 100 times larger in terms of gross output than their counterparts in Guinee. There is a significant wage labour force in the marketing systems (working for the owners of firms and in gangs in marketplaces) which is absent in the accounts of Guinee Forestière or of Hausaland. The classification of activity in markets does not correspond with types of firm. Firms can be very much bigger and more internally differentiated with tendencies towards uniqueness in the complex combinations of activities that each performs (Harriss-White, 1996). The patriarchal labour process in grain marketing is complex in ways different from that in West Africa. And female *traders* in India are much more homogeneous than their counterparts in West Africa.

Our evidence from West Bengal in the north-east (in 1990) and Tamil Nadu in the south-east (in 1980 and 1993–5) shows that in a typical firm owned by the males of a joint family and practising a diversity of trading and transformation activities, there are multiple relations of male labour. Male family labour (up to 13 members have been encountered) whose work is loosely specified, may work part-time or seasonally or as part of a multiple occupational profile. Permanent workers (averaging three but up to seven, whose task specification may be quite refined but whose terms and conditions are vague) may work at the simultaneous performance of more than one activity within the firm or on own account. Rates of pay are unsystematised, and accentuated by both patronage and debt bondage. Male casual labour (averaging 9 but up to 40) may be permanently attached to a trading firm but employed on a daily, weekly, seasonal, group contract or piece-rate

FEMINIST VISIONS OF DEVELOPMENT

basis for manual work. While tasks are highly specified, contracts, terms and conditions, and rates of pay vary greatly. Lastly, male child labour is underestimated,[9] used at key points in the grain marketing system (messages, carrying food and drink for negotiations, cleaning), and may be paid secure though very low wages. For some children, such work is an apprenticeship (though there is no reason why such apprenticeships should replace formal school because the children of rich traders participate in both activities).

Labour 'markets' in grain marketing are heavily structured by the assets distribution and by networks of gender, caste and locality. Markets are segmented spatially and socially. Large differences in contractual forms, in modes and levels of payment can obtain over short distances such that the very notion of a market in the restricted definition of Pandya and Dholakia is challenged.

Women participate in this grain trade in four ways, according to their caste and class position:

1   Directly (as in West Africa, but from a more restricted and poorer population segment), women from pauperised, female-headed and/or low caste households are confined to petty and often seasonal operation, to subsistence orientation and simple reproduction, to particular positions and activities within the system (especially processing and retailing), local territorial linkages, weekly marketplace sites and unlicensed and/or illegal transactions in cash. Their participation is conditioned by the life cycle, and when children are no longer dependent, these women tend to stop trading.

2   Female casual wage workers from the assetless class form the large substratum of labour in grain milling and pre-milling processing. Marketing systems rest on the backs of these women. The average mill employs 15, but up to 70 have been encountered.[10] Outcaste women are allowed to turn paddy on the large drying yards because the kernel is still protected from ritual pollution by its husk. As in Guinee and Hausaland women are debarred from being mill mechanics and it is unusual to find them handling heavy consignments of scalding paddy during the parboiling process. Female 'coolie' is prevalently but incorrectly regarded by mill owners as a household supplement for their employees.[11] Wage differentials of two thirds to a half that of male wages in rice mills in no way reflect productivity (which in any case would be tantamount to impossible to measure accurately since the division of tasks in milling is sex sequential). Female mill work is deliberately casualised and I have never encountered a unionised female labour force. The sexual exploitation of the mill workforce by management is not unknown.

3   In the recent past in smaller family firms, unwaged female family members have provided that part of the wage to labour in trading firms which takes the form of prepared food (though with the commercialisation of labour, this practice of payment in tea and meals is dying, or itself being commercialised). Female labour will then subsidise the firm. It has to be added that a large rice milling and trading firm will almost certainly 'subsidise' some of the costs of

FEMALE AND MALE GRAIN MARKETING SYSTEMS

reproduction of their male labour force such that the social reproduction of male labour is not entirely borne by female labour within working-class households. Accidents on site are usually compensated and medical expenses often paid at times of sickness. Both male and female labour receive at least one month's extra pay at a major festival. Often this is given in kind as cloth. It can also be argued, however, that such payments both retard the formation of labour markets (because of their informational opacity) and reflect 'backward' relationships of patronage rather than market exchange (by dint of their discretionary element).

4   Women in accumulating firm-families are used for the caste-based reproduction and expansion of firms first by means of their dowries on marriage and second through the (rare) practice of fictitious 'benami' registration of a trading company in a woman's name generally for the purposes of tax avoidance. In the first case, the higher education of such women is a good example of the economic inefficiency of gender institutions. For such women, education is a status good and leads neither to economic participation nor to control over assets or over major economic decision.[12] Educated mothers are thought better to educate their own children; but the structure of ownership of large mercantile companies, framed by the pre-emption of tax laws, frequently requires strong male control of young male adults and discourages migration for advanced education, so there exist constraints to education other than gender and other than its costs.

So the South Asian grains trade is also seen to be highly gendered. In turn, gender intersects with caste and class position. The lack of ownership or control over property, or any means of circulation (which determines creditworthiness), makes the economic role of women belonging to the accumulating oligopolies somewhat indirect, in contrast to the role of poor women in petty trade and the casual labour force.

Thus male marketing systems are dynamised by female wage labour and female marketing systems have male traders at their power points even if they also have a profusion of apparently independent female traders. The classification of marketing systems as male or female might be appealing but it is inaccurate as a generalisation and it obscures increasingly common characteristics of grain markets in these two regions. Both types of marketing system provide more livelihoods to women than they do to men, but women's livelihoods are on the whole relatively humble. We now turn to the thorny question of whether even these humble livelihoods can be emancipating.

Markets and gender subordination

Class societies which specialise, reproduce themselves through exchange. Just as social reproduction takes place within households so it takes place in markets. We have seen how marketplaces in certain parts of the world have been identified as

FEMINIST VISIONS OF DEVELOPMENT

female domains, as sites for the exercise of female autonomy. But equally, we have seen that market exchange is both complex and inherently riddled with ambiguity. It does not follow that processes of commodity marketing either ensure female autonomy and emancipation (within either the marketing system or the domestic unit) or remove the shackles from female property ownership or accumulation. Just as the household is a site for relationships which subordinate women so also, with subtlety, is the 'market' for wage labour and for grain.

In West African *rural* markets, despite the fame of the 'market queens', 'mama benz' or 'market mammies' and despite the undoubted greater freedom to trade and autonomous control over the returns to trade than in India, it seems the upward economic mobility of women is rarely achieved. Robson's work in Nigerian Hausaland rams home the point that, there, men do not share their control of agricultural production. Men have over the recent past come to engulf and to dominate periodic marketplace trade and even to share the village market with secluded women traders. The latter, for reasons of inheritance custom, access to capital and periodic taboos on trading based on life cycle events, are unable to accumulate (Robson, forthcoming).

In Guinee, the access of women to marketplaces and to commerce is restricted more often than not by the decisions of men about market supplies, which are frequently generated out of production processes centring upon the household. Women in marketplace trade may thus be prevented from buying and selling and constrained to selling. While market information is segmented by gender (and women are socialised and 'apprenticed' from childhood to appreciate better than men the subtle conventions surrounding volumetric measurements),[13] the economic resources necessary for the spatial and social mobility to amass wholesale consignments, command transport and/or own processing facilities are in the hands of men.

Inheritance down the female line is not possible, so the intergenerational transfer of commercial resources from mother to daughter has to be made early in the latter's maturity. Only petty quantities can be transferred in this way. The average capital of male traders is 27 times that of female traders. In Pujo's study only one woman trader gained returns greater than any male traders.

Once entry into trade is achieved, then gender-stratified access to technology and money means that processing costs for women are double those for men. Women's wholesale trading costs are 12 per cent higher than those of men; their transport costs are 55 per cent higher per unit distance; their storage costs are greater by a factor of three. Even the way trade is taxed disadvantages women in Guinee, the mechanism being gender specific because of the gender-geography of trade. On men tax is levied at a fixed rate per shop. On average it amounts to about 1 per cent of income. Women, by contrast, pay a tax every day they occupy a site in a marketplace – amounting to about 5 per cent of earnings. As a result male traders in Guekedou make $3,500 per annum to a weighted average of $820 for women (Pujo, 1997: 74).

Men exert other kinds of indirect control over female trading. In the forest

FEMALE AND MALE GRAIN MARKETING SYSTEMS

interior of Guinee, rotating credit associations among women traders facilitate accumulation and yet women traders' investments in cattle, houses and jewellery, and their savings, are still frequently controlled by men. The extent of economic and functional differentiation means that it is not to be assumed that women traders have any particular collective interest on account of their gender.

In South Asia, the same phenomena are writ large and much more intensely, it would seem. Roles within market systems are structured by non-market criteria. Control over capital is exclusively male while 55 per cent of the casual livelihoods comprising the physical work of marketing and post-harvest transformation are held by women. Casual female labour gets take-home pay based on piece rates which is on average about two thirds that of casual male labour. The subordination of women is extremely crude depending on the type and class of commercial firm. Petty trade admits low caste and poor women. Their 'independent' returns are rarely much more than can be got by wage labour in commercial firms and are on the poverty line: 2 per cent of the estimated average returns of a rice wholesale firm. But gender constrains entry into the permanent wage labour force where take-home wages including perks in kind average 20 to 300 per cent higher than earnings in the casual female labour segments.

Gender also constraints accumulation which is by men. In elite firms, the role of women is very rarely productive or managerial. Nor are women family members deployed in the firm. Instead women are constructed socially as vehicles for the transfer of commercial resources between kinship groups. The exploitation of low-paid casual female labour by this commercial class not only fuels capitalist profits but also in turn reproduces the educated, somewhat secluded, leisured state of women in the households of the 'rurban' elite. Indian grain markets reflect in vivid ways the gender subordination characteristic of Indian society as a whole. Resistance to these arrangements is rare and meets intense male hostility. The issue of resistance will be revisited in the concluding discussion of political organisation.

Not only is gender far from being a homogeneous category, but the extent to which gender divisions and ideologies structure and constrain individual or collective agency varies. While it looks as though what Folbre terms the 'structures of constraint' are less fortified in rural and 'rurban' West Africa, they are formidable in India. There, businesswomen and female entrepreneurs can be found. But(a) rarely in rural or even 'rurban' areas and(b) rarely in the grain trade.

The impact of market participation in domestic reproduction

It is a matter of debate whether intrahousehold activity is structured (and household resources are allocated) primarily by patriarchy without reference to markets (Baud, 1983) or by markets without reference to patriarchy (Haddad *et al.*, 1997) or whether the two interact. If it is the latter, the debate proceeds to tackle the question of whether household labour responds to labour markets or livelihood opportunities such as marketplace trade, where low wages or returns are gender

FEMINIST VISIONS OF DEVELOPMENT

neutral and reflect the low productivity of women, the terms and conditions of market participation of whom are conditioned by patriarchally determined work burdens within households. Or whether marketplace remuneration is independently patriarchally determined so that wages and incomes for women are low irrespective of their supply and their productivity.

Returns from trade, involving more or less autonomous action in public marketplaces (West Africa) or wage labouring in trading firms (India), insofar as it brings exchangeable income is argued to be empowering (Batliwala, 1993). By now it must be realised that if women are empowered or emancipated by the act of trading in the social arena of the marketplace, it is despite the fact that they face higher costs and lower returns and that gender ideologies compound female disadvantage by preventing challenge to the commanding heights of the wholesale trade. For women's income to empower them in the social arena of the household, their income has to remain in their control. Further, the consequences of this control have to matter to other household members. As Robson argues it is not control *per se* which denotes empowerment. Female earnings which release male income to enhance male private expenditure are disempowering (Robson, forthcoming, quoting Pahl, 1980: 322). Empowerment within the household also requires control over negotiations, discussions and decisions about the disposal and use of income (which means examining types and purposes of expenditure, savings, investment and transfers). Empowerment requires changes in the ideologies shaping norms and motivation, increased capacities to renegotiate the terms of market participation and the allocation of the burden of unremunerated, less-perceived and appreciated productive and reproductive work.

In the conventional model of a single stylised household, the possibility that gender relations within the household and in the market are class, regionally or ethnically specific is ignored. In focusing on one institution of culture and material economy (gender), the others have inevitably been put on hold. In Guinee, Pujo has found that the disposition of the returns from commercial activity of women traders with the same size of commercial enterprise will depend on the class position occupied by their husbands. The elasticity of relations of household reproduction (which may condition marketplace participation rather than be conditioned by it) is also a matter for empirical research. There is fragmentary evidence in South India that reproductive roles such as child care are not gender-rigid and that the elderly – even elderly males – may play an important reproductive role and condition the availability of adult women for remunerated economic activity (Gillespie and McNeill, 1992).

Although there is fragmentary research in this area, it would be cowardly not to summarise what is known (and not known) about the reproductive consequences of the gendering of trade. In Guinee, Hausaland and India, women are very rarely allowed land rights or ownership of tools or cattle.[14] So income from commodity trading is one of the restricted opportunities other than wage labour by means of which women may enhance a household's income. In Guinee and India decisions

FEMALE AND MALE GRAIN MARKETING SYSTEMS

on the disposal, household use or purchase of grain may be made by men (usually), by women and jointly (both much more rarely).

In West Africa there is significant variation between local regions in gender roles and burdens within households. The impact of female income from trade is added to the impact on the gendered control of the product of the labour process in production. In the Kissi region of Guinee women put in 40 per cent of the total labour in production but control 28 per cent of the product and perform all the reproductive labour, therefore having far less residual leisure than men. Even so women may sometimes be allowed to *manage* the granaries whose contents they do not *control*. Women traders keep separate accounts of expenditure and savings. But their lower returns and continual pressures by males to negotiate the appropriation of women's capital and the shedding of male expenditure responsibilities threatens this separate sphere. Further, the average income of a woman trader roughly equals her individual reproduction costs so, since women have obligations and dependants, they themselves are almost invariably thrown into relations of economic dependency (Pujo, 1997: 155–70, 209, 252).

In Zarewa village in Hausaland about one third of secluded women prepare and market cooked food. Women's incomes from grain and food marketing together with diverse other activities amount to about 13 per cent of household income: clearly much less than what men bring in and also much more unstable as a stream. While 85 per cent of household decisions are made by men, according to them, women reckon that 69 per cent are! One third of women's income goes on expenditure for the rest of the household, most of which is on food. Women spend less on themselves than do men and a smaller fraction of women than men reckon they have decision-making autonomy over matters of work, food or health expenditure (Robson, forthcoming).

From four pieces of field research into poor agrarian localities in Rajasthan (where female disadvantage is acute) in tribal Andhra Pradesh and in northern Tamil Nadu (where until recently female status has been relatively better: Agnihotri, 1996), it has been confirmed beyond doubt that female economic participation and the income derived from it does not by itself translate into greater decision-making power for women within their households, *except amongst the very poorest*. In labouring households the relationship is quite consistent.[15] For the rest, economic participation by itself does not enable a transformation of domestic control over resources and decisions. It does not lead inexorably to a change in the social relations of consumption inside the household (via the allocation of food) or outside it (via consumption expenditure). Within the household the significance of such earnings may be trivialised as 'pin money' or 'pocket money', appropriated or exchanged on more or less adverse 'terms of trade'. Independent female income may be a necessary condition for empowerment within the household but it is not sufficient. Other factors such as male outmigration, the consciousness-raising of an NGO, the extent of nuclear as opposed to joint/extended family forms, the particularities of joint family size and composition which affect relative status and the extent to which food needs were got from

FEMINIST VISIONS OF DEVELOPMENT

subsistence production were found to catalyse female income into female domestic power. In any case, neither resources nor decisions are to be assumed to be invariably in male hands. Resources may be controlled by one gender and decisions about their use by another gender or by joint negotiation. The degree of male control over expenditure decisions differs across commodity or type: health and agricultural inputs tend to be very male areas, food decisions tend to be much more female. But the degree of female control over household resources and decisions or even the intensity of female economic participation does not necessarily affect the political and social status of women in the public social territory outside the household.

With relevance to commodity market participation (though originally set out in relation to labour markets) Palmer has suggested four main considerations for the analysis of the intra-household impact of the participation of women in markets (1991: 11–15). By implication such factors may (individually or in combination) explain the varied relations already observed but they are not complete and their relative importance and role cannot be generalised:

1   the gender distribution of access to the means of production and distribution;
2   additional tasks faced by women in household reproduction and family maintenance and their gender elasticity);
3   the nature of the markets between the genders within the household (reflecting *inter alia* the extent to which a household is unitary or segmented);
4   norms governing the disposition of incomes between investment, savings and consumption between the genders and generations.

Palmer excludes from her list the crucial point of Sen (1990) that perceived contributions are as important as observable practices in the determination of relative status and welfare within households: that it is the relational quality of gender that counts as well as the material results of gendered transactions.

Despite the existence of returns from trading activity, gendered economic relations leading to subordinate status for *most* women and for *most* of their lives are associated with the subordinate status of women in marketing systems for staple foods – vividly in male marketing systems and even to be observed in female marketing systems. But with the evidence available it is just as plausible that both domestic and commercial relations are structured by the overarching forces of patriarchy. While commodity trading does not enhance the status of women within their households in any deterministic way, this does not mean that lack of independent income necessarily denotes low social or micro-political status within the household either. In Hausaland, for instance, age bears respect: 'women gain status with age' (Robson, forthcoming).[16]

Marketing systems show a certain idiosyncratic institutional autonomy, not only with respect to gender but in relation to most other social institutions, even including the social configuration of production over its spatial territory (Harriss-White, 1996). However, if, as Polanyi argued, markets destroy other forms of exchange

FEMALE AND MALE GRAIN MARKETING SYSTEMS

and replace social embeddedness and socially constituted forms of distribution by a cold commercial logic, we find that they carry out this historic mission over a very long time scale. What we observe commonly is that market exchange 'simply' reworks the social institutions through which it is constituted and that where forms of exchange moving towards a 'cold commercial logic' are found, they are on a very small scale indeed and they daub more complexity onto already highly institutionally complex relations of exchange. As with gender, so with caste in India and ethnic groups in Guinee, grain markets are reinforcing institutional inequalities and social territorialisation. Although sites and social arenas so generative of livelihoods for women lead the watcher to expect a politics of struggle, it is because marketing systems are quite remarkably *not* observed by field workers to be the site of individual, iconoclastic gender-agency, collective gender-struggle or social transformation that we now need to address 'policy'.

Policy issues

It is irresponsible to list 'policy issues' residually, as is conventionally done, as 'impediments to be removed' (caricatured by Rodgers, 1989: 1) by an equally analytically residualised state or policy process. The nature of the public policy process and all significant interests threatened by it need analytical specification in every case where the search for room for manoeuvre, for strategy and tactics for policy change is serious.

Here, instead of endogenising policy processes and situating policy advocacy, I shall restrict the discussion to a small set of social problems for women which arise from the conditions described earlier and which are relevant to the agenda-forming component of the policy process. These are principally relevant to the male marketing systems of South Asia but gain urgency from their bearing on the female marketing system of West Africa.

Technical change and livelihoods

Staple food marketing systems, even as they tend to subordinate women, nevertheless provide huge numbers of livelihoods. Eighty per cent of firms in Guinee Forestière were run by women. One hundred and forty-nine agrocommercial firms studied in South India generated jobs for 5,500 adults, of whom 72 per cent, or, 3,960, were for women (Harriss-White, 1996). That proportion would be higher if the invisible and unvalorised role of women from the families of elite firms were included.

Technical change in foodgrains (rice and oil) processing has involved (1) foreign imports of technology developed for the radically different 'factor endowments and ratios' of the US and Japan, (2) foreign technical assistance, the quality of whose scientific advice left a great deal to be desired and (3) protective domestic legislation outlawing the 'indigenous' technologies (Harriss and Kelly, 1982). Adoption of such imported packages was pressed on state institutions

205

FEMINIST VISIONS OF DEVELOPMENT

(co-operatives and parastatals) which were isolated from the other state and private institutions of finance, pricing, procurement and logistics upon which the package depended. Low capacity utilisation and higher per unit marketing and processing costs have resulted in chronic state subsidisation. 'The market' has resisted technical change in package form (a rational response) but has over the years adopted techniques in stages. This has resulted in economies of scale and accentuated the structural concentration of assets in marketing systems.

Each wave of incremental technical change has led to the net displacement of labour, but has been biased hugely against casual female labour. Whether or not this displacement destroys livelihoods or 'merely' reduces drudgery does not depend only on the degree of commercialisation of the product, it also depends on the extent to which the labour relations of post-harvest processing have become commercialised. The first mechanised technology (the Lewis Grant huller, adapted in the early twentieth century from a coffee grinder and now very widespread, cost effective and made illegal in India) is the most female-labour-displacing of all because it replaces hand- or foot-operated machines worked by women.[17] The latest components (husk-fired driers) substituting for the public good of sunshine pose very serious threats to large quantities of female livelihoods in marketing systems. While Douglass North has hypothesised that technology is generally adopted so as to maximise the use of lesser-skilled workers who do not have the bargaining power to disrupt production (1990: 65), here, technology is adopted which does away with precisely those people least capable of bargaining or of withholding labour – the cheapest factor of marketing – female labour. The newest technical components are only cost-effective at market prices under conditions of high capacity utilisation which are difficult to achieve. Yet, inexorably, they are being adopted in the very reverse of a green-revolutionary development.[18] Perhaps the employment of armies of low caste people who happen to be women is more of a status-reducing expression of the contaminating caste relations of a merchant than a status enhancing expression of patriarchy. Technical change can not only concentrate the economic asset structures of the marketing system but also reinforce their gender power relations.

Liberalisation and masculinisation

If liberalisation is successful, it results in the development of more integrated national markets, which in turn entail not just the commercialisation of production and the scaling-up of post-harvest technology but also an increase in specialisation and interregional wholesale trade, not the least in staples. The development of long-distance interregional trading in female marketing systems has been observed to be dominated by men. In parts of West Africa, masculinisation may substitute for female trading (e.g. in northern Nigeria) while elsewhere they may be complements (e.g. Guinee Forestière). Female marketing systems may be articulated with national territorial markets without a reduction in female

FEMALE AND MALE GRAIN MARKETING SYSTEMS

livelihoods. Indeed, these may very well expand. The point is that the integrated system as a whole is dominated, economically if not in numbers, by men. This domination places a new constraint upon female commercial accumulation. It is not necessary for a change in the gender division of work to occur. It is enough that there is expansion in precisely that type of work historically dominated by, if not entirely restricted to, men.[19]

The adaptive and productive inefficiency of gender roles in commerce

The most common question asked of markets concerns their efficiency. By virtue of there being no de-institutionalised marketing systems anywhere, efficiency is extremely difficult to evaluate. For the purposes of this discussion we can distinguish productive efficiency in which outputs from given inputs are maximised, from adaptive efficiency (North, 1990: 80–2) which involves judgements about the flexibility of the norms and institutions shaping the way an economy develops. In raising the issue of efficiency it does not follow that the World Bank's emphasis, particularly over the 1980s, on efficiency to the detriment of exploitation can be taken without question (see Elson, 1995). The point to be made here is that the economic consequences of the gendering of the rice marketing system reduces both sorts of efficiency in the examples we have used.

In Guinee, the gender division of labour has been calculated to cause losses in productive efficiency. Women face reduced incentives in production because of male control of the product of their labour, in processing because of the gendered stratification of technology and in trading because of the higher costs which were discussed earlier, which reduce their returns by 20 per cent.[20] The inefficient impact of these gendered relations is to raise consumer prices, leading to malnutrition, to raise the competitive advantage of imported over local rice (and imported rice is completely controlled by men) and to lead to massive female underemployment in the scarce season, which does not bode well for the nutritional status of their dependants (Pujo, 1997: 239–74).

In liberalising India, while gender roles, ideologies and the division of tasks in metropolitan conurbations may show considerable new elasticity (particularly among the 'middle classes') they seem to solidify with the inexorability of superglue outside such social territories, and are 'adaptively inefficient'. In a South Indian market town of some 100,000 people whose economy has been studied every decade from 1973, the adaptive inefficiency of the gendering of markets works differently from the West African case. Considerable strides have been made in female education and there is a small core of women doctors and lawyers. But women cannot own or manage commercial firms. The reasons given by the few women who want to enter trade are instructive. The state, in the guise of tax officials, blocks licensing on suspicion of bad faith and of intention to avoid tax by the family concerned. The state, in the guise of banks, also refuses to regard women as eligible for credit on the grounds that their registered collateral is 'benami'

FEMINIST VISIONS OF DEVELOPMENT

(bogus). With respect to the acquisition of skills and contacts, women's learning has to be confined to the domestic arena (to watching trade in a special room which can be a site – a private haven – for male business activity) and such women have faced male sanction on travel for purposes of commerce.

While there are no gender barriers to entry into high skill wage work such as computer programming in metropolitan cities and while the next stage of technical change in agro-commerce – automation – urgently requires computerisation, women in the marketing town who have somehow obtained relevant qualifications from the district capital's educational institutions are still debarred (on declared grounds of gender) from computer operation on commercial premises in the market town. The agro-commercial elite reject the female gendering of high-tech work, located socially (and physically) above their male labour force. The diffusion of computerisation is currently hindered and confined to the kind of simple accounting operations, which can be learned by trial and error by under-educated male family labour.

The commercial elite boasts many examples of what Sunder Rajan (1993) has ironically termed the 'new Indian woman': much more highly educated than their agro-commercial magnate husbands, these women have been imported for purposes of marriage from the metropolis. Their rare and always frustrated wish to enter commerce is seen as a natural outcome of a merchant capitalism construed everywhere as benevolent to them and massively reinforced in the popular English language media. Such 'modern women', confined to teaching the children of their elite peers and to philanthropic social work, with their roots in a carefully sanitised version of 'female tradition', accentuate the gap between their own apparent modernity and the alienated mass of women socially imprisoned by gender ideologies and by gendered material poverty.

Meanwhile, in this male marketing system the petty retail trade in staples which 20 years ago was an arena for women in the precincts of the Municipal Market has been taken over by men. Remaining women retailers are the most economically disavantaged – widows and abandoned women with children. The older generation of women traders ceased this activity once their children were no longer economically dependent upon them. While a few elite women see large scale commerce principally in terms of its profitability and contemplate entry, poor women experience marketplaces as public, physically dirty and ritually polluting places and contemplate exit. For this latter class the non-participation of women is what they mean by development and progress. For the rich and poor aspirant to commerce alike, information, contacts and credit are the *sine qua non* of the ability of contingent acts of individual agency to consolidate themselves into a successful patterned challenge to gender roles.

Political organisation

Our search for gender-empowering action in marketing systems revealed very little.[21] In Guinee, agency is expressed in achieving micro-monopolies under

208

FEMALE AND MALE GRAIN MARKETING SYSTEMS

competitive conditions, i.e. establishing niches, a regular clientele and repeated transactions so as to reduce competition. Otherwise gendered resistance and struggle is rare and is not acted out in the theatre of the marketplace. The division of labour in production and marketing is everywhere very close to ideological norms about the gendering of tasks and appropriate behaviour. If anything the measured input of women into rice *cultivation* is underestimated in normative statements.[22] This discrepancy between ideology and practice leads to men having greater control over the product than would be the case if tasks were actually performed according to gender norms. For women to take direct control of the means of production or the product is unusual. The resistance put up by women tends to take clandestine and petty forms: for instance hiding savings outside the home (part of the significance for women of gender-specific, rotating credit associations). But men also practise passive resistance in the same way. They also conceal savings and investments.

In India the micro-politics of casual male and female labour in marketplaces is quite different. Male casual labourers pull carts, load and unload, weigh and bag and act as millhands. Such labour tends to be permanent (albeit paid on piece rates or daily *coolie*) and unionised. Often casual male labour is organised in rival unions by competing political parties, unions run by professional politicians. Though this form of organisation smacks of 'divide and rule', unionised male labour has achieved some social change, e.g. the right to annual wage negotiations and the standardisation of piece rates in given localities.

By contrast casual female labour (which sweeps and cleans, dries and bags grain, separates and bags byproducts) is hardly organised at all throughout the subcontinent and even in states which have been ruled by the Communist parties. In fact their organisation is actively discouraged by the same mill owners prepared to negotiate with male unions. Over many years of fieldwork, I have encountered the stories of only two women 'foremen' who have sought to mobilise female casual labour. Both were harassed and sacked once the owners understood their purpose. Large unorganised female labour forces are *also* deliberately laid off by fractions in turn in order to avoid the welfare obligations towards permanent wage labour of the Factories Acts. Even in processing and trading firms which by dint of their male labour force are large enough to come under state regulation, there are no crèches, no sleeping areas for women, few latrines. Health and safety regulations are flouted. There are no muster rolls. Provident Funds, gratuities and lay-off compensations are ignored. The Factories Act inspectorate is widely co-opted and tends to collude with grain mill owners.

The working women forming the foundation of 'male' marketing systems are caught in a pincer. On the one side, technical change, on the other, the crudest of patriarchal commercial oppression threaten their livelihoods and their capacity collectively to improve their working conditions. Both in 'female' and 'male' marketing systems, and for a wide variety of reasons, it is no exaggeration to conclude that millions of female livelihoods worldwide are in jeopardy.

FEMINIST VISIONS OF DEVELOPMENT

Notes

1 These ideas have been developed in dialogues springing from a comparison of my work in South Asia with that of doctoral students Laurence Pujo, working in Guinea and Elsbeth Robson, working in Nigerian Hausaland, to both of whom I am very grateful. The response of QEH's Centre for Cross Cultural Research on Women's seminar, where an earlier version was presented, and of Cecile Jackson, have also been very helpful. The remaining weaknesses are my responsibility.
2 See Humphrey, 1987; Baud, 1983; Clark, 1993 and Pearson here.
3 See Harriss-White 1995,1996 for developments of this point.
4 Bohannan and Dalton, 1962; Lawson, 1971; Hill, 1977; Christiansen, forthcoming.
5 Koopmans, 1990; Bauer, 1992.
6 In societies where divorce is common, such independence is required of women.
7 The first view has been advanced and discussed by Cordonnier, 1987, the second and third by Hopkins, 1973.
8 c.f. Bain, 1959.
9 Male and female child labour is crucial for the perpetuation of secluded women's trade in Nigeria. Their education may be denied them for this reason, or they may trade with other pupils at school (Robson, forthcoming).
10 The female casual labour force can number up to 700 in cotton ginning and wholesaling firms (see Harriss-White, 1996: Ch. 7).
11 'Coolie' in Tamil means wages for casual labour.
12 Female education leads to the lowering of birth rates (though not to reduced gender discrimination in regions of South Asia where this is practised: Das Gupta, 1987; Jefferey and Jefferey, Ch. 11 of the present book). But it is primary rather than tertiary education which achieves this result.
13 See Christiansen, forthcoming, for a pioneering study of the volumetric conventions in price formation by women in marketplaces in Benin.
14 The exception is in Hausaland where women can own livestock, though its disposal requires the compliance of the husband of the owner (Robson, forthcoming).
15 The vast bulk of this female economic participation, however, was from artisan craft work and agricultural labour rather than from petty trade, least of all in grains. However, the results show how complex the issue of the gendered consequences of the gains from trade is likely to be. For the original research see Samuels, 1989 on three desert villages of Rajasthan; Gillespie, 1988 on four tribal villages in Andhra Pradesh; Gibbs, 1986 on one village and Harriss, 1991 on two other villages in northern Tamil Nadu.
16 This increasingly appears to be less the case in India: see Erb, 1996 and Vera Sanso, 1997 for evidence of secular decline in the relative status of poor elderly people in rural and slum-urban settings respectively.
17 The process of displacement is most backward (and therefore acute) in the north-east of the sub-continent: see Greeley, 1987.
18 A revolutionary component should increase output per unit of input and thus lower total costs per unit of output.
19 It is also the case that forces other than liberalisation and the formation of national markets may masculinise trade: the expansion of Islamic seclusion ideology and practice is one, the gender ideologies of the colonial and post-colonial state are another.
20 Not more because male traders have a wage labour cost component which female traders do not have (Pujo, 1997: 263).
21 None of the researchers upon whose work we have relied deliberately sought out institutions initiating change wherever they might have been located. NGOs such as SEWA in India, BRAC and the Grameen Bank in Bangladesh have a limited success with the collective organisation of women in rice processing (Rowbotham, 1997). In the regions on which we have focused here, there has been no such activity.

FEMALE AND MALE GRAIN MARKETING SYSTEMS

22 This is not unknown in India! See Mencher and Saradamoni, 1982.

References

Agarwal, B. (1995) *A Field of One's Own: Gender and Land Rights in South Asia.* Cambridge University Press, Cambridge.

Agnihotri, S. (1996) 'Juvenile Sex Ratios in India – A Disaggregated Analysis, *Economic and Political Weekly* December: 3369–82.

Bain, J. (1959) *Industrial Organisation.* John Wiley, New York.

Bardhan, K. (1993) 'Social Classes and Gender in India: The Structure of the Differences in the Condition of Women', in Clark (ed.) (1993 pp. 146–178).

Batliwala, S. (1993) *Empowerment of Women in South Asia: Concepts and Practices.* FAO, New Delhi.

Baud, I. (1983) *Women's Labour in the Indian Textile Industry: The Influence of Technology and Organisation on the Gender Division of Labor.* IRIS Report 23, Development Reseach Institute, Tilburg University, Netherlands.

Bauer, S. (1992) 'Action to Assist Rural Women: Marketing Approach for Income Generating Activities in Four African Countries', in Cammann (ed.) (1992), pp.10–20.

Bhaduri, A. (1986) 'Forced Commerce and Agrarian Growth', *World Development* 14, 2: 267–72.

Bohannan, P. and Dalton, G. (1962) *Markets in Africa.* Northwestern University, Illinois.

Boserup, E. (1970) *Women's Role in Economic Development.* Allen and Unwin, London.

Braudel, F. (1985) *Civilisation and Capitalism in the 15th to 18th Centuries: Vol. 2 The Wheel of Commerce.* Fontana, London.

Cammann, L. (ed.) (1992) *Traditional Marketing Systems.* German Foundation for International Development, Feldafing.

Christiansen, B. (forthcoming) 'Unstandardised Measures and the Analysis of Price Efficiency: An Application' in Benin, in B. Harriss-White (ed.) ch 3.1.

Clark, A. (ed.) (1993) *Gender and Political Economy: Explorations of South Asian Systems.* Oxford University Press, Delhi.

Cordonnier, R. (1987) *Femmes Africaines et commerce: les revendeuses de tissu de la Ville de Lome.* L'Harmattan, Série Villes et Entreprises, Paris.

Das Gupta, M. (1987) 'Selective Discrimination against Children in Punjab', *Population and Development Review* 13.

Davis, J. (1992) *Exchange.* Open University Press, Buckingham.

Elson, D. (1995) *Male Bias in the Development Process.* Manchester University Press, Manchester, 2nd edn.

Erb, S. (1996) *Outcast from Social Welfare: Adult Disability in Rural India: Report to the Overseas Development Administration.* Queen Elizabeth House, Oxford University.

Folbre, N. (1986) 'Heart of Spades: Paradigms of Household Economics', *World Development* 14, 2, pp.245–256.

Folbre, N. (1994) *Who Pays for the Kids? Gender and the Structures of Constraint.* Routledge, London.

Fourie, F. C. von N. (1991) 'A Structural Analysis of Markets', in G. Hodgson and E. Screpanti (eds) (1991).

Gibbs, C. (1986) 'Characteristics of Household Expenditure in a Tamil Village, South India. BA dissertation, Newnham College, University of Cambridge.

FEMINIST VISIONS OF DEVELOPMENT

Giddens, A. (1992) *Sociology: A Brief but Critical Introduction.* Macmillan, London.

Gillespie, S. (1988) 'Social and Economic Aspects of Malnutrition and Health among South Indian Tribal Groups.' Ph.D. thesis, London School of Hygiene and Tropical Medicine, University of London.

Gillespie, S. and McNeill, G. (1992) *Food, Health and Survival in India and Developing Countries.* Oxford University Press, New Delhi.

Greeley, M. (1987) *Post Harvest Losses, Technology and Employment: the Case of Rice in Bangladesh.* Westview Press, Boulder, Colorado.

Griffon, M. (ed.) (1990) *Economie des filières en régions chaudes: formation des prix et échanges agricoles.* CIRAD, Montpellier.

Guerrien, B. (1994) 'L'Introuvable Théorie du marché,' in Caille et al (eds).

Haddad, L., Hoddinott, J. and Adelman, I. (1997) *Intrahousehold Resource Allocation in Developing Countries: Models, Methods and Policy.* John Hopkins University Press, Baltimore, Maryland.

Harriss, B. (1991) *Child Nutrition and Poverty in Rural South India.* Concept, New Delhi.

Harriss, B. and Kelly, C. (1982) 'Food Processing: Policy for Rice and Oil Technology', *Bulletin of the Institute of Development Studies* 13, 3: 32–44.

Harriss, J., Hunter, J. and Lewis, C. (eds) (1995) *The New Institutional Economics and Third World Development.* Routledge, London.

Harriss-White, B. (1995) 'Maps and Landscapes of Grain Markets in South Asia', in J. Harriss *et al* (1995) pp.87–108.

Harriss-White, B. (1996) *A Political Economy of Agricultural Markets in South India: Masters of the Countryside.* Sage, New Delhi.

Harriss-White, B. (forthcoming) *Agricultural Exchange and Markets from Theory to Practice: Field Methods and Field Experience in Developing Countries.* Macmillan, London.

Hill, P. (1977) *Population, Prosperity and Poverty: Rural Kano 1900 and 1970.* Cambridge University Press, Cambridge.

Hodgson, G. (1988) *Economics and Institutions.* Polity, London.

Hodgson, G. and Screpanti, E. (eds) (1991) *Rethinking Economics.* Elgar, London.

Hopkins, A. (1973) *An Economic History of West Africa.* Longmans, Harlow.

Humphrey, J. (1987) *Gender and Work in the Third World: Sexual Divisions in Brazilian Industry.* Tavistock, London.

Jorion, P. (1994) 'L'Économie Comme Science de l'Interaction Humaine vue sous l'angle des Prix: vers une Physique Social', in Caillie *et al* (eds).

Kandiyoti, D. (1988) 'Bargaining with Patriarchy', *Gender and Society* 2, 3: 274–90.

Koopmans, J. (1990) 'Gender Issues in Food Production and Marketing: Core Issues in Africa's Food Crisis, in Griffon (ed.) (1990) pp.519–31.

Lawson, R. (1971) 'The Supply Response of Retail Trading Services to Urban Population Growth in Ghana', in Meillassoux (ed.) pp.377–99.

Meillassoux, C. (ed.) (1971) *L'Evolution du commerce en Afrique de l'ouest.* Oxford University Press, Oxford.

Mencher, J. and Saradamoni, K. (1982) 'Muddy Feet, Dirty Hands: Rice Production and Female Agricultural Labour, *Economic and Political Weekly Review of Agriculture* 17, 52: 149–67.

Moser, C. O. N. (1993) *Gender, Planning and Development: Theory, Practice and Training.* Routledge, London.

North, D. (1990) *Institutions, Institutional Change and Economic Performance.* Cambridge University Press, Cambridge.

FEMALE AND MALE GRAIN MARKETING SYSTEMS

Pahl, R. (1980) 'Patterns of Money Management within Marriage', *Journal of Social Policy* 9, 3: 313–35.

Palmer, I. (1991) *Gender and Population in the Adjustment of African Economies: Planning for Change.* International Labour Office, Geneva.

Pandya, A. and Dholakia, N. (1992) 'An Institutional Theory of Exchange in Marketing', *European Journal of Marketing* 26, 12: 19–41.

Penny, D. (1985) *Starvation: A Political Economy.* Australian National University, Canberra.

Polanyi, K. (1957/1985) *The Great Transformation: The Political and Economic Origins of Our Time.* Beacon Press, Boston, Mass.

Pujo, L. (1997) 'Towards a Methodology for the Analysis of the Embeddedness of Markets in Social Institutions: Application to Gender and the Market for Local Rice in Eastern Guinea'. D.Phil thesis, Oxford University.

Robson, E. (forthcoming) 'Gender, Households and Markets: Social Reproduction in a Hausa Village, Northern Nigeria'. D. Phil thesis, Oxford University.

Rodgers, G. (ed.) (1989) *Urban Poverty and the Labour Market: Access to Jobs and Incomes in Asian and Latin American Cities.* International Labour Office.

Rowbotham, S. (1997) 'Real Women of the Real World', *Guardian* 19 April: 21.

Samuels, F. (1989) 'Changes in Female Income and Status in Rural Rajasthan: a Survey of Three Villages'. MSc Dissertation, Queen Elizabeth House, Oxford University.

Sen, A. K. (1990) 'Gender and Co-operative Conflict', in Tinker (ed.) (1990) pp.123–49.

Shaffer, J. D. (1979) 'Observations on the Political Economics of Regulations', *American Journal of Agricultural Economics* 11, 2: 766–74.

Sunder Rajan, R. (1993) *Real and Imagined Women: Gender, Culture and Postcolonialism.* Routledge, London.

Tinker, I. (ed.) (1990) *Persistent Inequalities: Women and World Development.* Oxford University Press, Oxford.

Vera Sanso, P. (1997) 'Household Composition in Madras' Low-Income Settlements', *Review of Development and Change* 2, 1: 77–98.

Whitehead, A. (1981) '"I'm Hungry, Mum": The Politics of Domestic Budgeting', in Young *et al.* (1981) pp.54–68.

Young, K. Wolkowitz, C. and McCullagh, R. (eds) (1981) *Of Marriage and the Market: Women's Subordination in International Perspective.* CSE Books, London.

Part V
Institutional and Social Change

[24]

World Development, Vol. 13, No. 9, pp. 1037–1053, 1985.
Printed in Great Britain.

0305–750X/85 $3.00 + 0.00.

Rural Women and State Policy: The Latin American Agrarian Reform Experience

CARMEN DIANA DEERE*
University of Massachusetts, Amherst

Summary. — This review of 13 Latin American agrarian reforms shows that most have directly benefited only men. It is argued that this is largely because of the common designation of 'households' as the beneficiaries of an agrarian reform and the subsequent incorporation of only male household heads into the new agrarian reform structures. It is shown that a necessary, but not sufficient, condition for rural women to benefit on par with men is that they too be designated as beneficiaries. Women as well as men must be given access to land or the opportunity to participate within the agrarian cooperatives or state farms promoted by an agrarian reform. This comparative analysis of the Latin American agrarian reform demonstrates that this has happened only in countries where the incorporation of rural women to the reform is an explicit objective of state policy.

1. INTRODUCTION

In Latin America, agrarian reform has been the major state initiative in agricultural development and rural income redistribution over the last several decades. In some countries, agrarian reform fundamentally altered rural class structure and the national distribution of wealth and power. In other countries, efforts at reform were minimal, sometimes only involving colonization or resettlement schemes. Whatever the form or scale, each agrarian reform has involved state intervention in the redistribution of land to formerly landless or land-poor households.

The impact of an agrarian reform on rural women depends upon the class position of each woman's household, and whether that class, or segment of class, is a beneficiary of the reform. The broader the reform's redistributive thrust, the more women it should potentially benefit. It cannot, however, be assumed that the impact of an agrarian reform on rural households is gender neutral. An increase in the household's access to land or employment or in its level of income does not necessarily mean a positive change in women's socio-economic position. Processes of social change have complex economic, political and ideological effects which may alter the social status of rural women as well as their position relative to men.

The central thesis of this paper is that most Latin American agrarian reforms have directly benefited only men. It is argued that this is largely because 'households' are designated as the beneficiaries of an agrarian reform but only male household heads are incorporated into the new agrarian reform structures. It is shown here that a necessary, but not sufficient, condition for rural women to benefit on par with men is that they too be designated as beneficiaries. Women as well as men must be given access to land or the opportunity to participate in the agrarian cooperatives or state farms promoted by an agrarian reform. A comparative analysis of the Latin American agrarian reforms demonstrates that this has happened only in countries where the incorporation of rural women to the reform is an explicit objective of state policy.

This paper first presents a brief overview of 13 Latin American agrarian reforms as well as the available gender-disaggregated data on agrarian

* This paper was previously published as a Women in International Development Working Paper, No. 81 (Michigan State University, March 1985). This paper was presented to the Kellogg Institute of Notre Dame University workshop on 'Feminist Theory, State Policy and Rural Women in Latin America' (February 1985); an earlier version was presented to the Conference on 'After *The Second Sex*: New Directions' (University of Pennsylvania, April 1984). The author is grateful to Hannah Roditi for skilful research assistance and to numerous colleagues for supplying references for this undertaking.

reform beneficiaries. The following section presents an analysis of the mechanisms that have led to the exclusion of women among the beneficiaries of the agrarian reforms. It is argued that these mechanisms of exclusion are legal and structural as well as ideological. The two agrarian reform processes that have resulted in significant female participation — Cuban and Nicaraguan — are then examined. These cases illustrate how an explicit state policy favoring the incorporation of rural women is a necessary precondition for their participation. The next section considers why it is important, both for social equity and successful cooperative development, for women to be included as reform beneficiaries. The final section considers the barriers to women's effective participation as cooperative members.

2. AN OVERVIEW OF THE LATIN AMERICAN AGRARIAN REFORMS

To establish the context for the subsequent analysis, this section presents a brief overview of the principal features of 13 Latin American agrarian reforms. No attempt is made to analyze the efficacy of each of the agrarian reforms with respect to either its own goals or its actual impact upon the beneficiaries. Summarized in Table 1 are the year in which the agrarian reforms were initiated or subsequently modified, the most recent available estimate of beneficiaries as well as the proportion of rural households they represent, and the predominant form of tenure and productive organization in the reformed sector.

The potential redistributional impact of an agrarian reform largely reflects the political project that the reform represents.[1] The first three agrarian reforms carried out in Latin America — those of Mexico, Bolivia and Cuba — were the product of social revolutions. Through the agrarian reforms, the traditional *hacienda* was virtually eliminated and a major redistribution of landed property took place in favor of a significant proportion of the rural population.[2]

These three reforms differ, however, with respect to forms of tenancy and the organization of production in the reformed sector. The thrust of the Mexican agrarian reform was to constitute the *ejido*, a form of communal based property, with production carried out either collectively or individually. The Bolivian agrarian reform favored the creation of individual private holdings. While the Cuban agrarian reform also had a significant 'land to the tiller' thrust (every tenant, sharecropper and squatter was given ownership

of the land cultivated), the bulk of the expropriated land went to constitute state farms.[3] Only in the mid-1970s was emphasis placed on the promotion of production cooperatives based on peasants pooling their individual holdings.

The agrarian reforms initiated in the 1960s represent those of the 'Alliance for Progress.' United States development assistance in the 1960s was contingent on the Latin American countries' instituting agrarian reforms. United States policy clearly recognized that, if revolutionary social change was to be avoided in the Americas, the pressing issues of rural inequality and poverty had to be addressed.

Launched in the wake of the Cuban revolution, the Alliance for Progress agrarian reforms aimed both at containing the peasantry as a potential revolutionary force and at breaking the power of the Latin American landed élite. The traditional landowning class was viewed as an impediment to development and its hold on political power as a barrier to modernization. Moreover, it was argued, the redistribution of land would not only satisfy the peasantry's potentially revolutionary demands, but it would also spur growth by putting land into the hands of those who would work it most intensively. The higher incomes of these people would lead, in turn, to a larger internal market. A broader internal market would stimulate investment and hence the overall process of growth. Agrarian reform was thus the ideal mechanism both to contain the peasantry and to establish the preconditions for successful capitalist development.

Nonetheless, agrarian reform efforts in many Latin American countries were minimal, although agrarian reform laws were on the books. Considered in this analysis are only those countries where relatively serious attempts at reform were made. Of the agrarian reforms initiated under the Alliance for Progress, only those in Peru, Chile and Venezuela reached a significant number of beneficiaries. In the cases of Peru and Chile, this only happened after the initial Alliance for Progress reforms were modified and implemented by more progressive governments, the Allende government in Chile (from 1970 to 1973) and the revolutionary military regime in Peru (from 1969 to 1978).

The Alliance for Progress agrarian reforms generally favored the creation of individual private property, as Table 1 shows. Often this was accompanied by the organization of credit and service or marketing cooperatives among individual producers. In the 1970s, a number of countries gave priority to the organization of production cooperatives (based on collective or group farming), such as the *asentamientos* in

RURAL WOMEN AND STATE POLICY   1039

Table 1. *The Latin American agrarian reforms*

Country	Year	Beneficiaries	Rural households (%)	Organization of production
Mexico	1917, 1971	2,890,000 (1971)	69	*ejidos*
Bolivia	1952	217,000 (1970)	33	indiv.
Cuba	1959, 1963	260,000 (1963)	70	State, indiv. and prod. coops
Venezuela	1960	107,523 (1970)	17	Indiv. and prod. coops
Colombia	1961, 1973	135,000 (1975)	10	Indiv. and prod. coops
Costa Rica	1961	18,078 (1975)	9	Indiv.
Honduras	1962, 1975	33,203 (1978)	8	Indiv. and prod. coops
Dominican Republic	1962	11,000 (1970)	3	Indiv. and some coops
Chile	1962, 1970	58,170 (1973)	20	*asentamientos*
Peru	1963, 1969	359,600 (1975)	37	Prod. coops and some indiv.
Ecuador	1964, 1973	50,000 (1972)	7	Indiv. and some coops
Nicaragua	1979, 1981	72,072 (1983)	30	State, prod. coops and indiv.
El Salvador	1980	74,936 (1983)	12	Prod. coops and indiv.

Sources and notes: *Mexico:* Manzanilla (1977); percent of rural households benefited based on estimated 4,210,877 rural households in 1971. *Bolivia:* Jemio (1973), pp. 43, 73–74; based on estimated 668,597 rural households in 1970. In 1970, there were 587 production and marketing cooperatives in existence with 25,009 members. *Cuba:* Based on estimate of 110,000 new property owners as result of 1959 and 1963 laws, and permanent employment on state farms of 150,000 by 1963 (MacEwan, 1981, pp. 53, 56). Mesa-Lago (1972, p. 49) reports a somewhat higher figure, 200,000 new property owners by the end of the implementation of the 1963 agrarian reform. In 1983 there were 1400 production cooperatives with 78,000 members (Benjamin, Collins and Scott, 1984). *Venezuela:* Soto (1978), p. 80; based on estimated 625,144 rural households in 1970. The figures on the number of beneficiaries appear to be highly disputed; other sources put it closer to 95,000. In 1968 there were 210 production cooperatives with 78,000 members. *Colombia:* Blutstein *et al.* (1977), p. 354; based on estimated 1,305,582 rural households in 1975. The beneficiaries includes the *de facto* recognition of squatters. Anaya (1976) reports a much lower figure for 1970, 12,570 beneficiaries, amounting to only 1.1% of rural households. In 1982, there were 1284 *empresas comunales* with 12,300 households (Caro, 1982, p. 196). *Costa Rica:* Barahona (1980), p. 275; based on estimated 214,516 rural households in 1975. Seligson (1980, p. 152) reports a much lower figure, 11,306 beneficiary families in 1976, representing only 5.3% of rural households in that year. In 1977, 17 production cooperatives were reported in existence with 517 members. *Honduras:* Callejas (1983); Honduras (n.d., p. 7); based on 428,516 rural households. In 1976, 133 *empresas associativas* were reported, with 10,000 members. *Dominican Republic:* Weil (1973), p. 182; based on estimated 446,835 rural households. *Chile:* Cifuentes (1975); based on estimated 290,850 rural households. *Peru:* Caballero and Alvarez (1980). The number of beneficiaries is a bit deceptive, for over one-third of the beneficiaries enumerated in this estimate consists of households in the officially recognized peasant communities whose communities were adjudicated access to grazing land. Estimate based on 971,892 rural households in 1975. *Ecuador:* Franco Garcia (1976), p. 49; based on estimated 716,447 rural households. Blankstein and Zuvekas (1973, p. 81) report that 88% of *huasipungo* households (engaged in feudal relations of production on large estates) became landowners through the reform. *Nicaragua:* The estimate includes 22,072 individuals that have received land either as individual holdings or as part of a production cooperative as of December 1983, under the 1981 agrarian reform law, as well as 50,000 permanent workers on the state farms (Deere, Marchetti and Reinhardt, 1985). The figure underestimates the total number of beneficiaries since it does not include those who have gained access to land through the reform but who have not yet received land titles. In 1983, there were an estimated 238,602 rural households. *El Salvador:* The estimate includes 35,000 cooperative members on the Phase I estates and 39,936 applicants for individual land parcels under Decree 207 as of December 1983 (Deere, 1984). The figure probably overestimates the total number of beneficiaries since only 252 applicants under Decree 207 have actually received definitive land titles. The number of rural households in 1983 was estimated as 624,386.
Data on the number of rural households were estimated from *UN Demographic Yearbook* (1979); *1977 Compendium of Social Statistics* (1980); *OAS America en Cifras* (1977); and *Statistical Bulletin*, Vol. 3, No. 34 (1981).

Honduras or the *empresas comunitarias campesinas* of Colombia. The Allende reform in Chile and that of the Peruvian military favored collective forms of production, although in the latter case some land was also distributed individually.

The agrarian reform initiatives of the 1980s are the product of the revolutionary upheaval in Central America. The Nicaraguan and Salvadoran agrarian reforms represent quite different political projects. The Nicaraguan agrarian reform is being carried out in the context of revolutionary transformation, in the tradition of the first three Latin American agrarian reforms. Within the reformed sector, equal priority has been given to the constitution of state farms, production cooperatives and individual producers grouped in credit and service cooperatives (Deere, Marchetti and Reinhardt, 1985). In contrast, as a political project, the Salvadoran agrarian reform is being carried out in the legacy of the Alliance for Progress. Its primary intent is to contain the peasantry as a revolutionary force (Deere, 1982a and 1984). The reformed sector includes both production cooperatives and a 'land to the tiller' program.

All except the latter two agrarian reforms were initiated before feminism became an international force and women's participation in development a development concern. Since 1973, the Percy Amendment to the US Foreign Assistance Act has required all US financed development programs to take into account their impact upon women. Moreover, since 1975 when the UN Decade for Women was launched, many Latin American countries have created governmental women's commissions or bureaus to oversee state policy with regard to women. To what extent have these efforts brought state policy to bear positively on the position of rural women within the context of Latin American agrarian reforms?

(a) *Agrarian reform beneficiaries according to gender*

The majority of Latin American agrarian reforms have not produced significant numbers of female beneficiaries or even given attention to gender as a beneficiary category. As Table 2 shows, few Latin American countries report beneficiary data by sex. Even after a decade of 'women in development' efforts, the majority of countries still find it sufficient to publish beneficiary data according to the number of households or families benefited. For example, in the recent Salvadoran agrarian reform, potential benefi-

ciaries applying for land under Decree 207 (the 'land to the tiller' program) are not asked their sex.[4] The only country for which complete gender-disaggregated data on agrarian reform beneficiaries are available is Honduras. Data for Cuba and Nicaragua refer only to cooperative membership.[5]

The available national-level data suggest that only in Cuba do women represent a significant number of current agrarian reform beneficiaries. Women constitute 26% of the 78,000 members of the country's 1400 production cooperatives (Benjamin, Collins and Scott, 1984, Chapter 3). The available data on the Cuban state farms also suggest that women have been incorporated as wage workers in significant numbers on the state farms. By 1968, 44,000 women were employed as permanent workers on the state farms, and in the mid-1970s women represented 53% of the permanent workers in the state tobacco industry, 41% in the dairy industry, 19% in food processing and 7% in the sugar industry (FMC, 1975, p. 19).

The 1982 Nicaraguan Cooperative Census revealed that 20% of the production cooperatives and 60% of the credit and service cooperatives (based on individual private holdings) have at least one women member. However, in 1982 women represented only 6% of the total cooperative membership of 64,891. Rural women in Nicaragua fared somewhat better than their Honduran counterparts with women representing 3.8% of the agrarian reform beneficiaries.

A 1971 survey of 83 Peruvian agrarian reform cooperatives found that, of 724 members interviewed, approximately 5% were women (Buchler, 1975). But as a national estimate, even this figure may be high because the survey excluded the important coastal agro-industrial sugar cooperatives where membership was almost exclusively male. Moreover, regional studies in northern Peru, in the cotton-producing zone of Piura (Fernandez, 1982), and in the highland area of Cajamarca (Deere, 1982b), found that women comprised only 2% of cooperative membership.

The available studies of the agrarian reform processes of other Latin American countries also suggest that the overwhelming majority of the agrarian reform beneficiaries have been men. Garrett reports that in Chile few women were beneficiaries of the agrarian reform (1982a, b). Similarly, in the Dominican Republic, the vast majority of beneficiaries have been men (Castro, Grullon and Leon, 1983; CEDEE, 1983). In Colombia, women have been reported to be members of only two of 1283 collective enterprises organized between 1973 and 1982 (Caro, 1982, p. 196). No mention of women's

Table 2. *Women in the Latin American agrarian reforms*

Country	Women beneficiaries	Beneficiary criteria
Mexico	n.d.*	Individuals over 16; any age if have dependent; men or women farmers
Bolivia	n.d.	Individuals over 18 if *feudatario;* over 14 if married; widows with children may receive land
Cuba	26 (1983)	Individuals; state policy goal to incorporate women
Venezuela	n.d.	Individuals over 18; preference to household heads with most dependents and most efficient farmers
Colombia	n.d.	Individuals; point system favored farming experience, education
Costa Rica	n.d.	Individuals over 18; preference to household heads with most dependents and farming experience
Honduras	3.8 (1979)	If single male, 16; any age if married male; single or widowed women with children may apply
Dominican Republic	n.d.	Heads of household
Ecuador	n.d.	Individuals
Peru	n.d.	Heads of household with dependent children, agriculturalists over 18
Chile	n.d.	Married or effective heads of household; point system, favored 'aptitude' for agriculture
Nicaragua	6 (1982)	Individuals; an objective of agrarian reform to incorporate women
El Salvador	n.d.	Individuals

* n.d. = no data available.
Sources: *Mexico:* Anaya (1976), Chapter 9. *Bolivia:* Jemio (1973), p. 42, Article 78 of agriculture reform law. *Cuba:* Benjamin, Collins and Scott (1984), Chapter 13. *Venezuela:* Guerrero (1962), Articles 104, 63 of agriculture reform law. *Costa Rica:* Escoto (1965), p. 11. *Honduras:* Callejas (1983); Honduras (1976), pp. 237–288, Articles 97–125 of agriculture reform law. *Dominican Republic:* CEDEE (1983); Castro, Grullon and Leon (1983). *Chile:* Garrrett (1982b). *Ecuador:* Redclift (1978). *Peru:* Deere (1982b), Article 84 of agriculture reform law. *Nicaragua:* CIERA (1984), Chapter 2. *El Salvador:* Simon, Stephens and Diskin (1982), Appendix I.

participation could be found in the literature on the remaining agrarian reforms surveyed.

3. MECHANISMS OF EXCLUSION

The participation of rural women in the agricultural labor force in Latin America — both in peasant units of production and as seasonal wage workers — has now been well documented in the literature.[6] Yet, as the above data demonstrate, women have largely been excluded as agrarian reform beneficiaries. This section considers why and how women have been excluded from this major state initiative in rural areas.

The mechanisms of exclusion are legal, structural and ideological. In most of the Latin American agrarian reforms, the legal criteria defining beneficiary status have served to exclude the majority of rural women. This is often compounded by the structural characteristics of women's labor force participation. Moreover,

ideological norms regarding the 'proper' sexual division of labor often impede women from joining cooperatives even when it is legally possible.

Underlying almost all of the Latin American agrarian reforms has been the assumption that the rural househould is the primary social unit to benefit from the reform. But for purposes of implementation, in all except Cuba and Nicaragua, only one member of the household, the household head, has been officially designated the beneficiary. Hence, only the head of household has received land in his/her name or the right of membership in production cooperatives or credit and service cooperatives in the reformed sector.

Restricting beneficiaries to household heads discriminates only against women since throughout Latin America social custom dictates that if both an adult man and an adult woman reside in a household, the man is considered its head. Yet, in the majority of agrarian reforms examined, the beneficiary criteria either required or gave strong preference to heads of households. Even in those cases where beneficiaries were defined as individuals it was usually assumed, if not explicit, that only one individual per household could be designated a beneficiary, and that was to be the household head. As a result, the only women who could potentially be reform beneficiaries were either widows or single mothers with no adult male living in the household.

A related, structural problem is that many agrarian reforms have benefited only the permanent agricultural wage workers employed on estates at the moment of expropriation, excluding the often large seasonal labor force from cooperative membership. In both Peru and Chile, for example, the permanent agricultural wage workers on the expropriated estates were generally men, although women were often an important component of the seasonal labor force. Fernandez (1982) shows how on the northern Peruvian cotton plantations, although women represented up to 40% of the temporary labor force, few women held permanent jobs on the plantations and, as a result, women constituted only 2% of the cooperative membership.

For Chile, Garrett's (1976) analysis demonstrates how the process of modernization of the Chilean agriculture over the course of the twentieth century resulted in a sharp decrease in the number of permanent workers in agriculture. But women were displaced disproportionately from the estate's labor force as these estates were mechanized. At the time of the agrarian reform, these estates had few permanent workers relative to the total labor force employed during the year, and the permanent workers were largely males. As a result, the beneficiaries of the reform were overwhelmingly men (Garrett, 1982b).

The inability of these agrarian reforms to benefit the vast majority of seasonal agricultural workers was certainly prejudicial both to men and to women. But whereas men were found in both categories of workers, permanent and seasonal, the structural characteristics of women's labor force participation resulted in women's being excluded as a social group. The few women who were permanent workers on the estates, and thus potential beneficiaries of the reform, were then subject to the additional criterion of being household heads to become cooperative members. This, of course, reduced their participation still further.

Many of the reforms instituted in the Alliance for Progress period, besides prioritizing landless workers and tenants, selected potential beneficiaries on the basis of a point system. In the case of Colombia, for example, the point system favored those whose history of residence or work was in or near the farm being redistributed, and those peasants with more education, larger family size, good reputations and farming experience (Edwards, 1980, p. 59). Women would certainly be at a disadvantage compared to men in terms of educational attainment. Moreover, female heads of household might also suffer under the reputation criterion if nonconformity with the patriarchal nuclear family norm lowered their status in the eyes of the community. Women would also be disadvantaged by the farming experience criterion if, socially, men are considered to be the agriculturalists and women, as unremunerated family labor, simply the 'helpers.'

Ideological norms governing the proper sexual division of labor — that a woman's place is in the home while a man's is in the fields — appear not only in the content of agrarian reform legislation, but also constitute a significant barrier to the incorporation of women as beneficiaries in reforms that explicitly provide for the inclusion of female-headed households.

Inheritance provisions in the agrarian reform laws demonstrate that it was often explicitly assumed that beneficiaries would be male. Article 83 of the Venezuelan agrarian reform, for example, provides that in case of death or abandonment by the beneficiary: 'the Institute will adjudicate the parcel to his wife or concubine, or in third place to the son' (Guerro, 1962). Similarly, the only mention of women in the Costa Rican agrarian reform law is the provision to give the land title, should the owner abandon the farm, 'to the wife or the other person(s) who has lived permanently with the title owner' (Escota, 1965, p. 12).

Only three agrarian reforms — those of Mexico, Bolivia and Honduras — made explicit provision to include female household heads as potential beneficiaries. The 1942 Mexican agrarian code provided for either single or widowed women to receive land in the *ejido* as long as they had dependent children. Nonetheless, the law also discriminated against women since men could apply for land irrespective of their family position if they were over 16 years of age or at any age if they were married. Single women without dependents and married women could not (Chavez de Velazquez, 1960, p. 240). Moreover, if a female household head with land in the *ejido* married another *ejido* member she automatically lost her right to *ejido* land. While the apparent intention of this clause (Article 171) was to prevent land concentration within the *ejido*, its consequence was to dispossess married women of land rights.

The revised 1971 Mexican agrarian reform law improved on the earlier agrarian code by stipulating that beneficiaries could be 'male of female, above 16 years of age, or of any age if they have dependent children' (Anaya, 1976, p. 75). Moreover, it allowed women with land rights to preserve them if they married another *ejido* member (Alcerreca, 1974, p. 77). However, Article 200 requires beneficiaries to be agriculturalists and implicit in the law is that women are not. The assumption that women's primary responsibility is to the home and children is clear in the provision requiring *ejidatarios* to work the land directly. Only a female household head is exempted from this provision because of being 'constrained by domestic work and the attention to small children who depend upon her' (Anaya, 1976, p. 77).

The 1952 Bolivian agrarian reform law considered eligible for land 'those older than 18 who have been exploited (under feudal relations of production). . . , those older than 14 and married, and widows with dependent children' (Article 78, in Jemio, 1973, p. 42). While the rights of widows were protected in this law, it is unclear whether single mothers could claim beneficiary status. And once again, married women appear to be precluded from acquiring land through the reform. However, the 1965 Law of Indigenous Communities did provide for 'either men or women' to receive land in indigenous cooperatives (Urquidi, 1971, p. 233). The few references to women in the literature suggest that few married women or even female household heads have availed themselves of this opportunity (McEwen, 1969, p. 88; Iriarte, 1980, p. 86).

The 1962 Honduran agrarian reform law, like the 1942 Mexican agrarian code, guaranteed the rights both of widows and of single female household heads but discriminated against single women without dependents as compared to single men. In order to qualify as a beneficiary it was required to: 'Be Honduran by birth, male, over 16 years of age if single or any age if married, or a single woman or widow if in charge of a family' (Article 68 in Escoto, 1956, p. 46). In terms of preference ordering, the Honduran law does give female household heads priority over male heads and single men, unless the men exploited land under indirect forms of tenancy, had been previously dispossessed of their land, or had access to insufficient land as established by the zone (Article 68, in Escoto, 1965, p. 47). Apparently, the overwhelming number of rural men fell into one of these categories, for Youssef and LeBel (1981, p. 57) report that 'in existing *asentamientos* women have last priority in being

allocated land; they follow male-headed households, and single males.' Yet, in 1974, 18.7% of Honduran rural households were headed by women (Callejas, 1983).

An in-depth study of four Honduran *asentamientos* illustrated how the implementation of the law had resulted in the virtual exclusion of female household heads (Safilios-Rothschild, 1983, p. 19). Women were simply not considered to be agriculturalists. While women's participation in certain agricultural tasks was recognized, women were not considered capable of carrying out the 'heavier' agricultural tasks that required greater physical strength. Male cooperative members felt that women could join the cooperatives only if they had sons, and preferably adult sons, to replace them in agricultural field work. Thus, the predominant norms of the sexual division of labor served as a barrier to women's incorporation in the agrarian reform, although the law explicitly provided for at least female heads of household to be potential beneficiaries of the reform.

4. THE PRECONDITIONS FOR FEMALE PARTICIPATION

Cuba and Nicaragua, are the only two countries in which neither sex nor kinship position has been a legal barrier to the inclusion of women in the agrarian reform process. In both countries, not only female heads of household, but also wives and daughters can qualify as agrarian reform cooperative members. Moreover, in both countries, the incorporation of rural women is an explicit policy goal of the state.

In terms of rural women's participation, the Cuban agrarian reform process began along a road similar to that just described. The numerically important small farm sector created through the first agrarian reform law (1959) was considered to benefit household heads. The National Association of Small Producers (ANAP), the principal organization charged with developing credit and service cooperatives and other associations among private producers, was constituted by household heads who were primarily men. Within the state sector, the agricultural unions that were formed were also overwhelmingly male since they organized the permanent workers on the former sugar and cattle estates, who were generally men. Although the number of permanent workers within the state sector increased steadily, particularly after the 1963 agrarian reform law was promulgated, few women were employed on a permanent basis until the late 1960s.

The development of an explicit state policy with regard to the incorporation of rural women into the agrarian reform process was a response to both ideological and economic considerations. As the Cuban revolution began to develop its explicitly socialist character, the issue of equality, not just between social classes, but also between men and women, had to be addressed. Drawing on the Marxist classics, the Cubans accepted the theoretical premise that women's equality with men required their incorporation into the social labor force (Engels, 1975). The incorporation of women into productive labor was seen as a necessary step not only for women's own social development but also for the transformation of the social relations of Cuban society (Castro, 1981; PCC, 1976).

This theoretical position was complemented in the late 1960s by the economic imperative of increasing rural women's agricultural participation. The expansion of sugar cane production in the late 1960s significantly increased the demand for temporary labor. It was at this time that a concrete policy to integrate rural women into the labor force took form, and it was largely the result of the joint efforts of ANAP and the Cuban Women's Federation (FMC). In 1966, these two mass organizations joined to promote what were known as the FMC–ANAP brigades of rural women (FMC, 1975). At first consisting of volunteer labor, they provided the mechanism for thousands of rural women to participate in social production for the first time (Bengelsdorf and Hageman, 1977).

These female brigades were responsible for solving the seasonal labor shortages within the state sector and on private farms. It was estimated that by the mid-1970s women constituted over half of the seasonal labor force for the sugar cane, coffee, tobacco and fruit harvests (FMC, 1975). An important change, which explains the steady increase in women's participation, was that by the mid-1970s brigade work was no longer unremunerated. The FMC was successful in assuring that women were paid a wage for their work and that they received the same pay as men for equal work. Moreover, in order to encourage women's participation in the brigades, it was necessary to attend to women's reproductive roles. The FMC played a central role in promoting the development of child care centers in the countryside as well as the expansion of communal eating facilities at rural work centers.

The organization of rural women by FMC–ANAP was not limited to women's role in the seasonal labor reserve. It also promoted the incorporation of women as permanent workers on the state farms and as members of the credit

and service cooperatives of private producers. In the 1970s, eligibility for cooperative membership was changed from household heads to individual membership for all adults in the farm household. The FMC–ANAP brigades became the channel for the provision of technical assistance specifically for women so that they could develop the general agronomic and veterinary knowledge required for modern farming as well as specific skills for their own income-generating projects (FMC, 1975). They also promoted women's participation in decision-making in the farm household and in the credit and service cooperatives.

The FMC–ANAP brigades proved an important mechanism for organizing rural women and, by taking into account their specific needs and interests as women, integrated them into the national project of revolutionary change. This is seen in terms of the role that rural women have played in the development of production cooperatives in the post-1975 period (FMC, 1975). In that year, production cooperatives received official endorsement for the first time; state incentives were given for private farmers to voluntarily collectivize their holdings. Among the incentives was the possibility of constructing a new agricultural community that allowed the socialization of many women's domestic tasks. Of equal importance was women's right of membership and guaranteed employment in the production cooperatives. As noted earlier, women now constitute 26% of the cooperative membership.

In contrast to the Cuban case, where women's participation in the agrarian reform evolved over the course of the revolution, the Nicaraguan agrarian reform included the incorporation of women among its objectives from the beginning. In the 1981 agrarian reform law, neither sex nor kinship position is a limitation on being an agrarian reform beneficiary. And the incorporation of women into the agricultural cooperatives is an explicit objective detailed in the 1981 Agricultural Cooperative Law (Chapter 2, Article 2). Moreover, the legislation requires women to be integrated into the cooperatives under the same conditions as men, with the same rights and duties. The agrarian legislation conforms to the Statute of Rights and Guarantees of Nicaraguans (Decree 52, 1979, Article 3) which establishes the equality of the sexes before the law and requires the state 'to remove by all means all obstacles that impede the equality of its citizens and their participation in the political, economic and social life of the country.'

Interestingly, in a recent study of women's participation in the Nicaraguan agrarian reform cooperatives it was found that many women did not await the passage of the agrarian reform legislation to begin joining the agricultural cooperatives (CIERA, 1984, Chapter 3). In the majority of cases studied, women joined the cooperatives as they were being constituted in the 1979–81 period. This reflects the important participation of women in Nicaragua in the struggle that defeated the Somoza dictatorship; women felt that they 'had won their right' to participate in the cooperative movement. Nonetheless, the study also showed that the law has been an important armament in breaking down traditional views of the proper sexual division of labor and male resistance to female participation in the cooperatives.

Even in a revolutionary setting, cooperatives continue to be organized without considering the possible participation of women. In interviews with all-male cooperatives, members often asserted that women were not interested in cooperatives because they did not perform agricultral work. In fact, in several cases women had demonstrated their interest in joining these cooperatives but the male members had ignored them (Deere, 1983; CIERA, 1984). As is the case in Honduras (Safilios-Rothschild, 1983), male cooperative members were often reluctant to admit women as members since they did not believe that women could carry out a sufficient number of agricultural tasks. Nonetheless, case studies of 10 cooperatives with women members revealed that women participated in productive activities on par with the men. Moreover, men in cooperatives with women members were much more positive about women's participation and contribution than men in cooperatives without women members. This has also been reported in Honduras (Safilios-Rothschild, 1983). It suggests that a positive state policy with regard to women creates the necessary preconditions for women's participation and that giving women a chance to participate has important effects on ideological norms regarding the gender division of labor. This, as will be discussed later, has important implications for successful cooperative development.

The importance of a clear and vigorous state policy with respect to women's participation is illustrated by a contrasting example to the Cuban and Nicaraguan cases, that of the Chilean agrarian reform. Upon taking office in 1970, the Allende government broadened the criteria for defining beneficiaries because redistribution of access to resources as well as the generation of increased employment opportunities in the countryside were explicit policy goals of the Popular Unity government. The imbalance between the

situation of permanent and temporary workers on the asentamientos (who were, respectively, the members and non-members) was seen to be particularly problematic, so the asentamientos were reorganized to facilitate the incorporation of temporary workers.

In this broadening of the potential beneficiaries of the reform, the legal–structural impediments to women's participation within the new agrarian reform structures were eliminated (Garrett, 1982a,b). Neither sex nor marital status were to constitute criteria for membership, and all individuals over 18 years of age were eligible to become members of the general assembly of the new Centers of Agrarian Reform (the CERAs). As Garrett shows, the conditions were in place for women to be able to participate in the agrarian reform, but the new regulations did not result in the incorporation of a significant number of rural women. This was partly because the Popular Unity government lacked clarity on the role of women in the agrarian reform.

Garrett's analysis shows how ideological and political factors worked against women's incorporation into the reformed sector even after their participation was made legally possible. She agrues that women's participation in the CERAs was resisted both by men and by women. This reflected the conservative influence of what was the strongest women's organization in the countryside, the Centros de Madres (mothers' centers) organized by the Christian Democratic party under the Frei administration. The centers focused on and promoted women's domestic role much as they did in the Dominican Republic, Honduras and Venezuela. They gave little attention to women's role in production or to social problems since these were considered inappropriate activities for women. But they did provide rural women with a social outlet that drew them out of their homes into a forum where they could discuss their own everyday problems. At their heyday, the centers had some 10,500 members in the Chilean countryside.

The centers were apparently never integrated into the structure of the asentamientos. The Popular Unity government recognized this as a problem and proposed to organize rural women into Social Welfare Committees linked to each CERA. The Social Welfare Committees were intended to find collective solutions to social problems. But as Garrett illustrates, neither men nor women were in agreement that women should be concerned with problems that went beyond their own domestic units. Few rural women joined the Social Welfare Committees of their own volition, and the Allende government neither had nor directed the human resources required to organize rural women along lines different from those that had been traditionally successful. This was partly because of the difficult political conjuncture with which the Allende government was faced by 1973, but it also reflects the lack of a clear state policy with regard to the incorporation of women. In other words, the explicit absence of a state policy *vis-à-vis* women's participation in the agrarian reform was a source of confusion and acted as a barrier to women's actual incorporation.

5. THE IMPORTANCE OF INCORPORATING WOMEN

It is important for women as well as men to be included among the direct beneficiaries of an agrarian reform to ensure both social equity and the success of cooperative development. The exclusion of women not only has high costs for women, in that their position can be harmed both relative to men's and absolutely; it also has costs for cooperative and rural development programs in general. If the goal of an agrarian reform is to foster a process of social transformation, as was the case in various of these reforms, then the exclusion of one social group on the basis of gender or family position certainly limits the breadth and depth of the reform process.

Social equity criteria would require that, at the very least, if both men and women are permanent agricultural workers, both be entitled to become beneficiaries of an agrarian reform. An example from the dairy region of northern Peru, the province of Cajamarca, illustrates the discriminatory nature of constituting production cooperatives on the basis of only those permanent workers who are household heads (Deere, 1977). In this region, women made up from 30 to 50% of the permanent workers on the dairy farms since milking (which is still done manually) was considered a strictly female task. But of the 15 agrarian reform production cooperatives in the province, only five had female members and, overall, women constituted only 2% of the total cooperative membership. The women workers were excluded from cooperative membership primarily because they did not qualify as household heads because of their kin relationship to a male permanent worker on the farm. The result was that the only women who became cooperative members were widows or separated women who did not live with an adult man and who had children under 18 years of age.

If a goal of state policy in creating production cooperatives is to allow the participation of workers in the decisions concerning their labor process and in the allocation of the surplus which they produce, the exclusion of one group from membership on the basis of sex and kinship is, at best, discriminatory. At worst, it creates the conditions internal to the cooperative for the exploitation of one social group by another.

This is also the case in the relationship between permanent workers (the cooperative members) and temporary workers. In the Peruvian reform process, few temporary workers were incorporated into the cooperatives; they were not covered by social benefits, and their wages were usually lower than those of the cooperative members. Fernandez (1982) and Chambeu (1981) report that, in the cooperatives in Piura and Cuzco that they studied, not only were the majority of women working on the cooperatives temporary workers, but the women earned wages lower than did the male temporary workers. Moreover, women's wages relative to both male temporary workers and the cooperative members declined over the reform period. In the case of the Piura cotton cooperatives, work opportunities for women also declined over the reform period (Fernandez, 1982). Since the women had been excluded from cooperative membership, they had no recourse in this deterioration in their economic position.

The only reference to women's participation in the Ecuadorian agrarian reform is Article 8 of the 1973 Statutes of Production Cooperatives. The Statutes list as a condition for the official recognition of the cooperative that a cooperative employ outside labor only 'occasionally . . . and then only when preference has been given to the wives and families of members' (Redclift, 1978, p. 154). The analysis of the fate of female temporary workers in Peru suggests how marginal this institutional recognition is to women's labor force participation.

Another way in which processes of agrarian reform may be harmful to women is in terms of the changes introduced in traditional patterns of land rights. In most Andean highland areas, land inheritance has been bilateral. Women's ownership of land has assured them of participation in both agricultural decision-making and the allocation of household income. Land ownership has also given women a modicum of material security because they have not been totally dependent on their spouses. If a woman was abandoned or separated from her spouse, her inheritance assured her of a means of maintaining her family as a single woman.[7] Not surprisingly, a woman's status within the household and community is closely related to her ownership of land.

The Peruvian agrarian reform process represented a real setback for rural women. While the objective of the reform had been to promote production cooperatives on the estates that were expropriated, in many cases this was impossible due to peasant resistance and, in the post-reform period following the election of Belaunde, these peasants received individual titles to their plots. But since only male household heads were designated the potential beneficiaries, the land titles issued by the reform agency generally have been given to men.

It cannot be assumed that indirect participation in a reform process (through the head of household) is the equivalent of direct participation. The organization of credit and service cooperatives among independent producers on the basis of only male household heads may have important consequences for women's agricultural productivity. Providing technical assistance only to men will not necessarily result in women gaining access to the information or guarantee that they will take it into account and put it into practice. For example, if women are traditionally charged with seed selection in the peasant household, it cannot be assumed that training men in the benefits of new varieties will result in the information being passed on to and accepted by the women.

The Nicaraguan cooperative study found an impressive disparity in the level of technological knowledge of women members and women non-members (CIERA, 1984, Chapter 5). Male cooperative members rarely shared with their non-member wives what they were learning. On one credit and service cooperative with a significant number of female members, one male member admitted to this author that he was worried that his non-member wife knew so little compared to the female members because, if anything happened to him, she would take over management of the farm. But this reflection only took place because women had already been incorporated as cooperative members.

The 1979–83 Honduran National Development Plan appears laudatory in that it calls for the incorporation of 5625 peasant women who are 'direct or indirect' beneficiaries of the reform in activities leading to the economic diversification of the cooperatives (Honduras, n.d.). But incorporating women as temporary wage workers or into special income-generating projects does not necessarily lead to an improvement in their material well-being or status. Without the status of cooperative membership, the women are assured neither control of the resources necessary to carry out complementary income-generating activities (Garrett, 1982b) nor participation in the decisions governing labor allocation, wages, or the surplus produced.

The 1971 Mexican law is also unusual in providing women who are non-*ejido* members access to one parcel of land for collective agro-industrial activities. Article 103 indicates that the land should be of the best quality and adjacent to the urbanized area with 'child care centers, centers of sewing and education, *nixtamal* mills, and in general, all those installations destined specifically to be at the service and protection of the peasant woman' (Anaya, 1976, p. 79). Whether these actually materialized is unknown. While it is commendable that the law gives some attention to women, it must be kept in mind that these rights are not the equivalent of having access to land in one's own name or the right to participate in the decisions of the *ejido*.

Moreover, all too often these special projects aimed at women fail to recognize women's role as agricultural producer and serve to reproduce the idealized sexual division of labor with women as housewives and mothers. This has been the case not only in Honduras and Mexico, but also in Chile, Venezuela and the Dominican Republic. Since the 1960s in all of these countries, the wives of beneficiaries have been organized into 'mother's clubs' or 'mother's centers' where they are taught skills that are an extension of their domestic roles: cooking; sewing; flower arrangement; etc. (Challejas, 1983; Garrett, 1982a,b; Soto, 1978; CEDEE, 1983; Castro *et al.*, 1983).

When an agrarian reform directs state efforts and resources to benefit one group of the population through access to land, credit, technical assistance, marketing channels, etc., it is concentrating resources on only one specific group with socio-economic consequences for those who are excluded. It cannot be assumed that, by benefiting the male head of household, all household members will be benefited as well. Neither can it be assumed that, by organizing women into their own gender-specific activities, women will not lose out relative to men. The household is not gender neutral and neither are the effects of a process of state intervention.

(a) *Women as a positive force for cooperative development*

The Nicaraguan experience thus far seems to show that the incoporation of women to the agrarian cooperatives has been beneficial for cooperative development. In the cooperatives with women members, women are considered to be excellent agricultural workers, and they are a force of cohesion and stability in the cooperatives. In one study, it was found, for example, that proportionately more men than women had left the production cooperatives for reasons of personal feuds with other cooperative members or because they did not like collective work. The relatively few women who had abandoned the cooperatives were more likely to have left because of family problems such as jealous husbands (Deere, 1983).

In the few cooperative enterprises with women members in Colombia, women have also been noted to be a force of stability and cohesion. Lodono (1975, p. 144) reports that 'the integration of the woman and family has proven itself of real influence in the cohesiveness of the *empresa*. When the family lives on *empresa* land, when the woman participates in the assemblies and in the committees, with voice and even with vote, when she is listened to on problems of management and administration, the whole group feels itself more rooted in the *empresa*.'

In Nicaragua, as in Cuba, women appear to be a favorable force behind collectivization. In Nicaragua, the strong commitment of the women members of the production cooperatives to collective work is in many ways explained by the history of discrimination against women in rural Nicaragua. The majority of women members were previously landless wage workers and, as women, they had fewer agricultural employment opportunities open to them than did the men. Moreover, in the past, women were always paid less than men, even for the same tasks. Today they earn the same wage as men irrespective of the task performed, and the cooperatives offer them security of employment for the first time (Deere, 1983).

The discrimination women have traditionally faced also explains why women seem less prone than men to dream of their own private plots, and why, in some cases, women have voluntarily pooled their private land parcels to form a production cooperative. Because women had not been taken seriously as agricultural producers in the past, they had been excluded from access to credit and technical assistance. Moreover, female household heads often found it more difficult than men to acquire sufficient labor for certain agricultural tasks and to acquire male labor for the key 'male only' tasks. Pooling their land offers them the security of permanent employment and income.

In the Cuban case, female support for collectivization seems to be particularly tied to the advantages offered women in the realm of reproduction. Up through the 1970s, Cuban policy greatly favored workers on state farms through the development of what are known as the agricultural communities. The new communities offer modern housing, guaranteeing the provision of potable water, sanitation and electricity; moreover, they offer health centers, schools and day care centers, communal eating facilities, and stores provisioned with basic necessities. The principal change in policy with respect to the formation of production cooperatives was that, for the first time, the facilities for the construction of similar agricultural communities would be offered to farmers that pooled their land to form such a cooperative. The state would provide the materials and technical assistance if the new cooperative members provided the labor.

The rural women interviewed by this author in 1981 were quite clear as to the benefits offered them by the new agricultural communities. They all emphasized the increase in their families' standard of living and well-being and the importance of having convenient child care. Moreover, the improved housing greatly reduced the drudgery of housework. It was quite clear that women's enthusiasm for the new agricultural communities had been a central factor in the successful development of the production cooperatives and that this enthusiasm was tied to the benefits offered women with respect to their responsibility for household reproduction.

Both the Nicaraguan and Cuban experiences demonstrate that social equity and successful cooperative development are not a trade-off. Moreover, these positive experiences suggest the costs of excluding women in the other Latin American agrarian reforms.

6. THE PROBLEM OF ASSURING WOMEN'S EFFECTIVE PARTICIPATION AS COOPERATIVE MEMBERS

The analysis of women's participation in the Latin American agrarian reforms has demonstrated the importance of an explicit state policy with regard to the inclusion of women as reform beneficiaries. Legal reforms, however, only clear the way for women to claim beneficiary status. They are a necessary but not a sufficient condition to ensure women's effective participation within the reformed sector. In this section, the difficulties that rural women have experienced in exercising their full rights of membership in the cooperatives are examined. It is argued that, for women to achieve full equality with men as cooperative members, state attention must also be given to the material and ideological aspects of women's subordination.

A fairly common observation among those who have studied agrarian cooperatives with women members in Latin America is that, while women may participate in the productive activities of the cooperatives on par with men, they play a much reduced role with respect to cooperative decision-making. In the Peruvian cooperatives, female members usually attended cooperative meetings, but rarely did they actually participate in the discussions (Deere, 1977; Fernandez, 1982; Chambeu, 1981).

Buchler (1975, p. 50) describes Peruvian women's participation as follows: 'At the cooperative meeting the woman member is expected to be more reserved than the men. She usually sits on the floor in peasant society while the men take up any of the chairs available. Nevertheless, she can speak up when her interests are endangered. Her opinion will be listened to, but she seldom has much effect unless seconded by some important male leader.'

Fernandez (1982) reports that, in northern Peru, women as well as men viewed women's lack of education as a central factor in their inability to participate as effective cooperative members. In rural Peru, illiteracy falls disproportionately upon women. The men reportedly viewed this as the principal reason women were unqualified to participate in decisions regarding the cooperative. The women viewed their illiteracy as the primary reason that men showed little respect for their views and they were afraid to speak at cooperative meetings. But it should also be noted that women constitute a minority of the membership of these cooperatives, and the sheer power of numbers might explain the women's reluctance to participate in the meetings.

In the Nicaraguan cooperatives, the women members were also less likely than the men to offer their opinions in cooperative meetings and to be actively involved in the affairs of the cooperative (CIERA, 1984). Women's lower degree of education as compared to the men was often cited as the reason for their reduced participation in cooperative decision-making. While the majority of women members in Nicaragua are literate (most as a result of the 1980 literacy campaign), few have confidence in their ability to deal with the complex affairs of cooperative management. Moreover, household responsibilities often limit their ability to participate in the ongoing adult education program, thereby reproducing the inequality in functional literacy levels.

The responsibility of women for domestic chores and child care limits their ability to participate as effective cooperative members in other ways. The working day of women members is much longer than that of their male counterparts. The women members commonly spend two to three hours in domestic labor before going out to the fields and, after a six- to eight-hour day

working for the cooperative, return home to resume their domestic tasks. In contrast, the men usually socialize with the other male cooperative members after work, time often spent discussing cooperative business (CIERA, 1984).

The problem of 'the double day' also affects the ability of women to meet their full membership responsibilities in the cooperatives. It also explains, in the Peruvian case, the poor retention rate of women members. Chambeu (1981) reports that in a Cuzco cooperative that she studied the male members felt that women were not serious about their commitment to the cooperative since they often could not work a full day because of family problems. If the children are sick, it is usually women who must leave work to care for them. Rather than viewing this as a social problem, the response in this cooperative in 1980 was to vote not to accept any more women as members. The cooperative had already lowered women's wages with respect to men's contrary to Peruvian minimum wage provisions. With these impediments to participation, it is not surprising that half of the original eight women members resigned, and were replaced by their husbands.[8]

Childbearing is another factor that sometimes places women cooperative members at a disadvantage. In few countries have cooperatives made provisions for paid maternity leave. Only in Cuba are women cooperative members covered by a national social security system that includes paid maternity leave among its benefits. In the Peruvian case, cooperative members were covered by the labor legislation that stipulated a woman worker's right to paid maternity leave, but the costs fell on the individual cooperative. The male cooperative leadership considered it unjust for the cooperative to bear such a cost. On one cooperative, in Cajamarca, a woman who had demanded her legal right to paid maternity leave was pressured to resign. She was subsequently replaced in the cooperative by her husband.

The responsibility of women for domestic labor and child care, as well as their relatively lower educational attainment and lack of authority over men, are among the principal reasons cited for women's not being elected to leadership positions in the cooperatives. In Peru, only a handful of cooperatives with women officers have been reported (Bronstein, 1982). Chambeu (1981) reports the negative and short-lived experience of a Cuzco cooperative that elected a woman to a leadership position. Because of family responsibilities, the woman was unable to effectively carry out the work that she had been assigned, confirming the view of the majority of men that women are not suited for leadership positions. This experience suggests that women's responsibilities in the household do constitute a barrier to their effective participation within cooperatives. This problem must be directly addressed.

In Nicaragua, the data on women in cooperative leadership positions are more encouraging. A study of 10 cooperatives with women members showed that half of them had a woman as a cooperative officer (CIERA 1984). In most cases a woman had been elected to a leadership position as a result of an explicit concensus in the cooperative that the women members should have a representative. This was itself the product of the explicit state policy, actively promoted by the peasants' organization, to assure women's full participation within the cooperatives.

While gender-disaggregated data on cooperative leadership is not available for Cuba, the data on women in leadership positions in the peasant organization responsible for organizing the production cooperatives are quite favorable. In the mid-1970s, 16% of the local leadership positions in ANAP were held by women (PCC, 1976, p. 30).

Of all the Latin American agrarian reforms, the Cuban agrarian reform process is the one in which women have made the most impressive gains. But even these women still do not participate in production on equal terms with men (Croll, 1979). Women are still disproportionately represented among the temporary workers who provide seasonal labor to the state farms and to the production cooperatives. Benjamin, Collins and Scott (1984) also report that women's earnings on the cooperatives are substantially lower than men's. They note that there is still a marked sexual division of labor in productive tasks, and men's tasks are often better paid. Further, women cooperative members often work fewer days and fewer hours per day than men because of household responsibilities.

Cuban state policy has recognized the burden of the double day for women and its role in limiting women's full participation in production. The Family Law, promulgated in 1975, requires men to share equally in child rearing and in domestic maintenance tasks when the wife works in social production (see Stone, 1981, Appendix 2).

This is a most innovative step in social policy. Its importance lies in state recognition of the fact that women's participation in social production alone is not enough to guarantee women's equality with men as long as women alone carry the burden for reproduction. If domestic labor cannot be fully socialized, the only alternative, if

women's equality is to be achieved, is for men to share the reproductive burden. While Cuban society has not yet eradicated the subordination of women, important legal and economic preconditions, necessary to achieve the goal of social equality, are in place.

7. CONCLUSIONS

This comparative analysis of the Latin American agrarian reform experience has demonstrated that processes of socio-economic change are not gender neutral. It cannot be assumed that state policies designed to benefit rural households will necessarily benefit women.

Rural women in Latin America have not benefited from agrarian reform on par with men. Lack of attention to the incorporation of women as direct beneficiaries has resulted in women losing access to resources and/or being displaced from productive activities. The consequences are both economic — leading to lower female productivity or lower incomes — and social — contributing to a decline in female status and well-being. The lack of inclusion of women in new agrarian reform structures has also created new barriers to achieving male–female equality, barriers that serve to reproduce women's subordination. Moreover, the lack of female participation has also led to less successful processes of cooperative development, agrarian reform, and certainly of social transformation.

This comparative analysis of agrarian reform processes suggests that how rural women fare in an agrarian reform is closely tied to state policy. The inclusion of women in a process of socio-economic change does not happen automatically. At a minimum, it requires state attention to the legal and structural barriers that preclude female participation. As demonstrated, the criteria for selection of agrarian reform beneficiaries is most important in this regard. A crucial precondition for an egalitarian agrarian reform is that all adults in the targeted group be legally entitled to be beneficiaries.[9]

The right to acquire land in one's own name or the right of cooperative membership is a necessary but not sufficient condition for women to participate on par with men in an agrarian reform. State policy must also be directed towards creating the incentive and support structure for women to want to participate, to be able to overcome the possible resistance of men, and to be able to participate effectively. Attention to women's domestic responsibilities and making these compatible with productive work are important components of both the incentive and

RURAL WOMEN AND STATE POLICY   1051

support structure. Other policies that enable women to participate more effectively in the new agrarian structures include adult literacy programs and agricultural and leadership training courses specifically for women.

This comparative analysis of the Latin American agrarian reforms also suggests the important role that rural organizations can play in either promoting or discouraging women's participation in the new agrarian structures. The Cuban experience is most instructive, for here the mass organizations provided the crucial mechanism to link macro-policy with local level processes of change. Moreover, the coordination between the women's organization and the small farmers' organization proved effective in integrating women to the overall process of agrarian reform while paying attention to the specific needs of women.

NOTES

1. An excellent class-analytic overview of the Latin American agrarian reforms is provided in de Janvry (1983, Chapter 6).

2. The short-lived Guatemalan agrarian reform also fits into this category. Between 1952–54, 33% of the peasantry benefited through the reform (de Janvry, 1983, Table 6.1); the reform was subsequently undone.

3. After the implementation of the Cuban 1963 agrarian reform law, 63% of the cultivable land was in the state farm sector and 37% within the private, small farm sector (MacEwan, 1981, Chapters 6 and 8).

4. See Beneficiary Application Form, Appendix 3 in Simon, Stephens and Diskin (1982). The Agency for International Development, currently funding this agrarian reform, informed the author that data according to the sex of beneficiaries was not available for either Phase I or Phase III of the reform. Nevertheless, compliance with the Percy Ammendment requires that all US foreign assistance programs take into account the impact of such programs on women.

5. In both the Cuban and Nicaraguan reforms, land has been distributed in the form of individual private holdings to peasant households which have not necessarily joined cooperatives. Moreover, also excluded from this estimate are female permanent workers on the state farms. As a result, the available data underestimate the proportion of women benefited through the reform.

6. See Leon (1982) for a compilation of recent writings on women's agricultural participation throughout Latin America. A measure of women's agricultural participation in the Andean region is provided in Deere and Leon de Leal (1982).

7. Data for the Peruvian province of Cajamarca illustrate the importance that women have placed on owning land. In this area, many of the large estates were subdivided by the landlord class in the 1950s and 1960s and the core of the estates converted into modern dairy enterprises (Deere, 1977). Peasant households were given the opportunity to purchase the more marginal hacienda lands. An analysis of the property registers of the province showed that 40% of these land sales to the peasantry were registered in the name of both husband and wife. In the remaining 60% land was registered in the name of only one person, but almost as many women as men purchased land in their own names.

8. Structural problems, related to beneficiary criteria, are also important in explaining why the few women cooperative members in Peru have gradually been displaced. In one of the Peruvian dairy cooperatives studied by this author, the majority of women members in 1976, had been young single women who subsequently married in the 1976–82 period. Since, according to cooperative laws, only the head of household could be a member of the cooperative, as these young women married they ceded their positions to their husbands. This was also the only way that their husband could obtain full-time employment in the countryside. Chambeu (1981) reports a similar phenomenon in the Cuzco region.

9. A few Latin American countries have recently begun to take into account women's role as agricultural producer in designing agricultural sector strategies. For example, in Colombia, a recent policy document recognized the importance of removing barriers with respect to women's access to land; moreover, it recommended that state agricultural resources be directed specifically to rural women (Colombia, 1984).

REFERENCES

Alcerreca, L., *Analisis Critico de la Ley Federal de Reforma Agraria* (Mexico: 1974).

Anaya, P., *Los Problemas del Campo* (Mexico: Editorial Jus, 1976).

Barahona Riera, F., *Reforma Agraria y Poder Politico, el Caso de Costa Rica* (San Jose: Editorial Universitaria de Costa Rica, 1980).

Benglesdorf, C. and A. Hageman, 'Emerging from underdevelopment: Women and work in Cuba,' in Z. Eisenstein (Ed.), *Capitalist Patriarchy and the Case for Socialist Feminism* (New York: Monthly Review Press, 1977).

Benjamin, M., J. Collins and M. Scott, *No Free Lunch: Food and Revolution in Cuba Today* (San Francisco:

Institute for Food and Development Policy, 1984).

Blankstein, C. S. and C. Zuvekas, Jr., 'Agrarian reform in Ecuador: An evaluation of past efforts and the development of a new approach,' *Economic Development and Cultural Change*, Vol. 1, No. 2 (1973), pp. 73–94.

Blutstein, H. I., *et al.*, *Area Handbook for Colombia* (Washington, D.C.: American University Press, 1977).

Bronstein, A., *The Triple Struggle: Latin American Peasant Women* (Boston; South End Press, 1982).

Buchler, P., *Agrarian Cooperatives in Peru* (Berne: Sociological Institute, 1975).

Caballero, J. M. and E. Alvarez, *Aspectos Cuantitativos de la Reforma Agraria (1969–79)* (Lima: Instituto de Estudios Peruanos, 1980).

Callejas, R. Cecilia, 'Examination of Factors Limiting the Organization of Rural Women in Honduras,' M.A. Thesis, (University of Florida, 1983).

Caro, E., 'Programas de desarollo y la participacion de la mujer en Colombia,' in M. Leon (Ed.), *La Realidad Colombiana* (Bogota: ACEP, 1982).

Castro, A., N. Grullon and M. Leon, *Instituto Agrario Dominicano*, Report prepared for the 'Primer Seminario Nacional de Metodos y Tecnicas de Investigacion sobre la Mujer Rural,' (Santo Domingo: CIPAF, August 1983).

Castro, F., 'The revolution within the Revolution,' in E. Stone (Ed.), *Women and the Cuban Revolution* (New York: Pathfinder Press, 1981).

CEDEE, 'Historia y Situacion de la Organizacion de la Mujer Campesina en R. D.,' Paper presented to the Segundo Encuentro Nacional de Educacion Popular, (Santo Domingo: CEPAE, December 1983).

Chambeu, F., 'Participacion de la Mujer Rural en Acciones y Cambios Ideologicos en un Contexto de Reforma Agraria,' Unpublished research report (Lima: 1981).

Chavez de Velazquez, M., 'La Mujer y la Reforma Agraria,' *Filosofia y Letras*, Vol. 60 (1960–62), pp. 235–244.

CIERA, *La Mujer en las Cooperativas Agropecuarias en Nicaragua* (Managua: CIERA, 1984).

Cifuentes, E., 'Land reform in Chile,' Background paper, *Studies in Employment and Rural Development* No. 15 (Washington, D.C.: International Bank for Reconstruction and Development, June 1975).

Colombia, Republica de, 'Politica sobre el Papel de la Mujer Campesina en el Desarrollo Agropecuario,' Mimeo. (Bogota: Departamento Nacional de Planeacion, May 1984).

Croll, E., 'Socialist Development Experience: Women in Rural Production and Reproduction in the Soviet Union, China, Cuba, and Tanzania,' *Discussion Paper* (Institute of Development Studies, University of Sussex, September 1979).

Deere, C. D., 'Changing social relations of production and Peruvian peasant women's work,' *Latin American Perspectives*, Vol. 4, Nos. 1–2 (1977).

Deere, C. D., 'A comparative analysis of agrarian reform in El Salvador and Nicaragua,' *Development and Change* (Winter 1982a), pp. 1–41.

Deere, C. D., 'Rural Women and Agrarian Reform in Peru, Chile and Cuba,' Paper presented to the Second Annual Women, Work, and Public Policy Workshop, Harvard University (April 1982b).

Deere, C. D., 'Cooperative development and women's participation in the Nicaraguan agrarian reform,' *American Journal of Agricultural Economics* (December 1983).

Deere, C. D., 'Agrarian reform as revolution and counterrevolution: El Salvador and Nicaragua,' in R. Burbach and P. Flynn (Eds.), *The Politics of Intervention* (New York: Monthly Review Press, 1984).

Deere, C. D., and M. Leon de Leal, *Women in Andean Agriculture: Peasant Production and Rural Wage Employment in Colombia and Peru* (Geneva: ILO, 1982).

Deere, C. D., P. Marchetti, and N. Reinhardt, 'The peasantry and the development of Sandinista agrarian policy, 1979–1989,' *Latin American Research Review* (Forthcoming, Fall 1985).

de Janvry, A., *The Agrarian Question and Reformism in Latin America* (Baltimore: Johns Hopkins University Press, 1983).

Edwards, W. M., 'Ten issues in carrying out land reform in Colombia,' *Inter-America Economic Affairs* Vol. 34, No. 3 (1980), pp. 55–68.

Engels, F., *The Origins of Private Property, the Family and the State* (New York: International Publishers, 1975).

Escoto, Leon, *Leyes de Reforma Agraria en America Central* (Bogota: IICA-CIRA, 1965).

Fernandez, B., 'Reforma agraria y condicion socioeconomica de la mujer: El caso de dos cooperatives agrarias de produccion peruana,' in M. Leon (Ed.), *Las Trabajadoras del Agro* (Bogota: ACEP, 1982).

FMC (Federacion de Mujeres Cubanas), *Memories: Second Congress of Cuban Women's Federation* (Havana: Editorial Orbit, 1975).

Franco Garcia, J. M., 'Nueva ley de reforma agraria en el Ecuador,' *Derecho y Reforma Agraria*, Vol. 7, No. 7 (1976), pp. 35–54.

Garrett, P., 'Some structural constraints on the agricultural activity of women: The Chilean hacienda,' *Land Tenure Center Paper* No. 70, (Madison: University of Wisconsin, 1976).

Garrett, P., 'Women and agrarian reform: Chile 1964–1973,' *Sociologia Ruralis*, Vol. 22, No. 1 (1982a), pp. 17–28.

Garrett, P., 'La reforma agraria, organizacion popular, y participacion de la mujer en Chile,' in M. Leon (Ed.), *Las Trabajadoras del Agro* (Bogota: ACEP, 1982b).

Guerrero, T., *La Cuestion Agraria* (Caracas: 1962).

Honduras, 'Ley de Reforma Agraria: Decreto Ley No. 170,' *Derecho y Reforma Agraria*, Vol. 7, No. 7 (1976), pp. 237–288.

Honduras, Secretaria Tecnica del Consejo Superior de Planificacion Economica, *Plan Nacional de Desarollo 1979–1983* (n.d.).

Iriarte, G., *Sindicalismo Campesino Ayer, Hoy y Mañana* (La Paz: CIPCA, 1980).

Jemio, A. E., *La Reforma Agraria en Bolivia* (La Paz: MNR, 1973).

Leon, M. (Ed.), *Las Trabajadoras del Agro* (Bogota: ACEP, 1982).

Lodono, A., *Las Empresas Comunitarias Campesinas, Realidad y Perspectivas* (Bogota: Centro de Investigaciones y Accion Social, 1975).

MacEwan, A., *Revolution and Economic Development in Cuba* (London: Macmillan, 1981).

Manzanilla, V., *Reforma Agraria Mexicana* (Mexico: Editorial Porrua, 1977).

McEwen, W., *Changing Rural Bolivia* (Reasearch Institute for the Study of Man, 1969).

Mesa-Lago, C., *The Labor Force, Employment, Unemployment and Underemployment in Cuba: 1899–1970* (Beverly Hills, CA.: Sage Publications Professional Paper, 1972).

Organization of American States, *American en Cifras* (Washington, D.C.: OAS, 1977).

Organization of American States, *Statistical Bulletin*, Vol. 3, No. 34 (Washington D.C.: OAS, 1981).

PCC, Comite Central del Partido Comunista de Cuba, *Sobre el Pleno Ejercicio de la Igualdad de la Mujer, Tesis y Resolucion* (Havana: 1976).

Redclift, M. R., *Agrarian Reform and Peasant Organization on the Ecuadorian Coast* (London: Athlone Press, 1978).

Safilios-Rothschild, C., 'Women and the agrarian reform in Honduras,' in FAO, *Land Reform: Land Settlement and Cooperatives* (Rome: 1983), pp. 15–24.

Seligson, M., *Peasants of Costa Rica and the Development of Agrarian Capitalism* (Madison: University of Wisconsin Press, 1980).

Simon, L., J. Stephens and M. Diskin, *El Salvador Land Reform, Impact Audit* (Boston: Oxfam America, 1982).

Soto, O.D., *La Empresa y la Reforma Agraria en la Agricultura Venezolana* (Madrid: 1978).

Stone, E. (Ed.), *Women and the Cuban Revolution* (New York: Pathfinder Press, 1981).

United Nations, *Demographic Yearbook 1979* (New York: 1979).

United Nations, *1977 Compendium of Social Statistics* (New York: 1980).

Urquidi, A., *Las Comunidades Indigenas en Bolivia* (Cochabamba: Editorial Universitaria, 1971).

Weil, T. E., *et al.*, *Area Handbook for the Dominican Republic* (Washington, D.C.: American University Press, 1973).

Youssef, N. and A. LeBel, 'Exploring Alternative Employment and Income Generation Opportunities for Honduran Women: Analysis and Recommendations' (ICRW Report to USAID/Honduras Mission, October 1981).

[25]

Review of Radical Political Economics   Vol. 23(3 & 4)174-197(1991)

Peasant Patriarchy and the Subversion of the Collective in Vietnam

Nan Wiegersma

ABSTRACT: The Vietnamese peasant family economy operated according to its own dynamic, which sustained itself and undercut the collective economy. Although the Workers' Party was successful in some early aspects of collectivization, peasant patriarchs ultimately challenged collective institutions, forcing a return to family farming. The mechanism of this success was their careful control of the labor of women and children in small plot, kitchen garden and handicraft activities that, because of socialist pricing policies, were more profitable than the collective production of staples.

The contradiction which arises in every socialist revolution around the family and preconditions for women's liberation involves considerable fear of disrupting that basic institution, the patriarchal family. There has been so much concern about social disruption that each socialist revolution has been severely limited to measures which combat feudal forms but support a modernized patriarchal family structure. Since the social turmoil caused by experimentation with dissolving the legal and economic basis of male dominance following the Soviet Revolution in 1917, no group of Marxist-Leninist revolutionaries has been willing to go very far along the road of dissolving the patriarchal family unit. The Vietnamese Communists clearly fit into this reticent group.

This paper explores one of the most fundamental aspects of the Vietnamese collective experience, that which has been termed the "family economy problem." The analysis links this problem to an issue which has received more attention in the literature, "the middle peasant problem." The argument identifies patriarchy as the underlying cause of private interests becoming predominant and middle peasant men gaining control of collective politics. Village study materials on the Northern village in the early 1960s show that these trends were present before Northern involvement in the war with the United States and before the reconstruction period.

Patriarchy is seen here as more than a form of male-dominant family structure. It is also an independent political-economic system of production. In the basic unit of patriarchy, household production is organized and directed by the male head of the extended family or in his name. Production is generally directed by the woman only in the male's absence. In Vietnamese society, as in most societies, the basic unit of patriarchy is

Fitchburg State College.
I would like to thank Carol Brown, Laurie Nisonoff and the New England Women and Development Group for their contributions to this article.

supported by male dominance in the political structure. The patriarch acts as the family's representative to the local, regional and national political hierarchy, which in most cases reinforces his prerogatives.

The Communist Party in Vietnam underestimated the importance of the patriarchal family economy at the village level when they tried to introduce a socialist system from above. Since patriarchy was seen as a remnant of feudalism or capitalism and not as a political-economic system of production in itself, the strength and durability of patriarchy was undervalued.

In the traditional Vietnamese village, an oligarchy of notables was elected to village office. These notables were chosen among the males of the village according to wealth, age and mandarin title. The traditional village had significant collective institutions, including communal land comprising 35 to 50% of the village lands. Communal institutions existed side-by-side with the patriarchal extended family, controlling 50 to 65% of village land. A patrilocal residence pattern insured the continuance of patriarchal control. In addition, individual patriarchs, through long life, good luck and good management techniques, could move up the traditional village hierarchy and influence communal institutions. The power and wealth of the rich peasant and landlord elite in the village had grown during the colonial period as collective institutions crumbled and communal property was usurped by elite families or by French or Chinese outlanders (Wiegersma 1988: 51-86).

By Vietnamese Communist definitions of class, the middle peasants owned land but did not employ others or rent out land, and the rich peasants worked their land but also hired laborers and/or rented land. Poor peasants were landless laborers or tenants. Landlords rented out land and did not work their own land. Class lines were fuzzy, however, because older people without descendants were *expected* to rent rather than farm land themselves, and there was a differentiation made by the peasants, which arose in the colonial era between traditional landlords and modern (sometimes absentee) Westernized landlords.

The traditional village oligarchy was wiped out during the land reform in North Vietnam in the 1950s. Middle peasant leadership asserted itself in the 1960s village. The Party's policies pushed for poor peasant leadership, but these policies were never fully successful. The Workers' Party had in mind a gradual transformation from a collective economy, which had a supplementary family economy, to a totally collectivized economy. The actual process was quite the reverse, and the Party and State were forced to accept the *fait accompli* of a rural economy controlled by middle peasant patriarchs in the 1970s, since the patriarchal family economy had increasingly taken over collective responsibilities.

The contradiction involving the non-socialist family economy and middle peasant leadership are not linked together by Vietnamese sources. The family economy and the problem of continued class division in the countryside are seen as relics of a feudalist past and as separate problems. Vietnamese socialists, by largely ignoring the "family economy problem," missed the connection between the control of prosperous family economies and the public positions of some patriarchs. The private motivations of these patriarchs subverted collective organization.

We will see that the Workers' Party was largely successful in its goals in the land reform and collectivization campaigns. Despite adverse publicity about peasant violence against landlords at the time, the Party was successful in its goal of creating a socialist revolution in the countryside which displaced landlords and rich peasants. The party then galvanized collective labor to improve water control and thereby increasing agricultural production. Nevertheless, with time the patriarchal family economy eventually undercut the collectivized economy. This paper will show how the patriarch could control family labor more precisely because of his day-to-day association with family members. This precise patriarchal control of labor was very important in day-to-day production activities, and it became even more important with the green revolution.

LAND REFORM

Policy errors which resulted from a lack of analysis of peasant patriarchy predated the collective experience. Errors were made even in the land reform campaigns because of the "invisibility" of patriarchal forces.

In 1954, the government of the Democratic Republic of Vietnam needed the support of the poor peasant majority in the countryside in order to carry out its programs. Although much of the top layer of very rich or absentee landlords had been removed in the process of the previous struggle, the village oligarchies made up of traditional landlords and rich peasants were either still intact or could reconstitute themselves. Social change in the countryside depended on the support of the government by the poor peasants. This was a lesson which had been learned from the previous Rent Reduction Campaign and its positive impact on soldiers in fighting the French at Dien Bien Phu.

Decisions about the land reform program were made at the top party levels. The idea was not only to change production relations among the rural population but also to change the structure of the party in rural areas. In all subdivisions of the country, including zones, provinces, districts and villages, a land reform hierarchy was set up that was separate from the existing administration and party committees. The basic land reform hierarchy was recruited from the most committed party members. Their numbers were supplemented by party members from the recently demobilized military and from the urban working class. This meant that the cadre were generally younger than the peasants they were organizing. Although many of these committed cadre were from petty-bourgeois backgrounds and had rich peasant or landlord relatives in the countryside, they were intentionally not assigned to the areas they came from (White 1981: 318, 326).

In the periods that the Workers' Party had emphasized a united front policy against the French and then later the Americans, many landlords had joined the Vietminh and some had joined the Party. Some of these landlords were using their positions in the Vietminh and in the Party to maintain control over their tenants and their dominance over local government. Land reform cadre were instructed to remove these elements from the Party and from all positions of authority in the village. The land reform cadre were taught to be wary of the official party hierarchy existing in the countryside, and they were even given the impression that the existing organizations might be "organizations of the enemy" (Moise 1976: 79-82).

The object of the land reform was to create a rural revolution in which the country and the Party would be rid of the landlords and rich peasants who exploited others' labor. The land distribution was to be carried out by the poor peasant non-owners, with the Party's help, and the poor peasants were to make an alliance with the middle peasant self-supporters. The existing majority of Party members in the countryside, however, were from middle peasant backgrounds and, except for mistakes in classification, care was taken by the land reform cadre not to alienate the middle peasant class. While landlords were treated harshly, middle peasants were supposed to be given preferential treatment. They were allowed to keep more land than the poor peasants (White 1981: 364). The anger of the poor peasants was directed, by the cadre, toward the landlords and away from the middle peasants. The resulting actions against rich peasants, landlords and sometimes misclassified middle peasants were later to be considered errors in need of rectification.

Reformed village political organizations were set up in the midst of the land reform campaign. Open meetings of local party branches were held where poor peasants and landless laborers could bring evidence. This process led to the expulsion of rich peasants and landlords from the Party and often poor peasants were recruited to join village administration to replace those deposed. These poor peasants were promoted rapidly, despite often lacking experience for the jobs they were supposed to handle (Moise 1976: 81).

In theory, the structure of the land reform was supposed to leave the landlords with about as much land as their former tenants plus their houses and most other goods. In practice, the landlords were typically left with less land than anyone else in the village, and they often lost their houses, too. The vengeance of former tenants developed its own momentum and the land reform hierarchy, at least to some extent, lost control of the situation. Many landlords were beaten or killed for past sins against their tenants, and these killings made international news as being the fault of the Communists. Some rich peasants and landlords who were loyal to the Vietminh, and even experienced cadre, were taken before land reform committees. These resistance landlords were stripped of their former positions and often also imprisoned.

Party leaders reacted to the disruption in the countryside, and the trials of cadre, by instituting a "Rectification of Errors" campaign. During the Rectification of Errors, many members of the resistance who had been labeled as rich peasants and landlords were reclassified as middle peasants, and they resumed their former positions in the Party and in the village administrative hierarchy.

Christine White believes that patriarchal behavior was the reason for some of the mistaken categorization during the land reform campaign. The class categories used in the land reform did not recognize the existence of patriarchy. Those who engaged in "feudal" behavior such as wife-beating and gambling were sometimes wrongly classified as "feudal landlords" (White 1984: 17-20).[1]

The land reform had important but mostly unintentional effects on women in the patriarchal family structure and in the village. Men and women were all divided into the same class categories: landlord, rich peasant, middle peasant and poor peasant. Women officially had a share in the land distribution, although the land usually went to their families and, therefore, in effect, to the male family heads. Women were active in the land reform trials because crimes of "cruel landlord notables" had often been against women. Women were not among the old ruling elite, since they had been excluded from village administration. They were not, therefore, likely to be the primary targets of the land reform reorganization. Women nevertheless suffered the economic restrictions doled out to patriarchs on whom they were dependent.

In Hoa Xa village, in Ha Tay Province, for example, a man named Nhuan, who was owner of six mau (5.4 acres), was charged with being a landlord. His wife and children were among those who brought the charges. All of Nhuan's land and his house was taken from him and distributed to tenants and landless laborers. He was left with only one room which he shared with the wife and children who had accused him! The so-called landlord did not protest, according to a peasant from the village, but a year later a group of party officials arrived in the village and declared that an error had been committed. Nhuan was given back two mau of land and his house (Chaliand 1969: 223).

Nhuan's family must have been greatly relieved after the overcrowding that they had to endure with the man that they had helped to sentence. One wonders whether they had realized at the time of accusation that they would share his sentence. Chaliand mentions that the family was on good terms, so we can probably presume that the patriarch had changed his "cruel landlord" behavior. But this is an excellent example of the massive confusion between "cruel landlord" and "cruel patriarch" behavior in the land reform campaign.

AGRICULTURAL COLLECTIVIZATION

In the post-land reform period, there were many reasons why the North Vietnamese began thinking of building cooperatives in the countryside. Socialist ideology, and specifically the ideology coming from China before the China-Soviet split, favored collectivization. Pro-Mao cadres in the rural areas pushed for cooperatives, and then later for "higher level" cooperatives (collectives), before the Central Committee of the Workers' Party was ready to move on these issues.

Politically, the collectivization campaign was seen by the more radical cadres as a means of continuing class struggle in the countryside. Collectivization would benefit poor peasant households more than middle peasant households, and political control of the collective could (theoretically) be put in the hands of the poor peasant class by regulations which favored this class for leadership positions.

Collectivization of the Soviet type which would modernize agriculture was not possible in underdeveloped North Vietnam. Nevertheless, there would be other positive effects of collectivization on productivity. Hydraulic advances could more easily be made, especially at the village level, when there were no objections to new canals being built because of private property rights. Channels could be built straighter and fields could be larger, maximizing the usefulness of available cultivable land. Cooperative labor could also be more easily organized for construction projects.

The most frequent argument in favor of cooperatives and one which moved the North Vietnamese leadership the most was that the rural class structure was reasserting itself through the contingencies of the market. Poor peasants, after a bad crop year, were selling their land or parts of their land to "middle" peasants. (There were supposedly no "rich" peasants left, so the euphemism for what used to be called rich peasants was "upper middle" peasants). The "upper middle" peasants were gradually acquiring land in the post-land reform North.

Collectivization also enabled the state to gain control of any agricultural surplus (although this was small) for the purpose of financing the country's industrialization. The price of rice for city dwellers and workers in the new industries could be kept low if deliveries (requisitions) to the state were made by collectives instead of individual farmers. Individual peasants would tend to eat much of their own surplus or feed it to farm animals rather than sell to the state at a low price. The collective had no choice; it had to sell.

Mutual aid teams or neighborhood self-help groups, in the traditional pattern, had been set up throughout North Vietnam prior to the cooperative movement. It is not clear how much of the initiative for these teams came from the Party. Most likely much of the impetus for their establishment came from the peasantry's tendency to carry on with traditional communal institutions essential to production. It seems that the Party and the State tried to change the functioning of traditional, neighborhood mutual-aid teams by making them more permanent and by adding a new function — that of teaching new techniques to the team leaders.

Between 1958 and 1960, cooperatives were first developed and the cooperative debate continued. The movement to form lower level cooperatives took place fairly rapidly, once it was underway. In 1959, 45% of peasant families joined cooperatives and in 1960 another 41% joined (Gorgon 1981: 21). The already formed neighborhood mutual-aid teams were transformed, wherever possible, into production cooperatives. Village-level credit cooperatives and sales and purchase cooperatives that purchased inputs and sold outputs were simultaneously formed in the villages.

Cadres recruited the poor peasants for early participation and then later turned to the middle peasants. Membership was supposed to be voluntary, although ideological and political pressure was put on peasants to volunteer for membership quickly. There was a peaceful transition, however, with little vehement opposition. The rental payments that middle peasants received for their land, water buffalo and implements certainly alleviated some negative feelings about the movement.

Patriarchal Family Economy and Collectivization

Unlike collectivization in China, the North Vietnamese collectivized economy was not designed to supplant the peasant family economy at any time in the foreseeable future. The collective sphere did not provide more than half, and it often provided less than half, of the family's resources (Lam 1961: 9). In China, the collectives were in a stronger position vis-a-vis the family economy because the collective provided 90% of the family's resources, including extensive collective childcare facilities and there were some experiments with collective eating arrangements (Hewlett and Markie 1976: 43-45).

There were two rationales for the preservation of the patriarchal family economy in North Vietnam and both reasons were indicative of the limits of socialist planning in the Northern countryside. In the first place, the collective economy did not have the administrative capacity to provide many of the basic necessities for cooperative members. A sub-economy, run by the family patriarch, was deemed necessary for the provision of these necessities. Secondly, the family economy was needed to harness "surplus labor" that the collective economy could not absorb. The State saw that the family patriarch was able to organize the labor of young people and women for productive pursuits in the home and on the family plot (Duang 1962: 71-79). A minimum of 5% (but usually more) of the cultivable land available per capita was allocated to cooperative members, but it was controlled by the family patriarch, and the State took advantage of this patriarchal family structure. This land called 5 percent land, was used to grow vegetables, some rice and other high value crops. In addition to this source of income, families tended kitchen gardens and raised pigs and chickens for the market and they produced handicraft articles.

The basic subsistence food, rice, was mostly produced by the collective in this period as were other staples such as corn and potatoes. The staples were considered the central production activity, although the state provided a low price for these subsistence goods. The family economy was judged "supplementary," even when most income came from the family economy!

State pricing policies which kept the price of staples low aggravated the family economy/collective contradiction. Most income came from the family economy sector, *partially because* goods which were produced in this sector, like vegetables and handicrafts, sold at higher prices. The socialist goal of low-priced staples conflicted with the necessity of keeping the collective sector as the primary sector at the village level.

To summarize, although the families controlled only from 5 to 15% of the productive land area, they put intensive energy into high-value products from kitchen gardens, private orchards, and family plots and handicraft products which could be sold at high prices on the market. Meanwhile, the collective controlled 80 to 95% of the productive area, but this was less intensively cultivated and the prices of staples produced here remained low. The collective also retained some of its income from the collective property for itself. By the time the collective division of income was made to families, therefore, the average family received more income from family activities than from collective activities. The government failed to take into consideration these family economies and therefore continued to think of the family economy as "supplementary."

A number of cadres were concerned, during the collectivization campaign, that the family economy would be the seed of renewed capitalism in the countryside. These people were cautioned against this "leftist" deviation in the Party's theoretical journal, *Hoc Tap*:

> the contradiction between the supplementary (family) economy and the cooperative and the government is a minor one, not antagonistic in nature (Duang 1962: 76).

Since work was not performed by hired labor, but by household labor, the party argued that exploitation was not taking place. However, some cadres were so concerned that capitalism would rear its head, despite these arguments, that they did not initially distribute 5 percent land in villages for which they were responsible.

THE PATRIARCHAL/COLLECTIVE
COMPETITION FOR LABOR

Village study materials from the early 1960s in North Vietnam show the details of the restructuring of rural Vietnamese society. A study of Nam Hong village by Pham Cuong and a study of the Ngo Xuyen cooperative by Pham Toan form the basis of these observations (Pham Cuong 1976 and Pham Toan 1971).[2] Nguyen Yem's study of Thanh Oai District and Gerard Chaliand's interviews of peasants throughout North Vietnam were also useful (Nguyen 1971 and Chaliand 1969).[3]

Peasants in North Vietnam were not all equally receptive to cooperatives. Because of voluntary membership in cooperatives, the poorest villagers and women were usually the first to join. Some peasants in Dai Lai, for example, joined because they had more labor than could be utilized on their very small plot. One woman joined in order to get food for her family. Women in Nam Hong joined the collectives because they preferred the sociability of collective work over individualized family work. When only the wife wanted to join, sometimes the family's possessions were divided and each spouse was free to join or not (Pham Cuong 1976: 35).[4]

Middle peasant men initially feared losing power and wealth through collectivization, and other peasants feared collectivization because of inefficiency and unfairness. The old people without descendants and the sickly worried about being at a disadvantage in terms of work points. Others were concerned that differences about how to organize production would require endless hours in acrimonious meetings. These problems were resolved, at least partly, through the process of collectivization. Old and disabled people were cared for with the cooperative's "social fund." Efficient collective management remained a problem for many years, but the training of elected managers by the state improved efficiency somewhat.

Passing to a higher level of collectivization meant gradually reducing the rents which the village was still paying individual owners for land and equipment and the fusion of smaller units, often hamlets, into a larger unit, usually the former village. This consolidation often brought arguments because the hamlets were not equal in soil fertility or in land area. Close neighbors with a history of solidarity often took the step of forming a small cooperative quite easily, but identification with villagers who lived at a distance was much less and many arguments ensued.

> Between the hamlets, there were inequities with regard to cultivable acreage and available funds. Each one felt himself wronged when he got into a single co-op [collective] with others. Moreover, problems of organization and management were given rise to by the broadening of the co-op ... . Faced with these difficulties, peasants asked to get out of the co-op (Pham Toan 1971: 212).

These arguments about unequal benefits and obligations were often eventually worked out through improved management, but this was an arduous process.

The private-public division of land in the villages did not adhere to the formula of 95% public and 5% private set up by the State. Nam Hong had 6.7% of cultivable land in private hands, and this figure did not include kitchen gardens, orchards or fish ponds. In Ngo Xuyen, 13.2% of the land was held in private fields, private orchards and fish ponds. Since these particular villages were being observed carefully by the state and still had more than 5% of their lands in private hands, it is reasonable to assume that other villages probably had at least as much private land, if not more.

The most important aspect of this division is that the private fields were farmed much more intensively than the public fields. In the 1960s Nam Hong yields were twice as high in the private fields. The crop rotations involved two or three vegetable crops and one or two rice crops on these fields. A lot more labor and fertilizer was used on the private fields than on the public fields.

Sixty percent of the labor force in the northern villages of the late 1960s was female. Many of the men in the middle age range had lost their lives in the First Indochina War. Other men of this age and younger men were away from the village, fighting in the Second Indochina War. More than half of the men between the ages of 16 and 30 were missing from Nam Hong village. Most men missing from the villages were in the military, but some were working in the cities in government administration or in manufacturing industry.

In Nam Hong, 14% of working age women did not participate in cooperative work regularly. Women with several small children often did not participate. In addition, when these women did some cooperative work, they were often given less physically strenuous tasks which earned fewer work points. Women who were older, in their fifties and sixties, and had many sons and daughters-in-law in their households also sometimes elected not to participate and to instead do childcare and household tasks at home (Pham Cuong 1976: 36).

Cooperative members were organized in production brigades which ranged from 20 to 60 people for the planting, weeding and harvesting work. There were specialized work teams for tree planting, machinery work, fish breeding, brick making, water control, plowing and harrowing, etc. Men and women were often in different work teams, doing different specific tasks and accumulating different amounts of work points even when they were part of the same brigade.

Many male tasks, such as plowing, harrowing, manuring, clearing and lifting water, were awarded the maximum amount of work points per day. Another important task earning high points, but which women also participated in, was harvesting. The female task of planting-out rice often received fewer daily work points, but in one cooperative, in Hung Yen, it was given maximum points (Chaliand 1969: 122-125).

Other tasks which females usually participated in, such as weeding, hoeing, sweeping yards and making baskets, were awarded fewer work points. Women could expect to accumulate fewer work points than men, even if they worked the same number of hours. Women often did not work as many hours because of their family responsibilities. Thus their accumulation was usually lower (Chaliand 1969: 124-125).

The late 1960s was an unusual time in that labor resources were sent to the front and women were forced to take over male tasks in the village. Women took over jobs such as manuring and plowing when male labor was extremely short. The usual six -man plowing teams continued their work as much as possible, but where plowing teams were in short supply, strapping younger women formed teams (Chaliand 1969: 177). There was, nevertheless, little chance of this temporary work assignment permanently affecting the division of labor in the countryside. When the men returned home from war and the young women married, they were given easier tasks because of their childbearing status.

Older people did different work from the rest of the villagers and the gender division of labor in this group particularly reflected traditional values. Grandmothers retired to tend to the running of the household and to childcare responsibilities, often even when there were nursery schools available. In Nam Hong, for example, only 13% of women over 60 worked in the cooperative although over half of the men that age did cooperative work. Older men were assigned tasks such as planting and caring for cooperative fruit trees. They were also often given tasks which respected their age and status as household heads. For example, they discussed electrification with each household in the village in Nam Hong.

Children were sometimes auxiliary workers on the collective. They minded the buffalo or did other small jobs. Most of the children's labor, however, was used in the family economy.

All villagers were active in the private family economy which, as we have seen, accounted for a considerable amount of production in the rural economy. Women especially and also children were the most active participants. Women with the help of older children cooked, sewed, did laundry, reared the children and tended the kitchen garden at home. Women also worked extensively on the family plot. They did collective work as well, although significantly less than men. It made more economic sense for the family to send mostly male labor into the collective because male tasks were generally better remunerated.

There were problems with the quality of work done on the collective vis-a-vis work done in the family economy. Trees planted in family orchards did well while those planted in the co-op often did not (Pham Cuong 1976: 90). In the early stages of collectivization in Nam Hong, cooperative pigs died due to lack of care, and buffalo were "entrusted to whoever came along first each day." Many of these particular problems were dealt with eventually in Nam Hong. The quality of labor in the fields continued to be a problem, however. That private plots yielded two to three times what the collective was able to produce speaks for itself in describing the labor quality problem in the collective.

CONTROL OF PRODUCTION

Collective

Responsibility for collective production was not actually held at the village or collective level, but it was, instead, maintained at the production-brigade level. The production brigades were usually former hamlets and composed of from 40 to 70 people. Through a system of contracts with production brigades, production control responsibilities were essentially contracted out to the heads of these brigades. The three parts of the contract between the collective and the brigade specified (1) the volume and quality of goods to be delivered to the collective, (2) the deadlines by which these deliveries should take place, and (3) the general expenses of the brigade in carrying out their production responsibilities.

Collective leadership was more often male than female, despite the majority of female labor in the 1960s' collectives. Women were usually relegated to lower level leadership positions despite state regulations requiring a one-third minimum of female leadership, and a rule that a woman should be among the top leaders when there was over 50% of female workers. These regulations were usually not enforced in the countryside.

The village-level collective management was in charge of social service and water control activities. In larger cooperatives, there were teams which specialized in water conservancy: in smaller co-ops temporary teams were set up. In Ngo Xuyen a "water conservancy team" was set up during each crop, comprised of a member of the management committee of the village-level collective and the leaders of the production brigades. The team then saw to it that the fields were adequately irrigated or drained during the crop's growing season. The public works projects for improvements and upkeep of the irrigation system were closely directed by the collective management.

The purchase and sales cooperatives and the credit cooperatives were organized at the village level and administered by village officials. The credit cooperatives were like village savings banks. The villagers were encouraged to save their money in the credit cooperatives, and the village used the lands for collective investments. The sale and purchase cooperatives were developed to replace some private markets and also to integrate each village into a national distribution network. Village officials were directly responsible for the running of these co-ops and for the training of technicians to handle their accounting and day-to-day responsibilities. Village officials were also responsible for social services such as education, health and childcare. There were primary schools, nurseries, and kindergartens and health facilities in both Nam Hong and Ngo Xuyen. In Nam Hong, however, the childcare workers were paid by the production cooperatives at the hamlet level at different rates, causing problems since workers with similar village responsibilities receive a different wages (Pham Cuong 1976: 66).

Problems of adaptation of the peasants to socialism in the villages were seen by the State as problems in cooperative administration, rather than as competition with the family economy. Examples of the problems of collectivization abound in the villages studied. The peasants sometimes even abused collective property:

> common property was not adequately taken care of. Farm tools lay about in the fields after a day's work, even during months at times. Of the 18 improved carts, there remain only a few usable ... . Hence frequent and great waste ... This is one of the causes of the high cost of production and the low pay for a workday (Pham Toan 1971: 221).

With enough training in planning and scientific agriculture, the State believed that lack of enthusiasm for collectivization would be eliminated and peasants would contribute more work days to the collective.

Underemployment was specifically linked to deficiencies in management by the authors of both the Ngo Xuyen and Nam Hong village studies. Pham Toan claims that Ngo Xuyen had failed to work out a judicious plan for the use of manpower. In Nam Hong, there were no handicrafts practiced in the off-season. The collective administration recommended taking up such activities, but nothing happened (Pham Toan 1971: 119; Pham Cuong 1976: 45).

The fact that some production cooperatives were well managed and productivity was high, and in others, management was poor and productivity low, encouraged the Workers' Party to blame this on poor management. Two of the production cooperatives in Nam Hong were well managed, one of these had been better managed but the efficient cadre had been promoted to higher level jobs, leaving less efficient management to take over. One of the cooperatives was poorly managed and "conservative" and "narrow-minded" attitudes among the older cadre were seen as the reason. Nam Hong, located 20 km. from Hanoi, had many more party members than the average village. It can probably be accurately assumed that if there were traditional attitudes here, then they were even more abundant in the more remote areas (Pham Cuong 1976: 55-56).

Patriarchal Control of Family Economy
The "family heads," who were virtually always male, controlled the family economy, and the patriarchal family was at the root of the traditional

attitudes that undercut the collective. Even when a woman (a daughter-in-law) was the only able-bodied full-time worker in the family in Nam Hong, the father-in-law was considered the "head of household." There was actually a strong competition between a collective economy and the family economy, and even collective officials were sometimes not above putting the family economy first:

> It is deplorable that co-op members, even some brigade leaders sometimes busy themselves with more profitable jobs rather than work for the co-op. At the time of longan harvest, for instance, they prefer going to town to sell their fruit (Pham Toan 1971: 220).

In the 1960s (continuing in the 1970s) many cooperatives contracted work out to the family economy instead of the production brigades. Study and criticism sessions evidently put an end to these practices in Nam Hong because they "infringed on the very principle of collective agriculture" (Pham Cuong 1976: 61). In a neighboring province, however, this practice continued.

The family patriarchs differed considerably in their ability to organize their family labor force, usually composed of a wife, sons, daughters-in-law, and their children (or just wife and children, if the patriarch was young). In Pham Cuong's study of Nam Hong, he compares three family economies and finds one much more efficient than the others. The most efficient family economy is headed by a former village administrator who is "accustomed to planning his work" (Pham Cuong 1976: 107).

Despite the large-scale hydraulic work in the villages in the 1960s, tendencies stemming from the conflict between socialism and the patriarchal economy prevented full utilization of increased capacities because people devoted more attention, and qualitatively better attention, to the family economy. Since the (more than) 5 percent land yielded double what the collective land yielded, the rest of the land could presumably be brought up to nearly the level of the 5 percent land, with more fertilizer and better attention. The patriarch clearly had a firmer control over the labor force than the collective did, and this fact limited collective influence and collective production in the 1960s' village.

WOMEN IN THE COLLECTIVE

Markets set up and run by women merchants continued in socialist rural Vietnam, but the socialist rural market cooperatives were set up in competition, in order to put many of the traditional markets out of business. It was state policy that traditional markets took up too much of the peasants' time and therefore should be discouraged (Pham Toan 1971: 132-133).

The purchase and sales cooperatives were set up on the level of the production brigade, but they were directed by the collective. The usually male head of the purchase and sales cooperative groups periodically attended meetings of the cooperative's administrative committee. The cooperative acted as an agency for retailing State industrial products and as a purchasing agency for agricultural produce on behalf of the State, and it bought and sold local goods. Shops were set up in the various localities to replace most of the markets. In the district where Nam Hong was located, seven private markets were discontinued, leaving four. The purchase and sales co-op thereby took over about two-thirds of the market trading. Fifty "reformed" traders in Nam Hong returned to the land and agricultural production as a result of these changes. Since nearly all of the traders were women and since most of the village officials replacing them were men, this shift from private to public trading was a shift between women's and men's work.

From the beginning of the land reform and throughout the collectivization campaigns, women in the north Vietnamese villages saw these socialist movements as an advance for themselves. Despite the fact that most of the socialist cadre were men, women strongly identified with the socialist political-economy. In the first place, the socialists freed women from child marriages, concubinage, polygamy and arranged marriage. Secondly, although most women's children were still cared for by their mothers-in-law, some women in the village could take advantage of the nurseries and kindergartens that were set up. Thirdly, although women could not earn as many points in the collective as men because of women's additional household responsibilities, earning income from the collective gave women more power than merely working directly for their fathers-in-law or their husbands.

As a patriarchal system of production reestablished itself in the socialist environment of the North Vietnamese villages, however, women were probably taken by surprise. For example, what village woman would have realized that shops managed by the collective would replace their markets?

The young women who were active in the land reform and collectivization campaigns took their places in the lower levels of the village administrative hierarchy if they did not marry and move to another village. Meanwhile, many former middle peasant men were able to establish themselves as leaders in the village hierarchy by the middle sixties. The surpluses which were accumulated in the villages in the late '50s and early to mid-'60s were used almost exclusively either (1) for socialist accumulation, such as hydraulics, or (2) for patriarchal accumulation in the form of new brick houses. Women benefited from both kinds of accumulation in that they lived in the new houses and ate some of the increased food production. But women were not in charge of either the socialist economy or the patriarchal economy. They were participants in the new system and enjoyed a better status than under the old system but this was not equality.

Women's position in the North Vietnamese village changed again in the late '60s, but the cause of this change was predominantly the war with the United States, not the effects of socialism in the village. Women moved into village administration in North Vietnam in the late '60s and early '70s because so many men had been taken off to war or to higher level administration. Women made similar political moves in the south, however, even in areas controlled by the U.S.-sponsored regime. The women's plowing teams, on the other hand, may have been a uniquely socialist phenomenon. This participation in high status work, however, was temporary, since it was only allowed during a woman's young, pre-childbearing years. Women's participation in village administration was in a sense temporary, too. When the war was eventually over, women were expected to resume their prewar positions.

TECHNOLOGICAL CHANGE AND PRODUCTION INCREASES

New seed varieties were adopted in the northern villages in this period, more for their short growing span than for their high yields. In the production conditions of north Vietnam, yields of the new seed varieties were only marginally greater than the old varieties. The shorter growing season, however, combined with better water control resulting from hydraulics work projects permitted third crops in areas where there were formerly only two per year. The new varieties also allowed for changes in the crop mix. Very high value crops, like vegetables, were grown near cities, replacing some staple and industrial crops.

Chemical fertilizers were also introduced into northern villages, although not to nearly as large an extent as in some parts of the south. Producers increased the production of *azolla* (green manure) and the use of restorative crops and pig manure. The state had to persuade the peasants about the usefulness of chemical fertilizer, but by 1970 peasants were competing for those goods in the distribution in Ngo Xuyen.

The patriarchal family economy had an advantage over the cooperative with respect to the new technologies. The new rice varieties and additional fertilization increased the labor inputs needed to succeed in high yields of multiple crops. Since the patriarchs had a tighter control over labor, these very intensive labor techniques were more suited to the patriarchal family economy than the cooperative economy. New technologies could be added, despite traditional values, because of the existence of the collective, but once accepted, these particular technologies advanced the family economy more readily than the collective.

Throughout the period of land reform and in the first part of collectivization, there were significant increases in agricultural production in North Vietnam. There was a 47% increase in the production of staple crops

Table 1
Production of Staple Crops in North Vietnam

Year	Production of Staples*
	m. ton
1955	3.94
1956	4.79
1957	4.39
1958	4.96
1959	5.79
1960	4.70
1961	5.20
1962	5.17
1963	5.01
1964	5.52
1965	5.56
1966	5.10
1967	5.40
1968	4.63
1969	4.71
1970	5.28
1971	4.92
1972	5.74
1973	5.19
1974	6.28
1975	5.49

* Staples include rice paddy, maise, manioc and potatoes. Secondary crops are calculated in paddy rice equivalents. Source: Fforde 1982: 318 and Wickerman 1982: 486.

(rice, potatoes and corn) in the 1955-1959 period. Using the very unusually high 1959 production figure for staple crops of 5.8 million metric tons, however, exaggerates production increases in the '50s. Weather conditions that year were particularly good. It took the North Vietnamese until 1972 to again reach the high output rates achieved for staple crops in 1959, and until 1974 to pass this production mark (Fforde 1982: 379-83; Wickerman 1982: 486).

There are readily apparent reasons for the lack of staple crop production increases for the Vietnamese in the 1960s, apart from any possible good or bad effects from collectivization. Bad weather conditions in the early '60s, especially in 1960 and 1963, the effects of war on the agricultural labor force and bombing the dike system slowed production for the rest of the decade. As a result, generalizations about the effects of collectivization and land reform on production seem tenuous.

Production increases in the '50s were achieved mainly through small-scale water control projects. The Northern Communists argued that without changes in the relations of production, these projects would not have been possible. Getting rid of landlordism and the private property rights which interfered with canal building was imperative. Land reform and cooperativization not only achieved collective property rights over the land in question, but also cooperative labor was more easily organized for water control projects because of these programs (Fall 1964: 163, 294).

North Vietnam could not mechanize agricultures in this period, but they did make some medium-term changes which they called semi-mechanization. Ninety-eight percent of the land was still plowed by water buffalo instead of tractors in the early '60s, but the plows themselves were improved. In addition, wheelbarrows were produced in Vietnam which "liberated peoples' shoulders."

Increases in staples production in the late '50s and continued growth in production for market of vegetables, pigs, poultry, and handicrafts in the 1960s, enabled many formerly poor families to accumulate surpluses. As a result, housing construction boomed throughout the countryside. Kilns were built, and families collected bricks until they could build themselves new substantial houses to replace their mud huts.

Allowing for some heightening of the contrast for effect, the following Vietnamese source gives us a picture of changes in the countryside in North Vietnam in this period:

> The recent changes in the appearance of the rural areas is full of promise. The spectacle of desolate, muddy villages with a few ancient tile palaces of lords interspersed with rows of obscure thatch and mud houses and clusters of flimsy, twisted huts exists no longer. In its place is the spectacle of well lighted, attractive new brick houses belonging to the agricultural cooperative workers (Canh 1963: 53).

PATRIARCHY LIMITS SUCCESS

The North Vietnamese dilemma, which has been called the "middle peasant problem," persisted in Vietnam despite considerable attention by the government and the Party. After the land reform and at the beginning of the collectivization movement, middle peasants generally dominated lower level government positions. In the structure of cooperative leadership, therefore, there was a one-third *upper limit* put on middle peasant men. In addition to this, a one-third *lower limit* was put on the participation of women in cooperative management. These limits were not always adhered to, however, especially after the slowdown in cooperative organizing in 1961. Party politics tended to shift to the right and toward greater acceptance of the middle peasants as part of a "homogeneous" collectivized peasantry.

A problem of middle peasant domination also manifested itself in the Party. A Party member in Bac Ninh Province reported at the end of 1962:

> we failed to hold fast to the class policy of the party in the countryside, the ratio of party members coming from the middle peasant class greatly increased. ... party members coming from the poor peasant class were gradually eliminated (*Hoc Tap*, December 1962, JPRS 17666: 10).

The middle peasants initially showed less interest in collectivization than the poor peasants, but the middle peasants were eventually able to work within the new structure in ways which tended to preserve their positions and status. If they achieved positions of leadership in the collective, they received extra shares of collective returns. Also, they could best preserve their family economy interests by being aware of collective policies and the "contracting out" of some collective responsibilities such as rice drying.

Both the family economy and the problem of continued class division in the countryside were seen as relics of a feudal past which would be gradually overcome, but they were seen as separate problems. The Vietnamese did not recognize patriarchy as a system of accumulation, and therefore, they did not see how economic differences could be preserved and encouraged through the family economy.

A patriarch with a larger family and more enterprising or skilled family members was in a good position for economic betterment in the collective village in the '60s. If he could also earn extra shares of the cooperative's product through participation in management, this would further benefit his position. Having more children of working age improved his position, and this was not limited by biology since it could be altered by adoption. If the patriarch had a number of older male children, he could do particularly well in the cooperative work-point distribution, since mate cooperative jobs, like plowing, often earned more work points than female cooperative jobs, like weeding or transplanting. In the patriarchal family economy, on the other hand, older relatives, younger children and females could be put to work raising vegetables on the 5 percent land or raising pigs and chickens. They worked on sewing, weaving and handicraft items as well and selling these items on the private market. These opportunities encouraged considerable variation in households' standard of living. This inequality could be preserved and increased over time. There was no mechanism in the rural economy for these differences to decrease without an increase in collective responsibility vis-a-vis the patriarchal family economy.

Cooperatives had internal contradictions which encouraged the restablishment of a patriarchal system of production in the collectivized village. Many of the resulting problems were never truly solved: (1) Cooperative members tried to minimize the number of work days expected of each member in order to keep the ratio of labor to payment up because they knew that more work days meant less payment per day. (2) More fertilizer and concentrated effort was often devoted to the 5 percent land than to the cooperative land. (3) Many cooperatives were not well planned or organized, as many cooperative managers operated in devious ways vis-a-vis the state.

In pre-colonial times, what happened in the village (now called a production brigade or a cooperative) did not always correspond to regulations from the higher echelons. Modern cooperative officials often continued to act like the village oligarchy of patriarchs in the past, i.e., treating state plans as mere formalities.

> many times the plan became a show for the approval of the superior level only but in reality another plan was followed or work was performed without a plan (Nguyen Dang Kiew 1962).

That very "family economy" that the Party officials thought of as "supplementary" and unthreatening to the cooperative system provided a foundation for continuing traditional patterns. The patriarchs who controlled their own family economies could not fail to have self-interest in mind when dealing with the cooperative, and since they did control women in their family economies, they could hardly be expected to act in egalitarian ways toward them in their roles as cooperative managers.

Despite the Workers' Party's attempts, through land reform, through collectivization and through the training of cooperative managers, to revolutionize the Vietnamese village, many very traditional attitudes remained. Traditional attitudes about appropriate roles for women and youth, for example, often prevented technical cadre from carrying out their missions in the countryside. When they returned from technical agricultural training, young women were assigned to be kindergarten and elementary school teachers, suitable professions for their age and sex. Similarly, young men were given jobs in the village office or in the police section. Neither was allowed to teach villagers about new techniques or to carry out experiments with new crop varieties. Although collectives were required to have some women leaders, women were often not given opportunities for more responsibility or were appointed with little or no training (Nguyen Thi Kim Oanh 1962; Nguyen Van Thai 1962).

The basis of traditional attitudes in the patriarchal family and the traditional family economy was not fundamentally changed by the land reform, the collectivization movement or the campaign to train cooperative leadership. A leveling of income was possible as was a move forward in water control and productivity. Through these movements, also, a move for even distribution of power, especially among males, was accomplished. Ironically, it was the war with the United States in the next period which challenged traditional attitudes and allowed for more female leadership than was possible in the collectivization period. Women were then the dominant labor force, and they became leaders when men were sent to the front in the South.

Collectivized agriculture in North Vietnam fed the war effort by providing a stable quantity of rice and other staple foods at a time when many, perhaps 25%, of the male labor force was at war. Although certainly aware of the lack of growth of staple foods production in the collectives, the North Vietnamese leadership could not deal with the situation during the war. Instead, they relied on rice imports from China.

Only in the late '70s would the Vietnamese leadership be forced to come to terms with contradictions within the collectives. The Party would then turn over much more of the organization and control of agricultural production to the peasant patriarchal family heads. In the late '70s and early '80s, peasants were encouraged to raise their own buffalo and rent them to the collective and to cultivate any fallow collective land. With the Final Product Contract Quota System first introduced in 1979, the cooperative makes a contract for the delivery of final products with groups of households or with individual households. The households keep the rest for their needs and for private market trading. In 1988, steps were taken to further privatize production by extending contracts to 15 years and providing for most means of production to be sold to individual families (*Nhan Don* 1988: 21-25). The State has found it necessary to accommodate the patriarch and these household heads are firmly in control in the countryside.

The impression I had gained from reading the literature, that women's position in the Northern village is still very much a product of patriarchal control, was, unfortunately, verified by my interviews with women in the villages in 1987. Patrilocal residence and the mother-in-law system are still very much intact in the villages. There are sometimes women leaders who are politically very active in the countryside, but usually they are single women or widows. Married women I talked with in the 25-40 group had an average of four children and women in the over-40 group had an average of five children. They were very much tied down by family responsibilities and very much tied to their husbands' families. When I asked where they lived after marriage, they thought that was a very strange question. The response was: "With our in-laws, of course, where else would we live?"

Women in the cities, on the other hand, seemed to have fewer children, and patrilocal residence did not seem to be the rule. The situation of families in the cities has been financially very difficult in the current period because of rising costs for basic foodstuffs, but it is in the urban areas where women are moving past patriarchal family constraints.

The other area of hope for women in the countryside is that party officials seemed to be very aware of some of the contradictions of the present policy with regard to the "family economy." One male commune official called the situation a "vicious cycle" of poverty because families with more children are given larger plots to farm, and this encourages more population growth. Although people from outside Vietnam may see the present rural policies as a permanent shift in the direction of private property values, the Vietnamese officials may see it as an expedient necessity, until more development is possible.

CONCLUSION

Judith Stacey (1983) calls the alliance between socialists and peasant patriarchs in China a patriarchal-socialist rural order. In Vietnam, the rural economy might even be called socialist-patriarchy because of the greater importance of patriarchy and family economy throughout the socialist period. How much this rural system influences the rest of the political economy is another question. In this time of retrenchment from socialism in order to build production, it is easy to find examples of patriarchal domination in other areas, even in small scale industry (Stacey 1983).

Vietnamese literature seems to indicate patriarchal influence in the Party, such as problems of party officials promoting family members. Nevertheless, there is socialist control of large enterprises and socialist institutions are dominant in the cities. Socialist ideology controls the Party and the government, although patriarchal ideology is a very strong undercurrent. Patriarchal authority is dominant in agriculture and in many of the new "cooperative" small industries that are flourishing in Vietnam today. Industrial "cooperatives" are often really family run, for example.

Stacey contends that patriarchy reached its developmental limits as a revolutionary force in China during the 1950s and became a constraining context limiting socialist development later. This work on Vietnam does not see patriarchy in quite the same terms. Patriarchy is seen here as a dominant force in organizing production in the countryside and a force that was strong enough to defeat collective institutions that socialists were trying to direct. The reasons for that "defeat from below" are developed in this analysis. The greater amount of control of the labor force by the patriarch, as opposed to the collective, is an important factor in predetermining patriarchal ascendance. The fact that cooperative officials were able to use their position for their families' betterment through contracting out of cooperative work was another factor. And finally, since very intensive and careful labor input applied to small areas (i.e., family plots) was essential for the success of the new seed varieties, the nature of new technologies contributed still further to patriarchal ascendence.

In the future, technological change may again challenge the rural patriarchal economy in Vietnam in a different direction. With tractors and consolidation of plots and with people again leaving rural areas for jobs in the cities, socialists may get another chance to create effective collectivization and state farms in rural Vietnam. Meanwhile, the State has been forced to rely on the family economy, which is sustained by the labor of women and youths, to bring domestic production up to a reasonable level.

NOTES

1. There was not usually a village-level women's organization, as there had been during the land reform period in China, which could have identified wife beating as a "feudal" behavior. Instead, landlords and rich peasants with little land, but who had cruel reputations, were given stiff sentences and were sometimes misclassified.
2. Pham Cuong's study of the collectivization process in the village of Nam Hong is the most detailed and complete study of a revolutionary Vietnamese village. Pham Toan's study of the Ngo Xuyen Cooperative, appearing in *Vietnamese Studies*, is more easily available although less detailed.
3. Gerard Chaliand (1969) interviewed peasants in villages and hamlets in four provinces in 1967. A picture of ordinary life in the villages emerges from his interviews.
4. Pham Cuong later judged this concept of dividing up the husband's and wife's interests and property as a negative solution. It was clearly the radicalism of the party's positions during the land reform period which allowed for such a result.

REFERENCES

Canh Sinh. 1963. Correctly Understanding the Problem of Improving the Standard of Living. *Nhan Don*, August 6, Joint Publications Research Service (JPRS) 21435, October 12, 1963: 53.
Chaliand, Gerard. 1969. *The Peasants of North Vietnam*. Baltimore: Penguin Books.
Dao Thi Dinh. 1963. Training and Promoting Female Cadres. *Nhan Don*, November 6, JPRS 16891, March 6, 1963: 3.
Duang Quoc Cam. 1962. Correct Solution of the Relationships Between the Collective Economy and the Supplementary Economy or the Families of Individual members. *Hoc Tap* October, JPRS 16815: 71-79.
Fall, Bernard. 1964. *The Two Vietnams*. Revised edition. New York: Praeger.
Fforde, Adam J. 1982. Problems of Agricultural Development in North Vietnam. Ph. D. Dissertation, Clare College, Cambridge.
Gordon, Alec. 1981. North Vietnam's Collectivization Campaigns: Class Struggle, Production and the 'Middle Peasant' Problem. *Journal of Contemporary Asia* 11(1): 19-43.
Hewlet, Robert and John Markie. 1976. *Cooperative Farming as an Instrument of Rural Development*. FAO Land Reform Paper #2.
Hoc Tap (Hanoi). Our Acute Lessons in Building the Party in Bac Ninh Province. December 1962, JPRS #17666, February 15, 1963: 10.
Lam Quang Huyen. 1961. Economic Activities of a Cooperative Household. *Nghien Coo Kinh Te*. August, JPRS #15066: 9.
Moise, Edwin E. 1976 Land Reform and Land Reform Errors in North Vietnam. *Pacific Affairs* 49 (Spring): 72-83.
Nguyen Dang Kieu. 1962. A Uniform Financial and Production Plan for Agricultural Cooperatives. *Nghien Cuu Kinh Te* (August), JRPS #16633, December 11, 1962.
Nguyen Thi Kim Oanh. 1962. Agricultural Technician Rears Children. *Tien Phong*, May 20, JPRS #14666, July 9, 1962.
Nguyen Yem. 1971. The Thanh Oai District. *Vietnamese Studies* 27. Hanoi: Foreign Languages Publishing House.

Peasant Patriarchy and the Subversion of the Collective in Vietnam   197

Nhan Don. 1988. New Regulations on Agricultural Cooperatives, Production Cooperatives. November 30, 1988, JPRS #SEA-89-010, March 2, 1989: 22-25.

Pham Cuong. 1976. *Revolution in the Village of Nam Hong (1945-1975)*. Hanoi: Foreign Languages Publishing House.

Pham Toan. The Ngo Xuyen Cooperative. *Vietnamese Studies* 27: 209-249.

Stacey, Judith. 1983. *Patriarchy and Socialist Revolution in China*. Berkeley: University of California Press.

White, Christine Pelzer. 1981. Agrarian Reform and National Liberation in the Vietnamese Revolution. Ph.D. Dissertation, Cornell University.

_____. 1984. Family, Class and Theory in the Practice of Marxism: The Case of Vietnam. Institute for Development Studies Conference, No. 133, University of Sussex.

Wickerman, Andrew. 1982. Collectivization in the Democratic Republic of Vietnam: A Comment. *Journal of Contemporary Asia* 12, 4: 484-496.

Wiegersma, Nancy. 1988. *Vietnam: Peasant Land, Peasant Revolution: Patriarchy and Collectivity in the Rural Economy*. New York: St. Martin's Press.

[26]

Pergamon

World Development, Vol. 22, No. 10, pp. 1455–1478, 1994
Copyright © 1994 Elsevier Science Ltd
Printed in Great Britain. All rights reserved
0305–750X/94 $7.00 + 0.00

0305–750X(94)00058–1

Gender and Command Over Property: A Critical Gap in Economic Analysis and Policy in South Asia

BINA AGARWAL*
Institute of Economic Growth, Delhi, India

Summary. — This paper focuses on a much neglected issue: the links between gender inequities and command over property. It outlines why in rural South Asia, where arable land is the most important form of property, any significant improvement in women's economic and social situation is crucially tied to their having independent land rights. Better employment opportunities can complement but not substitute for land. But despite progressive legislation few South Asian women own land; even fewer effectively control any. Why? A complex range of factors — social, administrative, and ideological — are found to underlie the persistent gap between women's legal rights and their actual ownership of land, and between ownership and control. The necessity of collective action by women for overcoming these obstacles and the aspects needing a specific focus for policy and action are also discussed.

1. INTRODUCTION

We want [arable] land, all the rest is humbug.
(Landless women in South India answering a query whether they wanted better houses)[1]

Please go and ask the *sarkar* [government] why when it distributes land we don't get a title. Are we not peasants? If my husband throws me out, what is my security?
(Message conveyed by poor peasant women to the West Bengal government in 1979 through their women representatives on the village council)[2]

Economic analysis and policies concerning women have long been preoccupied with employment, to the neglect of a crucial determinant of women's situation, namely the gender gap in command over property. This is especially (but not only) true in analysis relating to South Asia.

It is argued here that the gender gap in the ownership and control of property is the single most critical contributor to the gender gap in economic well-being, social status and empowerment. In primarily rural economies such as those of South Asia the most important property in question is arable land.

The discussion below, divided into six sections, focuses on the following dimensions of gender and rights in arable land. Section 2, traces the considerable neglect of this issue by policy makers, activists and

academics in South Asia. Section 3 examines some conceptual links between property and gender, while section 4 elaborates why it is important for rural women to have independent rights in land. Section 5 looks at gender relations historically in those South Asian communities in which women traditionally enjoyed rights in land. Section 6 identifies the obstacles women face in realizing effective land rights in most parts of South Asia today, and illustrates how women's command over economic resources is crucially mediated by noneconomic factors. Finally, section 7 highlights some aspects of the interventions needed for change.

---

*This paper draws substantially on the author's forthcoming book: *A Field of One's Own: Gender and Land Rights in South Asia* (Cambridge: Cambridge University Press), especially Chapter 1. A version of the paper was presented at the Conference on "Feminist Perspectives in Economic Theory," Dept. of Economics, University of Amsterdam, June 1993. I am grateful especially to the following persons for comments on the material presented here: Janet Seiz, Amartya Sen, Michael Lipton, Nancy Folbre, Lourdes Beneria, Gillian Hart, Geoffrey Hawthorn, Raghav Gaiha, and the two anonymous reviewers of the journal.

Final revision accepted: May 14, 1994.

2. THE BACKDROP

The assumption that the household is a unit of congruent interests and preferences, among whose members the benefits of available resources are shared equitably, irrespective of gender, has been a long-standing one in economic theory and development policy; and one which, until recently, has been shared widely by governmental and nongovernmental groups, institutions and individuals. The process by which this assumption of a unitary household, and more generally of the gender-neutrality of development, has come to be challenged over the past 20 years is a complex one. It has been a process of negotiation and struggle involving multiple actors — academics and researchers, women's activist groups, government policy makers, and international agencies.[3] Today, as a result, the idea that development is not gender-neutral has gained fairly wide acceptance in development enquiry and policy, even though there is no consensus on the causes of the gender gap or on how it could be bridged.

Typically, policy directives and programs treat gender as an *additive* category, to be added onto existing ones, with women as a special target group, rather than gender as a lens through which the approach to development should itself be reexamined. The programs are essentially couched in welfare terms, under the umbrella of the "basic needs" approach that gained currency in development thinking in the mid-1970s. This approach emphasizes the provision of "basic" goods and services (such as food, health care, literacy) to the economically disadvantaged, without seriously questioning the existing distribution of productive resources and political power, or the social (gender/class/caste) division of labor.

In this scenario, the issue of women's land rights has, until recently, received little attention in policy formulation in South Asia. For instance, in India, it is only in the Sixth Five Year Plan (1980–85) that we see the first limited recognition by the government of women's need for land (and only in the context of poverty): the Plan stated that the government would "endeavor" to give joint titles to spouses in programs involving the distribution of land and homesites to the landless. In the Seventh Five Year Plan (1985–90) the directive on joint titles was not restated, while the recently formulated Eighth Plan (1992–97) makes only two specific points in relation to women and agricultural land: one, it recognizes that "one of the basic requirements for improving the status of women" is to change inheritance laws so that women get an equal share in parental property, but it lays down no directives to ensure that this is implemented. Two, it asks state governments to allot 40% of surplus land (i.e. land acquired by the government from households owning more than a specified maximum) to women alone, and to allot the rest jointly in the names of both spouses (GOI, 1992a, p. 34).[4] This

sounds good in principle; in practice only about 1.04 mha of surplus land remains to be distributed, constituting a mere 0.56% of the country's arable land (GOI, 1992a, p. 34).

The situation in other South Asian countries is even more discouraging. Nepal's Eighth Five Year Plan (1992–97) Summary highlights women's employment and the need to encourage women's participation in various activities, but contains no reference to their need for land. Bangladesh's Fourth Five Year Plan (1990–95) again emphasizes issues such as female employment, literacy, health, nutrition and credit, but makes no mention of land for women (Government of Bangladesh, 1990). Similarly, although Pakistan's *Report of the Working Group on Women's Development Program for the Sixth Plan (1983–88)* recommended that all land distributed under the land reform program should be jointly registered in the names of both spouses, this recommendation was not incorporated into the formal plan document. In addition, Pakistan's Eighth Five Year Plan (1993–98) Approach Paper promises women preferential treatment in education and employment, but does not mention property rights; it also casts gender relations in traditional terms, with the State explicitly undertaking "to protect the marriage, the family, the mother and the child . . ." and to forgo any approaches "which (could) antagonize male members of the community . . ." (Government of Pakistan, 1991, pp. 22, 24).

In other words, the issue of women and land, even today, remains one of marginal, not central concern to development policy in South Asia. What is especially striking is the disjunction between public policy formulation and the rights encased in personal law. The idea of women having independent property rights (including rights in land) was accepted by most South Asian countries in laws governing the inheritance of personal property when gender-progressive legislation was passed in the 1950s[5] (and even earlier in traditionally bilateral and matrilineal communities).[6] But such legislation remained confined to inheritance laws on private land; in policies governing the distribution of public land the issue of women's land rights was not discussed till the 1980s. Hence the redistributive land reform programs of the 1950s and 1960s in India, Pakistan and Sri Lanka, and of the 1970s in Bangladesh, continued to be modeled on the notion of a unitary male-headed household, with titles being granted only to men, except in households without adult men where women (typically widows) were clearly the heads. This bias was replicated again in resettlement schemes, even in Sri Lanka where there has been a long-standing practice of bilateral and matrilineal inheritance.

The possible factors underlying this disjunction between government policy in relation to public land distribution and the legal rights in private land granted to women under inheritance laws, cannot be traced here. But among the factors underlying the reluctance to change public policy and the tardy implementation of any changes would certainly be the following: the (noted) assumption of gender-congruence in intra-family interests; the dominant view that men are the breadwinners and women the dependents; strong male vested interests in all land, including public land; gaps between the central government's policy directives and the shape these are given at the state/provincial level; and the belief that land distribution to women will further reduce farm size and fragment cultivated holdings, thereby reducing agricultural productivity. The farm size and fragmentation arguments (discussed in section 4) have also been used in many regions of India to undercut post-Independence gender-progressive personal laws, by retaining age-old customary laws that disadvantage women in relation to agricultural land.

An ambiguity toward this issue is also found among those who have otherwise been strong advocates of redistributive land reform, namely Marxist political parties and left-wing nongovernmental organizations, but who still see class issues as primary and gender concerns as divisive and distracting.[7] At the same time, most women's organizations (whatever their political persuasion), with some recent exceptions, have been preoccupied with employment and nonland-related income-generating schemes as the primary means of improving women's economic status and welfare, paying little attention to property rights.[8]

This neglect of women's land-related concerns by both governmental and nongovernmental institutions mirrors a parallel gap within academic scholarship, where the relationship between women and property has remained virtually unattended and little theorized. For instance, a vast body of economic development and political science studies document a strong interdependence between the rural household's possession of agricultural land and its relative economic, social and political position. But characteristically these studies focus on the household as the unit of analysis, ignoring the intrahousehold gender dimension. Again, a substantial body of sociological and anthropological literature on South Asia, especially that relating to kinship and marriage, helps us construct a picture of some aspects of women's position; but even in the best of ethnographies up to the 1970s, the analysis is typically ungendered. Women appear mainly as objects of study and exchange, not as subjects; their presence is registered, seldom their perspective; and gender relations are depicted as essentially unproblematic. Often implicit in these descriptions is the assumption that underlying women's social subordination are the cultural values of the community to which they belong; and the possible material basis of women's subordination, or the dialectical link between their material context and gender ideology is

seldom recognized. Over the past decade and a half, however, a body of work has emerged which does incorporate gender analysis in diverse ways. This includes some gender-sensitive ethnographies which fill critical gaps (mainly on women's work and roles), and a spectrum of studies that could loosely be termed "women and development" literature. This literature examines gender biases in economic development, often giving primacy to women's economic position as a significant indicator of gender inequality and sometimes also as a causal factor underlying noneconomic dimensions of that inequality. But the measure of women's economic status is still typically employment and labor force participation, not property rights.[9]

In my giving centrality to the gender gap in command over landed property, a question that assumes significance is: Why do women in South Asia need independent rights in land? An answer to this question is attempted in section 4 below. Before "making the case," however, it is useful to consider some of the wider conceptual links between gender and property, why a focus on *landed* property is important, and what I mean by "rights" in land.

3. GENDER, PROPERTY AND LAND: SOME CONCEPTUAL LINKS

Consider first the relationship between gender and property. In the present discussion, five interrelated issues need particular focus: gender relations and a household's property status; gender relations and women's property status; the distinction between ownership and control of property; the distinctiveness of land as property; and what is meant by rights in land. The first three issues are discussed in the subsection below, and the last two in separate subsections.

(a) *Household property and women's property*

The links between gender subordination and property need to be sought in not only the distribution of property between households but also in its distribution between men and women, in not only who owns the property but also who controls it, and in relation not only to private property but also to communal property. Further, gender equality in legal rights to own property does not guarantee gender equality in actual ownership, nor does ownership guarantee control. The distinctions between law and practice and between ownership and control are especially critical: most South Asian women face significant barriers to realizing their legal claims in landed property, as well as to exercising control over any land they do get.

This formulation departs significantly from standard Marxist analysis, particularly from Engels's still-influential, though much-criticized, *The Origin of the Family,*

Private Property and the State, where intrafamily gender relations are seen as structured primarily by two overlapping economic factors: the property status of the households to which the women belong, and women's participation in wage labor. Engels argued that in capitalist societies, gender relations would be hierarchical among the property-owning families of the bourgeoisie where women did not go out to work and were economically dependent on men, and egalitarian in propertyless proletarian families where women were in the labor force. The ultimate restoration of women to their rightful status, in his view, required the total abolition of private property (i.e. a move to socialism), the socialization of housework and childcare, and the full participation of women in the labor force. In the context of industrializing Europe, Engels (1972, pp. 137–138) argued: "the first premise for the emancipation of women is the reintroduction of the entire female sex into public industry."[10]

In his analysis, therefore, the presumed equality of gender relations in a working class family rested on *both* husband and wife being propertyless and in the labor force, and the inequalities in the bourgeois family rested on men being propertied and women being both propertyless and outside the labor force. This underlying emphasis on the *relational* aspect of gender is clearly important. So is the emphasis on women's economic dependency as a critical constituent of the material basis of gender oppression. By advocating the abolition of all private property as the solution, however, Engels bypassed the issue of women's property rights altogether, and left open the question: what would be the impact on gender relations in propertied households if women too were propertied as individuals? Entry into the labor force is not the only way to reduce economic dependence; independent rights in property would be another, and possibly the more effective way.

Engels's emphasis on women's entry into the labor force as a necessary condition for their emancipation has been enormously influential in shaping the thinking of left-wing political parties and nonparty groups, including left-wing women's groups in South Asia.[11] They too give centrality to women's employment, but the necessary accompaniments emphasized by Engels, namely the abolition of private property in male hands and the socialization of housework and childcare, have largely been neglected, as has the question of women's property rights.

A critical additional point (missed in Engels's analysis and associated discussions) is that of property control. Property advantage stems not only from ownership, but also from effective control over it. In societies which underwent socialist revolutions, while private property ownership was legally abolished, control over wealth-generating property remained mainly with men; any positive effects on gender relations that could have stemmed from the change in ownership, if accompanied by gender-egalitarian mechanisms of control, thus went unrealized.[12] Indeed in most societies today it is men as a gen-

der (even if not all men as individuals) who largely control wealth-generating property, whether or not it is privately owned, including as managers in large corporations. Even property that is under State, community, or clan ownership remains effectively under the managerial control of selected men through their dominance in both traditional and modern institutions: caste or clan councils, village elected bodies, State bureaucracies at all levels,[13] and so on. Moreover, in most countries, men as a gender exercise dominance over the instruments through which their existing advantages of property ownership and control are perpetuated, such as the institutions that enact and implement laws,[14] the mechanisms of recruitment into bodies which exercise control over (private or public) property, the institutions which play an important role in shaping gender ideology, and so on.

A second issue concerning the relationship between gender and property is: how do we define a woman's class? Marxist analysis, for instance, implicitly assumes that women belong to the class of their husbands or fathers. Hence women of propertied "bourgeois" households are part of the bourgeoisie and those of proletarian households are counted as proletarian. As is now well-recognized, however, there are at least two problems with this characterization. (i) A woman's class position defined through that of a man is more open to change than that of a man: a well-placed marriage can raise it, divorce or widowhood can lower it. (ii) To the extent that women, even of propertied households, do not own property themselves, it is difficult to characterize their class position;[15] some have even argued that women constitute a class in themselves.[16] In fact, neither deriving women's class from the property status of men nor deriving it from their own propertyless status appears adequate, although both positions reflect a dimension of reality. Women of rich households do gain economically and socially from their husbands' class positions. But women also share common concerns which cut across derived class privilege (or deprivation), such as vulnerability to domestic violence; responsibility for housework and childcare (even if not all women perform such labor themselves — the more affluent ones can hire helpers); gender inequalities in legal rights; and the risk of poverty with marital breakdown. This ambiguity in women's class position impinges with critical force on the possibilities of collective action among women. On the one hand, class differences among women, derived through men, can be divisive. On the other hand, the noted commonalities between women's situations and the relatively vicarious character of their class privilege make class distinctions between them less sharp than those between men, and could provide the basis for collective action on several counts (as discussed in section 7).[17]

A third aspect of the relationship between gender and property concerns the links between gender ideology and property. For instance:

— Gender ideologies can obstruct women from getting property rights. Assumptions about women's needs, roles, capabilities, and so on, impinge on the framing and implementation of public policies and property laws. Again, ideas about gender underlie practices such as female seclusion, which restrict women's ability to exercise their existing property claims and to successfully challenge persisting gender inequalities in law, policy, and practice in relation to such claims. Hence ideological struggles are integrally linked to women's struggles over property rights.

— Those who own and/or control wealth-generating property can directly or indirectly control the principal institutions that shape ideology, such as educational and religious establishments and the media (defined broadly to include newspapers, TV, radio, film, theater, as well as literature and the arts). These can shape views in either gender-progressive or gender-retrogressive directions.

— The impact of gender ideologies can vary by a household's property status (given the household's religion, caste, etc). For instance, both propertied and propertyless households may espouse the ideology of female seclusion, but the former group would be in a better economic position to enforce its practice, and in so doing reinforce its emulation by unpropertied households as a mark of social status. At the same time, gender ideologies and associated practices are not derived from property differences alone, nor can they be seen in purely economic-functional terms. They would tend rather to change in interaction with economic shifts.

A fourth issue that arises in relation to women and property is the possible links of women's property rights with control over women's sexuality, marriage practices, and kinship structures. For instance, would women with independent property rights be subject to greater or lesser familial control over their sexual freedom than those without them? It would also be important to examine whether societies which historically recognized women's inheritance rights in immovable property, in order to keep the property intact and within their purview, tended to control women's choice of marriage partners and postmarital residence (as discussed later).

(b) *The significance of land as property*

Thus far our discussion has revolved around property in general, but not all forms of property are equally significant in all contexts, nor equally coveted. In the agrarian economies of South Asia, for instance, arable land is the most valued form of property, for its economic, political and symbolic significance. It is a productive, wealth-creating, and livelihood-sustaining asset. Traditionally it has been the basis of political power and social status. For many, it provides a sense of identity and rootedness within the village; and often in people's minds land has a

durability and permanence which no other asset possesses.[18] Although other forms of property such as cash, jewellery, cattle, and even domestic goods (the usual content of, say, dowry in rural India and Nepal) could in principle be converted into land, in practice rural land markets are often. constrained, and land is not always readily available for sale (Rosenzweig and Wolpin, 1985; Wallace, Kempler and Wilson-Moore, 1988). In any case, ancestral land often has a symbolic meaning (Selvaduri, 1976) or ritual importance (Krause, 1982) which purchased land does not. Hence in land disputes people may end up spending more to retain a disputed ancestral plot than its market value would justify (see examples in Selvaduri, 1976). In addition inheritance systems usually have different rules for the devolution of ancestral and self-acquired land. In other words, both the form that property takes and its origin are important in defining its significance and the associated possibility of conflict over it.

(c) *What do we mean by rights in land?*

Rights are defined here as claims that are legally and socially recognized and enforceable by an external legitimized authority, be it a village-level institution or some higher level judicial or executive body of the State.[19] Rights in land can be in the form of ownership or of usufruct (that is rights of use), associated with differing degrees of freedom to lease out, mortgage, bequeath, or sell. Land rights can stem from inheritance on an individual or joint family basis, from community membership (e.g., where a clan or village community owns or controls land and members have use rights to it), from transfers by the State, or from tenancy arrangements, purchase, and so on. Rights in land also have a temporal and sometimes locational dimension: they may be hereditary, or accrue only for a person's lifetime, or for a lesser period; and they may be conditional on the person residing where the land is located, e.g., in the village.

As distinct from rights in land, we could speak of "access" to land, a term used very loosely in the development literature. Access can be through rights of ownership and use, but it can also be through informal concessions granted by individuals to kin or friends. For instance, a man may allow his sister to use a plot of his owned land out of goodwill, but she cannot claim it as a right and call for its enforcement. There are thus several ways by which a woman may, in theory, have access to land, but of these, having "rights" provides a measure of security that the others typically do not.

In relation to land rights, four additional distinctions are relevant. First we need to distinguish between the *legal* recognition of a claim and it *social* recognition, and between recognition and enforcement. A woman may have the legal right to inherit property, but this may remain merely a right on paper if the law is not enforced, or if the claim is not socially recognized as legitimate and family members exert pressure on the woman to forfeit her share in favor, say of her brothers. Second, as noted earlier, is the distinction between the ownership of land and its effective control. (Control itself can have multiple meanings, such as the ability to decide how the land is used, how its produce is disposed of, whether it can be leased out, mortgaged, bequeathed, sold, and so on.) It is sometimes assumed incorrectly that legal ownership carries with it the right of control in all these senses. In fact, legal ownership may be accompanied by legal restrictions on disposal: for instance, among the Jaffna Tamils in Sri Lanka, under the *Thesawalami* legal code a married woman needs her husband's consent to alienate land which she legally owns. Or there may be no legal restriction on disposal but social constraints on doing so: for instance, the sale of ancestral land to strangers is often socially disapproved by kin and the village community. Third, it is important to distinguish between ownership and use rights vested in individuals and those vested in a group; and fourth, one might distinguish between rights conferred via inheritance and those conferred by State transfers of land.

Given the different forms (ownership and usufruct, as vested in individuals or in groups, etc.) that land rights can take, and given the variation in the organization of production and distribution that can accompany them, it is not possible to specify with any precision for all contexts, what may be the most desirable form for women's land rights to take. But a broad specification can be attempted here. When speaking of the importance of women having "independent rights in land" I mean *effective* rights, that is rights not just in law but in practice. When referring to legal rights alone I will say so explicitly. By "independent rights" I mean rights independent of male ownership or control (that is excluding joint titles with men). Independent rights would be preferable to joint titles with husbands for several reasons: first, with joint titles it could prove difficult for women to gain control over their share in case of marital breakup. Second, women would also be less in a position to escape from a situation of marital conflict or violence: as some Bihari village women said to me, "for retaining the land we would be tied to the man, even if he beat us." Third, wives may have different land use priorities from husbands which they would be in a better position to act upon with independent land rights. Fourth, women with independent rights would be better placed to control the produce. Fifth, with joint titles the question of how the land would be inherited could prove a contentious one. This is not to deny that joint titles with husbands would be better for women than having no land rights at all; but many of the advantages of having land would not accrue to women by joint titles alone.

Here the distinctions mentioned earlier between rights vested in individuals and those vested in groups, and between privatized land transfers via inheritance and land transfers by the State, need elaboration. In relation to privatized inheritable landed property, by effective land rights for women today I mean inheritance as individuals linked with full rights of control over land use (*viz.* sale, bequest, etc.) and over the disposal of its produce. Where land transfers by the State to women are involved, effective land rights could either mean individual titles conferring ownership and control rights exactly as with private land; or they could take the form of land transfers to groups of women (say of landless households) who would hold it in joint ownership or long lease, having full control over its use and over the disposal of its produce, but excluding the right to sell or bequeath it. Although many of the potential advantages of having rights in land would accrue to women whichever of the above forms those rights take, some advantages are specific to the form. For instance, individually owned land can be mortgaged or sold, which could be advantageous in distress circumstances. But group rights could protect the land say from scheming relatives and enable its more productive use through group investment (as elaborated in section 7). Where such specific issues are involved, the discussion will seek to clarify what form of rights I mean.

With the decline in communal land in South Asia, access to privatized land acquires a critical importance today which it did not have even a century ago. In India, for instance, by a rough estimate about 85.6% of arable land is likely to be in private hands.[20] Hence the importance of women's land rights spelt out in the next section, while couched in general terms, is especially focused on rights in privatized land, with two caveats: one, given the importance of communal land (e.g., village commons) to the rural poor, and especially to poor women (who depend on it for gathering firewood, fodder and a range of items basic for survival; see Agarwal, 1992), there is a strong case for protecting the communal nature of any land which still exists in that form. Two, it is necessary to explore the possibilities of new institutional arrangements for jointly owned/controlled land holdings by groups of women, rather than by groups of households (as is the usual focus). Joint ownership need not, however, imply joint cultivation.

In *legal* terms women's property rights in South Asia are governed by personal laws which vary a good deal by religion and region, forming a complex mosaic (as detailed in Agarwal, forthcoming). Most of these legal systems give women considerable inheritance rights; and in traditionally patrilineal groups much greater rights than they enjoyed by custom, as a result of legal reform, especially after 1950. For instance, in India, the Hindu Succession Act (HSA) of 1956 gave the daughters, widow and mother of a Hindu man dying intestate equal inheritance rights to sons in his property. These were rights of absolute ownership and not just a limited interest for life (as had been the case earlier). In Pakistan, the West Pakistan Muslim Personal Law (Shariat) Application Act of 1962 extended the Shariat as the basis of personal law to the whole of West Pakistan, except to the "Tribal Areas" in the North-West Frontier Province.

This Act abrogated custom (which typically gave women few rights) as the basis of law and legally entitled Muslim women to inherit agricultural property (again as full owners and not just as a life interest) as prescribed by the Shariat. For Muslim women in Bangladesh again, the Shariat applies also to agricultural land. In Nepal the *Maluki Ain* Code of 1854 continues to be valid, but with later amendments which have made it somewhat less gender unequal than the original Code. In Sri Lanka, even traditionally (as noted) virtually all communities practiced bilateral or matrilineal inheritance laws, and modifications in the postcolonial period have been in the direction of furthering gender equality.

In virtually all the legal systems, however, some gender inequalities remain. For instance, some systems prescribe lower shares for women (Islamic law, e.g., prescribes a daughter's share as half that of a son); some others restrict the conditions under which women can inherit and retain that inheritance (e.g., the *Maluki Ain* in Nepal only allows daughters to inherit if they are unmarried and over 35 years of age, and they have to forfeit their claims if they subsequently marry). Yet other legal systems restrict women's freedom to dispose of their inherited land (as noted for the Jaffna Tamils in Sri Lanka). Inequalities also stem from gender discriminatory land reform enactments which affect women's rights specifically in agricultural land. In India, for instance, these inequalities are especially of two kinds. First, agricultural land subject to tenancy rights is exempt from the scope of the HSA of 1956, and is governed by the rules of devolution specified in state-level enactments. In a number of states, mostly in northwest India, succession rules relating to such land date back to customs prevailing before the HSA was passed, and which give priority to male agnatic heirs. Moreover, in some states (such as Uttar Pradesh) the definition of tenancy is very broad and effectively includes all agricultural land. Second, in the fixation of ceilings under the land reform laws, there are at least two serious anomalies: one, in many states, additional land is allowed to be retained by the cultivating household on account of adult sons but not on account of adult daughters. Two, in most states, the holdings of both spouses are aggregated in assessing "family" land, and there is considerable arbitrariness in deciding whose portion will be declared surplus and forfeited. As a result, there have been several cases where the wife's land (and not many women have some) was declared surplus and taken over by the government, while the husband's land remained untouched (Saradamoni, 1983).

Even more critical than the persisting legal inequities is the gap between women's legal rights in land and its actual ownership, and between ownership and effective control. Although economic surveys typically do not collect gender-disaggregated data, village studies (especially anthropological accounts) indicate that in most parts of South Asia women do not own land and even fewer are able to exercise effective control over it.[21] These gaps are especially apparent in communities which customarily practiced patrilineal inheritance, that is where ancestral property passed through the male line. Communities traditionally practicing matrilineal or bilateral inheritance were few and confined to northeast India, parts of south India, and to Sri Lanka. Before examining the nature of gender relations in the latter communities, consider below why having independent rights in land is important for women's well-being and overall empowerment.

4. WHY DO WOMEN NEED INDEPENDENT RIGHTS IN LAND?

The importance of South Asian women having independent rights in arable land rests on several interconnected arguments which can be grouped into four broad categories: welfare, efficiency, equality, and empowerment.[22]

(a) *The welfare argument*

To begin with, especially among poor households, rights in land could reduce women's own and, more generally, the household's risk of poverty and destitution. The reasons for this stem partly from the general positive effect of giving women access to economic resources independently of men; and partly from the specific advantages associated with rights in land resources.

Consider first the general case. There is considerable evidence of intrahousehold gender inequalities in the sharing of benefits from household resources. For instance, in large parts of South Asia a systematic bias is noted against women and female children in intrahousehold access to resources for basic necessities such as health care, and in some degree, food.[23] This is revealed in gender differences in one or more of the following indicators: malnourishment, morbidity, mortality, hospital admissions, health expenditures, and female-adverse sex ratios (females per 100 males), although the evidence on food allocation *per se* is less conclusive.[24] The extent of this anti-female bias varies regionally, but it exists in some degree almost everywhere, particularly as revealed by the sex ratios which are female-adverse across all of South Asia, except Kerala in southwest India. The bias is strongest in northwest India, Pakistan and Bangladesh,[25] and much less stark in south India and Sri Lanka, where the sex ratios, although still female-adverse, are closer to parity.

Further, notable differences have been found in how men and women of poor rural households spend the incomes under their control: women typically spend almost all their incomes on the family's basic needs; men usually spend a significant part on their personal needs (tobacco, liquor, etc.).[26] A corollary to these gender differentials in spending patterns are research findings which suggest that children's nutritional status tend to be much more positively linked to the mother's earnings than the father's (Kumar, 1978).

In other words, the risk of poverty and the physical well-being of a woman and her children could depend significantly on whether or not she has direct access to income and productive assets such as land, and not just access mediated through her husband or other male family members. For female-headed households with no adult male support, the link between direct access to economic resources and physical well-being needs no emphasis. Such households constitute an estimated (and by no means negligible) 19–20% of all households in India and Bangladesh.[27]

Moreover, as noted earlier, a woman's economic status cannot be judged adequately by the economic status of her family. Even women from rich parental or marital homes can be economically vulnerable without independent resources in case of marital breakdown or widowhood. In parts of western and northwestern India, not uncommonly, women — divorced, deserted or widowed — can be found working as agricultural laborers on the farms of their well-off brothers or brothers-in-law (Omvedt, 1981, and personal observation). Elsewhere, in east India and Bangladesh, there are many cases of women, married into prosperous households, being left destitute and forced to seek wage work or even to beg after widowhood (Cain, Khanam and Nahar, 1979, and Vina Mazumdar, personal communication). "This fact," as Omvedt (1981, p. 21) observes, "perhaps . . . more than any other, shows the essential propertylessness of women *as women*."

Within this general argument for women's independent access to economic resources, the case for their having effective rights in *land* is especially strong. Consider, for a start, the relationship between poverty and a household's access to land. In India, in 1982 an estimated 89% of rural households owned some land (GOI, 1987, p. 9), and an estimated 74% operated some (GOI, 1986, p. 12).[28] In Bangladesh, in 1978, the percentage of rural households owning some land (arable or homestead) was 89, and those owning arable land was 67 (Jannuzi and Peach, 1980, p. 101). In Sri Lanka, in 1982, 89% of agricultural operators owned some land (including home gardens) (Government of Sri Lanka, 1984, p. 17). Although, given high land concentrations, the majority of these households across South Asia only have marginal plots, they face a significantly lower risk of absolute poverty than landless households: a negative relationship between the incidence of absolute poverty and land access (owned or operated) is noted in several studies.[29] Land access helps in both direct and indirect ways. The direct advantages stem from production possibilities, such as of growing crops, fodder, trees, or a vegetable garden (unless of course the land is of very poor quality), or keeping livestock, practicing sericulture, and so on. In addition, land provides indirect benefits, such as increasing access to credit, helping agricultural labor maintain its reserve price and even push up the aggregate real wage rate,[30] and, where the land is owned, serving as a mortgageable or saleable asset during a crisis.

Moreoever, for widows and the elderly, ownership of land and other wealth strengthens the support they receive from relatives, by increasing their bargaining power within the household (Caldwell, Reddy and Caldwell, 1988; Sharma and Dak, 1987). As an old man put it: "without property, children do not look after their parents well" (Caldwell, Reddy and Caldwell, 1988, p. 191).

However, given the noted biases, in the intrafamily distribution of benefits from household resources, exclusively *male* rights in land, which would render the *household* less susceptible to poverty by some average measure, will not automatically benefit all its members. Moreover, on grounds of both women's and children's welfare, there is a strong case for supporting women's effective rights in private or public land, independently of men. Although such rights are especially important as a poverty-alleviation measure for women in poor rural households, they are also relevant for those of better-off households, given the risk of poverty following marital breakdown faced by all rural women.

It needs emphasis here that the welfare case for women's land rights stands even if the plot is too small to be economically viable on its own. Indeed those opposing female inheritance in land often emphasize that women might end up inheriting economically nonviable holdings. In my view, this could be a problem where cultivation is seen as the sole basis of subsistence, but not where land-based production is one element (although a critical one) in a diversified livelihood system. For instance, a plot of land which does not produce enough grain to economically sustain a person or family could still support trees or provide grass for cattle. Moreover, although forced collective farming is likely to be inefficient, cases of people voluntarily cooperating to undertake land-based joint productive activities also exist: there are several successful instances of small groups of women doing so in India and Bangladesh (as discussed in section 7).

Of course, as the countries of South Asia develop and the industrial and service sectors expand, arable land would become less significant as a source of livelihood and a form of property. But today the majority of South Asia's population still depends on agriculture as a primary or an important supplementary source of sustenance. To this may be added the dependence on village common land and forests for fuel and other basic necessities, even among villagers whose income derives mainly from the nonfarm sector. In none of the South Asian countries do projections predict a rapid absorption of labor (especially female labor) into urban industry in the foreseeable future. Furthermore, since it is predominantly male workers who migrate from rural to urban areas (Bardhan, 1977), women's dependence on the rural/agricultural sector remains greater than men's. Although the rural nonfarm sector holds potential, its record in providing viable livelihoods has been mixed: there are some regions and segments of high returns/high wages (such as the Indian Punjab), but many others that are characterized by low returns and low wages.[31] In particular, women's nonfarm earnings (to the limited extent this has been studied) appear characteristically low and uncertain.[32] Hence, although there is clearly a need to strengthen women's earning opportunities in the nonfarm sector, especially by ensuring their entry into its more productive segments, for most women nonfarm livelihoods cannot substitute for land-based livelihoods, although they could supplement them. It is also noteworthy that those who do well in the rural nonfarm sector through self-employment are usually those who have land as an asset base (Islam, 1986; Chadha, 1992). Effectively, therefore, land will continue to occupy a place of primacy in South Asian livelihoods in general and female livelihoods in particular, for quite some time.

In addition, with sectoral shifts, although the importance of land as property may decline, income-generating property *per se* is likely to remain a significant mediator of social relations and an important determinant of social status and political power. Who owns and/or controls property would therefore still be a relevant consideration; and many of the arguments in favor of gender equality in ownership and control of landed property could also be extended to other forms of property.

(b) *The efficiency argument*

Tracing the likely efficiency effects of women having land rights is much more difficult than tracing the potential welfare effects. Consider the issue situationally.

In several contexts, women are operating as household heads with primary and sometimes sole responsibility for organizing cultivation and ensuring family subsistence, but without titles to the land they are cultivating. For instance, due to long-term male outmigration many women are serving as *de facto* household heads, especially but not only in the hill regions of the subcontinent. There are widows cultivating plots given to them from joint family estates (as part of their inheritance claims to their deceased husbands' lands), but the plots are still in their in-laws' names. Again, tribal women cultivating communal land rarely get titles to their fields, which are typically given out by the State only to male farmers. Titling women in these circumstances and providing them infrastructural support could increase output by increasing their access to credit,[33] and to technology and information on productivity-increasing agricultural practices and inputs (in the dissemination of which both a class and a gender bias prevails).[34] Land titles could both motivate and enable women to adopt improved agricultural technology and practices and hence increase overall production. This is not dissimilar to the argument made in land reform discourse favoring security of tenure for tenants to encourage technical investments in land by increasing the tenants' incentive and capacity to invest.

A more general issue, however, is the likely efficiency effect of women inheriting land. Female inheritance is often opposed in South Asia on the grounds that it will further reduce farm size, increase land fragmentation, and thus reduce output. Is this fear valid? The efficiency implications of female inheritance can be separated analytically into three: a farm-size effect (the average size of ownership holdings will be lower than if only men inherit); a land-fragmentation effect (fragmentation could increase insofar as the land is parcelled out to heirs, say according to land quality)[35]; and a gender-transfer effect (some of the land which would have gone only to men would now go to women).

The concerns surrounding the farm-size effect are similar to those arising from redistributive land reform, namely the effect of redistributing land from big to small farmers on farm output, on the adoption of new technology, and on marketed surplus. Those opposing redistribution argue that the impact would be negative on all three counts. Existing evidence from South Asia, however, indicates otherwise. For instance, small-sized farms typically have a higher value of annual output per unit cultivated area than large-sized ones: this inverse size productivity relationship which was strong in the 1950s and 1960s (the pre-Green Revolution period) has sustained in the post-Green Revolution period, even if somewhat weakened, as studies for India, Bangladesh and Pakistan bear out (Berry and Cline, 1979; Agarwal, 1983; Boyce, 1987). Small farmers have adopted the new technology in most areas where large farmers have done so, although after a time lag[36]; and the evidence on marketed surplus does not bear up to the skeptics' claim that this will decline because small farmers will tend to retain a larger percentage for self-consumption.[37] In any case, an improvement in the consumption of the poor in the farm sector cannot, in itself, be seen as an inefficient outcome. Indeed, a dietary improvement among the very poor may add to labor productivity.[38]

The existing evidence thus gives no reason to expect that land distribution in favor of women would reduce output on account of the size effect. Moreover, the problem of land fragmentation again is not unique to female ownership, but can arise equally with male inheritance: in both cases it calls for land consolidation. There could, of course, be a negative output effect of female inheritance through what I term the gender-transfer effect, insofar as women usually face the earlier-noted gender-specific disadvantages as managers of farms, when operating in factor and product markets. But again the answer lies in easing these constraints by institutional support to women farmers, rather than in disinheriting them.

Indeed the experience of nongovernmental credit institutions such as the Grameen Bank in Bangladesh suggest that women are often better credit risks than men (Hossain, 1988). In addition, supporting women as farm managers would enlarge the talent and information pool; and in very poor households allocating resources to women could increase their productivity by improving their nutrition.

The provision of land to women could have other indirect benefits as well, such as reducing migration to cities, both by women themselves and by family members dependent on them; and increasing farm incomes in women's hands, which in turn could generate a higher demand for nonfarm goods that are produced locally and labor-intensively, thus creating more rural jobs.[39]

(c) *The equality and empowerment arguments*

Equality and empowerment concerns, unlike welfare and efficiency considerations, stem less from the implications of land access or deprivation in absolute terms, and more from the implications of men's and women's *relative* access to land, and they affect particularly women's ability to challenge male dominance within the home and in society.

The equality argument for land rights can be approached in several different ways, but two aspects are especially important here. One is the larger issue of gender equality as a measure of a just society, in which equality of rights over productive resources would be an important part. Two, there is a specific aspect of equality in land rights as an indicator of women's economic empowerment and as a facilitator in challenging gender inequities in other (e.g., social and political) spheres. In the present discussion, the links between gender equality in land rights and women's empowerment are especially important. But first, what is meant by empowerment? The term has been used variously (and often loosely) in academic writing and by social action groups across the world, including South Asia. In the present context, it could be defined as a process that enhances the ability of disadvantaged ("powerless") individuals or groups to challenge and change (in their favor) existing power relationships that place them in subordinate economic, social and political positions. Empowerment can manifest itself in acts of individual resistance as well as in group mobilization. Entitling women with land could empower them economically, as well as strengthen their ability to challenge social and political gender inequities.

A telling illustration is provided by the Bodhgaya movement in Bihar (eastern India) in the late-1970s, in which women and men of landless households jointly participated in an extended struggle for ownership rights in the land they cultivated, which was under the illegal possession of a local *math* (a temple-monastery complex). During the struggle, women raised a demand for independent land rights, not only for reasons of economic security but also because this impinged on marital relations. They feared that if land titles went only to husbands, wives would be rendered relatively even more powerless, and vulnerable to domestic violence. Their fears proved correct. Where only men got titles there was an increase in drunkenness, wife-beating and threats: "Get out of the house, the land is mine now" (Manimala, 1983, p.15). Where women received titles they could now assert: "We had tongues but could not speak, we had

feet but could not walk. Now that we have the land, we have the strength to speak and walk." Similar responses were noted in China, when the Chinese Communist Party promulgated the Agrarian Reform law in 1947, which entitled women to hold separate land deeds for the first time (Hinton, 1972).

Land rights can also improve the treatment a woman receives from other family members, by strengthening her bargaining power.[40] Although employment and other means of earning could help in similar ways, in the rural context land usually offers greater security than other income sources — at the very least, a space of one's own. In the Bodhgaya case, for instance, the women were already wage laborers and were therefore not economically dependent; but their husbands were still able to threaten them with eviction. It is notable too that the Bodhgaya women saw intrahousehold gender relations being affected not just by their own propertyless state, but by their remaining propertyless while their husbands became propertied. In other words, land titles were important to women not only for improving their economic well-being in absolute terms (the welfare argument), but also for improving their *relative* bargaining position *vis-à-vis* their husbands: their sense of empowerment within the home was linked to economic *equality.*[41]

Outside the household as well, land ownership can empower women by improving the social treatment they receive from other villagers (Mies *et al.*, 1986), and by enabling them to bargain with employers from a stronger fall-back position. Land ownership is also widely linked to rural political power.[42] Of course, there can still be social barriers to individual women's participation in public decision-making bodies, even for women endowed with land, but land rights could facilitate such participation. Group solidarity among women would also help. For instance, an individual woman with landed property may find it difficult to assert herself politically or socially in the village, especially where social norms dictate seclusion, but a group of women acting in unity could do so (see examples in Chen, 1983). (Here there could be some congruence of interests even between women of diverse class and caste backgrounds.)

Indeed in a limited sense, collective action may itself empower women by enhancing their self-confidence and their ability to challenge oppression, although in a larger sense it is a means to empowerment, wherein empowerment lies not only in the process of challenging gender inequity but in eliminating it. And collective action is likely to prove a critical means for effecting change toward greater gender equality in land rights (as elaborated later).

(d) *Practical v. strategic gender needs*

While each of the above arguments for women's independent rights in land is important, are they of comparable weight? Or do some merely serve to further what have been described as "practical" gender needs, while others serve "strategic" gender needs? This distinction between practical and strategic needs, first made by Molyneux (1985) and elaborated by Moser (1989), is worth exploring since it also appears to define where, in public policy itself, a line is drawn on questions of gender. Practical gender needs, as defined by these two scholars, are the needs of basic subsistence (such as food, health care, water supply, etc): to satisfy them does not challenge women's position within the gender division of labor, or a given distribution of property or political power. By contrast, strategic gender needs, they argue, are those needs that would help overcome women's subordination, including transforming the gender division of labor, removing institutionalized forms of discrimination, such as in rights to own and control property, and establishing political equality. In these terms, land rights would fall under strategic gender needs.

However, the apparent analytical neatness of this distinction is confounded when examined from the perspective of *practice*, on several counts: first, certain strategic gender needs, such as for land rights, are also, in specific contexts, necessary for fulfilling practical gender needs, as evidenced from the welfare and efficiency arguments spelt out earlier. For instance, land titles for poor rural women may be a necessary component for improving female nutrition and health. At the same time, we also noted the significance of land in "empowering" women to challenge unequal gender relations within and outside the home. In other words, the case for women's land rights has both a welfare-efficiency ("practical") component and an empowerment ("strategic") component.

Second, even meeting subsistence needs often requires challenging existing political–economic structures. For instance, a demand for wage increases by poor women workers is a practical need in that it would improve their living standards, but it is strategic in that it challenges existing production relations and requires confronting the opposition of employers. Third, and relatedly, the same process, *viz.* group organization, is often necessary for fulfilling both practical gender needs (such as increasing women's wages), and strategic gender needs (such as securing land rights). Fourth, action in pursuit of "practical" needs may easily turn into action to meet "strategic" needs. Group organization around economic issues often opens the door for women to question other aspects of their lives. For instance, poor women organized into groups for the better delivery of credit or other economic programs by the Grameen Bank in Bangladesh, or the Bangladesh Rural Advancement Committee (BRAC), or the Self-Employed Women's Association in north India, have in many cases also been able to challenge gender violence or restrictive social practices such as female seclusion. Indeed even to participate in group meetings often requires women to overcome social constraints, or to negotiate childcare responsibilities with husbands and other family members.

In other words, the *process* of fulfilling "practical" gender needs cannot always be delinked from that of ful-

filling "strategic" gender needs.[43] That it is often more "politic" to couch gender concerns in terms of practical rather than strategic needs because welfare and efficiency arguments resonate more with State planners, should not detract from this linkage.

We might of course ask why welfare and efficiency arguments resonate more with State planners. Part of the answer certainly lies in the fact that these arguments (especially those concerning welfare) focus especially on poor women, and can be subsumed within the poverty-alleviation component of planning, with special targeting toward "the most vulnerable" groups, identified as women and female children. But part of the answer must also lie in deep-rooted notions of appropriate gender relations shared by many men who make and implement policy, for whom empowering women to transform those relations into more equal ones would appear inappropriate and even threatening to existing family and kinship structures. Hence it is easier to push for changes where the goal appears to be to give poor women a slightly better deal, than where the goal is to challenge basic inequities in gender relations across classes. It is also the case that programs for health and nutrition are more readily perceived in welfare terms than programs which call for gender-redistributive land reform. It is not a coincidence that *land rights* have yet to become a necessary component even of women-directed poverty-alleviation programs.

Consider now what can be learned about the association between land rights and gender relations from communities where women historically had significant rights in land.

5. GENDER RELATIONS IN TRADITIONALLY MATRILINEAL AND BILATERAL COMMUNITIES

Historically, in some South Asian communities, women enjoyed significant rights in land, and even today do so more there than elsewhere. These are communities traditionally practicing matrilineal or bilateral inheritance and concentrated in parts of northeast and south India, and Sri Lanka, as follows.[44] Northeast India: the home of three matrilineal tribal communities, the Garos, Khasis and Lalungs; south India: here the Nangudi Vellalars of Tamil Nadu practiced bilateral inheritance, and several other groups in and around Kerala practiced matrilineal inheritance, including the Nayars of north and central Kerala, the Tiyyars and Mappilas of north Kerala, and the Bants of Karnataka; and Sri Lanka: here all major communities practiced bilateral or matrilineal inheritance — the Sinhalese and Jaffna Tamils were bilateral, and the Muslim "Moors" were matrilineal.[45] Historical and ethnographic evidence (examined in Agarwal, forthcoming) suggests that in regions other than these, inheritance practices were essentially patrilineal.

The land rights that women enjoyed in matrilineal

and bilateral communities fell broadly into three categories. First are communities (such as the Garos) among which land was a clan's communal property and could not be inherited either by individuals or by joint family units. All clan members resident in the village had use rights to this land as individuals. Responsibility for land management vested with the husband who took up residence with his wife, but a woman's field labor was critical and she controlled the produce. Second are communities (such as the Khasis, Nayars, Tiyyars and Mappilas) among which land, although inherited in the female line, was held as joint family property, and women had no individual rights of alienation. Responsibility for land management vested principally with older men (usually brothers or maternal uncles). In decisions concerning the partition or transfer of landed property, however, women's concurrence was necessary. Finally there are communities (such as the Sinhalese and Jaffna Tamils) where both women and men had individual inheritance rights in land.

The picture of gender relations among these groups is a mixed one. On the positive side, women enjoyed considerable social independence and relative equality in marital relations. Indeed, in all the groups, a daughter's rights in land, and the fact that she either remained in her natal home after marriage or had inviolable rights to return to it if she so chose, provided her with a strong fall-back position within marriage. Women could choose their husbands (although heiresses faced some constraints) and initiate divorce. Where uxorilocality or matrilocality were the norm, as it was in many of these groups, marital breakdown led to the husband departing, sometimes (as among the Garos) with only the clothes on his back.[46] (In contrast, in patrilineal, patrilocal contexts, it was women (especially if they violated sexual norms) who faced the very real risk of being evicted and being left with little means of support.) Norms of sexual behavior outside marriage ranged from relatively gender egalitarian (as among the matrilineal tribes of northeast India and among the Sinhalese), to restricted for women (as among the Jaffna Tamils). But in comparison with Hindu and Muslim women of patrilineal groups, especially those shackled by seclusion practices in northern South Asia, women among all the matrilineal and bilateral groups enjoyed greater sexual freedom.

They also had considerable freedom of movement and of public interaction. Even among the Muslim Moors, Munck (1985, pp. 8, 108) remarks: "Women move freely about the village without veils covering their faces . . . Interaction between men and women is frequent and casual and often sexual comments are exchanged publicly." This is strikingly different from women's situation among most patrilineal Muslims of the subcontinent. Daughters were also specially desired among groups such as the Nayars,[47] in marked contrast to the strong preference for male children found in patrilineal communities across South Asia.

These favorable features, however, were counterbalanced by less favorable ones. First, women's property rights in the matrilineal and bilateral communities did not alter the overall gender division of labor: domestic work and childcare were still a woman's responsibilities. Second, the range of sexual mores found among these communities indicates that rights in land did not guarantee women the same sexual freedom as men. Third, formal managerial authority over land in a number of matrilineal communities lay with men (as husbands, brothers and maternal uncles). In practice, this would have worked in various ways depending on the role women played in the household's economy, the form (individual or joint) in which property was held, and the size of the estates involved. Where women's role in production and market activities was important (as among the northeastern tribal groups), and/or where women held individual rather than joint property rights (as among Sri Lanka's bilateral groups), they exercised greater control over the land. But where women played little role in farm production, and property was held in large joint family estates collectively owned by several generations of a woman's matrilineal descendants, as among the Nayars of central Kerala and the wealthy Mappilas of north Kerala, men's managerial control over property and their overall authority in the household and in public dealings appears to have been especially strong. This also highlights an important difference between matrilineal and patrilineal inheritance systems: in the former there is often a gender divergence between property ownership and its control, while in the latter there is convergence: men (as a gender) own as well as control the property.

Finally, and most importantly, in all the groups, customary institutions with jural power (such as the tribal and caste councils) were monopolized by men and typically excluded women. Among matrilineally inheriting communities, this meant that despite men's restricted access to property ownership, their rights (as a gender) of control over that property on the one hand, and their access to public bodies on the other (with links between the two domains), often enabled them to consolidate substantial social prestige and political power. The Nayar *karanavans*[48] of wealthy households and the Khasi chiefs commanded local influence in ways that the women heiresses of these communities appear not to have done as a rule. In addition, among all groups, men's control of the public decision-making domain gave them critical influence over the modification of legal and social rules when external conditions began to change in significant ways, especially under British colonial rule.

In short, ownership rights in landed property clearly conferred important benefits on women, but their virtual exclusion from property management (in some groups) and from jural and overall public authority (in all groups) circumscribed the power they could derive from those rights. This holds lessons for women's struggle for land rights today, namely that the full advantages of land ownership cannot be derived by women if they continue to be excluded from managerial control and jural authority. And the arenas of contestation over effective land rights for women will therefore need to extend much beyond the courtyards of the household to encompass the complex institutions of community and State — the arenas where legal, social, and political rules are made and unmade. This is further illustrated below.

6. OBSTACLES TO ACHIEVING EFFECTIVE LAND RIGHTS

Today, most arable land in South Asia (as noted) is in private hands, access to which is mainly through inheritance. Although women enjoy considerable rights in landed property, gender inequalities and anomalies in land-related laws remain. Moreover, there is a vast gender gap between law and practice. Most women do not own land, and few among those who do are able to exercise full control over it. A range of factors — social, administrative and ideological — severely restrict the effective implementation of inheritance laws. These obstacles, examined in detail in Agarwal (forthcoming), are summarized below.

First, in most traditionally patrilineal communities, there is a strong male resistance to endowing women, especially daughters, with land. This resistance was clearly apparent when progressive legislation in the 1950s gave women in patrilineal communities the right to inherit land. Several ethnographers who undertook village studies soon after the passing of such laws, commented on this.[49] For instance, every single household surveyed in Jhatikra village near Delhi, after the 1956 Hindu Succession Act was passed, disapproved of its provisions allowing daughters to inherit the patrimony (Freed and Freed, 1976). In Himachal Pradesh, the inheritance law "struck the valley as so unfair that they petitioned the government not to introduce the law, but without avail" (Newell, 1970, p. 51). In Uttar Pradesh, the Rajputs felt that the Act was "a very serious breach of village customary law, which has always held that no wife, daughter, or daughter's husband could inherit land. This rule was a very important one and still is adhered to with deep emotion" (Minturn and Hitchcock, 1966, p. 28).

Quite apart from the reluctance to admit more contenders to the most valuable form of rural property, one of the important factors underlying such resistance is a structural mismatch between contemporary inheritance laws and traditional marriage practices.

Among the matrilineal and bilateral communities discussed earlier, historically families sought to keep the land within the purview of the extended kin either by strict rules against land alienation by individuals, or where such alienation was possible (as among the bilateral communities), by other means: these included post-marital residence in the village, and often an emphasis on marriage with close kin, especially cross-cousins. In fact proximity of the postmarital residence to the natal home appears to have been virtually a necessary condition for recognizing a daughter's share in landed property. Contemporary laws as framed by the modern State, however, give inheritance rights to daughters as individuals among most communities, including in traditionally patrilineal, patrilocal ones, but marriage customs are still under the purview of local kin groups and, on the relevant counts, have remained largely unchanged. In India this mismatch between inheritance laws and marriage practices is greatest among upper-caste Hindus of the northwest who forbid marriages with close kin and practice village exogamy, preferring marriage alliances in distant villages. Many such communities, moreover, have social taboos against parents on the economic support of married daughters even during crises. Hence, in the northern states (and especially the northwestern ones) endowing daughters is seen by Hindu parents as bringing no reciprocal economic benefit, while increasing the risk of the land passing out of the hands of the extended family. Resistance to entitling daughters tends to be greatest here. Resistance is less in south and northeast India where marriages within the village and with close kin are allowed and sought, and seeking the help of married daughters during economic crises is also possible.

Second, women in many parts of South Asia tend to forgo their shares in parental land for the sake of potential economic and social support from brothers. A visit by a brother is often the only regular link a woman has with her natal home where she is married into a distant village, and especially where there are social taboos against parents accepting the hospitality of a married daughter. After the parents' deaths the brother's home often offers the only possibility of temporary or long-term refuge in case of marital breakup or widowhood. A woman's dependence on this support is directly related to her economic and social vulnerability. Economically, limited access to personal property (especially productive assets), illiteracy, limited training in income-earning skills, restricted earning opportunities, and low wages for available work, can all constrain women's access to earnings and potential for independent economic survival. Socially, women's vulnerability is associated partly with the strength of female seclusion practices and partly with the extent of social stigma attaching to widowhood or divorce. Both economic and social factors vary in strength by community, region, and circumstance. But typically, rather than risk losing such support women give up their claims on parental land. Cultural constructions of gender, including the definition of how a "good" sister should behave, the widespread feeling that it is "shameful" for a sister to claim her share, also discourage women from asserting their rights (Hershman, 1981; Westergaard, 1983). In practice, the evidence on the support that brothers actually provide is mixed: enthnographies give examples both of brothers helping a sister in need, and of their neglect and duplicity.

Third, dependence on brothers is part of a larger social context in which many aspects of rural women's relationship with the world outside the family is typically mediated through male relatives: fathers, brothers, husbands and extended male kin. Such mediation is necessitated by a variety of factors (the nature and strength of which vary according to region, class and caste), but particularly by the physical and social restrictions on women's mobility and behavior. In many South Asian communities these restrictions are explicit in the norms and ideology of purdah or female seclusion; in many others, they are implicit and subtle, but nevertheless effectively confine women. These restrictions are manifest not just in the veiling of women, but more commonly in the gender segregation of space and the gendered specification of behavior. In fact, strict veiling is limited to some communities and regions — being stronger among Muslims in northern South Asia and among upper-caste Hindus in northwest India, than elsewhere; and even here it varies in extent by the woman's caste, class and age. More pervasive are the behavioral strictures imposed upon and internalized by women from late childhood, which define where women can go, whom they can speak to and in what manner, how they should dress, and so on. Although such gendering of space and behavior is strongest in communities which explicity endorse purdah, its more subtle manifestations constitute an implicit code of expected female behavior in large parts of the subcontinent, even where (as in south India and Nepal) purdah is not endorsed. This circumscribes rural women's interaction with men and institutions, their physical and social mobility, their domain of activity and knowledge, and their access to education and to economic (markets, banks, etc), judicial and administrative institutions. All this severely limits women's ability to claim and control land.

Fourth, male relatives often seek to take preemptive steps to prevent women from getting their inheritance: for instance, fathers have been found to leave wills favoring sons and disinheriting daughters; and brothers have been known to forge wills or manipulate statements before the revenue authorities to make it appear that the woman has relinquished her right.[50] Natal kin are especially hostile to the idea of daughters and sisters inheriting land, since the property can pass outside the patrilineal descent group. A widow's claims are often viewed with less antagonism, since with a widow there is a greater chance of the land remaining with agnates: she can be persuaded to adopt the son of the deceased husband's brother if she is sonless, or to enter into a leviratic union with the husband's (usually younger) brother, or made to forfeit the property if she remarries outside the family.

Where preemptive methods fail, intimidation is attempted. A common tactic is to initiate expensive litigation which few women can financially afford (Kishwar, 1987). Some women drop their claims, others press on with the risk of having to mortgage the land to pay legal fees, thus possibly losing the land altogether. Land disputes involving women were rising in parts of the subcontinent even in the late 1950s (Mayer, 1960). Today direct violence is also increasingly used to deter women from filing claims or from exercising their customary rights: beatings are common and murder not unknown. Indeed in eastern and central India, the murder of women who have some land, through accusations of witchcraft, is on the rise.[51]

Fifth, the logistics of dealing with legal, economic and bureaucratic institutions are often formidable and work against women staking their claims; and they may only decide to do so if they have male relatives who can mediate. Village women's typically low level of education, and the noted restrictions on women's interaction with the extra-domestic sphere and with institutions constituted principally of men, the complicated procedures and red tape involved in dealing with judicial and administrative bodies, and so on, all work to women's disadvantage, as does women's relative lack of financial resources.[52] As a Pakistani woman lawyer notes: "lack of knowledge of the assets, the stamp duty, the cost and length of litigation and customary stigma, usually deters the sharer [who has been] denied her rights from going to court" (Patel, 1979, p. 139). The problem is especially acute in communities with high female seclusion, but it is not absent even where seclusion is not prescribed.

Sixth, local-level (largely male) government functionaries, responsible for overseeing the recording of inheritance shares, often obstruct the implementation of laws in women's favor. Social and official prejudice tends to be particularly acute against inheritance by daughters; widows' claims (as noted) are somewhat better accepted in principle, although often violated in practice. A survey I conducted in March 1993, of land records in three Rajasthan villages showed that of the women whose names were registered, 36 were widows and only two were daughters. Of the registered widows, 27 were registered jointly with their sons; and the popular perception was that this land was for the widow's maintenance and not for her independent use, bequest or transfer. Even such registration is a recent practice and only goes back 4–5 years. A village council secretary in Rajasthan clearly told me in 1987 that he usually pressured daughters to sign away their shares in favor of their brothers, but sought to persuade widows to keep their shares. In many other regions, even widows' shares are not registered. Indeed male bias on these counts is found in greater or lesser degree at all levels of legal and administrative institutions (see examples in Agarwal, forthcoming).

The gap between legal ownership rights and actual ownership is only one part of the story. The other part relates to the gap between ownership and effective control, especially managerial control, attributable to a mix of factors. Patrilocal marriages in distant villages make it difficult for women to directly supervise or cultivate any land inherited in the natal village. But problems of directly managing land inherited even in the marital village (say as a widow) are compounded in many areas by factors such as the practice of purdah or the more general (implicit or explicit) gender segregation of public space and social interaction; high rates of female illiteracy; and high fertility (which increases women's childbearing and childcare responsibilities). Moreover, male control over agricultural technology, especially the plough (there are cultural taboos against women operating the plough), and (the noted) male bias in the dissemination of information and technological inputs disadvantage women farmers and increase their dependence on male mediation. Often added to this is the threat and practice of violence by male relatives and others interested in acquiring women's land. Pressure on women to sharecrop their land to relatives (at below market rates) is usually high, as are the difficulties of ensuring that they get their fair share of the harvest. Some of these factors, such as gender bias in access to production inputs and information, constrain women farmers even in traditionally bilateral and matrilineal contexts.

However, the strength of these constraints to women claiming and managing land varies considerably by region. There are geographic differences in the social acceptance of women's land claims (stemming in part from differences in traditional inheritance rights); in prevailing marriage practices; in the emphasis on female seclusion and control over female sexuality; in women's freedom of movement and labor force participation; in women's literacy and fertility rates; and in the extent of land scarcity. Obstacles stemming from these factors are greatest in northwest India, Bangladesh and Pakistan, and least in south India and Sri Lanka. In fact four geographic zones can broadly be demarcated, ordered in terms of the strength of resistance women are likely to face in exercising their legal rights: Pakistan, northwest India and Bangladesh fall at the high resistance end of the spectrum, and south India and Sri Lanka at the low resistance end; while western, central and eastern India, and Nepal and northeast India, come in between.[53]

Over time, there is likely to be an increase in gen-der conflict over private land with its growing scarcity and skewness in distribution. On the one hand male family members will be increasingly reluctant to part with this land. On the other hand, the importance for women of asserting their inheritance rights will grow for several reasons, including the limited expansion of economic opportunities for nonland-related earnings, and the erosion of kin-support systems, as brothers and other relatives become less able and less willing to economically provide for female kin. Bangladeshi evidence suggests that gender conflict over land is indeed on the rise, with an increasing number of women asserting or planning to assert their claims[54], and we can expect this also to be the case in other acutely land-scarce parts of South Asia.

In the case of public land, that is land which is under government or community jurisdiction, the obstacles are of a somewhat different nature. Here women's struggle is more directly against the consistent male bias in the distribution of land under land reform programs, resettlement schemes, and various land development schemes, and only indirectly against individual family members who may be rival potential beneficiaries. Government officials typically resist the allotment of public land to women on the grounds that allotments can only be made to heads of households who are assumed to be men (Lal, 1986; Agarwal, forthcoming). This bias is found not only in government programs which affect patrilineal groups, but even when land titles are distributed in traditionally matrilineal and bilateral communities (Agarwal, 1990; and Schrijvers, 1988). And it is found in the policies and programs of all the political regimes in the subcontinent, including communist ones.

7. INTERVENTIONS FOR CHANGE: SOME CONSIDERATIONS

The discussion above indicates that today for women to gain effective rights in land will require not only removing existing gender inequalities in the law, but also ensuring that the laws are implemented. It will involve strengthening women's ability to claim and retain their rights in land, as well as their ability to exercise effective control over it. In other words, it will involve contestation and struggle at every level — the household, the community and the State — and on both economic and noneconomic fronts. The complexity of the noted obstacles preclude any simple prescriptions on how this could be achieved. In addition, given the regional variability of these obstacles, specific strategies to overcome them can only evolve through the process of localized campaigns. This section, therefore, does not attempt to outline strategy, but only to highlight some of the issues that will need particular attention from gender-progressive groups and policy makers.

To enhance women's ability to claim and keep control over their rightful inheritance shares, several aspects are likely to need attention: establishing the legitimacy of the claim; reducing gender bias in village land registration practices and village council rulings; enhancing women's legal knowledge and literacy; improving women's fall-back position so that they are better able to deal with the ensuing intrafamily conflict, including providing external support structures that would reduce women's dependence on brothers and close kin, and so on. In all this the role of collective action is likely to be primary.

For instance, the local bureaucracy is more likely to accurately register individual women's claims in family land (whether as daughters, widows, or in other capacities) if there were collective pressure on them to do so, say from gender-progressive groups, especially women's organizations. Such organizations can play a vital supportive role too in providing women with information on laws and contacts with legal experts, should legal action be necessary. A significant female presence in local decision-making bodies such as the village *panchayats* (village councils) could also strengthen the hands of rural women. Although women's presence in such bodies need not guarantee more gender-progressive programs, the record of elected all-women panels in village *panchayats* in parts of India (such as Maharashtra and Madhya Pradesh), and of field-level development administrators in Bangladesh, leave room for optimism: women in these bodies are found to be more sensitive to women's concerns and to give priority to local women's needs in ways that male *panchayat* members and bureaucrats typically do not.[55] The presence of women in decision-making roles and positions of authority also has a wider ideological impact; and South Asian women, especially but not only in purdah-practicing communities, are more likely to take their grievances to women representatives than to all-male bodies.

Local gender-progressive organizations could similarly strengthen women's fall-back position in case of intrafamily conflict over women's land claims, through economic and social support networks and programs which could reduce women's dependence on male relatives, especially their brothers in whose favor women often forfeit their claims. As a woman member of BRAC (a Bangladeshi development non government organization (NGO) which provides production credit and technical support to poor village women and men, organized separately into small groups) tellingly asserted: "Well the Samity is my 'brother'" (Hunt, 1983, p. 38). It is notable too that women after joining BRAC have been able to challenge purdah practices in their villages:

We do not listen to the *mullahs* [Muslim clergy] anymore. They did not give us even a quarter kilo of rice (BRAC women in Chen, 1983, p. 176).

They said . . . [w]e are ruining the prestige of the village and breaking *purdah* . . . Now nobody talks ill of us. They say: "They have formed a group and now they earn money. It is good" (BRAC women in Chen, 1983, pp. 176–177).

However, the obstacle posed by the practice of patrilocality-*cum*-village exogamy, to women claiming, retaining their claims, and self-managing land, does not lend itself to obvious solutions, given the rigidity of social norms and ideologies justifying such practices. We might expect, though, that as some success is achieved in establishing daughters' inheritance rights, postmarital residence patterns could become more flexible. For instance, uxorilocal residence by the son-in-law is an accepted practice among patrilineal communities where a brotherless daughter inherits her father's estate. In this context, a more gender-progressive approach by the State in the distribution of public land to women could also be helpful.

Apart from asserting their inheritance rights in private land, the most important other means of land acquisition for women (especially of poor rural households) in South Asia today is through the State. In the postcolonial period South Asian governments have distributed individual titles under various land reform and resettlement schemes, leased out public land under wasteland development and reforestation schemes, and legalized the distribution of land claimed by a peasant group through a land struggle. But as we had noted, there is a systematic male bias in all such allocations. Collective action by women again appears necessary for challenging these biases.

In this context, it is worth considering what institutional form of land ownership and management would be most desirable for women. For instance, should land be owned and managed individually or in some collective way? Consider first the issue of ownership. Although individual ownership gives a woman greater control over land use and the freedom to bequeath, mortgage or sell it as she wishes, it also carries the risk of the land being appropriated by a rapacious moneylender or by male relatives. In addition there is the dilemma of who would inherit the land from the woman — her sons or her daughters? An alternative arrangement to individual titles in the transfer of State land, or of land acquired by a peasant organization through a land struggle, could be for poor peasant women belonging to a set of households to seek rights as a group — women of each participating household having use rights in the land but not the right to individually dispose of it. The daughters-in-law and daughters of such households who are resident in the village would share these usufructuary rights; daughters leaving the village on marriage would lose them, but could reestablish their rights should they need to return to their parental homes on marital breakup or widowhood. In other words, land access could be linked formally to residence, as was the case under some tribal land use systems (such as among the Garos), the difference being that here the land would belong not to a clan but to a group of poor peasant women. This would strengthen women's ability to retain control over the land. Collective ownership would also be a means of creating a more communal and egalitarian basis of land access. More generally, containing the trend toward the individual privatization of what is currently communal land, especially village common land, would help protect the welfare interests of poor households, and especially of women in these households.

Group ownership of land need not of course imply joint management, just as individual ownership need not preclude joint management. Women jointly holding ownership rights could cultivate the land either in separate plots allocated on a household basis or cooperatively as a group, with each woman putting in labor time and sharing the returns. Or there could be some combination of individual and group management, such as family-based female cultivation along with joint investment by the women's group in capital equipment and cooperation in terms of labor-sharing, product-marketing, etc. Group investment could be advantageous even when women individually inherit land from parents or husbands, or receive titles in government land on an individual basis. There are many examples of groups of male farmers jointly investing in, say, an irrigation well. In women's case, group investment may be especially beneficial since individual women would not usually have enough economic resources for investing in irrigation and other inputs. Women functioning in groups would also be in a better position to mobilize resources either from among themselves, or through available governmental and nongovernmental schemes. Group investment when linked with group management could further strengthen women's hands in this respect.

Some cases of joint land management by groups of women already exist in South Asia. For instance, in Bangladesh some groups of landless women organized by BRAC are jointly cultivating plots of private land that they have leased in (Chen, 1983); and in India under the Bankura project in West Bengal and the Sewa Mandir project in Rajasthan, poor women's groups are jointly managing village wastelands (N. Singh, 1988; Lal, 1986).

In initiatives like these, and more generally to enhance women's ability to function as independent farmers, infrastructural support for women is critical, in the form of access to credit, production inputs, information on new agricultural practices, and so on. Existing systems are known to be extremely male biased. While a greater female presence in agricultural

input and information delivery systems (women extension agents are often recommended for the latter) would probably help in reducing existing male bias in such systems, it appears equally necessary to reorient these systems so that male functionaries too recognize the importance of assisting women farmers. A systematic promotion of women's cooperatives for production inputs and marketing (both by the State and by gender-progressive NGOs) would also be very important.

Indeed, building group support among and for women, both locally and nationally, appears to be crucial for an effective struggle for land rights. Group support can take at least two forms: through separately constituted groups which provide specialized legal and other services to village women, and through organizations comprised of village women themselves. Initiatives of both kinds are likely to be important in the struggles not only of women from landed households seeking their inheritance claims, but also of landless or near-landless women seeking rights, say, in public land.

How and under what conditions solidarity for collective action may emerge among women is too large a question to be answered here adequately. But a number of complexities will need to be addressed, especially those posed by class (and caste) differences in the households to which women belong, and the associated conflict of interests among women.

There are, however, significant areas of mutual benefit which could serve as starting points for collective action by women across class/caste lines. One is legal reform: women of all classes with a stake in family land (or more generally in family property), whatever its size, stand to gain from more gender-egalitarian personal laws governing the inheritance of landed property. (And the percentage of such women in South Asia is not small: despite the highly skewed distribution of land in the region, a large majority of rural households, as noted in section 4, do own some.) Again a wide spectrum of peasant women (even if not agricultural laborers) would benefit from certain changes in land reform legislation, such as (in India) bringing tenancy land under the purview of contemporary inheritance laws, and treating adult daughters on a par with adult sons and recognizing the wife as a separate unit in land ceiling laws. That women with divergent concerns can cooperate strategically for some types of legal reform is borne out by recent struggles to amend dowry and rape laws in India, for which women's groups, despite significant differences in their ideologies, agendas and social composition, successfully came together to form common fronts.

Similarly ideological contestations against existing social constructions of gender (including assumptions about women's needs and roles) offer potential benefits to a very broad range of women. As noted, whatever their class/caste, such contestation is intimately connected with women's ability to gain effective rights in economic resources, especially land. The issue of purdah is a case in point. Protests against the practice have come both from well-off upper-caste Hindu women in India (including those who campaigned against it in the 1930s), and from poor Muslim women in contemporary Bangladesh.

Some optimism on the possibilities of cross-class/caste action is also generated when we consider the important role played by many urban middle-class women activists in promoting issues affecting rural poor women. Indeed the role of such activists has been critical in catalyzing a focus on women's independent rights to land within mass peasant organizations and struggles such as the Bodhgaya movement in Bihar in the late 1970s, and the Shetkari Sanghatana's Mahila Aghadi in Maharashtra in the 1980s.

In this context, locationally separated efforts can gain and have gained from the emergence of countrywide women's movements in South Asia, espe-

cially over the last decade and a half. In India, for instance, the emergence of women's groups across the country and the spread of public awareness about gender concerns, even though not yet focused on the issue of property or land rights, have fertilized the soil on which the struggle for land rights can grow. Such developments enable the question of women's land rights to be placed in the arena of public debate — something which was not easy to do a mere two decades ago. At the same time, so far, the campaigns that have transcended local contexts and developed into national ones have been mainly around legal change, such as the noted campaigns in India on rape and dowry laws, and in Pakistan against gender-discriminatory Islamic injunctions and legislation. But the issue of gender equality in land rights — not only in law but in practice — calls for a much more multipronged and sustained effort than has been attempted so far on any gender-related issue in South Asia.

NOTES

1. See Mies, Lalita and Kumari (1986, p. 134).

2. Personal communication, Vina Mazumdar, Center for Women's Development Studies, New Delhi.

3. For a discussion on this see Agarwal (forthcoming).

4. In India, the term "state" relates to administrative divisions within the country and is not to be confused with "State" used throughout the paper in the political economy sense of the word. In Pakistan and Sri Lanka these administrative divisions are termed provinces.

5. The term "gender-progressive," as used here and subsequently, relates to those laws, practices, policies, etc., which reduce or eliminate the inequities (economic, social, political) that women face in relation to men. Individuals and organizations that work toward this end are also so described. "Gender-retrogressive" has the opposite meaning.

6. Bilateral inheritance: ancestral property passes to and through both sons and daughters; matrilineal inheritance: ancestral property passes through the female line; patrilineal inheritance: ancestral property passes through the male line. On the specific complex workings of these inheritance systems in South Asia, see Agarwal (forthcoming).

7. In West Bengal when the CPI (M) (Communist Party of India (Marxist)) government carried out "Operation Barga" (launched in 1978), a major land reform initiative which sought to provide tenants with security of tenure by systematically registering them, primarily men were registered. A similar bias has prevailed in the programs of most left-wing nonparty groups, one notable exception being the Bodhgaya (Bihar) peasant movement initiated in 1978 by

the Chatra Yuva Sangharsh Vahini, a Gandhian-Socialist Youth Organization which also took up the issue of women's land rights (see Manimala, 1983).

8. Among the exceptions is the Shetkari Sanghatana's Mahila Aghadi, the women's front of the Shetkari Sanghatana — a farmers' organization founded in Maharashtra (west India) in 1980. Also noteworthy is the role played by *Manushi* (a women's journal from India) in reporting such initiatives, and by one of the journal's founders, Madhu Kishwar, who in 1982 filed a petition in the Supreme Court of India challenging the denial of land rights to Ho tribal women in Bihar (see Kishwar, 1982).

9. Two notable exceptions are Sharma (1980) and Kishwar (1987).

10. This is not meant as a summary of Engels's complex thesis, but merely of one part of his argument. Critiques of different aspects of Engels's analysis abound: see especially Sacks (1975), Barrett (1980), Delmar (1976), Molyneux (1981), and various articles in Sayers, Evans and Redclift (1987) and in *Critique of Anthropology*, Vol. 3, Nos. 9–10 (1977). In particular, Engels's assumption that gender relations within propertyless groups such as the industrial proletariat or under socialism would necessarily be egalitarian has been widely criticized: see Delmar (1976), Molyneux (1981), and Barrett (1980).

11. In socialist countries also (including those which were socialist until recently), the influence of Engels's analysis led to a similar preoccupation with women's employment as the primary means of eliminating gender oppression (Molyneux, 1981).

12. Women's representation in top political and economic

decision-making bodies in such countries remained minimal. For instance, in the late 1970s, in the USSR, Czechoslovakia, Poland, and Yugoslavia under 5% of government posts were filled by women (Molyneux, 1981).

13. In India, for instance, male dominance is apparent in the judiciary (in 1985, women constituted only 3.6% of the state bar council advocates, and 2.8% of High Court and Supreme Court judges), the government administration (in 1987 only 7.4% of the Indian Administrative Service Officers, and 5.8% of all central government service officers taken together, were women), and the legislature (in 1984 only 8% of elected candidates in the Lok Sabha were women). All figures are taken from GOI (1988, pp. 119, 126–127, 173).

14. Scandinavian countries have a better record than most others on this count: in Norway and Finland, for instance, women constituted 34% and 32% of all elected and appointed members of national legislative bodies in 1985–87, in sharp contrast to analogous figures for India, Bangladesh and Pakistan which ranged between eight and 10, and even those for the United States and United Kingdom which were 5.3 and 6.3, respectively (United Nations, 1990).

15. Also property differences alone do not distinguish classes. Education, lifestyles and so on, help forge class distinctions as well (see e.g., Bourdieu, 1984). For a useful discussion on some of the characteristics of "class" within Marxist and non-Marxist literature, see Wolff and Resnick (1989).

16. E.g., Millet (1970), Firestone (1970), and Delphy (1977) all deny the significance of class divisions between women, but from different standpoints (for elaboration see Agarwal, forthcoming).

17. Of course aspects of a person's identity other than class can also be divisive or adhesive, such as caste, ethnicity, and religion.

18. See e.g., Selvaduri's (1976) observations on a Sinhalese village in Sri Lanka.

19. Also see Bromley (1991) and Feder and Feeny (1991) for some useful discussions on property rights, as well as on rights in land.

20. This was calculated from India's land use statistics for 1987–88 (GOI, 1992b) as follows: Total arable land comes to 184.73 mha by aggregating the net sown area, area under current fallows and other fallows, culturable wasteland, and land under miscellaneous tree crops and groves. This tallies with the Ministry of Agriculture's method of estimating arable land. Of this, 158.09 mha, which is the aggregate of net sown area, land under current fallows, and land under miscellaneous tree crops and groves, could broadly be assumed to be in private hands.

21. There is little quantitative data by gender on land ownership and management in South Asia. None of the countries in the region, with the exception of Sri Lanka, collects gender-disaggregated land ownership and use data

in its agricultural and centennial censuses or in its large-scale rural surveys. In Sri Lanka, although such data were collected in the 1981 agricultural census, they were limited to agricultural operators (these included cultivators as well as purely livestock and poultry operators) and did not cover all rural households. Moreover, the published data do not give a gender-wise breakdown of land ownership even among agricultural operators. Again, most South Asian village studies by economists that have focused on questions of agrarian structure, have (as noted earlier) confined themselves to the household unit. Hence to gain an idea of where women have been given or have claimed their shares in landed property and under what circumstances, I have drawn on anthropological, historical, and legal sources, supplemented by my fieldwork observations.

22. The discussion here will concern land linked in one way or another to rural livelihoods, especially arable land, but will exclude homesites, even though the available data on land ownership do not always separate land under homesites from the rest.

23. For details see Agarwal (1986, and forthcoming).

24. Harriss's (1990) literature review and detailed data analysis on intrahousehold food allocation in South Asia illustrates the difficulties of arriving at firm conclusions on this count. Nevertheless, her tentative conclusions include the following: (a) "discrimination in energy and protein intakes through the allocation of food within the household seems to be greater in the north [of the subcontinent] than in the south"; (b) "in the north it is least 'fair' for very young and very old females, and probably for adult women with special needs associated with pregnancy and lactation" (p. 405).

25. According to Dreze and Sen's (1989, p. 52) estimate, India, Pakistan and Bangladesh respectively would have some 36.9, 5.2 and 3.7 million more women today, if these countries had the same sex ratios as sub-Saharan Africa, namely 102. As they note, for most of Europe and North America the sex ratio averages about 105, essentially indicative of women's survival advantages over men in the absence of serious anti-female bias in the distribution of food and health care.

26. See especially Mencher (1988) and Per-Lee (1981) for South Asia, and the literature surveys by Blumberg (1991) and Hoddinott (1991) for other regions.

27. See Buvinic and Youssef (1978) for India, and Safilios-Rothchild and Mahmud (1989) for Bangladesh. According to the Indian census some 10% of households are headed by women, but this is a significant underestimate (see Agarwal, 1985, on reasons for the undercounting).

28. The estimates are based on the 37th round of the National Sample Survey (NSS) carried out in 1981–82. The figure for land ownership covers all land owned by the household, whether or not cultivated, including that used for nonagricultural uses.

29. See, Ali *et al.* (1981), Sundaram and Tendulkar (1983), and Gaiha and Kazmi (1981).

30. See e.g., Raj and Tharakan (1983).

31. See e.g., Islam (1986), Hazell and Haggblade (1990), and Basant and Kumar (1989).

32. See e.g., various case studies in Singh and Kelles-Vitanen (1987), *Shramshakti* (1988), and Islam (1987).

33. There is considerable evidence from Asia that titling can critically enhance a farmers' access to credit (in terms of sources, amounts and terms) by enabling them to use land as collateral (see e.g., Binswanger and Rosenzweig, 1986, and Feder, 1989). See also Saito and Weidenmann (1990) on the problems women farmers face in getting credit in the absence of titles.

34. For class bias in agricultural extension see Dasgupta (1977) and on gender bias see Kilkelly (1986).

35. The term "fragmentation" as used here relates to the division of a farm into several noncontiguous parcels of land, and farm size relates to the aggregate area of such parcels held by the cultivator. The analytical distinction between the farm-size effect and the fragmentation effect is important, as will be seen from the discussion which follows. In popular parlance the term "fragmentation" has come to be used rather loosely (and incorrectly) to refer also to the process of declining farm size.

36. See the considerable evidence for India, Pakistan, Bangladesh, and several other countries in Lipton and Longhurst (1989).

37. For nonfood crops the marketed surplus is found to be very high on farms of all size groups (Lipton, 1992) and for foodcrops the higher productivity effect of small farms may well outweigh their higher propensity-to-consume effect, as found, for instance, in Kenya (Lipton, 1992).

38. See e.g., Struass (1986) and Deolalikar (1988) on the positive association between nutritional intake and labor productivity, although admittedly the interaction between nutritional intake and human functioning could be subject to interpersonal and intrapersonal variation (Dreze and Sen, 1989).

39. This is partly because women's lesser mobility would confine them more than men to local markets; and partly derivative of the more general observation that villages with greater equality in land (and farm income) distribution in South Asia tend to generate more demand for local nonfarm products, especially through consumption linkages (Islam, 1986).

40. Personal observation in Rajasthan (northwest India); also see Dreze (1990) for similar observations on some other parts of India.

41. For further elaboration on the importance of women's rights in land in strengthening their overall bargaining position, and for a conceptual framework for characterizing gender relations, see Agarwal (forthcoming).

42. See e.g., Solaiman and Alam (1977), Merry (1983) and R. Singh (1988).

43. To some extent even elements in the State apparatus are beginning to realize this: in India a recent government attempt to promote adult female education (the *Mahila Samakhya* [Education for Women's Equality] Program launched in 1989) is not only couched in terms of female "empowerment" but recognizes that organizing rural women into groups to discuss gender relations can be a necessary first step toward that end (GOI, 1991).

44. For detailed case studies of these communities, see Agarwal (forthcoming).

45. Although the nomenclature "Moor" (given to the Sri Lankan Muslims under Portuguese rule) has today largely been subsumed under the general category "Muslim," I have retained the term to distinguish the group both from other Muslims in Sri Lanka who did not traditionally practice matriliny, and from the matrilineal Muslims (such as the Mappilas) of southwest India whose inheritance practices were different.

46. *Uxorilocality* implies that the husband takes up residence with the wife and (with or near) her parental family. Where this is a regular practice dictated by a preferred custom, this results in institutionalized *matrilocal* residence, where the normal residence of most husbands is with or near the matrilineal kin of the wives. *Patrilocal* implies that the wife takes up residence with the husband and (with or near) his patrilineal kin.

47. Personal communication, Joan Mencher, New York, 1992.

48. The *karanavan* was the head of the *taravad* and manager of the joint family estate; he was usually the seniormost male member of the *taravad*. *Taravad*: the matrilineal joint family, holding property in common and often sharing a common residence.

49. See e.g., Mayer (1960) for Madhya Pradesh (central India); Newell (1970) for Himachal Pradesh (northwest India); Freed and Freed (1976) for a village near Delhi; Beck (1972) for Tamil Nadu (south India); Ishwaran (1968) for Karnataka (south India); and Elgar (1960) for Pakistan Punjab.

50. See e.g., Parry (1979), Mayer (1960), Jansen (1983), Alavi (1972), and Elgar (1960).

51. See Chaudhuri (1987), Kishwar (1987), and Kelkar and Nathan (1991).

52. Although some of these constraints are also faced by poor rural men, women face them in greater degree; and several constraints are gender-specific.

53. For a mapping of these cross-regional patterns, see Agarwal (forthcoming).

54. See e.g., Abdullah and Zeidenstein (1982), Jansen (1983), Nath (1984) and Taniguchi (1987).

55. See Gandhi and Shah (1991) on the functioning of

some all-women village *panchayats* in India, and Goetz (1990) on the functioning of male and female field-level development administrators in Bangladesh.

REFERENCES

Abdullah, T., and S. A. Zeidenstein, *Village Women of Bangladesh: Prospects for Change* (Oxford: Pergamon Press, 1982).

Agarwal, B., *A Field of One's Own: Gender and Land Rights in South Asia,* (Cambridge: Cambridge University Press, forthcoming).

Agarwal, B., "The gender and environment debate: Lessons from India," *Feminist Studies,* Vol. 18, No. 1 (1992), pp. 119–158.

Agarwal, B., "Tribal matriliny in transition: Gender, property, and production relations in Northeast India," World Employment Programme Research Working Paper No. WEP 10/WP 50, (Geneva: International Labour Office (ILO), 1990).

Agarwal, B., "Women, poverty and agricultural growth in India," *The Journal of Peasant Studies* (July 1986), pp. 165–220.

Agarwal, B., "Work participation of rural women in the Third World: Some data and conceptual biases,"*Economic and Political Weekly* (December 21, 1985), pp. A155–A164.

Agarwal, B., *Mechanization in Indian Agriculture: An Analytical Study of the Indian Punjab* (Delhi: Allied Publishers, 1983).

Alavi, H., "Kinship in West Punjab villages," *Contributions to Indian Sociology,* New Series, No. 6 (December 1972), pp. 1–27.

Ali, I., B. M. Desai, R. Radhakrishna and V. S. Vyas, "Indian agriculture at 2000: Strategies for equality," *Economic and Political Weekly,* Annual Number, Vol. 16, Nos. 10–12 (March 1981), pp. 409–424.

Bardhan, K., "Rural employment, wages and labour markets in India: A survey of research," *Economic and Political Weekly,* Vol. 12, Nos. 26–28 (1977).

Bardhan, P., "Analytics of the institutions of informal co-operation in rural development," *World Development,* Vol. 21, No. 4 (1993), pp. 633–639.

Barrett, M., *Women's Oppression Today: The Marxist/Feminist Encounter* (London: Verso Books, 1980).

Basant, R., and B. L. Kumar, "Rural agricultural activities in India: A review of available evidence," *Social Scientist,* Vol. 17, Nos. 1–2 (1989), pp. 13–17.

Beck, B. E. F., *Peasant Society in Konku: A Study of Right and Left Subcastes in South India* (Vancouver: University of British Columbia Press, 1972).

Berry, R. A., and W. R. Cline. *Agrarian Structure and Productivity in Developing Countries* (Baltimore: Johns Hopkins University Press, 1979).

Binswanger, H. P., and M. Rosenzweig. "Credit markets, wealth and endowments in rural South India," Paper presented at the Eighth World Congress of the International Economic Association (New Delhi: December 1–5, 1986).

Blumberg, R. L., "Income under female vs. male control: Hypotheses from a theory of gender stratification and data from the Third World," in R. L. Blumberg (Ed.), *Gender, Family and Economy: The Triple Overlap* (Newbury Park: Sage Publications, 1991), pp. 97–127.

Bourdieu, P., *Distinctions* (Cambridge: Harvard University Press, 1984).

Boyce, J., *Agrarian Impasse in Bengal: Institutional Constraints to Technological Change* (Oxford: Oxford University Press, 1987).

Bromley, D. W., "Property, authority systems, and the artful state," Paper presented at a conference on "Common Property, Collective Action and Ecology" held at the Center for Ecological Sciences, Indian Institute of Science (Bangalore, India: August 19–21, 1991).

Buvinic, M., and N. H. Youseff, "Women-headed households: The ignored factor in development planning," Report submitted to AID/WID, International Center for Research on Women (Washington, DC: ICRW, March 1978).

Cain, M. T., S. R. Khanam, and S. Nahar, "Class, patriarchy and the structure of women's work in rural Bangladesh," Working Paper No. 43, Center for Population Studies (New York: The Population Council, 1979).

Caldwell, J. C., P. H. Reddy and P. Caldwell, *The Causes of Demographic Change: Experimental Research in South India* (Madison, WI: The University of Wisconsin Press, 1988).

Caplan, P., *Class and Gender in India: Women and their Organizations in a South Indian City* (New York: Tavistock Publications, 1985).

Chadha, G. K., "Non-farm sector in India's rural economy: Policy performance and growth prospects," Mimeo (New Delhi: Center for Regional Development, Jawaharlal Nehru University, 1992).

Chaudhuri, A. B., *The Santals: Religion and Rituals* (New Delhi: Ashish Publishing House, 1987).

Chen, M. A., *A Quiet Revolution: Women in Transition in Rural Bangladesh* (Cambridge: Schenkman Publishing Co, Inc., 1983).

Dasgupta, B., "Agrarian change and the new technology in India," Report No. 77.2 (Geneva: United Nations Research Institute for Social Development, 1977).

Delphy, C., *The Main Enemy: A Materialist Analysis of Women's Oppression* (London: Women's Research and Resources Center, 1977).

Delmar, R., "Looking again at Engels's origin of the family, private property and the state," in J. Mitchell and A. Oakley (Eds.), *The Rights and Wrongs of Women* (Harmondsworth: Penguin Books, 1976).

Deolalikar, A. B., "Nutrition and labour productivity in agriculture: Econometric estimates for rural South Asia," *Review of Economics and Statistics,* Vol. 70, No. 4 (August 1988), pp. 406–413.

Dixon, R., *Rural Women at Work: Strategies for Development in South Asia* (Baltimore: Johns Hopkins University Press, 1978).

Dreze, J., "Widows in India", Discussion paper No. DEP 46 (London: The Development Economics Research Programme, London School of Economics, 1990).

Dreze, J., and A. K. Sen, *Hunger and Public Action* (Oxford: Clarendon Press, 1989).

Elgar, Z., *A Punjabi Village in Pakistan* (New York: Columbia University Press, 1960).

Engels, F. A., *The Origin of the Family, Private Property and the State* (Harmondsworth: Penguin Books [1884], 1972).

Feder, G., "The economics of land titling in Thailand," Mimeo (Washington, DC: World Bank, April 1989).

Feder, G., and D. Feeny, "Land tenure and property rights: Theory and implications for development policy," *The World Bank Economic Review*, Vol. 5, No. 1 (1991), pp. 135–153.

Firestone, S., *The Dialectic of Sex: The Case for Feminist Revolution* (New York: Bantam Books, 1970).

Freed, S. A., and R. S. Freed, *Shanti Nagar: The Effects of Urbanization in a Village in North India*, Anthropological Papers of the American Museum of Natural History, Vol. 53, Part 1 (New York: American Museum of Natural History, 1976).

Gaiha, R., and N. A. Kazmi, "Aspects of rural poverty in India," *Economics of Planning*, Vol. 17, Nos. 2–3 (1981), pp. 74–112.

Gandhi, N., and N. Shah, *The Issues at Stake: Theory and Practice in the Contemporary Women's Movement in India* (Delhi: Kali for Women, 1991).

Goetz, A. M., "Local heroes, local despots: Exploring field-worker discretion in implementing gender-redistributive development policy," Paper presented at the Development Studies Association Conference (Glasgow: 1990).

Government of Bangladesh, *Fourth Five Year Plan (1990–95)* (Dhaka: Ministry of Planning, 1990).

Government of India, *The Eighth Five Year Plan: 1992–97, II* (Delhi: Planning Commission, 1992a).

Government of India, "Land use statistics, 1987–88, Mimeo (Delhi: Directorate of Economics and Statistics, Ministry of Agriculture, 1992b).

Government of India, "Mahila Samakhya: Education for women's equality, national overview report" (New Delhi: National Project Office (Dept. of Education, Ministry of Human Resource Development, 1991).

Government of India, *Women in India: A Statistical Profile — 1988* (New Delhi: Ministry of Human Resource Development, 1988).

Government of India, "A note on some aspects of household ownership holding: NSS 37th Round (January–December 1982) and results on some aspects of household ownership holding: NSS 37th Round (January–December 1982)," *Sarvekshana, A Journal of the National Sample Survey Organisation*, Vol. 11, No. 2, Issue No. 33 (October 1987), pp. 1–18, S1–S175.

Government of India, *Thirtyseventh Round Report on Land Holdings — 2: Some Aspects of Operational Holdings*, Report No. 331 (New Delhi: National Sample Survey Organisation, Dept. of Statistics, 1986).

Government of Nepal, *Eighth Plan, 1992–1997: Summary* (unofficial translation) (Kathmandu: National Planning Commission, 1992).

Government of Pakistan, *Eighth Five-Year Plan (1993–98) Approach Paper* (Islamabad: Planning Commission, 1991).

Government of Sri Lanka, *Sri Lanka Census of Agriculture 1982* (Colombo, Dept. of Census and Statistics, Ministry of Plan Implementation, 1984).

Harriss, B., "The intrafamily distribution of hunger in South Asia," in J. Dreze and A. K. Sen (Eds.), *The Political Economy of Hunger* (Oxford: Clarendon Press, 1990), pp. 351–424.

Hazell, P. B., and S. Haggblade, "Rural-urban growth linkages in India," Working Paper WPS 430, Agriculture and Rural Development Department (Washington, DC: World Bank, 1990).

Hershman, P., *Punjabi Kinship and Marriage* (Delhi: Hindustan Publishing Corporation, 1981).

Hinton, W., *Fanshen: A Documentary of Revolution in a Chinese Village* (Harmondsworth: Penguin Books Ltd. 1972).

Hoddinott, J., "Household economics and the economics of households," Draft paper presented at the conference on Intra-Household Resource Allocation, International Food Policy Research Institute and World Bank (Washington, DC: February 12–14, 1991).

Hossain, M., "Credit for women: A review of special credit programmes in Bangladesh," draft paper (Dhaka: Bangladesh Institute for Development Studies, 1988).

Hunt, H. I., "Intervention and change in the lives of rural poor women in Bangladesh: A discussion paper," (Dhaka: Bangladesh Rural Action Committee, December 1983).

Ishwaran, K., *Shivapur: A South Indian Village* (London: Routledge & Kegan Paul, 1968).

Islam, R., "Rural industrialisation and employment in Asia: Issues and evidence," in *Rural Industrialisation and Employment in Asia* (New Delhi: International Labour Organisation, Asian Employment Programme, 1987), pp. 1–18.

Islam, R., "Non-farm employment in rural Asia: Issues and evidence," in R. T. Shand (Ed.), *Off-Farm Employment in the Development of Rural Asia* (Canberra: Australian National University, 1986), pp. 153–173.

Jannuzi, F. T., and J. T. Peach, *The Agrarian Structure of Bangladesh: An Impediment to Development* (Delhi: Sangam Books, 1980).

Jansen, E. G., *Rural Bangladesh: Competition for Scarce Resources* (Oslo: Norwegian University Press, 1983).

Kelkar, G., and D. Nathan, *Women, Land and Forests: A Study of the Jharkhand Adivasis* (London: Zed Books; New Delhi: Kali for Women, 1991).

Kilkelly, K., "Women's roles in irrigated agricultural production systems during the 1985 Yala Season: Parakrama Samudra Scheme and Giritale Scheme, Polonnaruma District," Report (Colombo: United States Agency for International Development (USAID), 1986).

Kishwar, M., "Toiling without rights: Ho women of Singhbhum," *Economic and Political Weekly*, Vol. 22, Nos. 3–5 (1987).

Kishwar, M., "Challenging the denial of land rights to women," *Manushi* (November–December 1982), pp. 2–6.

Krause, I.-B., "Kinship and economics in North-West Nepal," Ph.D. dissertation (London: London School of Economics, University of London, 1982).

Kumar, S. K., "Role of the Household Economy in Child Nutrition at Low Incomes," Occasional Paper No. 95 (Ithaca: Dept. of Agricultural Economics, Cornell University, 1978).

Lal, I., "Goats and Tigers," a video film by Ian Lal (Delhi: International Labour Organisation, 1986).

Lipton, M., "Land reform as commenced business: The evidence against stopping," Draft paper (Brighton: Institute of Development Studies, Sussex, 1992).

Lipton, M., and R. Longhurst, *New Seeds and Poor People* (London: Unwin Hyman, 1989).

Manimala, *"Zameen Kenkar? Jote Onkar!:* Women's participation in the Bodhgaya Land Struggle," *Manushi,* Vol. 14 (1983), pp. 2–16.

Mayer, A. C., *Caste and Kinship in Central India — A Village and Its Region* (London: Routledge & Kegan Paul, 1960).

Mencher, J., "Women's work and poverty: Contribution to household maintenance in two regions of South India," in D. Dwyer and J. Bruce (Eds.), *A Home Divided: Women and Income in the Third World* (Stanford: Stanford University Press, 1988).

Merry, D. J., "Irrigation, poverty and social change in a village of Pakistani Punjab: An historical and cultural ecological analysis," Ph.D. dissertation (Philadelphia: University of Pennsylvania, 1983).

Mies, M., K. Lalita and K. Kumari, *Indian Women in Subsistence and Agricultural Labour* (Geneva: International Labour Organisation, 1986).

Millet, K., *Sexual Politics* (New York: Doubleday, 1970).

Minturn, L., and J. T. Hitchcock, *The Rajputs of Khalapur* (New York: John Wiley, 1966).

Molyneux, M., "Mobilization without emancipation? Women's interests, the state, and revolution in Nicaragua," *Feminist Studies,* Vol. 11, No. 2 (Summer 1985), pp. 227–254.

Molyneux, M., "Socialist societies old and new: Progress towards women's emancipation, *Feminist Review,* Vol. 8 (Summer 1981), pp. 1–34.

Moser, C. O. N., "Gender Planning in the Third World: Meeting practical and strategic gender needs," *World Development,* Vol. 17, No. 11 (1989), pp. 1799–1825.

Munck, V. C. de, "Cross-currents of conflict and cooperatives in Kotabowa, Ph.D. dissertation (Riverside, CA: University of California at Riverside, 1985).

Nath, J. N., Dynamics of socio-economic change and the role and status of women in Natunpur: Case study of a Bangladesh village," Ph.D. dissertation in sociology (Dhaka: University of Dhaka, 1984).

Newell, W. H., "An Upper Ravi Village; the process of social change in Himachal Pradesh," in K. Ishwaran (Ed.), *Change and Continuity in India's Villages* (New York: Colombia University Press, 1970), pp. 37–56.

Omvedt, G., "Effects of agricultural development on the status of women," Paper prepared for the International Labour Office Tripartite Asian Regional Seminar on Rural Development and Women (Mahabaleshwar, India: April 1981).

Parry, J. P., *Caste and Kinship in Kangra* (Delhi: Vikas Publishing House, 1979).

Patel, R., *Women and Law in Pakistan* (Karachi: Faiza Publishers, 1979).

Per-Lee, D. A., "Employment, ingenuity and family life: Rajasthani women in Delhi, India," Ph.D. dissertation (Washington, DC: American University, 1981).

Raj, K. N., and M. Tharakan, "Agrarian reform in Kerala and its impact on the rural economy — A preliminary assessment," in A. Ghose (Ed.), *Agrarian Reform in Contemporary Developing Countries* (London: Croom Helm, 1983), pp. 31–90.

Rosenzweig, M. R., and K. I. Wolpin, "Specific experience,

household structure, and intergenerational transfers: farm family land and labour arrangements in developing countries, *Quarterly Journal of Economics,* Vol. 100, Supplement (1985), pp. 961–987.

Sacks, K., "Engels revisited: Women: The organization of production, and private property," in R. R. Reiter (Ed.), *Toward an Anthropology of Women* (New York: Monthly Review Press, 1975), pp. 211–234.

Safilios-Rothschild, C., and S. Mahmud, "Women's roles in agriculture: Present trends and potential for growth," Paper produced for the Bangladesh Agricultural Sector Review, UNDP/UNIFEM (Dhaka: 1989).

Saito, K. A., and C. J. Weidenmann, "Agricultural extension and women farmers in Africa," World Bank Working Paper WPS 398, Population and Human Resource Department (Washington, DC: World Bank, 1990).

Saradamoni K., "Changing land relations and women: A case study of Palghat District, Kerala, " in V. Mazumdar (Ed.), *Women and Rural Transformation* (Delhi: Concept Publications (1993), pp. 35–171.

Sayers, J., M. Evans and N. Redclift (Eds.), *Engels Revisited: New Feminist Essays* (London: Tavistock Publications, 1987).

Schrijvers, J., "Blueprint for undernourishment: The Mahaweli River Development Scheme in Sri Lanka," in B. Agarwal (Ed.), *Structures of Patriarchy: State, Community and Household in Modernising Asia* (London: Zed Books; New Delhi: Kali for Women, 1988), pp. 29–51.

Selvaduri, A. J., "Land, personhood and sorcery in a Sinhalese Village," in L. Smith (Ed.), *Religion and Social Conflict in South Asia* (Leiden: E. J. Brill Publishers, 1976), pp. 82–96.

Sen, A. K., *Poverty and Famines: An Essay on Entitlement and Deprivation* (Delhi: Oxford University Press, 1981).

Sharma, M. L., and T. M. Dak (Eds.), *Aging in India: Challenge for the Society* (New Delhi: Ajanta Publishers, 1987).

Sharma, U., *Women, Work and Property in North-West India* (London and New York: Tavistock Publications, 1980).

Shramashakti: Report of the National Commission on Self-Employed Women and Women in the Informal Sector (New Delhi: 1988).

Singh, A. M., and A. Kelles-Vitannen (Eds.), *Invisible Hands: Women in Home-based Production* (Delhi: Sage Publications, 1987).

Singh, R., *Land, Power and People: Rural Elite in Transition, 1801–1970* (Delhi: Sage Publications, 1988).

Singh, N., *The Bankura Story: Rural Women Organise for Change* (New Delhi: ILO, 1988).

Solaiman, M., and M. Alam, "Characteristics of candidates for election in three union parishads in Comilla Kotwali Thana" (Comilla: Bangladesh Agency for Rural Development, 1977).

Strauss, J., "Does better nutrition raise farm productivity?" *Journal of Political Economy,* Vol. 94, No. 2 (April 1986), pp. 297–320.

Sundaram, K., and S. Tendulkar, "Towards an explanation of inter-regional variation in poverty and unemployment in Rural India," Working Paper No. 237 (New Delhi: Delhi School of Economics, May, 1983).

Taniguchi, S., *Society and Economy of a Rice-Producing Village in Northern Bangladesh,* Studies in Socio-Cultural Change in Rural Villages in Bangladesh No. 6,

Institute for the Study of Languages and Cultures in Asia and Africa (Tokyo: Tokyo University of Foreign Studies, 1987).

United Nations, *The Situation of Women: Selected Indicators 1990* (Vienna: Dept. of International Economics and Social Affairs, Statistical Office, 1990).

Wallace, B. J., R. V. Kempler and M. Wilson-Moore, "Land acquisition and inheritance in rural Bangladesh," *South Asian Anthropologist,* Vol. 9, No. 2 (1988), pp. 111–118.

Westergaard, K., *Pauperization and Rural Women in Bangladesh: A Case Study* (Comilla: BARD, 1983).

Wolff, R., and S. Resnick, "Power, property and class," Discussion paper No. 21 (Amherst, MA: Dept. of Economics, University of Massachusetts, 1989).

[27]

Pergamon

World Development, Vol. 25, No. 8, pp. 1205–1223, 1997
© 1997 Elsevier Science Ltd
All rights reserved. Printed in Great Britain
0305–750X/97 $17.00 + 0.00

PII: S0305–750X(97)00033–8

Gender, Development and Urban Social Change: Women's Community Action in Global Cities

AMY LIND*

Arizona State University, Tempe, Arizona, U.S.A.

Summary. — This article addresses the gender dimensions of women's community action in global cities. It focuses on two types of women's organizations (food provision and anti-violence) and draws out their implications for community and national development frameworks in the context of economic restructuring and urban poverty. The article undertakes three tasks: First, it rethinks frameworks of development and urban social change from a gender perspective. Second, it analyzes the ways in which local women's organizations have acted proactively—rather than merely reactively—to processes of urban restructuring. Third, it proposes an approach in which women's informal political and economic participation is better accounted for in national development frameworks and related community development initiatives. © 1997 Elsevier Science Ltd

Key words — gender, development, structural adjustment, urban poverty, women's movements, Latin America

The world is in dramatic flux. Global concerns force themselves on people's everyday lives at the same time that local events, with unprecedented speed and frequency, become global matters (Fisher and Kling, 1993, p. xi).

1. INTRODUCTION

In the past two decades, countries throughout the world have adopted neoliberal development policies and initiated dramatic restructuring processes of state, economic and civil institutions. In North America and Western Europe, traditional welfare states have been downsized and restructured, with the goal of decentralizing local services and redistributive subsidies, along with decision-making authority and accountability, from federal to municipal levels and from public to community organizations (Clavel *et al.*, 1997). In many developing and post-Soviet countries, this process has been initiated through structural adjustment policies (SAPs), and through the general adoption of neoliberal policy agendas by national governments (Smith *et al.*, 1994). One obvious outcome of this process has been that local communities have had to seek independent survival and development strategies.

Many have observed communities' responses to urban poverty in this context (see Fisher and Kling, 1993; Pickvance and Preteceille, 1991). What has been less observed is the global emergence of women's grassroots efforts to confront economic restructuring and poverty, despite the fact that women have participated massively in urban social movements and have created their own organizations and survival networks to address the social reproduction of their communities (Rowbotham and Mitter, 1994; Basu, 1995b; Walton and Seddon, 1994). This oversight can be partly explained by the general difficulty in accounting for volunteer action, yet it is also due to conceptual biases in development frameworks which overlook women's crucial yet unaccounted for roles in social reproduction and in urban social change (Elson, 1991; Benería, 1992 and

*I thank Martha Farmelo for her participation, support and encouragement throughout initial stages of this project. This article is derived from a study of women's volunteer action in global cities, based on a collaborative project of United Nations Volunteers (UNV), United Nations Research Institute for Social Development (UNRISD), and the Inter-American Foundation (IAF). At UNRISD, I wish to thank David Westendorff, Carol Miller and Shahrashoub Razavi for comments on earlier drafts. My thanks also to Lourdes Benería, Jo-Marie Burt and an anonymous referee for their helpful comments. Final revision accepted: March 15, 1997.

Benería, 1995; Cagatay *et al.*, 1995; Moser, 1993; Corcoran-Nantes, 1993). Women's organizations have been the first to point out the gender impacts of state development policies on local political, economic and family structures, and the first to make connections between global development and everyday life (Benería, 1989). In addition, they provide examples of how women have responded collectively to the (often hidden) transfer of welfare responsibilities to the community level—something which remains largely unexamined in the planning and development literature—and of how women have integrated themselves into local decision-making and planning processes.

This paper addresses the gender dimensions of women's community action in the context of economic restructuring and urban poverty. As I will show, the gender dimensions of urban structural change are far-reaching, and while initial research documents the potential gender effects of macroeconomic frameworks with "male biases" (Elson, 1991; also see Cagatay *et al.*, 1995), less has been done to understand the nature of women's collective participation in the reorganization of social reproduction at the community level, and to draw out the implications of this type of collective action for neoliberal development frameworks and practices. In some cases, women have acted based on their traditional gender roles—as in the case of "mothers' movements" against violence and human rights abuses, and in the process have transformed public understandings of women's participation in the development and political process. These organizations have made public a set of issues about violence and its impacts on family structures as well as about the (historically invisible) roles of women in local development and urban social change.

In other cases, women's organizations have participated actively in local initiatives which stem from policies of decentralization and state downsizing—through municipal planning structures, non-governmental organizations, and grassroots movements. Supporters of these policies often herald increases in local power on the basis that "more people are participating—more effectively, and more democratically"[1] however, as I argue in this article, increases in local power may not automatically transfer more power for women if and when the "hidden" transfer of welfare responsibilities to community organizations and households is left unexamined, and for as long as women's community participation is perceived as "outside" the planning and development process.

Local women's organizations are at the forefront of challenging these biases as they affect the participants' everyday lives and their surrounding urban and policy environments. This holds true comparatively among the cases in this study, despite

important cultural, political and historical differences among the organizations and cities. The similarities and differences in local movements within a global context depend upon a number of related factors that reflect both the organizations' and the participants' locations within community and urban structures; their institutional networks; and their roles in the household and family, and by extension, in their communities—roles which are often unacknowledged because they are not accounted for in the market and have been undervalued culturally (see Heyzer, 1995; UNDP, 1995). Whether it be through participating in one of the more than 2,000 communal kitchens in Lima, in neighborhood women's organizations in Quito, or in mothers' anti-violence movements in US cities, women's organizations have played key roles in generating women's involvement in community decision-making and addressing the daily impacts of economic restructuring: in this sense, both their community involvement and the implications of their action for policy frameworks merit further attention if we are to promote more equitable national and urban policies. Section 2 addresses some important conceptual issues related to gender and community action and serves to put into context the case studies presented in later sections. In it I discuss different types of women's organizations and movements, and the specific ways in which gender motivates, shapes and constrains women's local participation. This is analyzed within the context of neoliberal reform, when various sectors of poor women have been forced—or have felt compelled—to create their own, relatively autonomous strategies for survival and social change.

Sections 3 and 4 analyze two examples of women's community action (neighborhood and anti-violence) and their gender implications for state policy. It discusses the diverse ways in which organizations have confronted structural economic inequalities and more pervasive forms of gender, ethnic and racial discrimination in these countries. Section 5 addresses the strategic and conceptual implications of these forms of women's community action for community development and for broader policy processes, focusing on issues of sustainability, institution-building and the gender effects of decentralization measures on community action—all issues of great importance in the current context of neoliberal reform and economic restructuring at a global level.

2. STRUGGLES FOR LIVELIHOOD: WOMEN'S ORGANIZATIONS IN COMPARATIVE PERSPECTIVE

In fighting for what appear to be particularistic goals—finding their voices, setting their own agendas, and creating their own social spaces—women's movements are seeking the most universal objectives. But note that at such moments when the particular and the universal coincide, the subject may no longer be women. Thus, the tensions between local and global feminisms reverberate within the relationship between women's movements and the movements of other oppressed groups. The strengths of women's movements lie in their insights into that which distinguishes them and that which joins them to others who have suffered. And from these encounters come the most exquisite knowledge, vitality and power (Basu, 1995a, p. 20).

Much research has been conducted on women's organizations and movements in western, industrialized countries; until recently, much less so has been conducted on developing regions (see Basu, 1995b). The literature on Western women's movements has tended to focus on middle-class movements, although many studies document the important contributions of poor and working class women's organizations and movements in the United States, Canada and Western Europe (Katzenstein and Mueller, 1987; Lovenduski, 1986; Wolfe and Tucker, 1995; Bookman and Morgen, 1988). These and other studies point out that poor women's and other urban social movements have arisen in response to deindustrialization, massive unemployment, and struggles for decent living spaces in deeply segregated and economically overburdened cities. For many, this is coupled by a lack of citizenship rights, insufficient health and educational systems, and growing rates of political and racial violence in urban areas. In contrast to other urban social movements, women's organizations and movements address a set of gender-specific issues including: violence against women, their roles as mothers and as working women, gender-based discrimination in the workplace and/or in the informal sector, the gender impacts of social policies, and children's rights. To my knowledge, many studies which focus on community development and local power often overlook women's protagonistic roles in these processes (see, for example, Fainstein and Fainstein, 1982, 1985; Fisher and Kling, 1993; Logan and Swanstrom, 1990; Pickvance and Preteceille, 1991). Studies that focus specifically on women's organizations provide an important basis for explaining why women choose to create their own organizations and movements, and how gender-specific forms of community action might inform local government, urban and national policy.

Studies of poor women's movements in developing and in post-Soviet countries focus attention on their relationship to processes of development, democratization, and state formation. This is due to concrete historical reasons—such as the fact that many countries in these regions have undergone state transitions—as well as to the trajectory of scholarship on movements in these regions (Basu, 1995a).

In Latin America, a large number of poor women's organizations emerged during the period of economic crisis and democratic transition in the late 1970s and 1980s. These movements have been explored extensively (see, for example, Jaquette, 1994; Jelin, 1990; Alvarez, 1990; Schild, 1991; Radcliffe and Westwood, 1993; León, 1994; Friedmann et al., 1996). While original research focused on women's struggles against military authoritarianism and participation in processes of democratization, more recent scholarship has focused on the dynamics of power and structural inequalities which emerge and become consolidated under formal democracy (Alvarez, 1996). In the 1990s, further attention has been placed on women's collective responses to economic crisis and structural adjustment policies (Friedmann et al., 1996; Barrig, 1996; Benería and Feldman, 1992). This literature discusses the political potential and limitations of contemporary women's organizations, including their long-term impact on institutional and social change. In many countries where structural adjustment and/or neoliberal social and economic policies have been introduced, scholars and policy makers have begun to analyze women's collective survival strategies in this context: in Africa (Parpart and Staudt, 1989; Tripp, 1992), Latin America (Benería, 1992), South Asia (Feldman, 1992); Eastern Europe (Moghadam, 1994); and North America and Western Europe (Gordon, 1990; Bookman and Morgen, 1988; Cohen, 1994).

In Latin America, a proliferation of research has documented women's collective responses to urban poverty and economic restructuring; this is due in part to the rich tradition of women's collective organizing, and to the explicit responses many women's organizations have made to adjustment measures (Lind, 1995). In this section I draw from this literature and suggest its relevance for other regions undergoing similar processes. An initial question is the extent to which grassroots women's organizations are likely to sustain themselves through crisis periods, and influence state policy agendas in the long run. Alvarez (1996) argues that neoliberal development policies have served to institutionalize what were once viewed as spontaneous strategies to cope with a momentary crisis. Alvarez contends that women's organizations are increasingly placed in a paradoxical position under neoliberal development policies. On one hand, many community-based women's organizations were initiated in the late 1970s/early 1980s to confront the economic crisis and the negative impacts of structural adjustment policies. Their struggles therefore emerged out of economic necessity, although many developed more complicated critiques of power and structural inequalities through the process of organizing, and their political demands, similar to those of traditional party politics and class-based movements, were directed at the state. Under neoliberal reform, as the welfare state is dismantled, poor women's organizations have lost crucial state funding—as well as access to state welfare services—and have become even more dependent on an "undependable" state.[2] Women's organizations are therefore left with little recourse but to continue their efforts on their own or to seek funding elsewhere—primarily from international NGOs, bilateral and multilateral agencies. Alvarez's paradox, therefore, refers to the institutional crisis that organizations face as they are no longer certain where to direct their demands.

Indeed, many organizations have had to develop new strategies in order to secure funding and maintain their institutional structure. In the context of state retrenchment, as international donors increasingly channel funds to local NGOs and grassroots organizations in their new roles as service providers, Alvarez's paradox holds true. Women's organizations may in fact benefit from donors' emphasis on NGO participation if they are incorporated into the new local structures. Most development frameworks However, either do not account for gender or assume that women have indefinite time to participate in volunteer-based community groups. This being the case, despite donor's intentions to promote the participation of NGOs, strengthen civil society, and build democratic practices, women's organizations are likely to lose out entirely or continue serving in their roles as unpaid managers of social reproduction. This depends, to a large extent, on country-specific neoliberal measures as well as on the policies which preceded them and the effects of the shifts in welfare provision on local communities.

A related problem is the extent to which people will seek collective answers or retreat to the private realm of the family and other informal networks for survival. Benería (1992) found that there has been a "privatization of the struggle" for daily survival along with the broader process of privatizations taking place in Mexico. In her study of 55 households in Mexico City, Benería concludes that poor households are increasingly responsible for social reproduction, with little or no help from the state, or even from private organizations or informal networks. Thus Benería's work suggests that, in the case of Mexico City, rather than becoming more dependent on the state, poor women and their families have become more reliant on direct family networks than on any other form of welfare provision and/or social support. Benería observes a lack of collective action; Alvarez observes that women are acting collectively and have no alternative but to continue doing so, even if funding is scarce. Both analyses reflect accurately the dilemmas faced by neighborhood and other local women's organizations (and individual households) in cities throughout the world.

Studies of household survival strategies indicate that women's motivations for participating in organizations depends not only upon their poor economic situations but also upon the particular relationships they develop with public institutions and social movements (McFarren, 1992; Moser, 1989b; Lind, 1995). This observation merits further attention as it remains unclear why some women choose to participate and others do not. Research which focuses on the political, institutional context within which community-based women's organizations develop their strategies is one way to address why certain groups of women initiate organizations and what relationships they develop, over time, with public and community organizations. It also sheds light on why some groups deeply influence policy agendas while others do not. Barrig (1996) argues that the communal kitchen movement in Lima, Peru is a "needs-based" movements. She draws from Fraser's (Fraser, 1989) original work on needs-based discourse[3] and argues that members of communal kitchens in Lima position themselves politically as "consumers" and/or as "clients" of the state, rather than as a political class pushing for more fundamental institutional change. Specifically, Barrig argues that as kitchen members struggle for their rights and needs as poor women, mothers, and members of collective kitchens, they compete with other kitchens for scarce state resources. This has led to a situation in which the kitchens position themselves, hierarchically, as "clients" of the state and fail to make strategic connections between their own struggles and those of other kitchens, organizations and movements. Barrig suggests that these organizations are increasingly isolated from other movements, and often do not build coalitions nor envision a broader transformation of society (a situation, she suggests, which results both from institutional constraints and from the organizations' inability to conceptualize new political strategies). Thus, communal kitchens are largely reactive and unable to influence state policy in meaningful ways.

Other research concludes more positively, although cautiously, about the potential of women's organizations to influence policy agendas and negotiate power in their local communities—through interactions with neighborhood associations and/or cooperatives, political parties, municipalities, religious institutions, and NGOs. Schild (1991) analyzes women's roles in local (mixed) organizations in authoritarian Santiago, Chile (1973–80). She contends that women's participation in these organizations—and their struggles to establish their own, gender-specific organizations—deeply engendered the traditional arena of class politics and human rights struggles in Santiago. Their participation, therefore, must be viewed not only in terms of their actual involvement, but also in terms of how they negotiate gender and class relations, and political ideologies, in their daily lives and the consequences of these actions for changing consciousness. She contends that much of what is decided politically within the organizations depends upon their relationships to, and interpretations of, state development practices in Chile. Thus women's struggles for the seemingly most basic needs—such as the basic right to life and the right to a decent living space—are often ideological struggles over gender (and other) inequalities deeply engrained in state policy frameworks, in the law, and in community structures (also see Lind, 1995; Alexander, 1991).

Schild's analysis allows us to make connections between women's political identities and state development policies. Poor women's massive participation in (both mixed and gender-specific) organizations in Santiago, and social solidarity networks established between middle-class and poor women's organizations, contributed a great deal to the incorporation of gender issues into the state policies developed by the transition government of President Patricio Alwyn (1990–1994). This assertion is confirmed by other researchers such as Valdés (1994) who argues that the wide production of knowledge about Chilean poor women through grassroots, anti-authoritarian political activism in the 1970s provided the basis upon which policy makers could make a case for incorporating gender issues into the public agendas of the 1980s and 1990s. While important criticisms have been made of studies which contribute the emergence of urban social movements directly to international solidarity and development policies (see Mohanty, 1991; Basu, 1995a), these historical factors in Chile exemplify the complicated and intertwined relationships that women's organizations in poor countries have had with public institutions since the inception of their collective strategizing.

All of these studies provide important examples of the transformative power and limitations of local women's organizations in the 1980s and 1990s. They also point out that women's struggles for livelihood are often determined as much by their dire economic needs as by their positions, roles and relationships in family and political structures. In the remainder of this paper I examine some regional cases and draw out their gender implications for state policy and economic restructuring.

3. SHARING THE COSTS OF SOCIAL REPRODUCTION: COMMUNAL KITCHENS IN LIMA, PERÚ

In Peru, the state has undergone a series of measures to liberalize the economy, decrease state spending and transfer the responsibility of social reproduction to the private realm of the family, economy and civil society. Unlike most other Latin American countries they were originally carried out in a highly unorthodox fashion—one which differed from the recommendations of the International Monetary Fund (IMF). Breaking somewhat with Peru's heterodox policy tradition, the administration of President Alberto Fujimori (1990–present) applied an IMF-inspired structural adjustment program which has escalated the cost of living and doubled poverty rates according to important indicators of social crisis (see Barrig, 1996). Throughout the past 12 years, the Peruvian state's project has been implemented during a period of intense civil war, promulgated by Shining Path, which has cost over 25,000 lives (Barrig, 1996).

One result of these measures has been that poor neighborhoods have organized to collectivize costs and confront the economic and political crisis in Lima, the capital city of seven million inhabitants. Lima's *pueblos jovenes* (literally "young towns," or poor neighborhoods) have increased in population from 1.5 million in 1981 to approximately 3.5 million in 1993 (Burt, 1997), In this context of increased urban poverty, communal kitchens are one example of how women have developed a strong activist network to address the problem of poverty—in particular, food consumption and distribution. Every morning, some 40,000 low-income women belonging to the *Federación de Comedores Populares Autogestionarios* (FCPA, or Federation of Self-Managed Popular Kitchens) gather at 2,000 sites throughout Lima's poor neighborhoods, pooling their human and material resources to feed their families, some 200,000 persons. Twenty to 30 female friends, relatives, churchmates and neighbors participate in each *comedor*. Women are joined by shared concerns and are welcomed, in theory, regardless of political positions or religious affiliation. The women rotate in positions of leadership and all take turns collecting dues, buying foodstuffs, and preparing the meals, usually in one of the member's kitchens. The kitchens accept donations, and continue to be dependent on them to varying degrees.

The first kitchens were organized during 1979–86 as a response to the impact of structural adjustment programs which drastically cut—or eliminated— both real income and public food subsidies. Until 1990, participants were mainly middle aged women migrants seeking to escape rural poverty and violence. Rather than directly demand social benefits from the state, the women designed autonomous, self-help solutions based on their own resources.

Between September 1988 and March 1989 alone, the number of kitchens jumped from 700 to more than 1,000 in response to implementation of a structural adjustment package implemented by the administration of President Alan García (1985–90).

A similar surge took place in 1990, this time a result of a particularly drastic structural adjustment package commonly referred to as President Alberto Fujimori's *paquetazo*, incorporating thousands of younger, newly impoverished Lima residents into the kitchens. A combination of intense economic reforms, coupled with historically unprecedented levels of violence associated with Peru's internal war, led to the growth of new forms of poverty among Lima's settlers and to the emergence of the "new poor." Many women in this group sought refuge in the communal kitchens that already existed in their neighborhoods, or followed the example of other communities to create their own. Organizational support for some of the kitchens has come from the Catholic Church, political parties, or the state; other "autonomous" kitchens receive support elsewhere. There are many differences between these kitchens, including their levels of democratic structure and participation, reliance on external funding, self-sustainability, and quantity and quality of food served. Much debate has taken place about the relative autonomy of the different types of kitchens, and two major studies concluded that those kitchens organized in a "top down" fashion by the church or state were less likely to transform gender roles and consciousness than were autonomous organizations. In autonomous kitchens, members participated more actively in decision-making and became more active in broader community planning processes (see Sara-Lafosse, 1984; Blondet, 1991; Delpino, 1991; Barrig, 1996).

Today the communal kitchens are organized into federations and confederations, including the FCPA, which represents the movement to government officials, purchases wholesale inputs, organizes microenterprise activities, and elaborates and transmits a broader view of gender and women's community participation. In December 1988, the FCPA's predecessor, the *Comisión Nacional de Comedores* (CNC), achieved passage of a law which called for the creation of a fund to support the kitchens, and a new legal status for them (as a "social base group"). This achievement resulted from the efforts of the CNC leadership, the base group membership, professionals from local support organizations, and sympathetic government officials.

The communal kitchens serve as a powerful example of women's community action. Fifteen years of successful results, despite the political and economic odds, demonstrate the kitchens' sustainability; their expansion also demonstrates their replicability. Members of the organizations have gained a new awareness of their roles not only in social reproduction, but also in community and civic action. The kitchens constitute an important part of the broader "popular" women's movement in the country.[4] Their perspectives and demands have generated a great deal of attention from NGOs, political parties, feminist activists, church groups and other base groups who work in poor neighborhoods.[5] This was particularly evident when María Elena Moyano, ex-Vice Mayor of the municipality of Villa El Salvador, and ex-President of the Federación Popular de Mujeres de Villa El Salvador (FEPOMUVES), a women's federation which has organized several communal kitchens in Villa El Salvador, was assassinated by Shining Path in front of a local fundraising event on February 15, 1992 (see Miloslavich, 1993). For many neighborhood and feminist activists, her death represented the severe contradictions that local communities had faced since the inception of heavy political violence and economic crisis. In this context, communal kitchens in this slum area and in others came to represent much more than a struggle to put "bread and butter" on the table. Rather, members of the kitchens were forced to deal with the infiltration of violence, and particularly death threats from Shining Path, were they to take an explicit stance against Shining Path's presence in their community (Moyanon, 1991; Burt, 1995). This led to a situation in which members of communal kitchens were forced to strategize even the most seemingly mundane or "basic" aspects of their daily lives—the provision of food—under highly adverse, difficult and often dangerous conditions.

Moyano's death brought about an even stronger awareness of the strength and persistence of women's community action in Lima and in other cities of Latin America. While the kitchens continue, the political violence has undoubtedly served to atomize collective efforts within the local communities, as well as between the communities and middle-class NGOs and other women's organizations in Lima. In this context, researchers and activists have debated whether these organizations provide long-term solutions (see, for example, Barrig, 1994; Alvarez, 1996). Indeed, many women who participate in these organizations are doing so out of economic necessity, and some comment that, once they enter the organizations, they cannot afford to leave them. In a sense, they are structurally bound by the space and resources that the kitchens provide. As long as the crisis persists, they can find no other alternative.

But there are other reasons, as well, for women's long-term participation in these kitchens. While these reasons are not easily generalizable, and much depends on their relationships with other actors such as the Catholic Church, NGOs and donor agencies,[6] it has been argued that these organizations provide an important political base for members to debate community and national issues. Comparative results from studies on women's organizations demonstrate that women contribute in important ways to challenging gender inequalities and misconceptions in local planning processes and in national development (Benería and Roldán, 1987; Schild, 1991; Rodríguez, 1994; Valdés, 1994; Basu, 1995b). These studies argue that even the poorest women, once collectively organized, tend to question basic structural relations such as gender and class (among others) which shape and constrain their daily lives, their communities and countries. This is true for communal kitchens in Lima as well, such as the case of FEPOMUVES where women necessarily have become involved in issues of political violence and women's rights as well as urban poverty.

The fact that younger, Lima-born women are currently participating in the kitchens may also point toward a broader understanding of women's community action. Their participation may be purely out of economic necessity, but it also may be due to the fact that the kitchens have become an accepted practice in daily life for young Lime-ñans or, most positively, that they provide a sense of empowerment for many of their members. It is clear from the UNRISD case study and the other cited research that while the struggle for survival is a key motivating factor, the organizations have become an accepted means to raise awareness about other community issues. The perseverance of members to keep the kitchens active, despite the political and economic odds,[7] testifies to the fact that there continues to be a broad need for more adequate distribution of social welfare. In addition, the participation of many members has transformed their own understandings of domestic labor as well as the broader community's understandings of the shared costs of reproduction, something which has proved invaluable for the efforts of poor women in Lima.

The weaknesses in this form of organizing lie in the fact that women members may become "burnt out" from participating for so many years. After 15 years, the original excitement about the kitchens has worn off; many women are tired and would prefer to seek employment opportunities elsewhere rather than participate as volunteers in the kitchens (Barrig, 1996). Their volunteer participation, furthermore, is above and beyond their already strenuous (unpaid) domestic workloads. While in general the kitchens remain a successful survival strategy, there are nevertheless many constraints that the women members face. To begin with, women are the primary, if not exclusive, members of the kitchens. While awareness of the shared responsibility of reproduction has increased, it is women who remain responsible for food preparation and distribution in the kitchens. In this regard, the fact that communal kitchens have become accepted practices may not mean that they are desired, but rather necessary for survival.

Policies and projects which support the kitchens often exacerbate this problem by leaving unexamined women's unequal burdens in community food provision and by assuming that women have expendible time and energy to participate in social reproduction. Economic restructuring and social policies deepen gender inequalities when and if the hidden transfer of reproduction to families is left unexamined (Folbre, 1994; Elson, 1992). Communal kitchens exemplify contradictions in women's entry into community decision-making: on one hand, women have organized a massive movement which has transformed how central governments, local municipalities, and NGOs understand women's traditional, "private" role in food provision. It has politicized the women around issues of class and gender inequalities as well as political violence—a public awareness which cannot be removed from the historical record, neither for the participants themselves nor for the communities in which they live.[8]

This, however, is not enough to change important policy and political approaches which continue to reinforce gender inequalities by excluding gender as a variable in their frameworks, although initial efforts have been made to engender development frameworks by feminists and other social scientists.[9] Nor is it enough to improve the lives of the participants and their families in significant ways. The new economic and social policies of the Fujimori administration offer little hope for extremely poor communities in Lima who have little access to the benefits of the new state policies. For communal kitchens, this seems to imply a long-term struggle to provide for their families and seek basic levels of dignity in an urban system characterized by deep-rooted structural inequalities.

Other Latin American countries have undergone similar measures, and women's organizations have provided crucial networks for community survival. Ecuador, for example, has undergone a series of restructuring measures since 1981 which fall within the general recommendations of the IMF and World Bank. The government of President Sixto Durán-Ballén (1992–96) accelerated this process through its "modernization plan," a plan which included economic liberalization and the further dismantling of the welfare state. The Durán administration significantly reduced trade barriers, promoted export-led development, and decreased social spending. It restructured and downsized social and economic ministries, laid off 20,000+ state employees, centralized social policy concerns in the President's Office, and implemented a World Bank/IMF-designed Emergency Social Investment Fund (ESIF, or *Fondo de Inversión Social de Emergencia*) to address the social costs of structural adjustment. These measures were a response largely to the growing economic crisis which, in the case of

Ecuador, had its origins in the Ecuadorian state's reliance on its leading export product, oil, and the global oil crisis of the late 1970s and early 1980s, coupled with the military governments' overspending in that same period.

In this context, and in response to state authoritarianism and to the lack of conventional forms of democratic representation, neighborhood women's organizations emerged throughout Ecuador, although primarily in its two largest cities, Quito and Guayaquil. A conservative estimate of organizations with *personería jurídica*, or legal status, may be 80–100 at a national level (Centro María Quilla/ CEAAL, 1990). If one includes all types of grassroots women's organizations, both those with *personería jurídica* and those without, in rural and urban areas, there may be as many as 500 or 600 groups (Rosero, 1993, interview, November 21). Unlike the Peruvian case, these organizations have not made the transition into a massive movement; rather, they remain relatively small-scale and isolated instances of women's community action. In Quito, there are over 50 neighborhood women's organizations, all of which have distinct relationships with other women's organizations, traditional (male-based) neighborhood associations or cooperatives, the Municipality of Quito, political parties, the church, and NGOs. While their impact is less dramatic in terms of actual numbers, their emergence and presence is nevertheless significant for current policy discussions on state reform (Rodríguez, 1993). This is particularly true in regard to the new Emergency Social Investment Fund, which replaced an important institutional structure and funding source for community daycare centers and women's organizations throughout the country without providing a comparable alternative (Delgado, 1992; Ojeda, 1993).[10] In this context, neighborhood women's organizations in Quito have served as crucial providers and distributors of social welfare during a period of intense crisis, exacerbated in early 1995 by the Ecuador–Peru border war, in which the Ecuadorian government prioritized its' costly military defense over other policy concerns (Lind, 1995).[11]

While little research has been conducted to analyze whether Ecuadorian families are becoming increasingly self-reliant—rather than seeking collective answers—existing studies indicate that while many women and their families rely upon community organizations and informal networks, in contrast to Lima there is another largely unrecognized group which has retreated to the private realm rather than seek community support.[12] These results reflect the trend toward "the privatization of women's struggles" found in other countries such as Mexico (see Benería, 1992), where women have relied upon individual rather than collective forms of action to confront the process of economic restructuring and crisis.

4. URBAN POVERTY AND VIOLENCE: MOTHERS MOVEMENTS

In other cases, women have not mobilized directly to confront the economic crisis, but their efforts reflect related issues of urban violence and poverty. Mothers' movements, or movements of women to combat violence and human rights abuses against their families, have emerged throughout Latin America and other regions in the past 20 years (Jelin, 1990; Navarro, 1989; Schirmer, 1993; Taylor, 1994). These movements must be understood in the context of authoritarianism—both under military and democratic states—as well as in the context of rising rates of random violence in urban areas. The Maes de Acari, a mothers' movement in the Acari slum neighborhood of Rio de Janeiro, highlights one example of this type of mobilization.[13] This organization began when Marilene de Souza and five other mothers learned that their children had been abducted and "disappeared" in July 1990. Motivated by extreme distress and indignation, the mothers began a long process of investigation and protest of the "Acari Eleven" case. They carried banners before the Police Secretariat building, and made appointments for interviews with the Secretaries of Justice, Public Safety, and the Civil Police. With the participation of local government officials, they organized public rallies. These efforts led them to coalesce with the *Centro de Articulacao de Populacoes Marginalizadas* (CEAP, or Center for the Articulation of Marginalized Populations). CEAP mobilized support for the mothers from local and international human rights organizations such as Amnesty International, which continues to pressure the Brazilian government on this case.

Despite the fact that the mothers have not learned what happened to their abducted and missing children, the fact that two lawsuits are in process for such a politically loaded case involving indigent slumdwellers is an impressive victory. In the press, the Acari Eleven are no longer considered criminal youngsters, but 11 citizens—even if second class citizens. The murders are now appropriately treated as a political event, rather than a common crime, by activists, the media, and even by some state officials.

Most positively, the struggle of the Mothers of Acari has contributed to greater solidarity among the members of the Acari community, encouraging them to fight more strongly for their social, economic and political rights. The Acari slum has become a symbol of resistance to arbitrary government abuses and associated forms of systemic violence, and the Mothers of Acari have become a reference and a motivator for the broader human rights movement in Rio de Janeiro.

An interesting factor is that the mothers attribute the violence and the disappearances of their children to the conditions of poverty that they face as poor people, and not explicitly to their gender roles and their conditions as Afro-Brazilians (da Silva, interview, July 20, 1995).[14] They perceive themselves as constituting an economic class, rather than a class of women and/or a racial class. Nevertheless, they play increasingly strong public roles as women and continue to organize for a less violent society (da Silva, personal interview, July 20, 1995). For the Mothers of Acari, this includes a fundamental transformation in class relations.

The themes of urban poverty and violence appear in women's community strategies throughout the world. In postcolonial states of Africa and South Asia, women's organizations often address these issues in relation to their struggles for cultural, religious and ethnic survival (Moghadam, 1994; Basu, 1995b). In these cases, their survival often depends as much upon securing material needs as it does on changing discriminatory laws and policies that reinforce one religious/cultural perspective over another. Indeed, this is true for organizations such as Rah-e-Haqq in Bombay, a Muslim women's organization which has struggled to reform both Muslim personal laws and to oppose the proposed uniform civil code (UCC); a proposal spear-headed by the ruling Hindu party which, if passed, would establish universal family laws for all Indian citizens, regardless of their religious and cultural beliefs (Kapur and Cossman, 1993). Likewise, in the new South Africa, women's organizations are fighting not only for material needs, but also to restructure the law in the aftermath of apartheid and to broaden people's understandings of the relationships between racism and sexism (Kemp *et al.*, 1995).

Increasingly, mothers' anti-violence movements have emerged in US cities. In the United States with a current uneven income distribution which only compares to the Great Depression of the 1930s, poor communities have been faced with growing sets of problems related to poverty, housing, homelessness, racial violence, domestic violence and lack of affordable healthcare. In the midst of deep racial tensions in urban areas, some women have acted in their roles as mothers to combat violence and reclaim their urban spaces. New York City-based Mothers Against Violence (MAV) is one such organization which was created to address neighborhood violence at a city-wide level. Mothers Against Violence was created in 1991 to focus attention on the multiple dimensions of the problem of violence, its impact on individuals, families and communities, and to develop practical community responses to this complex problem. In New York City alone, violence

is the leading cause of death for young people ages 15–19, and the fourth ranked cause of death for children ages 5–14. MAV is unusual in that it was initiated by City Hall staff, but immediately became an independent nonprofit organization in which the power and decision-making emanate from the neighborhoods. The Deputy Mayor and a number of city commissioners supported the creation of a new nonprofit because they did not believe that government policy was the right vehicle for addressing racial violence.

Members of MAV are victims of violence from diverse cultural, ethnic, and socioeconomic backgrounds. They share the understanding however, that the criminal justice mindset with which the problem was usually addressed had to be changed to a public health mindset, seeing violence as a disease rather than a crime. MAV seeks to increase community-based violence prevention programs, to advocate for better services for victims and survivors, to raise awareness of the extent of the problem, and to reduce the presence of violence in the media. Pain, trauma, fear and apathy have been transformed into effective local prevention and advocacy strategies for program and policy reforms at the city-wide level. MAV's proactive role in mobilizing the community against violence is key in healing the mothers themselves, and also enables young people, parents, and others affected by violence to have similar opportunities, promoting community activism in the process.

MAV activities include public advocacy, providing safe havens for youth, memorial events, and a youth leadership project that involves peer counseling and youth employment initiatives. MAV develops gun violence elimination strategies, convenes annual conferences and publishes conference proceedings and other reports to disseminate information about the problem and what communities and individuals can do to prevent it. The youth in the program have articulated that they need a safe place to come together with their peers, so MAV facilitates recreational programs that keep youth off the streets. MAV has reached over 2,000 people through their chapter activities in seven neighborhoods, and thousands more through the media.

Like the Mothers of Acari and other mothers movements, MAV members originally acted out of sheer anger, frustration and pain at the disappearance of their children; through the process, however, they have become important public voices in neighborhood and city-wide decision-making processes. From their inception, MAV has addressed an intersection of issues ranging from violence to economic poverty to the stigmatization of working class and minority communities. This perspective on violence has led MAV through a transformative process, from a purely reactive movement to a proactive one where they lead citizen actions to promote positive institutional and policy reforms such as youth leadership training and public advocacy for underrepresented groups.

5. ENGENDERING COMMUNITY ACTION

Women's responses to urban poverty and their entry as a visible political class into community decision-making often occurs indirectly, through their struggles for seemingly non-gender specific needs. Mothers' movements against violence and neighborhood organizations are two such catalysts for women's active involvement in local development. Basu describes poor women's movements as processes of "shared oppression," in which women mobilize around certain issues, only to later discover the gender dimensions of their actions and/or be described as "women's movements". She argues that it is less important whether a particular movement defines itself as a "women's movement," and more important if it responds to the women's concerns and to those of external actors:

What initially motivates many women to organize is not necessarily a belief in the distinctive nature of their problems but rather a sense of shared oppression with other groups that have been denied their rights. Patriarchal domination is no more apt in and of itself to provide a catalyst to women's activism than class exploitation is likely in and of itself to stimulate class struggle....whether women organize on their own or as members of a larger group is not really what determines whether their activism is likely to endure. The more important issue is whether women's activism responds to their own concerns or to those of external actors, such as political parties and the state (Basu, 1995a, p. 10).

These types of women's organizations—neighborhood and anti-violence—reflect the diverse ways in which women coalesce around a shared sense of oppression to meet their needs and those of their communities. They, along with other types of movements such as housing,[15] provide a starting point from which women have entered community decision-making and in some cases, influenced state development policies. They therefore raise a series of questions about the significance of women's organizations for community development schemes and for overcoming gender inequalities in local and national development practices. For example, how do these organizations' relationships with public and community institutions—including local and national governments, political parties, NGOs, international organizations, and urban social movements—contribute to their success or failure? How does this relate to their sustainability? To what extent have these forms of community action engendered broad-

er political and policy arenas? To what extent have their efforts been acknowledged by their families and communities? How does the (often hidden) transfer of welfare responsibilities to the community level overlook—and perhaps deepen—women's unequal burden in community and household work? How does this process serve as a catalyst for women's collective action? Conversely, when does it serve to dissolve organizational networks and lead to women's retreat from community action? In this section I will address these questions and make some suggestions for future research and policy.

(a) Sustainability and community development approaches

The UNRISD study and other research on communal kitchens in Lima (as one example) indicates that the success or failure of the kitchens depends at least as much on institutional relationships and networking as it does on the kitchen members' will or desire to continue collective food provision (see especially Barrig, 1996). Changes in state development policy—such as decreases in social spending and in welfare programs—directly affects the kitchens economically and institutionally. Economically, the members are forced into a situation of permanent dependence, in which they rely upon the relatively inexpensive provision of food for their families and, in some cases, for the small salaries that their participation provides. Institutionally, the kitchens are constrained by the types of available funding and by the guidelines they must follow to receive it. An emphasis on vertical relations between local organizations, NGOs, national governments and international organizations often preempts local attempts to forge new, horizontal alliances between local groups. In this respect, the fact that communal kitchens are part of an umbrella organization (the FCPA) suggests that they have been successful at bridging local concerns against the odds of time, space, and institutional constraints, although as mentioned earlier, Barrig (1996) warns us of the structural and ideological dilemmas faced by these types of consumer-based or needs-based struggles. Neighborhood women's organizations in Quito, in contrast, have not been as successful at creating institutional links with other grassroots organizations. The successes or failures of community organizations therefore depends upon a number of related factors, including institutional constraints as well as their ability to address and/or cooperate with broader constituencies such as local governments, religious communities, urban social movements, and business and nonprofit sectors.

This is directly related to the sustainability of women's community organizations and to their long-term impacts upon urban policy, community and state development. Organizational sustainability is a tricky issue as it implies that very informal, grass-roots, often activist-oriented organizations must somehow integrate themselves into the official political and economic system to survive over the long term. Some organizations do not have the skills or resources to do this; others do not want to compromise their ideological principles to work within the official system; yet others find it essential and necessary to do so, even if at political or personal costs, as was the case of the Mothers of Acari, some of whom lost personal family support due to their increased visibility and participation in public arenas and decision-making (da Silva, 1995, personal interview, July 20).

Sustainability is even more complicated in the context of state restructuring, as the decentralization of local services and redistributive subsidies, along with decision-making authority and accountability, leads to the double-bind that Alvarez (1996) discusses in relation to Latin American women's organizations: on one hand, decentralization measures provide opportunities for previously unacknowledged groups to participate in community development and decision-making, thereby giving historically marginalized groups such as women an entry into planning and political processes. On the other hand, the most disenfranchised groups—immigrants, racial minorities, recent urban settlers, and poor women and men in general—are forced into mobilizing for resources in contexts in which funding, training and skill-building are difficult to acquire, and urban inequalities make it increasingly difficult for marginalized groups to feel they can promote change.

Despite these difficulties and contradictions, many seemingly disenfranchised groups have developed integral, comprehensive approaches to community development, even when their organizations focus on a "single issue" such as food provision, human rights, or daycare. New York's Mothers Against Violence, the Maes de Acari, and Lima's communal kitchens all testify to this fact in varying degrees. In each case, the participants have developed strategies to address the immediate problems of violence and access to community resources such as food, water and housing, but with a broader perspective on citizen rights and responsible community development.

Neighborhood women's organizations in Quito have also developed an integral approach to community development. From the beginning, they have focused on establishing daycare centers as well as on numerous other projects to enhance women's community involvement, their political participation, and their economic empowerment. These contributions to the local development process have been invalu-

able, despite limited documentation and conceptual biases in analyses of planning and development. Such biases overlook local development strategies that do not operate entirely through conventional institutional channels, as is the case of most of the organizations examined in this paper.[16] In fact, these community-based approaches deeply influence electoral and official planning processes, and this is clear when one considers the fact that IULA's (International Union of Local Authorities) six-year project on women and local power has observed that the majority of elected local women politicians in Ecuador and in seven other Latin American countries gained political recognition and support through their previous (informal, unpaid) community activism. IULA's finding and the UNRISD cases I analyze begin to break down conceptual biases in studies of women's "formal" and "informal" community participation (indeed, the emphasis on community and local power—as opposed to local government, electoral politics and/or official planning institutions—implies a breakdown of traditional categories of political participation and of public/private relations from the start, as politics are defined more broadly to include women's "community" and "official political" roles; see Arboleda, 1993). These cases also suggest that women's locations in community structures remain largely unexamined due to conceptual, methodological and cultural biases, and that uncovering these biases in future research and practice is key to understanding the effects of economic restructuring and decentralization measures on local communities and households, and ultimately, to promoting self-sustainability and integrating women into decision-making processes.

(b) *Gender, structures of constraint, and local power*

The examples discussed in this paper suggest that what catalyzes women's collective action (or conversely, what prevents women from participating at the community level) stems from the ways in which gender is structured into families and communities, development frameworks, and political and ideological movements (among others), and from how specific groups of women perceive and respond to these structures and practices. One way to understand why community action is (or is not) important to women is by analyzing local power in terms of gender. This includes an analysis of power relations within households, an approach developed in the feminist literature on household survival strategies. Despite the fact that this literature has focused largely on intrahousehold relations and has not theorized the community or larger public sphere (see, for example, Benería and Feldman, 1992), it

WORLD DEVELOPMENT

has nevertheless positioned the household as a central analytical category and has analyzed the links between households and broader institutions and structural changes (Moser, 1989a, b; Sen, 1990; Folbre, 1988). Disaggregating the household on the basis of gender and identifying it as a site of conflict and cooperation, as socially constructed and as an essential part of the economy, rather than as a nonmarket, natural unit characterized by altruism, provides a different—and indeed complementary—starting point for understanding why and how women develop strategies and approaches to community development that broaden our understandings of economic and political participation. As opposed to studies which posit households *vis-à-vis* the economy or civil society without analyzing power relations within them (as in conventional neoclassical and Marxist analysis—see Folbre, 1988), the feminist critiques suggest that households, like broader societal institutions, are not neutral, safe or cohesive with respect to gender. Women in particular observe this in their daily lives, and in cities where there is severe economic crisis or restructuring measures, gender inequalities in family structure, job opportunities, household maintenance and childcare tend to increase, often catalyzing women's collective action.

These examples and several others demonstrate this point and suggest, at the very least, that men and women experience and interpret urban poverty differently, according to their roles in everyday life: their perspectives on parenting, violence, safe living environments, the provisioning of food, schooling, health care, etc. Benería's (1992) Mexico study, for example, demonstrates how the Mexican debt crisis and subsequent structural adjustment policies also led to the "restructuring of everyday life," including an intensification of domestic work; changes in purchasing habits; and changes in social life. The particular ways in which women experience these effects contributes to the survival strategies they develop—whether they be individual (i.e. family/household-based) or collective (i.e. through community participation). The UNRISD studies suggest a similar process in other cities and demonstrate that community participation can empower women, yet also increase their reproductive workloads if and when community participation is not analyzed in terms of gender. This is especially evident in the communal kitchens, where women complain of being "burnt out" and of their unequal burden in food provision, despite increased community awareness of the shared costs of social reproduction, and in the case of the Mothers of Acari, where members have had great difficulties in balancing their activism with their family responsibilities. Thus the restructuring of everyday life is both an effect of broader restructuring measures and structural inequalities, as

well as of communities' locations in that process and the distributive and decision-making mechanisms they develop, both formally and informally.

The general move toward welfare deregulation in many countries—and the specific decentralization measures that emerge from the new policy frameworks—make it even more urgent to understand the gender dimensions of community action. For example, national policy proposals such as the so-called community option in the United States (Clavel *et al.*, 1997) and "laws of popular participation" in some Latin American countries may potentially shift major distributive and decision-making responsibilities to local communities,[17] potentially shifting responsibilities to households—and therefore to women. In Bolivia, the new Ley de Participación Política, initiated in 1995, has been passed in conjunction with a decentralization policy which promises to shift federal responsibilities to the local level and to incorporate indigenous and other community groups into the planning and political process. This law is quite dramatic when one considers the fact that over 300 of the local municipalities that have acquired this new responsibility were created for the first time with the passing of this bill (Albó, 1996). Prior to this legislation, local decision-making structures were defined by the residing indigenous communities; these local and historically resilient structures are now being replaced by the new municipalities—based on one universal model. Most positively, this new law may integrate historically unrepresented communities into the official political system. If this occurs indigenous, women's and other community organizations will acquire new political and advocacy roles in local planning processes, although much of this depends upon the decisions that are made at local leaderships levels; levels which are still highly marked by indigenous male leaders concerned primarily with preserving indigenous communities *vis-à-vis* the modern state.

In Bolivia, the tension between prioritizing ethnicity over gender in policy debates is reinforced by intellectual debates on gender relations in Andean *vs.* Western cultures. Many have argued, for example, that gender relations within Quechua and Aymara communities are complementary, rather than dichotomous and unequal as in Western traditions (on the notion of complementarity see Harris, 1978; Silverblatt, 1987). Based on this notion, many policy makers assume that gender is not a problem (or at least is not the most crucial problem) and overlook the important need of discussing gender relations within indigenous communities, both in rural and urban areas. Despite this, Bolivian women's long history of activism in anti-authoritarian, indigenous, leftist, and anti-poverty struggles cannot be ignored (see, for example, Zabala, 1995; León, 1990; THOA/Rivera

Cusicanqui, 1990), and many women's organizations have actively worked to incorporate gender into the local planning and political agendas that result from this law. In addition, feminist policy makers have worked to incorporate gender into development frameworks, primarily by emphasizing gender equity, a development concept which has many parallels in the Andean concept of complementarity, and therefore has been politically salient in Bolivian policy circles (see, for example, Montaño, 1993). In general, women's organizations and the Sub-secretaria de Género, the state office designed to integrate women into development, have addressed two issues in regard to the new decentralization laws: the potential gender impacts of the *Ley de Participación Política* in local communities; and the incorporation of women, and women's organizations, into the new planning structures (Bejarano, 1995, personal interview, November 28).

These two issues are deeply related, as the successful incorporation of women into the new structures and the acceptance of gender-aware planning agendas would most likely transform the outcome. The literature on urban social movements tends to overlook the important questions of how gender inequalities are reproduced in community structures, why more men are in community leadership roles than women, and how this determines policy agendas in general and women's participation in particular. Urban planners may applaud increases in local power—such as in the role of community development corporations (CDCs), local governments and social movements—without considering how local power is structured along gender lines, and what differential effects the restructuring of communities have for women and men. In other words, increases in local power may not automatically translate into power for women; at the very least, this needs to be explored in future research.

An analysis of gender in this context would include the assertion that (i) gender is an analytical category affecting the allocation of political, social and economic resources; (ii) perceived sex differences help determine patterns of social, political, and economic organization; and (iii) the concept of gender is used to assign men and women to different areas of the economy and society and thus contributes to the distribution of power in both public and private spheres (Fernández-Kelly, 1994). The gender dimensions of decentralization measures and shifts in local power depend largely upon the structures of local production, local government, civic organizations, and family networks (among others), and on the nature of the shifts that take place and their resulting gender impacts. In terms of economic development, what policy makers may

regard as a more productive local economy may instead be a shifting of costs from the paid to the unpaid economy, much of which falls upon women (see Elson, 1992). In terms of local power and community action, it is important to engender analyses of local power structures as well as broaden the scope of the question: for women and women's organizations, empowerment begins with addressing inequalities within their families as well as in society at large. The example of the new decentralization laws in Bolivia demonstrates the tensions that local communities face when they must both develop a cohesive strategy *vis-à-vis* the national state and address unequal power relations within the communities themselves. One way to understand the gender aspects of this process is to broaden working definitions of community development and planning to encompass both formal and informal, or both institutionalized and grassroots, planning practices. Indeed, Bolivian feminist policy makers and activists have been at the forefront of pushing for this type of definition in the new laws and planning practices in the country; the gender effects of these laws will depend largely upon the ways in which local communities negotiate and implement this process, and upon the extent to which women integrate themselves into decision-making positions and/or influence local leadership.

6. CONCLUSION

This paper shows that shifts resulting from economic restructuring, combined with the demands generated by increased urban poverty, have catalyzed women to organize collectively, ultimately contributing to new gender-based understandings and community practices in global cities. Women's organizations have responded to the local effects of globalization by creating their own organizations which reflect their gender locations in family structures and in the broader political economy. Throughout the world, women have played protagonistic roles in anti-violence and neighborhood movements (among others) and have engendered the landscape of urban social movements and change. Despite this, the roles of grassroots women's organizations in community development and planning processes remain largely undocumented, and both their collective work and the private household work of women in general have yet to be more fully incorporated into analyses of restructuring, decentralization and other measures associated with the new neoliberal policy frameworks. One way to overcome these conceptual biases and and the resulting gender impacts of development policies is by integrating feminist approaches to development and to urban social movements.

More integral community development approaches combined with gender analysis may provide some answers to how gender serves as a structure of constraint for many women (Folbre, 1994), and how this does (or does not) catalyze women to participate in local organizations and decision-making processes. The cases in this paper suggest that mobilization is possible; the extent to which these types of organizations sustain themselves and become more influential actors in the public sphere has yet to be determined. This depends upon how planning and political processes are defined, and whether local power is understood to include power relations within households or not. Women's roles in reproduction—in the family, household and community—are, after all, what characterize all of the movements cited in this paper and serve to guide the organizations in developing their strategies, their networks, and their perspectives on community in the context of structural change and urban poverty. Household relations therefore provide a starting point for understanding both the diversity and the similarities in local women's approaches to mobilizing for resources and responding to global change.

It is clear that the move toward integrating nation-states into the global economy and shifting welfare responsibilities to local (public and private) levels are not likely to subside or be reversed. Given these circumstances, it is especially important that researchers and policy makers begin to address the gender dimensions of this process in order to prevent further structural constraints and burdens for women and to integrate them into community development. What kind of strategies can be supported and/or developed to foster this process? Below are some suggestions.

—Gender analysis of neoliberal policies and their impacts upon local communities: on households, on community organizations, on local power (governance and private organizations), and on production structures, to name a few examples.

—Urban policies need to account for "male biases" in their frameworks by examining more systematically the relationship between formal and informal community development and the gender dimensions of these processes. Women's active participation in decision-making should be promoted and, given the fact that many women enter decision-making arenas through their participation in informal community organizations and

networks, these organizations and networks should be incorporated more fully into planning initiatives from the start.

—More support could be given to local women's organizations and horizontal networks among them and with other urban social movements. A broader understanding of community development and citizen participation could be fostered, in part by bringing public awareness to seemingly "private" issues such as women's roles in social reproduction and by increasing awareness of communities' locations in national, regional and global contexts and their ability to foster social change in restructuring processes.

—National governments and international organizations could promote the engendering of all social and economic policy frameworks rather than designing specific frameworks for addressing "women's issues." Initial efforts to do so include the UNDP 1995 *Human Development Report*, which incorporates gender as a variable in the human development index, and UNIFEM's proposal for the Beijing conference (see Heyzer, 1995). Engendering mainstream development frameworks, programs and projects will better lead to policies which promote and sustain more equitable development along gender lines from the beginning. Initial conceptual work has been done to engender macroeconomic frameworks and models (see Cagatay *et al.*, 1995), although as discussed throughout this article much needs to be done to examine empirically the "hidden" dimensions of neoliberal policies, and to translate these ideas into practice, particularly in regard to local development and urban policy.

These measures respond to some of the immediate problems of daily survival, although they do not address the root of the problem (Benería, 1992). Long-term solutions would include a reevaluation of international, national and urban policies that support the transfer of responsibilities, authority, decision-making and redistributive mechanisms to local communities without considering the parallel transfer to (and increased burden upon) poor households and poor women in particular. Viewing this process through the lens of gender could lead to more equitable policies and could provide a different outcome, one more beneficial to women's organizations and to poor communities in general.

NOTES

1. This includes both advocates of neoliberal models and advocates of "new social movements" (NSMs); two groups whose otherwise divergent views on the state's role in facilitating the development process converge in discussions on the participation of civil society in local development strategies. Neoliberal advocates, by support-

ing privatization strategies and state retrenchment, assume that the costs of restructuring will be "absorbed" by civil society through (among others) the increased participation of NGOs and neighborhood organizations in managing and facilitating policies related to social reproduction. Many advocates of NSMs who strive for a more participatory democratic process, while critical of the general trend toward "free-market" economies, view the increased role of local communities in the planning and political process as a small step towards achieving the goal of radical democracy. They therefore tend to support some aspects of the decentralization policies derived from neoliberal development frameworks—a strategy which, if it overlooks the broader process of neoliberal restructuring and state formation, may lead to negative consequences for local communities in the long run (Schild, forthcoming).

2.   In many cases, neighborhood women's organizations have received state funding to manage and facilitate state-designed projects, such as daycare centers, local stores, communal kitchens, and educational programs. Many of these projects have been discontinued as states decrease social spending, eliminate their direct support for community-based projects, and promote the role of private organizations in development. In Ecuador, for example, 300 local organizations lost funding for daycare centers when the government of Sixto Durán-Ballén (1992–96) eliminated the earlier Rodrigo Borja administration's (1988–92) social policies, including the Community Network for Child Development, a program designed to address the needs of children under the age of six, primarily through the daycare initiative. The Durán administration initiated an Emergency Social Investment Fund, designed to address the direct costs of adjustment measures, and many local women's organizations lost their only source of funding (see Delgado, 1992; Ojeda, 1993). This has occurred in many other Latin American countries as well, where traditional welfare states have been downsized and community-based projects (such as daycare centers) are de-prioritized. Thus, following Alvarez's argument, the crucial funding that many women's organizations have depended upon disappears, the general economic situation has not greatly improved for poor sectors, leaving women's organizations and poor sectors in general dependent upon an increasingly "undependable" state.

3.   Fraser's (1989) work analyzes the political arena in which "basic needs" are defined, operationalized and contested by different political actors. In particular, she analyzes the ways in which "poor black women" have been constructed as the stereotypical welfare recipients in dominant political discourse in the United States (also see Fraser and Gordon, 1994).

4.   Vargas (1992a) and Vargas (1992b) distinguishes between three streams of the Peruvian women's movement: feminist (e.g. self-defined feminist organizations that maintain autonomy from traditional male-based parties and institutions), political (i.e. those women's organizations allied with traditional political parties and institutions), and popular (e.g. poor, working class, indigenous women's organizations).

5.   Communal kitchens and other popular women's organizations in Lima have developed strong ties with outside professionals and activists who dedicate themselves to popular education and/or political organizing in marginalized neighborhoods in Lima. In general, there has been a strong tradition of solidarity work, as well as of charity work, by political parties, feminist and labor organizations, church groups, and other NGOs in Lima's poorest neighborhoods. While communal kitchens and other popular women's organizations have different perspectives and agendas than, for example, middle-class feminist research centers, and while there have been many divisions and conflicts among these groups, they nevertheless have negotiated relationships and collaborated in many political struggles, projects, and planning processes. This type of collaboration, however, has become more difficult since the surge of political violence in the 1980s and 1990s. (For more information, see Burt, 1995; Blondet, 1991, 1996.)

6.   For an historical analysis of communal kitchens and their relationship to the Catholic Church and NGOs, see Sara-Lafosse (1984); Barrig (1994), Barrig (1996); and Blondet (1996).

7.   In some poor neighborhoods in Lima, such as Villa El Salvador, communal kitchens have been under direct attack from Shining Path. Despite Moyano's death and the temporary dismantling of FEPOMUVES during 1992–95 due to Shining Path infiltration, kitchen members continue to struggle to maintain the kitchens and the broader organization.

8.   For an analysis of women's collective responses to political violence in Lima with examples of communal kitchens, see Wappenstein (1992).

9.   For example, the United Nations Development Programme's (UNDP) *Human Development Report 1995* focuses exclusively on gender as a variable of human development indexes. This report will undoubtedly influence future research and policy agendas. Likewise, UNIFEM's (Heyzer, 1995) publication prepared for the Beijing conference introduces the gender dimensions of new development issues such as international trade, global markets, and social policy. The concept of gender equity is centrally integrated into the Declaration and Programme of Action of the World Summit for Social Development (WSSD), held in March 1995, indicating a fundamental shift—an engendering—of Realpolitik (Somavia, 1995). In addition, many feminist economists have begun to integrate gender into economic models and theoretical frameworks (see, for example, Ferber and Nelson, 1993; Kuiper and Sap, 1995; Bakker, 1994; Kabeer, 1994; Moser, 1993; Benería, 1995). Also see the special issue of *World Development* entitled "Gender, Adjustment and Macro-economics" (Cagatay et al., 1995) and the journal *Feminist Economics* of the International Association for Feminist Economics (IAFFE).

10.   Specifically, the Emergency Social Investment Fund replaced an earlier program initiated under the Rodrigo Borja administration (1988–92), the Community Network for Child Development, a program which provided funding for 300 local organizations (see footnote 2).

11. Ecuador and Peru have disputed 78 km of frontier, along the southeast border of Ecuador and northeast border of Peru, which was never determined after the Rio Protocol ended a short war between the two countries in 1941. The border area has been a point of contention in relations between Peru and Ecuador ever since. In January 1995, open hostilities broke out, leading to the eventual death, on official count, of at least 28 Ecuadorian soldiers and 46 Peruvian soldiers, with an additional 100+ wounded. Unofficial estimates are much higher, putting the overall toll at 500 dead (see EIU, 1995).

12. There are unrecognized groups of poor women—and poor sectors in general—in Quito, Lima and cities throughout the region and world. In the cases of Peru and Ecuador, there is a stronger tradition of collective action in Lima than in Quito, which is explained by a number of related political, institutional, social and cultural factors (see Lind, 1992). In the case of Ecuador, Moser's (1989b) research on survival strategies in poor neighborhoods in Guayaquil is one example which begins to analyze women's different (collective and individual) responses. Moser concludes that the women she interviewed fall into three general categories: (i) those who are coping; (ii) those who are hanging on; and (iii) those who are burnt out. In her study, those who are "burnt out" have become increasingly isolated from collective efforts to deal with the crisis. While it is difficult to estimate the size of the most marginalized groups of women, it is clear from Moser's study and from others that this sector is growing (see for example Benería and Roldán, 1987; Friedmann *et al.*, 1996).

13. This section is based on an UNRISD/UNV case study. Unlike other mothers' movements such as the Madres de la Plaza de Mayo (a well-documented case), this organization and others examined in this section emerged in formal democratic contexts (as opposed to emerging under military authoritarian rule). They therefore have struggled under different conditions and have utilized distinct political strategies from those mothers' movements which emerged in the context of military authoritarianism, a topic which goes beyond the scope of this paper. For further analysis see Navarro (1989); Jelin (1990); Schirmer (1993); Taylor (1994).

14. Joselina da Silva observes that in general, Afro-Brazilians do not identify themselves as constituting a racial minority. Relatively few Afro-Brazilians coalesce politically around a shared sense of racial identity or oppression, and economically marginalized Afro-Brazilians (including the Mothers of Acari) attribute their social and economic conditions to the fact that they are poor, rather than explicitly to racial factors (da Silva, personal interview, July 29, 1995). This phenomena contrasts starkly with countries such as the United States, where many African-Americans are identified, and self-identify, as African-American or "Black", etc., or South Africa, where the legacy of apartheid has led to rigid, offical racial categorizations in which people have come to identify themselves much more explicitly along racial lines.

15. The case of housing is discussed at length in an earlier version of this article. See Lind and Farmelo (1996).

16. For a history of alternative planning practices and a reconceptualization of planning from the perspective of marginalized groups such as African-Americans, women, and sexual minorities, see Sandercock, 1995.

17. On the community option in urban policy in the United States, see Clavel *et al.* (1997). On decentralization measures and laws of political participation in Latin America, see Arboleda (1993); IULA/CELCADEL/US AID (1991).

REFERENCES

Albó, X. (1996) Making the leap: From local mobilization to national politics. *NACLA Report on the Americas* 29, 15–20.

Alexander, M. J. (1991) Redrafting morality: The post-colonial state and sexual offences bill of Trinidad and Tobago. In *Third World Women and the Politics of Feminism*, eds. C. T. Mohanty, A. Russo and L. Torres, pp. 133–152. Indiana University Press, Bloomington.

Alvarez, S. (1990) *Engendering Demomcracy in Brazil: Women's Movements and Transistion Politics*. Princeton University Press, Princeton, NJ.

Alvarez, S. (1996) Concluding reflections: 'Redrawing' the parameters of gender struggle. In *Emergences: Women's Struggles for Livelihood in Latin America*, eds. J. Friedmann, R. Abers, and L. Autler, pp. 137–151. UCLA Latin American Studies Center, Los Angeles.

Arboleda, M. (1993) Mujeres en el poder local en Ecuador, Proyecto "Mujer y desarrollo local". Quito: IULA/CELCADEL, unpublished paper.

Bakker, I. (1994) Introduction: Engendering macro-economic policy reform in the era of global restructuring and adjustment. In *The Strategic Silence: Gender and Economic Policy*, ed. I. Bakker, pp. 1–32. Zed Press, London/North-South Institute, Toronto.

Barrig, M. (1994) The difficult equilibrium between bread and roses: Women's organizations and democracy in Peru. In *The Women's Movement in Latin America: Participation and Democracy*, ed. Jaquette, pp. 151–175. Westview Press, Boulder.

Barrig, M. (1996) Women, collective kitchens and the crisis of the state in Peru. In *Emergences: Women's Struggles for Livelihood in Latin America*, eds. J. Friedmann, R. Abers and L. Autler, pp. 59–77. UCLA Latin American Studies Center, Los Angeles.

Basu, A. (1995a) Introduction. In *The Challenge of Local Feminisms: Women's Movements In Global Perspective*, ed. Amrita Basu, pp. 1–24. Westview Press, Boulder.

Basu, A. ed. (1995b) *The Challenge of Local Feminisms: Women's Movements In Global Perspective*. Westview Press, Boulder.

Bejarano, M. E. (November 28, 1995) Personal interview.

Benería, L. (1989) Gender and the global economy. In *Instability and Change in the World Economy*, eds. A. MacEwen and W. Tabb, pp. 241–258. Monthly Review Press, New York.

Benería, L. (1992) The Mexican debt crisis: Restructuring the household and the economy. In *Unequal Burden: Economic Crisis, Persistent Poverty, and Women's Work*, eds. L. Benería and S. Feldman, pp. 83–104. Westview Press, Boulder.

Benería, L. (1995) Toward a greater integration of gender in economics. *World Development* 23(11), 1839–1850.

Benería, L. and Feldman, S. eds. (1992) *Unequal Burden: Economic Crisis, Persistent Poverty and Women's Work*. Westview Press, Boulder.

Benería, L. and Roldán, M. (1987) *The Crossroads of Class and Gender: Industrial Homework, Subcontracting and Household Dynamics in Mexico City*. University of Chicago Press, Chicago.

Blondet, C. (1991) *Las mujeres y el poder: una historia de Villa El Salvador*. Instituto de Estudios Peruanos, Lima, Peru.

Blondet, C. (1996) The impact of political violence on women's organizations in Lima's poor neighborhoods. In *Emergences: Women's Struggles for Livelihood in Latin America*, eds. J. Friedmann *et al.*, pp, 79–90. UCLA Latin American Studies Center, Los Angeles.

Bookman, A. and Morgen, S. eds. (1988) *Women and the Politics of Empowerment*. Temple University Press, Philadelphia.

Burt, J.-M. (1995) Perú: Shining Path after Gúzman. *NACLA Report On the Americas* 28(3), 6–9.

Burt, J.-M. (1997) Political violence and the grassroots in Lima, Peru. In *The New politics of Inequality in Latin America: Rethinking Participation and Representation*, eds. D. Chalmers *et al.* pp. 281–309. Oxford University Press, London.

Cagatay, N., Elson, D. and Grown, C. eds. (1995) Gender, adjustment and macroeconomics. Special Issue of *World Development* 23(11), November.

Centro María Quilla/CEAAL (1990) *Mujeres, educación y conciencia de género en Ecuador*. Centro María Quilla, Quito, Ecuador.

Clavel, P., Pitt, J. and Yin, J. (1997) The community option in urban policy. *Urban Affairs Review* 32(4), 435–458.

Cohen, M. (1994) The implications of economic restructuring for women: The Canadian situation. In *The Strategic Silence: Gender and Economic Policy*, ed. I. Bakker, pp. 103–116. Zed Press, London.

Corcoran-Nantes, Y. (1993) Female consciousness or feminist consciousness? Women's consciousness raising in community-based struggles in Brazil. In *'Viva': Women and Popular Protest in Latin America*, eds. S. Radcliffe and S. Westwood, pp. 136–155. Routledge, London.

da Silva, J. (July 19, 1995) Personal interview conducted by Martha Farmelo.

Delgado, E. (1992) Ecuador: balance de las políticas para pagar la deuda social 1987–1990, Programa 'Red Comunitaria para el Desarrollo Infantil'. unpublished paper.

Delpino, N. (1991) Las organizaciones femeninas por la alimentación: un menú sazonado. In *La otra cara de la luna: nuevos actores sociales en el Perú*, eds. L. Pásara *et al.*, pp. 29–72. CEDYS, Buenos Aires.

Economist Intelligence Unit (EIU) (1995) *Country Profile: Ecuador, 1994–1995*. Economist Intelligence Unit, London.

Elson, D. (ed.) (1991) *Male Bias in the Development Process*. Manchester University Press, Manchester.

Elson, D. (1992) From survival strategies to transformation strategies: Women's needs and structural adjustment. In *Unequal Burden: Economic Crisis, Persistent Poverty and Women's Work*, eds. L. Benería and S. Feldman, pp. 26–48. Westview Press, Boulder.

Fainstein, N. and Fainstein, S. eds. (1982) *Urban Policy Under Capitalism*. Urban Affairs Annual Review No. 22. Sage Publications, Beverley Hills, CA.

Fainstein, S. and Fainstein, N. (1985) Economic restructuring and the rise of urban social movements. *Urban Affairs Quarterly* 21(2), 187–206.

Feldman, S. (1992) Crisis, Islam and gender in Bangladesh: The social construction of a female labor force. In *Unequal Burden: Economic Crises, Persistent Poverty and Women's Work*, eds. L. Benería and S. Feldman, pp. 105–130. Westview Press, Boulder.

Ferber, M. and Nelson, J. eds. (1993) *Beyond Economic Man: Feminist Theory and Economics*. University of Chicago Press, Chicago.

Fernández-Kelly, M. P. (1994) Political economy and gender in Latin America: The emerging dilemmas, Woodrow Wilson International Center for Scholars, Latin American Program Working Paper Series No. 207, Woodrow Wilson International Center, Washington DC.

Fisher, R. and Kling, J. eds. (1993) *Mobilizing the Community: Local Politics in the Era of the Global City*. Urban Affairs Annual Review No. 41, Sage Publications, Beverley Hills, CA.

Folbre, N. (1988) The black four of hearts: Towards a paradigm of household economics. In *A Home Divided: Women and Income in the Third World*, eds. D. Dwyer and J. Bruce, pp. 248–264. Stanford University Press, Stanford.

Folbre, N. (1994) *Who Pays For the Kids? Gender and the Structures of Constraint*. Routledge, London.

Fraser, N. (1989) *Unruly Practices: Power, Discourse and Gender in Contemporary Social Theory*. University of Minnesota Press, Minneapolis.

Fraser, N. and Gordon, L. (1994) A genealogy of dependency: tracing a keyword of the U.S. welfare state. *Signs* 19(2), 303–337.

Friedmann, J., Abers, R. and Autler, L. eds. (1996) *Emergences: Women's Struggles for Livelihood in Latin America*. UCLA Latin American Center, Los Angeles.

Gordon, L. ed. (1990) *Women, the State, and Welfare*. University of Wisconsin Press, Madison.

Harris, O. (1978) Complementarity and conflict: An Andean view of Women and men. In *Sex and Age as Principles of Social Differentiation*, ed. J. LaFontaine, pp. 21–40. Academic Press, New York.

Heyzer, N. ed. (1995) *A Commitment to the World's Women: Perspectives on Development for Beijing and Beyond*. UNIFEM, New York.

IULA/CELCADEL/US AID (1991) *Mujer y municipio: una nueva presencia comunitaria en el desarrollo local de América Latina*. Workbook No. 7, IULA, Quito, Ecuador.

Jaquette, J. ed. (1994) *The Women's Movement in Latin America: Participation and Democracy*. Westview Press, Boulder.

Jelin, E. ed. (1990) *Women and Social Change in Latin America*. Zed Books Ltd./UNRISD, London.

Kabeer, N. (1994) *Reversed Realities: Gender Hierarchies in Development Thought.* Verso, London.

Kapur, R. and Cossman, B. (1993) On women, equality and the constitution: Through the looking glass of feminism. *National Law School Journal,* Special Issue on "Feminism and Law," National Law School of India University, Bangalore, 1–61.

Katzenstein, M. and Mueller, C. eds. (1987) *The Women's Movements of the United States and Western Europe.* Temple University Press, Philadelphia.

Kemp, A., Madlala, N., Moodley, A. and Salo, E. (1995) The dawn of a new day: Redefining South African feminism. In *The Challenge of Local Feminisms: Women's Movements in Global Perspective,* ed. A. Basu, pp. 131–162. Westview Press, Boulder.

Kuiper, E. and Sap, J. eds. (1995) *Out of the Margin: Feminist Perspectives on Economics.* Routledge, London.

León de Leal, M. ed. (1994) *Mujeres y participación política: avances y desafíos en America Latina.* Tercer Mundo Editores, Bogotá, Colombia.

León, R. (1990) Bartolina sisa: The peasant women's organization in Bolivia. In *Women and Social Change in Latin America,* ed. E. Jelin, pp. 135–150. Zed Press/ UNRISD, London.

Lind, A. C. (1992) Gender, power and development: Popular women's organizations and the politics of needs in Ecuador. In *The Making of Social Movements in Latin America,* eds. A. Escobar and S. Alvarez, pp. 134–149. Westview Press, Boulder.

Lind, A. (1995) Gender, development and women's political practices in ecuador. Ph.D. Dissertation, Cornell University.

Lind, A. and Farmelo, M. (1996) Gender and urban social movements: Women's community responses to restructuring and urban poverty. Discussion Paper No. 76, UNRISD, Geneva, Switzerland.

Logan, J. and Swanstrom, T. eds. (1990) *Beyond the City Limits: Urban Policy and Economic Restructuring in Comparative Perspective.* Temple University Press, Philadelphia.

Lovenduski, J. (1986) *Women and European Politics.* University of Massachusetts Press, Amherst.

McFarren, W. (1992) The politics of Bolivia's economic crisis: Survival strategies of displaced tin-mining households. In *Unequal Burden: Economic Crises, Persistent Poverty and Women's Work,* eds. L. Benería and S. Feldman, pp. 131–158. Westview Press, Boulder.

Miloslavich, D. ed. (1993) *Maria Elena Moyano: en busca de una esperanza.* Ediciones Flora Tristan, Lima, Peru.

Moghadam, V. ed. (1994) *Identity Politics and Women: Cultural Reassertions and Feminisms in International Perspective.* Westview Press, Boulder.

Mohanty, C. T. (1991) Under Western eyes: Feminist scholarship and colonial discourses. In *Third World Women and the Politics of Feminism,* eds. C. T. Mohanty *et al.,* pp. 51–80. Indiana University Press, Bloomington.

Montaño, S. (1993) *Invertir en la equidad: políticas sociales para la mujer en Bolivia.* UDAPSO/ONAMFA, La Paz, Bolivia.

Moser, C. (1989) Gender planning in the Third World: Meeting practical and strategic gender needs. *World Development* **17**(11), 1799–1825.

Moser, C. (1989b) The impact of recession and structural adjustment policies at the micro-level: Low-income women and their households in Guayaquil, Ecuador, UNICEF-Ecuador, Quito.

Moser, C. (1993) *Gender Planning and Development.* Routledge, London.

Moyano, M. E. (1991) Testimonio: la mujer en los gobiernos locales. *Mujer y municipio: una nueva presencia comunitaria en el desarrollo local de América Latina.* Programa "Mujer y desarrollo local," Cuaderno #7, pp. 24–31. IULA/CELCADEL/US AID, Quito, Ecuador.

Navarro, M. (1989) The personal is political: Las Madres de Plaza de Mayo. In *Power and Popular Protest: Latin American Social Movements,* ed. S. Eckstein, pp. 241–258. University of California Press, Berkeley.

Ojeda, L. (1993) *El descrédito de lo social: las políticas sociales en el Ecuador.* Centro para el Desarrollo Social (CDS), Quito, Ecuador.

Parpart, J. and Staudt, K. eds. (1989) *Women and the State in Africa.* Lynne Reinner, Boulder.

Pickvance, C. and Preteceille, E. eds. (1991) *State Restructuring and Local Power.* Pinter Publishers, New York.

Radcliffe, S. A. and Westwood, S. eds. (1993) *'Viva': Women and Popular Protest in Latin America.* Routledge, London.

Rodríguez, L. (1993) *Género y desarrollo: nudos y desafíos en el trabajo no gubernmental en el Ecuador.* CEPAM, Quito, Ecuador.

Rodríguez, L. (1994) Barrio women: Between the urban and the feminist movement. *Latin American Perspectives* **21**(3), 32–48.

Rosero, R. (1993) Personal interview, November 21.

Rowbotham, S. and Mitter, S. eds. (1994) *Dignity and Daily Bread: New Forms of Economic Organising Among Poor Women in the Third World and the First.* Routledge, London.

Sandercock, L. ed. (1995) Making the invisible visible: New historiographies for planning. Special issue of *Planning Theory,* **13**, Summer.

Sara-Lafosse, V. (1984) *Comedores comunales: La mujer frente a la crisis.* SUMBI, Lima, Peru.

Schild, V. (1991) *Gender, Class and Politics: Poor Neighborhood Organizing in Authoritarian Chile.* Ph.D. Dissertation, University of Toronto.

Schild, V. (forthcoming) New subjects of rights? Women's movements and the construction of citizenship in the 'New Democracies'. In *Cultures of Politics/Politics of Cultures: Revisioning Latin American Social Movements,* eds. A. Escobar, E. Dagnino and S. Alvarez. Westview Press, Boulder.

Schirmer, J. (1993) 'Those who die for life cannot be called dead': Women and human rights protest in Latin America. In *Surviving Beyond Fear,* ed. M. Agosín, pp. 31–57. White Pine Press, Fredonia, NY.

Sen, A. (1990) Gender and cooperative conflict. In *Persistent Inequalities: Women and World Development,* ed. I. Tinker, pp. 123–149. Oxford University Press, Oxford.

Silverblatt, I. (1987) *Moon, Sun and Witches: Gender Ideologies and Class in Inca and Colonial Peru.* Princeton University Press, Princeton, NJ.

Smith, W., Acuña, C. and Gamarra, E. eds. (1994) *Latin American Political Economy in the Age of Neoliberal Reform.* Transaction Publishers, New Brunswick, NJ.

Somavia, J. (1995) The World Summit for Social Development: engendering realpolitik. In *A Commitment to the World's Women*, ed. N. Heyzer, pp. 178–184. UNIFEM, New York.

Taller de Historia Oral (THOA) and Rivera Cusicanqui, S. (1990) Indigenous women and community resistance: History and memory. In *Women and Social Change in Latin America*, ed. E. Jelin, pp. 151–183. Zed Press/ UNRISD, London.

Taylor, D. (1994) Performing gender: Las Madres de la Plaza de Mayo. In *Negotiating Performance*, eds. D. Taylor and J. Villegas, pp. 275–305. Duke University Press, Durham, NC.

Tripp, A. M. (1992) The impact of crisis and economic reform on women in urban Tanzania. In *Unequal Burden: Economic Crises, Persistent Poverty and Women's Work*, eds. L. Benería and S. Feldman, pp. 159–180. Westview Press, Boulder.

United Nations Development Programme (UNDP) (1995) *Human Development Report 1995.* Oxford University Press, New York.

Valdés, T. (1994) Movimiento de mujeres y producción de conocimientos de género: Chile, 1978–1989. In *Mujeres y participación: avances y desafíos en America Latina*, ed. M. León, pp. 291–318. Tercer Mundo Editores, Bogotá, Colombia.

Vargas, V. (1992a) Como cambiar el mundo sin perdernos. Ediciones Flora Tristan, Lima.

Vargas, V. (1992) The feminist movement in Latin America: Between hope and disenchantment. *Development and Change* 23(1), 195–214.

Walton, J. and Seddon, D. (1994) *Free Markets and Food Riots: The Politics of Global Adjustment.* Blackwell Publishers, Cambridge.

Wappenstein, S. (1992) Women, violence, and the politics of daily survival: The formation of a gender-based culture of resistance in Lima, Peru;. Master's Thesis, Cornell University.

Wolfe, L. and Tucker, J. (1995) Feminism lives: Building a multicultural women's movement in the United States. In *The Challenge of Local Feminisms: Women's Movements in Global Perspective*, ed. A. Basu, pp. 435–462. Westview Press, Boulder.

Zabala, M. L. (1995) *Nos/otras en democracia: mineras, cholas y feministas (1976–1994).* ILDIS, La Paz, Bolivia.

[28]

IMAGINED AND IMAGINING EQUALITY IN EAST CENTRAL EUROPE

Gender and ethnic differences in the economic transformation of Bulgaria

Mieke Meurs

Introduction

Clearly, the transformation currently under way in East Central Europe (ECE) is offering very different opportunities to different groups of people. Some individuals have quickly and easily become fantastically rich, while others find themselves struggling to find any employment sufficient to pay for heating and bread. Patterns in the distribution of these opportunities continue to be an under-analysed aspect of the economic transformation. The emergence of classes has been little examined. A literature on the impact of the transformation on women has begun to emerge, although data limitations have made early conclusions somewhat tentative. Furthermore, the differential impact of restructuring across ethnic groups has only just begun to be examined.

In this chapter I use Bulgarian data to examine the relative economic status of men and women and of Bulgaria's three main ethnic groups (the majority ethnic Bulgarians, and members of the minority ethnic Turkish and Roma populations) just prior to the transformation, by examining patterns of occupational segmentation and earnings. Using information on the early dynamics of economic restructuring, I suggest how the transformation is affecting the relative position of the various groups. Finally, I contrast the political responses of two groups, women and the Turkish population, to their changing economic position and suggest ways in which economic and political equality might be expanded.

Prior to 1989, women across East Central Europe faced similar patterns of occupational segmentation to those faced by Bulgarian women, and since that time they have also experienced similar dynamics of economic

GENDER AND ETHNICITY IN TRANSFORMATION

restructuring. As a result, the findings presented here may generalise to women in other ECE countries (see, for example, the work of Monica Fong and Gillian Paull 1993). Data on the position of ethnic minorities in other ECE countries before and after 1989 is much more limited, however, and generalisations must therefore be approached more cautiously.

Background: equality and inequality prior to 1989

Prior to 1989, social groups in ECE coexisted in a kind of 'imagined equality'. On the one hand, women and ethnic minorities were offered greatly expanded opportunities for education, paid employment and participation in institutionalised politics. The state's need to fully employ all available labour in order to achieve industrialisation goals and Stalin's policy of dealing with the 'nationalities question' through co-optation ensured this expansion of opportunities.

It would be hard to defend this increase in opportunity as equality, however. Recently, authors examining socialist policy on women have argued that the state provided 'too much' formal equality to women, and in doing so undermined the achievement of real equality between women and men. In a 1993 essay, Zuzana Kisczkova and Etela Farkasova illustrate the problem metaphorically, describing the reactions of women who are permitted, even forced, to enter the hallowed (but male-constructed) buildings of employment, politics and the democratic centrist state. Having been excluded from the design of the buildings, however, these women found the buildings alien and uncomfortable structures. Unable to choose the conditions of their emancipation, women experienced formal equality not as emancipation so much as a change in the conditions of oppression (albeit in some cases this change did offer some improvements in quality of life).

Another critique of women's emancipation in ECE argues that policies of increased employment and political participation reinforced or even increased inequality, by ensuring women's access to the workplace without challenging essentialist conceptions of the 'correct' division of household labour (a traditional patriarchal division of domestic activity). What had previously been a division of labour became, for women, a double burden, which prevented them from really participating equally in the workplace or in the political realm (Einhorn 1993a).

In the case of minority ethnic groups, similar sorts of formal equality were offered in workplace and political organisation, with a similar lack of recognition of distinct needs for expression of the cultural minorities. Official policy also failed to challenge existing conceptions of cultural hierarchy, such as the superiority of western 'civilisation' over oriental 'backwardness'. This expansion of certain formal equalities of opportunity within a structure organised and controlled by ethnic Bulgarian men resulted in clear patterns of occupational segregation for women and minorities.

MIEKE MEURS

The data presented below illustrate these patterns. The data are drawn from a 1986 survey of 6,000 Bulgarian households carried out by the Institute of Sociology of the Bulgarian Academy of Sciences. The sample is representative for the nation as a whole, but only the data on the 4,350 rural households have been analysed here. The survey is unusual in that it allows for the identification of ethnicity through the question of which languages the interviewee speaks fluently (including Bulgarian, Turkish and Roma). Language, of course, captures only one facet of ethnic identity. Individuals could identify themselves as members of a minority group without speaking the language, or members of one ethnic group could speak another ethnic language fluently. To eliminate the latter source of error, fully bilingual individuals (twenty-six people) have been dropped from the sample. In addition, social prejudices against minority groups might encourage under-reporting of minority language skills. Surprisingly, 18 per cent of rural households responded that they did speak Turkish in the home, while 4 per cent claimed to speak Roma (Institute of Sociology 1986). These data are approximately consistent with official data on the ethnic makeup of the population, which listed Turks as making up approximately 20 per cent of the rural population in 1992 and Roma as about 5 per cent. Turkish and Roma households are concentrated in rural areas – nationally they make up 10 per cent and 3 per cent of the population respectively (NSI 1993: 92). The derivation of ethnicity from language data prevents us from examining the economic situation of the Pomak ethnic group, which consists of ethnic Bulgarians who have converted to Islam. Members of this group made up approximately 3.5 per cent of the population in 1989 (Ilchev and Perry 1993).

With truly equal access to education and employment, all ethnic groups and both sexes would be expected to be relatively equally distributed across sectors of the economy. As can be seen from Table 14.1, there was a significant clustering of women and ethnic minorities in certain economic sectors prior to 1989. Members of the Turkish ethnic group tended to be clustered in agriculture (42 per cent of Turks worked in this sector, compared to 27 per cent of the sample), in part due to their residence in rural areas. Roma also held slightly more than their share of jobs in this sector in 1989, for the same reason. Women were particularly overrepresented in the low-paying service and commercial sectors. In the government sector, which offered the highest average wage, both minority groups and women were significantly underrepresented. All three groups are also underrepresented in the high-paying transport and industrial sectors, although to varying degrees.

Within each sector, women and members of ethnic minorities tended to be concentrated in the jobs that do not demand high qualifications, with some noteworthy exceptions. While 4.2 per cent of the sample worked in jobs requiring high qualification, only 3.1 per cent of Turks and 1.2 per cent of Roma held these jobs (Table 14.2). In particular, women and ethnic

GENDER AND ETHNICITY IN TRANSFORMATION

Table 14.1 Sphere of employment by language competence and gender (figures as percentages)

Sphere	Turkish	Roma	Female	Sample	Av. wage 1989
Industry	15.4	6.9	15.3	16.2	3,475
Construction	4.5	3.1	0.8	3.6	3,670
Agriculture	41.7	27.7	23.6	27.3	3,033
Commerce	2.3	3.1	3.9	3.1	2,788
Service	4.4	1.9	7.4	5.3	2,702
Science and culture	0.2	0.0	0.4	0.4	2,944
Government	1.3	0.6	1.2	2.7	3,767
Transport	2.7	2.5	0.5	2.9	3,580
Private	0.4	1.3	0.2	0.5	
Retired	27.0	52.8	45.8	38.0	

Sources: Institute of Sociology 1986; CSO 1988.

Table 14.2 Qualification level by language competence and gender (figures as percentages)

Qualification	Turkish	Roma	Female	Sample
Industrial workers				
Low	18.2	13.8	18.1	16.9
Medium	19.3	13.2	15.6	22.0
High	1.3	0.6	0.7	2.1
Agricultural workers				
Low	19.2	56.0	50.3	39.9
Medium	6.1	10.1	4.6	7.9
High	1.3	0.0	0.3	0.8
Service workers				
Low	1.4	0.0	2.5	2.7
Medium	2.7	5.7	6.6	6.3
High	0.5	0.6	1.3	1.3
Total				
Low	68.8	69.8	70.9	59.5
Medium	28.1	29.0	26.8	36.2
High	3.1	1.2	2.3	4.2

Source: Institute of Sociology 1986.

MIEKE MEURS

minorities were underrepresented in the category of highly qualified industrial workers, some of the most lucrative jobs under central planning. In the sectors where they made up more than their share of employees, however, women and minorities were slightly more likely to have jobs requiring more qualifications. In the service sector, where women were concentrated, women gained equal access to the highly qualified jobs. Likewise, members of the Turkish-speaking group controlled more of the highly qualified jobs in the agricultural sector, where they were concentrated. Roma speakers were absent from highly qualified jobs in all sectors, but did achieve significant representation among workers in agriculture with middle-range qualifications.

Finally, Table 14.3 illustrates the participation of the three groups in enterprise decision-making. In the firms which were considered important enough to be kept under central state control, rural women and ethnic minorities held no positions of responsibility, although they were employed by these firms. In municipally controlled firms, the three groups again held no positions of high authority, but some did hold positions of some responsibility. Most notably, Roma speakers made significant gains and were significantly overrepresented in municipal jobs with some responsibility. In locally controlled firms, women and ethnic minorities also held some positions of responsibility, but were still greatly underrepresented.

To some extent, these patterns of occupational segregation can be linked to differences in schooling. Among those with post-high school education, women and members of the Turkish and Roma-speaking minorities were

Table 14.3 Firm leaders by language competence and gender (figures as percentages)

Leadership level	Turkish	Roma	Female	Sample
Firm under national control				
Highest	0.0	0.0	0.0	0.0
Lower	0.0	0.0	0.0	0.2
No leadership responsibility	0.9	3.2	0.8	2.3
Firm under municipal control				
Highest	0.0	0.0	0.0	0.1
Lower	0.0	3.2	0.2	0.5
No leadership responsibility	2.6	1.6	0.9	2.7
Firm under local control				
Highest	0.5	0.0	0.3	8.0
Lower	1.5	3.2	1.3	4.8
No leadership responsibility	94.6	88.9	96.5	89.1

Source: Institute of Sociology 1986.

GENDER AND ETHNICITY IN TRANSFORMATION

significantly underrepresented, although people with post-high school education made up only 5 per cent of the entire sample. Those having completed primary school (eight years of schooling) or less made up 72 per cent of the sample, but 75 per cent of women had only this level of education, as did 82 per cent of Turkish and 84 per cent of Roma speakers. At the middle levels of education, groups also differed somewhat: 23 per cent of the sample had some middle-school or vocational education, as did 20 per cent of women, 16 per cent of Turkish speakers and 13 per cent of Roma speakers (Institute of Sociology 1986).

Surprisingly, the combination of concentration in sectors of the economy with lower average wages and in the less skilled and less responsible jobs in these sectors did not result in significant differences in average wages between Bulgarian and Turkish speakers (145.5 and 143 leva/month respectively).[1] This may be explained by the high prices the government offered for tobacco, produced mainly by Turkish agricultural workers, and by high wages in the construction industry, where Turkish speakers were also concentrated. The pattern of occupational segregation also did not result in statistically significant differences between Bulgarian and Roma speakers, although this is probably due to the small number of Roma speakers in the sample (110 of the total 4,350), since the wage gap was quite large (145.5 versus 132 leva). Between men and women, however, the wage gap was large and statistically significant (175.5 versus 118.2 leva) (Institute of Sociology 1986). Overall household incomes followed the same pattern as average wages: an average of 5,362 leva per year for all sample households, 5,362 for Turkish speakers and 5,128 for Roma speakers (Institute of Sociology 1986).

Impact of the transformation

Given these distinct patterns of pre-transformation employment, the current economic restructuring is likely to have very different effects on the three social groups analysed here. One of the most significant impacts of the restructuring has been the rise in unemployment. In 1995, unemployment stood at 16 per cent, down from a peak of 20 per cent in 1994 (European Commission 1996).

Early predictions were that unemployment would have a greater impact on women than men, as the light industries and government-run services where women were concentrated would be among the first businesses to close (Ciechocinska 1993). In addition, women were expected to be dismissed in larger numbers than men and to be re-hired more slowly because of their continued legal rights to maternity leave, leave to care for sick children, and other benefits in the state sector which made women relatively more costly to employers (Einhorn 1993a; Fong and Paull 1993).

The unemployment rates of men and women have not differed significantly in Bulgaria, however. In 1993, 22 per cent of Bulgarian women were registered as unemployed compared to 21 per cent of men. In 1995, the difference remained small: 16 per cent for women, 15.5 per cent for men (European Commission 1996). Nor have women left the labour force in significantly larger numbers than men, unlike in the Czech Republic, where the low level of national unemployment can be attributed to the withdrawal of women from the labour market. Despite a certain amount of popular pressure to spend more time in their 'natural' role caring for their families after the experiment with socialist equality, and despite the rapid decline in the availability and quality of child-care services, labour force participation rates fell almost equally for women and men. Ninety per cent of both men and women participated in the labour force in 1989, while 78 per cent of men and 75 per cent of women did so in 1995 (European Commission 1996).

The unexpectedly equal impact of restructuring on men's and women's employment may be explained by the rapid growth of new service industries. Light industry and state-run services, which had employed the majority of women before 1989, did indeed experience collapse or privatisation more rapidly than the heavy industry, transport, or construction sectors where the majority of men worked. But at the same time, nearly all new private sector jobs have been concentrated in the service sector – banking, restaurants and cafés, and retail stores. The majority of these new jobs have gone to women, especially young and attractive women. So while men have been slower to lose their jobs, some women have more easily found new jobs in the growing private sector.

The impact of restructuring on the relative earnings of women and men is harder to judge. Overall, real wages fell almost 50 per cent in 1991, recovered somewhat in 1992 and 1993 (about 20 per cent), and then fell another approximately 20 per cent in 1994 (European Commission 1995: 40). Data are not currently published on wages in the newly emerging private service sector where many women have found employment, however. Given the high unemployment rates and lack of unionisation or labour regulation in the private sector, we might expect low wages in that sector. But wages in the state sector have also fallen, and many state firms pay wages only intermittently, when cash flow permits. The overall impact of restructuring on relative wages is thus difficult to gauge without further data.

The traditional division of household labour has meant that restructuring has another difficult-to-measure impact on women's work. As fiscal and foreign exchange crises have created shortages of medicines, high prices for food, and decline in child-care services, women have carried much of the burden of searching for alternatives or preparing home-produced substitutes. Freed from the burden of standing in long lines for goods in the socialist economy, they now face a new set of tasks which detract equally from their ability to advance in paid employment.

336

GENDER AND ETHNICITY IN TRANSFORMATION

Comparing the impact of economic restructuring across ethnic groups is complicated by the fact that unemployment data are not published for individual ethnic groups. However, some aspects of the ethnic distribution of unemployment may be inferred from electoral support for the Movement for Rights and Freedoms Party in the 1991 parliamentary elections (Figure 5.3, Begg and Pickles in this volume). This party is supported mainly by members of the ethnic Turkish minority.[2] Comparing this map with Figure 5.2 (Begg and Pickles in this volume), which illustrates regions of highest unemployment, suggests that the Turkish-populated areas face levels of unemployment well above the 16 per cent reported nationally. Many areas face levels from 25 to 90 per cent.

In part, the high regional unemployment rates can be explained by the importance of agriculture in Turkish areas and the particularly rapid collapse of collective tobacco production, which Turkish speakers dominated. The small, disbursed tobacco plots had never been effectively collectivised in any case, and were quickly returned to their previous owners after 1989 (Meurs and Begg 1998). De-collectivisation eliminated many of the skilled jobs in management and technical support, while dispersed land was far from adequate to support the population in private farming. In addition, much of the industrial employment in the Turkish-speaking regions was subsidised by a government anxious to offer year-round employment to members of tobacco farming households, thereby ensuring the continued production of this foreign exchange-earning crop. After 1989, such subsidies were no longer available and much of the industrial production collapsed.

Comparing data from Smolyan, one of the counties (*okrug*) in the Turkish-populated regions for which data are published, with national data, indicates that nominal wages in this region have increased much more slowly than the national average (NSI 1995: 99). Combining this with the high unemployment rates has certainly caused average household incomes to fall significantly, although regional data are not available on this issue.

Political reorganisation

Women were not permitted to vote in Bulgaria until after the socialists took power in 1944, and thus had little pre-war experience in organising political parties. Middle-class urban women were, nevertheless, an organised political force in Bulgaria prior to the Second World War. The Bulgarian Women's Union was formed in 1901, and by 1931 the national organisation had 8,400 members (Todorova 1993: 34).

A certain level of political participation continued under socialism, where some participation in party life was often a requirement for job advancement. Women never attained the official target of 15 per cent of state and party jobs, however (Petrova 1993). Of rural women surveyed in 1986, 1.1 per cent had been elected to some party or state position, compared to 3.3

MIEKE MEURS

per cent of men (Institute of Sociology 1986). Instead, women enjoyed a token level of representation in most political organs and were encouraged to participate in the separate women's organisations, which advised women on how to manage their joint duties of socialist worker and socialist mother.

Political activity across ECE in the years leading up to 1989 gave some hope that women would play an important role in the reorganisation of society after state socialism collapsed. In the German Democratic Republic, feminist women's organisations played an important role in the green and anti-nuclear movements which challenged the socialist government in the 1980s (Einhorn 1993a). In Poland and Czechoslovakia women were active in anti-government movements, although they did not put forth a feminist agenda (Siklova 1993). In Bulgaria, women took to the streets of the northern city of Ruse in 1989 to protest environmental problems in a demonstration which signalled the beginning of the end for the socialist government. The ECE experience is similar to that seen in Latin America in the 1970s and 1980s, where women used the conservative, state-espoused ideology of women as mothers, subject to special protections, in order to challenge state actions (Noonan 1995).

In the GDR, the feminist Independent Women's Association (UFV) of the GDR did play an important role in 1990 in the organisation of the Roundtable, a grouping of socialist and opposition forces which governed the GDR in the period between the collapse of the socialist state and the first free elections. The UFV won the right for women to sit at the table as an interest group, alongside unions and political parties. Once seated, the UFV insisted on certain feminist democratic processes, such as shifting from majority voting to an increased emphasis on discussion, compromise and decentralisation (Bohm 1993: 156). With unification, however, the Roundtable was dissolved, and the UFV (along with most other East German political forces) lost much of its influence, although it did continue to support two representatives in Parliament in the mid-1990s.

In Bulgaria, like most other ECE countries, women disappeared from the political scene even more quickly. The reformed Communist Party women's organisation remains the only mass membership women's organisation, but continues to limit its focus to homemaking issues (Panova, Gavrilova and Merdzhanski 1993). Oppositional politics are mainly limited to mainstream struggles for parliamentary seats and cabinet appointments, where women are decreasingly represented. Whereas women made up approximately 21 per cent of national legislators in Bulgaria before 1989, in 1990 they made up only 8 per cent of the Great National Assembly (formed in 1990 to pass basic reform legislation) (Kostova 1993: 107) and in 1991 they made up less than 12 per cent of Parliament (Todorova 1993: 36). Unsupported by a strong women's group, the few women legislators continue to avoid 'women's issues', such as defence of equal employment opportunities, preferring to focus on the more widely accepted 'family issues', such as poverty relief. Women do

GENDER AND ETHNICITY IN TRANSFORMATION

turn out in approximately equal numbers with men when demonstrations are called by trade unions or other organisations, but explicitly women's organisations do not play a role in the organisation of such events.

The history of organising among the Turkish minority in Bulgaria is distinct from women's experience in a number of ways. Members of the minority remaining in Bulgaria at the turn of the century enjoyed full voting rights.[3] While a separate national Turkish organisation or political party did not exist, members of the Turkish minority participated actively in local and national politics. In 1923, there were ten (male) Turkish members of Parliament. This number declined to four in 1933, however, with the rise of fascism in Bulgaria, and Turkish political organisations were banned altogether by the fascist government in 1934 (Stoyanov 1994: 270).

From 1944 to 1956, separate Turkish organisations enjoyed renewed life with support from the new socialist government. A Turkish Department was created in the Central Committee of the Communist Party, Turkish language schools and newspapers were expanded through a policy of cultural autonomy under the guidance of the socialist state (Moutafchieva 1994: 32).

After 1956, however, state policy shifted. The very existence of separate ethnic groups was increasingly denied, and the separate organisations were gradually eliminated. This did not prevent the participation of Turkish speakers in politics, however. In 1986, 1.1 per cent of rural Turkish speakers interviewed reported that they had been elected to a local or national office. This level of participation equalled that reported by women, despite the fact that the Turkish-speaking population made up only about 10 per cent of the population. In contrast, none of the Roma speakers interviewed had been elected to any office.

In the period just prior to 1989, over 350,000 ethnic Turks (about 40 per cent of the ethnic Turkish population) were expelled from Bulgaria (Vasileva 1991) in an apparent effort by the government to distract the Bulgarian population from pressing economic problems. This fiasco may have contributed to the discrediting of the socialist government, but during this period ethnic Turkish organisations were not an active force in Bulgarian politics.

Despite this, the ethnic Turkish minority has emerged as a clear political voice in the post-1989 period. With the political opening of 1990, almost half of the expelled ethnic Turkish population returned to Bulgaria (Vasileva 1991), and one of the many new political parties formed that year was the Movement for Rights and Freedoms (MRF). This organisation won 12 per cent of seats in the Great National Assembly in 1990. In 1991, the MRF won 10 per cent of seats in a Parliament dominated by the two main political forces, the reformed Communist Party (BSP), which won 44 per cent of seats, and the neo-liberal coalition of opposition parties (UDF), which held 46 per cent of seats. In the 1994 parliamentary election, the MRF won 8 per cent of seats to the 29 per cent held by the UDF and 52 per cent held by

MIEKE MEURS

the BSP (Koulov 1995). In both Parliaments, MRF delegates voted as a bloc under the tight control of the central party organisation, and this allowed the MRF rapidly to become the critical swing vote and a powerful voice in national politics.

Although the party has been very active in cultural and political issues at the local level, to date the MRF has not often exercised this parliamentary power to pursue issues of specific interest to the ethnic Turkish minority. Between 1990 and 1992, the MRF did set improvement of economic conditions among the Turkish and mixed populations as a condition for supporting the government (FBIS 21 October 1990: 12; 27 October 1992: 1). But in more recent years there is little evidence that such demands have been forcefully pursued.

The contrast between the experiences of women's and of Turkish organising is striking. Why have the political experiences of interest group organising been so different for women and members of the Turkish-speaking minority in Bulgaria? One source of the difference may lie in the perceived potential for interest group politics to address the problems of the transition. While economic devastation is clearly concentrated in the regions populated by ethnic Turks, asymmetric economic impacts on women are harder to capture. The biggest economic hardship for women may well be the increased time and effort needed to assure household reproduction. This hardship appears in the first instance to affect the family as a whole, however, and the concentration of its impact on women is hard to measure. Organising specifically as women may not immediately emerge as a solution to these problems, whereas organising under the banner of the MRF may appear a more direct response to the problems faced by Turkish speakers.

Another explanation may lie in the differences in the cultural resources available to the two groups for use in organisation in 1989. The pre-1989 attack on members of the ethnic Turkish minority served to heighten their own awareness of their distinct culture. In the period just following the collapse of state socialism, language and religious freedom became prominent issues in the local politics of Turkish regions. This cultural mobilisation was also aided by sympathetic Turkish and Islamic organisations abroad, which donated resources for the construction of mosques, religious schools and the printing of ethnic and religious publications. The increased cultural mobilisation contributed to, and was in turn fed by, successful political organising by the MRF.

Women, in their protests against the state in 1989, mobilised under the conservative, state-sponsored rubric of women as mothers. In Latin America, some similar movements managed to transform the conservative identity into a more feminist one in the process of successful protest (Noonan 1995). The independent political action of Bulgarian women lasted only a few months, however, and was too short-lived to achieve such an evolution. After 1989, the very identity which had served to mobilise women contributed

340

GENDER AND ETHNICITY IN TRANSFORMATION

to their demobilisation, as women/mothers turned their attention to the overwhelming task of household reproduction in a time of economic crisis.

This reaction was reinforced by the ideology of East European dissident movements, which emphasised the importance of the unified family as the realm of anti-politics under state socialism. As the writings of Mikhail Gorbachev or Vaclav Havel on women illustrate, opposition movements conceptualised individual rights only in the public sphere and did not extend them to the household (Todorova 1993; Eisenstein 1993). In many places (the GDR is an interesting exception), this context undermined the development of women's consciousness of themselves as a group with distinctive interests. Examining the lack of political organising among Czech women, Hana Havelkova notes: '[w]henever the serious problems of women are debated in the Czech lands, someone, usually a woman, raises the question: "What about the problems of men?"' (1993: 62). Women continue to act mainly in the name of the family unit.

Another explanation for different levels of political response may lie in the form of political organisation which emerged after 1989. During the socialist period, women in East Central Europe mainly participated in mainstream politics predominantly at the local level (Einhorn 1993b: 56, 1993a), where they addressed concerns of immediate relevance to their families and daily lives – schools, transport, food distribution and environmental problems. Such local problems were also the basis of the anti-state organising of 1989, in which women participated quite actively. In the period immediately following 1989, a variety of forms of local participatory governance emerged spontaneously to fill the vacuum left by the collapse of the state. These forms of governance did not conform to the basic liberal conception of democracy based on hierarchical structures in a well-defined public sphere. Instead, they were decentralised and participatory (and sometimes chaotic). Local women often continued to participate in these structures.

The development of institutionalised ('normal') politics quickly eclipsed these experiments, however. True to the liberal conceptions which inspired the dissident movements, institutionalised politics was hierarchical and increasingly limited to 'public' issues. Local institutions were stripped of resources as changes in tax policy shifted the increasingly limited resources to the national level (Martinez-Vasques 1995), centralising institutionalised politics. This form of liberal politics may have contributed to emancipation from the all-controlling state, but it did little to promote women's expression of their common interests. Instead, post-socialist politics became a male domain. With women's opportunities to participate in the building of new (less alien) social institutions diminishing, they may have little motivation to remain in the hallowed 'buildings' of politics and the state.

This lack of political participation does not mean, of course, that women are not fighting back. Many struggle daily in their homes and communities

MIEKE MEURS

to retain jobs, protect access to child care, or simply hold on to the idea that they have a right to participate as full citizens in the emerging economy. Under the right conditions, such unorganised efforts may provide the basis for more structured actions.

The new institutionalised politics, in which two monolithic parties were locked in a relative stalemate, was a much more hospitable context for organising by the MRF. Male organisers in the MRF easily exploited the existing hierarchical structures of the religious community and territorial government to mobilise voters behind a hierarchical and centralised political party. This form of mobilisation contributed to electoral successes and parliamentary power.

Ironically, however, this 'successful' strategy seems to have yielded little in terms of protecting the interests of the ethnic Turkish minority. While before 1989 members of the Turkish-speaking minority enjoyed little access to the best paid and most responsible jobs, government policies assured individual and household incomes nearly equal to those of ethnic Bulgarian house- holds. In the post-1994 period, the MRF has given the Turkish minority a disproportionately important voice in Parliament, but members of the ethnic group have experienced the most severe and concentrated economic devastation in the country. The MRF has created strength as a voting bloc, but it has not used this strength to support policies to prevent or address this devastation. In part, the MRF may be trapped in its own rhetoric, in much the same way as Bulgarian women. While women organised under the conservative banner of wives and mothers, as a political party the MRF faced a legal ban on the organisation of ethnically based parties and thus organised under a universalist banner of internationally established human rights. This claim to universalism may now complicate MRF claims for special attention to the economic and cultural problems of the ethnic minority which supports it.

Imagining increased political and economic equality

To date, Bulgarian women's apparent preference for decentralised, local, political organising has contributed to their relative exclusion from political power. Ironically, however, this preference could hold the key to more effective political organising against the increasing economic hardships faced by Bulgarian women and ethnic minorities

The centralised, hierarchical political organisation of the MRF has not met the needs of the ethnic Turkish population which has supported it. On the contrary, the centrist, urban-focused political model which it supports would appear to have contributed to the economic devastation of regions with high concentrations of ethnic Turks. Local branch plants have been closed in the interests of the central firms, and tobacco prices have been driven to new lows in what appears to be a scheme to privatise the tobacco

342

GENDER AND ETHNICITY IN TRANSFORMATION

monopoly cheaply to government insiders (see Begg and Pickles in this volume). The Sofia-based MRF leadership has done little to resist these processes and has done little else to protect the economic interests of its rural supporters.

The potential of alternative forms of organising to better address local economic needs is illustrated by Hillary Wainwright in her study of successful forms of democratic governance in Western Europe. The organisations which Wainwright examined were like the early forms of post-socialist organising – decentralised, participatory, with decisions based on discussion and compromise. These organisations are examples of 'democratic management of public provision, co-ordination, and regulation of the economy', in which local organisations use local expertise to meet local needs (1994: 10).

Clearly, in 1989 much of the population of Eastern Europe was in no mood to experiment with radical new forms of democracy, despite the claims of leaders of the democracy movements, particularly in the GDR. The attitude was one of 'You rich countries experiment, give us something that works!' and what worked may seem to many to be liberal democracy in its traditional form.

Still, a revitalisation of decentralised, local forms of government might offer greatly expanded opportunities for expression by women and ethnic minorities, both of whom have a strong history of local political participation. At the same time, by focusing political control at the local level, such organisation would provide an institutional base for expanded control of economic resources. Villagers across Bulgaria have used local political structures to co-ordinate the collective purchase of liquidated collective farm assets for co-operative use (see Meurs and Begg 1998 and in this volume). Expanded local governments in de-industrialising regions might co-ordinate collective purchase of other local assets slated for liquidation if the population were mobilised for activity at this level,[4] or women might use local political structures to co-ordinate continued child-care services. Such a change in the focus of political organising would not change the fundamental conditions of the current transformation. Unemployment levels would remain high and government spending greatly restricted. But a change in the form of organising might permit greater equality of political expression and greater control of policy by those most negatively affected by the transformation. Imagine!

Acknowledgements

The author wishes to thank the International Research Exchanges Board, the John D. and Catherine T. MacArthur Foundation, and the US National Science Foundation Social and Behavioral Research Program (Grant 9515244) for supporting the research on which this chapter is based.

MIEKE MEURS

Notes

1 The hypothesis that the population means are equal is not rejected at p = .01 using a separate-variance t-test. This same standard is used for other findings of significance reported here.
2 Parties purporting to represent the interests of separate ethnic groups are illegal. The MRF thus formally defines its goals in terms of national development and cultural understanding. Nearly all of the party's supporters are ethnic Turks, however.
3 Most of the Turkish population left Bulgaria when it was freed from Ottoman control in the late 1800s, but some ethnic Turks chose to remain.
4 These assets may be subject to liquidation by central firms, which perceive a negative rate of return on the assets. Local populations may include employment and other positive externalities in their valuation of potential returns, and thus find it economically beneficial to purchase these assets, which in any case are liquidated at fire sale prices.

Bibliography

Bohm, T. (1993) 'The women's question as a democratic question: in search of civil society', in N. Funk and M. Mueller (eds) *Gender Politics and Post-Communism: Reflections from Eastern Europe and the Former Soviet Union*, New York: Routledge: 151–159.

Ciechocinska, M. (1993) 'Gender aspects of dismantling the command economy in Eastern Europe: the case of Poland', in V. Moghadam (ed.) *Democratic Reform and the Position of Women in Transitional Economies*, Oxford: Clarendon Press: 302–326.

CSO (1988) *Statistical Yearbook of the People's Republic of Bulgaria*, Sofia: Central Statistical Office.

Einhorn, B. (1993a) *Cinderella Goes to Market: Gender, Citizenship, and Women's Movements in East Central Europe*, New York: Verso.

Einhorn, B. (1993b) 'Democratisation and women's movements in Central and Eastern Europe: concepts of women's rights', in V. Moghadam (ed.) *Democratic Reform and the Position of Women in Transitional Economies*, Oxford: Clarendon Press: 48–74.

Eisenstein, Z. (1993) 'Eastern European male democracies: a problem of unequal equality', in N. Funk and M. Mueller (eds) *Gender Politics and Post-Communism: Reflections from Eastern Europe and the Former Soviet Union*, New York: Routledge: 303–317.

European Commission (1995) *Employment Observatory: Central and Eastern Europe*, 7.

European Commission (1996) *Employment Observatory: Central and Eastern Europe*, 8.

FBIS (Foreign Broadcast Information Service) (1990, 1992, 1993) Daily Report. Washington DC.

Fong, M. and Paull, G. (1993) 'Women's economic status in the restructuring of Eastern Europe', in V. Moghadam (ed.) *Democratic Reform and the Position of Women in Transitional Economies*, Oxford: Clarendon Press: 217–247.

GENDER AND ETHNICITY IN TRANSFORMATION

Hauser, E., Heyns, B. and Mansbridge, J. (1993) 'Feminism in the interstices of politics and culture: Poland in transition', in N. Funk and M. Mueller (eds) *Gender Politics and Post-Communism: Reflections from Eastern Europe and the Former Soviet Union*, New York: Routledge: 257–273.

Havelkova, H. (1993) 'A few pre-feminist thoughts', in 'Eastern European male democracies: a problem of unequal equality', in N. Funk and M. Mueller (eds) *Gender Politics and Post-Communism: Reflections from Eastern Europe and the Former Soviet Union*, New York: Routledge: 62–73.

Ilchev, I. and Perry, D. (1993) 'Bulgarian ethnic groups: politics and perceptions', *RFE/RL Research Report* 2, 12 (March): 35–41.

Institute of Sociology (1986) *Town and Village Study Survey Data*, Sofia: Bulgarian Academy of Sciences.

Kisczkova, Z. and Farkasova, E. (1993) 'The emancipation of women: a concept that failed', in N. Funk and M. Mueller (eds) *Gender Politics and Post-Communism: Reflections from Eastern Europe and the Former Soviet Union*, New York: Routledge: 84–94.

Kostova, D. (1993) 'The transition to democracy in Bulgaria: challenges and risks for women', in V. Moghadam (ed.) *Democratic Reform and the Position of Women in Transitional Economies*, Oxford: Clarendon Press: 92–109.

Koulov, B. (1995) 'Democratization "from above" and its limitations', Mimeo, Washington DC: American University.

Martinez-Vasques, J. (1995) 'Central and local tax relations', in Z. Bogetic and A. Hillman (eds) *Financing Government in the Transition: Bulgaria*, Washington DC: World Bank.

Meurs, M. and Begg, R. (1998) 'Path dependence in Bulgarian agriculture', in J. Pickles and A. Smith (eds) *Theorizing Transition: The Political Economy of Change in Central and Eastern Europe*, London: Routledge.

Moutafchieva, V. (1994) 'The Turk, the Gypsy and the Jew', in *Relations of Compatibility and Incompatibility between Christians and Muslims in Bulgaria*, Sofia: Intercultural Centre for Minority Studies and Intercultural Relations Foundation: 3–63.

Noonan, R. (1995) 'Women against the state: political opportunities and collective action frames in Chile's transition to democracy', *Sociological Forum* 10, 1: 81–111.

NSI (National Statistical Institute) (1993) *Demografska Kharakteristica na Bulgaria*, Sofia: National Statistical Institute.

NSI (National Statistical Institute) (1995) *Statistical Yearbook*, Sofia: National Statistical Institute.

Panova, R. Gavrilova, R. and Merdzhanski, C. (1993) 'Thinking gender: Bulgarian women's im/possibilities', in N. Funk and M. Mueller (eds) *Gender Politics and Post-Communism: Reflections from Eastern Europe and the Former Soviet Union*, New York: Routledge: 15–21.

Petrova, D. (1993) 'The winding road to emancipation in Bulgaria', in N. Funk and M. Mueller (eds) *Gender Politics and Post-Communism: Reflections from Eastern Europe and the Former Soviet Union*, New York: Routledge: 22–29.

Siklova, J. (1993) 'Are women in Central and Eastern Europe conservative?' in N. Funk and M. Mueller (eds) *Gender Politics and Post-Communism: Reflections from Eastern Europe and the Former Soviet Union*, New York: Routledge: 74–83.

MIEKE MEURS

Stoyanov, V. (1994) 'The Turks in Bulgaria', in *Relations of Compatibility and Incompatibility between Christians and Muslims in Bulgaria*, Sofia: Intercultural Centre for Minority Studies and Intercultural Relations Foundation: 268–271.

Territorial Statistical Bureau-Smolyan (1995) *Statistical Handbook Smolyan 1994*, Smolyan, Bulgaria: Statistical Publishing and Printing.

Todorova, M. (1993) 'The Bulgarian case: women's issues or feminist issues', in N. Funk and M. Mueller (eds) *Gender Politics and Post-Communism: Reflections from Eastern Europe and the Former Soviet Union*, New York: Routledge: 30–38.

Vasileva, D. (1991) 'Bulgarian Turkish emigration and return', *International Migration Review* 26, 2: 342–352.

Wainwright, H. (1994) *Arguments for a New Left: Answering the Free Market Right*, Oxford: Blackwell.

[29]

GENDER AND ECONOMIC REFORMS:
A FRAMEWORK FOR ANALYSIS AND EVIDENCE FROM
CENTRAL ASIA, THE CAUCASUS, AND TURKEY

VALENTINE M. MOGHADAM

Introduction and overview

Since 1990, a now prodigious body of literature has examined and often debated various aspects of the market reforms implemented in the former centrally-planned economies. Questions have centered around the nature of the crisis that precipitated the collapse of the communist system and launched the market transition; the timing, pace, and scope of the reforms; the effect of initial conditions; and the social impacts of the restructuring process. What was the relation between the decline in economic performance in the former communist countries and the global economic crisis? Was the gradual approach to market reforms that was taken by some countries preferable to the "shock therapy" applied in others?[1] How can privatization and the emerging private sector be evaluated? Have the reforms been poverty-inducing? Have social indicators deteriorated? What explains differences in levels and rates of unemployment across the transition economies?[2] Economists have been deeply divided over these issues.[3]

A parallel body of literature has focused on the gender aspects of the transition from centrally-planned to market economies,

---

[1] "Shock therapy" involves a sharp cut of budget deficits, liberalization of prices and imports, devaluation of exchange rates, interest rate increases, and tight control of money supply growth.

[2] Economies in transition include the countries of East Central Europe (Albania, Bulgaria, Croatia and Slovenia of the former Yugoslavia, the Czech Republic, Hungary, Poland, Romania, Slovakia), the republics of the former Soviet Union now cooperating within the Commonwealth of Independent States, and the Baltic states of Estonia, Latvia, and Lithuania. China and Vietnam are the two main Asian transition economies, although geographically speaking the Central Asian republics of the former Soviet Union, including Uzbekistan, belong to the category of Asian transition economies.

[3] For a pro-"big bang" perspective, see Sachs 1992. For the gradualist view, see Rana 1993. See also Economic Commission for Europe 1993.

24   VALENTINE MOGHADAM

examining in detail the impact of the reforms on women's labor-market positions, their social entitlements, and their place in the emerging political structures. Here there is more consensus among the feminist scholars and the gender-and-development specialists who have contributed to this scholarship (Moghadam 1994; Einhorn 1994; Rai, Pilkington, and Phizacklea 1992; Rueschemeyer 1994; Tokhtakhodzhaeva 1995b). The transition to a market economy has proved to be costly in terms of real income and output decline, loss of employment and security, a rapid deteriora-tion in social conditions, and deepening gender inequalities. Although privatization of state-owned enterprises and encour-agement of private-sector growth hypothetically offers women (and men) opportunities for higher incomes and for entrepreneurship, in fact it has tended to increase women's chances of being laid off, worsened their conditions of employment, and minimized their social entitlements. Whatever comparative advantage women had at the start of the reforms—in particular, the feminized nature of occupations such as trade, banking, insurance, financial services, and accounting—it was quickly overcome by a pervasive gender bias in favor of male recruitment in these now lucrative fields of employment. Women's position in the new labor markets has been further complicated by a resurgence of the stereotyping of gender roles, the growth (and export) of prostitution, a decline in the availability of social services (particularly in childcare), and the political powerlessness of women's organizations. It should be noted that these changes occurred in regions previously char-acterized by high rates of female employment, diversified occu-pational distribution, very high levels of educational attainment, and strong representation in political structures.

There is some analogy with the experience of gender and structural adjustment in developing countries. Economic reforms in both the transition economies and developing countries are motivated by the same neoliberal economic philosophy, and their adverse social and gender effects have been very similar. Most of the evidence on structural adjustment and women comes from Latin America, Sub-Saharan Africa, and Southeast Asia (Afshar and Dennis 1992; Bakker 1994; Beneria and Feldman 1992; Elson 1991; Sparr 1994; Tanski 1994). Countries in West Asia, including Tur-key, have had a more recent experience with structural adjustment, although in Turkey economic liberalization has been proceeding since the early 1980s (Moghadam 1998). We may ask, however, whether the socio-economic changes in Turkey—liberalization, privatization, and integration into the global economy—have had or will have the same negative effects that women have been experiencing in the transition economies, or whether given different initial conditions, the outcomes could also be different. We will return to this question later in the paper.

Gender and market reforms in Central Asia and the Caucasus

Until recently, international attention was focused on the transition in East Central Europe, Russia, and the Baltic states, but now the former Soviet republics of Central Asia—especially Kazakhstan, Kyrgyzstan, and Uzbekistan—are receiving attention, in terms of both research and policy. These and other countries of Central Asia and the Caucasus are not only experiencing the difficulties of a transition from central planning to a market economy but, as newly independent states, they are also engaging in state-building. Moreover, some of them have seen the revival of Islamist movements. As such, the implications of the transition for women go beyond the labor market and into the realm of culture and national identity (Moghadam 1994, 1995; Tokhtakhodzhaeva 1995a).

A quick glance at some statistical facts is instructive of the severity of the problems in the transition economies of Central Asia and the Caucasus. These problems include unemployment, poverty, deteriorating wages, rising prices, and a resurgence of patriarchal attitudes. In particular, we notice a trend toward a feminization of unemployment. Post-communist Uzbekistan has experienced declining output, falling incomes, high unemployment, and deteriorating social indicators. As reported by Marfua Tokhtakhodzhaeva, the majority of unemployed in the capital city of Tashkent are female (Tokhtakhodzhaeva 1995c). Most are women of secondary education or less, suggesting the impact on working-class women. Furthermore, as a predominantly Muslim country, Uzbekistan has experienced a post-Soviet resurgence of Islamist politics with distinctly gender-specific effects. Interest in Islamic culture and politics has emerged, with its accompanying pressures on educational institutions, the media, and women's

26   VALENTINE MOGHADAM

comportment. But as one enlightened, Soviet-educated Uzbek professor notes: "I support revival of spiritual values, but am against conservative traditions and customs, which hinder active creative life" (Tokhtakhodzhaeva 1995c).

Anyone who has read Gregory Massell's classic book, *The Surrogate Proletariat*, has some idea of the enormous advances made by the women of Central Asia since the early Soviet days (Massell 1974). One of the greatest achievements was the feminization of education and of science. As one author has noted, "in Soviet Central Asia industrialization, collectivization and cultural revolution resulted in new professions. One can say that socialism was built by women. Some occupations, such as health care, education, parts of the service sector, etc. were completely feminized. In schools male teachers are an exception" (Tabyshalieva 1995). This makes their current difficulties all the more poignant. At the same time, available evidence suggests that patriarchal gender ideologies were never eliminated, and these have merged with the new political economy to create an environment very unfavorable to women's equality and empowerment.

In Uzbekistan, a former Soviet republic, there is no *de jure* discrimination against women, who continue to enjoy the same legal rights as men. As seen in Table 1, they have high life expectancy (71 years), relatively low maternal mortality (55 per 100,000 live births), very high adult literacy rates (97 percent), good educational attainment, and considerable labor force participation in agriculture, industry, and services. Unlike many developing countries, including Turkey, gender gaps in literacy and educational attainment are not wide. (See Table 1.) Women's access to the professions and occupations was such that they were even a respectable 31 percent of the labor force in the mining, energy, and chemicals sector—sectors that are non-traditional, as far as women's employment is concerned. Some 40-45 percent of scientists in Uzbekistan were women. On average, women earned about 40 percent of all income and were about 46 percent of the total labor force (see Table 2). Uzbekistan inherited an extensive system of social protection characterized by child allowances, old age pensions, disability benefits, and subsidies on consumer goods and services. Given the generous benefits and the relatively easy access women had to employment, it is no wonder that Uzbek

women are reluctant to leave the shrinking state sector and work in
the growing private sector.

However, the collapse of trade and enterprise restructuring have
resulted in the deterioration of wages and the real value of cash
benefits, worsening working conditions, and rising unemployment.
According to the ILO, wages in Uzbekistan fell by 31 percent in
1991, increased by 6 percent in 1993, and fell again by 42 percent
in 1994.[4] Moreover, due to the persistence of tradition, women still
marry young and family size tends to be relatively large. As seen in
Table 1, the fertility rate in Uzbekistan was as high as 3.7 in 1994.
This has serious implications for the future expansion of the labor
force, especially in a low-growth market context. A World Bank
country study speculates that many women may opt for domestic
responsibility or part-time work (World Bank 1993, 98). On the
other hand, the departure of non-Uzbek women (mainly Russians
and Armenians) from factories, offices, educational institutions,
and hospitals may open up more employment opportunities for
Uzbek women. In any event, the transition and its difficulties seem
to have reinvigorated patriarchal views of women and gender relations and exacerbated the cultural constraints on women's
equality.[5] How the Uzbek government will address the issues of
unemployment, growing poverty, the needs of children, Islamic
revival, and pressures on women, is not yet known. It is clear that
women's organizations in Uzbekistan, whether they be the
successors to the Soviet-era women's organizations or the new
independent women's groups, will be required to play a leading
role in monitoring the situation and in bringing problems and
solutions to the attention of the government and international
organizations.

In a number of the countries of Central Asia and the Caucasus,
the problems of gender and the market transition have been
exacerbated by civil strife and conflict. These countries include
Armenia, Azerbaijan, Georgia, and Tajikistan, where the increase
not only in the number of refugees but also in the number of
prostitutes is said to be related to both the conflicts and the
economic difficulties of the transition. Tajikistan was long among
the most rural and least developed of the republics within

[4] ILO 1996, Table 4.3, p. 114.
[5] See Tokhtakhodzhaeva's (1995c) interviews with Uzbek women professionals.

Table 1. Women and Capabilities: Health and Education

| | Life expectancy at birth (years) 1994 | | Total Fertility | | Maternal mortality rate (per 100,000 live births) 1990 | Adult literacy rate (%) 1994 | | Tertiary students (per 100,000 people) 1992 | Female tertiary students (per 100,000 women) 1992 | Combined primary, secondary and tertiary gross enrollment ratio (%) 1994 | |
	Female	Male	Rate 1994	Index (1970=100) 1994		Female	Male			Female	Male
Armenia	74.5	67.1	2.0	63	50	98.8	98.8	3,711	:	83.0	74.0
Azerbaijan	74.9	66.8	2.5	55	22	96.3	96.3	2,323	2,453	71.0	74.0
Georgia	77.2	68.8	2.0	79	33	94.9	94.9	2,710	:	69.0	68.0
Kazakstan	72.3	62.6	2.3	66	80	97.5	97.5	3,433	:	75.0	71.0
Kyrgyzstan	72.1	63.3	3.4	71	110	97.0	97.0	1,837	:	74.0	71.0
Tajikistan	70.0	63.7	4.0	59	130	96.7	96.7	2,298	:	67.0	70.0
Turkey	70.6	65.9	1.9*	36	180	71.1	91.7		1,111	55.0	70.0
Turkmenistan	68.1	61.3	3.8	60	55	97.7	97.7	2,078	:	90.0	90.0
Uzbekistan	70.7	64.2	3.7	60	55	97.2	97.2	3,054	:	71.0	75.0

Source: UNDP, *Human Development Report 1997.*
* 2.7 World Bank, 1997

the former Soviet Union, and its social indicators did not compare well to those of Uzbekistan, Kazakhstan, Kyrgyzstan, or Armenia (see Tables 1 and 2). It then became a low-income country with internal conflicts tied to Islamism and a growing refugee population. The civil war ruined the social and physical infrastructure, with especially adverse effects on women, pensioners, and children. It remains to be seen whether the Economic Reform program for 1996-2000, which aims to create a "socially-oriented market economy for growth of the economy and welfare" will succeed in achieving its goals.[6]

Armenia and Azerbaijan are neighboring republics that progressed considerably during the socialist era. Women's capabilities were well developed. Life expectancy was high, fertility rates were relatively low in 1990 (having declined considerably since 1970), maternal mortality rates were low, and the literacy rate of adult women was very high. Indeed, Armenian women surpassed men in educational enrollments (see Table 1). In Azerbaijan, women's political participation has been quite respectable (see Table 3). However, the two countries have been at war with each other, and this has exacerbated the problems emanating from the collapse of the socialist economy and system of trade. Both economies have experienced considerable negative growth, and unemployment has grown.[7] An official report from Azerbaijan states that two-thirds of the unemployed are women.[8] In Armenia, although women were 47 percent of the labor force in 1995, they were 64 percent of the total persons unemployed. According to an official report, the duration of unemployment is longer for a woman than for a man, and her situation has been made more difficult by the shutting down of many pre-school and after-school facilities and programs.

---

[6] See "Republic of Tajikistan National Report" (by B. Dodkhudieva), background paper submitted to the Subregional Conference of Senior Governmental Experts on the Implementation of the Platform for Action Adopted by the 1995 Fourth World Conference on Women in Beijing, in Central and Eastern Europe, Bucharest, 12-14 September 1996, p. 2.

[7] The unemployment rates in Table 2 are the official rates of the registered unemployed only. The figures do not reflect the extent of job loss. See ILO 1996 for a discussion.

[8] "Report on Azerbaijan", background paper submitted to the Subregional Conference, Bucharest, 12-14 September 1996.

30   VALENTINE MOGHADAM

Table 2. Income, Employment, and Unemployment

	Real GDP per capita (PPP$) 1994	GDP Growth rate (%) 1990-95	Labor force (as % of total population) 1990	Percentage of labor force in			Women's share of adult labor force aged 15 and above		Female economic activity rate (as % of male) 1995	Earned income share (%) 1994		Un-employed people (thousands) 1993	Total unemployment rate* (%) 1995
				Agriculture 1990	Industry 1990	Services 1990	1970	1990		Female	Male		
Armenia	1,737	-21.2	48	18	43	39	46	47	87	40.3	59.7	..	8.1
Azerbaijan	1,670	-20.2	42	31	29	40	45	43	75	36.8	63.2	19	1.1
Georgia	1,585	-11.9	49	26	31	43	48	46	79	39.3	60.7	..	3.4
Kazakstan	3,284	-14.7	47	22	32	46	47	46	82	39.2	60.8	78	2.1
Kyrgyzstan	1,930		41	32	27	41	49	46	84	39.5	60.5	3	3
Tajikistan	1,117		36	41	23	36	45	42	76	36.4	63.6	..	1.8
Turkey	5,193	3.2	44	53	18	29	38	33	57	33.2	66.8	..	
Turkmenistan	3,469	3.2	41	37	23	40	46	45	81	38.2	61.8	..	..
Uzbekistan	2,438	-4.4	39	35	25	40	48	46	84	39.0	61.0	..	0.3

Sources: UNDP. *Human Development Report 1997.*

World Bank, *World Development Report 1997*

Women's wages are about one-third less than men's earnings; in the highly feminized sector of education (77.2 percent female), teachers' salaries are "a nominal $4.50 per month." As in other former Soviet countries, the high rate of abortion is considered a social problem and a reproductive health issue, reflecting lack of information about, and access to, family planning and contraception.[9]

As in other transition economies in the Caucasian and Central Asian republics, the transition from communism in Armenia seems to have exacerbated latent and manifest patriarchal attitudes, especially within households, to result in growing disadvantages experienced by women and girls. An interesting commentary on the "mixed signals" that girls received during the Soviet era comes from an official Armenian report:

> "Having been a former Soviet Republic for seventy years our society has been educated by communist principles which stressed equal opportunities of education for all men and women. For over seventy years now Armenian girls have attended public schools and have enjoyed the best educational opportunities that that system had to offer without being discriminated against. Most women have received higher education and have been employed. Gender inequalities in Armenia stem mainly from culture. As a result, practices at home and in society in general are more favorable to men than women. Armenians do give equal opportunity of education to both girls and boys, but very early in life girls learn that women's main function in life is to become a loyal wife and a devoted mother. Everything else is secondary . . . Armenian culture shares most of the attitudes of patriarchal cultures toward gender . . . As a result, women became educated, many of them reached higher level positions in their professional fields especially in education and health care but at home they continued to perform all of the household chores and childrearing was mainly their responsibility . . . Girls in our society grow up with conflicting and confusing messages."[10]

Georgia, Kazakhstan, Kyrgyzstan, and Turkmenistan exhibit patterns and trends similar to those of their neighbors. Except for Turkmenistan, GDP growth has fallen in all of the countries, although Kazakhstan has seen growth in industry and services, according to the World Bank (see Table 2). Wages have fluctuated

---

[9] "Armenia National Plan of Action (Background and Summary)", background paper submitted to ibid.
[10] Ibid.

32   VALENTINE MOGHADAM

wildly, according to the ILO. In Kazakhstan, they declined by nearly 11 percent in 1991, increased by the same amount in 1992, and then fell again, by 11.6 percent in 1993 and 31.3 percent in 1994. In Kirgizistan, wages rose in 1991 but then fell by 30 percent in 1992, 51.5 percent in 1993, and 25.8 percent in 1994. At the same time, the rate of inflation has been exceedingly high (e.g., 1,880 percent in Kazakhstan and 280 percent in Kyrgyzstan in 1994).[11] What is more, in the Kyrgyz Republic, 69 percent of people with higher education are women, and yet women made up 59.3 percent of the unemployed in early 1996. Women's average wages were 25 percent less than men's.[12] According to one study, more and more women are becoming poor, and infant mortality and maternal mortality are increasing. Violence against women is becoming more apparent. Although women's participation in government is higher than in neighboring countries (see Table 3), there has been a reduction in the percentage of women in the parliament. Finally, there is "the weakness of women's non-state social organizations" (Kenenbaeva, Tabyshalieva, and Karasaeva 1995).

What this brief survey has shown is that from a gender perspective, the market reforms that have been adopted in Central Asia and the Caucasus, prescribed and underwritten by the international financial institutions, and endorsed by neoliberal thinkers and policy-makers in Western countries, have been deeply flawed. The social costs of the transition have been far higher than expected, and the burden borne by women has been especially onerous. Seven years after market reforms began, not only are the majority of women not better off than they were before, but the adverse effects of economic restructuring have hit women harder than men.

Why is this the case? Why should the effects of market reforms be differentiated by gender? Why should women be more vulnerable than men? There are many reasons for this, but they may be distilled into two major causes, one "cultural" (that is, the

---

[11] Data from ILO 1996, Table 4.3, p. 114 and Table 4.4, p. 118.
[12] "National Report of the Representative of the Kirgiz Republic", background paper submitted to the Subregional Conference, Bucharest, 12-14 September 1996.

Table 3. Women's Political Participation

	Parliamentary seats held by women (as % of total) 1996	Women in Government		
		Total (%) 1995	At ministerial level (%) 1995	At sub-ministerial level (%) 1995
Armenia	6	2.0	0	3.1
Azerbaijan	12	5.3	4.0	6.0
Georgia	7	3.3	0	4.7
Kazakstan	11	1.1	2.7	0
Kyrgyzstan	5	8.0	4.3	11.1
Tajikistan	3	4.0	6.9	2.9
Turkey	3	3.9	4.3	3.6
Turkmenistan	18	3.9	4.3	3.6
Uzbekistan	6	2.9	2.8	2.9

Source: UNDP, *Human Development Report 1997.*

persistence of traditional gender ideology regarding men's and women's roles), and the other "economic" (that is, the nature of the reforms themselves and the assumptions in neoliberal economic thinking that inform the policies). In the section below, we consider a framework for understanding and explaining gender-differentiated outcomes.

A framework for analysis: Gender ideology and political economy

The position of women—their legal status and their access to economic resources and political power—has varied across historical eras and types of social formations. Scholars have variously identified political, economic, ideological, or cultural factors as the major determinants, or they have emphasized the class system, the mode of production, or "patriarchy" as the most critical factor in explaining stability and change in the position of women. In the

framework suggested here, the structural factors which seem to consistently shape
women's specific positions across history and different societies are the following: (a) class (which determines women's life-options, as well as access to economic and political power); (b) the nature of the state and the orientation of the leadership (which shapes the opportunity structure for women, including the legal framework); (c) the system of production (which determines the resources and kinds of work available to women); and (d) cultural understandings of men's and women's roles (which may be widely shared in the society or differentiated along class and ethnic lines). For the sake of analytic clarity and for ease of exposition, we may consider class, state, and production as three dimensions of political economy, while cultural understandings of men's and women's roles may be understood as gender ideology.

The concept of gender, now widely used by feminists and social scientists, has material and symbolic dimensions. It refers to a fairly universal pattern of relations between men and women, in which women are subordinated to men within the household, in the economy, and in the polity—relationships that are often codified in law. The asymmetrical relations between men and women often have been justified in terms of both divine law and natural law (Moghadam 1994a).

Understanding why gender matters and how it operates is facilitated by analogy to social class. The concept of class refers to asymmetrical relations between groups of people based on differential access to and ownership of the means of production, and is reflected in the labor-capital contention. Gender refers to asymmetrical relations between women and men based on reproduction, specifically, on women's childbearing and child-rearing capacities, and is expressed in the sexual division of labor. Just as class shapes opportunities and options, so does gender. And in the same way that societies everywhere have developed ideologies concerning the roles and prerogatives of certain categories of people, so too have gender ideologies emerged to explain, justify, and perpetuate the positions of men and women. Traditional gender ideology has rendered women's reproductive capacity into a subordinated social position for women and a privileged position for men in productive spheres. This ideology ties women to family roles and considers them secondary breadwinners at best. The persistence of traditional gender ideology explains why women have lower-paid and lower-status jobs compared with men, why women are most vulnerable to restructuring and workplace retrenchment, and why there is so much resistance to measures that allow women to combine work and family responsibilities. During times of crisis or austerity which necessitate cutbacks in social spending or public services, gender ideology holds that women will extend their care-giving inclinations to compensate for the losses. Where economic restructuring entails job losses, hiring freezes, new jobs that are precarious and low-paid, and other measures to cut costs and increase efficiency, gender ideology renders women an expendable or cheap supply of labor.

Is gender ideology stable, or is it subject to change? Let us now turn to political economy. The various dimensions of political economy—the class structure, the nature of the state, and the system of production, as well as specific economic policies and economic conditions—have powerful effects on women's access to economic resources, to political representation, and to social entitlements. Political economy also plays a part in shaping aspects of the prevailing gender ideology—hence the different kinds of gender arrangements that have existed historically in kinship-ordered, agrarian, developing, and advanced industrialized settings. In the twentieth century, women's rights to education, employment, and social policies enabling them to combine productive and reproductive activities have developed in quite distinct ways, reflecting the different forms of state and economic systems. States that are guided by central planning (for example, Cuba or the former German Democratic Republic), states that are theocratic and rich in oil (Saudi Arabia), states that are liberal-capitalist (the United States), and states that are social democratic (the Nordic countries) have had quite different laws concerning women, policies on the family, and concepts of women's rights and entitlements. A country's wealth and income does not guarantee a more advantaged position for women, as any comparative analysis of high-income Saudi Arabia and low-income Vietnam will reveal.

Thus far in our discussion of political economy, we have referred to structural factors that explain the position of women. Proximate causes that affect their economic status include economic policies and economic conditions. Economic policies may hinder or facilitate the well-being and advancement of women, and economic

36   VALENTINE MOGHADAM

conditions may be detrimental or conducive to improvements in the position of women. But the impact of proximate factors, such as an abrupt change in economic policies or an economic recession, are largely shaped by the structural factors mentioned above. That is, how well women (or children or working-class men) are cushioned in a period of economic crisis or restructuring will depend to a great extent on the nature of the state. But it will also depend on another, crucial factor—the ability of women to organize on behalf of their own interests, whether in their own organizations or within existing political parties.

The nature of the market reforms

Like structural adjustments in developing countries, the economic reforms implemented in the former socialist countries have been guided by the neoliberal economic philosophy which privileges the operation of a free market unencumbered by state interventions, and which tends to favor the accumulation of capital over and above the well-being of labor.[13] Individuals and institutions associated with neoliberal policies generally concede that the burden of adjustment falls on those on the lower rungs of the occupational ladder who are dependent on wages and who receive benefits that supplement those (usually low) wages. However, they are of the opinion that the pains of adjustment are both transitory and necessary to achieve macroeconomic stabilization and respectable rates of growth (World Bank 1990, 1995b). The elimination of subsidies—not only for food, utilities, transportation, housing, and vacations, but also social services such as health care, schooling, and childcare—is invariably part of the neoliberal prescription package. Here the gender bias reveals itself in the presumption that social and public services are monetized extensions of women's "natural" care-giving functions, and that during periods of crisis and contraction women can be relied upon to utilize their available time to compensate for the loss. In the transition economies the elimination of subsidized childcare has hit women

---

[13] This does not mean that social safety nets or policies targeted at poor households are not considered. Indeed, what distinguishes the neoliberal approach to welfare is precisely its preference for means-tested and targeted programs rather than universal programs based on notions of solidarity and equality.

especially hard, as they have depended on this service, subsidized by the state or the enterprise, to facilitate their employment.

The neoliberal philosophy does not recognize structural forms of disadvantage which circumscribe people's positions in the labor market. Stratification and the occupational hierarchy are presumed to be based on different skill levels and educational attainments, as well as varying forms of demand for and supply of labor, rather than more profound forms of disadvantage which may necessitate interventions. Feminist economists have pointed out that with respect to women, the neoliberal policy regime does not recognize legal, cultural, institutional, and reproductive constraints on women's mobility across sectors, jobs, and employers.[14] It assumes that men and women compete fairly in the labor market, that women's labor-market disadvantages are explained entirely in human capital terms, and that compensatory measures are not necessary. As argued earlier, however, gender is itself a powerful predictor of labor-market positionality. How else is it possible to explain the fact that among the pool of unemployed in Russia, women are more likely than men to be highly skilled? (Bodrova 1995; World Bank 1995a, 32).[15]

Economic policies may serve to attenuate or intensify gender ideology and may lessen or increase asymmetrical relations between men and women. For example, a human resource-driven strategy for economic and social development may recognize the significance of women and lead to investments in women's education and training, along with various forms of childcare and family support. Such a strategy is associated with the Nordic countries and the former centrally-planned economies, and this strategy led to high female labor force participation, a rise in the age of marriage, lower fertility rates, important economic and social contributions by women, and a lessening of gender inequality. Conversely, a strategy for economic growth that calls for

---

[14] For detailed information on "feminist economics," the feminist critique of neoclassical economics, and an argument for integrating the gender dimension in economic analysis and macroeconomic policy formulation, see the symposium in *World Development* 23(11) (1995), especially articles by Diane Elson, Nilufer Çağatay and Sule Özler, Lourdes Beneria, Ingrid Palmer, and Maria Sagrario Floro.

[15] It should be noted that this calls into question the widespread view that women's greater vulnerability to economic restructuring and their higher unemployment rates is a function of their lower skills levels and educational attainment.

cutbacks in the areas of health, education, and welfare could constrain the availability of women for work, limit their productive capacity, or over-extend their labor time. It could also revive traditional gender ideology and increase rather than decrease gender asymmetry. Because of household-based gender biases in many developing countries, public education and health services are key resources for women's advancement. Any negative impact of public expenditure cutbacks on these sectors will have a stronger negative impact on female than on male human-resource development. Recent evidence from Vietnam and China, among other countries, suggests that the introduction of user fees in health-care and schooling has forced a resurgence of son-preference among poor rural families. This could occur in poorer regions in Central Asia and the Caucasus as well.

Changing identities and roles: The case of Turkey

If market reforms have led to economic and labor-market losses on the part of women in the former centrally-planned economies, and if structural adjustment has similarly led to increased burdens on women in their productive and reproductive activities, can we expect to see similar losses in Turkey, as neoliberal policies proceed and liberalization and integration into the global market are deepened? Or, conversely, can we expect different outcomes in Turkey, given that the initial conditions are different?

It should be noted that Turkey lags behind the countries of Central Asia and the Caucasus on nearly all social indicators, including the pattern of female labor force participation. Not only is the literacy rate of adult Turkish women far lower, but the gap between men and women is much wider than in Central Asia and the Caucasus. The same pertains to combined school enrollments (see Table 1). Moreover, the female share of earned income and the female share of the adult labor force are lower in Turkey than in the other countries we have been considering. And this is despite the respectable economic growth rates Turkey has experienced.

The vast majority of the Turkish female labor force is in agriculture, and this sector is indeed feminized, as men are distributed more evenly across the occupations. Female labor force participation rates are very low, especially in urban areas, and women represent under 20 percent of the salaried workforce. Most employed women are found in professional jobs; a smaller percentage are found in manufacturing and lower-skilled service jobs. Gender ideology has not been entirely supportive of female employment, despite the legacy of Kemalism. The high wages obtained for men during the era of import-substitution industrialization were perhaps a disincentive for increased female participation in the formal sector. Thus, in contrast to many of the centrally planned economies, including some Central Asian and Caucasian countries, the non-agricultural labor force in Turkey was predominantly male, and a patriarchal gender contract assumed—and reinforced—the male breadwinner/female homemaker roles, in which men had control over the means of production and direct access to wage employment, and in which women were economically dependent.[16]

In such a context, how might the changing political economy affect women's educational and economic prospects? Could economic liberalization affect the gender composition of the labor force in Turkey? Might it even weaken the patriarchal gender contract? Women's employment could increase for the following reasons:

- Policies of export-oriented manufacturing are known to raise the demand for women in such industries as textiles, garments, and electronics;
- In the current era of globalization, countries are forced to make their industries—and their labor forces—more competitive, partly by raising skill levels. This could favor increased attention to more education, vocational training, skills-upgrading, and entrepreneurship for women;
- Structural reforms often call for fiscal changes and the mobilization of domestic resources, through such measures as expanding the tax base and making taxation more efficient. Governments may reason that in order to increase the income tax-paying population, policies would be needed to increase the size of the female labor force;

---

[16] The "patriarchal gender contract" is discussed in Moghadam 1998.

- The number of women could rise in such expanding occupations as banking, insurance, accounting, computing, and so on, which are indeed becoming feminized internationally;
- The expansion of tourism could break down cultural proscriptions against women's employment in sales and service occupations;
- As governments relinquish control over economic enterprises to focus on expanding and upgrading health, education, and social services, this could enhance the participation of women in the social sectors;
- The emphasis on private-sector development could encourage women-owned or managed businesses.

Available data suggest that aspects of the above scenario are being realized. The numbers of self-employed women in manufacturing, sales, and service occupations doubled between 1980 and 1990. The mean age at first marriage for all married women rose to 22 in 1990, up from 17.6 in 1983. Women are also responding to demand in the manufacturing sector (mainly in privately-owned enterprises in the textiles, garments, and leather industry) and in public and private services. In every type of economic activity and occupation, the number of women workers increased between 1980 and 1990, as employee and as self-employed. Women are seeking work because of personal aspiration, educational attainment, and economic need. A study of female migrants to a dam site in Elazig, eastern Turkey, found that 48 percent of the sample of young women and their mothers who joined the urban labor market cited economic factors as the main reason, including the unemployment of male family members and the family's poverty (Moghadam 1998, chapter 4).

If economic liberalization continues to bring about such labor-market changes, we can expect to see a change in the identity and roles of women: as their integration deepens in the formal labor force, they could be seen not only as wives and mothers but as workers, citizens, colleagues, and contributors to economic growth and social development. This process, and women's own activism, could bring serious pressure to bear on the patriarchal gender contract.

Of course, there could be quite negative results as well. The contraction of the public sector and the expansion of a private sector that is "unfriendly" to women and that otherwise offers undesirable working conditions could dissuade educated women from entering the labor force and increase "housewife-ization" among middle-class women. For women from working-class and lower middle class families, economic need and household survival could propel them towards the labor market, but the job opportunities could be mainly in the informal or unregulated sectors, including home-based activity through subcontracting arrangements, and without the security provided by work in the formal sector. Recent data show that although the female share of the labor force has been increasing, women's unemployment has also been increasing, a sign that there continue to be barriers to women's integration into the paid labor force despite the growing supply of job-seeking women and the growth of the economy. The employment costs to women are still great, while the poor nature of the social and physical infrastructure and of social policies may act as a disincentive for women to enter the labor force. The reluctance or inability of many private-sector employees to provide women workers with maternity leave benefits or childcare facilities creates a labor-market constraint for women workers with family responsibilities. It should be further noted that the changing political economy in Turkey is occurring against the backdrop of growing religious conservatism. In this respect, Turkey shares at least one of the problems of its Central Asian and Caucasian neighbors.

Summary and conclusions

In this paper I have endeavored to show the relationship between women's positions and the changing political economy, particularly in the context of socio-economic transition, with a focus on Central Asia, the Caucasus, and Turkey. Using data from official reports and international yearbooks, I have drawn attention to the gender-specific outcomes of the market transition in Central Asia and the Caucasus up to the mid-1990s. I have also compared and contrasted the situation of Turkey to that of its neighbors. I have suggested that whereas women in Central Asia and the Caucasus seem to have lost ground, women in Turkey may benefit from the economic reform process. This proposition, however, remains to be tested.

42   VALENTINE MOGHADAM

Gender relations and political economy are interactive and inextricably linked, and they affect the formation or transformation of identities and roles. Exactly how economic imperatives will interact with and attenuate the effects of gender ideology in the current context of liberalization and globalization in Turkey remains to be seen. Much will depend upon the mixture of policies and the role of collective action—on the vision of Turkey's policy-makers and the activities of the women's organizations.

REFERENCES

Afshar, Haleh and Carolyne Dennis, eds. 1992. *Women and Adjustment Policies in the Third World.* London: Macmillan.

Bakker, Isabella, ed. 1994. *The Strategic Silence: Gender and Economic Policy.* London: Zed Books.

Beneria, Lourdes and Shelley Feldman, eds. 1992. *Unequal Burden: Economic Crises, Persistent Poverty, and Women's Work.* Boulder, Co.: Westview Press.

Bodrova, Valentina. 1995. "Employment, Unemployment, and Working Women in Russia: Survey Results." Paper prepared for UNU/WIDER Helsinki.

Economic Commission for Europe. 1993. *Structural Change, Employment and Unemployment in the Market and Transition Economies.* Proceedings of a round-table discussion held under the auspices of the Senior Economic Advisers on 7 June 1993. Discussion Papers 3, no. 1. Geneva: ECE; New York: United Nations.

Einhorn, Barbara. 1994. *Cinderella Goes to Market: Citizenship, Gender and Women's Movements in East Central Europe.* London: Verso.

Elson, Diane, ed. 1991. *Male Bias in the Development Process.* London: Macmillan.

International Labour Office (ILO). 1996. *World Employment 1996/98: National Policies in a Global Context.* Geneva: ILO.

Kenenbaeva, Camilya, Anara Tabyshalieva, Altynai Karasaeva. 1995. "Women of Kirgizistan: Traditions and New Realities." In *Assertions of Self: The Nascent Women's Movement in Central Asia,* 28-34. A publication of Shirkat Gah and Women Living Under Muslim Laws. Lahore, Pakistan: Shirkat Gah.

Massell, Gregory. 1974. *The Surrogate Proletariat: Muslim Women and Revolutionary Strategies in Soviet Central Asia 1919-1929.* Princeton, N.J.: Princeton University Press.

Moghadam, Valentine M. 1998. *Women, Work and Economic Reform in the Middle East and North Africa.* Boulder, Co.: Lynne Rienner Publishers.

———. 1994a. "Women in Societies." *International Social Science Journal* 139: 95-116.

———, ed. 1995. *Gender and National Identity: Women and Politics in Muslim Societies.* London: Zed Books.

———, ed. 1994b. *Identity Politics and Women: Cultural Reassertions and Feminisms in International Perspective.* Boulder, Co.: Westview Press.

———, ed. 1993. *Democratic Reform and the Position of Women in Transitional Econ-omies.* Oxford: Clarendon Press.

Rai, Shirin, Hilary Pilkington and Annie Phizacklea, eds. 1992. *Women in the Face of Change: The Soviet Union, Eastern Europe and China.* London and New York: Routledge.

GENDER AND ECONOMICS REFORMS   43

Rana, Pradumna B. 1993. *Reforms in the Transitional Economies of Asia.* Manila: Asian
    Development Bank Occasional Paper, December.
Rueschemeyer, Marilyn, ed. 1994. *Women in the Politics of Postcommunist Eastern
    Europe.* Armonk, N.Y.: M. E. Sharpe.
Sachs, Jeffrey. 1992. "Accelerating Privatization in Eastern Europe: The Case of
    Poland." In *Proceedings of the Annual Conference on Development Economics 1991,*
    World Bank Conference on Development Economics. Washington D.C.:
    World Bank.
Sparr, Pam, ed. 1994. *Mortgaging Women's Lives: Feminist Critiques of Structural
    Adjustment.* Atlantic Highlands, N.J.; London: Zed Books.
Tabyshalieva, Anara. 1995. "Traditions and Women." In *Assertions of Self: The Nascent
    Women's Movement in Central Asia.* A publication of Shirkat Gah and Women
    Living Under Muslim Laws, 36-38. Lahore, Pakistan: Shirkat Gah, 1995.
Tanski, Janet. 1994. "The Impact of Crisis, Stabilization and Structural Adjustment
    on Women in Lima, Peru." *World Development* 22(11): 1627-42.
Tokhtakhodzhaeva, Marfua. 1995a. *Between the Slogans of Communism and the Laws of
    Islam: The Women of Uzbekistan,* translated by Sufian Aslam. Lahore, Pakistan:
    Shirkat Gah Women's Resource Centre.
———. 1995b. "Women and Law in Uzbekistan." In *Assertions of Self: The Nascent
    Women's Movement in Central Asia.* A publication of Shirkat Gah and Women
    Living Under Muslim Laws. Lahore, Pakistan: Shirkat Gah.
———. 1995c. "Working Women and Market Reforms in Uzbekistan: A Study of
    Tashkent Enterprises". Paper prepared for UNU/WIDER, Helsinki.
World Bank. 1995a. *Poverty in Russia: An Assessment.* Washington, D.C.: World Bank.
———. 1995b. *World Development Report 1995: Workers in an Integrating World.*
    Washington, D.C.: World Bank.
———. 1993. *Uzbekistan: An Agenda for Economic Reform.* Washington, D.C.: The
    World Bank.
———. 1990. *World Development Report 1990: Poverty.* Washington, D.C.: The World
    Bank.

Name Index

The International Library of Critical Writings in Economics

Forecasting Financial Markets
Terence C. Mills

New Developments in Exchange Rate Economics
Lucio Sarno and Mark P. Taylor

The Economics of Migration
Klaus F. Zimmermann and Thomas Bauer

Speculation and Financial Markets
Mark P. Taylor and Liam Gallagher

Macroeconomics and the Environment
Mohan Munasinghe

The Economics of Language
Donald M. Lamberton

The Economics of Poverty and Inequality
Frank A. Cowell

The Economics of Structural Change
Harald Hagemann, Michael Landesmann and Roberto Scazzieri

The Economics of Labor Unions
Alison Booth

Path Dependence
Paul David

The Economics of Crime
Isaac Ehrlich

The Economics of Organisation and Bureaucracy
Peter Jackson

The Economics of Business Strategy
John Kay

Alternative Theories of the Firm
Richard Langlois, Paul Robertson and Tony F. Yu

New Institutional Economics
Claude Ménard

Forms of Capitalism: Comparative Institutional Analyses
Ugo Pagano and Ernesto Screpanti

The International Economic Institutions of the Twentieth Century
David Greenaway and Robert C. Hine

The Economics of the Mass Media
Glenn Withers